THE LIMITS OF FEROCITY

THE LIMITS OF FEROCITY

SEXUAL AGGRESSION AND MODERN LITERARY REBELLION

DANIEL FUCHS

DUKE UNIVERSITY PRESS
DURHAM AND LONDON
2011

© 2011 Duke University Press
All rights reserved
Designed by Amy Ruth Buchanan
Typeset in Minion by
Keystone Typesetting, Inc.
Library of Congress Cataloging-
in-Publication Data appear on the
last printed page of this book.

IN MEMORY OF MY WIFE, CARA,
HUMANIST, FRIEND, LOVER,
AND MY SISTER FRAN,
CLINICAL PSYCHOLOGIST AND
LIFELONG BUDDY, WHO OPENED
MY TEENAGE LITERARY EYES
TO THE THEORETICAL SUBTLETY
OF PSYCHOLOGICAL CONSIDERATIONS.

CONTENTS

ACKNOWLEDGMENTS ix

INTRODUCTION 1

1. Freud and the Postwar Temper 11
2. Freud and Others on Aggression 24
3. Wilhelm Reich 40
4. Norman O. Brown 53
5. Deleuze and Guattari 67

  INTERCHAPTER *Deleuze and Guattari
on Lawrence and Miller* 88

6. The Marquis de Sade 102
7. D. H. Lawrence 145
8. Georges Bataille 194

  INTERCHAPTER *Bataille on Sade* 224

9. Henry Miller 232

  INTERCHAPTER *Miller on Lawrence* 271

10. Norman Mailer 293

  INTERCHAPTER *Mailer on Miller* 332

CONCLUSION: The Naked and the Clothed 346

NOTES 363

INDEX 391

ACKNOWLEDGMENTS

I am grateful to the readers of this study, from whose insights and encouragement I have benefited. My thanks to Reynolds Smith of Duke University Press for his editorial help.

I also wish to thank the Yaddo Corporation, in Saratoga Springs, New York; the Rockefeller Foundation, at Villa Serbelloni Bellagio, Italy; and the Wurlitzer Foundation, in Taos, New Mexico, for giving me ideal space and landscape to nurture my reflections. Thanks, too, to the College of Staten Island, City University of New York, for granting me released time toward the beginning and in the middle of my labors, and to the City University Research Foundation for grants during the same periods.

The following were venues for trial-run lectures on material for this book: the John F. Kennedy Institute for American Studies, Free University of Berlin; Humboldt University, Berlin; the City University Graduate Center, New York; Kansai University, Osaka; and Kansai Gaidai University, Osaka; Beijing Foreign Studies University; and Jagellonian University, Krakow. I am grateful to them.

The dedication to this book could have been extended to include my daughters, Margot and Sabrina; clinical psychologist and literary critic, respectively, they carry on a second generation of such compatible activity in our family. These are professions that put character first. Even more valuable than Margot's and Sabrina's reality as thinkers is their reality as daughters.

INTRODUCTION

The turn in American consciousness from the period after the Second World War to the late 1960s and 1970s is vividly reflected in the literature of sexual aggression. It is reflected as well in the ascendency and decline of Freud. This interdisciplinary study is an analysis of these related cultural phenomena. During this period the Marquis de Sade, D. H. Lawrence, Georges Bataille, Henry Miller, and Norman Mailer emerged as exemplars of significant aggression. Freud represents the humanist counterargument to this literature of ferocity. A number of theorists, both American and European, respond to Freud in favor of liberating violence. These theorists include Wilhelm Reich (post-Freudian), Norman O. Brown (meta-Freudian), and Gilles Deleuze and Felix Guattari (anti-Freudian). I am skeptical of this violence and want to show the limits of ferocity. By *limits* I mean powers as well as limitations. By *ferocity* I mean a loathing of middle-class culture—or, as the case may be, society itself—so intense that it can only be satisfied by the undoing of that culture. The undoing is artistic or ideational rather than political, though most of the writers in both sections of this study have some past connection to political revolution, usually through Marx and through Mao. So one of the key resonances of *ferocity* is, one may say, being rebellious or revolutionary by temperament. This study is, then, a critique of the revolutionary mentality as it manifests itself in literary and related intellectual texts: its utopianism, its violence, its assault on the liberal moderation that, ironically, much of the currently developing political world is trying in its own way to imitate. A viable middle class is a social condition that this developing world aspires to. For the writers of ferocity, *middle* is a dirty word (or they ignore the middle and consider only extremes), like the expression *common sense*. For them, these words only conceal the brutal truth, the shackles of a bourgeois culture that can be undone only by rebellion, which is exemplified in its first and purest form in literature and ideas. This is a large subject; the aspect of ferocity I am concerned to illuminate is the moment when social, political, or metaphysical aggression expresses itself as the fiction of sexual aggression. In examining the literature of ferocity, I seek to offer a counterbalance to the mentality of excess and to preserve the contours of a civilization based on civility.

This study is a chapter in the literary criticism of modernism—that is, modernism in its broad sense, the proliferation of artistic and intellectual consciousness from about the 1870s to the 1970s. So my experimental, avant-garde writers are Henry Miller and Georges Bataille, not T. S. Eliot and James Joyce. This book is not about the modernism of the religion of art, the idealism of the word issuing into the monumental aesthetic icon, or the godlike artistic impersonality. Its one fictional representative from the period of high modernism, D. H. Lawrence, has often been considered a modernist against modernism. Further, Miller self-consciously writes what is ostensibly an anti-literature in the backwash of high modernism. So does Bataille, in the sense that his pornography is a repudiation of Flaubertian aesthetic realism, or indeed any realism. And Mailer bursts onto the scene with a novel of dogged naturalism. Anarchic, aggressive, the writers of ferocity concern themselves more with sex than with art, giving us a modernism of the body where classic modernism is more likely to be a modernism of the mind. Where the body is prominent in classic modernism it is likely to be representative of a larger meaning, a symbolic pattern. When the mind is prominent in the fiction of ferocity, the focus is very likely to be on the body. Both modernisms are motivated by a sense of crisis, stemming from a realization that the major problem is civilization itself.

It is not possible, in my view, to perceive this subject in anything like its true depth without including European influences and illustrations. Economic globalization may be a recent phenomenon, but literary globalization has been going on for a long time. It is called comparative literature. It may seem paradoxical, but some aspects of American literary culture can be best explored by going beyond it. In addition, some of the works under consideration were not written in the period being defined but are instrumental to its definition. It is well to recall that part of the definition of the period concerns the pornography trials of *Lady Chatterley's Lover*, *Tropic of Cancer*, and *Naked Lunch*, a triumph over censorship. The trials were a cultural as well as a legal triumph, since a major part of literary expression experienced a new freedom. Legal immunity, of course, does not grant immunity to what in the case of novelists is the higher judgment of literary criticism.

That wary humanist, Saul Bellow's professor Moses Herzog, speaks of transcendence downward, a form of romantic rebellion in which "the inspired condition" or transcendence "is thought to be attainable only in the negative and is pursued in philosophy and literature as well as in sexual experience, or with the aid of narcotics, or in 'philosophical' 'gratuitous' crime and similar paths of horror."[1] Herzog is identifying the literature of ferocity, a cultural situation that has its literary roots in Sade—for example, the excremental vision, the apocalyptic orgasm.

Though the rest of this study is concerned with twentieth-century authors (Freud's early work was published in the last decade of the nineteenth century), Sade is the indispensable antecedent. All of the novelists considered have commented on Sade in some form. Two of them, Miller and Mailer, were thinking of writing books on Sade; a third, Bataille, wrote three essays on Sade and alludes to him in other works as well. So, although Sade essentially antedates the assault on middle-class culture, this avatar of sexual rebellion is the beginning of the tradition I am trying to define. A certain kind of tradition nourishes a certain kind of individual talent. As erotic blasphemer, Sade intended to strike a blow against the pillars of the ancien régime. As a libertine, however, he was a pillar of the ancien régime. Often classified with the *philosophes*, in his pursuit of a negative transcendence this exponent of the cult of energy can also be viewed as a pre-Romantic, even as a founder of the avant-garde. Though an eighteenth-century writer, Sade reaches his critical apogee in the period we focus on, mainly in France but in the United States as well.

In *Beyond Culture*, Lionel Trilling has written about the "adversarial" quality of modern high culture, which defines itself in opposition to "the specious good" (Wallace Fowlie's phrase, from his book on Rimbaud) that middle-class life represents.[2] This is a distinction that transcends our assent to the realm of everyday custom, says Trilling, in a problematic caveat. For how much assent can we give to this realm without actually believing in it? Trilling, in any case, is ambivalent about both of the aforementioned categories. In explaining this ambivalence, he invokes Hegel's distinction (in *The Phenomenology of Mind*) between the "honest consciousness" and the "disintegrated consciousness," between rational decency and noble baseness. Hegel, in my view, sees decency too easily as simple, placid, middle-class, and disintegration too readily as daring, viable, artistic. Paradoxically, it appears to Hegel, the deepest, most complex qualities of mind, most notably those that are produced by art and concerned with this production, involve baseness—a negative, unsavory, even violent quality, which may emerge as what I call ferocity. Though the disintegration is of norms, it is also of the self, disintegrated in the creative destruction of those norms. Trilling cites the hero of Goethe's *Sorrows of Young Werther* as an early prime, chaste instance, noting that the critics of this early romantic novel suggested that childish things should give way to maturity. Maturity is a serious concept in the period of American life we are considering, though it is most often used contemptuously by cultural radicals, who consider it a synonym for conformity. The novelists of ferocity do not think much of it. Much better the adult as wild child. These novelists have little to say about children as such. An exception, Mailer's child seductress in *Barbary Shore*, proves the rule.

Nor do they think much of psychoanalysis. Freud is the dark genius of honest consciousness—of rational decency and general civility—and therefore a prime target for most writers of ferocity and the rebel theoreticians of psychoanalysis. As Trilling notes, "the bias of psychoanalysis, so far from being Dionysian, is wholly in the service of the Apollonian principle, seeking to strengthen the 'honest soul' in the selfhood which is characterized by purposiveness and a clear-eyed recognition of limits."[3] That is, finally, Trilling's bias as well. It is also the bias of this book, which is why I consider the assault on Freud relevant to the fiction of ferocity. In attacking, if not destroying, the idea of limit, this fiction pronounces clear limits of its own. Of course, the attack is done differently by each author, and sometimes differently within the development of an author's career, so that what this study gives the reader is a variety of ferocious experiences, constituting a tradition or subtradition. It is a tradition in which the self, ideally, goes beyond all bounds, a self that seeks erotic transcendence. When bounds dramatically emerge to complicate the narrative, great literature may be written, as is the case with Lawrence. But, on the other hand, the frustrated quest for primitive redemption can issue into a tedious or pernicious violence. There is a conformity of rebellion just as there is a conformity of middle-class life. This study explores the possibility that, as the expression goes, the cure may be worse than the disease. It argues that modern literary culture has overvalued the tradition of extremity that the fiction of ferocity incarnates, and it suggests a reconsideration of the honest consciousness that artist-rebels consider square. My hope is that this book may help to bridge the gap—often, but not always justified—between literary culture and middle-class realities.

I have focused on a select number of writers and thinkers. Anyone might think of others. My concern is to describe an arc. Relating so directly yet so differently to Freud over a period of time, the figures I have chosen seem to me to do this most clearly and, by and large, most significantly. I have deliberately chosen writers who are household words (Bataille is the exception, although his top-drawer pornography, considered here, was well known to the cognoscenti during this period), at least if one considers one particular room of the household.

Topographically speaking, there are two main sections to the study. The first is theoretical, dealing with Freud's ideas and how they are viewed by other thinkers. This section begins with two chapters on Freud: "Freud and the Postwar Temper" and "Freud and Others [including Foucault] on Aggression." The next chapters, in varying degrees critical of Freud, delineate the thought of Reich, Brown, and Deleuze and Guattari. This part of the book is prolegomenal, serving as a cultural backdrop and analogue to the main part of it, which is a literary critique of the fiction of sexual aggression. The first part describes the cultural assault on the Freudian superego and the humanistic sense of limits that goes with it. Freud, who thought much about aggression, sexual and otherwise, becomes an object of utopian transformation. The second and main part of the book is composed of essays on the major fiction and relevant nonfictional prose of the writers of ferocity. Some of these writers have been considered together before, most notably in Kate Millett's broadly anti-patriarchal *Sexual Politics*, where Freud, Miller, and Mailer are all on the same side.[4] None has been considered collectively from the point of view elaborated in this book. In addition to the chapters on these novelists, there are a number of interchapters, where I consider what they write about another writer in this group (for example, Miller on Lawrence). Finally, there is a conclusion, a discussion of Burroughs's *Naked Lunch*, Ellis's *American Psycho*, and Rieff's *Fellow Teachers*, which extends the polarities of the rest of the book.

The first section of this study seeks to delineate Freud's ideas and the movement away from them. Freud's ego-id-superego paradigm is an affront to the self that concedes no limit to the id. His radical imperfectability, his tragic vision, stands in opposition to the revolutionary utopian element. Bersani, a deconstructionist, speaks for the limitless as in the "limitless" narcissism of infancy. For this liberationist, sexuality is intolerable to the structured self. He especially rejects the "policeman" of Freud's *The Ego and the Id*, which, Bersani holds, tends to reduce psychoanalysis to ego psychology. Bersani is attuned to ferocity; Freud is not. Foucault and his followers reject Freud's insistence on genital primacy, his positing of a virtual sexual normalcy. Foucault holds that sadomasochism is illustrative of the desexualiation of pleasure—that is, the degenitalization of pleasure. So, though Foucault admired Freud for opening up "the possibility of a dialogue with unreason"—not only with the unconscious, but with what Foucault calls "the serene world of mental illness"—he regrets that Freud became a medical personage, a judge who punishes and rewards, and that cure became a conformist disaster. Sade is Foucault's example of the "natural." The Oedipus complex is a straitjacket. Foucault wants a "non-disciplinary eroticism," a sadomasochism without pain.[5]

Reich dissents from the Freudian view that civilization is worth the price of repression. He will not recognize the Freudian sense of limits. All superego should be abolished—except his. For Reich, civilization is a prison and nature is a paradise. A Freudo-Marxist, Reich derives much of this sense of imprisonment from capitalist social corruption. A utopian, he violently proclaims nonviolence. A psychoanalyst, he believes apocalypse must begin on the couch. This will result in Dionysian release. The authoritarian grip of the Oedipus complex will be shattered by the sexual revolution. Like Lawrence, he argues that Freud does not see the purity of the instincts. That is why Freud is a mere compromiser, particularly in the way that he constructs the ego as mediator between superego and id. For all this, Reich does not want to get back to the pregenital.

Brown does. He wants the polymorphous perverse, a regression to primary narcissism, an undifferentiated ego and id. He sees civilization as a dead loss, a product of sublimation. He thinks Freud is too involved in the ego project to value the Dionysian highly. Diminishing the Dionysian makes for the mixture of sensuality we get in Sade and Hitler. Dionysus freed gives us Blake and Nietzsche. For ecstasy, for Bacchic frenzy, we need derangement. The Orphic Brown wants transgression, so that we can establish "the natural limits of intelligence."[6] Even insanity leads to liberation.

Deleuze and Guattari are proclaimed enemies of the Oedipus complex because it internalizes limit. It places a limit on the illimitable. There is no Oedipal unconscious. Not that they want the id; the id never existed. Neither did the unconscious. It is a bourgeois-capitalist fantasy, like the Oedipus complex. There is no moral reality but a "schizophrenic" (or schizo) indeterminacy characterized by fragments, flows, desires. Deleuze and Guattari utopianize experience without pain. Their schizophrenia is not an illness but a process. The schizo's fragmented life of multiple personalities undergoes a transformation into the exemplary desiring machine, which works only when it breaks down. Like Bersani, they are deconstructionists. Their schizo is a deconstructed subject—there is no ego, there is no individual. The breakdown of boundaries, limits, characters, and genres that we see in Burroughs and in postmodernism generally is a literary analogue. What emerges is a psychic anarchy.

The second section of this book looks at the literature of ferocity. Sade is its originator. Antinomian, he transvalued values before Nietzsche, who read him. Modeling his characters on what he calls "Nature," he is an avatar of the cult of energy and the morality of impulse. The energy is aggressive and uninhibited, an energy of destruction. In his assault on superego, he embodies the imagination as libertine. It exceeds all limits, dissipates all conditions. In the extremity of his posture, Sade anticipates modern, not just Romantic, criminality. Crime is a form of genius, a transformer of worlds. There is nothing that his master characters are not permitted. Cruelty is a positive energy, since it is the only thing that civilization has not yet corrupted—a virtue, not a vice. Sade's characters, then, are doubly (and contradictorily) cruel, by civilization and by nature. Among other things, his imagination is a justification of his own proclivities. It is also the origin of sexual modernism.

Though Lawrence repudiated what he saw as the endless, minuscule psychologizing of modern literature, he is very much the modernist in his embattled extremity and salvationary primitivism. His major surrogate, Birkin in *Women in Love*, rebels against a society he finds loathsome but also against the idea of society as such—much of the time. There is, as well, something in Birkin that rebels against the nature of things, even sex, for example. But sex is needed to support the individuality in togetherness that must characterize the man and woman relation. He thereby transcends the Sadean solipsism, in which the object is a matter of indifference. Lawrence has no illusions about sex being easy. It is a psycho-metaphysical experience often within a sadomasochistic context. Its enactment may lead to a qualified wholeness or to disintegration. His darkened world celebrates a difficult beauty. Mistrustful of Freudian motive, Lawrence rescues for his preferred lovers a final purity.

Bataille too is explicitly anti-Freudian, critical of the sublimations and repressions that inhibit. He is a disciple of Sade. He is one of those who speaks of "the Divine Marquis"—that is, a figure whose passion transcends the world of social values. Bataille is an eroticist *maudit*; eroticism exists only in the violent, angry gesture. Like Barthes, he distinguishes between *plaisir*, the usual affectionate sexual pleasure, and *jouissance*, the shocking, ego-disrupting sexuality that reflects a violent conflict with culture and nature. Despoiling woman's beauty is the essence of eroticism. Anthropologically, Bataille sees the need for *potlatch*, the need for expenditure to the point of ruin. Marxist surplus is a utilitarian reduction, since our deepest need is for conspicuous outlays that exhaust as they ennoble us. Limit, project, deferred gratification, the myth of the moral life—these give the lie to the agony of living. Nothing is useful; everything is waste. Only transgression is real. We are near the solipsistic world of Sade. Only convulsive laughter will save us from solipsism, Bataille holds. *Story of the Eye* is a perfect expression of these views as it concerns youth, *Madame Edwarda* as it concerns middle age. The first is episodic, racy, juvenile; the second metaphysical, lyrical, and hysterical.

Miller wrote his most important work in Paris and was much influenced by French literature. Rimbaud, about whom he wrote a book, is the first of his French culture heroes. With Rimbaud, he agrees that we must be absolutely modern, that chimeras are out of date, that we must renounce all that civilization has stood for. We must, in other words, resist the world of cowardly compromise and limitations known as society. Like Rimbaud, Miller resists "maturity." He announces at the beginning of *Tropic of Cancer* that his liberation as a writer came when he cast literature aside, and that his desire is to record "all that which is omitted in books."[7] Obscenity, then, may be ultimate honesty. Miller is the master of nihilistic sexual comedy. Lawrence's cosmic energy gives way to immediate gratification. He admittedly wants to go back to "a superinfantile realm," a resurgence of id at all costs.[8] His egomania is inseparable from a contempt for superego.

Mailer's sexual radicalism evolves from a dissolving political radicalism. In *The Naked and the Dead*, he denies the politics of civility, the reality of a liberal center. But since it is a naturalistic novel (at least in part), sexual aggression in this book is not yet self-conscious. In *The Deer Park* it is, one might say to a fault. In Marion Faye, Mailer gives us his first portrait of the hipster, whose Romantic satanism—Mailer quotes Sade (without acknowledgment) —strikes the apocalyptic note familiar to the literature of ferocity. Hollywood, like the army, gives us what Mailer considers American totalitarianism. The nihilism of hip, as Mailer conceives it, goes back to Sade, with every social restraint removed—even murder, as we see in "The White Negro." Like Sade, Lawrence, and Miller, Mailer moves to a negative transcendence. Rojack in *An American Dream* is a later version of the hipster, a man who follows his impulses no matter how destructive they may be. D. J.—the "I" of *Why Are We in Vietnam?*—is a reader of Sade by the age of fifteen and a follower of Burroughs. He is illustrative of Mailer's view that through obscenity a man can discriminate between himself and society. Mailer's journalism succeeds to a considerable degree because of its dramatization of a new, liberal persona. But fiction releases the sexual demons when, after a long absence, he comes back to it in *Ancient Evenings*. In this world without superego, Mailer leaves no phallus unadored, no incest uninhibited. Mailer's Egypt is a place sated and diminished by its own fulfillments. Ferocity, contingent to some degree on outrage, has lost its place.

This study's conclusion shows that the culture of extremity creates a bifurcation in the general culture. Burroughs and Ellis illustrate strains of the postmodern expression of contemporaneity, the sociology of Rieff a traditionalist counterargument. In *Naked Lunch*, Burroughs gives us a Sadean work, an antinomian explosion of fantasy that has appropriately been described as the literature of delirium. For Burroughs, civilization and destruction are equivalent. The id, then, must subvert the ego, since all civilized forms are sadistic. One of Kermode's "neo-modernists," whom we now call postmodernist, he is anti-language (words being the primary form of repression), anti-art, anti-ethics, anti-form. Like Miller, he is a Deleuze and Guattari schizo. His moral nihilism extends to characters who have no inner life. Sadomasochism is the truest relation.

Ellis presents radical sexual aggression not as rebellion but as a logical consequence of conformity. Charisma has been translated to the material world *faute de mieux*—there is no inner world. In the new blank fiction, commodities have taken over. In Ellis, only sadism and the sartorial are obsessively real. Realism becomes a form of surrealism. Disillusion with civilization is his credo and his rationale. But where the negative credo of Hemingway's Frederick Henry or Lawrence's Connie Chatterley reflects a complex irony deeply felt, Ellis's Bateman gives us an anesthetized heart. Modernism rises above capitalism; postmodernism inhabits the air it breathes. Heroic isolation, the elegiac tone, the monument have all morphed into phantasmagoria, parody, pop culture, aesthetic fragmentation. Sometimes the fragmentation is the very principle of composition, as in Burroughs's cut-up "method." Ellis uses a cut-up method applied to bodies. For him, the precincts of high seriousness are no longer inhabited.

But they are very much so by Rieff, a cultural critic who sits in angry lamentation at the spectacle. His *Fellow Teachers* addresses the problem of moral exhaustion, or, as it may be, vacuity raised by the tradition of ferocity, as well as modernism and postmodernism generally. Just as many formal aspects of postmodernism originate in modernism, where they take on a different emphasis, so do many of its moral weaknesses. Rieff laments the loss of authority, how the Nietzschean transvaluation of values has become in its recent American expression a valuation of all sexuality. To praise the infantile, to glorify the polymorphous perverse and immediate gratification, is to praise criminality. We know that everything is not permitted. High culture, which must be restored, is an establishment of limits. Rieff wishes to rescue pleasure from itself. "In superego," he holds, "we see the ghost of sacred order."[9] Some may regard Rieff's view as an extremity that extremity produced and may feel closer to writers who mediate between eroticism and morality, but his cry in the wilderness is necessary.

At issue in this period, as in high modernism, is the viability of civilization. Is it worth the price? The novelists of ferocity, like the psychoanalytic Left, say in essence that it is not—at least, not in any present or foreseeable form. Civilization *is* the problem. It must die to be resurrected. Hence the positive value, the creativity, of destruction. But there are those who are, as Bellow has put it, on the side of civilization. Freud is preeminent among them. W. H. Auden, in his powerful poem entitled "In Memory of Sigmund Freud," speaks of "Eros builder of cities," suggesting that the price we pay for civilization is worth it. Since its inception, I have thought of this study as the cultural alter ego of my book on Bellow,[10] a moderating cultural figure, a humanist. He shows an attenuated respect for custom, a partial appropriation of tradition. American literary and psychoanalytic culture of the postwar period can well be understood in terms of this cultural agon. This study expresses a skepticism about creative destruction, subjecting ferocity to a humanistic critique.

1

FREUD AND THE POSTWAR TEMPER

"He saw Americans one and all as victims of an anal-sadistic retentiveness hostile to pleasure but conducive at the same time to the most aggressive conduct in business and politics. This was why American existence was marked by 'haste.' That, too, was why the nonutilitarian aspects of life, whether innocent hobbies or the higher reaches of culture, were unavailable to Americans... worst of all America was enslaved to that favorite product of anal adults, money. For Freud, the United States was in a word, 'Dollaria,' " an acerbic pun that equates a symbolic (and real) currency with a common medical disorder. So writes the American historian and Freudian Peter Gay,[1] outlining the aggression that in time made an American reading public ready for the counter-aggression described in this study. Freud did not realize that at the very time he was thinking these adverse thoughts, American writers and bohemians of the 1920s agreed with him and were making use of his psychoanalysis to support a rebellious hedonism. If this cultural appropriation of Freud often lacked depth —it was sometimes nothing more than an extension of a nineteenth-century mind cure—it nonetheless served to reestablish a more serious attitude toward inner experience. In fact, as the historian Eli Zaretsky informs us in *Secrets of the Soul*, "by World War I the United States had the largest number of analysts in the world" (fifty-three), even if they were all medical doctors and "technique driven ... with little interest in psychoanalytic theory."[2] Freud's books sold poorly in the United States until the 1930s, when Americans made more serious evaluations of his work. Freud had been more concerned about the American medical resistance to lay analysis. Writing to Sandor Ferenczi in 1929, he considered this "the last mask of resistance against psychoanalysis and the most dangerous of all."[3] Some of this concern as well may have been misplaced. Zaretsky informs us that there were 2,295 psychiatrists in the United States by 1940, and 4,700 by 1948. Much of their work was clinical (as was most of the newly established profession of clinical psychology), but much of this was a sort of Carl Rogers counseling and psychotherapy rather than classical Freudian analysis. Because of this and because of the increasing dogmatism of the entrenched Freudians, Freud would have had some difficulty in recognizing his profession. In any case, psychoanalysis, as well as psychiatry and clinical psychology, was mostly in the service of war veterans. Zaretsky tells us that in 1945, 60 percent of veterans who were patients were confined for psychiatric reasons, 50 percent of disability pensions were psychiatric, and by the mid-1950s half of the hospital beds in the country were occupied by mental patients. By 1976 there were 27,000 psychiatrists, dominated to a significant extent by the 400 psychoanalysts who had established a practice before the end of the 1940s. Some of the analysts were Freudian, and some emphasized the social and interpersonal. A troubled inner life had become a widespread American characteristic. Maturity was the coin of this realm.

America has taken Freud more seriously than he ever took America, and in a more sophisticated way than he ever imagined. History helped. Along with the sharp decline in radical hopes that began just before the Second World War, the war itself helped bring an end to innocence that was conducive to the absorption of anti-Utopian Freudian realities. Americans in the 1920s may have expressed a more obvious enthusiasm for Freud's ideas, motivated by the bohemian fantasy of sexual liberation, but in the late 1940s and 1950s, despite the period's tendency to conformity, Americans were more appreciative of what Freud really meant. If this elevation of Freud had its downside in a retreat from personal responsibility on the part of parent-blaming analysands and their analysts, and from political responsibility on the part of conformists who were too quick to convert legitimate criticism into neurosis, it had its notable upside in a self-awareness and an ethic of honesty, a clear-eyed truth telling, that was, in terms of psychodynamic motive, firmly established in American experience. And even if the beneficiaries of Freudian analysis were the unhappy few, the influence of Freudianism extended far beyond the couch into the great world itself. Freud mattered, partly because he did not make great claims. He sought only partial cure. As he put it, with memorable tartness, from the start: "Much will be gained if we succeed in transforming your hysterical misery into common unhappiness."[4]

Freud's stoic disposition found fertile ground in the anti-millenarianism, the revisionist liberalism, of the postwar period. Not that the aftermath of the Second World War equaled the disillusionment that followed the First World War. In the 1920s, there was a sense of civilization's collapse. The Second World War, on the other hand, a "good" war in the European theater at least, gave a sense that evil had been vanquished. Still, the very epitome of this evil (the Holocaust), combined with the unique expression of explosiveness of even the good guys (the atomic bomb), was cause for reflection about the aggressive nature of man. It was not long before the popular joy at the war's being over gave way to a more sober assessment of human possibility. Freud's complex pessimism proved not to be alien to a country whose optimism he had trouble taking seriously. One recalls the anecdote of the American lady who protested, "My dreams are altruistic!" Maybe not.

Many Americans accepted the reality of man's radical imperfectability and were ready for, as some put it, Freud's tragic vision. The neo-Freudians (like Karen Horney and Erich Fromm), with their optimistic cultural determinism, and Harry Stack Sullivan, with his vague interpersonal relations—both denying Freud's sexual aetiology of the neurosis—were subject to scrutiny in the hard, economic light of Freud, which saw that the price for selfhood was invariably paid. In response, the dynamics of biological limitation was seen by the cultural critic Lionel Trilling to be the irreducible advantage against the tyranny of culture.

This turn paralleled the critique of Emersonian personalism or part of it—what the literary critic Quentin Anderson called "the imperial self," that self which knows no limits to its power or authority, in its rhapsodic quest for what Tocqueville called "infinite perfectibility."[5] In its place stood the tough structural dramatics of Freud's ego, id, and superego. In this sense, the postwar era represented America's coming of middle age. Writers of tragic dimension—such as Eliot and Faulkner—were central, though rebels like the Beats were soon to assert a neo-Romantic version of the imperial self.

While the hedonistic 1920s enlisted psychoanalysis in the war against Puritanism, by which it usually meant middle-class Victorianism amounting to Babbittry, the 1950s took Puritanism, by which it meant Christianity, quite seriously. Perry Miller's work, groundbreaking in itself, was a symbol of a larger religious viability. Freud's tough-mindedness lent itself to comparison with religious thought. Reinhold Niebuhr, for example, notes that before Freud, "prevailing philosophies of Enlightenment had practically eliminated pessimistic conclusions about the inevitability of egoistic corruption in all forms of human creativity which had been preserved in the Christian doctrine of original sin."[6] Niebuhr sees that, really, "Freud had no interest in original sin" but that he rejects a rational optimism. This endears him to the theologian, a former Marxist turned anti-Utopian known for, among other things, his rejection of what he calls soft Utopias, those envisioning progress without conflict (a simplified version of the Enlightenment), and hard Utopias, those in which an idealized future justifies present cruelty (deriving from Marxism). Niebuhr shared with Freud a tragic sense of life. For both, proximate change may be effected but there is no perfectability. Problems remain, finally, unsolvable. This is the nature of things.

Niebuhr admires Freud's psychodynamic structural paradigm because it "shattered the simple mind/body dualism"[7] of Western philosophy, including the work of Plato, Aristotle, Spinoza, Descartes, and Kant (for example, Kant's version of the intelligible and sensible self). In this dualism, the mind controls the impulses of nature. In Niebuhr's view, Freud rightly invalidates the Kantian idea of godlike reason, the reason that imposes duty on inclination. And in Freud, as in Niebuhr, there is no nature to go back to; that is, there is no salvationary nature. In Freud, nature is always roilingly there, struggling with conscience—or, in Freudian terms, the id is always struggling with the superego, with the ego as mediator. There is no split between reason and emotion, but rather a dynamic dualism of rational and irrational emotion.

So far so good, for Niebuhr. But, he must conclude, Freud's "mistake" was to equate the self too simply with its "natural impulses and necessities." For this theologian, Freud cannot do "full justice to the transcendent freedom of the spirit of which the self is capable." Niebuhr thinks that "the primary problem" of Freud's "determinism is that he finds the causative factors in a too narrow rage of subconscious motives."[8] The word *subconscious* is a giveaway, implying as it does the subordination of libidinal to rational or spiritual motive, something that the Freudian *unconscious* does not do. But Niebuhr is essentially simpatico with Freud, especially when he regards Freud's ideas as a plausible secular equivalent to original sin. He explicitly notes that Freud's realism is "regarded by many as a welcome scientific substitute for the prematurely discredited traditional doctrine of original sin" (272). Regretting that neither myth nor dogma has much relevance in today's progressive world, that Christian religious thought today is viewed as morbid in defining every form of self-concern as sinful, Niebuhr finds that Freud fills the darkness gap. But he considers Freud's realism to be defective in not seeing a self-regard originating beyond the id, and in corrupting the freedom of a "coherent and organized" ego (274). Niebuhr allows for some self-transcendence (and does not see that Freud does as well, for example in sublimation), while he rejects, like Freud, the self-deification or Promethean illusion of the imperial self. Niebuhr thinks that Freudian impulses do exist but are "subject to historical elaboration" (275). There is no reason to assume, then, that the

Oedipus complex is nature rather than culture. It is characteristic of the conservative turn of the 1950s that the Protestant theologian finds in Freud something of a kindred spirit. Both represent what was called moral realism.

The sociologist and cultural critic Philip Rieff, perhaps Freud's best expositor, describes skeptically Freud's somewhat surprising significance in the turn to religion of the 1950s: "Whatever is serious in the current revival of religion is evocatively, if not substantively, Augustinian in temper . . . it proclaims the wretchedness of the human condition and rather muffles the voice of God." He adds that "for this sort of religiosity Freud performs a delicate service. His atheism being dismissed as a personal aberration, Freud's psychology has been pressed into service, mainly as independent testimony to the religious 'depth' for those no longer persuaded of its existence by theological rhetorics."[9] Freud is thereby also made to support those who recoil from the optimism of liberal religion, to affirm "the habitual pronouncement of the pious: we are all miserable sinners," as he says in *Totem and Taboo* (*SE* 13:72). Freud's description, they understood, is ironic. So is a master of psychological need put to attenuated uses; so is a rationalist put to the uses of faith.

Freud does not tell us much about original sin, but he does speak for a sense of limit. Rieff rightly says that "despite his criticisms, Freud was not unsympathetic to the old moralities. As a man of culture, he could admire the repressions. But, as a man of science, he had learned from case after case that 'what the world calls its code of morals demands more sacrifices than it is worth.'"[10] (This man of culture was a paterfamilias who lived by the clock, paid all his bills punctiliously, and kept working into his eighties, though he was hampered for years by cancer.) In this sense, his invention, psychoanalysis, is or was a bargain. For, as Rieff says, "his therapy of honesty came modestly priced in a culture where all prices are too high" (323).

One must agree to limitations of instinct, but not too much. In the common parlance of the 1950s, one should be "well adjusted," an expression that Freud never used. The language comes from therapy, but the submerged technological metaphor suggests a tiny, functioning cog in a great industrial wheel, with Charlie Chaplin frantically tightening loosened psychological nuts, as in *Modern Times*. It suggests Freud Americanized. In reaction, there was a song popular among college students, "I Don't Want to Be Well Adjusted," and some idealistic young people did odd things, like choosing the life of ideas—academic life—despite its genteel poverty, to mention only one mild, middle-class form of rebellion in the land of Dollaria. Freud was ambivalent toward repressive culture and so were we. Like Freud, we were "its major critic and yet defender of its necessity."[11] Whether this is considered the higher ambivalence or just being mixed up, it was never a matter of—to quote the 1930s folk song—"Whose side are you on?" That question, once stirring, now seemed simplistic. Rather, as most of the New York intellectuals now understood, it was a question of self-definition in the face of society. Zaretsky is surely right in saying that it is a mistake to read the history of the period as "bad rationalizers versus good heretics" or "play off the conformist 50s against the rebellious 60s," arguing that even the ego psychologists appealed to charismatic sources of sexuality, individuality, and the personal unconscious; that charisma and rationalization were always intertwined; and that there was a continuity between 1950s domesticity and 1960s liberation—namely, "new possibilities for personal life."[12]

Some did not make this argument; indeed, some repudiated it, like the Beats and, more grandly, Norman Mailer, who keys into the tradition of rebellion described in this book. Here is the conundrum. "If," as Rieff puts it, "every limit can be seen as a limitation of personality, the question with which we may confront every opportunity is: after all, why not? While Freud never committed himself, the antinomian implications are there . . . those who have interpreted Freud as advocating, for reasons of health, sexual freedom—promiscuity rather than the strain of fidelity, adultery rather than neurosis—have caught the hint, if not the intent, of his psychoanalysis."[13] This is a fine distinction indeed. But it separates cultural figures as different as Norman O. Brown and Lionel Trilling, Herbert Marcuse and Philip Rieff, the first member of each pair catching the hint and the second the intent, the first in synch with the late 1960s, the second repelled by them.

Trilling points to the paradox that limit brings the greatest freedom. In *Freud and the Crisis of Our Culture*, he gives credence to Freud's description of himself as "a conservative, a conserving mind."[14] By that Freud meant that the work of ego building, that dike against the restless ocean of id, is essential to the shaping of culture. If culture makes man, man makes culture. But if culture saves man, it also imprisons him. This is the democratic version of the tragic flaw. In thrusting himself into the labor of culture, man falls because of his very strengths—a case of, in the vernacular, "doing better and feeling worse." Since the Romantics, the self has been more powerful and vulnerable because, as Trilling puts it, "in the degree that society was personalized by the concept of culture, the individual was seen to be far more deeply implicated in society than ever before." One can, therefore, speak of the style of the culture, its unexpressed, unconscious assumptions. But if man is seen to be conditioned by culture, Trilling points out, one "can more easily envisage a beneficent manipulation of his condition" (47). This part of the equation gives us, among other possibilities, the neo-Freudian view. Freud's emphasis on his structural paradigm is, in this view, considered "reactionary." Trilling considers the Freudian dynamics liberating, precisely because of the limits it sets on culture in setting limits for the self. In forging ego, Freud's structural paradigm "proposes to us that culture is not all powerful. It suggests that there is a residue of human quality beyond the reach of cultural control, [which] elemental as it may be, serves to bring culture itself under criticism and keeps it from being absolute" (48). One need not be Socrates or Giordano Bruno to illustrate this point. There is no modern writer, Trilling holds, who "has not expressed the bitterness of his discontent with civilization, who has not said that the self made greater legitimate demands than any culture could hope to satisfy. This intense conviction of the existence of the self apart from culture is, as culture well knows, its noblest and most generous achievement" (58). These stirring, paradoxical accents define the heroism of essentialist struggle.

They also define the temper of Freudian humanism. Trilling rightly pronounces Freud "one of the very greatest of humanist minds" (15). He holds that "the complex accuracy of Freud's view of culture may best be spoken of in terms of his affinity with the tradition of literary humanism." For literature, as for Freud, "the test of culture is always the individual self, not the other way around" (33). Freud would have gratefully accepted the mantle of humanism. Ernest Jones, who knew him well, tells us that "he never felt at home in the medical profession . . . he did not seem to himself to be a regular member of it."[15] And Peter Gay quotes from Freud's letter to Paul Federn in which he states: "As long as I live, I shall balk at having psychoanalysis swallowed by medicine."[16] Jones knew that Freud was most interested in "the unraveling of cultural and historical problems,"[17] despite having done some excellent medical research early in his career. Jones informs us: "He might have become a creative writer, perhaps not a poet but a novelist—in fact he said so himself more than once." This may prove only that Freud had an active fantasy life, but Jones seems right to aver that "it was in this wider bearing of his work that he was primarily interested." As Jones notes, Freud wrote Arthur Schnitzler, the celebrated Viennese dramatist and novelist, that "he felt his [Schnitzler's] mind to be more akin to his own than anyone else's he had come across" (432). (Schnitzler, a physician-turned-writer with an eye for pathology, is known for a sophisticated, tender cynicism commonly called Viennese. Freud was faithful[18] and strait-laced according to most accounts. So this remark may give one pause.) There is, too, Freud's special admiration for Shakespeare, his reading of the classics, his Goethe Prize for literature, and his well-known statement that he learned more from the drama and the novel than from academic psychology. Jones speculates that Freud might have been a philosopher. It is relevant to recall that when Freud was in school, the humanities were considered the best preparation for the study of science. Renaissance concepts of education were still prevalent. Nor was the psychoanalysis that Freud developed a hard science, subject to experimental physical laws. In the postscript to *An Autobiographical Study*, Freud speaks of "a lifelong *détour* through the natural sciences, medicine and psychotherapy . . . to the cultural problems which had fascinated me long before, when I was a youth scarcely old enough for thinking." Freud thinks of this with good-natured irony as a "regressive development" in that he knows that he is first and foremost a psychoanalyst: "No personal experiences of mine are of any interest in comparison to my relations with that science" (*SE* 20:71–72).

Freud is far from being the traditional humanist. For him, there is no Platonic right reason. In fact, the rational self or ego must struggle with moral reason or the superego in the process of self-definition. Moreover, the discovery of the determining unconscious denies the primacy of reason or intellect. This circumspect rationalist understood perhaps too well the respect that the rational must pay to the irrational. Still, science was rational, as was society to some degree. But society could not be rational enough. A certainty was gone, if it ever really existed. For Freud, unlike a more typical humanist such as Matthew Arnold, culture could not have the moral certitude that religion once possessed (if only in an illusory way). In these ways, Freud helped to steer the postwar divergence from traditional humanism, while supporting a humanism characterized by anxiety and amenable to therapeutic consolations. The Oedipal paradigm dramatized in a distanced storm-and-stress way the essential humanistic quality, the sense of becoming, even if in its biologically determined character it minimized the most dramatic quality deriving from this sense, the pull of moral indeterminacy. More liberal humanists would not do so.

The postwar period in literature (say 1945 to 1965) has been described, sometimes pejoratively, as an age of criticism. We are concerned here with its literary and psychological manifestations. It was an age of criticism, not only in the sense that there were direct Freudian critiques of literature, but also, and more important, in that the age demanded interpretation. It believed in meaning; it believed that the truth about literature could and must be rationally articulated. The zeitgeist married literary criticism and psychology. The age was for, not against, interpretation, in Susan Sontag's resonant expression.[19] Meaning was the bridge between reason and the unconscious. Like Freud, the postwar age saw the imagination as a symptom of the unconscious. In the minds of some analysts, then, literary criticism was more compelling than fiction or drama—and certainly more than narcissistic poetry, with what they considered to be its regressive sucking of consonants and vowels—in a sense similar to the one in which psychoanalysis was more compelling than being neurotic. Thus criticism could be seen to be not merely necessary to the illumination of artistic motive but also superior to it. Both literary criticism and psychoanalysis were, ideally, attuned to the analysis of language and symbol, though this did not mean that the best literary criticism was Freudian in itself. Meaning *meant* because a humanistic or psychoanalytic truth existed. The thrill of illumination could actually transcend what was to be illuminated, which was fantasy or neurosis or a combination of the two. The shards of dark history and bright hope were treasures to these archaeologists of the intelligible self. Psychoanalysis, in its interpretive power, was the science of humanists. Poor Freud! To this day he is a scientist of sorts more admired by humanists than by scientists. The literary and psychoanalytic cultures have always been linked by a fascination with what is now called, pejoratively, "the anecdotal," the uniqueness of individual experience, something beyond data to make known.

These are some of the reasons why the postwar period is one, unlike the immediate present, in which art is more central than politics to the consciousness of the intelligentsia. The history of the first half of the twentieth century was often chaotic to the point of being unreal. As modernists know, this chaos put the onus of reality on private life. The middle of the century was capable of being, in a mass society, a particularly individuated interregnum. High culture came as close as it could to replacing the authority once held by religion, the cure of souls. Yet it could not possibly achieve the Arnoldian hope of doing so.

If art was central to informed consciousness it could not be simply a byproduct of neurosis. If art was, as Freud thought, an instance of the ego's being taken over by the unconscious, this was a game in which the ego colluded. Freud sees art in its civilizing function even when he denigrates it somewhat. He says, in *The Future of an Illusion*, that "art offers substitute gratifications for the oldest cultural renunciations, still the ones most deeply felt, and for that reason it serves as nothing else to reconcile men to the sacrifices made on behalf of culture" (*SE* 21:14). Freud's ambivalence about artistic genius—in one sense infantile, in another sense awesome, beyond the purview of psychoanalysis—is well known. In the end, art serves a moderating Freudian function. As the art critic Jack Spector says, "just as a successful composition would . . . stay on a humane middle ground between abstraction and excessive emotionalism, so the healthy ego would function as a synthesizer of divergent and swarming energies."[20] So, for example, though the surrealists liked Freud, Freud did not like the surrealists. Of surrealism he writes in a letter to Stefan Zweig in 1938, "the concept of art resists an extension beyond the point where the quantitative proportion between the unconscious maternal and preconscious elaboration is not kept within a certain limit" (SE 21:141–42). The ego, as Spector suggests, seemed to blend the neoclassic (order and beauty) and the romantic (originality and uninhibited expression). This balanced quality says something about the postwar period in literature and psychoanalysis as well. The more extreme eruptions of the unconscious, including sexual eruptions—the literature of ferocity—were often viewed from a skeptical perspective.

Part of Freud's appeal in the postwar era was his focus on myth, Oedipus being the most obvious example. His archaeological interest brought a number of archetypes to life. In his review of Joyce's *Ulysses*, T. S. Eliot said that mythical method organized the chaos of contemporary experience.[21] Freud was part of that contemporaneity. The postwar period could easily accommodate what could in a cultural sense enhance its religiosity. Freud's appropriation of Moses is a case in point. It emphasizes the integration of unconscious and humanistic motives, a meeting of aggression and limit. In *Moses and Monotheism*, Freud reenacts the Oedipal drama of *Totem and Taboo*, where the killing of the primal father by the primal horde eventuates in the return of the repressed through the miracle of guilt. Conscience thereby establishes culture. The end result for the ancient Jews is the worship of God, the father of fathers, and the cherishing of the Ten Commandments, including "thou shalt not murder." This is morality as an imaginative achievement.

A more impressive encounter with Moses, and almost equally original, is Freud's essay on Michelangelo's Moses. It is no exaggeration to say that Freud was obsessed with this statue. His description of his feelings in approaching the statue is an indication, it seems, of his identification with it. Again contrary to the biblical account, Freud thinks that Michelangelo's formidable hero will not destroy the tablets but will refrain from doing so. This figure of potential aggression subdues himself to the imperatives of limit. In so doing, he authenticates the authority of humanism. This is the general significance of

Freud's use of myth. And it is another instance of why the reading of Freud was characteristic of postwar intellectual life in America.

In his focus on the constant rhythms of experience; on the eternal recurrence, psychoanalytic style; and on the struggle between libido and aggression, Freud expressed an essentialist sense of things. Rieff says: "The popularity of psychoanalysis, in an age suffering vertigo from the acceleration of historical events, may be partly ascribed to Freud's rehabilitation of the constant nature underlying history."[22] Freud's truth lent an impetus to what liberal revisionist intellectuals called the end of ideology. Marx had subordinated nature to history, a skewed version of history at that. There was not an end to ideology in the sense of political and social outlooks, of course, but in the sense of exclusionary Marxist rigidity. Civility or civil politics is the alternative to ideology, implying individual political and moral agency and the subsequent consensus. This is not a simple process. For the postwar liberal, the awareness of complexity is the sign of wisdom. Like Freud, the liberal recognizes that every virtue must be paid for and that virtue is bound up with vice. Like Freud, the liberal believes that the ethic of civility will bring about a hoped-for self-sufficiency in a time of disillusionment. Utopia is not the place, even if it is nice to think about. Yes, there is civilization, but there are also its discontents. Rieff notes that "Freud had none of the enthusiasm that characterizes the antinomian temper . . . Sexuality for him is a force that permanently prevents any utopian transforming of the social order. Freud had no hope of transforming civilization. On the contrary, the great utopian possibility—insofar as he had any—is whether repressive civilization can permanently tame the instincts" (28). Freud's Utopia, in short, was anti-Utopian. Freud's revolutionary was a neurotic, pounding papa. Freud was a revolutionary only in the sense that he told the truth.

Freud's politics, like that of the postwar period generally, was of the center. And it was consonant with the time in that it was a subjective politics far more than an objective one. It focused on the individual far more than the collective, more on the private than the public. As Rieff says, Freud was too aware of the corrosive aspects of community to take political solidarity very seriously. In this respect, psychoanalysis was in the political vanguard, so to speak, of an apolitical era. Politics has for a long time been less real—less authentic—than the private life, especially in the postwar years. Whether it was because modernism had deeply discredited public language; because, after Armageddon, there was a recessional impulse toward the illusion of normalcy defined as peaceful privacy; or because the traditional American distrust of politicians had gained an unusual impetus from the coincidence of these developments, the general indifference to public life had a life of its own. Of course, there were still momentous public events. The negative ones—McCarthy, the Rosenbergs—were consequences of tensions implicit in the uneasy wartime alliance with the Soviet Union. The positive ones—economic recovery, the GI Bill, the democratization of elites, the beginnings of the civil rights movement, the publication of the standard edition of Freud—focused largely on individual redefinition. The civil rights movement, to be sure, involved the public issue of race, but it began with a single woman feeling a certain way about giving up her seat to someone else because of her color. Like the 1954 decision on segregated schools, it was decided on the basis of injury to self-esteem. Yet these were inevitably political events.

In any case, a related and significant cultural shift had been in the making for some time. It is well described by the political scientist Jeffrey Abramson: "As against an older republican tradition which identified freedom with public space, communal solidarity, and the activity of citizenship, freedom in modern society is most often envisioned as the personal achievement of individuals in private space—a matter of abolishing external constraints on the expression of one's inner or authentic self . . . In the older, republican vision of freedom, political liberation was basic to personal liberation, because it was the community itself—and the public loyalties and virtues it spawned—that gave the self its character as well as its aims and purposes in life. By contrast, among ourselves it is the act of dispossessing the self of community, of tradition and religion and family, that is commonly seen as therapeutic and liberating."[23] Freud's complex conception of the self shows that this desired dispossession is an ideal tendency, particularly with regard to family. It also shows that therapy is a stoic form of liberation.

Freud spoke to an anxious but not an alienated self. For, as Abramson says, he can be seen, paradoxically, "as contributing to a more communitarian vision of liberation and well-being. He does this by setting out in [an] unsurpassed manner the limits to the competing, atomized understanding of liberation."[24] Writing in the 1970s, Abramson sees with special clarity that "Freud foresaw and criticized the modern appeal of an ethic of self-assertion and spontaneity, an ethic that has its roots in Nietzsche but parades today under the banners of the permissive society and sexual liberation. Against any such easy understanding of liberty as license for naturalness and self-expression, Freud explored the internal contradictions of erotic life" (2). There is some question, though, about whether Freud foresaw the extent of sexual permissiveness or if he did not, from his Victorian perspective, exaggerate the repressiveness of society. But, as Rieff notes, "it was an accommodation to social authority that he envisaged not its abolition."[25] Abramson and Rieff give us an accurate picture of Freud as a liberal who accepts some repression. His solution too is liberal. Rieff points out that his "very aim, to educate the ruling ego, is a sure mark of Freud's classical liberalism. By enfranchising the uneducable populace of sexuality, Freud seeks to bring it into responsible relations with the ruling power. To the liberal political tradition, with its belief that the 'two nations' could be brought together, Freud offered a supporting parallel in psychological and moral theory, for he desired, as far as possible, to bring the instinctual unconscious into the rational community" (345). In other words, through analysis, or just growing up, Freud hoped for a mediating moral agency in the face of determining factors. This conservative liberalism, this resolution, was one of the conspicuous possibilities of the postwar period. If the culture of psychoanalysis intensified the American indifference to practical politics, its doing so was political in its own way.

2

FREUD AND OTHERS ON AGGRESSION

The concept of aggression evolved in Freud's palimpsest mind. Freud is always a dualist; he always sees psychology in terms of dynamic struggle. But the terms of the struggle change. For two decades, instinctual conflict meant the struggle between erotic and self-preservative instincts. The essay "On Narcissism" (1914) breaks this dualism in focusing on self-love. Conflict is now seen between two forms of sexual instinct. A year later, in "Instincts and Their Vicissitudes" (1915), he went beyond the sexual to say that the ego contained what he came to call an aggressive instinct. Manifested as a drive for mastery, it was, in part, self-preservative. For the first time aggression is equated with health, though war is soon seen to be a perversion of developmentally necessary aggression. So the new opposition was between the sexual and aggressive drives, one which mainstream psychoanalytic theory stayed with for a long time and still finds durable, to the extent that it still deals with drive theory. This change was clarified in Freud's *The Ego and the Id*, in which aggressive trends are, as Edward Bibring says, "no longer primary attributes of the ego instincts" but "independent instincts of aggression and destruction" existing side by side with the ego instincts.[1] Freud no longer sees ego instincts as independent entities but as derived partly from libidinal and partly from aggressive instincts, from eros and death,[2] which he later called primal instincts. In *Civilization and Its Discontents*, Freud meditates on the outward effects of the death instinct.

The ego psychologists Heinz Hartmann, Ernst Kris, and Rudolph Loewenstein focus on the structural theory advanced in *The Ego and the Id*, emphasizing that the ego has no drives of its own.[3] Drives are the motor force of the id, but unlike the instinct, the drive cannot reach its goal without the ego's intervention. The ego is a learning process, and the gratification of drives is guaranteed by learning. The ego psychologists consider that they clarify rather than modify Freud, eliminating contradictions rather than supplying redefinitions.

Aggression has to be distinguished from the drive to mastery. Some kinds of mastery are correlated to the ego. Some types of mastery are manifestations of aggression, which means that aggressive impulses may be seen as manifestations of an innate destructive drive. Freud had elaborated on the life and death instincts in *Beyond the Pleasure Principle*, where he said that there are ego and object instincts that were not libidinal. Later, in *Civilization and Its Discontents*, he writes: "I can no longer understand how we can have overlooked the ubiquity of non-erotic aggressivity and destructiveness" (*SE* 21: 120). Freud here considers this inclination to aggression "the greatest impediment to civilization" (*SE* 21:122). Those who dismiss Freud's dualism of eros and death instincts tend to dismiss the existence of a primary drive toward aggression as well. Ego psychology does not, though it leaves proof of a death instinct to biology; that is, it never affirms it.

Albert Solnit puts the basically Freudian ego psychology view clearly: "Aggression and libido coexist and are viewed in terms of ego's relationship to id. When this coexistence is characterized by what is termed fusion, aggression can be influenced and channeled into constructive expressions; where it is defused, as in aggressive states, aggression becomes destructive and hinders developmental advances." Of course, fusion depends on "a satisfactory relationship to the love object, i.e., libidinal ties promote the availability of aggressive-drive energies so they can be modified and subject to the dominant role of the ego."[4] At its most sustaining, Hartmann's adaptational ego psychology married aggression to assertiveness and what it called self-actualization. In any case, aggression may be seen as destructive or as constructive. Freud said that the man who first flung an epithet instead of a spear at his enemy was the true founder of civilization. Two cheers for civilization and aggression.

How about three cheers for aggression? Opposed to ego psychology accommodation is the Freud scholar and deconstructionist literary critic Leo Bersani. In *The Freudian Body*, he maintains that the aggressive instinct derives from the death instinct, and in this he is closer to some of Freud's insights, those that have generally not been accepted. To Bersani, aggressiveness evokes the oceanic feeling described in *Civilization and Its Discontents*, traceable to what Freud calls the "limitless narcissism" (*SE:* 21,72) of infancy. Bersani is attracted to the limitless. He seems to forget that Freud is talking about the indirect influence of infancy. And although Freud points to the bonds between love and hate, libido and aggression, he does not say, as Bersani does, that destructiveness "is identical with love."[5] Rather, as Philip Rieff has it, Freud holds that "the law of 'primal ambivalence' . . . provides every strong hate with a counterpart of love, and hobbles every act of aggression with a subsequent burden of guilt."[6] Ambivalence inserts, then, into the social contract, "a reassertion of the will of the father against the rebellious impulses of a chastened sonship" (223). But Bersani is interested neither in the social contract nor in guilt. For him, the process of maturation is "biologically dysfunctional."[7] Indeed, sexuality "is intolerable to the structured self" (38), so Freud's psychology is rigid rather than flexible. Bersani thinks that masochism, for example, is not grounded in "parental vicissitudes" but in an ontology of sexuality itself. That is, sexuality "could be thought of as a tautology for masochism" (39). Sexuality, after all, is not an exchange between individuals but "a condition of broken negotiations with the world" (40), a choice for extinction rather than survival. For Bersani, masochism is both relieved and fulfilled by death. Life is a sort of snuff film. Forget reproduction, forget the unification of the sexes, forget nirvana in its aspect of tension reduction. Forget Freud?

Deconstruction runs the risk of doing just that. Bersani thinks it "naive to take what might be called the official Freud literally, to assume he is saying what, for the most part, he obviously thought he was saying" (1–2). In other words, Freud did not understand his own ideas. Bersani wants "to celebrate a kind of failure in Freud's thought." To do so he advances the deconstructionist gestalt: "the psychoanalytic authenticity of Freud's work *depends* on a process of theoretical collapse" (3). While it is true that Freud was often engaged in the process of refining his concepts, it is not true to say, as Bersani does, that he was engaged in the process of subverting his principal arguments. In psychoanalysis Freud shows how the unconscious subverts the conscious, but there is always something beyond the subversion. Bersani exaggerates Freud the theoretician at the expense of Freud the empiricist. He cites Beckett's Molloy as an exemplar in the battle against "thought," which "far from providing a guarantee of being in this radically non-Cartesian world, is the excrement of being" (11). But he invokes the shit standard too quickly, for the thrust of Freud's system is non-Cartesian. For Bersani, Freud's failure resides in his putative timidity to live by the radicality of *Three Essays*. Instead he became the moral policeman of *The Ego and the Id*, "relentlessly pursu[ing] the project of domesticating and rationalizing the sexual in a historical narrative and a psychic structure" (102). In thus repressing the eroticized psychoanalytic text, Freud invited the reduction of psychoanalysis to ego psychology.

Freud does say that even with complete sexual liberation, something he considers only hypothetically, the indestructible destructiveness of human beings would still be with us. But Freud, unlike Bersani, derives no satisfaction from this. Freud is thinking at this point in *Civilization and Its Discontents* of the corrosive effects of the superego, which he considers tragically. The central conundrum of civilization and the cause of our discontent is the guilt it imposes on the ego for its Oedipal aggression, even when this aggression is renounced. The superego is not, as Bersani says it is, "merely a cultural metaphor for the psychic fulfillment in each of us of a narcissistically thrilling wish to destroy the world."[8] Nor is "necessity" in Freud "at least implicitly, an *apology for violence*" (24). Bersani is attuned to ferocity; Freud is not.

Bersani and Norman O. Brown are drawn to the nirvana principle as an expression of the limitless. As an expression of the death instinct it, too, abolishes the ego, dissipates the pull of self-preservation and self-assertion. It smiles at the civilizing principle of Apollonian restraint and proportion. Rieff argues that pleasure to Freud "was just the sense of transition from an excess to a deficiency of mental energy. It was a decline in the tension of life, involving a regret as great in its way as the one involved in pain. It followed, then, that death might be the greatest pleasure."[9] So much for transfiguration through destruction. Freud's positing of a nirvana principle causes Rieff to say: "There is something Oriental in the Freudian ethic." He sees that, for Freud, "only one way lies open to escape the dissatisfactions inherent in every satisfaction, and that is to grow equable." With none of the Buddhist supreme liberation and bliss, there is neither the sense of perpetual bondage that the desires have imposed, nor its attendant asceticism. It is nonetheless puzzling to reflect on the evolution of ideas in a thinker so attuned to the determined and subsequently so drawn to the unconditioned. It may, however, be the perfectly logical or, rather, psychological sequence, like taking a week off to do nothing after a year of working in the mines. Still, the expression on the face of the Buddha experiencing nirvana in, say, the Ajanta Caves of India, is nothing like the expression of the later Freud. And the long-term New York analysand may appear more like a desensitized tooth than a reclining Buddha. The Western appropriation of ancient Far Eastern motifs is generally problematic, even in Freud. For ancient Buddhists, nirvana was a principle of belief. For Freud, it is the ultimate relief. A psychoanalyst once told me that the profession has never been the same since the introduction of Valium. And now there is Prozac.

The death instinct may be, as Rieff says, "the greatest pleasure." Rieff follows the path that others have taken when he goes on to suggest that the pleasure principle might be "more justly named the principle of pleasure-pain, for, conversely, pain was the transition from a feeling of deficiency to one of excess. Pleasure registers the decrease of pain, a temporary relief from the intensities of living."[10] But for Bersani and Brown it is not merely a question of relief but one of transcendence. Rieff is more true to Freud's intent; Bersani and Brown are saving Freud from himself.

Freud himself considered the death instinct speculative. It may have had a personal basis. Ernest Jones observes that Freud was preoccupied with death, "the dread of it and the wish for it."[11] Max Schur, Freud's physician and another biographer, confirms this.[12] Freud states in *Beyond the Pleasure Principle* that "everything living dies for internal reasons—becomes inorganic once again." Hence, "the aim of all life is death" (*SE* 18:39). Jones argues that Freud's idea that the fundamental aim of all the instincts is to revert to an earlier state, a regression, can receive no support from biology, that Freud confuses *telos* with finis. Jones remains skeptical about Freud's crossing from the mental to the inorganic.

Another telling argument from the mental to the inorganic is made by Otto Fenichel. He holds that the death instinct does not meet Freud's definition of instinct: the demand made by the body on the mind—that is, excitement and relaxation. Freud says that the erotic is to assimilation (creation) what death is to dissimilation (objective destruction). But the parallel is specious since "instinct aims at eliminating the somatic charge which we designate as the source of the instinct; but the death instinct does not aim to eliminate dissimulation."[13] So the eros-death juxtaposition does not work. For Fenichel, the death instinct is really not an instinct at all but a principle, the nirvana principle: it "permits a view of all psychological processes and all life processes in general." Fenichel does not completely deny the existence of a death instinct, only its symmetrical opposition to eros. Moreover, Fenichel holds, it is in the sexual instincts that the Freudian longing for quiescence and the conservative nature of the instincts can best be seen.

A more recent psychodynamic psychoanalyst, Robert Stoller, is appreciative of Freud as the first major thinker about early childhood but dismissive of Freud's dualism of the eros and death instincts. Stoller points out, as have some philosophers of science, that Freud's "predilection for biologizing had him reading primeval psychological motivation (for example, life versus death instincts) into such mechanistic processes as cell function and even molecular chemistry."[14]

Whether or not the love and death instincts are primary, whatever their validity as metapsychological determinants, the validity of libidinal and aggressive drives is sufficient unto the personal day—and night. This becomes evident in any ABC of S and M. Once we focus on these drives, Freud's analysis of sadism and masochism takes on considerable clarity. Freud becomes more cogent when we move from the cosmos to the bedroom. In the much revised *Three Essays*, Freud calls sadism and masochism "the most common and the most significant of all the perversions." He refers to "the desire to inflict pain upon the sexual object and the reverse" (*SE* 7:157).

Considering sadism, Freud says that "the roots are easy to detect in the normal," since "the sexuality of most male human beings contains an element of aggressiveness—a desire to subjugate" (ibid.). He notes that the "biological significance of it seems to lie in the need for overcoming the resistance of the object by means other than the process of wooing." There is implicit in sadism, Freud believes, the desire to tear down the civilized veil. With this, all of our novelists of ferocity would agree. Unlike these writers—in their various ways—Freud does not consider sadism honorifically. It occurs when "an aggressive component of the sexual instinct . . . has become independent and exaggerated and, by displacement, has usurped the leading position" (*SE* 7:158). Moreover, Freud distinguishes between "cases merely characterized by an active or violent attitude to the sexual object," which is the sadism of "ordinary speech," and cases "in which satisfaction is entirely conditional on the humiliation and maltreatment of the object." Strictly speaking, he notes, "it is only this last extreme instance which deserves to be described as a perversion."[15] Sade is the only one of our fiction writers to continually satisfy all criteria in his work (and to a lesser degree in his life). The other writers do so in varying degrees, with Bataille and Mailer representing something like discipleship. I am, of course, applying clinical terminology to art, which Freud considers a substitute gratification. I do not intend to treat writers as cases, or novels as case studies, but I do want to establish a connection between clinical categories and imaginative constructs.

Freud notes that perversions were first considered to be "indications of degeneration and disease," but he maintains that "most of these extensions, or at any rate the less severe of them, are constituents which are rarely absent from the sexual life of healthy people, and are judged by them no differently from other intimate events" (*SE* 7:160). He holds that the word " 'perversion' should not be used as a term of reproach." Time seems to have done him one better. It speaks to Freud's influence, unintended though it is in this case, that the word seems to have dropped out of the language. Like *nymphomaniac*. Freud did believe that "normal" people can, "under the domination of the most unruly of all the instincts" be sick in sex, as in necrophilia, and that "abnormality" in general "can invariably be shown to have a background of abnormal sexual conduct" (7:161). The crux is this: if a perversion ousts the normal sexual aim, if it is a fixation, then it is usually pathological. Freud is not a believer in the sexually normal but in the sexually normative.

Where sadism is active, masochism is passive, "the extreme instance of which," says Freud, "appears to be that in which satisfaction is conditional upon suffering physical or mental pain at the hands of the sexual object" (*SE* 7:161). Freud believes that "masochism is nothing more than an extension of sadism turned round upon the subject's own self" (7:158), and that a "sadist is always at the same time a masochist, although the active or the passive aspect of the perversion may be the more strongly developed in him and may represent his predominant sexual activity" (7:159). In *Three Essays*, Freud considers both sadism and masochism to be outcomes of the aggressive instincts. However, they are even more representative of "the opposing masculinity and femininity which are combined in bisexuality" (7:160) or of activity and passivity, a given in Freud's polymorphous perversity. Perversity in this sense is not perversion but a description of the infant's protean nature.

Freud's ideas on sadomasochism are considerably deepened in the landmark essay "A Child is Being Beaten." Here he focuses on the aetiology of aggression, leaning heavily on the Oedipus complex. Freud reasons that "a sense of guilt is invariably the factor that transforms sadism into masochism," though this is not "the whole content of masochism . . . a share must also fall to the love-impulse" (*SE* 17:189). Freud is speaking of children "in whom the sadistic component was able for constitutional reasons to develop prematurely," who therefore "find it particularly easy to hark back to the pregenital, sadistic, anal organization of their sexual life" (ibid.). He says that "where the genital organization is met by repression . . . every psychical representation of the incestuous love becomes unconscious" and "there is a regressive debasement of the genital organization itself to a lower level. 'My father loves me' was meant in a genital sense; owing to the regression it is turned into 'My father is beating me' . . . This being beaten is now a convergence of the sense of guilt and sexual love. *It is not only the punishment for the forbidden sexual relation, but also the regressive substitute for that relation*, and from this latter source it derives the libidinal excitation which is from this time forward attached to it . . . Here for the first time we have the essence of masochism."

Masochism is defensive, not just instinctual. The man can play the role of the mischievous boy going to be punished. In this example, masochism is a defense against castration and object loss, which turns a threatening parent into an accepting one. Oedipal balance is maintained, Oedipal guilt is assuaged. There is a parallel in religion where, say, a Christian may give dramatic proof of giving up forbidden sexual and aggressive tendencies, sometimes famously so—though, as Stuart Asch has remarked, it is difficult to conceive of Origen's self-castration as a defense against castration (clinically, gender identity disorder is involved).[16] Such are the vicissitudes of belief. This says something as well about the nature of God Almighty. In *The Ego and the Id*, Freud points out that the superego retains the character of the father. The more powerful the Oedipus complex, the more rapidly it succumbs to repression, "the stricter will be the domination of the superego over the ego later on" (*SE* 19:34).

The strict superego in connection with the strong ego gives rise to many related phenomena which are not sadomasochistic in the clinical sense. Arnold Cooper, for example, speaks of the pain that serves a need for self-definition—that is, mastery—giving as examples the pleasurable fatigue after a day's work, the ecstasy of the athlete's exhaustion, the dogged pursuit of a distant goal, the willingness to cling to an absurd ideal, and the hero's ordeal.[17] Cooper wants to present pain in terms of its defensive and adaptive functions, without recourse to a primary drive. It seems, on this view, that any worthwhile achievement has a sadomasochistic resonance. Perhaps, but this is not to be confused with sadomasochism as a sexual problem. And many would not conflate pain in Cooper's sense with sadomasochism at all.

More to the point, Anita Phillips says that "sexual masochism offers a way through for people who push themselves too hard, who overachieve, who are never good enough."[18] She notes that it is not just a cliché that formidable public figures seek private chastisement. And one can imagine types with a surfeit of superego—the military officer, the football coach, the business executive, the clergyman—who are sadists by day and masochists by night. Of course, one can equally well imagine such types in terms of sadism around the clock, depending on which parent is the tyrant or even just "wears the pants," real or fantasized. Phillips cites St. Theresa in her rapture—agony and ecstasy in one—with her fantasies of being lifted and pulverized. St. Theresa's revelation was accompanied by a pain so great that it made her moan. Who can doubt that Bernini's statue is, in addition to its primary spiritual meaning, an expression of orgasm? An aristocrat of Bernini's day remarked, "If this is spirituality, then I have experienced it."

Phillips regards commitment to a relationship as a form of bondage on the ethical level (though one may argue that the failure to commit is a deeper bondage). Phillips brings to mind the new *cogito* expressed on a bumper sticker: "I think, therefore I'm single." She seems to relish Bersani's Dionysian perception that being ruptured by something external is the essence of eroticism, which, if literally true, leaves the overwhelming majority of males innocent of the essence of eroticism. Bersani himself notes that "self-shattering may be intrinsic to the homo-ness in homosexuality."[19] But what, more broadly speaking, is Bersani's jouissance? It's fucking in modernese, sex as transformative gesture, if only on a personal, transient scale. Bersani modifies this idea by including as jouissance "any activities or mental states or affective processes that produce a certain degree of intensity in the organism and momentarily disturb psychic organization" (25). He includes "the transformations of sadism into masochism as an effect of such appropriations of the real as art and philosophy." Phillips holds that erotic fantasy rarely rakes up childhood events. It does, but she avoids the main question, that of aetiology. If we learn anything from Freud, it is that childhood events can be assumed to have taken place and can be uncovered. For Phillips, it is a question of master and slave, not of parent and child. Freud shows us how the two are inextricably bound.

In male masochism as it is ordinarily understood—in garden variety Freudian masochism—it is the woman who administers chastisement. But the fantasy of the mother beating is derived from the beating administered by the father long ago. In the fantasy of the male beating, according to Freud, "being beaten also stands for being loved (in a genital sense) though this has been debased to a lower level because of regression." So the unconscious "I am loved by my father" becomes the conscious "I am being beaten by my mother" (*SE* 17:198). In both the boy and the girl, the beating fantasy originates in an incestuous attachment to the father. In the boy, Freud calls it the negative Oedipus complex, denoting a feminine attitude toward the father. Freud concludes that "the boy evades his homosexuality by repressing and remodeling his unconscious fantasy: and the remarkable thing about his later conscious fantasy is that it has for its content a feminine attitude without a homosexual object-choice" (*SE* 17:199). There is often a delirious passivity involved. In D. H. Lawrence's *Sons and Lovers*, Paul Morel's anxious fantasizing about the voluptuous Clara Dawes as a larger-than-life figure at the theater is a case in point. Henry Miller's vivid masochistic delirium at the end of *Sexus*, in response to Mara's formidable dyke lover, is a related example, though here the masochism takes the form of dehumanization, with Henry barking like a dog. In Miller's life, the mother was the aggressive, threatening figure to begin with. Gudrun's sexual relation with Gerald in *Women in Love* is a female version of an intense, ambivalent masochism. Gerald is almost the perfect sadist, but he does not quite strangle her. The climax of "The Woman Who Rode Away" is self-destruction as transcendence. Frieda Lawrence has wisely observed that, in "The Prussian Officer," Lawrence is both characters. We may add that the woman who rode away is a Lawrence persona as much as the Mexican Indians who destroy her through sacrifice.

"The Woman Who Rode Away" is seen by some as an illustration of a moral masochism that originates in the death instinct but that has never made it outward as aggression. In "The Economic Problem of Masochism," however, Freud says that there is a mitigating factor in such aggression. Since "it has the significance of an erotic component, even the subject's destruction of himself cannot take place without libidinal satisfaction" (*SE* 19:170). In this connection, Otto Kernberg notes that sexual masochism may be severely destructive as well.[20] He is speaking of borderline personalities who regress from a neurotic to a psychotic state, with a consequent danger of mutilation and death. There is a lack of integration of superego functions; there is bisexuality and primitive aggression. In extreme forms there is self-castration, as in religious ritual or submission to an idealized, severely sadistic primitive object. The woman who rode away also crosses the border, which in its general sense, is a state that particularly fascinated Lawrence. Paradoxically, Kernberg says, there is in extreme submissiveness a sense of triumph over life and death, pain and fear, and unconsciously, the world of object relations, as there is in Lawrence's heroine. For Kernberg and others, Freud's later linkage of masochism to the death instinct dilutes the meaning, the personal significance, of masochism. Masochism provides narcissistic gratification.

Freud's "The Economic Problem of Masochism" (the word *sadism* does not appear in the title of any essay by Freud) defines aggression through the death instinct. The part of the instinct "placed directly in the service of the sexual function" is "sadism proper." When the libido directs the death instinct outward toward objects in the external world, the instinct is then called "the destructive instinct, the instinct for mastery, or the will to power" (*SE* 19:163). The part remaining "inside the organism" is "the original erotogenic masochism" (*SE* 19:164). We never have to deal with the pure life or death instinct but with a fusion or defusion of them, which means that the death instinct is "tamed" by libido. The exception is when it is not bound to the admixtures of libido, when it refuses to be tamed. The death instinct may present a non-erotic aggressivity, Freud says in *Civilization and Its Discontents* (*SE* 21:120).

Freud's later writings distinguish between a primary sadism and a primary masochism (the death instinct operative in the organism), both beyond the pleasure principle and tied into the death instinct. Primary masochism is one that no longer derives from sadism. The feminine and moral masochism derive from the primary or erotogenic masochism, reflecting the need for punishment stemming from an excessively hard superego. "Sadism which cannot find employment in actual life," Freud says, "is turned around upon the subject's own self and so produces a secondary masochism, which is superadded to the primary kind" (*SE* 7:158, note 2). The pleasure principle still obtains, but not in moral masochism where the pain is only suffering. The turning back of sadism against the self is a result of cultural suppression of the instincts. Conscience makes us see "that the destructiveness which returns from the external world is also taken up by the superego," without a transformation into masochism, and "increases its sadism against the ego. The sadism of the superego and the masochism of the ego supplement each other and unite to produce the same effects." We can then see that "suppression of an instinct" generally results "in a sense of guilt and how a person's conscience becomes more severe and more sensitive the more he refrains from aggression against others" (*SE* 19:170). The superego is that much more harsh, impelled as it is by the death instinct. The superego is both the origin of repression and the outcome of Oedipal resolution. In Freud there is no innate ethical sense. He transforms the traditional humanistic view. Renunciation creates the ethical sense, not the other way around.

Insightful though it is, Freud's account of sadomasochism does not include other major scenarios. The tyrannical mother or even just the bossy one typically engenders sadism in the son. Stoller thinks that this is the origin of all perversions. The unavailable mother is a similar problem. Sade's mother was unavailable, Miller's tyrannical. The smothering mother is often seen in combination with the inept yet threatening father, as in the Oedipal triangle of *Sons and Lovers*. In the cases of Miller and Mailer, the father seemed no threat at all. Sadomasochistic fantasy may be engendered as well in Bataille's combination of the castrated yet threatening father with the hysterical yet seductive mother. First there is the wound and then there is the bow, according to the Philoctetes myth, and the bow is literature. We are primarily interested in the bow, but we must remark on the connection. In every case there is a connection between eroticism and aggression. Moreover, for these writers sexual fiction is an aggression that is mastery. Sexual aggression is inseparable from their inspiration.

There remains the question of whether sadism and masochism are situations of great significance or just fun, or some combination of both—experiences of great intensity or routine descriptions of what happens in the bedroom. It seems that once we go past the horsing around common in the bedroom, the willing suspension of disbelieve that constitutes erotic faith, real sadism and masochism are serious matters that have deep personal and cultural ramifications. To say as John Noyes does that masochism is a "staged aggression"[21] distinct from truly aggressive or violent behavior and may therefore defuse violence is to speak a half-truth that, taken as total explanation, mocks Freud's profound analysis—particularly his conclusion that the roots of extremism go back to the Oedipal struggle for genital primacy. It is not surprising that Noyes thinks that the real is a construct. Freud, of course, did not. In his idea of genital primacy, he posited something like essentialist sexual normalcy. Noyes echoes Foucault in his resentment of Freud's judging forms of sexuality to be good, indifferent, or bad—which of course is what Noyes does in his emphasis on guiltless pleasures. Why bother with psychoanalysis? Bersani says: "Free association is an expensive bore; with the whip, *jouir* becomes identical to *durcharbeiten*."[22] He obviously takes issue with the idea that the masochist seeks only pleasure. But his idea of the self-shattered ego requires a deeper insight and feeling. Freud shows us that the roots of extremity, like the roots of normalcy, stem from a deeper set of scenarios.

In the recent discussion of sexual aggression, many roads lead to Michel Foucault, the un-Freud. Yet Foucault seems to have considered himself a psychologist first and foremost. He studied psychology formally, receiving a *license* in philosophy and psychology and two *diplômes* from the Institut de Psychologie de Paris, where he treated patients. He was an instructor of psychology between 1951 and 1955 and was for a long time involved with the Rorschach test. Foucault gave considerable thought to sadomasochism, which he considered inventive, creative, and illustrative of the sexualization of pleasure—that is, the degenitalization of pleasure. He wished to root out the notion of sex between a man and a woman as the norm, and to forget the idea that sex has much of anything to do with the idea of reproduction.

Foucault is known mainly for his political ideas. Oddly enough, what is sometimes crucially missing from his ideas on sexuality is the political dimension. Sadomasochism can involve the deepest psychological enactments of mastery and slavery. Even the sympathetic Bersani must say that while Foucault spoke "so brilliantly of the body as an object of power . . . we may fail to notice how little he spoke of the body as an agent of power."[23] Foucault's central idea—that reason is an expression of power—made liberals recoil and hasten to defend individual and political agency. What would power be opposed to? On what grounds could it be opposed? How do outlooks change? Is all belief illusion? Is language mainly self-referential? David Couzens Hoy points out that "if almost everyone is still talking in the vocabulary of modern enlightenment humanism, and arguably ought to do so, then the identification of that discourse as degenerating can result only by projecting backward from an as yet fictitious standpoint." Without ascertaining that standpoint, "the critique of current-humanistic discourse is empty."[24] What standards ought to judge the present? How is the normative to be avoided? In politics? In psychoanalysis?

Foucault's key images—for example, the panopticon and the gaze—are forceful. But they are at the same time the iconography of paranoia. Lawrence Stone has said that Foucault's "recurrent emphasis on central domination and punishment as the only mediating qualities possible in personal and social relationships (needs) a strong dose of skepticism, even a sense of humor."[25] Agreed.

Foucault thought of psychoanalysis as a major controlling discourse. Despite the key role that sadomasochism played in his life—or perhaps because of it—he had little interest in Freudian aetiology. He had the family experience but missed the meaning. The meaning was exactly what he wanted to miss. Still, in *Madness and Civilization*, Foucault says that "we must do justice to Freud" because "Freud went back to madness at the level of its *language*, reconstituted one of the essential elements of an experience reduced to silence by positivism." In doing so, "he restored, in medical thought, the possibility of a dialogue with unreason"[26]—that is, a dialogue not only with the energies of the unconscious but with what Foucault calls, in a notorious phrase, the "serene world of mental illness."[27] It is as if madness had no pain other than what society imposed on it after the fact.

Foucault argues that though Freud restored the possibility of a dialogue with unreason, though he was "the first to consent not to look away" and "silenced the instances of condemnation," he "exploited the structure that enveloped the medical personage . . . preparing for its omnipotence a quasi-divine status" (277–78). Whatever scattered truth may lie in this judgment, Freud generally thought of himself as human to the point of vulnerability. Foucault finally turns on Freud, who, it seems, fumbled the ball: "He focused on this single presence . . . all the power . . . of any asylum; he transformed this into an absolute observation, a pure and circumspect silence, a judge who punishes and rewards in a judgment that does not even condescend to language" (277–78). Foucault here makes his usual confusion between the authority and the authoritarian in melodramatic terms. Freud turns out to be another repressing normalizer, another establishment pillar, another phallocrat. For Foucault, it would be disastrous to "cure" a Nerval or an Artaud—or a Foucault.

The eponymous prince of sadism, Sade, is a more compatible thinker on the question of sexual aggression. Foucault considers Sade's to be "calm, patient language"(?), which "gathers up the final words of unreason" (282). In Sade, "man rediscovers a truth he had forgotten"—namely, the truth in the rhetorical question "what desire can be contrary to nature, since it was given to man by nature itself?" A legitimate question, but Sade as a writer is no psychologist, even though he is a prime subject for psychology. Then, too, how much can he laud Sade in these terms, since Foucault develops the idea that sex is an invention rather than a discovery, that basically everything is a construct? How can he grant Sade the privilege of "nature"? Because Sade is exemplary in his ferocity. For Sade, says Foucault, "everything that morality and religion, everything that a clumsy society has stifled in man, revives in the castle of murders." And where does Foucault's ferocity and sadomasochism revive? In the castle of cultural parricide.

In volume 1 of the later, more moderate *The History of Sexuality*, Foucault's ambivalent feeling toward Freud becomes even darker. Despite "some progress" made by Freud, "one denounces Freud's conformism, the normalization functions of psychoanalysis, the obvious timidity underlying Reich's vehemence."[28] Reich may have been ferocious, but his analytic orientation was, alas, genital. Still, Freud deserves some favorable acknowledgment because "until Freud . . . the discourse on sex . . . never ceased to hide the thing it was speaking about" (53). Freud's psychoanalysis also had the virtue of opposing "the political and institutional effects of the perversion-hereditary-degenerescence system" (119). Yet Freud does not satisfy the revolutionary Foucault, who holds that "we must conceive of sex without the law, and power without the king" (91).

Volume 1 of *The History of Sexuality* is another Foucauldian production designed to knock conventional wisdom into a cocked hat. The author holds that it is not talk about sex that was repressed; on the contrary, "the deployment of sexuality" was rampant but was turned into repression by "the deployment of alliance," which made the repression all the more onerous. In plain English, the family badly compromised sexual convention. Foucault resents the incest taboo because it "guaranteed" that "this deployment of sexuality . . . would not be able to escape from the grand and ancient system of alliance" (109). He does not consider the moral or psychological dimensions of incest—it is wrong, its inhibition is necessary to culture, it severely damages people—because he sees no moral or psychological dimension to it. Not that he is interested in incest as such. He is interested in sexual self-justification. Hence Foucault dismisses the explosive issue of juvenile consent or the permanent psychic damage that ensues from such encounters on the grounds that young boys have desires, too. For Foucault, Freud's Oedipus complex is a straitjacket: "If one considers the threshold of all culture to be prohibited incest," as Freud does, "then sexuality has been from the dawn of time, under the sway of law and right" (119–20). This, in his view, is a bad thing. What is the cause of all this villainy? "The family, the keystone of alliance," says Foucault, "was the germ of all the misfortunes of sex" (111). Although psychoanalysis brought sexuality to light and called family relations into question, it is through psychoanalysis that "sexuality gave body and life to the rules of alliance by saturating them with desire" (113). So sex is not autonomous, it is created by discourse. "By creating the imaginary element that is 'sex,' " says Foucault, "the deployment of sexuality established one of its most essential internal operating principles: the desire for sex . . . It constituted sex itself as something desirable" (156). Therefore, he argues, "We must not think that by saying yes to sex, one says no to power; on the contrary, one tracks along the course laid by the general deployment of sexuality" (157). There is a sexual politics, but Foucault gives us a caricature of intellectuality in saying that "sex is the most speculative, most ideal, and most internal element in a deployment of sexuality organized by power" (155).

Foucault's rationalization of sex gives it a primary authority, more than even it can bear. Over the centuries, he tells us, sex "has become more important than our soul, more important almost than our life." He is a knowing and willing (to the extent that he admits to the reality of will) participant in "the Faustian pact, whose temptation has been instilled in us by the deployment of sexuality," that is, sexual discourse, "to exchange life in its entirety for sex itself, for the truth and sovereignty itself" (156). Once upon a time, life could make death "acceptable"; now sex does. "Sex," says Foucault, "is worth dying for" (156).[29] Many a teenage Romeo has in effect said the same, but Foucault really means it.

What exactly does he mean? Foucault distinguishes between desire and pleasure. He sees these in historical terms. People have been talking about desire for centuries. It is the core of Western discourse, part of its power structure—the deployment of sexuality in the service of the deployment of alliance. As David Halperin puts it, to Foucault desire is "not an event but a permanent feature of the subject," determinative of normalcy. Pleasure, on the other hand, is almost devoid of meaning. Hence "there is no 'pathology' of pleasure, no 'abnormal' pleasure."[30] It is somehow outside the subject. So good drugs, for example, can give pleasure. And, better yet, so can "bad" sex. One should not want to be imprisoned in "one's identity . . . one's own face." Beware the dog that denies the individual face. What Foucault wants is intense sexual pleasure that decenters the subject and fragments personal identity. "Pleasure is something that passes from one individual to another," he says, "it is not secreted by identity. Pleasure has no passport, no identification papers" (quoted in Halperin 95). "Passport" is an eloquent metaphor, but expressive of what? Foucault's paranoid tendency to confuse a face with the formal administration of it.

Why run from personal identity? Why must Foucault conceive of it as "the law, the principle, the rule" (quoted at 95) in his crude melodrama of gay hero and straight villain? He considers the Freudian self the unitary self. This is something of a straw man, since Freud's dynamic structural theory undermines just this unitary self, while at the same time showing that a self exists. It is at least a failure of imagination for Foucault to characterize this self as an object of monolithic social regulation. And it is self-congratulatory for him to picture himself as the knight of "non-disciplinary eroticism" (quoted at 96), particularly when sadomasochism involves a much more obvious sort of discipline. What is most dubious about Foucault's argument is *its* claim to exclusive pleasurability and significance. Freud taught us more about the pleasure principle than Foucault and his followers seem willing to grasp. Foucault's later claims for sadomasochism without pain and narcissism without pathology—his bruited journey from Marxism to Maoism to Jismism—constitute a trivialization of a subject that Freud deeply, humanistically defines.

3

WILHELM REICH

If Georges Bataille is an essentialist of violence, Wilhelm Reich is a progressive. It is as if the medieval and Enlightenment mentalities assumed twentieth-century modernist incarnations. An influential psychoanalytic clinician and a theoretician whose influence carried over into the literary world, Reich put Freudian categories to his own significant use. Freud found in repression a necessary limit, the price one pays for a civilization that is ultimately worth it. Reich does not recognize this limit. Does he thus reject the idea of limit? Reich is a purer antinomian than Bataille, as for Reich the moral and the natural are clearly opposed. Morality is a prison, nature a paradise—an opposition familiar since Romanticism. Given this condition, Reich sees sexual failure—including its most spectacular manifestation, sexual violence—as a consequence of capitalist social corruption. He eventually comes to think that there is no contemporary society that is not corrupt, none that is not coercive to natural impulse. Reich is a utopian who sees nature as gentle, harmonious, rhythmic, orgastic. Man is here to redeem an original tenderness. Reich pursues these fugitive goals with a ferocity that rises to hysteria in his later work. He violently proclaims a world without violence, he fulminates against sadism, he tears cruelty to pieces. Reich himself, alas, is this side of paradise.

The manacles that Reich seeks to break are forged by the mind. Conscience is, as Philip Rieff puts it, "the first tyranny."[1] Reichian therapy aims for the abolition of the superego—except, of course, for his. For Reich, all moral authority is authoritarian. Even primitive law, or taboo, is in its service. On the individual level superego, on the familial level patriarchy, and on the political level the state—all must be overthrown. "The instincts and the proletariat must triumph together, or not at all," as Rieff says (*TT* 144). His self-styled Freudo-Marxism was more Marx than Freud in the sense that he was subverting psychoanalysis to the aim of revolution, something that Freud would never do. "Political questions could be treated psychoanalytically,"

Rieff notes, "but psychoanalysis could not be treated politically. This was Reich's original heresy; for this he was read out of the movement. Depth psychology, he insisted, needed the complement of radical politics" (143). But this was not politics in the usual sense, which was, after all, another form of authority, even if it was the authority of the proletariat. Reich was a moral revolutionary, and this undercut the idea of conventional politics itself, which is one way of defining Reich's ferocity. For, as Rieff says, "not merely institutions but sentiments must be liquidated" (149). For Reich, a moral revolutionary, morality or conscience, like the state, would wither away. So would therapy: in Utopia, no one would be repressed, no one would be sick. But before Dionysian release, there must be apocalypse on the couch.

Freudo-Marxism, then, was finally more Freud than Marx. Reich thought more in terms of the individual than the collective. Nor did class struggle fit well with freedom through individual sexual expression. "My arguments," Reich says, were not " 'dictated from Moscow,' as was contended by others ... I was using these arguments against the economic theorists in the socialist movement who, with their slogans of the 'inevitable course of history' and of 'economic factors' were destroying the very people whom they professed to liberate."[2] But since he held that all of humanity is remediably ill, there could be no question of dispensing with social measures to cure individual neuroses. His Freudo-Marxism is, then, as Rieff says, "something entirely different from being a Freudian or a Marxist ... The famous Oedipus complex is a mere symptom of the authoritarian social order and is removable by the surgery of revolution" (*TT* 150). This was, of course, the sexual revolution about which he literally wrote the book.

In his oracular late style, Reich says of Freud: "A great man came and showed you your soul, but wasn't able to tell you how this soul is anchored in the body" (*LLM* 89). Reich was able. Freud's unconscious exposed the superficiality of everyday life by uncovering the power of what Reich describes as "the inferno of antisocial and perverse impulses" (*FO* 187). Reich holds that Freud does not mention satisfaction of the instincts because he does not see their purity. Reich's argument is similar to that advanced by D. H. Lawrence in *Psychoanalysis and the Unconscious* and *Fantasia of the Unconscious*. It is repression that makes the unconscious sadistic; it is the superego that falsifies natural impulse. Rather than liberation there was adaptation, adjustment, compromise. Reich fancies that Freud wrote *Civilization and Its Discontents* to refute the radical thrust of his own work. He believes that Freud is wrong in saying there that the pleasure principle "simply cannot be put into execution" (quoted in *FO* 185). To admit happiness would have meant scrapping the death instinct. "It would have meant criticism of the social institutions which destroy happiness in life," Reich maintains (*FO* 185).

But even before the late *Civilization and Its Discontents*, the work of Freud that sticks in Reich's craw is *The Ego and the Id*. Freud's great discovery was the sexual aetiology of mental disease and disturbance, and he held, following Charcot, that anxiety and neurosis were caused by sexual failure. In *The Ego and the Id*, Freud reverses this, saying that it is anxiety and neurosis that cause sexual failure. Thus Freud undercuts libido theory and establishes the centrality of the ego in its mediating function between superego and id. For Reich this is a fatal compromise, a sellout to the powers of repression.

He paints a vivid portrait of what this Freudian change meant to him as a now-confused therapist. One did not know what to do with "superego" or "unconscious guilt feelings" (100). There were, he says, no technical procedures for dealing with these. He "preferred to deal with fear of masturbation or sexual guilt feelings." He laments that "those analysts who did not practice and those who were unable to comprehend the sexual theory, began to apply the new 'ego theory.' It was a sad state of affairs. Instead of sexuality, one now talked of 'Eros.' " The superego was no longer an "auxiliary theoretical concept" but "clinical fact." Reich becomes high-spirited in his denunciation: "The Id was 'wicked'; the Superego sat there with a long beard and was 'strict'; the poor ego tried to be a go-between. Living, fluent description of facts came to be replaced by a mechanical blueprint which made all further thinking unnecessary. Clinical discussions were fewer and fewer, and speculation took their place." The end result was that "sexuality became an empty shell, the concept of 'libido' became devoid of any sexual content and turned into an empty phrase." In other words, "they still spoke of sexuality but they no longer meant it" (100–101). But they did mean it. Freud was not happy about repression, nor was he some ascetic theoretician. As everyone but Reich knows, his view was ironic and tragic. Freud was working to define a stoic concept of character.

Reich mistrusted character. He saw it as a defense, a submission to moral authority, "the prison of impulses," as Rieff puts it (*TT* 171). Rather than spontaneity there is the muck of ambivalence—in political terms, liberalism. For Freud, defense was a neutral term. The ego puts defenses into place that will modify the problematic impulses of the id. This is character. Character is supposed to be a proof of sanity, but Reich came to prefer the wisdom of psychotics. They have the advantage of a disintegrated ego, enacting, as Frederick Crews says, "the buried self in vatic form . . . ego now being the servant of the divine."³ Though Freud does not grant the ego the independence that the ego psychology of Heinz Hartmann does, he treats it with far more respect than Reich will allow. Freud's well-known late characterization of the id, in *The New Introductory Lectures*, as "a cauldron full of seething excitations" (*SE* 22:73) leaves Reich dissatisfied as to what's cooking. For him, such a description inevitably leads to character as compulsive symptom.

The ideas of character as illness, however dubious, allowed for Reich's major contribution to psychoanalysis: character armor. Building on Freud's idea of the defense, Reich notes that "it is impossible to derive the dynamics of therapy from the process of making conscious alone" (*CA* 16). In ordinary life as in analysis, the individual is characterologically armored against the outer world and his or her unconscious drives. So the analyst must be observant not only of slips but of total bodily behavior.

The metaphor of armor implies a military encasement, a dramatic form of self-imprisonment. The situation of the individual is dire, for he is embattled against himself. The therapy is correspondingly violent, a violence begotten by violence. It is therapy by confrontation, involving provocation, loud repetition, poking, a sort of benign, necessary sadism. Reich admits that character analysis creates "violent emotional outbursts and often dangerous situations," for "a great many neuroses can not be overcome by mild means." The therapy will be "unpleasant for the patient" (47). As it will be for the doctor when the patient mounts a violent counterattack. The Reichian therapy is institutionalized ferocity. It normalizes romantic rebellion, but in a way that is paradoxically authoritarian. This scourge of authoritarian consequences, this prophet of release tyrannized his patients—all for the sake of deinhibition. As long as the armor was intact, the best the patient could achieve was an intellectual understanding. This has little therapeutic effect.

Reich's originality is to place the therapeutic emphasis not on the content of neurotic fantasy but on energy function, not on what the patient says but on his manner of saying it. The *how* is more important than the *what*, Reich emphasizes. Words can lie, but the mode of expression does not. "It is the immediate unconscious manifestation of character," says this seeker beyond the mask (*FO* 145). "For years," Reich boasts, "patients have not heard any psychoanalytic technical terms from me. They were thus deprived of the possibility of covering up an instinctual desire behind a word" (146). Is there no instinctual desire for verbal expression? Don't infants babble eloquently? Reich's method reflects his radical subordination of mind to body. In his own way, this monist expresses an inverse dualism. The Reichian ideal, Rieff notes, is not the man who thinks but the man who acts; we can, therefore, "see the revolutionary sentiment running counter to the entire Western intellectual tradition with its ideal of discursive rationality" (*TT* 164). This ideal has fallen on difficult times. As Rieff says, for Reich, "repression began the moment man made the mistake of thinking about himself, ceasing thus to trust his 'instinctual judgment.'" Man, like a Freudian analyst, "began to think when he felt threatened by his own instinctual energies." In short, Reich reverses the intellectualism of the liberal tradition "in which ignorance is blamed for the human condition" that "may be cured by self-knowledge only" (153). The wisdom of the Delphic oracle—know thyself—is supplanted by a clinical Orphism.

Reich accordingly rejects the invisible analyst—our Delphic oracle?—because he is objective, Olympian, sexless. How could the patient make critical remarks? The analyst should invite criticism, dramatizing the all-important transference. Patients should look at me, says Reich, in "an un-authoritative, *human* way" (*FO* 147). And this from an analyst given to tyrannizing, and with a host of patient followers! Still, many were independent. In any case, Reich's point is that the fear of sex that makes a patient ill must be overcome. "No patient was claimed to be cured," he informs us, "unless he was able at least to masturbate without guilt feelings" (148). The talking cure ideally became the fucking cure, the patient miming the sexual act, often, apparently, in nudity, all defenses stripped away. Reich had only a very occasional affair with a patient. But, with the exception of the one he married, this ended their connection—whether this was a matter of professional ethics or sexual cure is not clear.

Reich's "vegetotherapy," with its subliminal suggestion that healthy people aspired to be vegetables, indicated a Romantic primitivism so radical as to take the psyche out of psychoanalysis. The terms implies, as Charles Rycroft says, the vegetative nervous system or what is not subject to voluntary control —the heart, the intestines, the genitals, the organs not capable of being directly affected by acts of will. But, as Rycroft notes, Reich's use of the word was often arbitrary, meaning good, natural, spontaneous, or sexual, quite apart from the neurophysiological process he is describing.[4] Much vegetotherapy is concerned with "muscular armor" or voluntary muscles, such as the inhibition of respiration, a primary defense mechanism of neurotics. For Reich, the problem with psychoanalysis is that it has no physiological meaning. Psychoanalysis interprets, and Reich is one of the first to be, in Susan Sontag's expression, against interpretation.[5] Reich insists that the loosening of rigid muscular attitudes is not the result or the cause of psychic processes, "they were simply these processes themselves in the somatic sphere" (*FO* 242). What is Reich's therapy but a prioritizing of our animal nature? Even in the act of intercourse, animals are exemplary. Full orgasm should not involve the telltale effort of pelvic thrust, as animals show us in their quick, sleek movements. Man should ape apes. Reich's sentimental primitivism may have the virtue of restoring to us a sense of the value of humanism. It is probably better to be a human being than some fucking animal. What is most valuable in man is, often, the transcendence of nature that makes for civilization, expensive though it is.

Not all of Reich gravitates toward the extreme. Rycroft reminds us of what can easily be overlooked, that there is a "sensible" aspect to Reich's views about strict toilet training, for example, or the prohibition of childhood masturbation, as there is about the effects of poverty and the problems of inadequate privacy.[6] Among his enduring contributions are character classifications, most notably phallic narcissist, a category of particular relevance to this literary study. The phallic narcissist is the man with pride in phallus, real or fantasized. To this man's unconscious, Reich says, "the penis is not in the service of love but is an instrument of aggression and vengeance. This is the basis of his strong erective potency as well as his ability to experience orgasm . . . In men, one often finds that the mother was the stronger of the parents, or the father had died early or was otherwise out of the picture" (*CA* 203). This parental scenario obtains in Lawrence, Bataille, Miller, and Mailer. The instance of Sade indicates that the absentee mother (and remote father) can, by virtue of the logic of extremes meeting, have a similar effect. Reich seems to explain the link when he speaks of a "frustration of genital and exhibitionistic activity . . . by the very person toward whom the genital interest is displayed . . . the mother is retained as an object with only narcissistic attitudes and impulses of sadistic revenge." Reich concludes: "In such men, the sexual act has the unconscious meaning of again and again proving to the woman how potent they are; at the same time it means piercing, or destroying the woman, in a more superficial layer degrading her" (203). Sade's mother-in-law made her own vivifying contribution to this iconography. (The female phallic narcissist is castrating, taking vengeance on the man—in Sade's case, a justifiable vengeance.) The disturbed potency of the phallic narcissist manifests a labile mood in which there is "a rapid alternation of hypomanic self-confident phases and phases of severe depression" (204). Elsewhere, Reich says that "they are always found among army officers of the Prussian type, Don Juans and other compulsively self-confident individuals. They all suffer from a severe orgastic disturbance. To them, the sexual act is nothing but an evacuation, followed by a reaction of disgust. They do not embrace a woman, they 'make' her. Their sexual behavior creates among women an intense disgust for the act" (*FO* 139). If this sounds like a feminist critique on Sade, Miller, and Mailer, it is because Reich was a feminist. Even some of Lawrence's characters fit the description, notably, Gerald Crich. Reich says that "the phallic narcissistic character . . . wards off his anal and passive homosexual impulses with the aid of phallic aggression" (*CA* 204), though one particular Prussian officer, Lawrence's, is not capable of doing so. This critical characterization sounds like Mailer's Denise Gondelman, the feisty New York University sophomore of Mailer's "The Time of Her Time," lecturing her phallic-narcissist conquerer, Sergius O'Shaughnessy. She is presented satirically by Mailer, but what she says may be true.

On this subject, Reich goes even further. He says that the "relationship between genius and criminality . . . belongs . . . predominantly to the phallic-narcissist character. Most of the sex murderers of recent history . . . have suffered the most severe infantile disappointments in love and later realized their phallic-sadistic vengeance on the love object" (206). Mailer's Rojack is an insistent fantasy projection. Mailer himself had a finger in this pie. And his esteemed Marquis de Sade is *the* literary manifestation of genius as criminal. "The combination of phallic narcissism, phallic sadism and simultaneous compensation of passive and anal homosexual strivings makes for the most energetic characters," Reich maintains (206). This energy can become literary in one degree or another, and these writers share a cardinal characteristic: a tendency toward bombast, an indefatigable verbal sadism that realizes itself in tome after lurid tome spiked with tirades—a tendency they share with Reich himself, something of a stylist in his own right. It is almost as if the sexual interpretation of experience cannot seize reality without doing violence to it. Reich says that whether one is a genius or a criminal depends largely on the social atmosphere and the possibilities of the energy in sublimated form. These writers all found their forms. Reich helps to explain the propinquity of genius to crime. So much depends, in his view, on the level of genital gratification. He holds that "analysis is always successful if one succeeds in unmasking the phallic-narcissistic attitudes as a defense against passive-feminine tendencies and in eliminating the unconscious tendency of revenge against the other sex" (206). To be a man means to be spontaneously tender.

This is just what Reich's ideal man, the genital character (for example,

Lawrence's Mellors), is. Reich's world rests on a paradox. Can one have character and not be armored? The genital character is, of course, not the neurotic character. Yet Reich admits that none of his patients ever became genital characters. As Rieff notes, "even the therapists could not help but bring some repressions with them" (*TT* 173). But even an idealized character is a character and has qualities. Rieff explains Reich's idealized genital character (*CA* 169). He is " 'post-ambivalent' (meaning: free of the Oedipus complex and all other constricting conflicts and strains); 'aggression-sublimated' (meaning: cultured but quite able to use his fists and feet when provoked); 'sex-affirmative' (meaning: unfettered by the aspirations of his parents) and with a 'high degree of harmony between id and superego' " (*TT* 171). Having reached a neutral plateau of health, he is happy but angry, capable of love and hatred, childlike but not infantile. Androgyny, however, is not one of his qualities. Unlike Norman O. Brown, Reich does not want to get back to the Freudian pregenital. He is more than willing to pay the price of forgetting that for culture.

The genital character, however, is up against it. He is encumbered by the prevalence of what Reich calls the emotional plague, which is derived from the genital frustration that is very widespread in modern life. Hence the pervasiveness of schizophrenia, heart disease, and cancer. Reich does not distinguish here between mental and physiological illness, consistent with his view that the body is the mind. Still, there are particular consequences for human behavior. What we see in the grim first half of the twentieth century is "a pandemic, in the form of a gigantic break-through of sadism and criminality, such as the Catholic Inquisition of the middle ages or the international fascism of the present century" (*CA* 248). The pandemic is active in "mysticism in its most destructive form; passive and active striving for authority; moralism . . . party politics, the familial plague which I termed 'familitis'; sadistic methods of upbringing; masochistic toleration of such methods or criminal rebellion against them; authoritarian race hatred . . . or even the principle of politics in general . . . to wit, greed for power and advantage" (252). Moreover, for Reich, virtually everyone has made the putative Freudian error of confusing the genital with the perverse—even writers of serious sexual fiction, who dramatize an un-Reichian category, the orgastic neurotic.[7]

Reich notes that in full-blown cases of impotence, "sadism . . . is never absent" (*CA* 213). The plague-ridden individual is "always sadistic and pornographic." In him there is the "simultaneous existence of sexual lasciviousness (because of incapacity for sexual gratification) and *sadistic moralism*"

(260). Natural love life is persecuted under the guise of "culture" and "morals." All this makes for what he later calls "the pornographic flood of a free-for-all fucking epidemic" and "the fucker chaos" (*MC* 95), reminiscent of the declining Roman Empire. How these sexologues loathe promiscuity! It is the ultimate travesty of nature, the defacing of the inner sanctum. *Nature* is a key word in Reich, and he is hardly the first to ascribe his own values to it. Nature is the instincts, and the instincts are good. God is natural law. The "*unity of culture and nature*," he tells us, is contingent on "the biological demands of natural (orgastic) gratification" (*FO* xx). A good orgasm, as Mailer would put it, is a triumph of nature over corrupt convention. Orgastic patients no longer went to prostitutes. Women formerly promiscuous now wanted one lover who satisfied them (not necessarily the husband), though not a mate for life, not monogamy—which is not natural. Yet orgasm does not rout morality, Reich argues, only repressive morality. It subsumes the best of "official morality." So, for example, "one does not rape women or seduce children." This is moral but not the morality of "Thou shalt" and "Thou shalt not" (153). Freedom came into being when "the deep chasm between 'I want to' and 'I dare not' disappeared" (154). Chastity, for Reich, is not a moral possibility; there can be no healthy celibacy. It is unnatural, moral in the pejorative sense. Nor is it possible to be monogamous and genitally strong, though he later concedes that marriage can be a "decent bondage"—that is, in "every naturally growing marriage," which includes "love and contact and mutual surrender and body delight" (*MC* 28).

This quote is from *The Murder of Christ*, which really should be called *The Martyrdom of Reich*, the book that Reich considered his most important. The point of Christ's life is that "he knew love in the body and woman as he knew so many other things natural" (32). Reich's Christ, "who is nature himself," knows that "Nature and God are one" (20). Reich maintains that it was the women who loved Christ in the body, "and not his admirers and disciples who had only sucked life from his body" who were "present at the last agony"—that is, Mary Cleophas; Mary Magdalene; Joanna, the wife of Chuza; Salome; and others, according to Ernest Renan.[8] Reich notes with regret that there is "no trace of the very essence of Christ's life, of the women who had loved Christ's body" (151).

Like Jesus, Reich is persecuted by the sick, ungrateful little man—democratic man—for trying to make him a healthy genital character. People are just not big enough for the messianic. When Reich says that "a lonely, persecuted writer will, two thousand years later, understand this deepest secret and write a little book, 'The Man Who Died,'" he unites himself with Jesus and D. H. Lawrence to form an orgastic, salvationary triumvirate. In Lawrence, Reich found a kindred spirit, another utopian sexual visionary who in this work identifies with Christ, a role not unfamiliar to him. Reich and Lawrence felt that nature was good; they were Romantic vitalists who, like members of the early mystery cults, worshipped life. Both even tried to establish a Utopia, Rananim and Organon, respectively. Reich's rather simplistically emphasizes the obvious salvationary quality of orgasm, the ultimate act. For Lawrence sex was penultimate, the coming into man-and-womanness being primary—and difficult, since there is something in the narcissistic self that resists dual identity. Yet for both men nature or the cosmos—what Reich calls the "Cosmic Energy Ocean"—is primarily sexual, not moral. The universe is erotic.

The lack of living, mystical connection with this truth is what causes aggression. There is no primary destructiveness for Reich. "What I never could find in my clinical work," he says, "was a will to die, a death instinct as primary impulse, corresponding to the sexual instinct or the need for food" (*FO* 130). The death instinct is really the product of neurosis. Reich reduces the death instinct, in the sense of longing for dissolution or nothingness, to unconscious longing for orgastic release of tension. Reich holds, moreover, that there is no primary pleasure in destruction. We destroy in a dangerous situation because we want to live and do not want to suffer anxiety. An animal does not kill another animal for the pleasure of killing: "that would be sadistic murder for pleasure's sake" (131). It kills because it is hungry or threatened. But, as Rycroft argues, Reich is mistaken in thinking animals peaceful. He ignores the aggressiveness associated with territoriality (described by Konrad Lorenz and Robert Ardrey) and the establishment of pecking orders. Make love, not war—a perfectly Reichian slogan—ignores the realities of power, as Rycroft insists. Reich goes so far as to say that aggression in the strict sense of the word has nothing to do with either sadism or destructiveness. Its literal meaning is "approaching." The *Oxford English Dictionary* verifies this up to a point; the word means "approaching" in the sense of marching forward, and the illustration of that meaning happens to be from *Cambyses*, a bloody enough drama. All the other illustrations, including the dictionary's oldest one, give the meaning as "attack." So when Reich says that every positive manifestation of life is aggressive, "pleasurable sexual activity as well as destructive hateful activity" (131), he is playing word games.

Reich is somewhat more convincing on sadism, which occurs when the pleasure aim of love has been eliminated; then aggression becomes pleasurable in itself. The loss of the real love aim results in hatred; aggression assumes the character of destructiveness with sexual aims, as in sex murder. Its prerequisite is the complete inability to experience pleasure in a natural way. Reich holds that sadism does not exist in the animal kingdom. It is a recent acquisition of man, "*a secondary drive*" (*FO* 132). It does not exist in nature. Sadism assumes a civilized—that is, corrupted—psychology. But what is more corrupt than civilization? What is more pure than nature? What is more natural than orgasm? And what is more simplistic than the idea that destructive tendencies can be reduced "to disappointment in love or to loss of love," that "the destructiveness which is bound up in the character is nothing but anger about frustration in general and denial of sexual gratification in particular" (124)?

"WHY DID MAN LOSE PARADISE?" Reich asks in capital letters, indicating that this is *the* question (*MC* 14). Despite his practical side, despite his contribution to therapy, despite his saying of the way we live now that "pleasure and *joie de vivre* are inconceivable without fight, without painful experiences and without unpleasurable struggling with oneself" (*FO* 173), Reich remains an unreconstructed Utopian for whom all negative complication will somehow dissipate, given the realm of orgastic redemption. Reich makes fun of "Dolson," "the chemical promoted on the radio as a cure for everything" (*MC* 76), not seeing the parallel between it and his own orgone energy. In his later phase he became something of a Manichean, witnessing the cosmic struggle between good and evil orgone energy. His therapy at that point had nothing to do with psychoanalysis or rationality. Reich claimed to see the color of orgone energy and to see its vapors emitted from the lunatic box he constructed for the redemption of his hapless patients. They were the saved, unlike the godforsaken remainder of men who carry "within themselves a last little gleam of a lovely memory of a lost paradise forfeited by themselves" (158).

Reich actually found the prelapsarian only slightly marred by what he took to be an incongruous moralism in Malinowski's Trobriand Islanders. Reich writes: "The children engage freely in the sexual activities which correspond to their age . . . The socially accepted form of sexual life is spontaneous monogamy without compulsion, a relationship which can be dissolved without difficulties; thus, there is no promiscuity" (*FO* 201). Malinowski, however, found much difficulty among the Trobriand Islanders. Reich's Utopianism reaches fever pitch in his glorification of their matriarchy, which, as Rycroft holds, parallels Marx's era of primitive communism: no state, no private property, no sexual repression. These primitives were matrilineal, but Malinowski never said they were matriarchal, a significant blunder by Reich.

There was no evolution into matriarchy to speak of. Malinowski was a cultural relativist who explained things in terms of function. He observes that in matrilineal societies, women defer to men in questions of political and ethical, including familial, authority.

Passionate primitivists are often those out of touch with their own primordial impulses, hence their tendency to sentimentality. Reich is pursuing something long ago and far away. The peculiar attenuation of his thought is analogous to millenarianism. He castigates the democratic citizen in just such terms. "Little man," he says, "there has never been a human culture," lamenting that even his own vision "bears no more resemblance to the culture that will develop in a thousand or five thousand years than does the first wheel contrived thousands of years ago to a modern diesel locomotive" (*LLM* 98). It is ironic that the metaphor is mechanistic. Reich in old age is raging like a parody of a disintegrated King Lear who "will do such things, I know not what." Reich is a master of futuristic rage, which is what happens when one's superego is tied to the id, basically missing the middle of a mediating ego. No doubt changes will occur in a thousand years, but Reich will not be there to supervise them. Two thousand years will pass, he tells us in *The Murder of Christ*, "before men's minds will dare approach the Love of God again" (92). That love of God is, as we have seen, a Reichian telling of the tale. In Reich's world, orgasm is the once and future king.

Reich's deification of instinct may find him floating freely in time, but he is anchored in an act that demands the nitty-gritty of terrestrial space. No one knows this better than Reich, with his therapeutic prods, or his patients who have bruises to show for it. Who can forget his physical description of sexual intercourse as liberation: "One does not have sexual intercourse 'in order to produce children,' but because fluid congestion produces a bio-electric charge in the genital organs and presses for discharge" (*FO* 252)? At crucial moments Reich becomes the sadistic mechanist he excoriates, sounding like Bellow's Basteshaw, the Utopian maniac whom Augie March is stuck with in a lifeboat. Though Reich does speak about the tenderness, even the love, that comes with orgastic experience, to him as a thinker and person, the orgasm is far more real than the love. This critic of patriarchy lived the double standard, this advocate of sexual permissiveness was uncontrollably jealous. Rycroft is right that Reich leaves us with a "chilling explanation of sexual desire," elaborated "solely by subjects mounting internal tension without regard to the desirability—or desires—of the object." Indeed, solipsism is a problem with all ferocious sexual salvationists. And Rycroft is also right that Reich's cosmic longing for union "beyond" and his failure to say much "about longing for the person of the loved one" is chilling, too (91). This is analogous to the failure that the mature Clara Dawes finds in the young Paul Morel in Lawrence's *Sons and Lovers* and that, ultimately, Morel finds in himself. The sentimentalizing of instinct, Freud knew, confused freedom, to the extent that it was accessible, with determinism. Repression has its place because the instincts are difficult and recalcitrant. The mediating ego is another name for autonomy, a quality that is meaningful largely to the extent that it is inclusive. The subject should object.

4

NORMAN O. BROWN

Norman O. Brown mounts a critique of Freud from within. In Brown's work, Dionysus is the presiding god because "he affirms the dialectical unity of the great instinctual opposites: male and female, self and other, life and death."[1] Although "Freud saw that in the id there is no negation, only affirmation and eternity" (*LD* 175), he was too involved in the Apollonian ego project to hold the Dionysian id so highly. Brown is skeptical about any synthesis of the Apollonian and the Dionysian, concurring with Nietzsche that the Apollonian preserves and the Dionysian destroys self-consciousness. Brown's sympathy is with the later Nietzsche of the Dionysian ego. Without the Dionysian ego, there is the mixture of sensuality and cruelty "which is the revolt of the Dionysian against the Apollonian" (175–76). Nietzsche's witches' brew of cruelty and sensuality can be seen "in the sexology of Sade and the politics of Hitler," but the Dionysian ego proper can be seen in the romanticism of Blake, whose heir is Nietzsche. Brown's great hope is "psychoanalytic consciousness, which is not the Apollonian scholasticism of orthodox psychoanalysis" (176) but instinct affirming and freed of genital organization. Dionysus is the answer because our choice "is between holy and unholy madness," between Nietzsche and Freud. "It is not possible to get the illuminations without the derangement," Brown asserts. Ecstasy, Bacchic frenzy, transgression of "the natural limits of intelligence"[2]—this is what Brown was after in his well-known lecture at Columbia College in 1960, called "Apocalypse."

In assuming the role of inspired oracle, our Blake, Brown comes to us through aphorism—the fragmentary, Orphic "form of the mad truth, the Dionysian form."[3] (Has he ever heard of La Rochefoucauld, a master of Apollonian aphorism?) Brown's *Love's Body*, a *succès de scandale*, remains an eccentric book, full of pyrotechnics that fizzle. Frederick Crews has characterized admirably Brown's Dionysian style: "the form of the sentence, the proposition which freezes the content is abandoned; the words, freed from their enchaining form, recapture their explosive meaning, a hidden truth."[4] Of course, the hidden truth often remains hidden from Brown himself, whose mysticism is a form of obscurity. And if he gives us, as Crews characterizes it, thought as play, a *jeu interdit*, a Nietzschean gay science, full of drunkenness and laughter, we may want to hold him accountable to mere reason or common sense. Brown's peculiar weightlessness has been acutely accounted for by Crews: "Therapeutic Idealism, which has been out of favor with most intellectuals since the time of Mrs. Eddy, here undergoes another birth, in the guise of its opposite, total desublimation. Set free of all neurotic striving, Eros politely agrees not to be a nuisance any more and retires to the domain of symbolism" (38). Brown's "Dionysian Christianity" assumes that meaning is symbolic because it is a continual revelation breaking through from the unconscious. Brown's unconscious gives us the "noumenal" (*LD* 94) reality of ourselves, the metaphysical underpinning of what Crews calls his "inverted Transcendentalism."[5] But, as Crews puts it, Brown "goes wrong where all primitivism does, in making a static idol of the buried life." Brown thereby ironically subverts his own quest for symbolism, "turning what might have been a dynamic analysis into an ideological allegory" (38). Freud's dualism kept the founder of psychoanalysis from this most seductive form of sentimentality.

For Brown, sublimation is what distorts the emotional life, giving us a soul distinct from the body. In this sense, as Crews says, it is "the mode of an organism which must discover life rather than live, must know rather than be" (171). It is typical of Brown, but not of Freud, to set knowing and being at loggerheads. Sublimation in Freud leads to humanity's noblest achievements; it is what most makes us human, despite its cost. For Brown, as Crews says, sublimation distorts real "living-and-dying," and we are left with "the desexualized or deadened life." Sublimation and repression are "morbid forms of dying." Brown converts Freud's stoic insight about the ego's working in opposition to the purposes of Eros and thereby creating aggression into a triumph for aggression alone, neglecting Freud's emphasis on the gain in civilization. For Brown, civilization is not a gain but virtually a dead loss, the adjective in this case being literal. So Apollo, the god of sublimation, represents the Delphic wisdom of "nothing too much" and is the god of what Brown calls "deathly form" (quoted at 174). Apollo's symbol is the sun—not Lawrence's dark sun of repressed sexual energy unbinding itself, but the bright sun of sublimated eros, the sun of clarity, proportion, perspective, and all such fatal compromises.

Brown views the familiar Freudian terrain through a very special lens.

Some of his most original insights come in particularizing the corruption, the dirt, the excrement that civilization brings in its wake, as in his chapter on Martin Luther. "Since the Devil is lord of this world," says Brown, "Luther sees civilization as having an essentially anal-sadistic structure, as essentially constructed by the sublimation of anality . . . To see the Devil as lord of this world is to see the world as a manure heap, to see universal filth" (*LD* 225–26). The avarice of Leipzig—an esteemed locale in the history of capitalism—is the devil's filthy work. Luther is not deceived by sublimated anality. The Prince of Darkness may be a gentleman, but his clothing does not disguise the filth; it is its emblem. Luther equates Catholicism—with its Platonic-Aristotelian sublimation, its worldliness, its worship of mammon (for example, the sale of indulgences), and above all its pope—with the devil. Luther's obscenity is itself a prime example of the inevitable sublimated anality of this world. And his Christ will come "not indeed with gold, but with brimstone" (226). The sublimated excrement of the world must make way for the filthy aggression it deserves. Luther is, in this sense, sadistic, but he is not Sade. His obscenity resists the triumph of the devil. Christian eschatology, the belief that the fast-approaching end of time will bring release from Satan, radically distinguishes him from the Satanic Sade both ethically and historically.

Brown's chapter on Jonathan Swift, "The Excremental Vision,"[6] is another telling instance of the link between sublimation—or, as Brown says, all civilized behavior—and anality. For Swift, this is a theme with variations. He may take the view that the two are reconcilable. "Should I the Queen of Love refuse / Because she rose from stinking Ooze?," Cassinus rhetorically asks Strephon, in an acrid description of Aphrodite. Cassinus stays on the side of reconciliation to which his friend should submit: "such Order from Confusion sprung / Such gaudy Tulips rais'd from Dung."[7] Swift's poetry, however, notoriously explodes civilized compromise: "Oh! *Caelia*, Caelia, Caelia sh—." The heavenly and the excremental form a violent, witty dissonance. Freud is among those who trace the dissonance made by the juxtaposition of the coprophilic and the aesthetic back to man's development of the upright posture, when gamy smells began to be less available to the nose. Brown notes that on the two occasions when Freud refers to this subject, he quotes Augustine's observation about the genitals that man is born "*inter urinas et faeces*." Many resist this insight, Freud observes, thereby instancing repression of or resistance to full sexual satisfaction, notably in regard to the sadistic elements belonging to the erotic instinct.

Swift does not resist. Swift's Yahoos, Brown observes, "are distinguished from other animals by their attitude toward their own excrement. Excrement to the Yahoos is no mere waste product but a magic instrument for self-expression and aggression" (*LD* 190). Brown concludes that "the excremental vision of the Yahoo is substantially identical with the psychoanalytical doctrine of the extensive role of anal eroticism in the formation of human culture" (191). Brown follows the Freudian line here. In the anal stage, libido is concentrated in the anal zone. The anal product, in the infantile stage, is considered one's own child or creation which the infant may use in narcissistic play or to obtain love from another (feces as gift), assert independence from another (feces as property), or commit aggression (feces as weapon). These qualities originate in the anal phase and never lose their connection with it, despite sublimation. So, for example, "money is feces, because the anal eroticism continues in the unconscious. The anal eroticism has not been renounced or abandoned but repressed" (191).

Paralleling Freud but with a more radical emphasis, Brown says that the pregenital organizations "represent that distortion of the human body which is the human ego" (191). Both Freud and Swift agree, then, that anal eroticism, which Swift calls "a strange Disposition to Nastiness and Dirt," is characteristically human.[8] Both Swift and Freud emphasize the connection between anal eroticism and human aggression, deriving from the anal-sadistic phase. Brown concurs that "defiance, mastery, will to power are attributes of human reason first developed in the symbolic manipulation of excrement and perpetuated in the symbolic manipulation of symbolic substitutes for excrement" (for example, money) (*LD* 192). That the theory of anal eroticism depends on sublimation was anticipated with much anxiety by Swift; in William Empson's words, Swift held that "everything spiritual is really material . . . all religion is really a perversion of sexuality."[9] Further, when Swift says that "the corruption of the sense is the Generation of the Spirit," he is saying that repression causes sublimation.[10]

Brown's *Life against Death* is, among other things, a post-Marxist assault on capitalism, a meta-Freudian assault. *Homo economicus* is the ideal type of the prudential, calculating anal character. Not just the ridiculous miser but capitalism itself is anal, as is the related compulsion to accumulate money. Brown quotes Freud's well-known utterance about money: "Happiness is the deferred fulfillment of a prehistoric wish. That is why wealth brings so little happiness; money is not an infantile wish" (quoted in *LD* 254). (Freud is jejune in ignoring the many wishes that can be satisfied and desires that can be fulfilled by access to money.) And Brown notes that the psychoanalytic equation of money and excrement points to the "absolute worthlessness" (254) of money. His hostility to money carries over even to his discussion of primitive culture, where he sees the anal complex merged with the oral complex to make what he calls the superfluity complex. Superfluity is characterized by limitless consumer demand and luxury. Brown sees forms of conspicuous consumption negatively. "The neurotic perversion of needs," he says, "is not a child of civilization or class domination, but begins in archaic man" (257). Brown, then, is far from his later Battaillean sympathy with accumulation for purposes of waste, or inspired excess. He does not yet see what he later half-ironically calls the Dionysian energy of consumerism.

With his newly considered insight from his acknowledged kindred spirit Georges Bataille about expenditure, the later Brown becomes an unlikely admirer of capitalism. He holds that Schumpeter was right in saying that capitalism had proven itself more dynamic than socialism because it is Dionysian. "Its essential nature is to be out of control," Brown says, marked as it is by "exuberant energy, exploiting every opportunity, to extract a surplus." So "the self-destructive, ruinous process continues. Death and Dionysus get their due, deny them as we may . . . The forces not of production but of wasteful destruction have been unleashed and will not get back into the cage" (*AM* 189). Brown has nothing to say about the market as a self-regulating mechanism of supply and demand, or about the positive effects of sound monetary policy. No Friedmanite, Brown insists that "it is not so easy as bourgeois clerical optimists have imagined to distinguish gloriously from catastrophically" (189–90), which are Bataille's terms for two types of necessary spending. Brown resists Marcuse's vision of this world as one of "peace and pleasure," a dream of *luxe calme et volupté* (despite admittedly falling victim to it himself a bit in the last chapter of *Life against Death*), knowing that "the new truth that cannot be avoided is the advent of the spendthrift masses" (*AM* 190). Of course, there are some hitches. Because we do not really know how to consume, much energy is spent on accumulating excrement or money, which cannot be consumed. Clearly not focused on the bottom line, Brown misses something about capitalism here: the dream of material satisfactions. But he insists that "real consumption is inseparable from Dionysian violence, the consuming fire" (192), a transcendent Chapter Eleven. He underestimated the American character.

The discussion of money in his classic *Life against Death* does, nonetheless, take us toward the Dionysian by inversion, and it does so more persuasively than anything else he wrote. It serves as a wedge Brown can use to put a distance between himself and orthodox Freudianism. For Swift, Brown notes, "shame and repression of anality did not exist in the age of innocence," and he quotes Swift to prove his point: "That *golden* Age, to *Gold* unknown" (*LD* 200). The problem of corrupted anality is one of a kind greatly exacerbated by degree. Classic psychoanalytic theory, Brown holds, says that "possessive mastery over nature and rigorously economical thinking are partial impulses in the human being (the human body) which in modern civilization have become tyrant organizers of the whole of human life; abstraction from the reality of the whole body and substitution of the abstracted impulse for the whole reality are inherent in *Homo economicus*" (236). Instead of the prevailing morbidity, a new science in Brown's view "would presumably be erotic rather than (anal) sadistic in aim. Its aim would be not mastery over but union with nature. And its means would not be economizing but erotic exuberance," because—and here is Brown's triumphant conclusion—"it would be based on the whole body and not just a part; that is to say, it would be based on the polymorphous perverse body."

Brown is a sexual Utopian whose strength and weakness both rest on the notion of the polymorphous perverse. "What we call 'character,'" he tells us (as Reich did), "is really a disorganization or malfunctioning of the body" (*LD* 291). And he notes even more starkly (as Reich did not): "The pattern of normal adult sexuality [i.e., genital] . . . can be no clue to the essential nature of the erotic desires of mankind" (40). Clueless! Clearly, no one is more ferocious in theory than Brown. If civilization were such a disaster, one might be morally obligated to perish. Brown's point is that, short of a radical sexual restructuring, this is precisely what we are doing. His main point about polymorphous perversity is the cultural relativist one that "the pattern of normal adult sexuality is not a natural (biological) necessity but a cultural phenomenon" (24). But where is there a culture without this pattern? And how long could it last? Among other things, it is precisely "a natural (biological) necessity." Having destroyed nature, anything goes for Brown. There are no limits. There is no essence except as culture defines it. Brown can, therefore, dismiss the Freudian view that the free play of polymorphous perversity is incompatible with cultural order. This raises the possibility that Brown's Utopia would not be more than a form of anarchy, which is fine with Brown since order is by definition repressive and death dealing.

He puts a monumental premium on presumed infantile desires. *Love's Body* is, stylistically, his literary equivalent of infantile desire, with its chewing on vowels and consonants, its fragmented expressiveness, its logic of narcissistic explosion, its unconsciousness activated by puns, its uninhibited assertiveness, and its radical indifference to consecutive thought and mere linear rationality. *Love's Body*, which one may consider the logical extension of "the way out" and other metaphors of imprisonment promulgated in the closely reasoned *Life against Death*, is thought as poetry, Orphic poetry. Yet, as Crews says, "one may wonder about the accuracy or adequacy of Brown's representation of art, which stresses . . . its childlike aspect at the expense of the philosophic mind, and affirms Dionysus at the expense of Apollo."[11] Thinking is, after all, an emblem of anality, eros perverted. So the thought-laden *Life against Death* advocates polymorphous perversity and *Love's Body* attempts to embody it.

Life against Death found an advocate in Susan Sontag. Her review of it is an attack on genital sexuality as exhibited, say, in *Lady Chatterley's Lover*. Sontag is taken aback by the warm reception that this novel had in America in the early 1960s. "A country in which the vindication of so sexually reactionary a book as *Lady Chatterley's Lover* is a serious matter is plainly at a very elementary stage of sexual maturity," she maintains. Never mind that there were those who did not vindicate it. Sontag argues, more particularly, that Lawrence's "puritanical insistence on genital sexuality seriously mars his ideas on sex."[12] Calling insistence on genital sexuality puritanical shows that America had been transformed in the forty years since the 1920s, when such an insistence was an attack on Puritanism. The question now is not what comes out, but what goes in. It is not entirely clear whether, deep down, Sontag is attacking the insistence or the genital sex. One can only imagine her reaction to Mellors's tirade on "lesbian rampers." Beyond that, confining genital sexuality to sexual elementary school can only leave us wondering about the value of higher education. True, Lawrence's sense of heterosexual relations may be a stereotyping, but to attack him on grounds of genitality itself only gives more validity to his representation. Yet Sontag is right, as were many of Brown's readers, in seeing that Brown "invites us to accept the androgynous mode of being and the narcissistic mode of self-expression that lie hidden in the body" (258–59).

Love's Body illustrates this last insight in form as well as in content. For example, in a paragraph on—God help us—the Ark of the Covenant, Brown quotes the traditional priestly assertion that "God loves his people as a man loves a woman," a lovely, uncomplicated simile. Brown then quotes an elaboration of the traditional image to the effect that Jehovah in the temple is "a male within a female hid as in an Ark and curtains." Moreover, "the staves that were used to carry the Ark during the wanderings grew longer in the sanctuary, and caused the Veil to protrude as the two breasts of a woman." Brown comments: "Breasts, or penises—who knows?" (*LB* 59). Of course, pretty much everybody but the Dionysian Brown knows. Anyone beyond the infantile stage should know. But, ideally, there is no beyond the infantile for Brown. In a related aphorism in this passage, Brown says, "Father and mother together is mother with a Penis" (59), another case of forced androgyny.

Brown is now speaking in symbols and metaphors because, in his view, "symbolism is polymorphous perversity, the translation of all our senses into one another, the interplay between the senses, the metaphor, the free translation" (*LB* 250). Symbolism is generally thought of in terms of secular transcendence or of sociological nexus; Brown thinks of it as erotic release. Resisting his desired *déreglement des sens* brings on a virtual sterility analogous to the mere monosignificance of allegory.

What Brown wants, on the contrary, is "speech resexualized," which would bring "annunciations, messages, messengers, angels, having intercourse with the daughters of men, making pregnant through the ear; angels or birds, winged words or doves of the spirit" (*LB* 250). Lest the last metaphors bring us too much into the orbit of sublimation, Brown reminds us that "the flying bird is an erection or a winged phallus." What he wants is a word that is a penis, a sentence that is coitus, supernatural pregnancies. He wants an erotic cosmos. He is one with Bataille in this regard, who in his early work spoke of "the polymorphous and organic coitus of the earth with the sun" and who held that "the sea continually jerks off."[13] Brown notes that there has always been resistance to this freedom. "Speech resexualized," he tells us, was "abolished at Babel and restored at Pentecost," where there are "tongues of fire, a flame in the shape of a male member. Speaking with tongues is fiery speech, speech as sexual act, a firebird or phoenix" (*LB* 251). It is characteristic of Brown to embrace this marginal version of Christianity not for its fundamentalism but for its ego-dissolving, freaked-out style, as it is characteristic of him to see the phoenix of erotic spirit rising out of Lawrencean ashes. In the metaphor of speech resexualized, "two become one" (252). Brown conspicuously excludes irony in his description for that is essentially an ego quality that undercuts the erotic or Dionysian sense of reality; it comes from reason, proportion, and ambiguity rather than from union.

But this sense of merging or "fusion" that Brown seeks, where "the distinction between inner self and outside world, between subject and object [is] overcome" (253), is, in his usage, another name for solipsism. It is a good idea to know where you end and the world begins. Nor is he helping his cause much in pointing to a parallel with schizophrenia, where "what happens to the person's own body is identified with what happens to the universe" (*LB* 254). Brown is not above the sentimentalizing of mental illness. The insane may show the way out because "civilized objectivity is non-participating consciousness, consciousness as separation, as dualism"—as in Freud. It is, for Brown, "consciousness by negation, which is from the death instinct." As Brown puts it in *Life against Death*, Freud "did not abandon the illusion that Adam really fell and thus his allegiance to sublimation and civilization—the consequences of original sin" (270). Hence Brown's resistance. But there is a contradiction between Brown's complicity in the Freudian pessimism of unconscious determinism and his prelapsarian sense of the polymorphous perverse, as there is between his intellect and his prelapsarian dreams. The core of his weakness is the salvationary importance of a Utopian concept. "Polymorphous perversity," as Crews persuasively argues, "seems indeed to be the acme of quietism; it requires no partner, overburdens no organ, and entails no direct social consequence . . . [Brown] eliminates our problems by eliminating us."[14] Most bizarre of all, as Crews maintains, is the image created by *Love's Body* of "this self-castrating advocate of pregenitility going on to revel in the sacrificial imagery of the cross" (33). Brown, then, proves despite himself that humanity in culture cannot escape from sublimation. He believes that sublimation is a form of death. The story of Jesus shows that death may be a form of sublimation.

Brown is Freudian in seeing that psychological problems are not merely social but indicative of internal conflict. But where Freud stoically accepted man as the self-repressing animal, Brown's emphasis is on recapturing the sense of oneness with the world. What influences him most in early Freud is polymorphous perversity, in later Freud the death instinct. In both instances, Brown is seeking to deny the idea of limit. This can be done through uninhibited erotic fulfillment and through the nirvana principle, a key element of the death instinct, whereby one recaptures the oceanic feeling that makes no distinction between self and world, that recaptures the pleasurable calm of the womb. Nirvana is something positive, denying the anxieties of separation and the compromises of dependence. But it is a problematic sense of death that equates resurrection with denial of the human condition, as nirvana does.

The "restless pleasure-principle—which is the morbid manifestation of the Nirvana principle—is what makes man Faustian, and Faustian man is history-making man," Brown observes wistfully (*LB* 91). If repression were overcome, the restless career of Faustian man would come to an end, because he would be satisfied and could say, "*Verweile doch, du bist so schön.*"¹⁵ Brown is dedicated to the capturing of this moment, which would destroy time. Becoming, as Brown says, would yield to being. He is looking over the edge into "eternity . . . the mode of unrepressed bodies" (93). This is Brown's nirvana. No wonder he sees "no reason why" Freud insists on the term *death* in reference to the nirvana principle (99). In Brown's Utopian view, this principle is not a cessation from striving as much as it is an absolute fulfillment.

Brown sees pretty much the opposite when he views the actuality of Western culture. "It is hard," he says, "under conditions of general repression, to affirm the death instinct without becoming an enemy of life" (*LB* 106). Under such conditions, the death instinct operates malignantly. When it fuses dialectically with eros, says Brown, the death instinct "is a principle of restless negativity (like Goethe's Mephistopheles), but given the basic unsatisfactoriness of life under conditions of general repression, a defusion into a simple wish to die is always lurking in the background." For Brown, life as we know it is under the domination of the death instinct. Hence his empathy for Luther, whose devil "is ultimately personified death" (215). Luther, like Brown in theory, had to be born again, to find life in death beyond this death in life. Brown parts company sharply with Freud on this point. Brown, like Luther, wants the apocalypse and is sympathetic to Luther's eschatology—which, in Brown's words, "challenges psychoanalysis to formulate the conditions under which the domain of death and anality could be abolished" (232).

Most of us have to live with that domain, however. And some brilliant literary criticism has been written, not on the abolition of death and anality, but on the next best thing: living with sublimated aggression. Lionel Trilling's "The Fate of Pleasure" is an example. This essay describes the career of pleasure in Western culture from an ennobling harmony to a degrading dissonance. Trilling uses Dostoevsky's underground man, with his violent assault on false representations of the good and the beautiful, as a memorable instance. "There are human impulses," Trilling says, "which . . . repudiate pleasure and seek gratification in—to use Freud's word—unpleasure."¹⁶ Unpleasure, sublimated aggression, is a key to modern aesthetic essence.

Trilling traces this now typical aesthetic attitude back to, among other places, Augustine's stolen pears, an apparently gratuitous act. Trilling says that "in having no conceivable pleasure in view, it was a sort of negative transcendence—in effect, a negation—of his humanity." This incident is a resonant one because we have "been engaged in an experiment in the negative transcendence of the human, a condition which is to be achieved by freeing the self from the thralldom to pleasure. Augustine's puzzling sin is the paradigm of the modern spiritual enterprise." But where Augustine was critical of this transcendence, the modern view is likely to be sympathetic: "To be aware of this undertaking of negative transcendence is, surely, to admire the energy of its desperateness."[17] It may be ugly, but it is aggressively alive. And confession generally elicits empathy in a psychological age. "I have more life in me than you," says Dostoevsky's unsavory, mesmerizing underground man in his confession, and in this respect Trilling says he speaks for us—that is, for literary culture.

And we moderns are not even a unique case. For going beyond the pleasure principle is, as Trilling puts it, "a fact of the psychic life itself."[18] Therefore, "it has always been true of some men that to pleasure they have preferred unpleasure. They imposed upon themselves difficult and painful tasks, they committed themselves to strange, 'unnatural' modes of life, they sought out distressing emotions, in order to know the psychic energies which are not to be summoned up in felicity. These psychic energies, even when they are experienced in self-destruction, are a means of self-definition and self-affirmation . . . it is the choice of the hero, the saint and martyr, and, in some cultures, the artist." Trilling might have included the libertine and aggression outward as well as aggression inward. Clearly, as modern literature attests, we are one of those cultures. The difference is that "what was once a mode of experience of a few has now become an ideal experience of many" (85). We now confront the irony of "an accredited subversiveness, an established moral radicalism, a respectable violence" (86). The death instinct has established itself disproportionately over the pleasure principle. That is, pleasure itself is inseparable from a perversity or morbidness. Can we aspire only to a negative transcendence?

And so we read Bataille and Brown (and Sade, Lawrence, Miller, and Mailer)—and we are unshockable. Bataille the aesthetician says: "If beauty so far removed from the animal is passionately desired, it is because to possess is to sully, to reduce to the animal level. Beauty is desired in order that it may be befouled; not for its own sake, but for the joy brought by the certainty of profaning it."[19] Whether or not Bataille is building a theoretical structure to justify his own sadistic proclivities is immaterial to the odd aesthetic centrality of his view. Keats, a Romantic, gives us in *The Eve of St. Agnes* a scene of erotic fulfillment with death on the outside looking in. More than this, Keats felt, as Trilling puts it, "that there is something perverse and negating in the erotic life, that it is quite in the course of nature that we should feel 'Pleasure . . .

turning to Poison as the bee-mouth sips.'" This condition was once graced with the name of melancholy. Coleridge wrote an "Ode to Dejection," but things have become more clinical. Can one write an ode to depression? More typically, we now get the depression without the ode. Keats takes unpleasure even further in "La Belle Dame Sans Merci," where, as Trilling says, we see "the scene of erotic pleasure which leads to devastation, of an erotic fulfillment which implies castration" (66). What in the Romantics was an anxiety is often in the moderns a dogma. "There is no form of repulsion in which I do not discern an affinity with desire," says Bataille,[20] sounding much like Mailer's sadistic hipster, Marion Faye. Reticence has given way to ferocity.

The reversal of humanistic proportion reflects an age of narcissism. Narcissism, the fallen, grown-up kind, has typically been a problem for humanism. In *The Heresy of Self-Love*, a sympathetic account of the phenomenon in Western culture, Paul Zweig notes that the danger of narcissism has always been that the individual will become so enamored of his mind and flesh that society will go untended and God go unloved.[21] Zweig notes that the narcissist has always had a paradoxical status, deplored for his inhuman solitude, admired as a figure of fulfillment and transcendence—as in the Gnostics, medieval Brethren, the objectless love poetry of Provence, Adam Smith's theory of self-interest, and radical social criticism of the nineteenth century. Self-love was seen by the Romantics, as it is more radically by Brown, as a shield against the alienation imposed by society. The subversive egotism of Emerson and Nietzsche was a turning from social order and responsibility. Rousseau is a key figure for Zweig because in *The Confessions* Rousseau transformed objective into subjective reality, talking not about "man" but about "me." Brown talks about man as me, little me, which he wants back with a vengeance. He is a cardinal instance of contemporary narcissism. For—to use his Freudian terminology—he seeks a regression to the primary narcissism of an undifferentiated ego and id. Polymorphous perversity is ideally a form of self-love, appearing before the transformation of narcissistic libido into object libido. The superego is formed to replace the paradisical state of primary narcissism, a paradise lost. In this paradise, the body is its own object, the ego attributes pleasure to itself, indifferent to what is not itself. Having little use for the superego, Brown wants to recapture this self-indulgent state to whatever extent he can. His political indifference is not unrelated to that of the garden variety narcissist of recent vintage whose self-love is a form of isolation—the "me generation," for example, or Heinz Kohut's "narcissistic personality disorder." The latter stems from distant parents, unrealized Oedipal resistance, and superego inadequacy and produces emptiness rather than sharply defined neurosis. As critics have pointed out, this is the emptiness of minimalist fiction, the late 1960s "hangover," as Eugene Goodheart puts it.[22]

"It is precisely the elevation of sexual desire, indeed of desire as a supreme value, that entails as one of its consequences its enervation. What keeps desire alive is the sense of resistance, of the play of other values, energies, faculties," Goodheart rightly argues.[23] After *Life against Death*, Brown's hold on such complexities becomes increasingly loose. He argues that "the essence of man consists not, as Descartes maintained, in thinking but in desiring" (*LD* 7), unwittingly attributing a primacy to rationality by using the word *essence* in a particularly emphatic way. Furthermore, one may have a desire, indeed a passion, for the rational but not in the current critical usage of desire. Brown is interested in the triumph of subjectivity—something a first-person rationalist like Descartes helped to establish—in ways that the philosopher never could have imagined. But it was for the Romantics to establish its primary venue, imagination. Imagination has often been hailed as the haven of illimitable desire. Goodheart's caution on this point is salutary. We should not confuse the "valuable expansion of boundaries of desire and the self-destructive dream of an existence without boundaries. To choose illimitable desire is to submit onself to a destructive necessity."[24] Enter Norman O. Brown. Goodheart may well be speaking of him when he says that "illimitable desire may be a tendency of the revolutionary, expansive, and utopian ethos of modern life, an ethos that always promises more than it can deliver" (19). Witness the ominous vagueness of the magical realm of the polymorphous perverse. Illimitable desire can institute its own repressiveness. Brown's *Love's Body* is a *locus classicus*, along with Deleuze and Guattari's *Anti-Oedipus*.

There is one thing that Brown did not learn from Bataille: desire has its own limits. There is no flower-power fantasy, no androgynous wet dream in the mature Bataille. In Bataille you get a flamboyantly decadent version of "you get what you pay for." And odds are that you do not even get that. "We know that possession of the object we are afire for is out of the question," he maintains. "It is one thing or another: either desire will consume us entirely, or its object will cease to fire us with longing. We possess it on one condition only, that gradually the desire it arouses will fade."[25] This may be read as a partial gloss on his *Madame Edwarda*—or Faust in a whorehouse. Though Brown in his interpretation of Freud shows a complex grasp of the difficulty of being, his Utopian way out is largely an evasion of that difficulty. Bataille may be almost comically dire, but he is certainly not Utopian. To possess the object of erotic desire is to lose, sully, or profane it. Brown sees ultimate erotic desire as some illimitable experience. For Bataille, on the contrary, "desire in eroticism is the desire that triumphs over the taboo. It presupposes man in conflict with himself" (256). Brown envisions a tranquility either in nirvana or the realm of the polymorphous perverse. Bataille's will to expenditure encompasses violence. The former is passive and masochistic, the latter aggressive and sadistic. There is never any doubt of the erotic object in Bataille, tortured as that connection may be; Brown, on the other hand, often seems to be positing the self as the object. Bataille believes that taboo is proof of the sacred, Brown that it is proof of the disease called life that worships at the altar of death. Brown sees disorder in our erotic order; the mature Bataille sees order in our erotic disorder. It is remarkable that for all of Brown's ferocity, he sees its manifestation as sexual aggression only as an instance of disease and the triumph of death. That Brown does not deal with the erotic violence of his proclaimed ally is an astonishing omission. It is self-defeating for a man so dedicated to the exclusive salvationary power of the primordial body to be so mired in sublimation as to ignore this violence.

5

DELEUZE AND GUATTARI

Gilles Deleuze and Félix Guattari, the authors of *Anti-Oedipus*, are not—outside their Left Bank cadre—easily given to praise. So when they call Reich "the true founder of a materialist psychiatry," these embattled proponents of such a psychiatry are making a statement of some import. "The strength of Reich," they say, "consists in having shown how psychic repression [*refoulement*] depended on social repression [*répression*]."[1] For them, Reich "raised the most profound of questions—'Why did the masses desire fascism?'" (*AO* 30). He, alas, vitiated the force of his question by answering it like a psychiatrist interested in subjectivity, remaining "a prisoner of derived concepts," falling short of "the materialist psychiatry he dreamed of." He did so by introducing "precisely the line of argument he was interested in demolishing," distinguishing between the rationality of social production and the irrational element of desire, which is the subject of psychoanalysis. For Deleuze and Guattari, "everything is objective or subjective as one wishes." For them, "libidinal economy is no less objective than political economy, and the political no less subjective than the libidinal" (344–45).

Something seems to be missing: the self. But no, since "the self and the non-self, outside and inside, no longer have any meaning whatsoever" (*AO* 2). Deleuze and Guattari agree with Lacan that the coherent, autonomous ego is an illusion. Freud's famous dictum—where id was, there shall ego be—becomes, in them, where ego was, there shall id be. Though this is not quite right, since, as Guattari puts it elsewhere, "desire is not intrinsically linked to an individuation of the libido."[2] Like the ego, the id never really existed. "What a mistake to have ever said *the* id," they think. Why? Because "everywhere *it* is machines . . . The breast is a machine that produces milk, and the mouth a machine coupled to it . . . Hence we are all handymen" (*AO* 1). One may bridle at this confusion of the vital and mechanistic. If we are all handymen, how could *Anti-Oedipus* ever rise above the spirit's nuts and bolts? The answer is that it does not.

By adhering to the psychoanalytic, say Deleuze and Guattari, Reich fails to see that "desiring production is one and the same thing as social production," and that "fantasy is never individual: it is group fantasy" (*AO* 30). Reich did intuit a fundamental principle of their kind of psychoanalysis, provocatively dubbed schizoanalysis, in thinking that "the destruction of resistances must not wait upon the discovery of the material." He was right, in other words, to radically undercut the Freudian unconscious. "But the reason for this," they go on to say, "is even more radical than he thought: There is no unconscious material, so that schizoanalysis has nothing to interpret" (314). Moreover, though Reich does see that psychoanalysis is a force of social repression, he does not see its inextricable link to capitalism. Psychoanalysis "depends directly on an economic mechanism (whence its relations with money) through which the decoded flower of desire"—the energies released by capitalism, in this case—"must necessarily be reduced to a familial field." That is, Oedipus is "the last word in capitalist consumption." For this conjunction of capitalism and psychoanalysis, Deleuze and Guattari save some of their most inflamed rhetoric: "The whole of psychoanalysis is an immense perversion, a drug, a radical break with reality, starting with the reality of desire: it is a narcissism, a monstrous autism: the characteristic autism and the intrinsic perversion of the machine of capital" (312–13). Viewing sex in the context of Reich's much maligned orgone theory, therefore, seems to them "more adequate than the reduction of sexuality to the pitiful little familiast secret" (291). So speaks the voice of the anti-Oedipus, as in the antichrist. Yet if Reich is a father figure of the anti-Oedipus, there may be more to the Oedipus myth than the authors are willing to admit.

When Deleuze and Guattari say that there is no unconscious material they do not mean that there is no unconscious. They mean that there is no Oedipal unconscious. The unconscious is not a theater but a factory. They hold that "the unconscious itself is no more structural than personal, it does not symbolize any more than it represents; it engineers, it is mechanic. Neither imaginary nor symbolic, it is the Real in itself" (*AO* 53). A mechanical *Ding an Sich*, or at least one that does not have an Oedipal (Freudian or Lacanian) character. It actively relates to the material world. Oddly, these two mechanists want what religious humanists want in an unconscious: indeterminacy. But it is a totally different kind of indeterminacy, not one redolent of a moral reality but what they call a "schizophrenic" one, characterized by fragments and flows of desire. Desire, Guattari says, "passes over and under all barriers" ("Everybody" 81). Love laughs at locksmiths, as Joyce's Gerty MacDowell said in a kinder, gentler day.

Deleuze and Guattari are forever playing tennis without a net, Utopianizing experience without pain. They concede that Oedipus signifies responsibility rather than anarchy, but they claim that this is the problem. They "do not deny that there is an Oedipal sexuality, an Oedipal heterosexuality and homosexuality, an Oedipal castration, as well as complete objects, global images, and specific egos." What they deny is "that these are productions of the unconscious" (*AO* 74). That is, these realities have been imposed by certain social contexts. What is needed is a revolution to dispel or disintegrate these contexts so that we can "rediscover a transcendental unconscious defined by the immanence of its criteria, and a corresponding practice that we shall call schizoanalysis" (75). Is schizoanalysis possible? For now, we must note that "the unconscious of schizoanalysis is unaware of persons, aggregates, and laws, and of images, structures, and symbols." It is, in short, dehumanized. "It is an orphan," they say, not merely disinherited but disconnected from what most take to be human. It certainly has no parents, state, or God. It is "an anarchist and an atheist." Above all, it is a revolutionary. Its motto is: "Destroy, destroy." Modernism as psychological cartoon? Deleuze and Guattari are adamant: "The task of schizoanalysis goes by way of destruction—a whole scouring of the unconscious, a complete curettage. Destroy Oedipus, the illusion of the ego, the puppet of the superego, guilt, the law, castration" (311). Like Brown in *Love's Body*, they want to destroy us. René Girard observes that their unconscious "can assimilate almost anything, the whole universe if need be," rightly concluding that they are "all the while rejecting what solipsisms have always liked to reject, the existence of whole persons"—all of them.[3] For Girard, their unconscious "does so very cleverly, with no obvious resentment and we are supposed to believe that no hasty *exclusion* is intended." But the ego is excluded, as is memory. Freud was the genius of memory, the discoverer of repression. In giving us an impersonal, mechanistic unconscious, Deleuze and Guattari unwittingly make a case for the Freudian unconscious.

The nub of their assault on the Freudian unconscious and their preference for the Reichian unconscious is their rejection of the Oedipus complex. Their critique is essentially Nietzschean. What Christianity is to Nietzsche, psychoanalysis is to Deleuze and Guattari. The Oedipus complex posits an unconscious that is "dark and somber" (*AO* 112). The Reichian unconscious is generally thought to be merely "idyllic." But for Deleuze and Guattari, the unconscious is idyllic, it is "Rousseauistic." The monsters of the unconscious are not engendered by "the slumber of reason" but by "vigilant and insomniac rationality." Transgression, guilt, and castration are not determinants of the unconscious, but the way "a priest sees things." Deleuze and Guattari concede that "there are many other forces besides psychoanalysis for Oedipalizing the unconscious, rendering it guilty, castrating it." But psychoanalysis "reinforces the movement; it invents a last priest."

Not that psychoanalysis invented the Oedipus complex; it discovered it. Deleuze and Guattari give Oedipus some slack: "We are not saying that Oedipus and castration do not amount to anything. We are Oedipalized, we are castrated" (*AO* 67). The problem is that this silences "the outcry of desiring production," no matter what form it takes. For "we are all schizos! We are all perverts!" "Liberty! Equality! Perversity!" as Herzog ironically exclaimed. We need "schizophrenization that must cure us of the cure" (*AO* 68). They equate schizophrenia—as process, not as illness—with desiring production. Schizophrenia is the fragmented and salvationary impulse that is "the limit of social production," or socialized behavior. In other words, it is the advent of the illimitable; it transcends the Oedipal. This is a crucial distinction. Deleuze and Guattari can thus say that "we are now able to surmise what Oedipus signifies,"—namely, "it internalizes the limit." That is, it places a limit on the illimitable. And their illimitable tends to be ferocious, if only because of the current sick state of affairs—which is basically an aberration. Oedipus is a limit of ferocity. Deleuze and Guattari lament the current sad state of affairs. What they see is "a society of neurotics." What they want is "one successful schizophrenic who has not been made autistic." Instead there is merely Oedipus, "the incomparable instrument of gregariousness" (101)—and mediocrity. Yes, Oedipus wrecks. In these sentences they invoke Artaud, the world's most "successful schizophrenic." This is what romanticism has come to.

Perhaps the most extravagant claim made by Deleuze and Guattari is the equation of Oedipalization and fascism. Schizophrenia and paranoia as process are ideal polarities for them, and the first is to freedom what the second is to fascism. In his preface to "this great book," Foucault says that *Anti-Oedipus* could be subtitled "An Introduction to the Nonfascist Life," and that the essential energy of the book is "the tracking down of all varieties of fascism, from the enormous ones that surround and crush us," such as those of Hitler and Mussolini, "to the petty ones that constitute the tyrannical bitterness of our everyday lives," or "the fascism that causes us to love power," which is, of course, "the very thing that dominates and exploits us." Oedipus is the primary expression of our current "unity and totalizing paranoia" (xii)—the pot calls the kettle black.

Just how wide a berth may be given to fascism, conflating Hitler and the couch, is best seen in Guattari's essay "Everybody Wants to be a Fascist," where the antipsychiatrist removed his armor—the heavy encrustation of protective Deleuzian abstraction—and speaks his mind in relaxed, everyday prose. It is wrong, he says, to think that fascism is over. It continues to operate in the family, school, and trade union. But even the word *fascism* is not strong enough for Guattari, since the fascist, the Stalinist, and the domestic bourgeois are "modern forms of totalitarianism" ("Everybody" 92). He modifies the inclusion of the last member of the group, adding "in as much as one can speak of a sort of fascism of the superego in situations of guilt and neurosis" (93)—like Oedipus. Still, Guattari is not interested in drawing distinctions between fascism and totalitarianism. Indeed, he is skeptical about differences between the Axis and the Allies in the Second World War. This is not, as one might surmise, because of the disgrace of Vichy France, but because fascism "remained external to a certain type of bourgeoisie, which rejected it only because of its instability and because it stirred excessively powerful forces of desire within the masses" (95). Fascism became more of a threat to capitalism (more dangerous than Bolshevism) and to Stalinism because the masses invested a fantastic collective death instinct in it, fascism being a composite of love and death. So the bourgeoisie had to inhibit its own fascistic tendencies. Nonetheless Guattari insists that the fascism of the concentration camps (though here *totalitarianism* would seem to be a better word) parallels that of families and schools.

Peter Rudnytsky's assessment of *Anti-Oedipus* is sound. The work's putative integration of Freud and Marx is mainly about Marx. The emphasis is on the social and political, and Deleuze and Guattari's "schizoanalysis" is Marxist in orientation. Rudnytsky notes that Sophocles does not appear in the index to *Anti-Oedipus*, nor is there anything about tragedy, "Freud's inspiration."[4] There is nothing about the very will to be civilized, the *hamartia* of everyday life that brings with it resulting discontents.

Everyone knows more or less what psychoanalysis is, but Deleuze and Guattari's alternative, schizoanalysis, is hardly a household word. What, then, is schizoanalysis? Before we can answer this question, we must clarify what they mean by *schizophrenic*. We have seen that they are interested in schizophrenia as process rather than illness. So the broken, fragmented life of the sick man who assumes multiple personalities undergoes a magical transformation. "Schizophrenia," in the eyes of Deleuze and Guattari, "is like love." Their "schizophrenia" will be another chapter in the utopian id, another critique of the neurotic ego (not to mention the fascist superego). In pursuit of their definition, their dismissal of the consensus of the psychiatric and psychoanalytic profession is sweeping: "there is no specifically schizophrenic phenomenon or entity." We should think, instead, that schizophrenia is the universe of productive and reproductive desiring-machines, universal primary production as "the essential reality of man and nature" (*AO* 5). The idea of the quasi-Marxist, or at least materialist, "production" and "machines" is metaphor doing the work of argument. Nature and the human being, we know, are organic and individuated, as in Blake. Deleuze and Guattari's equation of the machine and desire is a futurist rejection of this cardinal aspect of romanticism.

Crucial to their concept of schizophrenia is the idea, taken from Artaud, of the body without organs. This is a state of biological nonfunctioning so intransigent that it makes for a condition of ideal disintegration. The body is preserved from nothingness by inevitable flows of energy and partial objects. Artaud imagined himself with "*No mouth. No tongue. No larynx. No belly. No anus.*" (*AO* 8). And, one might add, no penis, since Oedipal genitality, phallic intention, was an irrelevance to Artaud. For Deleuze and Guattari, the point is not simply that the schizo is bisexual. "He is," they tell us, "transsexual." Moreover, "he is trans-alivedead, trans-parentchild" (*AO* 77). He has, as Deleuze and Guattari put it, "carried his flows right into the desert," a sort of Alceste who never had a Célimène (67). Artaud found himself with no shape, illustrating the death instinct or desire desiring death "just as it desires life, because the organs of life are *the working machine.*" Similarly, Judge Schreber in Freud's portrayal lived for a long time without stomach or intestines, almost without lungs. "Desiring machines," Deleuze and Guattari tell us, "work only when they break down, and by continually breaking down" (8). Like Bersani, Deleuze and Guattari are faithful deconstructionists. Rather archly, though, they pull away from clarity on these important points: "We shall not inquire how all this fits together so that the machine will run." Perhaps they should inquire instead of retreating into obscurity, which they do from time to time. What is apparently clear to them, at any rate, is that the body without organs "has nothing whatsoever to do with the body itself, or with an image of the body," for "it is the body without an image." This is its advantage: "[It is] nonproductive . . . It is perpetually reinserted into the process of production." It is in conflict with desiring machines, resisting their connected flows with "a counterflow of amorphous, undifferentiated fluid." To resist using words, it utters, Artaud-like, "gasps and cries that are sheer unarticulated blocks of sound." It releases an energy that Deleuze and Guattari consider "divine" (12), which explains, for example, the strange relationship that Schreber has with God, fantasizing himself as God's female lover.

Above all, "the 'either . . . or . . . or' of the schizophrenic takes over from the 'and then'" (*AO* 12). Freud's reading of Schreber is the reductive, Oedipal "and then." He maintains "intact the rights of Oedipus in the God of delirium" (13). Oedipus to the contrary, the schizo would say, as Artaud does, "I, Antonin Artaud am my son, my father, my mother, and myself" (15). Schreber's fantasized breasts are "the actual lived emotion of having breasts" (19); his fantasy of having his anus "miraculated" by the sun is similar.[5] We must, say Deleuze and Guattari, ascend to "the code of delirium" and its "extraordinary fluidity." We must aspire to the reality of the schizophrenic, who "deliberately *scrambles all the codes* . . . never giving the same explanation from one day to the next" (15). For Deleuze and Guattari, it is intolerable that the schizophrenic has been reduced to autism when he has "sought to remain at the unbearable point where the mind touches matter and lives in every intensity" (19–20). So there we have it, the madman as hero, when the reality is that the schizophrenic has "sought" nothing of the kind. In ascribing a creative will to the schizophrenic, Deleuze and Guattari indulge, however tangentially, in the humanism they despise. It is as if they prefer Nietzsche mad to Nietzsche sane. They can then take his rantings on historical figures—"They're *me*!"—as an illustration of the idea that "no one has been as deeply involved in history as the schizo . . . He consumes all universal history in one fell swoop" (21). How would this go down at the Historical Association? But then what should one expect from a collection of Oedipalizing goons whose passion is circumscribed by mere fact?

Deleuze and Guattari anticipate psychiatric resistance—who would consent to his own dismemberment? "There are those who will maintain," they realize, "that the schizo is incapable of uttering the word *I*, and that we must restore his ability to pronounce this hallowed word. All of which the schizo sums up by saying" that "they're fucking me over again: 'I won't say *I* any more'" (*AO* 23). Here and elsewhere in the writings of Deleuze and Guattari—and those of other antipsychiatrists, like David Cooper—schizo intransigence is intensified by Oedipal pressure. Deleuze and Guattari hold, invidiously, that Freud does not like schizophrenics, in particular their resistance to Oedipalization: "They mistake words for things, he says. They are apathetic, narcissistic, cut off from reality, incapable of achieving transference" (23). Yet Deleuze and Guattari, in effect, make some of these points themselves—for example, that for the schizophrenic the word and the thing are one; saying is doing. While Freud considers this an ominous weakness, Deleuze and Guattari consider it a hopeful strength. For them, the personal is the social. It can ideally—and did in 1968 and in postmodern literature—lead to the breakdown of boundaries, limits, roles, functions, disciplines, and genres. Freud sees schizophrenia as a dissolution of epistemic order and a challenge to professional authority, or something bad; Deleuze and Guattari see it the same way and pronounce it good. For them the problem lies not in schizophrenia but in considering schizophrenia only as an illness, which, they say, it is or can be. In fact, they view it as "our characteristic malady"—and here they become subtler than some other French Marxists—not merely because "modern life drives people mad" with its social and economic inequity but because "capitalism, through its process of production, produces an awesome schizophrenic accumulation of energy or charge" (34). It does this because it avoids limits while tending toward limit—that is, repression. For Deleuze and Guattari, "the schizophrenic deliberately seeks out the very limit of capitalism: he is its inherent tendency brought to its fulfillment" (35).

This is an engaging idea that requires an explanation of their sense of the social consequences of capitalism. Like capitalism, the schizophrenic unscrambles the codes, pushes toward the illimitable, but seems to deflate in reality. Deleuze and Guattari see the affinity between the two as "great." Capitalism "sets into motion schizo-flows that animate 'our' arts and 'our' sciences, just as they congeal into the production of 'our own' sick, the schizophrenics . . . Our society produces schizos the same way it produces Prell shampoo or Ford cars" (*AO* 245). This is a wildly materialistic view of how art and science are produced, totally destructive of individual will, treating creativity and genius as if they had no reality of their own. How did "capitalism" produce a Henry James, a Wallace Stevens, or a Saul Bellow? Are these writers products? And even Deleuze and Guattari have to admit that capitalism did not invent schizophrenia. At their worst, Deleuze and Guattari are no different from other leftists who blame everything on social injustice. Are schizos a product? Deleuze and Guattari's very use of the words *product* and *production* begs the question of cure. Life is not manufactured, it is organic; it is not uniform, as production inevitably implies, it is individuated. Deleuze and Guattari are not romantics, they are a parody of romanticism, a grotesque distortion of Blakean energetics.

Respected psychiatric opinion (of course, Deleuze and Guattari would argue that there is no such thing) holds that schizophrenics are born, not made. For example, a study of the Holocaust that shows extreme stress produces neurotics, not psychotics. Deleuze and Guattari need psychotics, uncompromising heroes, intransigent enemies of the system, people whom they say Freud did not understand. They need the rebel against Oedipalization who will "no longer say me . . . no longer say daddy-mommy—and . . . he keeps his word" (*AO* 362). But this is one of the key places in which their conflation of real schizophrenia and the schizo, disease and inspired anarchy, breaks down. The real schizophrenic cannot keep his word. There is no word to keep. The schizophrenic *is* sick and no amount of cultural sophistry will change that. Why, Deleuze and Guattari ask, does "capitalist production . . . make the schizophrenic into a sick person?" And "why does it confine its madmen and madwomen instead of seeing in them its own heroes and heroines, its own fulfillment?" If there were ever questions that answered themselves, these do. Deleuze and Guattari are not interested in questions; they have all the answers. But the second question in particular is the acme of self-reference, and with it their system breaks down.

The idea of treating sickness as the real health is a form of romantic sentimentalism. Here we have a long, opaque, monumentally abstract, doggedly logical tome singing the praises of the true spontaneity: psychic anarchy. For this is what Deleuze and Guattari's schizophrenia is, ideally—flows, fragments, partial objects, the "nomadic self" finding its true home, nowhere in particular. They have the answer to the question why capitalism imprisons the mad who are in reality its very fulfillment. It brings about "the decoding of the flows that other social formations (the Primitive, the Despotic) coded and overcoded" (*AO* 246). This process of "deterritorialization" makes capitalism "the *relative* limit" of every society. Schizophrenia, they maintain, is "the *absolute* limit that causes the flow to travel in a free state on a desocialized body without organs. Hence one can say that schizophrenia is the *exterior* limit of capitalism itself and the conclusion of its deepest tendency, but that capitalism only functions on condition that it inhibit this tendency, that it push back or displace this limit, by substituting for it its own *immanent* relative limits . . . It axiomatizes with one hand what it decodes on the other." In other words, compared to social systems of the past, capitalism liberates libido, but since it commodifies all value—material and fantasy value—it inhibits its liberating tendencies. The ideal schizophrenic energy is released but then canceled by, say, the boss or the shrink. Health thereby is reduced to sickness.

Deleuze and Guattari's two poles of desire, schizophrenia and paranoia, are, roughly, the id and superego. The despotic or paranoid element in capitalist culture can be subjugated only by the triumph of the liberated or schizophrenic element. Because of this, schizophrenia "is not the identity of capitalism, but on the contrary its difference, its divergence, and its death" (*AO* 246). For capitalism to die, the individual subject must be displaced by the group subjects. Socially sensitive, schizoid, and revolutionary, these groups will transcend Oedipalization and subvert commodification. Potentially the most liberating of the social systems, capitalism is actually the worst because social repression is strongest in it. This explains the widespread freeing of a death instinct (in Deleuze and Guattari, a condition that is historically and socially determined) that "crushes desire" (262). When push comes to shove in Deleuze and Guattari, it is Marx who pushes and Freud who is shoved: "Individual persons are social persons first. Private persons are therefore images of a second order." Indeed, "private persons are an illusion," an illusion named Oedipus (264).

Deleuze and Guattari's loathing for capitalism climaxes in sheer hysteria in the concluding pages of *Anti-Oedipus*—perhaps an example of the delirium they cherish. For them, capitalism's "mode of subjugation has no equal" (*AO* 372). It "does not run the risk of becoming mad, it is mad from one end to the other and from the beginning, and this is the true source of its rationality." Furthermore, it "is defined by a cruelty having no parallel in the primitive system of cruelty, and by a terror having no parallel in the despotic regime of terror" (374). The few positive steps taken by capitalists—wage increases, improvements in workers' standard of living, the New Deal, the acceptance of strong unions—are merely steps to appease the Soviet Union. Deleuze and Guattari do not mention that these steps were partly the result of a viable, democratic, anti-Soviet Left in Western countries. Rather, "exploitation grows constantly harsher . . . final solutions of the 'Jewish problem' variety are prepared down to the last detail" (373). So capitalism and totalitarianism are moral equivalents. Indeed, capitalism is a holocaust. "The factories are prisons," Deleuze and Guattari aver. "Everything in the system is insane" (374). Given their universe of competing desires, they cannot even attack capitalism where it is most vulnerable to attack: its element of moral rot; the greed revealed in, for example, the obscene pay differentials between executives and workers (not to mention the threat of political oligarchy deriving from this); outrageous accounting practices to benefit the corporate elite; colossal scandals like the bipartisan subprime mortgage disaster. It is not so much the greed of capitalism but its "unconscious libido, a disinterested love" (374) that drives Deleuze and Guattari to distraction.

Seeing none of the positives in capitalism in itself, they will not settle for reform but remain intransigently revolutionary—in other words, ineffective. To the last, they say that "the revolutionary investment of desire . . . is indeed what undermines capitalism" (*AO* 378). They hope for the "one manifestation of desire, which would be enough to make its fundamental structure explode" (379). They wonder whether this will come from "a Castro, an Arab, a Black Panther, or a Chinaman [sic] on the horizon. A May '68, a home-grown Marxist?" Even they see a sadness to their fantasies: "Fascist colonels start reading Mao, we won't be fooled again; Castro has become impossible even in relation to himself" (378). This 1972 prognostication for capitalism could not have been more wrong. It seems that almost everybody wants to benefit from the system that Deleuze and Guattari despise. (Someone should have told them that capitalism has to do with economics. In an age of much creative economic thought, the one economic text they quote—besides Marx—is a Marxist study that has not generated much interest in decades.)[6] After Deleuze and Guattari, what? The new philosophers are a return, in a sense, to the anticommunism of Aron and Camus in the late 1940s.

Given the double-barreled hell of Oedipus and capitalism, is it any wonder that a good schizo would want to escape? This is the direction first sketched by R. D. Laing in *The Politics of Experience*. Deleuze and Guattari hold that Laing "is entirely right in defining the schizophrenic process as a voyage of initiation, a transcendental experience of the loss of the Ego, which causes a subject to remark: 'I had existed since the very beginning . . . from the lowest form of life [the body without organs][7] to the present time . . . ahead of me was lying the most horrific journey'" (*AO* 84). The adjective *horrific* is as important as the noun. To their credit, Deleuze and Guattari see the schizo as involved in a difficult journey, the journey to the interior. But this is not the subjective interior. The schizo "hallucinates and raves universal history, and proliferates the races." He does not represent races and cultures; they designate regions on his body without organs. Once again, Artaud is a model. "The theater of cruelty," Deleuze and Guattari note, "cannot be separated from the struggle against our culture, from the confrontation of the 'races,' and from Artaud's great migration to Mexico, its forces and its religions: individuations, not individuals, are produced only within fields of forces expressly defined by good vibrations, and that animate cruel personages only in so far as they are induced organs, parts of desiring-machines" (85). But can one speak of individuations and deny individuality?

The schizo is a deconstructed subject, and notions of individuality—ego—are irrelevant to Deleuze and Guattari. There is nonetheless "a season in hell," not to be "separated from denunciations of European families, from the call for destructions . . . from the admiration of the convict, from the intense crossing of the thresholds of history . . ." (*AO* 85–86). Deleuze and Guattari here invoke Rimbaud, another member of the schizo pantheon, and his sense of delirious denunciation: "I have never been a Christian . . . yes my eyes are closed to your light. I am a beast, a Negro" (quoted at 86). "Je suis un autre," said Rimbaud famously in another context, and this might be a motto for Deleuze and Guattari's schizo, who "has no principles: he is something only by being something else." Such, say Deleuze and Guattari, is "the 'historianism' of the schizophrenic . . . the true program for a theater of cruelty, the *mise-en-scène* of a machine to produce the real" (87). In the theater of cruelty, Deleuze and Guattari find an analogy to their own rage. Artaud's *Héliogobale*, in which the delirious hero is conceived in sperm and dies in shit, is a cherished masterpiece. The chronicled Caesar's rise and fall "into the latrines of the city" cause them to ask rhetorically: "Wasn't it already the anus that detached the object on high and produced the eminent voice?" (211). Didn't the transcendence of the phallus depend on the anus? That is, since the anus was "the first organ to suffer privation, removal from the social field," sublimation results from this. "*The whole of Oedipus is anal* and implies an individual overinvestment of the organ to compensate for its collective disinvestment" (143). The universal anality of culture is why the vanquished despot is nothing more than this "dead rat's ass suspended from the ceiling of the sky," an Artaud quote that is a favorite of theirs. "The entire history of the graphic flux," they say, "goes from the flood of sperm in the tyrant's cradle, to the wave of his shit in his sewer tomb—'all writing is so much pig shit [another quote from Artaud],' all writing in this simulation, sperm and excrement" (211). Deleuze and Guattari like this oracular utterance of Artaud's so well that they repeat it several times in their book. They cannot get enough of rubbing civilization's face in the mud. In reducing culture to pig shit, Deleuze and Guattari recall the worst days of 1968. They want to rethink toilet training. They want to rethink toilets. *Anti-Oedipus* is, among other things, an exercise in sadism.

Though they laud the schizo, they themselves are intentional. They are aware of this and somewhat embarrassed by it. They note, for example, that schizoanalysis has no political program to propose. This is because they are "still too competent" but "would like to speak in the name of an absolute incompetence" (AO 380). They must be aware of the irony: how can an absolute incompetence speak? Then again, that is what they want, speech unspoken. Grunts, perhaps, and other sounds. Artaud. Their concept of the schizophrenic remains vague and sentimental. Does anyone agree with them that "far from having lost who knows what contact with life, the schizophrenic is closest to the beating heart of reality, to an intense point identical with the production of the real" (87)? True disintegration cannot easily be equated with being free. Despite all their efforts, being bound is not being free. It was the sane Artaud who wrote his impressive essays—the White Period Artaud—though even these essays are somewhat ominous. Deleuze and Guattari's schizo is itself a problematic conception. "These men of desire," they say, "or do they not yet exist?—are like Zarathustra. They know incredible sufferings, vertigoes, and sicknesses . . . But such a man produces himself as a free man, irresponsible, solitary, and joyous, finally able to do something simple in his own name, without asking permission; a desire lacking nothing, a flux that overcomes barriers and codes, a name that no longer designates any ego whatever. He has simply ceased being afraid of being mad" (131). Rudnytsky rightly points out that the "sufferings, vertigoes, and sicknesses" of schizophrenia are undercut by Deleuze and Guattari's portrayal of "their imaginary egoless 'schizo' as 'free and joyous.'"[8] And what is this "desire lacking nothing," this doing conceived as illimitable desire? It would have to issue from beyond the reality principle, which includes lack. What is such a quality but another form of sentimentality?

Their claims for the schizo are often wildly extravagant. They ridicule the notion that "a little neurosis is good for the work of art, good material, but not psychosis, especially not psychosis. As if the great voices, which were capable of performing a breakthrough in grammar and syntax, and of making all language a desire, were not speaking from the depths of psychosis, and as if they were not demonstrating for our benefit an eminently psychotic and revolutionary means of escape" (AO 134). All modernisms, then, indeed all styles created in the rapture (or delirium) of an aesthetic bliss, are illustrations of madness. And how do such breakthroughs come about without the ego? Can style be egoless?[9] When they say that "the schizophrenic voyage is the only kind there is," crossing any limit becomes schizo, and the use of the word *schizo* becomes hopelessly vague. Is an ancestral voyage a schizo voyage? On the contrary. Deleuze and Guattari's use of the words *molar* and *molecular*, another way of stating their ideal polarity of paranoia and schizophrenia, gives rise to another bizarre judgment: "There is a whole biology of schizophrenia, molecular biology" (289). In their ideal molecular chain, "everything is possible" (328). They make neutral particles sound like nineteenth-century Russian nihilists. But molecular biology shows that this is not the case, that there is an order governing even the smallest particles. Scientists will be glad to know that Deleuze and Guattari consider them schizos.

Schizoanalysis can be understood only in the context of a redefinition of desire. This redefinition actually begins for Deleuze and Guattari with Freud, who "discovers the subjective nature or abstract essence of desire . . . who is thus the first to engage desire itself" (*AO* 299–300). Freud put the Cartesian cogito to rest by showing that the essence of man was desire not thought—and that desire is often bound to the unconscious. This is the meaning of Faust's modern restlessness, as Brown says, and of our fascination with Augustinian restlessness: "men are not satisfied by the satisfaction of their conscious desires; men are unconscious of their real desires."[10] Freudian sexuality, Brown notes, "is the energy of desire with which the human being pursues pleasure, with the further specification that the pleasure sought is the pleasurable activity of an organ of the human body" (25–26). It may be genital (the penis), oral (the mouth), or visual (the eyes), but it is always personal. And, as in the tradition of Western humanism generally, it always implies a lack. It is with these last two qualifications that Freud went wrong, say Deleuze and Guattari. For them desire is not personal, and it does not imply a lack.

The wedding of desire to lack is what makes desire personal, intentional. Instead, say Deleuze and Guattari, desire should be understood "in the real order of its production . . . as a molecular phenomenon devoid of any goal or intention" (*AO* 342). For them there is no such thing as independent spheres, no distinction between man and nature since both are within nature in the form of production. Borrowing from Marx and science, Deleuze and Guattari describe the hard facts of a material world. But *production* implies a product being produced, which itself is intentional. And it implies a factory, not the organic world. Deleuze and Guattari maintain that the world is a factory, that there is nothing organic in the sense of the living individual, the personal. Therefore, "desire is never signifying, it exists in the thousands of productive break-flows that never allow themselves to be signified within the unary stroke of castration" (112). If desire is repressed, it is because it is potentially subversive: "there is no desiring-machine . . . without demolishing entire social sectors," for "desire is revolutionary in its essence" (116). Political desire, a machine for repression, is still desire. Unlike Reich, they make no distinction between political economy and libidinal economy. Freud's erotic motive does not have to do with Oedipus but with the social field. "We believe in desire," Deleuze and Guattari say, "because it is the production of desire" (379). When in doubt, rely on the circular. Fluxes, planes, particles, molecules—Deleuze and Guattari give us metaphor masked as scientific fact. This is the essence of their denatured self. The erotic, if this word can be used in so random a context, is seen to be an impersonal mechanism that pleasures itself as it can. The coldness of this idea is so obvious that it can be reached best perhaps in the form of a junior high school limerick:

> There was a young man from Nantucket
> Whose prick was so long he could suck it.
> He said with a grin
> As he wiped off his chin
> If my ear was a cunt I would fuck it.

Not to worry. Nature is full of apertures with which to perform the schizo polka. Auto-eroticism in Deleuze and Guattari may mean a gas tank. In Brown's resexualized speech, angels impregnate *women* through the ear.

The metaphor of the machine is at the center of the elaborate rational fantasy that is *Anti-Oedipus*. Deleuze and Guattari's is a nonmechanistic machine because a real machine would imply mechanism, which "abstracts a *structural unity* in terms of which it explains the functioning of the organism" (*AO* 337). There is no such unity in the desiring machine. Real machines have an intention; the great thing about them is that they work predictably. Deleuze and Guattari's use of simile is flauntingly pedestrian: They will never issue upward comparisons. For example, the machine "functions like a ham-slicing machine, removing portions from the associative flow. . . . The mouth . . . cuts off not only the flow of milk but the flow of sound" (36). There is something grotesque in their schizo imagery. What about the mouth that speaks, that utters moving sentiments, that expresses passion—the personal mouth?

Their constant and perverse insistence on dehumanization yields one of the more remarkable images of the book. They cite as a model of their thesis Joey of Bruno Bettelheim's *The Empty Fortress*, who "can live, eat, defecate, and sleep only if he is plugged into machines provided with motors, wires, lights, carburetors, propellers, and steering wheels: an electronic feeding machine, a care machine that enables him to breathe, an anal machine that lights up" (37). This machine makes Deleuze and Guattari feel perfectly at home for, as they tell us, "there are very few examples that cast as much light on the régime of desiring production, and the way in which breaking down constitutes an integral part of functioning, or the way in which the cutting off is an integral part of mechanical connections" (37). They are serious, deeply ensconced in their own mythology of a body without organs. They do anticipate the obvious: "Doubtless there are those who will object that this mechanic, schizophrenic life expresses the absence and the destruction of desire rather than desire itself, and presupposes certain extremely negative attitudes on the part of his parents to which the child reacts by turning himself into a machine." But quite apart from the attitude of Joey's parents—perhaps we do not know enough about their particular trial to judge at this point—the fact that Deleuze and Guattari can use this contraption as an illustration of human possibility is staggering. From Dickens's Smallweeds family to Kafka's Gregor Samsa, the modern reader has become inured to downward comparisons. Yet the relentlessly perverse logic of Deleuze and Guattari makes this image particularly repellent. Of course, Bettelheim must have been confronted with an extremely difficult case. But Deleuze and Guattari set this up as a model of desire!

In another illustration, they say that "Moses flees from the Egyptian machine into the wild and installs his new machine there, a holy ark and a portable temple, and gives his people a new religious-military organization" (*Ao* 193). The holy ark and what it contains is, to say the least, a great work of imagination. Imagination, it is said, is the only home of illimitable desire. In this case we have proof that there may be an illimitable desire for the moral, the totalizing, the limiting. Deleuze and Guattari manage to reduce the ultimate father, God, to a machine. Of course it is a paranoiac, molar machine, barbarian and despotic, rather than a schizophrenic, molecular machine. The important thing to remember, they say, is that "desire is not in the subject . . . the real difference is not between the living and the machine, vitalism and mechanism, but between two states of the machine that are two states of the living as well" (206). This statement is logically consistent but a travesty of human creativity.

One final machine illustration from the schizo world: a schizo who does well in third grade, provided he works in mechanics. "The man in the garage has been his best therapist," says the psychiatric report that Deleuze and Guattari cite (*AO* 381). If we take the mechanics away, the report continues, the boy will be schizophrenic again. For Deleuze and Guattari, this "marks the point where the social machine, the technical machine, and the desiring machine join closely together . . . this is indeed the direction the social, technical, scientific and artistic machines take when they are revolutionary." Their ecstasy here suggests that this may be the answer—let's all be auto mechanics! To come up with such a small example as proof of their grandiose thesis is laughable. Deleuze and Guattari are breaking new ground here, the revolutionary auto mechanic. Maybe it is because of what the psychiatrist said to the auto mechanic: get under the couch.

Despite their round-the-clock cannonading, Deleuze and Guattari do have some respect for the couch. They do acknowledge its originality: "The great discovery of psychoanalysis was that of production of desire, the productions of the unconscious" (AO 211). But they do so in a way that unwittingly cancels the acknowledgment. Libido and the unconscious are not productions, not manufactured by Nature Inc., that material corporation. They are not assembly-line stuff, but individuated, organic, vitalistic. "Vitalism," Deleuze and Guattari say, "invokes an *individual specific* unity of the living, which every machine presupposes insofar as it is subordinate to organic continuance" (284). But this is not very far. Machines, as common wisdom has it, do not libidinally reproduce themselves, which in some of its most exalted moments is what libido is about. Deleuze and Guattari have no real way of dealing with creation, not to mention Creation. Machines, production—they are left with a series of metaphors of sterility.

Their infatuation with individuality is not long-lived. There is no individual, they tell us, "there is only desire and environments, fields, forms of herd instinct. Stated differently, the molecular desiring-machines are in themselves the investment of the large molar machines or of the configurations that the desiring-machines form *according to the laws of large numbers*" (AO 287). Let's not be anecdotal, they say in solid statistical fashion. But literature is anecdotal, as is the humanistic enterprise generally, including psychoanalysis. What genuinely reveals the true self is the prime subject matter of the humanities. Style is the avenue to this revelation, and it does not create itself.

In Deleuze and Guattari's gloss on Engel's reading of Balzac—unmistakably their gloss—they beg to differ with this view of style. They write: "Engels demonstrated how an author is great because he cannot prevent himself from tracing flows and causing them to circulate, flows that split asunder the catholic and despotic signifier of his work, and that necessarily nourish a revolutionary machine on the horizon. That is what style is, or rather the absence of style—asyntactic, agrammatical: the moment when language is no longer defined by what it says, even less by what makes it a signifying thing, but by what causes it to move, to flow, and to explode—desire. For literature is like schizophrenia: a process, and not a goal, a production and not an expression" (*AO* 133). Desire, then, has no aim. Balzac's style, therefore, must be characterized as stylelessness. So there is Balzac, going, as it were, with the revolutionary flow, despite himself—not an artist but a medium, an instrument of explosive desire; his work schizophrenic, not created, not individual, not an utterance but produced by an impersonal process. Balzac, the carrier of an indispensable delirium. "For the real truth of the matter," for Deleuze and Guattari, "the glaring, sober truth that resides in delirium"—a sober delirium? —"is that there is no such thing as relatively independent spheres or circuits: production is immediately consumption and a recording process. Everything is production: production of productions, of actions and of passions" (4). Somehow genius writes itself. "Production as process overtakes all idealistic categories," they say. The schizo is *Homo natura*. Integrity is not the word; it implies integration, wholeness, rationality. Deleuze and Guattari are for salvationary disintegration.

The schizo, then, "is not revolutionary, but the schizophrenic process—in terms of which the schizo is merely the interruption, or the continuation in the void—is the potential for revolution" (*AO* 341). Elsewhere they simply say that "the schizophrenic process (the schizoid pole) is revolutionary" (379–80), just as the paranoiac pole is reactionary and fascist. Their world is a struggle between polar opposites. There is no room for the middle. This is why Guattari can ridicule the labor movement for dealing with questions of family in the context of "'quality of life' and other nonsense." But mention homosexuality, delinquency, abortion "they call in the cops."[11] They will not, he complains, tackle "libido-revolutionary" problems.

Yet all of his pet issues have become "middle" issues. And despite himself, Guattari cannot get away from the pragmatism of reform. He avers that "much as I am against the illusion of a step by step transformation of society— 'small reforms which make up great transformations'—I believe that microscopic attempts at creating communities, setting up analytic groups among militants, organizing a day-care center at a university—are crucial."[12] In his mind, this sort of thing will lead to "a great big rip like May '68." But the opposite is likely to be true. Except for the word *militants*, he might be describing "middle" America. There is more resilience to reform in bourgeois society than Deleuze and Guattari could ever admit. Guattari himself complains that the weakness of neo-Marxism is its reductive dualism—class struggle, city versus country, peace camp versus war camp. The neo-Marxists are as molar as the fascists. Micropolitics, on the other hand, would not represent the masses. But it "would place itself in opposition to the Manichean dualism that presently contaminates the revolutionary movements" ("Everybody" 89). May 1968 is his illustration and his hope. But he is already indulging in nostalgia. There is a winsome sadness to the Deleuze and Guattari enterprise. Guattari knows that he is a radical talking to radicals.

May 1968, it can be argued, had something to do with changes in antinuclear policy and environmentalism—that is, reformist rather than revolutionary changes. Above all, it brought the Left from economics to a politics of anarchic impulse and personal revolution, "revolution for the hell of it," in Abbie Hoffman's phrase.[13] "Take your desires for reality," read a line of graffiti in the Sorbonne courtyard in 1968; "liberate psychoanalysis," read another, and they might have been written by Deleuze and Guattari or by Reich—who, as Sherry Turkle attests,[14] became a *maître à penser* during *Les Évènements*, the French student uprising. Deleuze and Guattari became symbols of 1968 and its "*spontenéism*," though this is not quite what they were about. And, according to Alice Jardine, they were "fervently worshipped by a vocal (male) student minority."[15] Although a failure in terms of practical politics, May 1968 did consolidate Marxism and antipsychiatry. The American turn toward psychoanalysis and self after 1968, as Turkle argues, was accompanied by a disillusionment with politics, but that was not the case in Paris where, it is said, it is always May 1968—at least in certain purlieus. The major result of Les Évènements in terms of practical politics was the de Gaulle landslide, the return of the repressed, Big Daddy. Not that the French take all this as solemnly or as melodramatically as some Americans do. To anyone residing in Paris at the time, as I was, it was obvious that there was skepticism about de Gaulle even at the moment of his ascendency as there was about the *dix huitards*. A certain subtlety of the historical dialectic was assumed. The French had a tolerance for revolutionary impulse in this country of 1789 because they seemed fated to repeat it (even if only in the diminished version delineated by Marx in his *Eighteenth Brumaire*). Revolution was somehow French. One had to love it as one would one's obstreperous child. Yet *plus ça change, plus c'est la même chose*—in a nation with a passion for paradox, this one is the most time honored and the most profound.

When *Anti-Oedipus* came out in 1972, it was a cause célèbre in Paris for those who still carried the revolutionary torch. Among other things, the book satisfied a need for those who felt that the revolution required the reinvention of language. The authors' perverse style, as T. J. Adamowski said in his review of the book, "seems intended to deny us the traditional language by which we speak of the self, a language that in the view of the authors has been corrupted by centuries of fear in the face of the impervious surge of desire."[16] I agree with those who consider it a paranoid style, illustrative of the totalizing mentality the authors purport to condemn. It is a style conspicuously conscious of its own brilliance, a style of so many provocative reversals that they become all but mechanical ("alphabetical writing is not for illiterates but by illiterates" [208]; "only the mind is capable of shitting" [143]), a style and a logic straining every nerve to astound ("There is no such thing as incest" [2]; "desire and its object are one and the same thing" [26]). And, for all its brilliance, it is a style of unsettling confusion ("but it seems that things are becoming very obscure" [330]; "the situation is completely muddled" [350]). It is an eclectic and sometimes raunchy, funny style as well, at those times, as Mark Seem notes in his introduction to the book, closer to Henry Miller than to Marx and Freud. There is something Falstaffian about this big book; it is not only a source of wit but a source of wit in others. Above all, as anyone who has actually read this opaque tome can attest—and its readers are certainly far fewer than those who talk about it—the style is an intensely academic style (my favorite word is *biunivocal*), casting doubt in its very incarnation on the authors' assault on reason. Indeed, it is a style, not—as they would ideally have it—a stylelessness.

For all its ponderousness, there is a weightlessness to *Anti-Oedipus*. The more we penetrate its logic, the more we see it as a work of mysticism. Like medieval monks, Deleuze and Guattari are transforming this difficult world, averting their gaze from it in favor of a Utopian vision, a Utopia without transcendence. "Someone asked us if we had ever seen a schizophrenic," they remark. But "no, no, we have never seen one" (*AO* 380). And, in their sense, they never will. As Jay Cantor has argued, "*Anti-Oedipus* lacks concreteness and the schizo is often a somewhat imaginary creation." How would schizo revolutionaries talk to each other? How "in the iridescent flux of constantly changing meanings would we make our lives together? How would the social and the unconscious coexist in the continuous transformations without either the disconnection of madness (they don't recognize this), or the flux giving rise to a social world that would crush it?"[17] We must be tough-minded. We cannot place responsibility for unhappiness exclusively on the social— Freudian and religious humanists are in agreement on this point—which, considering Deleuze and Guattari's conflation of Oedipus and capitalism is just what they do, if not so obviously as the kind of Marxism they transcend. "Desiring production is the utopia of a universe without conflict," as Girard says.[18] And Trilling has rightly criticized Deleuze and Guattari's fellow Utopian Laing for ruling out the possibility "that pain is inherent in the process of mind."[19] Sylvère Lotringer, a fellow traveler of Deleuze and Guattari and the editor of the issue of *Semiotext(e)* called "Schizo Culture," says that one "does not cure neurosis, one changes a society that cannot do without it."[20] The implication is that only then will neurosis be "cured"—homeopathically, in this case, by heavy doses of psychosis or at least a psychotic style. Neurosis, though, can be another name for what used to be called unhappiness. Neurosis can be the psychological documentation of the difficulty of being. Doubtless different cultures have different kinds of psychological problems, but wishing them away is an evasion. Like Marx, Deleuze and Guattari want a withering away of the human condition. The final words of *Anti-Oedipus* call for what Lawrence called for, a "new earth" (382). A new republic is possible; a new earth is an unfulfillable desire.

[INTERCHAPTER]

DELEUZE AND GUATTARI
ON LAWRENCE AND MILLER

Deleuze and Guattari seem rather shaky when it comes down to cases. Two of their exemplars, D. H. Lawrence and Henry Miller, are central figures in this study. Just how they are exemplary to Deleuze and Guattari and, indeed, whether they are really, is a matter of particular relevance. Lawrence is the first example to be considered here.

Deleuze and Guattari focus on *Aaron's Rod*. Though, understandably, they are more interested in Lawrence's ideas than in his fictional patterns, it is not accidental that they choose a novel in which the hero intransigently repudiates family—namely, his own. Lawrence himself was, at this stage, no respecter of family normalcy and decorum, yet the heartlessness with which Aaron walks out on it all—Lawrence has a woman do this too, in *The Woman Who Rode Away*—is about as stony as the novelist gets. The virtue of such hardness, with which the reader is invited to sympathize, the radical split or what Deleuze and Guattari would call the schizo break, makes Aaron an antihero close to their hearts.

Lawrence appears in three different guises in the novel: Aaron, Lilly, and the narrator. Aaron is the spirit of revolt manifested in a more or less ordinary man, or ordinary musician. Lilly is that spirit manifested in the Nietzchean superman as crank. Aaron and Lilly relate to each other as pupil and master in a sort of dialogue of mutual defiance. The third incarnation of Lawrence, the narrative voice, appears most conspicuously—and awkwardly—when Aaron is alone, especially when he is reflecting, to illuminate what Aaron deeply feels but cannot express.

It is from such a passage that Deleuze and Guattari select an exemplary quotation. The narrator tells us that since Aaron is "a musician . . . his deepest *ideas* were not word-ideas, his very thoughts were not composed of words and ideal concepts . . . I, as a word-user, must translate his deep conscious vibrations into finite words."¹ This is not quite convincing even in its own terms, since Aaron does well enough in other situations. Also, his job in the mining world might have given him some such facility. The problem is, additionally, that the line between Lilly's consciousness and Aaron's is occasionally blurred, even though they are usually more like leader and follower, a new Moses and Aaron. At times the Lawrencean message in this didactic book falls on Aaron, and it is the narrator who steps awkwardly into the breach.

Aaron, the unyielding male, has never worshipped women. He comes to the realization that he never intended to yield to Lottie, his wife, nor to his mother or to anybody else. This state of mind recalls the something in Paul Morel of *Sons and Lovers* that Clara can never reach, even in passion. But the theme is undeveloped in *Sons and Lovers*. Lawrence's power phase, of which *Aaron's Rod* is a major example, is a rejection of the Oedipally compromised Paul Morel in its insistence on the isolation of phallic manhood. Lawrence is working out Paul Morel's dependence on his mother with a vengeance. So much the better for Deleuze and Guattari. They would applaud Aaron's idea that "to fling down the whole soul in one gesture of finality in love was as much a criminal suicide as to jump off a church-tower or a mountain-peak" (*AR* 209). They would not use the word *soul* but would admire the deterritorialization and break-flows involved in Aaron's overcoming the despotic Oedipal pattern. The tragedy of modern man for Lawrence is that man, a victim of Oedipal idealization, makes a gift of himself to woman. And woman is nauseated by this gift. Deleuze and Guattari quote from *Aaron's Rod* on this point. Lawrence's narrator says of our distorted love: "We have pushed the process into a goal. The aim of any process is not the perpetuation of that process, but the completion thereof" (*AR* 210). This quotation accords with Deleuze and Guattari's idea of process insofar as it posits a fusion of man and nature, and insofar as love is not viewed as an end in itself. But they then skip over "love is a process of the incomprehensible human soul" and give the impression that Lawrence, like them, is talking not about people but about machines, desiring though they be. What Deleuze and Guattari omit undercuts their materialism. They then quote Lawrence to the effect that "the process should work to a completion, not to some horror of intensification and extremity wherein the soul and body ultimately perish," (210–11) apparently provisionally accepting both soul and the dualism of soul and body. But they leave out Lawrence's main point of emphasis, which contradicts their materialism quite directly: The completion of "the process of love is never accomplished. But it moves in great stages, and at the end of each stage a true goal, where the soul possesses itself in simple and gorgeous singleness. Without this love is a disease" (211). So there is a goal, a "true goal," possession of the self, which Deleuze and Guattari say does not exist. This goal derives from love, but love itself is not the goal. There is, then, a *telos*, an ego dimension to Lawrence's deepest feeling, that contradicts and transcends the idea of material production and process. When Deleuze and Guattari conclude from their use (or abuse) of Lawrence that "schizophrenia is like love: there is no specifically schizophrenic phenomenon or entity; schizophrenia is the universe of productive and reproductive desiring-machines" (*AO* 5), there is a great comedown, a falling away from Lawrence's teleological intensity into mechanistic metaphor.

Indeed, *Aaron's Rod* is an exaltation of a masculine intensity, a valiant ego that is foreign to the determinations of *Anti-Oedipus*. In Florence, Aaron is struck by the city's men who are redolent of "the only manly quality, unyielding, acrid fearlessness" (*AR* 270). This to him is "the eternal challenge of the unquenched human soul . . . men—who existed without apology and without justification." They stand out all the more in contrast to the English homosexuals whom Lawrence portrays mercilessly. (Yet Florence is the city of Michelangelo, whose *David* Aaron endlessly admires. And the somewhat misogynistic Lilly-Aaron relationship, almost a tutor-ephebe one, includes the scene in which Lilly—signifying woman as a first name—massages Aaron's lower body parts. This may suggest that the English homosexuals are only one side of the coin.) We are no longer in the depersonalized world of Deleuze and Guattari.

Aaron's intense attraction to the Marchesa cannot be described as that of a desiring machine. His passion is totally phallic. The narrator speaks of "the powerful male passion, arrogant, royal, Jove's thunderbolt. Aaron's black rod of power, blossoming again with red Florentine lilies and fierce thorns." This is the second and ultimate meaning of the novel's titular metaphor. While Lawrence tends to be ludicrously operatic in his description of phallic ecstasy, this is what he is describing. And Aaron's music is a reflection of this underlying meaning. Thus Deleuze and Guattari's musings seem bloodless: "Will Aaron leave with his flute, which is not a phallus, but a desiring-machine and a process of deterritorialization" (*AO* 357)? The experience described here is not material but religious: "He moved about in the splendour of his own male lightning, invested in the thunder of the male passion-power. He had got it back, the male godliness, the male godhead" (*AR* 326–27). Lawrence may be resistant to Oedipal mythology, but he is dependent on a mythology of his own: "The phoenix had risen in fire again, out of the ashes" (*AR* 327). Deleuze and Guattari's body without organs may be revived, but there is no resurrection in their neutral universe. And resurrection is the ultimate overcoming of a lack. Lawrence does, in his own mind, move away from Oedipal totalizing, but his famous "allotropic" self implies an ontology, an ascent to Being, that is foreign to the atomized universe of Deleuze and Guattari. Lawrence is in this way interested in the whole, not parts. He is a poet of the overcoming of disintegration. The fragmentary is equated with a loss of male status. "Much that is life has passed away from men," the narrator laments, "leaving us all mere bits" (*AR* 336).

Lawrence, in short, is a romantic, and Deleuze and Guattari are not. This is nowhere more apparent than in his affirmation of the organic universe that Deleuze and Guattari deny. "You can't lose yourself, neither in woman nor humanity nor in God," preaches Lilly to the already converted Aaron. Elaborating in terms that Deleuze and Guattari would find alien to their notion of process without goal, Lilly says: "There's no goal outside you—and there's no God outside you . . . There is only one thing, your very own self." In a telling metaphor, Lilly then likens the self to "a germinating egg, your precious Easter egg of your own soul." Resurrection is inextricably bound to biology in Lawrence. Lilly says of "the integral unique self" that "you've got to develop it from the egg into the chicken, and from the chicken into the one and only phoenix, of which there can be only one at a time in the universe." One might ask, how unique can you get? Here Lawrence is very far from the leveling of Deleuze and Guattari. Lilly's organic imagery culminates in an affirmation of the principle of individuation: "your own soul's self." The apparent redundancy indicates that self, or the psychological, is inseparable from soul, or the transcendent. Lawrence's view is basically religious, Deleuze and Guattari's a form of philosophical futurism. So when Lilly concludes that "the only goal is the fulfilling of your own soul's active desire and suggestion," Lawrence is using desire in a different sense from the material one that Deleuze and Guattari employ. Lilly's organic image of the tree—the soul "develops actions within you as a tree develops new cells," truly the "Tree of Life" (*AR* 372–73)—is, in its underlying Hebraic quality, light-years from the machine imagery that Deleuze and Guattari rely on.

Lilly is giving Aaron instruction, but it is not from the actual Hebraic Tree of Life, the Torah. Even in his most didactic moments, Lawrence remains rather Egyptian in his vision of an erotic universe. In *Aaron's Rod*, the Egyptian motif becomes pharaonic. "We've exhausted our love urge, for the moment," says Lilly, "We've got to accept the power motive . . . It was that great dark power-urge which kept Egypt so intensely living for so many centuries . . . the will-to-power—but not in Nietzsche's sense. Not intellectual power. Not mental power. Not conscious will-power. Not even wisdom. But dark, living, fructifying power" (*AR* 376). Despite Lilly's harangues, Aaron is resistant to the "deep, unfathomable free submission" (*AR* 376) that Lilly espouses. Deleuze and Guattari would consider such a submission a reterritorialization to despotic codes, an inevitable turn to Oedipalization. This possibility is part of the reason for Aaron's resistance, but Aaron is not the man of Deleuze and Guattari's figure. Lilly is even farther away.

The first positive task of schizoanalysis, say Deleuze and Guattari, is discovering in a subject how desiring machines function, "independent of any interpretations"—that is, Freudian or other categories except, of course, theirs. Their question is "what are your nonhuman sexes" (*AO* 322)? Hence the phallus is equated with Oedipalization, which means "one and the same penalty, one and the same ridiculous wound for all—castration" (323). They hold that "this whole conception of sexuality . . . horrifies Lawrence precisely because it is no more than a conception, because it is an idea that 'reason' imposes on the unconscious and introduces into the passional sphere . . . here is where desire finds itself trapped, specifically limited to human sex." They use Lawrence's *Psychoanalysis and the Unconscious* as evidence to clinch their argument. "As Lawrence said," they conclude, "analysis does not have to do with anything that resembles a concept or a person, 'the so-called human relations are not involved'" (*AO* 323). Lawrence does recognize the erotic element in nonhuman nature—in animals and even in landscape. But when Lawrence uses the word *phallic* he does not mean Oedipal. When he says that the so-called human relations are not involved, he means that analysis, the unconscious that it employs, should be transcendently directed—"by the unconscious we do mean the soul," he says[2]—that the phallus is first and foremost a religious term, and that Oedipalizing distorts its religious function. Lawrence's unconscious is pure but directed; it is not the amorphous unconscious of Deleuze and Guattari. What Lawrence means by *phallus* Deleuze and Guattari would consider anthropomorphizing.

Their reading of Lawrence's essay "We Need One Another" is equally slipshod. While it is true that, as they say, "Lawrence shows in a profound way that sexuality, including chastity, is a matter of flows" (*AO* 351), he means by *flows* something very different. Lawrence is not in favor of what Deleuze and Guattari call the molecular. His primary concern in this essay is not the part but the "whole," or "wholeness," words he uses eight times in the last ten paragraphs. He also makes use of words like *flow*, *river*, and *vibrations* a number of times in the essay, but they all work toward rather than against wholeness. That is, the piece is an example of Lawrence's personal dialectic, in which the most authentic togetherness respects separation. Lawrence is not talking about a desiring machine but "a vital relationship," not about schizo but "soul." He says: "The wholeness of my soul I must achieve,"[3] a sentiment that could have come from a Midland's chapel. Lawrence does not want fragments. These he is likely to associate with negativity, as when he says: "All I see in our vaunted civilization is men and women smashing each other emotionally to bits" (*Ph* 194). He does, as Deleuze and Guattari say, want to change the existing pattern, "break up this fixity" of woman's roles, "sweetheart, mistress, wife, mother" and "realize the unseizable quality of real woman," her uniqueness, difference, and spontaneous complementarity. Lawrence does not, however, simply blame woman's current roles on the Oedipal triangle. Rather it is a question of man's failure to be in touch with his cosmic roots. Nor does Lawrence repudiate family. Next in importance to the relation of man to woman is that of "man to man," and "a long way after," but specifically included, are "all the other relationships, fatherhood, motherhood, sister, brother, friend" (*Ph* 193). Like the relation between man and woman, these are all essential to "actual human life." It is not clear that Deleuze and Guattari are talking about actual human life.

In all these ways, Deleuze and Guattari misread Lawrence's sense of Oedipalization, but they do not entirely misread it. Lawrence lives the Oedipal pattern in his own way, just as he resists it. The question is defining what there is about it that he resists. The best illustration of this in *Aaron's Rod*, an illustration Deleuze and Guattari use, is the scene in which Jim Bricknell is rambling on about self-sacrificial love. Lilly is physically repelled and regards Jim's physical awkwardness to be a consequence of his feelings. "Look at you," says Lilly, "stumbling and staggering with no use in your legs . . . And it's nothing but your wanting to be loved which does it. A maudlin crying to be loved which makes your knees all go rickety" (*AR* 103). For Deleuze and Guattari, this is desire turning back on itself, Nietzsche's "Ananke of the weak and the depressed, the contagious neurotic Ananke" (*AO* 334). They see this "desire to be loved . . . a desire that is reborn of its own frustration: no, daddy-mommy didn't love me enough." Lilly's view is consonant with this idea, but it takes a different, again Nietzschean, emphasis. Jim had said that "the greatest joy is sacrificing oneself to love . . . Christ is the principle of love" (*AR* 97–98). He does not speak of *someone* to love. Lilly responds, "I think Love and your

Christ detestable . . . *You want to be loved* . . . a man of your years. It's disgusting . . . It wouldn't matter if it did you no harm. But when you stagger and stumble down a road out of sheer sloppy relaxation of your will" (98, 103), it is too much for Lilly to bear. Lilly's argument depends upon a belief in will, consciousness, ego—this is not Deleuze and Guattari's emphasis. Lilly tells Jim: "Stiffen your backbone . . . You should stand by yourself and learn to *be* by yourself" (102). Such individuality to the point of self-reliance is not what Deleuze and Guattari are about. Such individuality is another name for Oedipal resolution, whether Lawrence is consciously aware of it or not. (That Bricknell does have the use of his arms—he knocks the wind out of the haranguing Lilly, to Tanny's apparent satisfaction—is one indication among others that even Lawrence is aware of Lilly's strident quality.)

Lawrence's own resistance to the Oedipus complex is, many concur, a classic case of someone who denies the reality he illustrates. All of Lawrence's work after *Sons and Lovers* can be read as a resolution to the Oedipal crisis dramatized in that novel. Lawrence directly takes on Freud, or what he takes to be Freud, in *Psychoanalysis and the Unconscious* and *Fantasia of the Unconscious*, a confrontation that interests Deleuze and Guattari, although they quote only the first.

Deleuze and Guattari are relentless in exposing what they take to be the "bizarre Freudian mania" of seeing an Oedipus complex behind every tree (*AO* 114). They enlist Lawrence as a like-minded self who agrees that "Oedipus is not a state of desire and the drives, it is an *idea* . . . In the service of repression." Lawrence, after all, speaks of "the flows of sexuality and the intensities of the unconscious" (115). And he does consistently characterize the Oedipus complex in negative terms, simplistically assuming, for example, that Freud says inhibition of the craving for incest is the cause of neurosis. On that ground, Lawrence holds, incest should be accepted as normal sexuality. Again simplistically, Lawrence interprets the Freudian logic to be that any inhibition must be wrong.

Yet there are times in *Fantasia of the Unconscious* where he reads Freud more sympathetically, and this may be why Deleuze and Guattari do not quote from what Lawrence considered to be a subtler book. For example, he speaks of "love-bullying" as a form of spiritual incest (as the author of *Sons and Lovers* knew well), and he says that psychoanalysis has "proved" that love-sympathy between parent and child can lead to incestuous feeling, that "lower involvement" was inevitable. He notes with the wisdom of experience that it is the unhappy woman who turns to her child. Yet he says cavalierly, almost in the same breath, that the "father complex, mother complex, incest dreams"[4] are forgettable, despite making the acolyte feel a false thrill of immorality. Broadly speaking, though, Lawrence softens his anti-Oedipal animus in *Fantasia of the Unconscious* in his general view of the family. He sees the family as "a group of wireless stations, all adjusted to the same, or very much the same vibration." He notes that "between child and parents, the first interplay of primal, pre-mental knowledge and sympathy" takes place, that "it is a great and subtle interplay, and from this interplay the child is built up, body and psyche," and that "any lack of vital interchange between father and child . . . means an inevitable impoverishment to the infant" (72). The importance Lawrence places on the parent-child relationship and the necessity for family warmth, including the vital interchange between father and child, runs counter to Deleuze and Guattari's gestalt.

Lawrence's argument with Freud centers on a rejection of the Freudian unconscious. Freud was mistaken, he says, in seeing there "nothing but a huge slimy serpent of sex, and heaps of excrement, and a myriad of repulsive little horrors spawned between sex and excrement" (*PU* 5). Lawrence objects that psychoanalysis fails to determine "the nature of the pristine unconscious in man" (8). Man's unconscious is where knowledge mainly comes from. That is why knowledge "is always a matter of whole experience," never "a matter of mental conception merely" (15). Because the unconscious contains nothing ideal, nothing conceptual, it contains "nothing in the least personal, since personality, like the ego, belongs to the conscious or mental-subjective self. So the first analyses are, or should be, so impersonal that the so-called *human* relations are not involved" (30).

Deleuze and Guattari seize on this last point, but in a way that distorts Lawrence's intention. Analysis, in their view, should deal mainly with "the mechanic arrangements grasped in the context of their molecular dispersion" (*AO* 323). It must deal with partial objects of desiring machines, not the Oedipal phallus—that "anthropomorphic representation of sex," an idea that reason imposes on the unconscious. Oedipalization limits desire to human sex, unified in the molar constellation, with its fictions of masculine and feminine.

But surely if Lawrence insists on anything, it is the distinction between male and female. He does not equate the Oedipal with the phallic, which he sees as a positive category. Far from molecular dispersion, Lawrence universalizes this central opposition. Far from materialism, Lawrence sees it as mysticism. "Through imagination," Lawrence says, "a man may in his time add to himself the whole of the universe, by increasing pristine realization of the universal," by which he means "a truly male mysticism" (*PU* 40). He rejects Deleuze and Guattari's favored notion of androgyny, maintaining that "every single cell in every male child is male, and every cell in every female child is female. The talk about a third sex, or about the indeterminate sex, is just to pervert the issue" (*FU* 131). That man is to the volitional what woman is to the sympathetic has been reversed by Christian love, as in the case of Bricknell. Still, Lawrence holds, "the gulf between Heliogabalus, or the most womanly man on earth, and the most manly woman, is just the same as ever" (132). This would have to include Judge Schreber. Man is male, woman female. Man is "the eternal protagonist" (133). The hand that rocks the cradle rules the world—this he considers "the hermaphrodite fallacy" (134). In a well-known formulation, Lawrence proclaims that "it is the pure and disinterested craving of the human male to make something wonderful, out of his own head and his own self, and his own soul's faith and delight, which starts everything going" (80).

Lawrence denigrates personality but not character, because the latter reflects a transcendent dimension. Lawrence's male wonder tells us that "the essentially religious or creative motive is the first motive for all human activity" (*FU* 60). He thereby presents us with a purified, if sexist, unconscious. Yet he fails to see the complexity of the Freudian ego and its access to the unconscious as a mediator; he fails to see the sense of moral being in Freud, or that his own sense of male and female is a matter of the conscious as well as the unconscious life. Lawrence does reject the idealization of what he narrowly perceives to be the Oedipus complex but only in favor of a different idealization, which assumes, wrongly, that "psychoanalysis is out, under a therapeutic disguise, to do away with the moral faculty in man" (*PU* 4).

Deleuze and Guattari could never accept the fact that Lawrence's is a religious temperament. Because of this he can complain that Freud, in his neutrality, "can't get down to the rock on which he must build his church" (*PU* 4). Lawrence's church is not Christian but pagan, ancient Egyptian if you will, a religion of erotic relationship or "polarized unison" (*PU* 44), man and woman separately together. His emphasis is on wholeness, on the permanent uniqueness of the relationship, on "the effectual correspondent" (45). We are far from the partial objects of a schizo world. And he is emphatically anthropomorphic. He argues that "the cosmos is nothing but the aggregate of the dead bodies and dead energies of bygone individuals" (*FU* 182). He holds that "since Egypt the sun of creative activity beams from the breast, the heart of the supreme Man. This is to use the source of light—the loving heart, the Sacred Heart" (*PU* 36). We are far from poor Schreber's miraculating and perverse anal sunbeams. "From the sympathetic heart goes forth administering, like sunbeams" (37), says Lawrence. We are at a polar extreme from the fragmentation that Deleuze and Guattari pursue. Sounding positively humanistic, the renegade Lawrence concedes that "we must live by all three, ideal, impulse, and tradition, each in its own hour"—but not, as he sees it, the Oedipal ideal (*FU* 166). In *Fantasia*, Lawrence is given to a kind of rhapsodized totalizing that is remote from anything in Deleuze and Guattari. Lawrence implies the Oedipal resolution and occasionally all but makes it explicit, as when he says in reference to the religious and sexual motives: "The two great impulses are like man and wife, or father and son" (60). He concedes more to concept as well when he says that "even art is utterly dependent on philosophy: or if you prefer it, on a metaphysic" (57). For ballast there is his enduring imperial self, man as God: "For me there is only one law: *I am I*" (66). Could there be anything further from schizo fragmentation than this biblical grandiloquence, even if it is set in a romantic landscape of the self?

If the religious or creative motive is the first necessary thing, Lawrence tells us, "the sexual motive comes second" (*FU* 60). But by sex he does not mean the polymorphous perversity of Deleuze and Guattari. Lawrence means "coition," which he—along with a few billion other people—considers "the essential clue to sex." Without "the consummating act of coition," he avers, sex is "never quite sex . . . just as a eunuch is never a man." But do not talk to the apotheosizers of Artaud about eunuchs! And do not talk to Lawrence about sex that is not phallic. The reconstitution of the phallus is at the core of Lawrence's utopian desire for "a new heaven and a new earth" (140). It cannot be separated from its religious dimension any more than it can replace that dimension. Deleuze and Guattari speak only of a new earth.

Lawrence finds a limit to sexual desire, which he does not regard as self-sustaining. "With sex as the one accepted prime motive," he asserts, "the world drifts into despair and anarchy" (*FU* 144). Though coition is "the vital experience" upon which "the life and very being of the individual largely depends" for Lawrence (141), "sex as an end in itself is a disaster: a vice." Yet there is something worse, for "an ideal purpose which has no roots in the deep sea of passionate sex is a greater disaster still" (214–15). Now he sees only these two negative alternatives: sex as tragedy (think of *Carmen* or *Anna Karenina*) or Christianity. Unlike Deleuze and Guattari, Lawrence goes beyond Oedipalization in identifying the root causes of the modern malady.

Lawrence considers ideal control of the passionate soul "a supreme machine principle," or "the active unit of the material world" (*PU* 12). Psychoanalysis is his illustration, with its "automatic principles . . . like any little mechanic inside the works." Any word as origin "has all the mechanical force of the non-vital universe." One must struggle against "the mechanic-material reality" (47), as represented, say, by "the medicine man" who is "the archmechanic of our day" (*FU* 93). Deleuze and Guattari are also enemies of the ideal or, in their case, the Oedipal, but they are acolytes of the machine. Even though they try to deny that it implies mechanism as they use it, the metaphorical logic of their abiding materialism represents a deindividuation that is the opposite of Lawrence's central thrust.

Deleuze and Guattari say that they reject both mechanism and vitalism. But Lawrence comes, as he puts it, from "the chirpy land of the vitalists" (*FU* 62). Lawrence's "vital flux" is a concept inimical to Deleuze and Guattari, depending as it does on self and another, which brings about "the development and evolution of every individual psyche and physique" (*PU* 46). Nor are his "vital vibrations" in the womb (*FU* 107) the decentered vibrations of Deleuze and Guattari. For Lawrence, even the geological world reflects the vitalism of individuals, "even the sun depends for its heart-beat . . . on the beating hearts of men and beast, on the dynamic of the soul-impulse in individual creatures" (163).

Individuation—on this fundamental point, Lawrence and Deleuze and Guattari are polar opposites. Deleuze and Guattari regard coition as an almost random encounter. For Lawrence, it is momentous because it is the beginning of individuation, for, he says, "on this vital individual experience the life and very being of the individual largely depends" (*FU* 141). Love is "individual integrity"—wholeness—in the context of "interhuman polarity" (*PU* 45). And it is personal. "The face," Lawrence says, "is of course the great window of the self." It is also conventional: "The kiss of the mouth is the first sensual connection" (*FU* 98). Lips are not a partial object, but the beginning of a process of wholeness and completion. From a Lawrencean point of view, what Deleuze and Guattari are talking about is promiscuity or "non-individual connection" (203).

No one believes in the existence of a goal, then, more than Lawrence, and the goal is clear: "the perfecting of each single individuality unique in itself—which cannot take place without a perfected harmony between the beloved" (*PU* 22). Harmony is an ideal, not the built-in dissonance or atonality of *Anti-Oedipus*. Harmony, wholeness—Deleuze and Guattari make the modern Lawrence sound like a classical Greek or a teleologist touting "the whole goal of life," a rhapsodist of "the unconscious soul" (42). All of this is considered in a context of "responsibility" (*FU* 143), ethical rather than material. Lawrence is in the opposite of the poststructuralist schizo mode. For all his complexity, Lawrence is, in fact, Lawrencean. He may shake, but he does not tear down the beliefs he expounds. Lawrence is not the schizo turning on himself. He is not a serial being.[5]

Deleuze and Guattari are on much safer ground with Henry Miller. Indeed, one of the clearest ways of distinguishing between Miller and Lawrence—there are, as we shall see, many—is to use Deleuze and Guattari as an index. They misread Lawrence but rightly judge Miller to be a schizo example.

They recognize a kindred spirit in "the celebration of desire-as-flux expressed in the phrase . . . 'and my guts spilled out in a grand schizophrenic rush, an evacuation that leaves me face to face with the Absolute'" (*AO* 5, note). They like the schizophrenic rush, but they must have demurred at the Absolute, even Miller's. They especially like the flow metaphor, to which their desiring machine gives a binary twist. They write: "Desire causes the current to flow, itself flows in turn, and breaks the flows," like breast and mouth (5). Miller's flow, however, is unrestrained: "I love everything that flows, even the menstrual flow that carries away the seed unfecund."[6] Rather than "even," we might say especially such a flow, considering Miller's preference of process to telos.

Deleuze and Guattari mention Miller with Lawrence, Ginsberg, and Kerouac, among others, as "men who know how to leave, to scramble the codes, to cause flows to circulate, to traverse the desert of the body without organs" (*AO* 132). These writers elicit Deleuze and Guattari's key terminology because they "overcome a limit, they shatter a wall, the capitalist barrier." While this is putting things with a peculiarly Marxist rigidity, the point of romantic rebellion is clear enough. Deleuze and Guattari admit that "of course, they fail to complete the process, they never cease failing to do so. The neurotic impasse again closes—the daddy-mommy of Oedipalization, America . . . or else the perversion of the exotic territorialities, then drugs, alcohol—or worse still, an old fascist dream." They admit that "even those who are best at 'leaving' . . . those who set out in search of non-human sex—Lawrence, Miller—stake out a far-off territoriality that still forms an anthropomorphic and phallic representation: the Orient, Mexico" (315). Deleuze and Guattari will have to make do with what is available. "Never," they lament, "has delirium oscillated more between two poles" (133). It is also possible that cracking up is not all that it is cracked up to be. Can there be a continual, eternal delirium? Can any writer measure down to their schizo standard? Nonetheless, Deleuze and Guattari hold that despite the difficulties, "a schizophrenic flow moves, irresistibly." Sounding like Miller, they describe the flow as "sperm, river, drainage, inflamed genital mucus," or, more in their own argot, a stream of words "that do not let themselves be coded, a libido that is too fluid, too viscous: a violence against syntax, a concerted destruction of the signifier" (132–33). Not much of this pertains to Lawrence. And even Miller, despite his penchant for the fragmentary, somehow remains intact as the irrepressible Henry. But Deleuze and Guattari are right about the stream of words, the liquid libido, the violence against syntax, certainly as it applies to his best novel, *Tropic of Cancer*. However, they are too insistent on attributing bad conscience to capitalism and on attributing this view to Lawrence and Miller. While the latter two are no friends of capitalism, they would have the ferocious view of any modern technological state. It is not capitalism as such that motivates Lawrence and Miller, let alone its dubious links to Oedipus, but the organization and central thrust of mass societies and their impact on private life.

Yet Miller is perfectly representative of the rebellion against "the abject desire to be loved" and "the reduction of sexuality to 'the dirty little secret' "—which he makes the dirty open confession—as he is of "this whole *priest's psychology*" deriving, as Deleuze and Guattari see it, from Oedipus (*AO* 269–70). Deleuze and Guattari go so far as to say that Reich's orgone theory is better than "the pitiful little familiast secret," and they add: "We think that Lawrence and Miller have a more accurate evaluation of sexuality than Freud, even from the viewpoint of the famous scientificity" (292). Much of this is beside the point, since Freud's value is as much humanistic as it is scientific. Miller is seen as a better scientist than Freud because he is a better illustration of the materialism of *Anti-Oedipus*.

Perhaps the most unqualified, enraptured praise in all of *Anti-Oedipus* comes in Deleuze and Guattari's commentary on a passage from Miller's *Hamlet*, an epistolary dialogue with his friend Michael Frankel. They like the passage so well that they quote extensively from it twice in the text (*AO* 112–13, 298–99).[7] In this passage, Miller accuses his intellectual friend of archetypal determination, which is precisely what Deleuze and Guattari accuse the profession of psychoanalysis of. Miller is actually lamenting Frankel's parallel of himself to Hamlet and the negative consequences that entails. Miller never mentions Oedipus. But, in defense of Deleuze and Guattari, one can think of Hamlet as Oedipus, and many since Freud's *Interpretation of Dreams* and Ernest Jones's *Hamlet and Oedipus* have done so. Deleuze and Guattari assume the equation without even arguing in its favor or considering them as two different characters.

The nub of Miller's argument is his characterization of Frankel as a willed martyr: "the question . . . is this: are we *born* Hamlets? Were you born Hamlet? Or did you not rather create the type in yourself? . . . Why revert to myth?"[8] This is the central question of *Anti-Oedipus*, about one myth in particular. Miller proceeds to, in effect, outline the direction of schizoanalysis: "I believe with each line I write that I am scouring the womb, giving it the *curette*, as it were. Behind this process lies the idea not of 'edifice' and 'superstructure,' which is culture and hence false, but of continuous birth, renewal, *life, life*." These last few words are vitalistic rather than mechanistic. Still, Miller anticipates Deleuze and Guattari's diagnosis: "That is why, speaking of the *schizophrenic nature* of our age, I said—'until the process is completed the belly of the world shall be the Third Eye.'" That is, the new world must be conceived. "And to conceive," Miller concludes, "there must first be desire."

Deleuze and Guattari respond ecstatically to these words. "Everything is said in these pages from Miller," they aver: "Oedipus (or Hamlet) led to the point of autocritique; the expressive forms—myth and tragedy—denounced as conscious beliefs or illusions, nothing more than ideas; the necessity of scouring the unconscious, schizoanalysis as a curettage of the unconscious . . . the splendid affirmation of the orphan- and producer-unconscious; the exaltation of the process as a schizophrenic process of deterritorialization that must produce a new earth; and even the functioning of the desiring-machines against tragedy" (*AO* 299). Poor Frankel is caught in the humanistic web. "He talks like a psychoanalyst or like a nineteenth-century Hellenist," they assert. Frankel, they note, thinks Miller "is unaware of these things."

Their identification of Miller as the profound thinker of the age tells us more about Deleuze and Guattari than it does about Miller. Seem, in his introduction to *Anti-Oedipus*, unwittingly draws up the indictment when he happily characterizes the thought of Miller and Artaud—and Nietzsche—as "stoned thinking based on intensely lived experiences: Pop Philosophy" (xxi). For this, Deleuze and Guattari supply a formidable infrastructure.

6

THE MARQUIS DE SADE

The Pléiade edition of the Marquis de Sade's works, with its superfine "Bible paper," announces a singular canonization. Since the end of the Second World War, distinguished French intellectuals have cited Sade in various ways—not merely as a neglected case or a writer worth preserving, but as a central icon in the pantheon of literary modernism. And that is what he has become, for reasons that are not always persuasive. Sade's ascendency, his overvaluation as a major figure, rests on qualities that might be well scrutinized by the old criticism, a cultural critique, moralistic in tendency, that works toward a psychological analysis of image, language, theme, and form.

Sade's mind may be best understood as a part of the Gnostic tradition, whose roots go deep in Western culture.[1] Gnosticism began as a medieval religious movement that denies the biblical account of ex nihilo creation just as it denies the reality of an omnipotent, omniscient God. In the Gnostic account, the God of creation is evil or weak. Similarly, the idea of nature as telos, order, or plan is false; nature conceals a principle of chaos. The task of the Gnostic is to reunite his own small fragment of divine substance, hidden behind his social self, with the larger piece of divine substance hidden behind the apparently ordered phenomenal universe, thereby overcoming alienation from the true God. The boundaries of the old believers are seen by the Gnostic to be prison walls.

In some versions of Gnosticism, sex is sanctified rather than denigrated, as it is in Christianity; pornography becomes a sacred text. Anticipating Romanticism, the Gnostic must violate social rules to fuel sparks of the divine ensnared by the false structure of "nature" and "human nature" and unite with the trapped God. One Gnostic hoped to attain original purity by committing all possible crimes. Violence leads to authenticity or, rather, salvation. One Gnostic branch arrives at salvation through sex. The libertine, in this scenario, is the savior of the universe for man and godhead. Sex is especially appropriate for freeing entangled divine sparks because the supreme godhead of Gnosticism is essentially sexual.

The Gnostic Sade is the first modern antinomian, holding the rule of law to be inferior to that of anarchy. Before Nietzsche, who read him, Sade transvalued values. What society calls good is crucially bad, and what it calls bad is Sade's good. There can be no concept of law in the usual sense. Sade is for impulse no matter where it may lead, and impulse in his pornographic work is always violent. "We may kill, but we may not judge," notes Simone de Beauvoir in her essay on Sade. "The pretensions of the judge are more arrogant than those of the tyrant; for the tyrant confines himself to being himself, whereas the judge tries to erect his opinions into universal laws."[2] One may say, what price authenticity? But Sade is not the one. He values the language of impulse; indeed, for Sade impulse is the only freedom, and civility is merely a method of restraint. Though Sade is cognizant of the idea that, as Maurice Blanchot puts it (citing Durand of *Juliette* as an example), one may revolt "against the law—because one is too far beneath it to be able to conform to the law without perishing," he is far more attuned to the idea that one may be "too far above the law to be able to submit to it without abasement" (as in the case of St. Fond).[3] Law as consensual, as social contract—law as almost everyone else knows it—is an irrelevance in Sade. Yet he may have wondered about the value of law when he was victimized by the *lettre de cachet*, when his home was destroyed by irate peasants, when he had to bootlick and prevaricate like a Brechtian toady to survive the Terror of the French Revolution.

Sade was a coprophiliac, a lover of excrement. His Juliette, finding herself quickly on top of the heap, says, "I am rolling in gold, which for me, is the foremost of enjoyable things."[4] The ultimate shit fantasy, as Freud might have thought. Money in Sade is an aphrodisiac, a passport to endless indulgence and delirious aggression, a symbol of haves and have nots, masters and slaves. Preoccupied with money as individual freedom, Sade has no interest in making it and was unscrupulous, even fraudulent, in how he obtained it. "Denial of reality was a permanent trait of Sade's nature," says Maurice Lever in his admirable biography. "In monetary matters this denial took on truly insane proportions."[5] Relying on the privilege of aristocrats in the ancien régime, Sade would spectacularly not pay his debts; payment would have been an acknowledgment of the social contract, of the rights of the other, a restraint on one's own impulses and proclivities. Of this numerical calculation, the otherwise compulsively numerical Sade wanted no part. Sade loathed accounting for things—it assumes the approbative principle, being accountable

—but he had the temperament of an accountant on speed. *The 120 Days of Sodom* seems at times to be a work of arithmetic.

He did keep his own kind of accounts. In prison he received from his wife artificial organs for simulating sodomy and achieving orgasm. They worked. By December 1780, Sade had recorded 6,536 masturbations, almost thirty-four a month—more than one a day—for twenty-seven months. Poor imprisoned Sade had it all wrong. He had been a teenage orgiast and was now a middle-aged masturbator. Elsewhere he "computes" that 23,180,000 people had been murdered in cold blood (*Jul* 790, note 33). This is, of course, a speculative statistic, existing more for the sake of pleasure than of utility. Moreover, Lever says, Sade elaborated a "method of divination [that] extended to the most routine events of prison life."[6] Some call it divination, others paranoia. Incarceration brought out the anal compulsive in Sade. Most typically, enumeration was for him a form of control, a power fantasy in which the other is reduced to a number. Even in this meticulous guise, sadism is a variety of lawlessness.

Most often, Sade negates law in its metaphysical sense. If there is one idea he laughs to scorn, it is poetic justice. Should it exist, the universe would have meaning. Ethics would be the core of human relations. Throughout the novel *Justine*, Sade is at pains to have the righteous suffer and the wicked prosper: no happy ending here.

Sade was an atheist who intended blasphemy. Before he whipped Rose Keller, he offered to hear her Easter confession. He regarded Holbach's *System of Nature* as the basis of his philosophy—like many eighteenth-century French writers, he considered that he had one. Holbach abolished God, Condillac the soul, and La Mettrie any illusion that man was more than a machine. In Sade, man is a fucking machine, occasionally to the point of Rube Goldberg complexity. Sade found materialism consoling because it held that teleology had no application to nature's universe, any more than it did to God's. "If Nature permits anything," notes Beauvoir, "then the worst catastrophes are a matter of indifference."[7] Here Sade dutifully follows nature. But in its supreme lawlessness, nature has a superhuman freedom that surpasses his own and that he sometimes envies, sometimes hates. Nonetheless, he usually tries to imitate this freedom, even when—especially when—he acts in ways conventionally considered unnatural. There is a primal energy, and we should model ourselves on it. Sensation is the only measure of reality in Sade, as Beauvoir says, and since virtue is not a sensation, it has no real basis.

Sade lives because he was a writer, one who "actually made the imagination the mainspring of vice," Beauvoir says.[8] Sade's imagination is the imagination of disaster—somebody else's. Holbach thought that if vice made man happy, he ought to love vice. Sade found it easy to agree. But Holbach also thought that habitual debauchery extinguishes feeling and thought. Sade, as Ronald Hayman says, preserved the letter and subverted the spirit of Holbach.[9] Sade was both part of and at odds with the thought of his time. "The Enlightenment," as Alphonso Lingis observes, "had believed that the discursive movements of reason were also the advances of freedom, that the conclusions of reason were also the constructive achievements of the good."[10] Sade thought nothing of the kind. Unlike Hume, he did not believe in an innate benevolence. He accepted innate viciousness far more in his writings than in his life, but the two were bound together. It is difficult for the contemporary reader to imagine that the Sadean orgies were not wildly exaggerated. In our democratic propriety, we think of him as the Marquis de Sade, another dissolute, aristocratic libertine. One of his real-life orgies lasted a month and a half and included children. A disintegrating aristocracy, it seems, could still lord it in the bedroom. Louis XV, who saw the deluge coming *après moi*, carried on famously in his brothel, the Deer Park, an aspect of French royal history that elicited Norman Mailer's envy. Unbridled sexual and political license found a home in tyranny.

In embracing evil, Sade anticipates romantic criminality. He would agree with Milton's Satan: "Evil be thou my good." Sade was of the devil's party and knew it. A secularist, Sade embodied the devil without, of course, believing in him. Evil in Sade is essentially metaphysical. He will assault God and even nature, but he assaults the ethical or social as well. Sade is against society because it exists. It impedes his omnipotence; it violates the integrity of his solipsistic passion. "'Twas man's ingratitude dried out my heart," says Dolmancé in *Philosophy in the Bedroom*,[11] but Sade does not dwell on psychological complication. Dolmancé's utterance is better as rhetoric than insight, relevant though it is to Sade's particular psychomachia. Dolmancé does indeed resemble Sade in his brutal solipsism. But they are libertines not so much out of despair and resentment, as Beauvoir contends, but out of ecstasy and sovereignty, fornicating with the aid of a gaudy didacticism that in turn spurs them on. Self-confirmation through argument is as effective for the Sadean hero as Spanish fly. "He did not think," says Beauvoir, "that he was addressing only the members of the privileged classes, whose arrogance he detested."[12] And, one should add, embodied. Sade was a precursor rather than an example of romantic rebellion.

But a rebel he was. Which came first, his perversity or his didacticism? Beauvoir is right in saying that it was the former. "Sade tried to make of his psycho-physical destiny an ethical choice," she says, adding that "he erected these tastes into principles."[13] She is also right in claiming that "the aim of [his] system was precisely to justify the 'crimes' which Sade never dreamed of renouncing" (45). She admires his attraction to the concrete, his disrespect for conventional wisdom, his "ethic of authenticity," concluding that "Sade's desire to grasp the very essence of the human condition in terms of his particular situation is the source of his greatness" (62). This is surely the source of his (existential) importance. But questions arise. For example, can any psycho-physical destiny be transformed into ethical choice? Can an ethic of brutal self-indulgence be justified as authenticity? Sade's situation is eccentric, and his repudiation of abstraction engendered an abstraction of its own. There developed a conventional Sadean wisdom that no one could live by—except, perhaps, Sade.

Sade anticipates the villain-hero of Romanticism. Chronologically between Mozart's *Don Giovanni*, where the Don Juan figure is wistfully repudiated, and Byron, where he is a hero for the time, Sade stands ominously. As Caroline Lamb said of Byron, Sade was "mad, bad and dangerous to know."[14] They both inhabit the air of misogyny, incest, and "perversity." Masters of scorn, they both court isolation. Yet they diverge in transcendence, Byron's finally being upward and Sade's downward. Sade denies transcendence in the traditional sense; man does not ascend to the accepted notion of godliness. But Sade is inspired in his total mastery of a confined world, in his solipsistic emotion, in his fiction of limitlessness and lack of repression, and in his tyrannical sex. He is a pornographer who transvalues. He is inspired, one may safely say, as a sadist. He transcends downward into criminality. For Sade, transcendence is not an aspiration but an energy. Culture hero or schizophrenic? Or both? Is he, in Apollinaire's words, the most free spirit that has ever lived, or the prisoner of his id?[15]

"I am a libertine, but I am neither a criminal nor a murderer," says Sade in a letter that Lever quotes.[16] He was not a murderer, but in fact he was a criminal. It never occurred to Sade that forcing sex on a girl or woman was in any sense criminal. (Nor, apparently, did it occur to him that sodomy in eighteenth-century France was a capital crime—on the books, that is.) It did occur to an enraged father who wanted to kill him, and it did occur to the French criminal system. The main issue for the reader is Sade's writing, in which there are many sympathetic portrayals of the libertine, the criminal, and the murderer. Juliette tells Clairwil, after the latter had expressed the desire to commit an eternal crime, that she should try hard at a moral crime, the kind one commits in writing. French criticism has been notably Apollonian in describing these violent Dionysian outbursts. Blanchot writes: "Sade's heroes draw their sustenance from the death they cause, and there are times when, dreaming of everlasting life, he dreams of a death he can inflict eternally. The result is that the executioner and the victim, set eternally face to face, find themselves endowed equally with the same power, with the same divine attribute of eternity."[17] If this sounds like a refined version of Norman Mailer in "The White Negro," expounding on murderer, victim, and a dialogue with eternity, it is nonetheless true to Sade's spirit of negative transcendence. There is something bleak and repellent about this view of eternity.

"If Sade's heroes commit massacres, it is because none of them gives full satisfaction," says Beauvoir.[18] The poor man! Sade is the precursor of snuff films, movies in which actors are apparently literally murdered at the climax (the films have proved to be frauds). It is a sign of the developed American superego that *Screw* magazine came out against them. Of course, Sade's work is word and the snuff film is apparent deed, but history shows that there is often a connection.

Roland Barthes denies such a connection. He sees little interest in the mimetic or what has grimly come to be called the referential value of literature. "We can say finally," he holds, "that Sadian crime exists only in proportion to the quantity of language invested in it, in no way because it is dreamt or narrated, but because only language can construct it."[19] To be sure, literature is a linguistic medium, but language does not write itself. Literature is dream as much as it is word; it is psychological as well as verbal content, historical as well as stylistic. The writer has an inspiration and an intention. Tolstoy called truth the god of his desire. If, as Barthes holds, "practice follows speech, and is absolutely determined by it: what is done has been said" (35), he should apply more than an aesthetic standard to what is said. How can speech absolutely determine anything? Speech comes partly from a context of action. The monotony that many feel in reading Sade is cast aside by Barthes as aesthetic obtuseness. "Sade is boring," he says, "only if we fix our gaze on the crimes being reported and not on the performances of the discourse" (36). But we should fix our gaze on both word and event. There is language and meaning, form and content, image and idea. Ingenious discourse alone does not save us from boredom. What happens in a Sadean novel "represents," it "imitates," and imagination is fused with reality. "Incest," Barthes says archly, "is only a surprise of vocabulary" (138). "The victim," in his view, "is not *he* or *she* who submits, but *he* or *she who uses a certain language*" (144). For all his distinctive cerebral hedonism, for all the well-observed internalities, Barthes leaves an inkhorn residue. Goodheart says of Barthes's study *Sade, Fourier, Loyola* that "if one consults one's experience of the text, one must demur from Barthes's conviction that reality has been absorbed by the signifier. The essays on Sade have more power than the essays on Loyola and Fourier because the scandal of the referent informs the play of the discourse."[20] What suffers in Barthes is literature as experience.

Barthes wants a "total disengagement from value produced by the pleasure of the text."[21] But value is a prime pleasure in literature as it is in life. In *The Nicomachean Ethics*, Aristotle distinguished between pleasure as sensation and pleasure as activity. In the *Poetics*, he described literature as "an imitation of life," thereby placing value on the activity being imitated. Barthes will have none of this. But his criticism itself rests on moral assumptions. His aestheticism is, in his own view, a form of revolution. Within the rotted welter of bourgeois ideology, he sees "the victorious deployment of the significant text, the terrorist text, allowing the received meaning, the (liberal) repressive discourse that constantly attempts to recover it, slough itself off like an old skin" (10). Writing is by definition a "terrorist" activity—antinomian, violent—against the seductions of liberal civility. "The social intervention of a text," says Barthes, "is measured . . . by the violence that enables it to *exceed* the laws." Literature is by nature revolutionary, and Sade is an "exemplary hero" (177).

The failure of the uprising of 1968 in France took much of the edge off the literary Left. Philippe Sollers, another well-known Parisian literary figure and commentator on Sade, admits: "I had the utopian notion, which I no longer hold, that the revolution in language and the revolution as action should coincide absolutely . . . It's an illusion of the twentieth-century avant-garde that should be totally abandoned."[22] Agreed. But before Sollers abandoned the revolutionary perspective, he had made a more explicit defense of Sade's sexuality based on language. Sollers had believed that "what appears beneath the savage mask of perversion is the exact inverse of the neurosis instituted by a civilization based on the deification of speech." Like Barthes, he had wanted "the *natural*, and *norm*, to be forever undermined" (46). Man's "only choice," Sollers had said, "is between communal neurosis and perversion, between neurosis and what will be referred to as 'madness'" (48). So we have it. The "madness" within is always justified by the sickness without. With metaphorical perversity, the "old" Sollers regards the texts as "the primary crime" (60), thereby equating all literature with criminality, as Barthes did criticism with terrorism. The ideological tendency of these views is remarkable. What would the French intellectuals do without their monolithic bourgeoisie? And what would they be without their conformist rhetoric of transgression, their sexual psychodrama of the extreme?

So Sade has been made a hero. This uneven performer, this bizarre fantasist, who is at best a writer of the second rank and at worst a jerk-off curiosity, whom neither Swinburne nor I can read without laughing—is there a clearer example of Bergson's idea that the essence of comedy is a human being acting like a machine?—has been elevated to the French literary pantheon by the critical establishment. How can one be satisfied with the exquisiteness of verbal structures when Sade also focuses the contemporary reader on pressing issues of violence and misogyny? The referential quality of literature is central and unavoidable. Andrea Dworkin's ludicrous contention that, to the male, all sex is rape is perfectly reasonable if we apply it to the works that Sade is known for.[23]

Sade writes serious literature that is pornographic. The characteristics of pornography have been so well defined by Steven Marcus from a Freudian perspective, and in a way that dovetails with the interpretation of Sade given here, that it is worth giving a summary of the definition of pornography in Marcus's study, *The Other Victorians*.[24] He notes that although pornography appears to be the most concrete kind of writing, it is in reality very abstract, regularly moving toward independence of time, space, history, and even language itself. Pornotopia, the ideal realm posited, is outside time; it is always bedtime. Life does not begin with birth but with one's first sexual impulse. Others have noted as well that time is always sexual time, a mathematical function corresponding to the limited number of variables in a series of sexual combinations. There is no "out there" in pornography, which serves to indicate again in what phase of our mental existence this kind of thinking had its origins. Given its logic of fantasy, observation is incidental rather than organic. The governing tendency of pornography is the elimination of social and psychological reality. Marcus rightly observes that in Sade "the entire adult genital organization was dissolved back into the components of infancy" (173). The pornographic hero has the desire to have all sexual pleasures in all ways at once. This instability, connected with one's earliest experiences, is an effort to both reconstitute that early state of polymorphous perverse pleasure and overcome the anguish and frustration that our inevitable expulsion from that state brings about. There is a connection between the fact that the male is wholly concerned with his own response and his pronounced sadistic tendencies. (Krafft-Ebing thought that great frequency of sex was itself sadistic.)²⁵ Women are objects to be despised and violated. There is an emotional anesthesia and a compulsion to repeat actions. Since the unconscious is inaccessible to learning, sex exhibits a mechanical, monotonous variety. Also, it is the nature of instinctive drives to repeat themselves. Unpleasurableness, violence and aggression, and the impulse toward extinction are not explained by the pleasure principle alone but also by the death instinct. Gratification is excluded. Emotions are displaced onto organs. It is often difficult to distinguish one woman from another. It is sometimes difficult to distinguish women from men; clitorises become penises, anuses are common to both sexes, and everyone is everything to everyone else.

Pornotopia is a Utopia where reality is defined in exclusively sexual terms. Its qualities include a systematic violation of prohibitions and taboos. One breathes the air of infantile megalomania. Literary form is a casualty. There is generally an excuse for a beginning; once having begun, however, the work goes on and on and ends nowhere, really having no ending since its cardinal principle of existence is repetition. Pornography is in this sense anti-literature. Form implies moral expectation, the gratification of an ending. The ideal pornographic novel will go on forever. Language in pornography is generally a bothersome necessity; its function is to set going a series of nonverbal images. Taboo words, the linguistic core of pornography, are minimally verbal, still felt as acts; they are not dissociated from the unconscious impulses in which they took their origin. Metaphors are literal truths; everything is possible in this Utopia that recalls our original supremacy.

Pornotopia could only have been imagined by people who have suffered extreme deprivation, sexual but also literal starvation. The origins are visions of permanently hungry men. The Marquis de Sade took the matter to its logical conclusion: When his orgies include the eating of excrement, and then finally murder with the purpose of cannibalism, he was bringing to explicit statement the direction taken by all works of pornography. Inside of every pornographer is an infant screaming for the breast from which he has been torn. Pornography represents an endless and infinitely repeated effort to recapture that breast, and the bliss it offered, as it often represents as well a revenge against the world—and the women in it—in which such cosmic injustice could occur. The perpetual erection is a reflection of castration anxiety, a reassurance that one's penis is always there, not gone or taken away. The major Don Juans hate their mothers.

Sade has been fortunate in his choice of recent biographers, all of whom in different ways essentially support Marcus's view (thereby diminishing the hagiographic impulse of Maurice Heine and Gilbert Lély). Francine du Plessix Gray had the good sense to consult Freudian psychoanalysts in writing her biography—she cites Sheldon Bach[26] and Janine Chasseguet-Smirgel among others—which gives us the expected confirming scenario. Sade's well-known childhood fit of rage against the prince de Condé was motivated by the prince's being both an idealized self and a rival. Sade's mother was both a lady-in-waiting and governess to the prince. Sade's rage, Gray says, caused his traumatic banishment from court life and from the presence of his mother, "who would seldom reenter his orbit."[27] Exile at the crucial age of four to his doting grandmother in Avignon elicited Sade's grandiose, archaic self of early childhood, "a necessary stage in human development, which turns to megalomania if retained in adulthood" as a compensation for early trauma. With his parents long gone, Sade's overblown ego evolved as a defense mechanism. In addition, there are the erotic floggings of his school years, which complicate his masochism. The negative Oedipus complex emerges in adolescence, exhibiting, in this case, "a savage resentment toward the cold, neglectful mother and an equally fierce but frustrated love for the father." His father's rejection of him resulted in a personality that refused to endure renunciations essential to the reality principle, producing "an individual who, in order not to lapse into total psychosis, needed to retain the grandiose delusions of the very young child into adulthood." All this adds up to the crucial point: "Throughout his life as a free man, Sade's extravagant behavior was characteristic of an individual's struggling against the threat of psychic disintegration through the mechanism of regressive neurosis." His neurosis is marked by the following symptoms: narcissism (the universe flatters his whims, resulting in his accompanying sense of control over others); delusional identities (his illusory immunity to law, crime without punishment—transgressions incited by delusions of grandeur are improbably repetitive because the delusory self is perpetually threatened and must be continually affirmed); infantile anality (receiving and giving buttock flagellation and bisexual sodomy, anal sexuality being the principal site of a small child's pleasures); and exhibitionism (either to evoke punishment or to heighten power and control). The most profound point is that "the only constant" in Sade's offenses is that "they served to reassure him that *he was not being ignored*" (158).

Laurence L. Bongie, a biographer who describes himself as a classical moralist, also affirms Marcus's description of victimization. Sade's father, a courtier and a libertine with little personal integrity, married Sade's mother for her high social connections (she had little money, however) and for the opportunity to bed her good friend, the Princesse de Charoloais. Their wedding night was, so to speak, a delayed threesome. He had intercourse with the kitchen staff as well, both male and female. Sade's mother was aware, resigned, and virtually deserted. When he took a political post in Bonn for money, she left Sade, then only sixteen months old, to join her husband. He sent her back because she cramped his sexual style. Later, illness and probably pressure from her husband caused her to ship Sade off to Avignon at age four to live with his grandmother. Sade's father called his wife "the invalid." Bongie sympathizes with the mother, holding that the account of her abandoning her son is a fiction. She was, after all, so put upon by an impossible husband, even by ancien régime standards. But no one else sees the mother as a sympathetic figure. Indeed, Bongie himself recognizes in her the impossible hauteur of a fading aristocrat and is not uniformly sympathetic. He has far less sympathy for the father. In some ways, Sade identified with his father, the only family member he really cared for besides one of his sons before they fell out and his wife after they had been married a while, and then only intermittently. (Still, when a priest was called to give the last rites to his very sick father, Sade was not present. "My son has not missed a ball or the theater even once," his father complained.)[28] His father was a fatal ego-ideal, while being at the same time a conventional social type. He could be generous to his son. For Sade's thirteenth birthday, his father bought him a *petite maison*—in effect, a private whorehouse—for the Bar Mitzvah boy who has everything! By this age, in any case, Sade hated his absent mother. Whether she actively abandoned him and—if so—to what extent, or whether she just rarely noticed him, she was the mother who was not there. Gray tells us that Sade saw his mother "so seldom that he could barely describe her."[29] From a Freudian point of view, of course, the maternal absentee is a disaster, as *Inhibitions, Symptoms, and Anxiety* attests. Here, for the first time, Freud places the genesis of anxiety more on separation than on castration.

Bongie sees the substitute or *seconde maman* as a psychological necessity for Sade. His mother-in-law, the difficult Mme. de Montreuil, is the best known. For some time, they liked each other up to a point. Like Gray, Bongie considers Mme. de Montreuil much maligned. Most readers of Sade remember her as the mother-in-law from hell who had him incarcerated, without necessarily thinking of Sade as the son-in-law from hell, which he was. Sade's criminal sexual escapades—Bongie reminds us, if we need reminding, that forcing yourself sexually upon a woman against her will is a crime called rape, as is debauching resistant minors—were at first actually covered up by his mother-in-law for the sake of the family's respectability. Sade duplicated his father's contempt for his spouse. His too was a marriage of advantage—money, in this case. Sade did not want to marry his wife. Not that their marriage made much difference for a long time. His mother-in-law tried to cover things up to avoid scandal, even to the extent of keeping her plain-Jane daughter in the dark. But when Sade bedded his wife's younger sister, who was her parents' favorite as well as elegant and virginal, his mother-in-law could take no more. Sade may have had his double transgression but Mme. de Montreuil had her transgressor. Yet it was not she but the police, or the state, that was primarily responsible for Sade's incarcerations. His reputation was scandalous, for good reason, and he had been under surveillance for some time. So though it is true that once Mme. de Montreuil snapped and she became his relentless enemy, her effectiveness was secondary to that of the state. And though some of the accusations against Sade were exaggerated or even false, basically the authorities got the right guy. Even in a society ready to define crime in terms of class, Sade finally lost his immunity.

Sade's father was a man of elegant formulations. He guided his son toward a life of "virtue without austerity."[30] He wrote in a letter to a mistress: "If my son were to choose a life of constancy, I would be outraged. I would almost prefer to see him become a member of the Academy" (76). When asked about the necessity to live in Paris, he answered that Paris will not make you happy, but it will make you miserable to live anywhere else. Roué that he was, he admitted that one should not grow old in Paris. Sade's legacy on his father's side was an island of eloquence in a stream of cynicism. That and unlimited libertine license.

Bongie sees that, in a sense, Sade's father's infidelities were a just "punishment" for the straitlaced, icy mother. Combined with the impossible relationship that developed between Sade and his mother-in-law, the conditions for the emergence of Sade the sadist, the punisher of women, took root. Incarceration insured that fantasy would exceed reality in this matter. Feudal elitist that he was, Sade's specialty was, as Bongie says, "violence toward lower-class prostitutes, women he viewed as a necessary but contemptible form of subhuman life" (108).

Gray and Bongie benefit from Lever's earlier, influential biography, which is a savvy psychological and historical portrait. Lever presents Sade's father as "one of the most illustrious libertines of Louis XV's reign."[31] His father was not only a personal influence on Sade but, having written more than twenty literary and philosophical works, a literary influence as well. The son collected these with extreme care, annotating them in his own hand, writing between his father's lines.

Lever basically agrees with Pierre Klossowski's application of Freud's negative Oedipus complex. Klossowski holds that Sade, like other "homosexual neurotics . . . allies himself with paternal power and turns all his available aggressivity against the mother."[32] Sade bridles against the original gratitude of childbirth, against the sanctity of his mother's womb. His mother and wife are considered of little significance. For example, Bressac, in *Justine*, after his father's death, adapts his cruelty as if to avenge his absence. The suppression of mother carried out by father and son is recounted in the Brisa Testa story in *Juliette*. Sade repudiated the presumably maternal values: compassion, tenderness, consolation, sacrifice, and fidelity. In a proto-Nietzschean way, he considered them motivated by self-interest and fear. His wife's boundless devotion often met with his contempt.

Lever holds that the reason for Sade's rage is the mother's perpetual absence. None of Sade's other relatives were present at his delivery. The mother was, according to Lever, "virtually non-existent."[33] His "virgin mother" was first idolized, then repudiated by Sade. He hated his remote, indifferent mother. In the Freudian paradigm, Sade felt abandoned by her, and this helped fuel his infantile rage against woman. So mother is a source and an object of aggression. That she may have been her husband's victim never seems to have occurred to Sade.

Being raised as an ancien régime aristocrat only helped to crystallize these powerful tendencies in Sade. "Raised in the conviction that he was a superior species, [Sade] was soon schooled in that aristocratic haughtiness of demeanor known as *morgue*," Lever writes.[34] At age four, "his despotic nature was already formed." This all makes horrible sense. "Blind to the world around him," Lever says, "he soon shut himself behind a world of incommunicability and incomprehension, cutting himself off from others in his vicinity, even those he loved—especially those he loved. From earliest childhood his actions reflected a tragic inability to speak" (51). We may note that this inability to speak is a logical as well as psychological symbol of his almost lifelong solipsism. Sade came to tolerate almost no one else in his universe. Fate acceded to his disposition perhaps too well by granting him decades of incarceration. He was to expand on his infantile silence in many volumes.

In Provence, Lever tells us, eminent citizens bowed to the four-year-old child. The "apprentice tyrant" asked for everything and got it. Sade, this image for some of ultimate freedom, is a man whose life was in many ways determined—and by an awful scenario. "Taken from his mother at the age of four, transported to a princely palace on a rocky summit, imprisoned in a fortress with a libertine priest [his uncle!], and surrounded by debauched women: all the ingredients of a Sade novel are present in this early traumatic experience," Lever justly concludes (52).

Nor did things work out well with his father. As two egomaniacs sharing much of the same space, they did not get along. His father wanted to marry him off, especially to the *noblesse de robe*. "What made up my mind," says dad, "is that I'll be rid of the boy, who has not one good quality and all the bad ones" (quoted at 102). Sade's father was not an easy man to live with, and his wife (like Henry James's Claire de Cintré, another victim of family abuse, who, however, went all the way and became a nun) retired to the Carmelite convent on Paris's rue d'Enfer. Sade outdid his father in outrageousness. When his father and in-laws went to Versailles to have his marriage contract signed by no less a figure than Louis XV, Sade refused to go. Sade could have traveled in the king's carriage, but he did not even show up for his own wedding! So, the deed was done without him. Of course, individual preference had long had little to do with aristocratic royal marriages. It is possible to think that this and other details of his life are more interesting than anything in his work. Perhaps the critic may therefore be excused for dwelling extensively in this case on biography.

Sade's marriage was better than anyone could have predicted. The sadist found his ideal masochist. Lever speaks of how the "voluntary servitude" of Sade's wife was "strangely akin to love." She actually understood him: "She understood that behind the man of domination there lurked a helpless child, sometimes cruel and sometimes needy but always requiring unflagging support" (116). Helplessness, impotence, fear of castration—these are the underlying characteristics of the pornographer. "The vision of a grim, gray, and spiritless universe is common to pornography," Marcus maintains. The tone may be lighthearted, yet the "impotent quest for omnipotence" is the internal motivation.[35] The central paradox in Sade is that from this weakness, he achieved in his life and even more in his work a transcendent negativity that enabled even a humble René-Pélagie, his wife, to be lifted to what Lever surmises to be "incredible heights"—or is it depths? "For thirty years," Lever writes, "she had the feeling of being above the law, both human and divine,"[36] a feeling she would rather have done without and, in fact, eventually escaped.

It would be difficult to say whether Sade loved his wife. Moreover, it would be hard to establish that love is actually depicted in his serious work. Love implies a certain amount of idealization, dependence, and self-forgetfulness that Sade would not acknowledge. Love is an intrusion on his sovereign independence. La Rochefoucauld—how rich the French tradition is in cynicism!—said that few would fall in love if they had never heard of it. In a way, Sade had never heard of it, but it would not have made a difference if he had.

Hardly the ideal lover, Sade was never interested in vaginal intercourse but only in sodomy. His father described himself, and he might as well have been describing Sade, as playing the woman with the man but being all man with the woman, a euphemism for sodomy. Sexual heaven for Sade, he would clearly explain, is penetrating a woman anally at the moment that he is being penetrated by a man. The passivity, as Beauvoir suggests, is a desire to escape from the reality of the self and, one may say, bow to the reality of others. Summoning the antiself seems to be a prime sexual function. Yet his penetration of the other is accompanied by the power of transgression. Like his father, Sade thought it unmanly to possess a woman in the usual way. Manliness he equates with aggression toward women. "We may wonder," Beauvoir shrewdly observes, "whether Sade did not hate women because he saw in them his double rather than his complement and because there was nothing he could get from them. His great female villains have more warmth and life than his heroes, not only for aesthetic reasons but because they were closer to him . . . [Juliette] proudly and contentedly submits to the same treatment as her sister." Indeed, many readers think of Juliette as Sade in drag. Beauvoir concludes: "Sade felt himself to be feminine, and he resented the fact that women were not the males he really desired." She notes that "he endows Durand," whom Beauvoir considers "the greatest and most extravagant of them all, with a huge clitoris which enables her to become sexually like a man."[37] In all this inversion, there is some difference of agreement as to what Sade's sexual preference was, though there is agreement in seeing it as a function of transgression. Beauvoir says he preferred boys because the crime of sex with them was greater. But stating sexual preference in terms of idea, even though Sade seems to do this himself, is putting things too abstractly. As Beauvoir herself states, first came the preference. In any case, Barthes, who ought to know, takes issue with Beauvoir on this point. He claims that pederasts, "who are usually loath to recognize Sade as one of theirs, are not mistaken [because] only women offer the choice of two sites of intromission: in choosing one over the other *in the area of the same body*, the libertine produces and assumes a meaning, that of transgression."[38] The Sade male does seems to derive more emotion from his encounters with women, which would make him primarily heterosexual, but whatever that emotion may be, it is always—as Barthes implies—part of something else. We now turn to the major illustrations of this something else.

....

The masochist says to the sadist, "Beat me," and the sadist says, "No." So goes one of our psychologically attuned jokes. Curval, one of the four major male characters of *120 Days of Sodom*, did not know this bit of wisdom. He can find no answer to the question, How can you punish a masochist? Nor can his fellow libertine, the Duc de Blangis. " 'Oh, what is this glory, jest, and riddle of the world,' sighed the Duc, Hamlet-like. 'Yes my friend, an enigma above all else,' said the grave Curval. 'And that perhaps is what led a very witty individual to say that better every time to fuck a man than to comprehend him.' "[39] So much for the wisdom of the *philosophes*! Never mind that Curval is an old, skeletal buggeree who eats shit and drinks piss. He has given the answer, the ultimate answer in Sade. The marquis's world is informed by a paradoxical didacticism, as we are introduced to a community of fornication. Community implies something like Rousseau's general will; fornication, in Sade's world, implies tyranny. Sade's isolism, his belief that all men are alone and that no real contact is possible between people, is a doctrine consonant with and doubtless originating in his erotic solipsism, not to mention his infancy. Yet claims of friendship have been made for the four leads of *120 Days of Sodom*, beginning with Beauvoir and enlarged recently by Jane Gallop. Beauvoir acknowledges the lack of permanent bonds between Sade's libertines, but sees a "genuine communion" among them in that each "perceives the meaning of his acts and of his own figure through the minds of others."[40] One may consider this an excessively generous description. It is as if there were some subtle dialectic unfolding before these fucking maniacs. Beauvoir contends that "eroticism appears in Sade as a mode of communication, the only valid one" (60). Where eroticism is the only valid mode of communication, a parody of communication exists.

Barthes too speaks of the "deep, ardent friendship" in the pact between Juliette and Clairwil, which joins them "for life"[41] but is somehow revocable from one day to the next. Barthes then points out that Juliette poisons Clairwil, saying nothing about the ensuing sense of moral vacuum. How deep, how ardent could this friendship have been? But the attempt to supply Sade with a moral resonance he does not possess is made most extravagantly by Gallop, building her argument on the aforementioned precedents. The four friends, in her view, "display unfailing loyalty and candor in regard to each other, never betraying the pact implied by friendship."⁴²

The description of the four libertines is done with more care for individuality than Sade usually allows, and he thereby gives us some insight into, for example, the variety of passive sodomy (a characteristic that they all share). But rather than giving us insights into friendship, the quadrapartite division is basically a fine device to reflect sadistic sex in nearly infinite variety. What we get from *120 Days* is not psychological depth or moral communion, but a spectacularly choreographed set of orgies that brings to mind nothing so much as Busby Berkeley gone ape.

Gallop even makes the case for Sade as an example of community: "The subjection of even the most outrageous libertine to a social contract is a moment found in all of Sade's works."⁴³ But Sade gives us political inversion rather than an elaboration of Rousseau. To be sure, there is a language of law, even regulation, in Sade, but it is incongruous and ultimately parodistic, a Ubuist conception. "The orgies shall cease at precisely two in the morning" (*D* 247) is a bit of sublimated anality that is a shadow of the real unsublimated thing, a loony injunction imposed on sober chaos. It is from the section called statutes, which includes "wives shall . . . be treated with a maximum of rigor and inhumanity, and . . . shall be frequently employed upon the vilest and most painful enterprises, such as for example the cleaning of the private and common privies established in the chapel [a double satisfaction here, both wife and religion reduced to shit]. These privies shall be emptied only once a week, but always by them, and they shall be severely punished if they resist the work or accomplish it poorly" (249). Similarly in *Juliette*, the "Statutes of the Sodality of the Friends of Crime" stipulated that "the sodality . . . considers itself above the law because the law is of mortal and artificial contrivance." The Sodality "respects Nature only" (*Jul* 418). Sadism, the sexual enactment of a master-slave relationship, has its own farcical sense of theatricality. For the libertines, *law* usually means what most people think of as delayed gratification, a generally alien concept in Sade. One puts up with it so that the orgy can proceed at full force. There is an undercurrent of bogus legalism in Sade that in almost anyone else would be intentional parody, but that in Sade may be unintentional. There is no general will in Sade; rather, there is a virtually unanimous will of the autocrats playing at community. And there are the many victims, a disembodied community of pain.

Law as it applies to the four men means rules and regulations; as it applies to women, humiliation and threat. For example, in what amounts to an urversion of Justine, "tender and melancholic" Zelmire, a relatively individualized character, resists frigging the four friends. In despair, she "had besought God to deliver her from perils wherewith she was beset, and had above all prayed that help would come before her virginity were lost." The duc says that she should die. Zelmire replies: "Kill me, at least the God I invoke shall have pity on me, kill me before you dishonor me." The duc, rather than having her punished more severely, "reminding his cohorts of their inviolable contract ... was content to propose—and his suggestion was unanimously approved— that she be condemned to be punished very violently the following Saturday and that, in the meantime, she kneel and for fifteen minutes take into her mouth and suck each friend's prick, and that she be warned that the penalty is death if her error were to be repeated. She would in that case be judged and punished to the fullest extent of the law" (D 366–67). The law here is an intensification of male sovereignty and female victimization. There is an ecstatic, phallic quality to "fullest extent," and the duc is quickly eroticized by his own peculiar version of social contract. In short, there is no social contract in Sade, but an anal compulsive fantasy on it given with jerk-off precision.

What one gets in Sade is not community but psychotic fantasy, the lunatic logic of sexual permutations. The duc says to Curval, "You resemble a great many other of Justice's servitors whose pricks, they say, rise up every time they pronounce the death sentence" (D 484). This is funny, and it is probably unfair to Sade to say that he does not realize the humor. Sade's wild but typical way of juxtaposing death and eroticism tells us more about where he stands than his pages of advanced but generally specious argument. It is as a lunatic fantasist that Sade is most original and most valuable. He has the humor of sexual disproportion, and if one reads his tedious volumes—as I do—for the comedy he intends and even more for the comedy he does not, one can laugh oneself to sleep. And have nightmares, for Sade's humor, particularly as applied to women, is more brutal than the laugh allows. In Sade there is an excessively narrow community of assent: a community of one, perhaps. When Sade gets to the "murderous passions," he writes: "He used to like to slap the whore's face; as a mature man, he twists her head around until it faces backward. When so adjusted, one may simultaneously look at her face and her buttocks" (630). The ramifications of artful sodomy are, one may say, endless. One can see why the surrealists deified Sade, considering him "the divine marquis." For those of a nonrevolutionary disposition, the joke may not be funny. Sade seems aware of this, and at some of his most brutal moments, he explicitly reminds us to laugh. The duc cuts through the partition dividing the anus from the vagina of one of his victims. Sade writes: "He throws aside the scalpel, reintroduces his hand, and rummaging about in her entrails, forces her to shit through her cunt, another amusing stunt" (659). They were hard, those long prison years in Vincennes and the Bastille. They were also, it turns out, influential. Sade could never have imagined, for example, that he was paving the way for the presbyter of Beat rebellion, William Burroughs.

Sade shows originality in his cataloging ability as well, his energy of nomination. He antedates Krafft-Ebing. We have the saliva swallower, the frigging bum licker, the peeping Tom, the armpit fucker, the cripple humper, the belch swallower, the cunt-juice gourmet, the thigh fornicator, the man who feeds Duclos a certain diet to impart an "exquisite taste" (*D* 394) to her turds (he tells us that poultry, especially chicken breast, is best), the man who cannot crap until his ass is kissed, the man (Curval) who likes a "cunt to smell like a beach covered with dead fish," the man who can come only when the last nail in his coffin is hammered in (then he starts cursing and threatening), the man who howls like a wolf at the moment of orgasm. Sade proceeds with a thoroughness and dispassion that would do a bureaucrat proud. Of course, Sade need not trouble with data, which adds to the free-form energy of his display. Part fantasy, part observation, Sade's catalog anticipates later clinical truth. Annie Le Brun writes: "No one else will ever dare observe, from such close quarters, the volcanoes of our sexual night."[44] While one may find the histrionic tone of this statement risible, one must admit that there is a courage in Sade that makes him impossible to dismiss. His main virtue as a writer is to uninhibitedly present his strange predilections in concrete form.

Yet searching for redeemable nuggets in Sade is like looking for a rose on a dung heap. It's dirty work, and paralyzingly dull. While Sade is at his best in balancing the abstract tendency in his writing with a startling concreteness, the abstraction too often takes over. By abstraction I mean not only the discursive insistence in his work but, more centrally, the virtually arithmetical extension of his inspiration. Time in Sade is indeed sexual time, as Marcus says: "a mathematical function corresponding to the limited number of variables in series of sexual combinations."[45] And, he continues, "this is why *The One Hundred Twenty Days of Sodom* represents one kind of perfection in this genre. Pornography's mad genius, the Marquis de Sade, with psychotic rigidity and precision, and with psychotic logic, wrote his novel along strictly arithmetical lines." This view enables Marcus to suggest an interesting possible explanation for why Sade never completed the novel: "It is commonly believed that Sade did not finish this novel, since large parts of it exist only in outline, [but] such a conclusion is not acceptable. Having completed his outline, Sade had in effect written his novel—the rest is only filling in." Marcus concludes that "a pornographic novel might be written by a computer" (274), an ominous thought in this day and age. I have a different view as to why he did not complete this work: he could not finish out of boredom.

....

Sade's Ubuist examples of law remind us that parallels between Sade and the Nazis—particularly between Sade and Hitler—are not, as they are so often made out to be, irrelevant. Was Raymond Queneau wrong to see Sade as a striking prefiguration of the Gestapo and the concentration camps? Was Albert Camus wrong in saying that the history and tragedy of our times really begin with Sade—that two centuries in advance and on a reduced scale, Sade exalted the totalitarian society in the name of frenzied liberty? In fact, Sade tells us a great deal about the twentieth century's greatest monster, Adolf Hitler, particularly when we view Sade from a Freudian perspective.

Robert G. L. Waite's *The Psychopathic God: Adolf Hitler* shows that Hitler can be viewed as a Sadean character. Sade was not interested in politics, except in a precautionary way after the French Revolution. But politics, alas, seems to have been interested in Sade. Hitler is a prime illustration of sadism, or rather—like Sade himself—of sadomasochism. Like the child Sade, young Hitler had to have things his way. His half-brother recalls that as a boy of seven, "if he didn't have his way, he got very angry . . . He would fly into a rage over any triviality."[46] If Hitler got a tune wrong, it was the composer who had made a mistake. Hitler would stop playing a game of bowls if anyone else was winning. His temper could be volcanic in unusual circumstances. He could not believe, for example, that he did not win the lottery. In a rage, he considered it a fraud. A friend rightly surmised that the source of the explosion was that "he had been deserted by his will power" (177)—or his "will to power," in Nietzsche's phrase, an inner dynamism unfettered by the compromises of morality and politics. Nietzsche was thinking primarily of the aristocracy of art; Hitler, though also interested in the Romantic artist (e.g., Wagner), thought of power in political terms, indeed militaristic terms, which Nietzsche loathed. Like Sade, Hitler made an exception of himself in mundane, telling ways. Neither liked paying or, literally, being accountable. The question of back taxes due on sales of *Mein Kampf* was solved when Hitler declared himself exempt from taxation. He owed half a million marks in back taxes when he became chancellor, but he ordered this obligation cancelled and paid no taxes after 1934. But although he could exempt himself from taxes, death was another matter. As we shall see, he seemed to court that.

Hitler's temperament manifested itself politically in many ways. At his trial for high treason in Munich in 1924, he spoke, Castro-like, for four hours; future orations would be equally long. Under his picture in the Nazi Party's Munich headquarters were the words: "Nothing happens in this Movement, except what I wish."[47] This was no mere figure of speech. Hitler was unique; only he could be the *Führer*. His hold was more potent than mere royal absolutism, which depended on the institution of monarchy. In a mystical, Romantic idealism, he was the Idea made flesh. "He was Nazism," says Waite: "His whim, quite literally, became the law of the land" (81). When Hitler says, "Ich bein das deutsche Volk!" (I am the German people), he is not exaggerating. The well-known slogan of the Third Reich, "Ein Volk! Ein Reich! Ein Führer!" (one people, one country, one leader) replaced that of the Second Reich: "Ein Volk! Ein Reich! Ein Gott!" (one people, one country, one God) (329). Psychological solipsism can go no further: The *Führer* replaced God. Hitler's architectural drawings manifested a similar impulse aesthetically. They were, as Albert Speer says, "the very expression of a tyranny" (quoted in 66)—not as intimidating, perhaps, as a mountaintop castle, but more ominous.

Sade's defense of republicanism in *Philosophy in the Bedroom* is really a defense of Romantic individualism to the point of anarchy. No republican, Sade never even entertained the thought of being a democrat. "It is a terrible justice," Sade holds, "to require that men of unlike character be ruled by the same law" (*PB* 310). What he defends here is the impulse of the strong to murder and rape. This is not Blake's "one law for the lion and the ox is oppression," because there is no Blakean affirmation of the sanctity of individual life as such.[48] On the contrary, Sade avers that it is "beyond human powers to prove that there may exist anything criminal in the alleged destruction of a creature" (*PB* 331). The republican attitude toward murder, therefore, "calls for a touch of ferocity." This is necessary, for if the republican "grows soft, if his energy slackens in him, the republican will be subjugated in a trice" (333). Part of this desired hardness is a rigorous eugenics program, a harbinger of Nazi policy.

Hitler's *Volk* were no mere people, and his *Reich* no mere government, or so the Romantically mystical *Führer* assured his masses. The alternative to the *Führerprinzip* was the chaos of democracy. "It is madness to think," said Hitler, "and criminal to proclaim that a majority can suddenly replace the accomplishment of a man of genius";[49] of course, he had no doubt that he was this man. His cultural idol Wagner had called for an end to "the French and English nonsense" (113) of parliaments and constitutions and called for the establishment of a dictatorship under a heroic leader. And if Hitler carried out the Bismarckian Prussianism whereby the ruler rules and the subjects obey, he never understood one of Bismarck's favorite quotes from Goethe: "Genius is the art of limitation."[50]

Hitler's tyrannical disposition manifested itself sexually. His attitude toward women is in many ways that of a male chauvinist sadist. He believed that women "cannot think logically or reason objectively since they are ruled only by emotion." He held that "a woman must be a cute, cuddly, naive little thing—tender, sweet, and stupid."[51] In the presence of Eva Braun, his mistress, he said, "a highly intelligent man should take a primitive and stupid woman" (quoted at 52).

Hitler's Oedipal pattern gives us yet another instance of the universal tendency to debasement in erotic life. His father, Alois, was forty-six when he married Hitler's mother, Klara, then twenty-two. Husband and wife called each other uncle and niece. The father's portrait dominated the family's flat. Characterized by strictness, pedantic punctuality, a violent temper, a sense of petty address, Alois Hitler was the perfect cartoon German. He demanded silence and forbade back talk, a characteristic Adolf would pick up. Alois beat Adolf and whistled for him as he would for a dog—with two fingers in his mouth. Waite concludes: "This arbitrary and ferocious man . . . lived up to a little boy's dread Oedipal fantasy of a powerful and avenging enemy who launched sudden thunderbolts of terror, pain, and punishment" (135).

Oedipal conditions were in place for the Great Romance between the young mother and her son. The Hitler family doctor averred: "I have never witnessed a closer attachment between mother and son" (quoted at 141). "All his life," Waite tells us, "Hitler carried his mother's picture in his pocket. In all his bedrooms—in Munich, the Berlin Chancellory, the Obersalzberg—her portrait hung at the head of his bed." Hitler remembered the years just after his father's death in 1903, when he lived with his mother in a comfortable apartment in Linz, as the freest and happiest time of his life. Yet, as Waite notes, mother love of such intensity is never unalloyed with mistrust and hatred, and this hatred is usually camouflaged by extraordinary expressions of love and devotion. He cites Karl Menninger to the effect that this is not mature feeling but "an infantile attachment which is partly *dependence* and partly *hostility*, but very little love." As Menninger says, men with such feelings are not capable of normal sex: "If they consort with women at all, it is women who are much older or much younger than themselves and are treated as protecting mothers or as inconsequential childish amusements," masquerades of love (quoted at 143). Freud emphasizes the second option, and Hitler went mostly for that too.

Hitler told his friends that the only person he could have married was his niece, Geli Raubel. "She was much younger than he," Waite notes, "about as young as his mother had been when she married his father. And just as his own parents had called each other 'uncle' and 'niece,' Hitler asked Geli to call him 'uncle Alfi'"; he always referred to her as "my niece Geli" (224). But she did not reciprocate his affections. She "could not bring herself to do 'what he wants me to do,'" Waite informs us, quoting Geli. She committed suicide with a pistol. Waite notes: "With the single exception of his mother's death, no other event in his personal life had hit him so hard." Hitler "stayed in the death room in Munich just as in Linz, years earlier, he had spent Christmas time watching over the corpse of his mother . . . it seems likely that . . . in her death he suffered anew the death of Klara" (228).

But no one could talk about women the way Hitler generally did who had not had trouble with his own mother. Like Menninger, we must wonder what his mother did to him, considering his sadomasochism. We know what his father did. Just as Hitler's character reflects ambivalence toward his father, there was as well the other mother in his mind. He thought her eyes (and his) were like the Medusa's. His favorite visual artist was Franz von Stuck, whose portrait of Medusa of the terrifying eye he loved. He identifies these eyes with his mother's, which were, like Hitler's own, intense. The Medusa, of course, turns men to stone, makes them impotent. Hitler was certainly a study in castration anxiety, with his hands typically posed as if to protect his genitals, as Waite shrewdly observes, and his lifelong fascination with images of decapitation. "As a boy in Linz," Waite informs us, "he drew severed heads to entertain a schoolmate who was a boarder in his mother's home" (65). Hitler's favorite Englishmen were Cromwell and Henry VIII, both known for beheadings—"the only two positive figures in English history," in his judgment (22). He wanted to see the place where King Henry had decapitated his wives. But beheading could work both ways: "Politics is like a harlot," said Hitler; "if you love her unsuccessfully she bites your head off" (quoted at 21). And so she did.

The key behavior is Hitler's sexual reticence. Waite tells us that "the thought of getting married and of having genital sexual relations with a wife did not appeal to him" (234). On the basis of a passage from *Mein Kampf* and related material, Waite speculates that a brutal primal scene and its attendant castration anxiety (in conjunction with Hitler's monorchism—the condition of having one testicle), combined with the attraction and repulsion for him of incest fantasies in the Oedipal rivalry, induced the belief "that coitus is brutal, infectious, and dangerous." Waite adds that "his avoidance of genital intercourse with women may also have been a consequence of his unconscious association of all women with one woman—his mother—who yielded deceitfully to his father-rival, produced deficient children (who died early in life or were mentally or physically defective), and then nursed them at breasts that later became diseased" (167). So, Waite says, normal sexual intercourse seemed frightening and repulsive to Hitler. *Mein Kampf*, with its abundance of sexual imagery—notably, its excited allusions to rape, prostitution, syphilis, and "the most disgusting" sexual practices—suggests voyeurism. Hitler was fascinated by von Stuck's perverse, sensuous women consorting with a monumental snake, images of sexual anxiety if not terror. Hitler acquired one such painting, *Sin*, for his Munich apartment. He had a library of pornography, he had "blue" films made especially for his private viewing, and he drew pictures which, according to his intimate friend Ernst "Putzi" Hanfstaengl, "only a perverted voyeur could have committed to paper" (234).

In short, Hitler illustrates the Madonna-whore complex, in his case the "splitting" of a borderline personality. There was "his ethereal love for the inviolate Stephanie," Hitler's Beatrice. Through this young lady, this angel too good to be touched, "he could make a virtue out of his psychological necessity of avoiding physical relations with women" (180), as Waite notes. "Stephanie was the only creature on God's earth whom he excepted from this infamous humanity" (190), Waite says.

Often the sense of sexual infection that Hitler's friends remarked on necessitated no response. Waite holds that Hitler's disjunctive stereotyping of men and women, together with his paranoia, suggests a latent homosexuality. He rightly maintains that in Hitler "the fantasied tough male sex role developed into sadism, murder, and destruction." In psychodynamic terms, when the Oedipal rage is overwhelming, "the attempt to eroticize it fails and the individual turns to sadism" (236). This quality emerged in Hitler's public life as well as his private one. "Cruelty and brutal strength" is what the masses want to "make them shudderingly submissive" (quoted at 41), Hitler said, lauding terror as the most effective way in politics. The sexual metaphor is intended. For Hitler, the masses were "like a woman . . . who will submit to the strong man" (quoted at 53). His speech was often charged with an obvious sexual symbolism of hammers and doors. The eroticism in Hitler's stance as an orator is ingeniously described by Waite: "His speeches began as he stood erect, rocking back and forth slowly on his heels, his voice carefully modulated and deliberately low. After a period of gentle introductory foreplay, he would move with mounting excitement toward the climax. The last five minutes have been described as an 'orgasm of words.' He once told an intimate of the very great importance he attached to the delicate matter of sensing the precise climactic moment, which, he said must be . . . shared between himself and his audience. 'By feeling the reaction of the audience, one must know exactly when the moment has come to throw the last flaming javelin which sets the crowd afire'" (53). Hitler often said he was never so happy as after a good speech, an act which would leave him "physically and emotionally spent." His sadism was consonant with his belief that force alone is decisive. Brutality is a virtue in man, according to Hitler, since "man knows nothing but the extermination of his enemies in the world" (quoted at 77).

Waite holds that Hitler's demagoguery may be considered an oral aggression deriving from dislocations in the infant feeding process. This led to oral disturbances and fixations like his sucking his fingers in times of excitement, his inordinate craving for candy, his violent rages, poor appetite, books about food fads, and constant comments about diet. Waite says that Hitler was "a compulsive and aggressive talker even as a youth," noting that he "was friendly only with those whom he could dominate verbally" (147). Hitler put his military bona fides in order by saying: "You can fight with your mouth." (quoted at ibid.). Waite holds that his need to command, to conquer, reflects Melanie Klein's views on oral sadism.[52]

Once Hitler's father struck him 230 times. In "A Child is Being Beaten," Freud speaks of masochism as deriving from Oedipal guilt. So while hating his father consciously, Hitler may have desired punishment as a way of gaining his father's love and attention. The evidence supports the view that Hitler, like Sade, was sadomasochistic. In Freud, masochism is the obverse of sadism, aggression directed inward (or, as he later thinks, an extension of the death instinct). Sadomasochism reflects the confusion of love and hatred in Hitler and illustrates the "splitting" characteristic of his sexual behavior. According to Waite, Hitler used whips incidentally, mainly as a form of self-chastisement—one of many illustrations of his sadomasochistic tendencies. Other examples are more spectacular, all the way to coprophilia, the underside of his grandiose public image (237–38, 244–45) and the extreme expression of his castration anxiety.

Hitler's psychopathology became, as Waite says, "a political asset" (243).

He agrees with Erich Fromm that in Germany of the 1920s "something akin to group sadomasochism developed: the 'little man' [lower middle class] wanted to be dominated, but also wanted to dominate others, to hate and destroy" (329). It was easy for the masses to identify with Hitler, and he with them. Waite quotes one observer, who put it precisely: "He let them relax into a precivilized, presocial, infantile stage. He allowed them to hate and believe, to strike and obey, to march and feel as masters of the world" (quoted at 331). Impotence breeds its opposite. Violence, as many have said, is an expression of impotence.

Waite holds with Freud's view that "perverted sexuality is nothing else but infantile sexuality, magnified and separated into component parts," agreeing that "infantilism is clearly marked when, as with Hitler, the perversion involves a reversion to the anal stage" (242). Klara Hitler had the cleanest house in town, and Adolf had an overly stringent toilet training. To compensate for his anal fixation, Hitler practiced "the most punctilious personal cleanliness" (241). He shaved and changed his shirt twice a day. If the child is father of the man, in Hitler's case he appears to be the mother as well.

Perhaps the eccentricity most dangerous to himself was the necktie game he played with his valet. He would hold his breath and count to ten while the valet tied the knot, relieved when the task was done before he reached ten. This game of substitute suicide was playing with the ultimate masochistic resolution, whether one thinks of it as assuaging Oedipal guilt or experiencing a wish for death. Equally dramatic, suicidal women were an attraction to Hitler. Six of the seven women Hitler very probably engaged in intimate relations with committed suicide—or came close to doing so. His first encounter, not without its hilarious moments, occurred in 1926, when Hitler was already thirty-seven years old; the woman, named Mimi, was sixteen, a clerk in her mother's dress shop. Hitler "addressed her in language normally reserved for children" (224), playfully feeding her cake with his fork as if she were a small child. Hitler met her refusal of a goodnight kiss with controlled anger. Saving face, he shot up his arm and said, "Heil Hitler!," a unique option. The affair proceeded in his favor, but he had to cut it off for reasons of political expediency. Later in the year, Mimi unsuccessfully attempted suicide by hanging. Geli, as we have seen, did commit suicide. Hitler paid only occasional attentions to Eva Braun until she attempted suicide. It was only after her second attempt that Hitler showed real interest in her. Eventually, they were suicides together, in a grim parody of Wagner's "Liebestod," one of Hitler's favorite pieces of music.

In the case of the inviolate Stephanie, whom he never touched, *he* contemplated suicide, insisting, however, that she would have to die with him. The ultimate masochistic act is consonant with Hitler's inclination for self-punishment. It is sometimes suggested that the obviousness of his military blunders was itself an unconscious form of suicide. Waite paraphrases Menninger to the effect that "people who consider themselves unique, who refuse to be examined physically or to have their beliefs questioned, may find in suicide a confirmation of their omnipotence" (424). He might as well be describing Hitler, who fits all these categories. A person about to commit suicide may be in a state of ecstasy because, as Karl Wahl puts it, he "achieves, as does the infant, a kind of cosmic identification" (quoted at 426). Waite says in this connection that the suicide equates the world with himself, "sharing the delusion of the medieval mystics who said, with St. Eustace, 'Nothing outside my own mind is real; the world and all persons in it are, in reality, me.'" We see in this solipsism how close suicide is to murder. Thus, Wahl maintains, suicide may be "matricide, patricide . . . even genocide" (quoted at 426). Let the world perish, for it is not worthy of him. Hitler's Third Reich, then, is uncannily Sadean. Solipsism is the ultimate sadism. In Hitler, history—and the historian—has given us a Sadean character far more absorbing than anyone Sade could imagine. This is partly due to the Freudian perspective brought to bear on a historical figure. But it is also due to the fact that though Sade had an obvious pathology, he scarcely had a psychology at all.

Had there been an early reader of *Justine* who knew *120 Days of Sodom*, a book that was not published until the twentieth century, he would have been startled by the claims that Sade or the narrator makes for *Justine* in the prologue. Sounding very much the *philosophe*, Sade addresses himself to the burning question of poetic justice raised by the book of Job. The Bible presents the problem in religious or, one might say, metaphysical terms. Sade's emphasis is somewhat different. "If," he says, "though full of respect for social conventions and never overstepping the bounds they draw round us . . . it should come to pass that we meet with nothing but brambles and briars, while the wicked tread upon flowers . . . if misery persecutes virtue and prosperity accompanies crime [is it not] far better to join company with the wicked?"[53] Rather than a problem between man and God, Sade sees evil in terms of "social conventions." This suggests a problem remediable within man's purview alone. Unlike the author of the book of Job, Sade would never yield questions of sovereignty to God. Yet, like the religious man, the narrator of *Justine* rejects "these ... dangerous sophistries of a false philosophy," finding it "essential ... to show the spirit quite as surely restored to righteousness" (*J* 457). As a writer with something of a dialectical disposition, Sade asks "the reader's indulgence for the erroneous doctrines which are to be placed in the mouths of our characters, and for the sometimes rather painful situations which, out of love for truth, we have been obliged to dress before his eyes" (458). Sade clearly aligns himself with benevolence, exclaiming: "Oh, how these renderings of crime made me proud of my love for virtue! How sublime does it appear through tears" (456). Is this sheer hypocrisy, false consciousness, or the legerdemain of the narrative voice that the tale will expose? Whichever, it is impossible to take seriously the Sade who presents himself as "detesting the sophistries of libertinage and irreligion" (455).

Les Infortunes de la Vertu (the adversities of virtue) is the subtitle of the 1787 manuscript version of *Justine*. The longer, published version of 1791 is more sadistic and appropriately subtitled *Les Malheurs de la Vertu* (good conduct well chastised). Both titles emphasize the reversal of poetic justice, which is ostensibly what the book is thematically about—Job in pink tights, as it has been described. For Sade, such a reversal is not problematic but exulting. He never tires of trying to subvert Justine's faith in a spiritual rightness, never tires of asserting the primacy of a destructive material energy. There is a propriety to the simple picaresque structure of her adventures; it showcases a malevolence that is as likely to be random as it is inclusive. Poor Justine realizes that she is "destined, since childhood, to acquit myself of not a single virtuous deed or feel a single righteous sentiment without suffering instant retribution" (*J* 719). She lives in a world in which no good deed goes unpunished. So, for example, it is after doing a favor for a villainous merchant that she is hit over the head by him with a cane and finally loses her virginity (an echo of Richardson's Clarissa, who lost hers only when drugged). In the Sadean universe, Justine's fatal fault is never losing faith. "I put my faith in the God of Justice who will revenge me for your crimes," she tells the infamous Cardoville, himself a judge. Sade often singles out that profession for special mockery: as there is no justice in heaven, why should there be any on earth? After making this profession of faith, Justine (she who seeks the just) exclaims in utter disappointment: "And divine lightning strikes him not!" (736). Her question is basically Job's: "Why is it that this enlightened Providence whose justice I am pleased to worship, the while punishing me for my virtues, simultaneously shows me those who crush me with their crimes carried to the pinnacle of happiness?" Yet this is not quite Job's question. Nobody crushed him with their crimes. The Sadean twist speaks of violent human agency: the criminals crush the innocent, as they may even eventually crush themselves on occasion.

Justine (called Thérèse) is unknowingly telling her sad tale to Juliette (Comtesse de Lorsange), her sister; the recognition scene has not yet taken place. The worldly Juliette is another illustration of poetic injustice. In fifteen years she has accumulated a title, a fortune of thirty thousand pounds, jewels, houses in the country and city, and access to powerful men. Never mind that she started as a whore with "on sale . . . merchandise" (J 464), specializing as a faux virgin. Never mind that at twenty she married a rich man twice her age whom she killed, thereby inheriting all his wealth. Never mind her subsequent murders and infanticides, or the narrator's crocodile tears: "It is hence true that prosperity may attend conduct of the very worst" (466). With Sade's usual dramatic unbelievability there follows between the sisters a crescendo of the *larmoyant*. Justine's story has a great effect on Madame de Lorsange, "in whom . . . the monstrous errors of her youth had not by any means extinguished sensibility . . . she was ready to swoon" (738). Is it possible? Hardened Juliette! When the mandatory recognition scene breaks out, sobs are abundant. And Juliette's friend, Justice de Corville—a good Justice!—will take up Justine's cause. Juliette praises him for "true acquaintance with the human heart and the spirit of the law which is the avenger of oppressed innocence" (739). Dramatic effect momentarily overrides thematic plausibility. Here we have a Sade-sponsored equation of the good heart and the law. Both sisters weep on Corville.

Of course, it is the still melancholy Justine, not some villain, who is later struck by lightning. Such is the will of nature, both destructive and creative, which prevails over man-made convention. It does Justine little good that she stands "in the middle of the room" (J 741) in a thunderstorm, and that some of the shutters had been closed. Like a mockery of fertility, after entering her heart, the lightning "burst through her belly."[54] It is all too much for her sister, who will take the veil as a Carmelite nun. That is an unlikely concession, for to her rhetorical question—"Ah, what must be the punishment I have got to fear from Him, I, whose libertinage, irreligion, and abandon [sic] of every principle have stamped every instant of my life!" (742)—the answer must be "none."

Despite such lurid melodrama, there is a tendency in Sade criticism to attribute to him a moral and psychological unity, an aesthetic subtlety that he does not possess, a tendency to treat him as a self-conscious modern writer. He was not. In the vogue for Sade, everyone seems to have forgotten that despite his original fantasy logic, he was not a writer of the first rank. Sade is a writer who could scarcely build a scene, or could do so only melodramatically; who wallows in episodic and rhetorical repetition; who is lurid ad nauseam; whose major narratives go on interminably; and whose spirit is inseparable from psychosis. Sade has little sense of developed character and not much more of event. As Beauvoir puts it, we see "Sade's heroes only from without . . . That is why these perverse bucolics have the austerity of a nudist colony."[55] Moreover, as Edmund Wilson has said, Sade had neither the taste nor balance to produce a masterpiece like Laclos's *Liaisons Dangereuses*. Because there is no "real conflict between different moral values," Wilson believes, "there is no drama in Sade."[56] One may accept this sane, old-fashioned judgment. Sade is a gourmand, not a gourmet, of emotion.

Angela Carter is one critic who attributes overly complex motives to Justine. Criticizing her as a woman who will "never feel a moment's gratification," Carter condemns Justine's "chastity as frigidity."[57] For Carter it is not rape, which perpetually refreshes Justine's virginity, but seduction that the character fears. Justine cannot envision a benign sexuality. Carter wonders why she is such a prude. But since this is Sade's world and not some presumptive up-tight, middle-class community, it is much more likely the case that Justine simply does not encounter benign sexuality. Carter condemns her for accepting Dubreuil's proposal of marriage; she sees Justine accepting only because he has made her the offer, not because it was her sexual preference. But Justine is not a manipulating woman; she is an ingénue, a stock character whose nonexistent complexity is determined by the predictable exigencies of Sade's plot. She is an exercise in generic portraiture, not a character in the modern psychological sense. Consistent with this fallacy of misplaced subtlety, Carter holds that Justine's inability to be changed by experience is symbolized by her sterility. But one does not read *Justine* for symbolist depth. It is all too obvious: Justine is a tortured innocent, trying to survive. When Carter concludes by saying that "Justine's virtue, in action, is the liberal lie in action, a good heart and an inadequate methodology" (55), she is reducing *Justine* to postwar English politics.

Occasionally, *Justine* does show the depth that generic portraiture can give. The Comte de Bressac episode is a case in point. The sequence is unusual in that Justine falls in love with her victimizer. It is improbable in that the object of her affection is a passive, effeminate homosexual. Justine tells us that "nothing in the world was able to extinguish this nascent passion, and had the Count called upon me to lay down my life, I would have sacrificed it for him a thousand times over" (*J* 511). There she goes again, volunteering the ultimate submissiveness, self-destruction. Justine's passion is psychologically dubious and rhetorically unconvincing. The outcome is predictable. The more indifferent the count is—he has no idea of her passion—the more she loves him, until a murder-for-money plot sets her against him and brings about her ruin. There may be some psychological complexity here in that Justine feels passion for a being who is totally inaccessible, someone who is safely out of reach. Or in that, with her fear of men, she in effect falls in love with a woman. Needless to say, Sade minimizes the possible complexity and quickly converts the affair into a scene of victimization. Justine tips off the person who is to be murdered, is then accused of committing the crime, and is kicked out and denied her earnings. Another antinomian victory. "Here I am," laments the one who would be just, "a second time denounced to justice for having been overly respectful of the law" (532–33). So ends another tale of our strange stock character, recorded with what she calls "the eloquence of wretchedness" (464).

Justine's severely masochistic character is in play even in her piety. She is constantly praying for the favor of one sovereign master or another. Whether in prayer or fellatio, she is often on her knees. And, submissive, she is always "innocent and weak" (*J* 503). After having lost her vaginal virginity to St. Florent, she prays to God: "If . . . even I am to find naught but stings and nettles terrestrially, is it to offend Thee, O my sovereign Master, to supplicate Thy puissance to take me into Thy bosom, in order untroubled to adore Thee, to worship thee far away from these perverse men" (503). Justine seems born to the pleasure of desperate supplication. Here the wish for death is the ultimate masochistic satisfaction, which shows us the occasionally surprising range of stock portraiture.

Leon Charney observes that "psychological touches in the presentation of Justine show us novelistic possibilities that Sade could have exploited further but didn't. He is generally content to pursue Justine's adventures as a moral fable rather than a novel."[58] True, but Sade could not have exploited these possibilities further because his conception of character was not very deep. It is not a question of his being "content," but one of his being limited by nature and convention. In his desire to establish the seriousness of "sexual fiction," Charney avoids the obvious truth that Sade, though certainly a writer of serious fiction, is, above all, a pornographer.

Charney claims too much for *Justine* by way of her becoming "subtly involved in her own adventure." He says, dubiously, that "she usually falls in love with her inhuman but dashing and manly tormentor," and that she is therefore "not so completely a moral creature as she pretends to be; she has a definite emotional stake in the action and is filled with the profound ambivalence of Richardson's Pamela" (46). This is not the case. There is hardly ever any ambivalence at all. Justine quite clearly resists her victimizers in a book motivated by the dramatization of some monstrous lust or other with which Sade has a ghoulish, mocking sympathy. The character of Justine is largely—except for what is a given for the ingénue—the confluence of these happenings. She wants to get away but is unable to do so except in occasional, timorous flights. Charney misreads the episode of the blood-sucking (literally), phlebotomizing Gernande, a particularly loathsome monster with whom Justine is, in his view, "more than a little in love" (36). There is no irony, other than the obvious dramatic one, in the scene in which Justine fellates him to spare his sorely beleaguered, especially good, especially beautiful wife a drawn-out torture. (Like many of Sade's weirdos—like Sade himself, apparently—Gernande is barely potent.) For this reason, Justine says quite unambivalently that she became a whore from kindness, a libertine through virtue. Rather than profound ambivalence, what we have is a madman's soap opera. The melodrama here is so heavy, so campy, that Justine's supervirtuous utterance is unintentionally funny.

Justine *is* an open book. She *is* very much the moral creature she pretends to be. Though there have been sophisticated, perhaps cynical, interpretations of *Pamela* that make the heroine out to be a clever gold digger holding out for her price, she is, as Charney says, torn between "her honor and her passion."[59] Not so Justine. Richardson wants us to take Pamela's humility seriously. His audience understood that Puritan lowliness is God-given, not an expression of discontent. There is nothing in Justine like the constant emotional engagement of Pamela with her would-be lover. Sade is much too interested in the pyrotechnics of the sexual picaresque for that. Richardson focuses more on the description of character, Sade on the description of episode, which is partly why Richardson, in *Clarissa*, achieves a novel of real psychological complexity—one of the great English novels—and Sade never does. He is driven mainly by an ingenious proliferation of perverse incident. In making the novel an exhaustive commentary on the minutiae of daily conduct, Richardson defined a major, perhaps the major, strain of the novel. The crudeness of *Pamela* when the heroine accepts Squire B. and he converts is an aesthetic one. Richardson was to transcend this inadequacy of characterization in *Clarissa*. Sade never really develops as a writer; he just goes on and on, like an expanding bookcase.

It is not accidental that Richardson's Squire B., like Sade and many of his surrogates, was an indulged, aristocratic child. The middle-class reaction to the brutality of Restoration sexual mores was central to Richardson's popularity. In *Clarissa*, the novelist dissipated the dramatic awkwardness of *Pamela* —its contradictory condemnation of upper-class licentiousness and abject regard for upper-class status—by minimizing the social distance between Lovelace and Clarissa. Yet Lovelace remains the cavalier, Clarissa the Puritan. Like Sade, yet unlike Sade, Lovelace is somewhat sorry to find pleasure in playing the tyrant in love. Sade's tyrants express no remorse. And there is nothing in Sade to equal Lovelace's struggle with himself.

Though having neither the architectonics of *120 Days of Sodom* nor the relative literary proportion of *Justine*, *Philosophy in the Bedroom* can make its claim as a major Sadean text in its full-fledged assumption of the didactic mode. Structurally, the work is, as Gray says, "a pastiche of the conversational form long used in erotic literature, and also of eighteenth-century classroom didacticism."[60] So, for example, proscribe becomes prescribe. Eugénie's education gives us a somewhat sharper and more ambitious ideational context than the earlier works. The wit is as trenchant as in *120 Days*. Plato maintained that the best learning took place only when teacher and student were erotically linked. If so, Dolmancé's academy is a veritable palace of instruction. Despite its unity of time, place, and action, this dialogue resembling a play is, like all of Sade's major works, distinguished by the quality of obsession. This is why it is actually so much like the earlier works that it is said to barely resemble. Although it takes place in a single day, it is another *120 Days of Sade*. If all of Sade's pornography is a dialogue trying to escape fictional form, here he almost succeeds.

But a clear picture emerges. *Philosophy in the Bedroom* gives us the *philosophe* as pre-Romantic. Sade prefaces the work by remarks to "voluptuaries of all ages," indicating from the outset a world of no limits, a world in which the conditionality of nature is not a restraint. The voluptuaries are also "of all sexes," a curious conception. For Sade, there are not just two sexes but as many as one can fantasize or invent, which makes him the grandfather of the adult polymorphous perverse. "I am an amphibious creature," says his Mme. St. Ange, "I love everything, everyone . . . I should like to combine every species" (*PB* 187). Deinhibition is married to androgyny in Sade. In his exaltation of the morality of impulse, in his belief that "no voice save that of the passions can conduct to happiness," Sade anticipates and parallels Romantic morality. Of course, his idea of passion is sex, often violent. There is none of the idealizing element that one usually associates with Romanticism.

But Sade is Romantic, at least in tendency, in his espousal of a liberation psychology, an intransigence of the self versus society. He is an avatar of the cult of energy. His mouthpiece, Dolmancé, links energy with the devil. "Nothing can vanquish the hold this demon's energy has upon us," he says (*PB* 212). He and Mme. St. Ange—the instructors in this pedagogical work subtitled *The Immoral Schoolteachers*—launch a total assault on superego, even to the point of affirming that there is no general criminality, "none, not even theft, nor incest, neither murder, nor parricide itself" (218). Such is the logic of impulse. Society, not nature, is at fault. In stating the case so extremely, Sade anticipates notions of not only Romantic but modern criminality. The woman making this statement (that the speaker is a woman is modern in itself) is one of Sade's spectacularly liberated spirits. Married at the then-customary age of fourteen, she has in the twelve years since had sexual intercourse with upward of ten or twelve thousand people (not all men), or about a thousand a year or three a day, making Don Juan appear a slouch. Her justification is a peculiarly Romantic one: "Imagination," she maintains, "is so libertine nothing can restrain it; its greatest triumph, its most eminent delights come of exceeding all limits imposed on it . . . It worships disorder, idolizes whatever wears the brand of crime" (232). There is an almost Rimbaudian sense of honorable derangement in these remarks. Foucault has noted the emergence of a passional energy to the point of delirium in reaction to the Age of Reason. Broadly speaking, Sade is a case in point. Anticipating the underground man's rejection of utilitarianism, Sade holds that man often acts or should act in ways that are contrary to his social self-interest. In Sade's case, utilitarianism is easily transcended by passional self-interest. Social self-interest is the enemy of the more profound inner assertion, and one of the reasons for its violence. Nature is the other. Precisely the forbidden is sought by Mme. St. Ange, and in a perfectly Sadean way: "What is of the filthiest, the most infamous, the most forbidden, 'tis that which best rouses the intellect . . . 'tis that which always causes us most deliciously to discharge" (233). In Sade imagination and intellect serve the cause of libertinage.

The tail wags the dog in Sade, and there is always something ridiculous in his sexual myopia. Unintended hilarity results when Dolmancé affirms Sade's principles with historical evidence: "Nero, Tiberius, Heliogabolus slaughtered their children to cause an erection" (*PB* 254). Reading Sade's pedagogical sections is like attending a university lecture gone terribly wrong. Elsewhere, we are informed that "goat-fucking" is "very widespread" in Italy, that "the Syberites embuggered dogs; Egyptian women gave themselves to crocodiles," and—my favorite—"American women appreciate being fucked by monkeys" (*Jul* 189). When he isn't affirming instinct, he is parodying it. After justifying murder to Mme. St. Ange on the familiar ground that it alters forms, Dolmancé is lauded by her in Romantic terms: " 'Tis to the man of genius only there is reserved the honor of shattering all the links of ignorance and stupidity. Kiss me" (*PB* 239). Sade gives us an unintentional parody of the immoralist genius as a fantasy eroticist whose appeal as love object is seasoned by his effeminacy—think of Dolmancé as Dolly. It is all too human, all too Sadean. Like some Dostoevskian false superman, Dolmancé has done "everything," including murder and theft; he has "permitted" himself everything (279). Cruelty may be his sexual mask, but then "cruelty exists among savages" (253) who are so much nearer to nature than civilized men are. "Cruelty," Dolmancé opines, "is simply the energy in a man civilization has not yet altogether corrupted: therefore it is a virtue not a vice." The preference of nature over civilization is, once again, Romantic, and the identification of civilization itself with corruption is modern. The transvaluation of values here is Sadean rather than Nietzschean. Dolmancé's conclusion is, of course, antinomian: "Repeal your laws, do away with your constraints"—and cruelty will disappear? Not quite, not in Sade. "Cruelty will have dangerous effects no more," Dolmancé believes, "since it will never manifest itself save when it meets with resistance, and then the collision will always be between competing cruelties." In Sade's sophistic Utopia, then, there will be more, not less, unbridled cruelty, though the crushing of the weak will be called something else—perhaps nature. Sade was never able to demolish the world of law, and his convincing cruelty remained the easily recognizable kind that may be pleasurable to the sadist but is dangerous to everyone else.

From time to time, Dolmancé is confronted with a "moral" argument. As a *philosophe*, he may seem moral himself, arguing from nature: "All individuals being of uniform importance in her eyes, 'tis impossible that she have a predilection from some one among them" (*PB* 283). Not bad—it even sounds a little like the beginning of the book of Genesis—but this does not seem to be Sade. And the perverse Sadean logic follows: "Hence, the deed that serves one person by causing suffering to another is of perfect indifference to Nature." Sade really does not seem to see that the difference between victim and victimizer is not a matter of "uniform importance." Tactfully, civically, Eugénie questions this proposition: "But if the action were harmful to a very great quantity of individuals . . . and if it rewarded us only with a very small quantity of pleasure, would it not then be a frightful thing to execute it?" Dolmancé has the Sadean answer: "No more so, because there is no possible comparison between what others experience and what we sense" (283), *we* meaning we sexual supermen. It is comments like this that justify Hayman's tart comment that Sade's "achievement is that before the Romantic movement had been launched, he succeeded in making solipsism look like omniscience."[61] Sade's truest stance is solipsism. Therefore, do unto others before they do unto you. "Are we not," he asks, "come into the world all enemies, the one of the other, all in a state of perpetual and reciprocal warfare?" (*PB* 283). That thought left Hobbes with a powerful state, but it leaves Dolmancé against any political arrangement at all.

Later in *Philosophy in the Bedroom*, after the scene with the famous pamphlet on republican principle, the Chevalier notes that "cruel" Dolmancé's ideas would be very different were *he* to be crushed by misfortune. The Chevalier speaks of "benevolence," "virtues," "sensibility," and "heart" (341), but very briefly. Despite all the argumentation in his work, Sade is the last person in the world to be truly dialectical. Here and in one other abortive scene, he makes short shrift of the Chevalier's morality. Yet as if in recognition of the merit of the character's argument, Dolmancé says that " 'twas man's ingratitude dried out my heart." This ingratitude is never dramatized. And there is, to say the least, a contradiction between blaming society for his cruelty, as Dolmancé does here, and saying elsewhere that cruelty is a noble quality found in nature. Dolmancé does admit to his consequent coldness and—true Sadean hero that he is—defends it: "The delights born of apathy are worth much more than those you get of your sensibility" (342).

Apathy is precisely right, for it is, as Blanchot says, "the spirit of negation applied to the man who has chosen to make himself supreme."[62] Dolmancé moves with narcissistic logic from apathy to a defense of the flagrant use of subject as object: "What is it one desires when taking one's pleasures? That everything around us be occupied with nothing but ourselves . . . There is not a living man who does not wish to play the despot when he is stiff" (*PB* 344). Again we see the coincidence in Sade of tyranny and infancy. Sadean wisdom speaks with the confidence of the definitional. If you are not a despot at this time, you are not a living man. Dolmancé avers that men whose "behavior during copulation [is not] the same as behavior in anger" are mere "women-worshippers . . . prostrate at their insolent Dulcinea's feet . . . basely the slaves of the sex they ought to dominate" (345). For Sade, there is no relationship between the sexes other than that of master and slave. "He is the man of all passions," says Blanchot, "and he is without feeling."[63] Sade is certainly a man without feeling, but he is a man of narrow, obsessive passion made all the more hyperbolic by his years of incarceration. Blanchot is surely right—and psychoanalysis backs him up—in saying that "all these mighty libertines who live solely for pleasure are mighty only because they have eliminated in themselves all capacity for pleasure. This is why they resort to terrifying and hideous anomalies, for otherwise the mediocrity of normal pleasures would suffice for them" (68). For the libertine aristocrat or sexual superman, nothing is as dreary as the republic of tenderness.

Philosophy in the Bedroom is ostensibly a justification of republican principles. The best known of Sade's many digressions is "Yet Another Effort, Frenchmen, if You Would Become Republicans," the long essay that appears in this work. Whether or not it was arbitrarily inserted may not matter much, since the tract is very much a piece or extension of Sade's thought. The argument in the essay does not have an immediate historical reference in that its assault on a theistic virtue is, as Lever says, an attack on Robespierre as well as on Christianity. How much of a republican could Sade be? Lever is clear on Sade's being a constitutional monarchist, liberal in that restricted sense. Any republican political sentiment of his should be taken with several grains of salt. It was not difficult to appear antimonarchist after the French Revolution.

Despite its title, the central thrust of the essay is cultural, not political—scarcely republican in the usual sense. Sade remains the antinomian, anarchist, cartoon superman. Law, like republicanism, rests on the principles of divine command and universal reason, or at least consensus. Sade emphasizes only the limitations of law: "The law, cold and impersonal, is a total stranger to the passions which are able to justify in man the cruel act of murder" (*PB* 310). A republican Caligula! Sade is therefore against capital punishment, on the ground that he is for murder. The law, of course, does not understand this because it is "opposed . . . to Nature." Nature teaches murder: "Savages, the most independent of men, the nearest to Nature, daily indulge in murder which amongst them goes unpunished" (333). True, there are headhunter tribes with ritualized killing. This, however, is not murder in the eyes of the tribesmen, but either military necessity or a sort of reverse imperialism, where the virtue of the victim is literally absorbed, all to the glory of the victor. Acknowledging that his defense of murder may surprise the reader, Sade asks, "Have we not acquired the right to say anything?" (329). We may have come close to that, but we do not have the right to do anything. Moreover, in a republic where anything can be said, anything is subject to criticism. Murder precludes freedom of speech.

To justify criminality, Sade resorts to an apparatus of bogus scholarship, fantasy anthropology, kitsch history, and loony logic. Theft, we are told, was "permitted, nay, recompensed in all the Greek republics . . . it is certain that stealing nourishes courage, strength, skill, tact, in a word all the virtues useful to a republican system and consequently to our own" (*PB* 313). After this ethical justification, he gives us a political one: "What are the elements of the social contract? Does it not consist in one's yielding a little of his freedom and of his wealth in order to assure and sustain the preservation of each?" This almost sounds right, but Sade seems oblivious to the question of who is yielding what to whom. In his justification of theft, though, he approaches a Romantic argument. He is so against law and for impulse that his logic makes him an improbable defender of the weak. So he comes out for theft. "Consider," he says, "whether he who commits [theft] does any more than put himself in harmony with the most sacred of Nature's movements, that of preserving one's own existence at no matter whose expense" (*PB* 314). But Sade isn't Hugo defending the victimized Jean Valjean.

Apparently a justification of republicanism, the essay is most of all a justification of Sade's favorite things to justify: criminality and aberrant sexuality. He calls love "the soul's madness" and makes, of all things, an ostensibly utilitarian critique of monogamy (*PB* 320). Since love satisfies "two persons only, the beloved and the loving, [it cannot] serve the happiness of others, and it is for the sake of the happiness of everyone, and not for egotistical and privileged happiness, that women have been given to us." It is refreshing to see Sade come out against egotism and privilege. Of course, anyone who "possesses" a woman Sade wants is an egotist. It is equally refreshing to see him come out for the greatest happiness for the greatest number—which translates into sexist free love. "All men," he says, "have an equal right of enjoyment of all women; therefore, there is no man who, in keeping with natural law, may lay claim to a unique and personal right over a woman." Clearly, sexual rights are not reciprocal. This would not be in keeping with Sade's "natural law." Women, it seems, have the right to be sex objects, even professional ones. Accordingly, "the law which will oblige them to prostitute themselves . . . is thus one of the most equitable of laws." Thus Sade is for legal equity. Moreover, it does not matter how young the prostitute is. Since men have a "proprietary right of enjoyment . . . the issue of [the woman's] well-being . . . is irrelevant." Sade's republicanism is again inseparable from tyranny. "Ah, break those irons," he implores women—so that better ones can be forged. In a rare instance of awareness that he might be contradicting himself, Sade maintains that men "have the right to compel their [women's] submission, not exclusively, for I should then be contradicting myself, but temporarily" (319). Man has, then, the right to rape or to force into prostitution, but no right of to a permanent or even long-term relationship. Generally speaking, men have the right to live and women have the right to die in the Sadean republic.

In his contempt for marriage and family, Sade anticipates modern critiques of these venerable, hence vulnerable, institutions. This is another way in which he can be thought of as avant-garde, at least in the context of his more traditional time. Sade thinks that children "ought to belong solely to the republic" and not be "immured in their families" (*PB* 321). A champion of anarchic individualism, Sade is scarcely interested in collective child rearing. He does not want a program for children, he wants a dump. Sade himself was a virtually accidental father. Eventually, his sons barely recognized his existence. One of his daughters never lost her virginity. Poetic justice had the last laugh in his life, if not in his fiction. Sade again provides ballast for his sexual ship through a bogus pastiche of testimony and history. Sexual taboos yield particularly fantastic testimony. Regarding incest, for example, Sade says that "in Judea, the eldest son must marry his father's wife" (*PB* 24). He adds that "incest ought to be every government's law—every government whose basis is fraternity." So incest is all right, anything goes, as long as it's in the family. Perversions, Sade says, are determined by a man's constitution. Therefore, he argues revealingly, the pervert is not "any more guilty than the person Nature created deformed" (329). This simile, however generous in intention, would seem to be something of an admission of his own disadvantage or a concession to the normative. At the same time, though, it is a denial of all responsibility for breaking sexual taboos. His argument against guilt in perversion, if one may use his word, gained him many twentieth-century friends. Sade wrote volumes about his own sexual rights, but he had little to say generally about the rights of man.

If to be a writer of note means creating a world that is unique and indisputably yours in a series of works, Sade is such a writer. But his work (much of what he wrote has been lost) is such a turmoil of bombast and eloquence that the reader might anticipate a final, justifying masterpiece. In the logic of his career, *Juliette* should have been that book. But it is not. Immense in size, geographically and historically ambitious—the only one of his novels that he calls *histoire*—it is not immense in scope; rather, it is a never-ending repetition of his quirks, mannerisms, and obsessions. Sade never writes his *Clarissa*, and it seems that the narrowness of his vision precluded that breakthrough into major art.

This is apparently not the view of *Juliette* in Paris in recent times, even among critics not sympathetic to poststructuralism. Annie Le Brun makes the case for *Juliette*. Le Brun's Juliette is a character free from solipsistic tendencies, erotic or otherwise. Instead, she is a metaphysician of the body whose "unquenchable search for knowledge is equaled only by her sense of its physical origins."[64] There may well be a deep link between thought and sensation—there is in the Romantics Blake, Wordsworth, and Keats—but the depth of such a connection is not notably present in Sade, where the two exist in a topographical rather than a causal relation. Moreover, in Sade knowledge is the handmaid of sensation, not an illustration of the equality that Le Brun's formulation suggests. She attributes too much intellectual subtlety to Juliette as an anti-ideologist, one who views her masters' thought as jammed into a system. She notices that the self-contained Juliette "does not alter in any way" (189), but she sees this in terms of dialectical subtlety rather than a narrative necessity imposed by an obsessive theme and a monochromatic aesthetic. Le Brun insists on idealizing Juliette "as being in search of a form beyond forms, . . . the finest idea of freedom" (192). This platonizing seems far-fetched, as is Le Brun's more down-to-earth judgment that, unlike her friends, Juliette "has no special weirdness or strange tastes" (195). One is tempted to say that is because she has them all.

Juliette does give more female portraiture than Sade's other major works. What we largely see, though, are Sadean attitudes expressed by women. So Delbène refers to Moses as a "mountain-climbing madman" and Jesus as "Mary's meeching [sic] bastard" (*Jul* 3). We have the usual rhetoric of outrage and transvaluation of values. But the fact that Juliette is a woman produces what might be considered new insights as well. She identifies the clitoris as "the true seat of woman's pleasure" (7). She maintains that men have made women self-abnegating. Just when we are engaged by her feminist prescience on these points, Delbène says that whores as whores are "interested . . . in the welfare of others" (84). Not that Sade believes this—if he did, it would be an incentive to sadism—but his characters are imbued with a scattershot logic that may hit the mark and then, seconds later, miss by a mile. Clairwil, sometimes taken as a radical breakthrough in characterization for Sade, is not much more than another Sadean mouthpiece as woman, an inversion of the heroine of sensibility. Educated, wealthy, this Minerva is antireligious, child-hating, and libertine: "She prided herself on never having shed a tear" (274). A breakthrough in female psychology? In any case, the Sadean dialogue may take an incongruously feminine turn: Juliette asks: "Do you whip, my dear?" And Clairwil replies: "Until the blood flows, my darling" (287). Or Clairwil may be seen as another fantasy version of Sade in drag, as when she says, "Torturing males is still my favorite pastime" (359), or when she inspires Juliette to eroticized cannibalism. Juliette discovers that eating a man can be as much of a turn-on as lashing a woman and adds that "my very perverse soul revealed itself in its entirety."

Despite their intimacy, Juliette and Clairwil have a falling out, which comes as a surprise—if anything in Sade can be said to surprise. Were they not together in throwing their friend Olympia into Vesuvius, after sexually molesting her? This too comes as something of a surprise. Olympia is unconvincingly accused of lacking "depth and rigor in her principles" (*Jul* 1019). Character in Sade exists as a function of sadistic fantasy, and the everlasting tie between Juliette and Clairwil will soon dissipate. According to Durand—an ardent older lesbian who has an obstructed vagina, a clitoris "as long as a finger" (1032), and a bugger's passion for delectable Juliette—Clairwil is plotting Juliette's death to get her money. Instead, Juliette poisons Clairwil and inherits *her* money. Durand then admits to having lied about Clairwil, not having been able to tolerate her as a rival. Juliette loves Durand for this, so much so that she would now commit the murder unprompted. Again character is a function of Sadean spectacle, and of rhetoric. Juliette denounces a Neopolitan who refuses to marry off his daughters so that he and his wife can continue to live in luxury. Now she is for marriage and against self-indulgence! Her ideas, like her sex life, are polymorphous perverse—any position will do. Like Sade, she has postures rather than ideas. Sade's is the logic of denunciation. Juliette's rhetoric itself is properly coarse, the inverse of the dulcet, polite style of her sweet sister.

In a rare moment of potential psychological complexity, the worldly Juliette meets her daughter, now seven years old, in Paris. Unable to respond to her in anything like a motherly way, Juliette seems to recognize the tyranny of the id. "Nature was mute in me," she says, "libertinage had extinguished its voice ... taking a soul in its tyrant's grip" (*Jul* 1152). Nature is here considered sensibility; feeling is elicited by customary ties. It counts for nothing. "I am obliged to say," Juliette adds, "that in embracing Marianne I feel absolutely nothing stir in me but the pulsations of lubricity." This proves that one can be honest and corrupt at the same time. Thank heaven for little girls. It is the most engaging psychological moment in the book, though in a way Sade did not intend—for he cannot deal with the psychological rather than rhetorical or dramatic reversal; he cannot deal with turning, changes of heart. True, Juliettee does not bed her daughter. Rather than a shift into complexity, however, we are given Juliette's desire to educate her daughter in the "necessity for crime," the familiar Sadean retreat.

The female portraits in *Juliette* include complication, if not complexity. And this may be said for an occasional male figure as well. St. Fond (*fond* means bottom) is depicted in more than Sade's usual novelistic flatness. Proud and "very ferocious" (*Jul* 217), St. Fond has robbed the treasury and issued many *lettres de cachet*. He will not use the informal second person to Juliette and instructs her to "never say *thou* to me. Address me . . . as my Lord, speak to me in the third person as far as possible." Further, he informs her that "I like servants to kneel before me, [I] prefer always to employ an interpreter when holding parlay with that vile rabble known as the people." An extreme royalist, he likes dirty analingus—there must be a logical or psychological connection. On the other hand, he shits and pisses on Juliette and beats her as well. His discharges are accompanied by blasphemies (as were Sade's). Afterward, she must kiss his feet. Juliette helps him to destroy his friend's wife (actually, he says "I am a friend to no one" [246])—she is first burned alive, then literally fucked to death as punishment for her prudery—and then lives with him in Parisian splendor. She is seventeen to his fifty and must kneel to kiss his hand, but the money and power make it all worthwhile to Juliette. A biblical parallelism and repetition underscores her gracious state: "The contents of my wardrobe were worth well above one hundred thousand francs, a hundred thousand crowns was the value of the jewelries [sic] and diamonds I wore" (230). Under St. Fond's influence, Juliette becomes an expert poisoner and procuress. This would be a Faustian bargain if she had a soul to sell. St. Fond is a perfect ancien régime Mephisto. They eat each other's shit. He wipes her ass with his *cordon bleu*. His credo is: "Whatever originates in the heart is false; for my part, I believe in the senses alone, I believe alone in the carnal habits and appetites" (232). Like other Sadean libertines, St. Fond anticipates a modern moral, if not social, type: the moralistic villain.

There are these instances of aesthetic assurance in *Juliette*. There are also especially wild images (Minski eats "virgins-blood sausages" and "testicle patties" [603]; Mme. Zatta has a dildo with four stems [1147]) and ferocious wit (Minski points out that "as I eat what I fuck that spares me the wages of a butcher" [582]). But there is too a narrative tedium so great that even Juliette must say, "since I have a good many adventures of this kind to relate, rather than risk being tedious, I shall forego a description of this one" (249) and "further horrors were perpetrated, whereof I'll say only that they were ghastly" (251). No doubt. The attempt made by recent French critics to sanitize Sade by paradoxical praise is unconvincing. Le Brun's claim (echoing earlier ones), that Sade's erotic vision is determined by "the principle of delicacy"[65] and Alain Robbe-Grillet's contention (quoted by Le Brun) that "Sade likes what is *joli*... the trickle of blood is there to emphasize the perfection in the most delicate of curves" seem false. The blood is more like a flood than a trickle, and it is possible for a culture to develop hubris in respect to sexual expertise. Reading Sade is an exercise not in subtlety but in obviousness. Barthes says that "language has this property of denying, ignoring, dissociating reality: when written, shit does not have an odor."[66] Nor, however, does it have an aroma.

The prettification of Sade does not wash. Much better Beauvoir's point vis-à-vis the undercutting of a neoclassical conception of harmonious beauty. "His linking of eroticism with vileness," she says, "is as original as his linking it with cruelty."[67] Sade is original because he is dirty in his way. But claims made for his great insight in this matter remain primarily historical. Least valid of all, in terms of literary quality, is the overvaluation of Sade made by those looking for a symbolic liberator of the polymorphous perverse—Austryn Wainhouse, for example, Sade's admirable translator. In his view, Sade is the heroic revolutionary: "He wants 'a permanent insurrection of the spirit,' an intimate revolution, a revolution within. He wanted what today revolution no longer holds 'impossible' but holds to be a starting point as well as a final end: to change man. To change him through and through, cost what it may, be it at the price of his 'human nature,' and even at the price of his sexual nature—and above all at the price of that which, in our communities, has forged all relations between all men and denatured them, and merged love and continuity into one disaster, one humanity."[68] Such superheated idealism stems from a political rather than an aesthetic appropriation of Sade. But it is a characteristic of the Francophiliated literary culture of America in the late sixties and seventies to believe that revolution is an honorific, the life we live is loathsome, anything is better than the repressive bourgeois present, and every demon is an avenging angel screaming to be released.

7

D. H. LAWRENCE

The loathing of modern life has led to curious paths of redemption. To counter his unholy triumvirate of capitalism, industrialism, and democracy, Lawrence posits a saving sexuality, a pre-Judeo-Christian mystical eroticism. But residually a secular Protestant, Lawrence sees things in a Pauline light. Rather than a love of necessity—Nietzsche's *amor fati*, or the acceptance of life's neutral rhythm—we are offered an assumption of renewal. As Paul Delany notes, Lawrence's Puritan side manifested itself in the dark, recurrent image of the grain of wheat that must die before it can yield its fruit. "Life could only be affirmed," says Delany, "as correlative with death; creation with destruction."[1]

Delany makes the further biographical point that "in conducting his intimate relationships [Lawrence] knew no middle voice between adulation or vindictive contempt." With his preference for "simple positives and negatives," Delany holds, Lawrence made "no allowance for shades and gradations" (*LN* 205). Delany is speaking of the crucial period of 1915, but the characterization is valid for much of Lawrence's life and art. There is a missing middle in Lawrence, an assumed violence, a ferocity so pervasive that it elicits an inevitable skepticism. Antinomianism has its limits, self-appointed grace is always suspect. For all his attacks on the aesthetic of modernism as supersubtle psychologizing, Lawrence is very much the modern in his embattled extremity and salvationary primitivism. Saul Bellow has noted the similarity between Lawrence's views of sex and the modernist antinomian salvation through art: "There are the saved and the damned, the elect and the lost, the orgasmic and the impotent."[2]

Though not much interested in the aesthetic aristocrat, Lawrence is drawn by sexual immoralism. Adultery is so paradigmatic an act in his work that one might think it would undermine the value he places on true marriage. Of course, the adulterer is always right, because society is always wrong. Witness

Oliver Mellors, the gamekeeper of *Lady Chatterley's Lover*. But what if society is not only malevolent, partly insane, and bestial, as the intimidated Mellors thinks? What if tenderness is not exclusively antinomian? What if the riches of desire do not have to be preserved? What if they may be just out there? This is more than Lawrence will allow. As the Florentine printer of *Lady Chatterley's Lover* said about the fuss over the novel's subject, "*O! ma!* but we do it every day!"[3] Common life is not as decimated as Lawrence assumes it to be.

In Lawrence a risk of nihilism accompanies erotic situations where life may be at stake. Since life is a form of death, death may be a form of life. Death is therefore often thought of, and even imposed with Lawrence's sympathy. "The Prussian Officer" is an early case in point, even if it is not quite typical in its merely qualified sympathy. The revenged orderly "had gone out from everyday life into the unknown and he could not, he even did not want to go back."[4] To the extent that the simple man transcended his ordinary being, Lawrence sympathizes with his act of murder. But the narrator tells us that "here his own life also ended," acknowledging some moral cost—perhaps because it is still early enough for Lawrence to feel guilt. By the next year, 1915, he writes "The Crown," and says that "very few men have being at all . . . whether they live or die does not matter . . . Their death is of no more matter than cutting off a cabbage in the garden, an act utterly apart from grace" (*PII* 384). Again we have the saved and the damned. In Lawrence this dualism usually takes the form of sexual expression directed against the dead order and can be viewed as a form of Romantic criminality. "Psanek means outlaw,"[5] Count Dionys tells Daphne in *The Ladybird*. In *The Fox*, the powerful climactic struggle between Grenfel and Banford over the sexual life of March results in an immoralist moment: "In his heart he had decided her death . . . The inner necessity of his life was fulfilling itself, it was he who was to live" (*FSN* 173–74). Given the context of the story—the struggle between heterosexual love and lesbianism in the soul of March—and the clever dramatic situation, the reader is sympathetic to the fox, as he is for that matter to the orderly in "The Prussian Officer." Grenfel has no regrets about Banford's spectacular demise. March feels guilt but is gradually broken down by the heterosexual imperative. In *St. Mawr*, when Lou buys the stallion, she is well aware of what she is doing. She "was prepared to sacrifice Rico,"[6] though it turns out that she is not quite prepared after all. And in *The Plumed Serpent*, Kate Leslie is so thankful for her virgin girl reincarnation, as it were, that she thinks of Don Cipriano, "What do I care if he kills people? His flame is young and clean."[7] She is motivated not just by the Mexican blood-daze but by the adoration of the phallic. A similar passage occurs in *Lady Chatterley's Lover* when Mellors says of Clifford and Bertha to Connie, "I ought to be allowed to shoot them."[8] Granted there is a difference between deed and wish, but there is also some overlap: words may lead to deeds. Destruction is a luxury that few victims can afford.

In the modernist assault on authority, Lawrence has played a key role. As Philip Rieff maintains, Lawrence is "the most forthright of modern heresiarchs, chief and father—although only after his death—over all our little heresiarchs: all those professionally angry young father killers who march along the literary horizon looking for an older generation with some reserves of dignity that might be exposed as class discrimination and coldness; or what is even more Laurentian, the Angries, the Beats, and the Espressoists are looking for an older generation with some fixed ideals so long as they are fixed."[9] Perhaps these versions of the luxury of destruction have run their course. Lawrence is, of course, equally embattled. His insights into sexual aggression, both explicit and sublimated, and how it manifests a cultural attitude, as well as his honesty in assessing its powers and limitations, are memorable.

Beginning with *Women in Love*, Lawrence's most powerful works deal centrally with this subject, though it is important even in the relatively pastoral *The Rainbow*. Will Brangwen's vision of London is one that Rupert Birkin might have had. He contemplates "the ponderous, massive, ugly (how often does Lawrence give us three successive adjectives?) superstructure of a world of man upon a world of nature!"[10] With a somewhat assumed anger, Will thinks that "the works of man were more terrible than man himself." The novel does not dramatize Will's contempt for his fellow man, so his misanthropy is imposed. Yet Lawrence is quick to tell us that Will would "sweep away the whole monstrous superstructure of the world today, cities and industries and civilization," leaving what becomes in Lawrence an all-too-familiar landscape: "only the bare earth with plants growing and water running" (190). There are no people in the landscape.

Lawrence told Waldo Frank that he was writing "a destructive work" or he would not have called it *The Rainbow*, "in reference to the Flood."[11] The novel was written before the First World War. Lawrence wrote Frank that the revision of the book was a "working up to the dark sensual or Dionysic and Aphrodisic ecstasy, which does actually burst the world, burst the word-consciousness in every individual. What I did through individuals, the world has done through the war." This extraordinary description speaks to the joy of destruction to the point of apocalypse. That these remarks apply to *Women in Love* is clear. It is less clear how they apply to *The Rainbow*, considering its woman-blessing opening chapters, and even the marriage of Will and Anna as it develops.

Their sexual relationship is somewhat violent even before the late intensification of this violence in the revision, consisting of Will's London interlude and its aftermath. At first the violence is part of the power struggle between them. Resisting his smothering darkness, Anna strikes him and draws blood. In reaction he feels that "he must beat her" (166) but he does not. The battle is really over the pall of religion and Anna's disillusioned resistance to it. She wins, and Will is thereby diminished as a man. Although she believes in the "omnipotence of the human mind," as Lawrence's women at this stage of his writing are likely to do, she eventually becomes a mother—of nine! Her power then lies in womanliness. Diminished in moral stature, reduced in function, Will appears to be one of Lawrence's pathetic males: "What had he in life save her? Nothing" (234). An affair gives Will back some masculine independence, and Anna "saw she could not reduce him to what he had been before." She had lost "her old, established supremacy" (231–32). Their relationship goes beyond "tenderness"—or, to use a word that Lawrence comes to scorn, "love" —into "a sensuality violent and extreme as death" (234). Though Lawrence calls this "a passion of death," he concedes that the "shameful, natural and unnatural acts of sensual voluptuousness . . . had their heavy beauty and their delight," even concluding that "the secret, shameful things are most terribly beautiful" (234–35). Though the language of disintegration is employed here, the experience is one of integration. In this struggle between man and wife, a balance is restored. Anna regains respect for Will, and the new Will is liberated for public affairs. He wants to conduct a woodworking class. From anal intercourse to bore drilling is a benign, utilitarian turn. Lawrence, in short, is not yet moving to a new psychological perception brought on by his daring theme. Though there is a shift of consciousness resulting from the couple's sexual breakthrough, there is no corresponding enlargement, no elevation of the negative, having to do with their dark passion. Though there is indeed, in Lawrence's terms, a working up to the Dionysic and Aphrodisic ecstasy, the end result is not the bursting of the world that he describes. For that we must go elsewhere.

The relationship between Ursula and Skrebensky gives us a more characteristic view of apocalypse, in which social and sexual aggression are inextricably bound and destruction has a transcendent value. Late in the novel Skrebensky, rather sentimentally associated with the darkness of the Negro, makes what appears to be a serious impact on Ursula. "He kissed her," Lawrence writes, "and she quivered as if she were being destroyed, shattered . . . They were one stream, one dark fecundity" (*R* 446–47). This stream is to develop into the key "river of dissolution" image in *Women in Love*, where its significance is to be fully drawn. For the moment, it yields no decomposition. Still, sex has a potent effect. What art does for Stephen Dedalus, sexual potency does for Ursula and Skrebensky: it gives them a king's-eye view of ordinary life. Even the rather utilitarian Skrebensky, a military engineer, is given the gift of contempt: "He despised it all—it was all non-existent . . . He had no use for people, nor for words" (449). Words, after all, are a product of civilized life, not as significantly emotive as touch and other qualities more representative of unconscious reality. This is a fairly constant theme in Lawrence, part of his assault on ordinary perception. The feeling of the two lovers is an erotic solipsism: "They were perfect, therefore nothing else existed. The world was a world of servants whom one civilly ignored. Wherever they went, they were the sensuous aristocrats . . . They alone inhabited the world of reality. All the rest lived on a lower sphere" (454–55). Sexual Nietzscheanism has its price: the dehumanization of everybody else.

Indeed, for the more romantic Ursula, even Skrebensky "had never become finally real" (493). His mundane sense of vocation, his ultimate lack of masculine assertiveness, are measures of this unreality. Ursula has a wide and unfocused rebelliousness to which perhaps no male could measure up. Responding to the impersonal pull of the ocean, she says to him, "I want to go." "Where?" he asks. "I don't know," she replies, articulating the rebel without a cause rootlessness decades before James Dean. She has only a generalized contempt for what passes for life. Poor Skrebensky does not stand a chance. Their final kiss shows the souring of romantic vitalism and the reversal of the destructive element in their relationship. Ursula has aggressive potency, and the compromised Skrebensky does not: "She clenched hold of him hard, as if suddenly she had the strength of destruction, she fastened her arms around him and tightened him in her grip, whilst her mouth sought his in a hard, rending, everincreasing kiss, till his body was powerless in her grip, his heat melted in fear from the fierce, beaked, harpy's kisses" (479). All of this by the sea's edge, between time and eternity, and between either and or. Like Skrebensky, Lawrence sees in this display of womanly energy no two stars in one constellation. In the vacuum left by a man who does not lead, a woman will act accordingly; in this she reflects her own upbringing. In later works, the

Lawrence surrogate will be wary of the harpy. Here, however, he empathizes with this image of destruction because it is Ursula who expresses the author's alienation from a reality that includes the effective absence of man. It is a disillusioned, very Lawrencean heroine who says at the end of her adventures: "I have no father nor mother nor lover, I have no allocated place in the world of things, I do not belong to Beldover not to Nottingham nor to England nor to this world, they none of them exist" (492). Her complaint is the ultimate Lawrence complaint: "They are all of them unreal." And her extremity yields the ultimate Lawrence wish, the wish for a virtually religious transcendence, for "the man who would come out of Eternity to which she herself belongs" (493). Lawrence strikes a note that is to run through his work, even to *The Man Who Died*: the advent of the ontological lover. Ursula might be Isis in *The Man Who Died*—a vestal virgin anticipating her orgasmic messiah. In her eventual pregnancy Isis, like Ursula, "sat to watch a new creation" (*R* 493). Ursula is thinking of the rainbow, wishing for the recreation of the world. When she miscarries, it is a sign that the new creation cannot come from her disintegrated love.

The celebrated symbolism of the novel's concluding chapter indicates that there will be a collective dying into a new life. Ursula's dark night of the soul is defined by two images. In the first, the horses are symbolic of a frightening animal potency limited in its confinement, an apparent masculine threat to neutralize her assumption of the masculine role with Skrebensky. But romantic vitalism of either sort is not the answer. This is why Ursula has reached "the bottom of all things" (490) and falls into delirium. She expresses a nearly total alienation from an unreal world and has her miscarriage. She awakes to a transcendental God, and the man who "would come out of Eternity." Yet ordinary life is described in the harshest and most venerable of romantic metaphors ("They were all in prison, they were all going mad" [494]), and Ursula is a prototype of the alienated Lawrence protagonist. The rainbow, then, the second image, is transcendence over corruption; this rainbow, in ironic counterpoint to the biblical one, implies a flood to come, the old architecture swept away.

The Rainbow is a somewhat disjointed book, as criticism has often documented. For our purposes what needs to be noted is the contradiction between the family chronicle as a genre and Lawrence's famous loss of unitary character. The "allotropic states,"[12] or the forays from existence to Being that concern Lawrence, imply dramatic rather than chronological time, cosmic rather than familial or social unfolding. The apocalypse does not usually take generations to occur. When it does so aesthetically, as in Faulkner's *The Sound and the Fury*, a radical foreshortening of time takes place. This does not happen in *The Rainbow*. The matter in this sense contradicts the manner; Lawrence has the modern theme but is only groping toward modern form. Moreover, the book is not sufficiently anchored in a central symbolism to record consistently that drama of an alienated and transcendent subjectivity that is more successfully rendered in *Women in Love* for just these reasons. In that work, Lawrence found a form and style congruent to his meaning.

George Ford tells us that the title of *Women in Love* was originally to be *The Latter Days*, *Dies Irae*, or *Days of Wrath* (the English translation of *dies irae*), and that Lawrence finally chose a nonapocalyptic title evocative of the novel's second or positive rhythm.[13] The novel is Lawrence's fullest treatment of the complex meaning of sexual aggression.

From the very beginning of *Women in Love*, we are in the atmosphere of extremity. Normative connections are spent. Thinking of her home in the English Midlands, Ursula "loathed it . . . this obsolete life . . . the insufferable torture of these ugly, meaningless people, this defaced countryside"[14] Gudrun understands and, in language familiar from *The Rainbow*, says, "Everything is a ghoulish replica of the real world . . . It's like being mad, Ursula." Moderns both, the sisters have decided against marriage and children. When a voice in the marketplace says, "What price the stockings!" Gudrun responds with unexpected ferocity: "A sudden fierce anger swept over the girl, violent and murderous. She would have liked them all annihilated, cleared away, so that the world was left clear for her" (7). The emotional nexus is familiar—violence, death before life, solipsism.

When Birkin is introduced the dark tone does not dissipate. He is profoundly misanthropic: "His dislike of mankind, of the mass of mankind, amounted almost to an illness" (53). And his words to Ursula echo those of *The Rainbow*'s Ursula: "I abhor humanity, I wish it was swept away . . . don't you find it a beautiful clean thought, a world empty of people, just uninterrupted grass, and a hare sitting up?" (*WL* 119). Birkin shares the essential nihilistic wisdom: "Man is a mistake, he must go" (*WL* 120). He does not utter these words in unmitigated rage, however. The narrator describes his tone as "impatient fury . . . great amusement, and a final tolerance." But Ursula mistrusts the tolerance, not the fury. She knows the savior complex when she sees it. Even in his more buoyant moments with Ursula, Birkin's mental rhythm is a dying into life. For him, it is understood that our life is death. Nonetheless he says: "I want love that is like sleep, like being born again" (178). Like Birkin, Lawrence is altogether serious—evangelically so.

The assault on civilized value once again manifests itself as a mistrust of words. Ursula "knew, as well as [Birkin] knew, that words themselves do not convey meaning, that they are but a gesture we make, a dumb show like any other" (178). In a uniquely Lawrencean hyphenated construction, Birkin agrees: "I was becoming quite dead-alive"; he was becoming "nothing but a word-bag." He wishes to cast off this merely verbal self, but the "other hovered" (180). It may be possible for Lawrence's blind man or his woman who rode away to cast off this self, but the obvious Lawrence surrogate like Birkin cannot do it.

One of Birkin's most extreme acts is his rejection of Ursula's request to buy a chair. Merely doing so would be for him the equivalent of being tied down. "We don't want things at all," he tells her. "The thought of a house and furniture of my own is hateful to me . . . House and furniture and clothes, they are all terms of an old base world, a detestable society of man" (348). Even universally accepted accommodations to conditionality are to Birkin a capitulation to society. And at this point he is the relatively mellow Birkin who has established a relationship with Ursula.

Birkin's misanthropy, then, takes two forms: rebellion against his society and rebellion against society as such. After some amatory moments with Ursula earlier in the novel, we find him in a characteristic posture: "He lay sick and unmoved, in pure opposition to everything" (190). Though he wishes somehow to persist in life, "the thought of love, marriage, and children, and a life lived together, in the horrible privacy of domestic and connubial satisfaction, was repulsive." Yet "he hated promiscuity even worse than marriage." There seems almost no way out because "on the whole, he hated sex, it was such a limitation" in that one was merely a "broken half of a couple." He remains an erotic spiritual seeker who "believed in sex marriage" (191), which he defines as freedom together, as in the image of constellated stars. Such a relationship will define man as man and woman as woman in a togetherness that, paradoxically, must make for ultimate individuality. The Lawrence surrogate rebels, finally, against the nature of things, which imposes this subjection to sex so that one may be defined in mutual cosmic isolation. His eroticism will reflect these aggressive motives.

The relationship between Lawrence and Frieda, treated elegiacally in *Women in Love*, is reduced to an almost comic bickering in Somers and Harriet of

Kangaroo, where for a long time the hero is unable to transcend the domestic slough, even in an exotic locale like Australia. The Lawrence surrogate is familiar, even if the wife's accusations are more everyday. Of course Harriet is right about Somers's misanthropy. "You *don't* like people," she says. "You always turn away from them and hate them. Yet like a dog to his vomit you always turn back."[15]

Somers does not disagree. In a book with more than its share of volcanic images, he fights off the temptation to see himself as "a sort of human bomb, all black inside waiting to explode" (*K* 166). There are peaceful moments, but his usual temper is ferocious. His fulminations are so extensive that they sound like an anthology: "most men . . . are . . . ants . . . Like riffraff on the teeming absolute of the dung-heap or ant-heap. Sometimes the dust-heap becomes huge, huge, huge, and covers nearly all the world. Then it turns into a volcano, and all starts again" (288). Kangaroo thinks in similar terms; he too wants to "break down the anthill" (120). He is a "gentle father" of a Grand Inquisitor, willing to relieve the common man from the burden of responsibility. He will use his authority "in the name of living life" (110–11), the last words a typical Lawrence tautology. In antinomian fashion, Kangaroo views the "root of evil" to be "the principle of permanency, everlastingness." He is an improbable Jew. Though he views the "Ten Commandments which Moses heard" as "the very voice of life," his interpretation of their place is heterodox: "The tablets of stone he engraved them on are millstones around our necks." With more delicacy than many Lawrencean tablet breakers, he opines: "Commandments should fade as flowers do. They are no more divine than flowers are" (111). The end result is submission to the disintegrative flux. For Lawrence, morality and nature are in a loose equivalence. He rejects the conception of creation ex nihilo, a morally realized world. He dismisses both the biblical Word and the word. In the collapse of moral regeneration through politics that the novel unconvincingly dramatizes, Somers is left with the familiar Lawrencean disillusion with language itself: "Human beings should learn to make weird, wordless cries, like the animals, and cast off the clutter of words . . . nothing is so meaningless as meanings" (341). They are the detritus of civilization.

If this destruction has a whiff of nihilism, can the glorification of murder be far behind? In the struggle between workers and fascists, Jack kills three people on the workers' side. Anticipating Mailer's macho Rojack, he experiences this as an erotic thrill and then some. "*Nothing* backs you up sometimes like killing a man—nothing," he says. "You feel a perfect *angel* after it" (327). Though loving a woman does not compare, there is a certain equivalence:

"Killing's natural to a man . . . just as natural as lying with a woman." Though not the Lawrence surrogate in this work, Jack is a sympathetically drawn character. Somers's killings are more subtle and cerebral, the closest he comes to the impulse in his wish "to be cold, as sea things are cold, and murderously fierce" (124). *Kangaroo*, like *Aaron's Rod*, is often justifiably considered as minor Lawrence. This may be seen in its dramatization of ferocity. It is not that the novel is uniquely or particularly or excessively ferocious in its theme, but that Lawrence's ferocity is most meaningful and aesthetically complete when it offers insights into the erotic life of men and women, when it offers something more central than the bizarre shrillness of a latent homosexual who will not be examined naked in wartime.

Lawrence tries to organize the chaos of modern experience through myth in *The Plumed Serpent*, to use the T. S. Eliot formulation. But myth itself may be considered a consequence of the Lawrencean disgust. Kate Leslie—the Lawrence surrogate here is female, a feat he often manages with suspicious ease—strikes the familiar note of ferocity at the outset. Nauseated by the spectacle of Mexican bullfighting, repulsed by Mexico City, she reflects: "The longer I live the more loathsome the human species becomes to me. *How much nicer the bulls are*" (*PS* 24). In this novel, one must go far from contemporary Mexico to arrive at the primitive ithyphallic truth. The actual Mexico is a world of lice, garbage, and rabies. Even its socialist art (by Diego Rivera) is merely to *épater le bourgeois* and, for Kate, "the épateurs were as boring as the bourgeois" (54). Kate has the Lawrencean repulsion, which is again manifested in insect imagery: "Men today . . . and women . . . Half-made creatures, rarely more than half-responsible and half-accountable, acting in terrible swarms, like locusts . . . a collective insect-like will" (116). Kate does feel something positive in the "semi-barbarian men" (117), the Indians of the lake, which composes the domain of the rebellious Don Ramón and Cipriano. In their locale, she contemplates a Lawrencean version of the Aristotelian mean: "It is not too savage, and not ever civilized" (118). It is, as it were, properly savage. She feels the possibility, therefore, of transcendent birth, something "rich and alive" in these people who want to breathe "the Great Breath" (119). Kate surprises herself by this use of language, but Lawrence's mythic ontology has taken hold. Lawrence in capital letters always risks self-parody. At the least, capitals mean we are off on a peculiar journey. We have an indication of its direction in an earlier description of Cipriano, in which Kate notes the Indian's "intense masculine yearning, coupled with a certain male ferocity in the man's breast" (74).

Lawrence's last and best-known novel, *Lady Chatterley's Lover*, returns to the arena of English class life, a form of lovelessness. In a passage much like Hemingway's repudiation of glory, honor, and courage in *A Farewell to Arms*—Lawrence admired Hemingway's radical honesty—Lawrence expresses the modernist disillusion: "All the great words it seemed to Connie, were cancelled for her generation: love, joy, happiness, home, mother, father, husband, all these great dynamic words were half dead now, and dying from day to day . . . As for sex, the last of the great words, it was just a cocktail term for an excitement that bucked you up for a while, then left you more raggy than ever. Frayed!" (*LCL* 71). Poor Connie, choosing at this stage between active and passive impotence, has lost faith in language. She has become skeptical of words, especially the important ones. She is estranged from the glories of English. The Elizabethans are rather "upholstered," she holds. "Violets were June's eyelids, and wildflowers were unravished brides. [Romantics!] How she hated words, always coming between her and life . . . ready-made words and phrases, sucking all the life-sap out of living things" (108). Once again, Lawrence presents discourse as a form of irrationality. In this context, Mellor's four-letter words have a pristine, redemptive quality. Connie has the essential Lawrence insight: "Society was terrible because it was insane. Civilized society is insane. Money and so-called love are its two great manias; money a long way first" (112). Love is supposed to be true, but money is the unvarnished truth—an impotent truth, as Clifford's mine-managing life shows. Mine owners do not come off well in Lawrence, his way of keeping faith with his miner father. To the extent that the owners take pleasure in technology, they come off even worse. Every technical triumph for Clifford makes him even less of a man. The spectacle of his relaxing with his radio for hours on end elicits Lawrence's rage at what he calls, in an unhappy turn of phrase, "the unspeakable thing." Just the thought of it fills Connie with "terror of the incipient insanity of the whole civilized species" (128). What would Lawrence have made of television or the computer? One cannot think of a modern writer sent more rapidly whirling in his grave by the triumphs of technology. Surely it is a weakness in Lawrence not to admit the possible existence of any sort of technological poetry. Such resistance is, of course, his strength, but it is also a kind of imaginative failure to be so out of touch with one's century. He remains a proud Luddite, and his ferocity on this point is given voice by Mellors: "I'd wipe the machines off the face of the earth again, and end the industrial epoch absolutely." Yet Mellors's joy in destruction is modified: "But since I can't . . . I'd better hold my peace" (265).

The voice of romantic vitalism speaks with intransigent integrity in Lawrence to the last. In his final book, appropriately called *Apocalypse*, he intones: "Within the last fifty years man has lost the horse. Now man is lost."[16] The reader hardly knows whether to laugh or cry. But Lawrence is secure in the ferocious knowledge that "all of our present life-forms are evil" (95). And in a 1930 introduction to "The Crown," written in 1915, he affirms his earlier unyielding belief: "It is no use trying to modify present forms. The whole great form of our era will have to go." He adds, in his special form of attenuated hopefulness: "And nothing will really send it down but the new shoots of life springing up and slowly bursting the foundations" (*PII* 364).

In *The Rainbow*, where Ursula meets Winifred Inger's "strange" social milieu, which appears to her "like a chaos, like the end of the world" (*R* 342); *The Plumed Serpent*, where Don Ramón wishes that "the world would blow up like a bomb!" (*PS* 297) and hopes (with Queztlquoatl) "for the final day" (284); *Lady Chatterley's Lover*, where the narrator tells us at the outset that "the cataclysm has happened, we are among the ruins" (*LCL* 1); and in his letter to Waldo Frank that "there is a quality in your sky . . . that will, without the agency of man, destroy you all" (*LN* 306), Lawrence is a visionary of the apocalypse. Unlike the Christians who believe in the apocalypse, Lawrence judges from the point of view of lordship, not sainthood. His *Apocalypse* is a Nietzschean account of the book of Revelations that turns goodness into envy, since the Judeo-Christian tradition reduces the Great Mother to the Whore of Babylon. Frank Kermode rightly characterizes Lawrence's apocalypse as elitist, like that of the medieval Brethren of the spirit, sharply distinguishing between the chosen and the profane.[17] Lawrence gives these terms a distinctly modern significance.

Lawrence's elect is an erotic one in touch with transcendence. The godhead in Lawrence is erotic, hence that rare Lawrencean amalgam of intimacy and impersonality. The idea of impersonality is one of the more difficult aspects of his work, but it is fundamental to an understanding of the regenerative side of the apocalypse. The idea is an evolving one, not yet fully established in his first major work, *Sons and Lovers*. Paul Morel experiences passion with Clara, but it is qualified. Lawrence says: "Clara was, indeed, passionately in love with him, and he with her, as far as passion went" (*SL* 351). Passion, it seems, does not go far enough. From Clara's point of view, their love is merely impersonal. Paul, on the other hand, is content with "the tremendous living flood which carried them always [and which could] identify them altogether with itself," even if it "was something that happened because of her, but it was not her ... his experience had been impersonal, and not Clara" (354). Somewhat tentatively, Lawrence places priority on the cosmic nature of erotic relationship. Poor woman! With much justification, Clara asks Paul: "Is it *me* you want, or is it It?" (363). By placing so heavy an ontological emphasis on passion, Lawrence reduces the living particularity of love to secondary status, relying more on metaphor ("the tremendous living flood") than on character.

Lawrence is more certain of this emphasis in *The Rainbow*, where Will Brangwen is the peculiarly detached Lawrencean type: "He did not admit the immediate importance of mankind. He did not care about himself as a human being ... The verity was his connection with Anna and his connection with the Church, his real being lay in his dark emotional experience of the Infinite, the Absolute" (*R* 155). Anna, by comparison, is merely personal. Will is for a long time the ontological lover, thinking of his wife and the Church in the same way.

Ursula, their daughter, is afflicted with a similar malady. She considers her lover Skrebensky in this way: "The man, what was he?—a dark, powerful vibration that encompassed her ... She entered the dark fields of immortality" (451). Not *who* was he, but what. And once more that telling emphasis on metaphor, the lover as "vibration." Such immortality is dark indeed. Though she receives him, "her eyes were open looking at the stars, it was as if the stars were lying with her and entering the unfathomable darkness of her womb, fathoming her at last. It was not him" (473). This scene is something of a precursor to the remarkable finale of *St. Mawr*, as is Ursula's walk along the shore, where the sea in its "definite motion, its strength, its attack" beggars the masculine soul of Skrebensky (477). Clearly Ursula wants "something impersonal" (475).

Ursula's doubt about love as mere "personal gratification" (475), her restless and annihilating skepticism, is expressed in *Women in Love* by Birkin rather than the character named Ursula in that book. (The case for the two Ursulas being discontinuous is nowhere clearer than on this point.) Birkin does not believe in love but in "unseen hosts" (*WL* 121). His romancing of Ursula has the peculiar Lawrencean elevation. He tells her: "It is there I would want to meet you—not in the emotional, loving plane—but there beyond, where there is no speech and no terms of agreement" (137). Wordlessness is next to godliness, Lawrence tells us in thirty volumes. Birkin carries the logic of erotic impersonality one step further than the Ursula of *The Rainbow* ever did by making it a form of dying into life. "We will both cast off everything," he tells his prospective lover, "cast off ourselves even and cease to be, so that that which is perfectly ourselves can take place in us" (138). To be is to transcend. For Lawrence, to be is not to be. Birkin's relationship to Gerald is to transcend "sloppy emotionalism" and be part of "an impersonal union that leaves one free" (199). In this novel, Ursula typically makes the case for the more mundane personal demands, but (partly because she is changed by the Gerald-Gudrun-Loerke triangle) she is finally persuaded to Birkin's point of view. "Love is too human and little," she tells her sister. "I believe in something inhuman of which love is only a little part" (429).

The paradox of impersonality in Lawrence is that it establishes what is most profoundly personal, a masculine identity in proper relation to the feminine. This the Lawrencean cosmos reveals to the properly impersonal acolyte. So we are told of Grenfel, the assured, masculine "fox" in *The Fox* that "his sharp-eyed impersonal curiosity was insatiable" (*FSN* 129). Man the hunter—alone, free, indomitable—will be lover and loved. A somewhat comic but finally serious version of the Lawrencean impersonality is Captain Hepburn of *The Captain's Doll*. "Look at the moon," he tells Hannele. "It doesn't matter in the least to the moon whether I exist or whether I don't. So why should it matter to me?" (*FSN* 203). The incredulous Hannele has just been listening to an apparently excruciatingly self-abnegating account of his love life with his wife. Yet the very firmness of his indifference is one of the things that attracts her madly to him. For it belies an ultimate masculine strength, as Lawrence conceives it, the strength never again to be taken in by "love" or any other sentiment not proven in his blood. For Hepburn only one thing is necessary: being an independent, ideal-free man whose women will honor and obey him. And this apparently Hannele desires more than she is willing to admit. Hepburn's heroic impersonality is supported by his connection to the cold stars.

"The Woman Who Rode Away" is a story of a woman whose "kind of womanhood, intensely personal and individual, was to be obliterated . . . and the great primeval symbols were to tower once more over the fallen individual independence of women" (*SS* 2:569). If we think of this as Lawrence getting back at his mother with a passion, the exultant narrative voice underscores the point: "The sharpness and the quivering nervous consciousness of the highly bred white woman was to be destroyed again." For what purpose? A familiar one: "Womanhood was to be cast once more into the great stream of impersonal sex and impersonal passion." She wants to be ravished impersonally, ravished by the cosmic masculine spirit. After the long subversion of this spirit by white culture has been explained to her, and the sacrificial fate she has willingly assumed has been made clear, her young Mexican Indian interlocutor speaks to her gently. But "an unrelenting sort of hate came out of his words, a strange, profound, impersonal hate. Personally he liked her, she was sure" (2:576). The impersonal hate derives from the inversion of the cosmic order, the inversion of the masculine-feminine relationship, which to the Indian is the disaster of white culture. In the sacrifice itself, "the red sun should send his ray through the column of ice" in a cosmic dispersal of frigidity which reestablishes "the mastery that man must hold and that passes from race to race" (2:581). For Lawrence, this is the universal wisdom that must be purchased at all costs. Margarita Lederman willingly dies into symbolic life.

The ending of *St. Mawr* presents a landscape that impersonally gives Lou Witt a sense of male danger and potency that no man, least of all her husband Rico, can. Familiarly enough, Lou says that she wants to "give myself only to unseen presences" (*StM* 139). However, she wishes to do so not to enhance her sexuality but to dispense with it. Like the woman who rode away, she gives it all up. Like a vestal virgin—such as Isis of *The Man Who Died*—Lou is a "woman weary of the embrace of incompetent men." The astonishing yet inimitably Lawrencean denouement to the story posits a spiritual sex. The heroine says yearningly: "I am here, right deep in America, where there's a wild spirit that wants me, a wild spirit more than men . . . It needs me. It craves for me. And to it, my sex is deep and sacred, deeper than I am" (159). Can there really be an impersonal *sehnsucht*, and does she desire it? So she would have us believe. Again, the "deep and sacred" impersonality transcends mere personality.

Lawrence's concept of impersonality, visionary as it is and dismissive of the ordinary world, lends itself to mythological treatment, as we see in "The Woman Who Rode Away" and to a lesser degree in *St. Mawr* (in the horse itself—a symbol trying to be a myth—and in the denouement, an attempt at mythologizing landscape). We are prepared, then, for a character like the Mexican Indian Don Cipriano of *The Plumed Serpent*. Is Kate Leslie? "His desire seemed curiously impersonal," the narrator says, "physical, and yet not personal at all" (*PS* 259). The personal, white, Western Kate realized that "surely it would not be *herself* who could marry him. It would be some curious female within her whom she did not know and did not own" (260). Would this be the impersonal, mythological Kate? She has difficulty answering this question and dealing with the consequences of an affirmative answer:

"How could she marry Cipriano, and give her body to this death? . . . Die before dying . . . Ah no! Better to escape to the white man's lands" (269). But we are in Lawrence country, and escape is not a real option. Kate and Cipriano will soon marry. Even then, living with the master of fire and supremely passive, Kate remains "a little afraid of that flashing, primitive gladness, which was so impersonal and beyond her" (352). Their marriage is hardly anything a Western woman would describe by that word: "There was hardly anything to say to him. And there was no personal intimacy . . . He was a stranger to her, she to him . . . It was his impersonal presence which enveloped her." Kate is married to a myth, and the novel creaks with doctrine because (a) the doctrine, taken literally, is bizarre and (b) it destroys any sense of credible drama here. The great Lawrencean "mindless communion of the blood" is a crashing bore. Lawrence manages to make impersonality a form of narcissism. The reader cannot accept the assertion that "there was no need for emotions" (464). And Kate's realization that she is "like Teresa, really" is preposterous. Can anyone believe her conversion to pliant superpassivity? Or desire to emulate it? What works in "The Woman Who Rode Away" does not work in *The Plumed Serpent* because myth can succeed in Lawrence as lyricism, as symbol, image, or language—but not as a sustained novel with pretensions to dramatic intricacy.

The doctrine itself is ominous, a sentimental romanticism-cum-protofascism that Kate welcomes because of her "disgust of people," including her own ex-husband and children. Don Ramón is Lawrence's hieratic mouthpiece, a Mussolini with a Mexican accent proclaiming the higher impersonality: "One must be able to disentangle oneself from persons, from people . . . and see people as one sees trees in a landscape . . . to turn beyond them, to the greater life" (275). This metaphysical transformation of the human into the inanimate, this dismissal of ordinary life in favor of some nearly fascist sublimity, is Lawrence at his most dismal. Ramón shares Kate's disgust with "personal people" (276). This fatal tautology is something that only Lawrence at his most allotropic could have conceived. Of course, Ramón wants to transcend mere humanity "to meet them on another plane . . . without intimacy . . . The quick of a man must turn to God alone" (277). As ideas of God go, impersonal erotic transfiguration is rather thin. An impersonal eroticism is itself a dubious notion. Ramón recognizes that it poses problems because women want intimacy. He realizes with a great, absurd sadness, therefore, that "men and women should know that they cannot, absolutely, meet on earth" (277). Thank God for that thin margin of inabsoluteness.

While not so deeply involved with the higher impersonality in a realistic novel like *Lady Chatterley's Lover*, Lawrence still thinks in these terms in his last novel. After Mellors has intercourse with Connie Chatterley for the first time, Lawrence writes: "It really wasn't personal. She was only really a female to him" (*LCL* 143). In almost any neutral context, these words would mark the lover as a certified cad, but in Lawrence the reverse is true: "Perhaps that was better ... after all, he was kind to the female in her, which no man had ever been. Men were very kind to the *person* she was, but rather cruel to the female, despising her or ignoring her altogether." Mellors can never be accused of excessive politeness or of social deference, or of what Lawrence calls sex in the head: "He took no notice of Constance or of Lady Chatterley; he just softly stroked her loins or her breasts" (143). Though they are certainly representative of blood consciousness, of male and female as Lawrence created them, mellifluous, honey-tongued Mellors is so much the craftsman that the usual theological dimension of sex seems all but lost. If *The Plumed Serpent* errs on the side of vatic sex, *Lady Chatterley's Lover* may make too much of plumbing. In his commentary on the novel, Lawrence distinguishes between social superficiality and "the inner, impersonal great desires that are fulfilled in long periods of time" (*PII* 501). He warns us that sex will always be "in some way hostile to the mental, *personal* relationship between man and woman" (506). But the sex between Mellors and Connie seems personal enough, and touching for that reason. (Only Lawrence would equate the personal and the mental.) Perhaps one ought to be thankful for modest gains. For when Lawrence comes back to the vatic elevation of sex in *The Man Who Died*, Christ's rhetoric is reminiscent of Don Ramón's. He rejects the desirous peasant woman in familiar terms: "He could not touch the little, personal body, the little, personal life of this woman ... he had risen for the woman, or women, who knew the greater life of the body" (*MD* 177). He finds metaphysical sex in Isis, the vestal virgin, in a universe throbbing with phallic consciousness through a vision energized by blasphemy.

Given the nature of Lawrence's subject, the ontological dimension will take you only so far. What is Lawrence's view of "love," and how is it informed by his ferocity? His view of love, though not as dim as his view of marriage, is problematic. Perhaps the best that can be said about love is what Birkin tells Ursula: "I don't believe in love at all—that is any more than I believe in hate, or in grief. Love is one of the emotions like all the others—and so it is all right whilst you feel it. But I can't see how it becomes an absolute" (*WL* 121). Yet

Birkin does believe in "the unseen hosts." As it happens, Birkin does love Ursula, in the only way that Lawrence approves. "I love you," he says, "and I know it's final" (244). In her womanly way, Ursula believes that "love far surpassed the individual." However, "for him, the bright, single soul accepted love as one of its conditions, a condition of its own equilibrium" (258). So even in the relatively balanced *Women in Love*, love is anterior to self-emergence, which is as close to cosmic connection as man can come. As we have seen, Ursula eventually comes around to this point of view.

But we have noticed in the famous passage of denunciation from *Lady Chatterley's Lover* and from Captain Hepburn's remarks to an astonished Hannele that love is typically seen in Lawrence as a disintegrated ideal. This is because, as Somers of *Kangaroo* says, "human love without the God-passion always kills the thing it loves" (*K* 202). Love must have the element of cosmic transcendence, male and female separation in togetherness. Somers views the usual personal love with Nietzschean contempt: "It is a world of slaves: all love-professing" (138). Like Count Dionys, he nourishes the demon inside himself. Unlike the count, he is frustrated at not being able to express it. Perhaps Lawrence puts it most clearly in "A Propos of *Lady Chatterley's Lover*" when he says, "Above all things love is a counterfeit feeling today . . . And with counterfeit there is no real sex at all" (*PII* 195). Whether Lawrence in his own life embodied his difficult ideal is a problem for the biographer. Delany holds that "in describing the final harmony of Birkin and Ursula [Lawrence] was presenting a wishful fantasy rather than the actual state of his marriage in 1916" (*LN* 226). Delany adds that the rough-and-tumble Lawrence style is transferred to the relationship between Gerald and Gudrun; moreover, Hermione's breaking the dish on Birkin's head was actually something out of Frieda and Lawrence's relationship.

If love as it is customarily understood—a primarily personal emotion—is not what Lawrence is after, neither is sex *without* the personal element. "The Odor of Chrysanthemums" shows us that, even in early Lawrence, sex and procreation can exist without meaning. It is only one of the first of the failed marriages in Lawrence's work. Elizabeth Bates is noble in admitting the reality of her failure; yet the chrysanthemums recall the bittersweet of some sort of erotic life. Married sex in Lawrence is often an experience of emptiness, but with some redeeming quality. Even Gertrude Morel reflects the baptism by fire. Promiscuity, on the other hand, is purely negative. Phoenix of *St. Mawr* is simply "a sexual rat" (*StM* 157). In *The Plumed Serpent*, Don Ramón describes Mexico as "a country where men despise sex, and live for it . . . which is just suicide" (*PS* 143). Only the demon lover can reverse this reality. But the reversal in Don Ramon's words sounds like Lawrence at his most didactic, that pompous ontological insistence that barely conceals a feeling of repulsion about mere humanity. The point of the Indian dance, the narrator says, was that it sends "man into the greater manhood, woman into the greater womanhood. It was sex, but the greater not the lesser sex" (43). Kate, of course, has the "new secret . . . of her greater womanhood" (144)—which includes the transcendence of her orgasmic self. Lawrence oscillates violently between the poles of mere sex and mystical sex. The form that the former takes in society is a trivial game. In *Lady Chatterley's Lover*, Charlie May expresses this attitude: "I can't see I do a woman any more harm by sleeping with her than by dancing with her . . . or even talking to her about the weather. It's just an interchange of sensations instead of ideas, so why not?" (*LCL* 35, ellipsis in the original). Mabel Dodge Luhan reports that the free love of Hollywood people amazed and infuriated Lawrence.[18] And Aldous Huxley informs us that Lawrence "had a horror of Don Juans, all knowing sensualists and libertines," and that at about the time he was writing *Lady Chatterley's Lover*, he read Casanova's autobiography and was shocked.[19] Lawrence is not feigning when he says with some exasperation: "And I, who loathe sexuality so deeply, am considered a lurid sexuality specialist" (*CL* 2:xx). As Cornelia Nixon notes, he protests too much, though clearly he does indict modern sensation seeking.[20]

"A lurid sexuality specialist": not an altogether unfair description of Lawrence, if we dismiss sensation seeking as his motive and consider sexuality in its primary significance as a reflection of the striving, tormented modern spirit. The sensation seeking is, for Lawrence, a disturbance. He is nonetheless interested in disturbance in a broader sense, as symptom. His real subject is sexuality that transcends symptom—that transcends any sort of disturbance or perversion, even when it includes it, and is creative; or that fails to transcend it and is destructive. Sensation seeking is only one aspect of the dissolution that Lawrence takes as a central subject. Frigidity, impotence, and sadomasochism are others. Far from dismissing these lurid aspects of sexuality, Lawrence includes them in the very texture of the erotic experience rendered allotropically, simultaneously as being and Being. Accordingly, the strain of Lawrence criticism that treats him as a recent instance of the Romantic Agony[21]—George Ford, but more particularly Colin Clarke, Frank Kermode, Cornelia Nixon, and David Cavitch—has been the most engaging one since the era of F. R. Leavis. That strain is, of course, a refutation of Leavis's central tendency, which is to reserve Lawrence for the great tradition of English literature. What emerges in the new strain is a view of Lawrence in all his painful and heroic honesty, in all his ferocity.

With total moral seriousness, Lawrence confronts the eccentric, aggressive, even—as he says—corrupt elements of sexual life that pervade modern love life as he views it. Though the head-on confrontation with such corruption does not come until *Women in Love*, there is some of it in *The Rainbow*, as we have seen, in, for example, Ursula's assault on Skrebensky. Although the rainbow appears to her at the end of the novel, she knows that the "world's corruption" still lives (*R* 495). In the typical language of renewal, Lawrence sees that though the rainbow is "arched . . . in blood," it would "quiver to life," so that "sordid people" would "cast off their horny covering of disintegration, that new, clean, naked bodies would issue to a new germination, to a new growth." This rainbow, as Lawrence says, implies a flood in which the old architecture, "the old brittle corruption of houses and factories [will be] swept away." The biological metaphors, as well as the inclusion of the positive in the negative, convey the essentially romantic disposition that Lawrence still has in *The Rainbow*.

The relatively minor episode involving the marriage of Uncle Tom Brangwen to Winifred Inger suggests something more intractable and in this sense anticipates *Women in Love*. Tom looks at Winifred and "detected in her a kinship with his own dark corruption" (*R* 346). But here corruption remains *mere* corruption, a moral category, and the sexual eccentricity of her lesbian past remains submerged. In a key metaphor, Tom "had something marshy about him—the succulent moistness and turgidity, and the same brackish, nauseating effect of a marsh, where life and decaying are one" (350). The marsh, moist and turgid, comes to represent in "The Crown," that central essay, disintegrative sexuality itself. Ursula notices a "bitter-sweet corruption," but again it is *mere* corruption.

Women in Love gives us the full resonance of this bittersweetness. In a well-known passage, Birkin and Ursula are at a waterside party, and he lectures her on the meaning of the marsh, which he calls "the black river" (*WL* 164). He tells her that "we always consider the silver river of life, rolling . . . on to heaven, flowing into a bright eternal sea, a heaven of angels thronging. But the other is our real reality." Again tautology alerts us to a particularly insistent distinction. Birkin's thought now becomes complicated, for Lawrence's is an unanticipated ontology. The "other" is "that dark river of dissolution . . . that black river of corruption. And our flowers are of this—our sea-born Aphrodite, all our white phosphorescent flowers of sensuous perfection." The essence of eroticism, then, is indistinguishable from a quality of psychological disintegration. Lawrence is that much of a psychologist; you do not have the old stable ego of the character in his work, as he says in a famous letter to David Garnett, only the new unstable ego.[22] Since it is a psychological disintegration, it is perforce a social one as well. Our flowers, Lawrence says, stem from "all our reality, nowadays"—*Fleurs du Mal*, as Ursula interjects skeptically. Clearly this is a great age for sexual asymmetry, but equally clearly the modern age did not invent it. Forms of death—literal, psychic, and spiritual—have always been with us, and for Lawrence, Aphrodite "is the flowering mystery of the death process." Lawrence scripts an Eros-Thanatos scenario, with death understood as physical extinction, but more than that as well. "When the stream of synthetic creation lapses," Birkin says, "we find ourselves part of the inverse process, the blood of destructive creation." Lawrence—Birkin is surely his mouthpiece here—gives us his most profound turn on creative aggression, the inverse process manifested sexually. He thereby gives so-called perversity a psychological and metaphysical base. His imagery of snakes, swans, lotus, and marsh flowers suggests an eroticism inseparable from the swamp of dissolution. Ursula resists the formulation and accuses him of wanting us to know only death. But Birkin gives the modern rationale, heroic honesty: "I only want us to *know* what we are" (165).

The novel makes a dual presentation of the theme: as the critics have observed, two couples are illustrations of the same general principle but to radically different effect. Where Birkin and Ursula come to swim creatively on the river of dissolution as a couple, Gerald and Gudrun are destroyed.

Birkin and Ursula may be considered the only exemplary couple in Lawrence, all the more convincing in that they come through to harmonious being in a relationship marked by considerable complication. In *Women in Love*, symbols give substance to Lawrence's rather abstract didactic passages, producing an aesthetic balance rarely present in his later novels. One such symbol is Halliday's statuette of an African woman, the second such art object described. It is highly stylized: long body, short legs, beetle-browed face, protuberant buttocks. Birkin—who, like Lawrence, is very good at this—reads cultural significance into the work. He says that there is "purely sensual, purely unspiritual knowledge behind her," adding, "it must have been thousands of years since her race had died mystically: that is, since the relation between the senses and the outspoken mind had broken, leaving the experience all in one sort, mystically sensual" (*WL* 245). Far from being antagonistic, Birkin virtually identifies with the statuette: "That which was imminent in himself must have taken place in these Africans." Is Lawrence suggesting that the old mysticism is dying in Birkin as well, so that a new one can be born? Birkin sees that "the goodness, the holiness, the desire for creation and productive happiness must have lapsed, leaving the single impulse for knowledge in one sort, mindless, progressive knowledge through the senses"—which, he reiterates, is "mystic knowledge" but "in disintegration and dissolution, knowledge such as the beetles have." He adds that "this was why the Egyptians worshipped the ball-rolling scarab: because of the principle of knowledge in dissolution and corruption" (245–46). This is why the statue has a face like a beetle's. The scarab, in Birkin's words, lives "purely within the world of corruption and cold dissolution" (246); it lays its eggs in dung and was therefore taken as a symbol of life in death by the Egyptians.

It is significant that ancient Egypt lies at the heart of one of the most important passages in Lawrence. In his massive disaffection from the Judeo-Christian tradition, ancient Egypt is his ideal alternative. In "The Crown," written in 1915—the same period as *The Rainbow* and *Women in Love*—Lawrence is on the Egyptian wavelength. "In corruption there is divinity," he says (*PII* 402). "Aphrodite is, on one side, the great goddess of destruction in sex, Dionysus in the spirit. Moloch and some of the gods of Egypt are gods also of the knowledge of death." For "in the soft and shiny voluptuousness of decay, in the marshy chill heat of reptiles, there is the sign of Godhead."

The scarab serves a central symbol in *The Ladybird*, where the *Marienkäfer* or spotted beetle is noted as the descendant of the Egyptian scarab. "So I connect myself to Pharaohs," says Count Dionys. Lord Beveridge explains that the beetle rolling his ball of dung is the first principle that set the globe rolling, and that, according to Fabre, it became symbolic of the creative principle for the Egyptians.[23] If the Egyptians embodied a sublimated corruption, they also incarnated an erotic transcendence. When Daphne touches Count Dionys, "a flame went over him that left him no more a man. He was something seated in flame, in flame unconscious, seated erect, like an Egyptian King-god in the statues" (*FSN* 103). Birkin, too, after erotic bliss "sat still like an Egyptian Pharaoh" and "felt as if he were seated in immemorial potency, like the great carven statues of real Egypt" (*WL* 310). Consummated love makes him experience the "Egyptian . . . pure mystic nodality of physical being" (311). It makes no difference that he has had Ursula backward and forward. We are given to believe that this is the power of the Egyptian experience. Lawrence emphasizes the spiritual quality of this intensely physical experience, often with an embattled insistence. "Since Egypt," he tells us in *Psychoanalysis and the Uncon-*

scious, "the sun of creative activity beams from the breast, the heart of the supreme Man. This is to us the source of light—the loving heart, the Sacred Heart" (*PU* 54). This in contrast to the abdomen or female sympathetic center in his strange symbolic biology. "Ramses II was no doubt as pure in heart as John the Evangel. Indeed perhaps purer, since John was an insister," Somers tells us (*K* 273). Lawrence is firm in this preference even in his last book, asking rhetorically: "Have we anything as good as the Egyptians of two or three thousand years before Christ as a people?" (*A* 49). Anything Western is likely bad, even if it is pagan. When Lawrence compares Egypt and Greece as founders "of a science in terms of life," first prize goes to Egypt for having the true, or sexual, wisdom on which "great purposive activity" can alone be based (*FU* 145). Yet in his own work, the highest purposive activity that his characters express convincingly is the experience of sexual being.

Halliday's African statuette suggests something less buoyant and more mysterious than some of these Egyptian analogies might indicate. Birkin sees in it "mysteries . . . far beyond the phallic cult" (*WL* 246)—that is, presumably, beyond procreative sex. The statuette is a link to the prominent place that anal sex has in Birkin's life. Ursula understands that "he did not want an Odalisk. He wanted a woman to take something from him, to give herself up so much that she could take the last realities of him, the last facts, the last physical facts, physical and unbearable" (286). At first Ursula resists what Kate Leslie is later to welcome and Constance Chatterley to endure. Ursula is not willing "to give herself up so much." But Birkin is driven by a higher impulse: "There were depths of passion when one became impersonal and indifferent, unemotional. Whereas Ursula was still at the emotional personal level—always so abominably personal." The social character, Ursula, resists the sexual impulse driving Birkin from a deeper source. Lawrence writes: "He had taken her as he had never been taken himself. He had taken her at the roots of her darkness and shame—like a demon, laughing over the fountain of mystic corruption which was one of the sources of her being, laughing, shrugging, accepting, accepting finally" (296). Birkin from time to time deflates his cosmic self-importance and can do so even as demon lover. One can only speculate as to how he had never been taken himself in the same way—heterosexual style or homosexual substance? Whichever, Ursula is not amused: "As for her, when would she so much go beyond herself as to accept him at the quick of death?" She cannot yet feel good about wading in the river of dissolution. Her "unspeakable intimacies" seem to run to milder "perversities" like fellatio: "She wanted to have him, utterly, finally to have him as her own, oh, so unspeakable in intimacy. To drink him down—ah, like a life-draught" (257). This still involves the mystic fountain. Anal penetration carries negative meaning for her as it does for him.

Part of her resentment comes from her jealousy of his relationship with Hermione, broken though it already is. She sees Hermione relating to his soul as she relates to his body, and she bridles at this variant of the madonna-whore complex. So she berates Birkin: "Your spiritual brides can't give you what you want, they aren't common and fleshy enough for you . . . So you come to me . . . You will marry me for daily use . . . I'm not spiritual enough" (218). Birkin is in this sense another illustration of Freud's essay "On the Universal Tendency to Debasement in the Sphere of Love."[24] As Freud puts it, where they love they cannot desire, and where they desire they cannot love. Love must be tender and sexual, Freud tells us, adding that this is rarely the case. Though we know nothing of Birkin's familial past, it is easy to see that it was not the case with the typical Lawrence surrogates.

Ursula accuses Birkin of being what romantic, messianic types are often considered to be: holiness above, dirt below. Her jealousy is almost beside the point as a description of his already dead relationship with Hermione, but quite vivid as it affects Birkin's sexual relations with her. "You love the sham spirituality," she storms; "Why? Because of the dirt underneath. Do you think I don't know the foulness of your sex life—and hers?—I do" (*WL* 299). In fact, she does not, but she does know the dubious quality of her own experience with Birkin. She accuses him of a virtually homosexual narcissism in his sexual style: "You may well say, you don't want love. No, you want *yourself*, and dirt and death . . . You are so *perverse*, so death-eating." Birkin's response to this tirade is not embattled but rather cool and modern, with the sense of self-implicating acceptance. This is because he "knew she was in the main right. He knew he was perverse, so spiritual on the one hand, and in some strange way, degraded on the other. But was she herself any better? Was anybody any better?" (300). Lawrence's answer, of course, is no; what he is describing is a therapeutic world—therapy without the doctor—though he would never use this term. In any case, Birkin must live with his particular sexual nature and the knowledge of his inamorata's worldly wisdom. "He knew," writes Lawrence, "that his spirituality was concomitant of a process of depravity, a sort of pleasure in self-destruction . . . especially when it was translated spiritually." His physical life takes on a sort of spiritual anti-life (e.g., Hermione), enacting a self-lacerating guilt on his own sadomasochistic preferences. No one is immune from psychosexual quirkiness in his view:

"Was not Ursula's way of emotional intimacy, emotional and physical, was it not just as dangerous as Hermione's abstract spiritual intimacy?" Birkin's independence is threatened by any intimacy with woman, and he often considers this "fusion" of two beings "nauseous and horrible" (301). The nausea of the Lawrence surrogate, then, may extend to the physical act itself.

Birkin feels physical disgust partly in recoiling from Ursula's accusations. The success of their intimacy dissipates the vapors. Their intimacy remains, however, a curious one. Ursula is transported by caressing the back of Birkin's thighs—an anal caress, apparently. This brings her a deep wisdom: "She had thought there was no source deeper than the phallic source. And now, behold, from the smitten rock of the man's body, from the strange marvelous flanks and thighs, deeper, farther in mystery than the phallic source, came the floods of ineffable darkness and ineffable riches" (306). The second African statuette, we recall, also deals in the wisdom "far beyond the phallic cult" (246). Ursula responds to something statuesque rather than procreative, something aft rather than fore, an area whose life implies death in Lawrence, and whose creativity implies destruction. The phallic source is life and creation, and neither Birkin nor, it now seems, Ursula desire it most of all.

The scene is the transition between Ursula's resistance to anal intercourse and her acceptance of it. For Ursula undergoes a conversion in respect to this experience. The next time Birkin performs, her reaction is quite different: "How could anything that gave one satisfaction be excluded? What was degrading? Who cared? Degrading things were real with a different reality" (*WL* 403). Yet she still feels degraded and negatively toward Birkin for this act. "Wasn't it rather horrible," she thinks, "a man who could be so soulful and spiritual, now to be so ... bestial? So bestial, they two! So degraded! She winced." She then asks what Philip Rieff has called the central question in an age of permissiveness, of crumbling authority: "But after all, why not?" It is a question we understand all too well. The fact is that "she exulted as well. Why not be bestial, and go the whole round of experience? ... How good it was to be really shameful! ... no dark shameful things were denied her." The impulse toward complete sexual expression couched in the language of Victorian inhibition may make the reader smile. Birkin and Ursula proceed in innocence.

Partly because they come to terms with the element of dissolution, and partly because they seem to do well in the normative mode as well, Birkin and Ursula have come through. "Look! We Have Come through" is the bravado title of a poem (and a book) that Lawrence wrote in this period. One may find his pride on the subject wearing. As Bertrand Russell has remarked, "I don't mind his having come through, but why should I look?"²⁵ They have come through, above all, because their sexuality leads to the cosmic calm of sexual differentiation, the principle of individuation to which Lawrence believes sexuality should lead. Sex once more is the penultimate act, leading to the ultimate splendid separateness of man and woman in their primal cosmic identity.

But descent into dissolution may not bring transcendent peace in separateness. The love life of Gerald and Gudrun shows that agony is not enough. Immersion in the destructive element may cause drowning. Their relationship is a study in sadomasochism of a self-destructive sort. Gudrun is captivated by Gerald's masculine potency, particularly as it manifests itself in a sadistic way. In this Pussums is a foreshadowing, as she is in her masochistic desire for a promiscuous lover. Gerald's sadism appears first in the remarkable scene in which he violently restrains a mare from moving onto the train tracks. The scene is analogous to rape. "She's bleeding! She's bleeding!" cries Ursula as he digs his spurs into the mare (*WL* 104). Gudrun passes out at the sight of Gerald's "soft white magnetic domination . . . enclosing and encompassing the mare heavily into unutterable subordination, soft-blood-subordination, terrible" (106). This is the first of several such scenes, which usually but not always involve male aggression: the mare, the cat-cuffing female cat, the rabbit. After Gerald subdues the rabbit, Gudrun looks at him with "a smile of obscene recognition" (235). Lawrence gives this scene a religious resonance: "They were implicated with each other in abhorrent mysteries" (234). Gerald conceives of Gudrun's look paradoxically. He is implicated in the contraries by her "strange, darkened eyes, strained with underworld knowledge, almost supplicating, like those of a creature which is at his mercy, yet which is his ultimate victor." He feels "the mutual hellish recognition" (234). Sadomasochism is a game two can play.

While Gerald's sadism is fairly constant, Gudrun may, at the apex of erotic indulgence, feel something similar. As their relationship progresses, "both felt the subterranean desire to let go, to fling away everything, and lapse into sheer unrestraint, brutal and licentious. A strange black passion surged up pure in Gudrun. She felt strong. She felt her hands so strong, as if she could tear the world asunder with them. She remembered the abandonments of Roman license, and her heat grew hot . . . Ah, if that which was unknown and suppressed in her were once let loose, what an orgiastic and satisfying event it would be" (279). We get some indication of what the suppressed element might be later in an aggressive encounter with Gerald, but mostly this seems to be the fantasy of an alter ego. More ominous and authentic is Gerald standing "just behind her" (a significant position?), "suggestive of the same black licentiousness that rose in herself."

Still more typical of their sensual mood is an encounter explicitly expressive of Gerald's sexual ferocity (aroused, we are given to believe, by the ordeal of his father's death)—and Gudrun's masochistic passivity. A sort of sheik of Araby, at night when she's asleep into her tent he creeps: "Into her he poured all his pent-up darkness and corrosive death, and he was whole again . . . And she, subject, received him as a vessel filled with his bitter potion of death . . . The terrible frictional violence of death filled her, and she received it in an ecstasy of subjection, in throes of acute, violent sensation" (337). The reference to death implies anal intercourse, which Gudrun—unlike Ursula at first—willingly receives. The aggressive sexual release in Gerald brings on a tenderness: "He worshipped her. Mother and substance of all life she was." Yet tenderness never brings a desire for marriage, as it does with Birkin and Ursula.

In fact, the tenderness between Gerald and Gudrun is short-lived. The resolution of sexual aggression into harmonious relation never comes. What Gudrun's id desires, her ego cannot tolerate. She fears enslavement. Aware of Gerald's "impending figure standing close behind her"—a typical approach of Gerald's and a consequent uneasiness of Gudrun's—"she could not bear it anymore, in a few minutes she would fall down at his feet, groveling at his feet, and letting him destroy her" (405).

This particular motif—falling at the partner's feet, or clasping the knees—is a crucial one in Lawrence, indicative as it is of man-woman power relationships. Lawrence's view of this experience reflects a double standard. While it is fine for women to so express themselves, it is anathema for men. That Gudrun resists doing so indicates a resistance to being female, though in this case it also shows a justified fear, given Gerald's sadistic style. Ursula has no such problem, even though she is aware of Birkin's tendency to assume something of a master-slave relationship with women. Before she can exult in the area behind his thighs and down his flanks, and doubtless partly because of this, she descends to her knees. In his aura of masculinity she "was drawn to him strangely, as in a spell. Kneeling on the hearth-rug before him, she put her arms round his loins." She caresses the area in back of his thighs. At this moment of bliss Lawrence adds, almost unexpectedly: "He did not like this crouching, this radiance," qualifying it with "not altogether" (305). Presumably the development of their relationship makes him more sensitive to any master-slave imputation. But he does not change position. Since it is Birkin and Ursula, this particular bit of choreography has the maximum Lawrence complexity.

The case is usually simpler. For example, after Clara Dawes and Baxter reconcile, "she wanted to humble herself to him, to kneel before him. She wanted now to be self-sacrificial" (*SL* 384). In *The Rainbow*, Lydia kisses Lensky's feet like a slave, "embracing his knees" (*R* 254), though Lensky hardly knew her. And in the rainy marriage ceremony of *The Plumed Serpent*, Kate kisses the feet and heels of Don Cipriano, who kisses her brow and breast in return (*PS* 362). For the man to descend even in wish is disconcerting to Lawrence. It is an indication, for example, of Skrebensky's loss of the manly aura and a foreshadowing of his rejection: "In his dark, subterranean male soul, he was kneeling before her . . . He was waiting at her feet. He was helpless, at her mercy . . . If she rejected him, something would die in him. For him it was life or death" (*R* 443). In Lawrence, no man can exhibit such dependence and still be a man. Adrian, the eternal boy of "Mother and Daughter" and a failed suitor, "adored [Virginia] on his knees" (*SS* 3:813). Bertie, the sentimental barrister in "The Blind Man," is "on his knees before the woman he adored but did not want to marry" (*SS* 2:349). As he is a latent homosexual, for Bertie the position involves another form of unmasculinity.

Perhaps the most vivid representation of the act occurs in the powerful short novels. In *The Ladybird*, Basil Apsley returns from the First World War to his beloved Daphne, whom he has idealized out of sexual existence. Despite his rhetoric, Basil is all polite gesture (read mental consciousness), no match in his wife's eyes for Count Dionys. He says to the aliened Daphne: "I knew if I had to kneel, it was before you. I knew you were divine, you were the one—Cybele—Isis, I knew I was your slave . . . I had to learn to worship you." He kisses her feet "again and again" (*FSN* 79). He is finished! In *The Captain's Doll*, Hannele feels something like Daphne's repulsion as she thinks of Captain Hepburn and his horrible wife: "The picture of Alec at his wife's feet on his wedding night, vowing to devote himself to her life-long happiness" (*FSN* 214). It's just too much for Hannele. However, "if he had been at her own feet, then Hannele would have thought it almost natural." Later, responding to Alec's odd insistence that she honor and obey him without his expressing any love for her, she develops a somewhat different view: "He must go down on his knees to her if he wanted her love," for a "master and bully she would never have" (251). But his doing that is out of the question, and she realizes that his recalcitrance is part of the quality of masculinity that she must have. It is precisely this quality that is missing in Michaelis of *Lady Chatterley's Lover*, when "he kneeled down beside [Connie] and . . . looked up at her with that awful appeal in his full, glowing eyes" (*LCL* 27).

The essence of Mellors's appeal to Connie is his impregnability to such displays. Mellors is a usual Lawrence icon. Though somewhat delicate physically, he exudes a masculine aura—the Lawrence hero recalled to life. Connie responds to him as a usual Lawrencean woman: "She obeyed him. He had that curious kind of protective authority she obeyed at once" (101). Lawrence repeats the word "obey"—here and elsewhere in the novel—that Captain Hepburn insisted on. Connie is a relatively simple version of the woman that Lawrence wants after a lifetime of struggle. She "was gifted from nature with this appearance of demure submissive maidenliness" (151). The appearance does not belie the reality, provided that she feels a masculine presence. Lawrence usually distinguishes female submission from slavery. But it must be submission to a real, as opposed to merely a social, master. It matters little when, after their first lovemaking, a very English Mellors deferentially reminds Connie that "you've got to remember your ladyship is carrying on with a gamekeeper. It's not as if I was a gentleman" (146). Connie too feels this pull of class. At first Clifford "had seemed, in some way, her master, beyond her" (112). This feeling soon passes as Connie comes to equate mastery with masculine sexual authority. Like Ursula, the eventually sexually mature Connie sees lovemaking as "the sons of god with the daughters of men" (208), thereby giving ontological priority to the masculine principle. Clifford's mastery, by contrast is a perverse parody, a solipsistic regression into infancy: "Only when he was alone with Mrs. Bolton did he really feel a lord and master. And he let her shave him and sponge his body as if he were a child" (128). In Lawrence's world, there is nothing left for Clifford to do but become a master of coalmining technology. Politically, his sense of mastery takes on an even uglier form, protofascism. He opines that "the masses have been ruled since time began and . . . they will have to be. It is sheer hypocrisy and farce to say that they can rule themselves" (218). Lawrence must have had some difficulty in writing these words, since he is in political agreement with a character he presents as loathsome, a caricature of the lord and master type. While it is true that at about this time he wrote in a letter that "the hero is obsolete, the leader of men is a back number," and that tenderness, therefore, is the prime value (*CL* 2:1045–46), Lawrence never gave up his disgust with the common life. Nor did he give up on leadership in the bedroom, which is the one kind that he sees going hand in hand with tenderness.

Taken by itself, Gudrun's hysteria about falling at Gerald's feet is suspect in Lawrence's general view. Yet in this particular case it may well be justified. Gudrun finally wishes to destroy the threatening Gerald: "She had the whip hand over him now. She knew he had not realized her terrible panic" (*WL* 406). There is no trust in their relationship, no confirmation of their togetherness, no sublimation into tenderness of their primitive aggressions. Ironically, she comes to think of him in the same way that he thinks of his mining employees: "To her mind, he was a pure, inhuman, almost superhuman instrument" (408). Yet she still oscillates into tenderness, thinking of their "perfect moments" (409), like tobogganing, which she describes as "the complete moment of my life" (411). This is a telling example, suggesting as it does her full attraction to dependence and oblivion.

Drawn though she is to self-destruction, she remains distant to her tormentor. Gerald is this because his sexuality does not make the transference to love or marriage, its inevitable consequence in Lawrence. This is why "her pity for him was as cold as stone, its deepest motive was hate of him, and fear of his power over her, which she must always counterfoil" (434). She says to the stymied Gerald: "Try to love me a little more and want me a little less . . . there is so little grace in you, so little fineness. You are so crude. You break me—you only waste me—it is horrible to me." These are final words that no relationship can withstand. They point to an unsublimated and intimidating aggression, and they only can elicit polar power fantasies from Gerald: "He might give in, and fawn on her. Or, finally, he might kill her" (436).

Pathetic? Yet one might think that the murder fantasy is the ultimate in masculine sadism and feminine masochism, and in fact Lawrence comes close to playing it this way. Enraged with jealousy over Loerke's apparent advances to Gudrun, Gerald has a sudden desire to kill her. This is an act he sees in sexual terms: "What a perfect voluptuous consummation it would be to strangle her" (452). The situation is made more tense when Gudrun tells him: "You cannot love . . . I couldn't love you" (453). Gerald slugs Loerke twice, and then Gudrun hits him. He almost strangles her, a near consummation of his sadism: "What a fulfillment, what a satisfaction!" (463). Lawrence makes it clear that this violence has a sexual nature. Being nearly strangled is a consummation of Gudrun's masochism, and she reaches orgasm because of it. Lawrence writes: "Her reciprocal lustful passion in this embrace, the more violent it became, the greater the frenzy of delight, till the zenith was reached, the crisis, the struggle was overborne, her movement became softer, appeased." In this astonishing, violent climax to the affair, eros falls to thanatos.

Aggression contains eroticism and not the other way around, as with Birkin and Ursula. The sexual struggle between Gerald and Gudrun, then, ends in sickness rather than health. In the end, Gerald turns his aggression most definitively on himself in suicide. Gudrun survives in a way that tells us still more about perversity.

Loerke is one of Lawrence's most intriguing characters, and one of his most perverse. In accepting him, Gudrun embraces a subtler sadism. Gerald is fine, if severe looking; Loerke is *chétif* (puny)—one of Lawrence's favorite words to describe unprepossessing lovers, like Mr. Massy in "Daughters of the Vicar," Philip Farquar of "The Borderline," and, perhaps, Lawrence himself. Yet Gerald's "blind force of passion" is no match for "the subtle thrills of extreme sensation in reduction" (*WL* 442) Loerke can provide for the masochistic side of Gudrun. She seems eager for the confrontation of "an unbroken will reacting against her unbroken will in a myriad subtle thrills of reduction, the last subtle activities of analysis and breaking down, carried out in the darkness of her, while the outside form, the individual, was utterly unchanged, even sentimental in its poses." She is willing to play the game, present the face, for possession of the demiurge, "the obscene religious mystery of ultimate reduction, the mystical frictional activities of diabolic reducing down, disintegrating the vital organic body and life" (443). That she knows all this in her unconscious is no less a recognition of the power of negative transcendence. We are far beyond the phallic source. A sense of danger and destruction accompanies the male. She may be beaten by Gerald, but she will be cut by Loerke: "Where [Gerald's] ruder blows could not penetrate, the fine, insinuating blade of Loerke's insect-like comprehension could." The real penetration belongs to the subtler being, the only possible final penetration: "At least, it was time for her now to pass over to the other, the creature, the final craftsman."

One may wonder about the protean nature of feminine desire. Gerald and Loerke are physical opposites, but Gudrun is morally as well as physically masochistic, so her attraction to Loerke may seem plausible. He is certainly sadistic in style. Obviously homosexual, he is accompanied on his Alpine vacation by Leitner, a "large fair youth . . . too soft, too humble for Gudrun's taste" (*WL* 402), another indication that to Gudrun, style may be more important than substance. Although he is well built, the youth is "slightly abject . . . [with] a humility that covered a certain fear." When Leitner dances with the diminutive Gudrun, Loerke "felt a sardonic ruthless hatred for this young love-companion who was his penniless dependent." Lawrence is clear about Loerke's domineering nature, one qualified by a dependence on masculine strength. Both qualities become intensified by the next major example of Loerke's sexual preferences, all the more so because in this case they are artistic preferences as well.

Loerke has done a metal-plate engraving of a small, finely made girl—a Lolita nymph sitting "on a great naked horse . . . as if in shame and grief." Her legs are "scarcely formed" (*WL* 419). The horse is "a massive, magnificent stallion, rigid with pent-up power." Upon seeing the engraving, Gudrun falls into a spell usually associated with Gerald. She "went pale, and a darkness came over her eyes, like shame, she looked up with a certain supplication, almost slave-like" (420). The erotic element in Loerke's art possesses a fatal attraction for Gudrun. She identifies with the nymph. The maternal Ursula objects to the "so stiff" phallic quality of the horse, opting, as she essentially does in Birkin, for the "delicate and sensitive." Like Lawrence, like the Romantics, Ursula sees the artist in a symbiotic relationship to his art—"art for my sake," as Lawrence says—in this case realizing the artist's sadism. "The horse is a picture of your own stock, stupid brutality, and the girl was a girl you loved and tortured and then ignored," she tells Loerke. She dismisses Loerke's protestations about the world of art. As Lawrence would have said, she says that "the world of art is only the truth about the real world" (422). Although Gudrun is to side with Loerke in the argument, her response to the work is intensely subjective, intensely masochistic. The "darling . . . pretty . . . tender" feet of the nymph, an art student, make her look at Loerke's eyes "with a hot, flaming look" (423). The engraving, titled "Lady Godiva" and done six years earlier, shows a girl of seventeen who, now at a mature twenty-three, is in Loerke's eyes "no more good." (Seventeen is too old for Nabokov's Humbert Humbert in *Lolita*.) Loerke feels that "the Venus of Milo is a bourgeoise" (423). As a model, Annette von Weck was a nuisance who would not keep still for Loerke, "not until I'd slapped her hard and made her cry—then she'd sit for five minutes" (424). Gudrun makes a point of asking if he really slapped her. When Gerald points out that Annette is too small to be Godiva, "a queer spasm went over Loerke's face." Gudrun and Loerke, it seems, were made for each other.

Is their relationship sinister, or have they found an island of stability in the river of dissolution? Doesn't Loerke, like Birkin and Lawrence, admire "West African wooden figures" and presumably what we know they may signify? And isn't even the sense of election of Loerke and Gudrun analogous to that of Birkin and Ursula (and Lawrence)? "They alone," Lawrence writes, "were initiated into the fearful central secrets, that the world dare not know . . . they kindled themselves at the subtle lust of the Egyptians or the Mexicans" (*WL* 439). But the difference in the way they look at art underscores their difference in dissolution. Loerke and Gudrun are aesthetes, and Lawrence views their aestheticism as a negative aspect of disintegration: "Art and life were to them the Reality and the Unreality" (439). This is wrong to Lawrence, who likes to think that his art, however dissolute, is in the service of life. The aesthete Loerke says: "What one does in one's life, that is a bagatelle." Gudrun immediately thinks of Gerald as a "Bagatelle," something trifling to be used as a stepping-stone to a higher purpose. "What was the lover," she thinks, "but fuel for the transport of this subtle knowledge, for a female art, the art of pure, perfect knowledge in sensuous understanding" (440).

Birkin does not see Loerke's early work "Lady Godiva," but he does see a copy of the artist's Cologne factory frieze in which peasants move in an orgy of chaotic motion—"the machine works him [the worker] instead of he the machine" (*WL* 415), says Loerke—seemingly a negative form of energy.[26] As he witnesses Loerke's behavior to Leitner and Gudrun, Birkin is struck by his sinister quality though they are mired in a common element. Loerke "lives like a rat in the river of corruption," Birkin tells Gerald, admitting: "I suppose we want the same . . . Only we want to take a quick jump downwards, in a sort of ecstasy—and he ebbs in the stream, the sewer stream" (419). Birkin sees himself and Gerald as proponents of negative transcendence, whereas Loerke rests content in dissolution. There is a risk to such transcendence. Birkin and Ursula do come through; Gerald and Gudrun explode; Loerke and Gudrun will be in limbo. The apocalypse, for Birkin, leads to a new world; for Gerald, to the end of his world. For Loerke, playing at apocalypse with Gudrun, "one laughed out some mocking dream of destruction of the world by a ridiculous catastrophe of man's invention" (444). Loerke rarely sees beyond the cynical. Birkin, resisting it, falls in love; Gerald attempts love; Loerke denies it. He wants Gudrun to come with him to Dresden, the city of art, not Paris, the city of love. Loerke says that love "makes me sick. Pah—l'amour, I detest it . . . in every language," and he wishes to settle for "a little companionship in intelligence" (450). If Loerke's cynicism sounds like Birkin's, it is, in fact, distantly related. In a draft of the novel in which Loerke is just a drawing-room character, it is Birkin who is tired of l'amour. As we have seen, Lawrence always views it with some skepticism. But in the finished novel, Loerke's views cast those of Birkin and Ursula into a relatively bold relief. Loerke's sickness and Gudrun's consequent attraction is one of the ways of recording the health of Birkin and Ursula.[27]

Lawrence rightly considered *Women in Love* his most important work, and it is that because in it his most complex themes receive their fullest orchestration. The Romantic Agony line of Lawrence criticism is good at defining this complexity, yet it does so in ways that create additional complexity. Colin Clarke states the situation accurately when he says that George Ford makes a final opposition between corruption and noncorruption when he argues that Birkin must escape at all costs from a world in love with death. "That the corruption might also be life-giving is not recognized as a relevant possibility," says Clark. Ford does have a good deal to say about how the novel obscurely endorses the degradation of Birkin himself, but Ford "nowhere suggests that this equivocal tolerance is in any sense extended to the decadence of the world Birkin inhabits . . . The degenerated world which Birkin so reviled is beautiful as well as foul, and much of the novel is a haunting celebration of this beauty. The social decay, furthermore, is a potential source of life."[28] Clarke, of course, sees that Birkin does also save himself "by non-corruptive agencies," but his major point has to do with the nature of dissolution. He refutes Mark Spilka's contention that dissolution is limited to the excremental by pointing out that it functions as abstraction, organic (life-giving), trance, rapture of intense sensation, fusion, immersion, and fluidity.[29] Clarke brilliantly demonstrates Lawrence's turn on the Romantic Agony: the novelist affirms the demonic and paradisiacal simultaneously, endorses corruption as he judges it. In this respect, Clarke rightly holds, Lawrence is open to the charge he brought against Dostoevsky, of mixing God and sadism or creation and decomposition. Clarke points out that Lawrence mixes the two Romanticisms, demonic and organicist, in an audacious way, making the transition from Wordsworthian trance to Keatsian swoon in *Women in Love*, the book in which English Romanticism for the first time becomes self-conscious.

While *Lady Chatterley's Lover* and its precursor *The Ladybird* do not present dissolution with the same transforming complexity, one must take issue with Clarke's judgment that they are "concessions to the Paradisal myth . . . oversimple solutions" (*RD* 111). In Lawrence's later works involving sexuality, one does not find the transformation of dissolution into decomposition, the assumption that corruption regenerates. Though Clarke is right about the paridisiacal nature of *Lady Chatterlely's Lover* in this strict sense, looked at from the point of view of ferocity there is a thematic—and to a considerable degree even a psychological—continuum so pronounced that it minimizes the necessity for the sexual extremity that Lawrence considers ultimate in truth and sensation. The world is still well worth destroying, sex still represents psychological and social disintegration. Even when it springs phoenix-like from such ashes into fiery life, the phallic is tempered by anal compromise, and balance is achieved through a dominant-submissive relationship not without sadomasochistic elements. Moreover, it is arguable that this difficult paradise is finally lost. *The Ladybird*, to be sure, is not quite major Lawrence, but that is not because the tale does not face up to corruption. Clarke holds that for Birkin, to be conscious is an agonized privilege. But this holds true for Daphne Apsley as well. What could speak more to the disintegrated consciousness than her dying out of mental consciousness and receding sexuality into the life of blood consciousness of the dark Count Dionys? Dionys himself feels the full Lawrencean alienation, as a result of the collapse of civilization in the First World War. True, the mythologizing of their sexual encounter makes its high seriousness almost comic, and we are left wondering—though we may be able to imagine—what he actually did with her on that millennial night. But the disintegration of the civilized world (shown in the character of Lady Beveridge), Daphne's desperate assumption of the feminine role, the rejection of the attentive husband at her feet, and the presumptive salvation through primitive regression speak well enough to the ethic of dissolution. In *Lady Chatterley's Lover*, a greater work based on a similar triangle, there is again a loss of psychological and metaphysical complexity compared with *Women in Love*. But this novel holds its own in Lawrence's literature of disintegration. Clifford's impotence, Connie's early promiscuity, and Mellors's disastrous marriage are all signs of a universal dissolution. This stems from not just a flat Blakean, Carlylean opposition of the organic to the industrial, as Clarke argues, but from a profound sexual war typically involving reversal of the cosmic sexual roles. In the great scene (great even if influenced by sentimental fiction) in which the mother hen fiercely protects her vulnerable chicks, one of which Connie handles through Mellors's intervention, the heroine weeps at the rightness of nature "in all the anguish of her generation's forlornness" (*LCL* 135). The perception of the value of simplicity in not usually a simple thing, and the power in so plain a line can come only from emotional complication. Moreover, Connie's coming into mutual orgasmic being is something not so paradisiacally gained, but it is itself consistent enough with the establishment of the man-woman relation as Lawrence often conceives it, a pattern of obedience and submission that may not be everyone's idea of paradise.

After the first intercourse, where "the orgasm was his, all his," Connie thinks that "if she gave herself to the man, it was real. But if she kept herself for herself, it was nothing . . . She was to be had for the taking" (137). That may be paradise for readers of girlie magazines, but not for Lawrence. Connie expresses at the outset of her encounters with Mellors a reversal of her young woman's practice, where her style was going through the motions to finish solo. But the isolation persisting in her arrangements with Mellors brings tears in her second encounter. She is aware of a frigidity. Their third encounter is a prelude of things to come, but Connie is still passive and nonorgasmic. Mutual orgasm comes with the fourth encounter, but there is still no breakthrough into the mystery of womanly identity. In their fifth encounter, the ridiculousness of the physical procedure is what strikes her. Her ensuing panic, though, is what she needs to "let herself go" in the sixth and definitive encounter, where the phallic quality of the male and the passive, receptive quality of the female is emphasized as she dies into a new life—"she yielded with a quiver that was like death" (207). The metaphorical Lawrence asserts himself in an imagery of swelling and waves, but the cosmic *is* integrated with the individual. Connie's life is changed, and only Lawrence could have put it this way: "She was gone, she was not, and she was born a woman" (208). Nothing less than the passion that makes you a woman can destroy you into the new life. The ensuing coda, their seventh encounter, is a calmer replay of orgasm, the transforming sexual experience.

Lady Chatterley's Lover is Lawrence's last major statement on the corruption and renovation of man-woman relations. Clifford's is the familiar perversion: "He worshipped Connie, she was his wife, a higher being, and he worshipped her with a queer, craven idolatry, like a savage, a worship based on fear, even hate of the power of the idol" (29). Of course, he is impotent, and it is important to note that he was impotent before he went off to war and received his terrible wound. "He had been virgin when he married," Lawrence tells us, "and the sex part did not mean much to him" (10). His stories have "no touch, no actual contact" (16). His offer to let Connie have a child by someone else, "provided it doesn't touch your love for me," is to Connie "really the gabbling of an idiot" (130). By some standards, Clifford's offer is a generous one, but not by Lawrence's blood-consciousness standards. Clifford goes on in a way that is self-emasculating: "You are the great I-am, as far as life goes. . . . but for you I am absolutely nothing." More explicitly than Daphne Apsley listening to Basil, "Connie heard it all with deepening dismay and repulsion . . . What man with a spark of honor would put this ghostly burden of life-responsibility upon a woman, and leave her there, in the void?" There is a cause: "Because they were out of touch, he tortured her with his declaration of idolatry. It was the cruelty of utter impotence." So Lawrence attempts to absolve himself from the charge of cruelty in his delineation of Clifford.

Connie certainly understands Clifford's disintegration and comes to understand her own. Her new life comes with Mellors and it is not so easily gained, since it involves a growth in sexual consciousness—as is the case with a number of Lawrence's heroines, including Ursula in *Women in Love*. For Connie, too, consciousness is an agonized privilege. It may well be, as Clarke maintains, that Carlyle, say, flatly opposes the organic to the industrial, the paradisiacal to the mechanical, the machine to the sacred wood, and that therefore he can convey little sense of the inner life of which he speaks, little sense of ambivalence or complexity. But it is not true of Lawrence in *Lady Chatterley's Lover*. So Clarke's contentions, for example, that anal sex is divorced from the natural and cosmic context and that Lawrence does not prepare the reader for Mellors's sensual violence are not true. Connie's sexual conversion to a passive and receptive womanhood, her discovery of the element of manly danger, pride, and sexuality in Mellors, assumes a natural and cosmic context. What is Connie's desire for obedience and Mellors's sense of mastery, what is their ensuing tenderness, if not part of Lawrence's cosmic choreography?

Even figuratively the novel may occasionally sound like the darker part of *Women in Love*, as when Lawrence describes the Dubliner Michaelis's facial expression as "acquiescence in race destiny, instead of our individual resistance. And then a swimming through, like rats in a dark river" (*LCL* 24). Something of Loerke exists here. And Connie's reaction to this commercial literary artist is something like Gudrun's to Loerke in respect to Gerald: she "felt a sudden, strange leap of sympathy for him, a leap mingled with compassion, and tinged with repulsion, amounting almost to love. The outsider! And they called him a bounder! How much more bounderish and assertive Clifford looked! How much stupider!" (25). But Michaelis is a kneeler and a sexual soloist, leaving Connie to her own devices. Though Lawrence compares Michaelis with Clifford in saying that "sexually they were passionless, even dead" (57), he acknowledges that "on the far side of his supreme prostitution to the bitch-goddess [Michaelis] seemed pure, pure as an African ivory mask that dreams impurity into purity, in its ivory curves and planes" (58). Michaelis is complex enough to evoke something like the idea of African sensuality that Lawrence came fully to grips with in *Women in Love*.

Which brings us to anal intercourse. Some may smirk at the churchly solemnity in Lawrence's account of an act which more often in the United States today goes down lightly with other sexual patter, provided it is heterosexual. Maybe there is something in the American character that is relatively nonjudgmental about this act of adventure, in performance of which, like Columbus, one may discover a new world by going the wrong way. In three of his four major novels—*The Rainbow*, *Women in Love*, and *Lady Chatterley's Lover*—anal intercourse occurs, and in the last two it is prominent and treated similarly, as an act that requires the overcoming of shame.

It is worth emphasizing that in *Lady Chatterley's Lover*, Mellors initiates the night of shame after criticizing Connie's snobbish sister Hilda for being "stubborn" and self-willed (295). That he had spoken in dialect to Hilda underscores the class animosity that he brings to the evening tryst with Connie. Early in the novel, Mellors reacts to Connie in almost identical terms, thinking of "her will, her female will, and her modern female insistency." Even more he "dreaded her cool upper-class impudence and having her own way. For after all he was only a hired man" (103). Class is very important in this novel, and Mellors's sexual aggression that evening is a way of settling class differences, but this does not reduce the natural and cosmic elements. Given Clifford's brutal behavior to Mellors in the wheelchair incident, Connie herself would not mind this aspect of Mellors's behavior as part of the total picture, just as she does not mind it when Mellors switches into dialect and uses four-letter words.

But the main thrust, so to speak, of the event is precisely in terms of nature and the role playing that Lawrence links to abiding truth. For Connie, the thrills of sensuality are "more terrible than the thrills of tenderness, but, at the moment, more desirable . . . though a little frightened she let him have his way, and the reckless, shameless sensuality shook her to her foundations, stripped her to the very last, and made a different woman of her" (297). Lawrence thereby attributes a permanent quality to the event precisely in its aggression. Lawrence's thought about how man relates to woman is much of a piece. In *Fantasia of the Unconscious*, often taken like "The Crown" as a centerpiece of his ideas, he advises: "Take it all out of her. Make her yield once more the male leadership: if you've got anywhere to lead to" (218). Take the starch out of her— that is the male wisdom of any street corner. Mellors's act is something Connie understands in terms of his necessary aggression. Yet Lawrence is far from idealizing the event: "It was not really love. It was not voluptuousness. It was sensuality sharp and searing as fire, burning the soul to tinder. Burning out the shames, the deepest, oldest shames, in the most secret places" (*LCL* 297). What are the shames? The shame of swimming in the river of dissolution, the shame of consenting to masculine aggression, as Lawrence views it: "She had to be a passive, consenting thing, like a slave, a physical slave . . . she really thought she was dying: yet a poignant, marvelous death." The latter is what Eloise thought in being loved by Abelard. It seems that modernism must go to extremes to achieve what became the romantic norm. Yet there is a familiar element. Connie is, after all, dying into life—again. This is why Lawrence holds that the act is "necessary, forever necessary, to burn out false shames and smelt out the heaviest ore of the body into purity" (297–98). What is this if not, in Clarke's terms, reductive violence built into the nature of things just as certainly as creativeness and fecundity? Clarke is off the mark in saying, "if this sensual violence puts us in mind of anything it is the machine—within the universe of discourse the principle of the devil" (*RD* 140). Mellors's demon is hardly Clarke's devil. Connie feels a release: "Shame died . . . she felt, now, she had come to the bedrock of her nature . . . what a reckless devil the man was!" (*LCL* 298). Her demon lover has afforded her nothing less than revelation. Connie concludes: "What liars poets and everybody were. They made one think one wanted sentiment. What one supremely wanted was this piercing, consuming, rather awful sensuality," or, somewhat more fully, to know "tenderness . . . [and] sensuality with the same person" (304). Sensuality without tenderness is Lawrence's definition of Paris. Connie, on the other hand, has "the warm, flamy life" (320), the crucial Lawrence desideratum. Though the unregenerate decomposition is not as well developed as in *Women in Love*, it is present in Michaelis and Connie, in Mellors and his various women, including Bertha Coutts, who reach orgasm alone—"lesbian rampers," as he calls them—and, most dramatically, in Clifford's childlike surrender to the motherly ministrations of Mrs. Bolton. *Lady Chatterley's Lover* brings the cosmos into the bedroom, presents nature as explicit sex, and does so in the more or less familiar Lawrencean context of regeneration through dissolution. Often there is only the dissolution.

Paradisiacal or not, the novel faces up to the corruption of sexual roles and attempts to set things right. The source of its nonparadisiacal dynamic may be this: woman's authority has long been Lawrence's bugaboo. Another way of saying this is that man's authority has failed for him. Again origins are dramatized in *Sons and Lovers*. At the theater with Clara, Paul is transported by her luxurious physical presence and then by the play itself. Things take a peculiar turn: "Then he felt himself small and helpless, her towering in her force above him" (*SL* 331). Paul's submerged ambivalence toward his possessive mother manifests itself in a nightmare transformation of his desire for Clara. Harry T. Moore informs us that this episode was based on a real incident when Lawrence and Jessie Chambers saw Sarah Bernhardt in a performance of Alexandre Dumas's *La dame aux camélias*. Bernhardt's performance "terrified Lawrence and he rushed out of the theater. He wrote to Jessie that he was afraid that some day he might, like Armand in the play, 'become enslaved by a woman.'"[30] On first meeting Lawrence, Frieda reports: "He said he had finished with his attempts at knowing women. I was amazed at the way he fiercely denounced them... In after years he said: 'I would write a different *Sons and Lovers* now; my mother was wrong, and I thought she was absolutely right.'"[31] Frieda adds: "In his heart of hearts I think he always dreaded women, felt that they were in the end more powerful than men. Woman is so absolute and undeniable. Man moves, his spirit flies here and there, but you can't go beyond a woman. From her man is born and to her he returns for his ultimate need of body and soul" (55–57). Feminists may squirm. If Frieda is right, a consequent masculine aggression is implicit in heterosexual relationships as man struggles to deal with woman as authority, even though he does the creative work. There are many instances of such aggression in Lawrence. Birkin feels that women "wanted to have, to own, to control, to be dominant... It filled him almost with insane fury, this calm assumption of the Magna Mater, that all was hers, because she had borne it" (*WL* 192). Hermione is the *mater dolorosa*, Ursula "a Queen bee" who would worship a man "as a woman worships her own infant, with a worship of perfect possession." Luhan tells us that "Queen bee" is what Lawrence called Frieda. For what it is worth, Luhan claims that Frieda had complete control over him in human things "as though he had no will of his own." Luhan thinks of the real Lawrence as a dominant personality, but whenever he "reunited with Frieda, he capitulated to her and sank into the flesh," adding that "he beat her up for it afterwards."[32]

Though Birkin says he resents Ursula for being "the perfect womb, the bath of birth, to which all men must come" (*WL* 301), he does so just before she presents him with a flower as an emblem of simplicity. Birkin, bored for the time being by emotion and complexity, accepts her by embracing her. Hardly the passive type, Ursula "flung her arms around him... straining him close" (302). In the car, "she cried in sudden ecstasy, putting her arm round him and clutching him violently against her, as he steered" (303). It is not long before she is "kneeling on the hearthrug before him... her arms round his loins" (305), thinking of sons of God and daughters of men, experiencing something even deeper than the phallic source. Ursula's initiatory gestures, perhaps maternal, might even be necessary to elicit Birkin's erotic consent. She leads him into life, "he, who was so nearly dead." Marriage to her "was his resurrection and his life" (361). When a Lawrence hero literally comes back from the dead in *The Man Who Died*, the erotic figure of revival, Isis, also ministers to him in a maternal way: "suddenly she put her breast against the wound in his left side, and her arms round him, folding over the wound in his right side, and she pressed him to her, in a power of living warmth, like the folds of a river" (*MD* 206). Lawrence's Christ says to the crouching Isis: "On this rock I built my life." The relationship between Birkin and Ursula is Lawrence's most convincing representation of overcoming the fear of womanly authority. The early stoning of the moonlit water was an expression of this fear—whether of woman as fertility goddess or as castrating mother. For the time being, the fear is overcome as a delicate equilibrium is established between the couple. This is due, in part, as Clarke observes, quoting the novel, to Birkin's willingness "to smash the false integrity of the ego in order to make possible the true integrity of the blood" (*WL* 100). In Lawrence, relationship justifies. But sustained happiness between man and woman is not something that Lawrence could dramatize very often. Nixon points out that not long after his well-known remark about marriage to David Garnett—"Your most vital necessity in this life is that you shall love your wife completely and implicitly and in entire nakedness of body and spirit"[33]—Lawrence told a friend that, with his approval, Frieda was taking rooms in Hampstead and that they were going to live apart.

Some recent criticism has emphasized the negative aspects of dissolution in Lawrence to the extent that Nixon, for example, finds it "paradoxical" that Ursula and Birkin have genital sex, since in her reading of *Women in Love*, "the phallic relation is to be superseded, by a new relationship of separateness and touch."[34] She cites a list of earlier Lawrence male characters who are reticent about sex, including Paul Morel, Tom Brangwen, and Alfred Durant. But Nixon misreads *Women in Love* as a novel in which sex produces a permanent separation of male and female, due to what Lawrence calls the "horrible merging mingling self-abnegation of love" (*WL* 192). She quotes from what is perhaps the most obscure passage in Lawrence's fiction. What he is saying, it seems to me, is not that love is self-abnegating as such, difficult though that is, but that love is horrible when it is self-abnegating. In other words, when the man is not a man and the woman is not a woman, love is destructive of the differentiated self, which the narrator describes as "fulfilled in difference" (193). This is Lawrence's "two single beings constellated together like two stars," and it stands in opposition to some original ignoble androgyny from "the old age, before sex was." So much evolution Lawrence espouses, though he does not clarify whether it is a physical or cultural evolution that he has in mind. Clifford's relation to Mrs. Bolton is an extreme self-abnegating regression, though any failed self-abnegation—as in the cases of Clifford and Connie, Basil and Daphne, and Captain and Mrs. Hepburn—will do. *Women in Love* is not, as Nixon thinks, based on a transcendence of desire. The acceptance of "corruption" is a form of desire and not a precondition to its transcendence. It is excessive to say, as Nixon does, that in *Women in Love* the middle way to being is not sex, but stillness and an impersonal bond based on recognition of the partner's unreachable otherness—whereas sex is treated as destructive of self and others. Nixon misreads Birkin's being ill "in pure opposition to everything" as a result of having sex with Ursula, when in fact it is because Hermione has smashed him on the head with a statuette. Nixon holds that Birkin, Lawrence's hero, "rejects all female sexuality and does so, he says, because of woman's motherhood and her consequent assumptions of privacy."[35] But this is far from being Birkin's last word. He wants "a woman to take something from him, give herself up so much that she could take the last realities of him, the last facts, the last physical facts, physical and unbearable" (*WL* 286). The post-Brangwen saga Lawrence, woman-doubting though he may be compared to the author of *Sons and Lovers*, is not a writer who generally considers "female-desire . . . an evil force upon" men (132). Sex, as we have seen, may take disintegrative forms, but these may well be appropriate forms of eroticism. There is not much point to reading impotence as the dominant pattern in Lawrence when he is still writing of sexuality. Yet there are intimations of impotence everywhere in his work, even though it does not become his central theme until the mid-1920s.

This period includes "The Woman Who Rode Away," *St. Mawr*, and, in essential respects, *The Plumed Serpent*. These *are* works in which the fading of desire leads to the courting of aloneness. At first, Kate Leslie "was no longer in love with love. She no longer yearned for the love of a man, or the love even of her children" (*PS* 62). A "peace that passes understanding" took its place, where "she could escape into her true loneliness." For Kate, as for Margarita Lederman and Lou Witt, a disenchantment with white men leads to the death of the old erotic self. Unlike the other women, Kate did love a man, but he broke his soul and spirit in Irish nationalist politics. Lou Witt and Margarita

Lederman are left to a simpler disenchantment: perpetual absence. Kate and Elizabeth are healed by myth and ritual; Lou has no such luck.

St. Mawr is Lawrence's masterwork on the theme of impotence, and nowhere is his ferocity more transparent. The work deals with the disintegration of eroticism—albeit the mental disintegration—as disintegration alone. Hence the bitter, satiric narrative voice, approximated only in *Lady Chatterley's Lover* among his major works. The complexity of *St. Mawr* is partly confusion, but it is a great work, one whose greatness lies in an obvious brutality's becoming transcendent. It reflects a nearly mad logic carried to an impressive inevitability. Lawrence said that he worked out his sickness in his books, but the remarkable thing about *St. Mawr* is that the sickness is not worked out. It is one of the supreme modernist statements of hysteria. *St. Mawr* is fired by a savage misanthropy, the cause of which is the failure of manhood. With its mixture of apocalypse and elegy, *St. Mawr* is a bible for the impotent. "Most men have a deadness," Lou Witt tells her mother (*StM* 49). Her judgment hinges on the familiar Lawrencean antinomy of blood consciousness and mental consciousness. St. Mawr, a horse, symbolizes the former and men the latter. Reflecting a somewhat sentimental dualism, Lou says: "Why can't men get their life straight, like St. Mawr, and then think?" But St. Mawr's life is not all that straight. The story's main irony is that even this image of masculine potency is impotent. Raised for stud purposes, he cannot perform. His violence has no sexual function: it is merely lethal.

Yet as a piece of abstract sculpture, as it were, St. Mawr's function is not impaired. The groom is correct in saying to Lou: "If he was a human being, you'd say something had gone wrong in his life" (12). St. Mawr is the energy that has been injured. He has been involved in two deaths, one of which he caused. When we are told that "he looked like something finely bred and passionate, that has been judged and condemned" (13), we see him in relation to the romantic criminal, another instance of Lawrence's antinomianism. Like many women whose repressed lives draw them to images of masculine aggression, Lou is, as it were, spellbound: "Master of doom, he seemed to be!" (15). His impact on her is profoundly sexual, "as if that mysterious fire in the horse's body had split some rock in her" (14). For Lou, feeling his immense significance, St. Mawr is the ultimate stud, an inhabitant of the "heavily potent world . . . undominated and unsurpassed" (20). There is a cosmic shock of recognition: "It was as if she had a vision" (14). St. Mawr, in short, is everything her husband is not.

St. Mawr is driven by the prevalence of inversion. It is a world of apparently cocksure women and hensure men, to use Lawrence's terminology. The short novel begins with one of Lawrence's best opening sentences: "Lou Witt had had her own way so long that by the age of twenty-five she didn't know where she was" (1). She is spoiled sick, as if there were no masculine authority to contain her. Even the diminutive version of her name is an inversion from feminine to masculine. Her mother is described as "a smooth, leveled, gunmetal pistol" (9), indicating aggressive masculinity as does the submerged meaning of her name, Witt. Mr. Saintsbury, the owner of the mews, "flashed his old-maid's smile" (10). His name suggests a funereal goodness. Above all, inversion marks the marriage of what had already been a failed romance. Lou has a husband: "she had 'got' him. Oh, yes! You had only to see the uneasy backward glance at her, from his big blue eyes: just like a horse that is edging away from its master: to know how completely he was mastered" (3). So does Lawrence note an inverted relationship, though in this ghost sonata of a work, sexuality is a memory that informs behavior rather than behavior itself.

The climactic scene, therefore—in which the mounted Rico does not meet St. Mawr half-way in a moment of crisis and is therefore thrown and trampled—is one in which Lou's sublimated sexual feelings for the horse are at once expressed and destroyed. She had wanted St. Mawr to destroy Rico, true masculinity casting out false, and was "spellbound" (67) by their agon, where Rico's friend Flora was solicitous. Lou is shocked by her own feelings. Having once held the view that evil is privative, she now thinks it is positive and embodied in the reversed St. Mawr. This scene is the end of her romantic trust in nature. Her loathing for modern life, however, has not abated. Like the misanthropes, like the mystics, she will "retreat to the desert, and fight" (73)—a spiritual fight. Disillusioned, she attributes to St. Mawr a Dostoevskian servility, the animal domesticated. "Far better kicks and servility," she thinks, "than the hard, lonely responsibility of real freedom." Hence the horse's vengeance. Lawrence indulges here in what has been called anthropohorsizing—a play on anthropomorphizing about a horse. There is nothing so detestable as the maudlin attributing of human feelings and consciousness to animals, says Birkin (*WL* 130–31). Can one speak of a horse's "lonely responsibility of real freedom" (*StM* 73)? Lawrence has wrung animal nature for whatever it was worth and there is not much left, mainly a boomerang effect. Neither Lawrence nor Lou know quite what to make of this event—can nature be as bad as society?—so she concludes feebly that "she knew the horse was born to serve nobly, had waited in vain for someone noble to serve. His spirit knew that nobility had gone out of man. And this left him high and dry, in a sort of despair" (76). Of course, this describes Lou much better than it does the horse. St. Mawr, sent off to the southwestern United States, has his sexuality restored, saved apparently by this movement away from the apex of a castrating civilization. Lou, however, is no longer interested in even "the illusion of the beautiful St. Mawr" (137). Male sexuality appears to her through the accident of propinquity in the nihilistic guise of "a sexual rat" (137), Phoenix, the promiscuous, cocky male. In a bizarre turn of the story, she momentarily considers him a serious possibility.

In the denouement of this remarkable tale, Lawrence insists on attributing a human quality, sexuality itself, to the landscape. Like the woman who rode away, Lou finds herself ascending mountains to find an answer to her spiritual quest. She will give herself to the higher impersonality, "the unseen presences" (139). Anticipating Isis in *The Man Who Died*, she understands the psyche of the vestal virgin, of "woman weary of the embrace of incompetent men, weary, weary, weary of all that." Her revelation amounts to a sexual asceticism, leaving her with the knowledge that she "can never, never mate with any man, since the mystic new man will never come to me" (139–40). She is an Isis waiting for her sexual messiah.

A marked quality of Lawrence's Arizona mountainscape is that the far landscape is transcendently beautiful while the near landscape is a "debasing malevolence" (145) symbolized by rats, as if Lawrence doubted his own idealization. This malevolence has pithed or castrated the Mexicans and the white men and has humbled the New England woman (with her idea of a merciful God). The quality of disintegration that Lawrence's lovers confront and assimilate to their betterment in so many cases is here sublimated into a sense of sexual landscape, the most explicit of Lawrence's forms of impersonality. St. Mawr, after all, was animate and, finally, too closely allied to the neurotic distortions of men. Lou finds sexual solace—love, danger, mystical transcendence, the spirit of masculine nobility—only in the inanimate. "There's something else even that loves me and wants me," she tells her mother, who is nervous about her becoming a vestal spinster; "It's a spirit . . . in this landscape. It's something more real to me than men are, and it soothes me, and it holds me up. It's something wild, that will hurt me sometimes and will wear me down sometimes." The inviting poetry of pain, a familiar receptivity in some of Lawrence's heroines, is contained here by a rare transcendence: "But it's something big, bigger than men, bigger than people, bigger than religion . . . And I am here, right deep in America, where there's a wild spirit wants me, a wild spirit more than men . . . It needs me. It craves for me. And to it, my sex is deep and sacred, deeper than I am, with a deep nature aware deep down of my sex" (158–59). Only Lawrence could have written this astonishing passage. Can one be a sexual anchorite? Lou's consummation is another name for impotence, and sexual solipsism for a debilitating narcissism. Lawrence's mad logic of despair drives him to get semen from a stone. Lou is not an octogenarian whose age qualifies her for a melancholy neutrality. She is a woman in her prime, her neurotic prime. Yet Lawrence may be most memorable as a writer when he is dramatizing the sickness he has not worked out.

The Man Who Died is a coda to the symphony of Lawrence's erotic life, and the sense of physical resurrection is usually emphasized in the story's interpretation. While it is undeniably there, what is even more prominent than the night of symbolic love (reminiscent in this respect of Count Dionys and Daphne in *The Ladybird*) is the profound impotence and disgust from which Lawrence's Jesus is resurrected. He is imbued with a ferocity so paralyzing that sex appears as a miracle. Like a number of Lawrence's characters, the returned Jesus "lay overcome with a sense of nausea" (*MD* 165). He wishes for death, the ultimate impersonality, "the utter cold nullity of being outside." Jesus feels the familiar Lawrencean disgust with the common life. The sleeping soldiers "were repulsive" (166), the peasant "dirty and stupid" (172), and "he could not mingle with" the erotic thoughts of the peasant woman (177). Similarly, when Isis, "the lady of Egypt" (191), speaks to her slave, "she spoke coldly, for she found slaves invariably repellent, a little repulsive. They were so imbedded in the lesser life, and their appetites and their small consciousness were a little disgusting" (193). Jesus and even Isis are characters whose eroticism is an impotence denied. In this respect they are like Count Dionys and Lady Daphne, Captain Hepburn, and Mellors and Connie. Like Jesus, who has "the sickness of death in life" (177), an apparently Kierkegaardian malaise, Dionys says, "I have wished to die" (*FSN* 52); he too "lay for hours with black, open eyes, seeing everything around with a touch of disgust and heeding nothing" (55). He too sees the common life as a failure in itself. Common men have "only made themselves free in order voluntarily to saddle themselves with new lords and new masters" (90). In *The Captain's Doll*, Hepburn felt "a helpless disgust . . . he felt sick, even physically" when people approached him "to spread their feelings over him" (*FSN* 225). Mellors, as we have seen, needs also to be recalled to life. Jesus, of course, is particularly enervated by the moral compulsion he put on others in his first life. Yet he has died into life, into pagan, erotic, blasphemous life, and is to be reborn as the Egyptian god Osiris.

The eroticism he feels is more a function of nature, of the cosmos, more a mythological reality, than a feeling for any particular woman, despite the fact that Isis is like Ursula in *Women in Love* in her initiatory sexual style. Lady Chatterley was Lawrence's last woman lover. Now eros can live only in the rarefied atmosphere of the gods as the greater life of the body. The reassertion of the phallic in Lawrence brings a pregnancy in *Lady Chatterley's Lover* and in *The Man Who Died*, but not the child itself. That is just as well, since Lawrence had for so long at best a tangential relation to ordinary life. Here is a man who could say to Frieda that she "should leave [her] children alone till they are men and women. Then, if there *is* love, if there *is* a connection, it is undeniable: if there is no active love, nothing can create it" (quoted in *LN* 254). So much for child development! So much for family life! It was a great disappointment for Lawrence, an undermining of his potency, not to have had children. But who can doubt that it was far better for him—to say nothing of children—not to have to deal with these common realities on a long-term basis when his art reflects an estrangement from them.

The Man Who Died is a strained, impersonal work that calls to mind Nickolas Muray's searing photograph of a devitalized Lawrence. Is it the reassertion of a cosmic energy or the painful thrust of a rusty pump? Whichever, it manages a remarkable erotic landscape in the language of a surging natural energy that impersonality can realize, as in *St. Mawr*. The man who died looks on life and "saw a vast resoluteness everywhere flinging itself up in stormy or subtle wave-crests, foam-tips emerging out of the blue invisible, a black and orange cock or the green flame-tongues out of the extremes of the fig-tree. They came forth, these things and creatures of spring, glowing with desire and with assertion. They came like crests of foam, out of the blue flood of the invisible desire" (*MD* 171). As in *St. Mawr*, the phallic throbs in its cosmic element. But human sexuality is more like a once in a lifetime affair. Lawrence assumes too well the guise of the metafucker.

Lawrence's metaphysical insistence comes from a personal lack. His lifelong obsession with the phallic and beyond derives from a questionable sexuality. According to most accounts, Lawrence was often impotent. According to most recent accounts, he was a suppressed homosexual. John Middleton Murry, who held this view long ago, was much derided for it then. Lawrence's champions had for some time set up a protective veil around his difficult characteristics, as the examination of these qualities, or even the expression of them, was seen to be vulgarly reductive—as if a priestly immunity went with his sacramental task. But Murry has been read more seriously by the dissolution critics and other recent critics. Nixon holds that Lawrence's sexual orientation was primarily homoerotic, "but he was unable to accept it," that the "most secret and shameful desire" alluded to in the letters (*CL* 2:315) is homoerotic desire. Is *Women in Love* a working through of these feelings? Or is it a more innocent longing for a primitive *Blütbrudershaft*? Is Gudrun's response to Gerald and Loerke a thinly veiled version of Birkin's intoxicated response to these two types of men in the suppressed prologue? Cavitch holds that "Lawrence transferred to [Gudrun] the feelings that would have been Birkin's if his homosexuality had become explicitly the central issue in the fiction."[36] Delany says of Lawrence's images that the focus on "putrescence, snakes, the marsh—points to a special concern with anality and homosexuality" (*LN* 289). And Jeffrey Myers believes that Lawrence condemned in others what he wanted for himself, quoting what Lawrence presumably told Compton Mackenzie: "I believe the nearest I've ever come to perfect love was a young coal-miner when I was sixteen."[37] Myers points out that Lawrence's first plans for Rananim, his utopian colony, excluded women. The original of the homosexual reference in the prologue to *Women in Love* and the nightmare chapter in *Kangaroo* is William Henry Hocking, a Cornish farmer whom Lawrence knew. Was their relationship homosexual, sublimated or otherwise? The statement in the prologue is unambiguous: "It was for men that he felt the hot, flushing, roused attraction which a man is supposed to feel for the other sex" (*WL* 103–4). So is Jesus' recollection of Judas: "If I had kissed Judas with live love [the Lawrencean tautology again], perhaps he never would have kissed me with death. Perhaps he loved me in the flesh, and I willed that he should love me bodylessly" (*MD* 205). So Lawrence is Christ. Perhaps only an epicene can preach so effectively the virtues of heterosexual love. Such are the uses of dissolution.

"I shall change the world for one thousand years,"[38] said Lawrence, but he changed his mind a few years later. His idea of leadership crumbled. Erotic megalomania had ultimately to be a form of self-deflation for a man who for a long time had trouble sustaining an erection. And Lawrence was nothing if not iffyphallic. Though Lawrence would have been appalled by the promiscuity of the twentieth-century sexual revolution, who can deny that the sane lack of inhibition about sexuality deriving from that movement is a good thing that is partly attributable to Lawrence? The use of the word *good* reminds us that we live in an age where ethics has been preempted by sexuality. The reality of good and evil is often questioned, but what is unquestionable is that it is good to be "good" in bed. Lawrence gives us an ethical eroticism in the sense that he is sacramental. But civilizations based on the cardinality of sex have floundered, like ours to the extent that it is so based. There are higher sacraments, blessed though this one is. Lawrence is sometimes criticized for confusing the visionary and the ethical. "The visionary habit is alien to moral life, because it refuses to accommodate itself to anything different from it," says one critic.[39] True. But one must ask: Visionary about what? Visions are converted into actions, and the immoralist tendency in Lawrence's fiction is at least questionable. The visionary habit, it need hardly be said, may well be expressive of a moral morality, to counter tautology with tautology. Iconoclastic in its inception, moral morality involved the shattering of idols, some of which Lawrence wishes to restore.

Certainly Lawrence's vision has a rather specific content. He is a vitalist who has rediscovered life. As such, he is particularly susceptible to humanistic attack, and that attack has on occasion been well made. Eliseo Vivas points out that " 'life' that is not experience dominantly cognitive, moral, religious, or aesthetic, cannot be found, and it is indeed as much if not more of an abstraction than the shriveled, conceptual irresponsibilities of the idea-mongers whom Lawrence despised."[40] Vivas is right in saying that Lawrence is irresponsible for thinking that once "life" has been found, all other problems will solve themselves. And right again in saying that "we *know* the sun is a ball of gas. To assume we can go back to the Dragon Cosmos is on a level with the assumption that we can solve our sociopolitical or economic problems by going back to handicrafts and eschewing commerce and technology" (99). Lawrence is, as Vivas holds, an archaic mind who accepted what we moderns reject: "the ultimate relationship between the mystery of sex and the mystery of the cosmos" (222). Frank Kermode quotes Worringer to the effect that the novel as a kind belongs to humanism, not to mystery religion, and that consequently it cannot abandon empathy in favor of abstraction.[41] Kermode is essentially right in saying that *Women in Love* is the last novel in which Lawrence kept the balance, and that he progressively loses historical power (*Lady Chatterley's Lover* is the exception). This is also why Lawrence typically excels in the shorter forms of literature, where the net of social reality may be gracefully channeled or circumvented, and where lyrical, symbolic, or mythical effects may more easily prevail. Even now, one of the first words on Lawrence may be one of the last. His friend Aldous Huxley said that Lawrence, living in isolation, gives us a bird's-eye view; that he ignores the difficulties of the social life, judges too sweepingly, condemns too lightly; that, like Nietzsche, he is so wrong and so right.[42]

8

GEORGES BATAILLE

Norman O. Brown, metaphysical Pied Piper of the late 1960s, sees in Georges Bataille "a fellow traveler on the Dionysian path," or another ex-Marxist sympathetic to another form of revolution. In his revealing "Dionysus in 1990," the concluding essay in his 1991 collection *Apocalypse and/or Metamorphosis*, Brown pays his respects to a kindred spirit discovered by him in 1990. Bataille, says Brown, "in appropriately unruly ways bears precious testimony to the need for a Dionysian transvaluation of the Freudian revolution. Bataille's style and stance is almost as significant as his substance" (*AM* 182). Brown himself had long assumed the Orphic stance and found in Bataille's peculiar theater of cruelty something better than thinking. If Brown was enamored of Bataille's "style," he was even more taken with his content. Brown cites Bataille's 1939 manifesto, "The Practice of Joy before Death," which shows how "his lifelong obsession with violent death had been transfigured by the advent of World War II." Brown is taken particularly by the section called "Heraclitean Meditation,"[1] which "covers with exemplary candor and directness ground laboriously crawled in *Love's Body*."

Contemplating suicide in the manifesto, "a violent decision, which disrupts his repose," Bataille is "in rending agony."[2] Yet this preparation for death, this mystical exercise, is, Bataille says, a joy "to the person for whom there is no beyond, an ecstasy for the nihilist, the Dionysian" (236). Bataille takes Christian renunciation and reverses it. Moreover, he imagines that "limitless" possibilities "can only be appeased by war," an odd transfiguration in the political year 1939, the self-absorption of a remote man. He desires a transcendent aggression, envisions "an exhaustion charged with nausea," perceives "a succession of cruel splendors whose very movement requires that I die." Not to worry, for "this death is only the *exploding* consumption of all that was, the joy of existence of all that comes into the world" (239). In short, no cowardly sublimations, no civilized repressions should compromise the violent joy before death. Life is the ultimate gratuitous expenditure. Bataille opts for mystical indulgence in a time screaming for restraint and reason. Brown notices no incongruity. Nor does he find anything irresponsible—even in that fateful year—in a man's celebrating his own self-destruction "in a great festival of blood" (238). Brown attempts to clarify his views with regard to his own work: "As in *Love's Body*,[3] and whatever the laws of thermodynamics may say, Bataille finds in Heraclitean Fire the best metaphor for the universal unity of eternal creation and eternal destruction—Blake's tiger burning" (*AM* 184). But Brown's particular chapter selection underscores the apocalypse. His saying, for example, "the real prayer is to see the world go up in flames"[4] is far from Heraclitus and may even be a bit much for Bataille.

For Brown, Bataille is an emblem of the harmony of violent excess, who "helped me to reformulate the difference between the Freudian dualism and the Dionysian or Heraclitean principle of the unity of opposites" (*AM* 182). Brown condemns Freud for his "opposition to all forms of violent and excessive pleasure ... as counterproductive or pathological," his view that where id was, there shall ego be. Brown notes that in Freud "the good bourgeois principle of self-preservation, and the good rational (Apollonian) principle of moderation are in command." This, Brown holds, distorts life and death. In his questionable view, "the ironical effect, as Freud later came to realize, is to place the pleasure-principle, which Lucretius had celebrated as *dux vitae*, the guide to life, entirely at the service of the death instinct: it becomes, Freud says, a Nirvana principle, aiming at the reduction of the 'throbbing energy of life' to the lowest possible level."

For Brown, of course, Freud's Copernican revolution (the ego is not even master in its own house) is not complete until the "ego is forced to admit another master, the Dionysian principle of excess. Nietzsche called it drunkenness" (*AM* 183). In Bataille, Brown finds his own sense of the death instinct: "It takes a madman like Bataille, and a libertine like Bataille, to challenge the homeostatic pleasure-principle in terms of another definition of pleasure and another definition of life. In Bataille's Heraclitean vision we are suffering not from some repressed longing for death but from excess of life—the Dionysian principle of excess, Blake's principle of exuberance." This is why, Brown says, "in the last resort, there is only poetry." In other words, in Bataille, "Eros and Thanatos are one" (186), not in need of the Freudian compromise formations attributable to the contest between them. Freud's stability seems pale in comparison to Bataille's excess, "which must be spent gloriously or catastrophically." And since there is no distinction between wasteful and necessary expenditure, Marxist "surplus" becomes an irrelevance. The ex-Marxists Brown and Bataille are in agreement on this point.

Brown sees that Bataille's anthropological influences are Marcel Mauss and Roger Caillois and their idea of the gift, which lays the foundation for human culture by repressing Hobbesian human nature. Brown emphasizes that "the human tendency Bataille sees at work in the potlatch is not aggression but death: the need to lose, the need to spend, to give away, to surrender; the need to sacrifice; the need for ruin. Power is the ability to lose" (*AM* 187). Brown also sees the development of rivalries involving sovereignty, games of conspicuous waste and superiority. He sees the analogy between potlatch and male rutting rivalries—the aggressive element asserting itself. And he agrees with Bataille when the latter draws on the relevance of psychoanalytic interpretation emphasizing "the primordial connection between excrement and jewelry, between the worthless and the priceless, between anal eroticism and anal sadism." Brown also sees the connection between Bataille's anthropology and his psychology: "Bataille's personal erotic excesses are potlatches" (197), he says, understanding that the cruelty of his eroticism demands ruinous outlays.

Bataille is an eroticist *maudit*. For him, eroticism exists only in the violent, angry gesture. It is an expression of modern rebellion against an unreal, secular normalcy that contents itself with what Barthes calls *plaisir*, the warm, ego-caressing transactions that most people settle for. It is equally a rebellion against Christianity, "which eschewed the desire to use violent experience to probe the secrets of existence" by denying the likeness of "piety in sacrifice" and the "untrammeled eroticism" of the lover as "assailant."[5] Before the term took on its current clarity of connotation, Bataille's intellectual and fictional writings exemplified the meaning of *jouissance*. Orgasmic pleasure, yes, but it goes beyond that to become, as Jane Gallop holds, something shocking and ego-disrupting, in conflict with the canons of culture. Jouissance, in this sense, is consonant with the idea of ferocity. Though nondoctrinal, it has the power to unsettle ideological assumptions. It is presumably expressive of the deepest emotion.[6] And that emotion is likely to be deeply subversive. As Philippe Sollers has said, Bataille "associated *jouissance* with horror, Sade's 'delicacy.'"[7] Of the erotic woman, Bataille says, it is "as if some mad bitch had usurped the personality of the dignified hostess of a little while back" (*E* 116). Eroticism is a world beyond or beneath the social self.

Bataille distinguishes, then, between eroticism and sexuality (by which he means sex). "Eroticism," he tells us, "unlike simple sexual activity, is a psychological quest independent of the natural goal: reproduction and desire for children" (11). Unlike the sexual liberationists, Bataille is not merely lauding sexual experimentation at the expense of the benighted family. No, he says, "I am not in the least inclined to think that physical pleasure is the most important thing on earth. Man is not to be identified with the organ of pleasure" (269). What is he to be identified with? What is the proper context of eroticism? Here Bataille makes a substantial claim: "Eroticism cannot be discussed ... independently of the history of religion" (8).

His physical has a metaphysical base, if one can apply such a conventional philosophical word to Bataille. Man is born alone and dies alone. Between one being and another there is a gulf, "a discontinuity" (13). And for us, "discontinuous beings that we are, death means continuity of being." All try to replace discontinuity with continuity. This nexus is "the dominant element in eroticism," whether physical, emotional, or religious.

Bataille, a former Catholic who in his youth had wanted to enter a monastery and later did, brings his sense of original sin to the bedroom—or the taxi, or wherever. Peter Tracey Connor gives us an excellent account of Bataille's relationship to Christianity and mysticism and points to the wry affinity that Bataille has to "the exquisitely obscene representations of which Christianity alone was capable." Connor argues that "in its art and in its texts, Christianity represented eroticism and spirituality conjoined in equal intensity, even if only to condemn a seriousness it held to be base. Perversely then, Bataille's reading of Christianity is an affirmation of its clearest yet most repressed projections: what is more Bataillean today than the image of the mutilated, naked body crucified in transcendent abjection?"[8] The agony of the "Chinese Torture of the Hundred Pieces" described in *Tears of Eros*, particularly the morbid photographs taken of the torture of Fou-Tchou Li in 1905 (tied to a stake, naked, both sides of his chest flayed, yet with what might be an enigmatic smile in one photograph—which Bataille interprets as ecstasy but may simply be the effects of opium given to prolong the torture) replaced in Bataille's private iconography the agony of Christ on the cross. By his own account, Bataille took no physical (sadistic) pleasure in this representation but rather a moral one, to ruin in himself that which was opposed to ruin. Bataille, but no one else, considered *Tears of Eros* his most important book.

Bataille sees the notorious Gilles de Rais from a Christian perspective, noting that he was "up to the end—naively a good and devout Christian."[9] How so? "Perhaps," Bataille argues, "Christianity is even fundamentally the pressing demand for crime, the demand for the horror that in a sense it needs in order to forgive ... Perhaps Christianity is above all bound to an archaic human nature, one unrestrainedly open to violence?" It would not be difficult to find a better example of Christianity than Gilles de Rais, who came on the bodies of the young boys he was murdering. Yet, at the very least, Bataille shares with Christianity a sense of what he considers irremediable insufficiency. This is a physical consideration as much as an ideational one. His biographer Michel Surya has it right in saying that "he never loved the flesh, at least never in the sense that he could imagine it without repugnance, in any case never in such a way that he could not see the kind of death to which it, and whoever was wedded to it, was consigned."[10] Rejecting revelation, accepting sin, Bataille is—as Connor says—"neither a fanatic anti-Christian crusader nor a lapsed Catholic recovering from the fall."[11] Still, Bataille threatened to kill the Catholic cleric who would dare to say mass at the funeral of his second wife, Laure.

Bataille is a secular believer. He regards Gilles de Rais as a sacred monster in the same sense that some French critics have for some time considered Sade "the Divine Marquis." Living in a world of passion, de Rais and Sade transcend the social values that had sacrificed their countervalues. They transcend the homogeneity of convention for the inflamed, base adventure of the heterogeneous. Transcendence for Bataille is a negative transcendence, involving eroticism in a context of dirt, excrement, violence, delirium, and crime.

Perhaps the culminating devolutionary image in Bataille is that of the ass-headed god, which becomes the headless god of his magazine *Acéphale*, symbolic of its assault on rationalism and the authority of God. Philosophically, Bataille is in the Gnostic tradition, which, as he puts it in "Base Materialism and Gnosticism," conceives "of matter as an *active* principle having its own eternal autonomous existence as darkness ... and as evil (which would not be the absence of good, but a creative action)" (*V* 47). This tradition is in contradiction to "the profoundly monistic Hellenistic spirit, whose dominant tendency saw matter and evil as degradations of superior principles." For the Greeks, Gnosticism was "a nauseating, inadmissable pessimism." In this sense, Bataille's work can be seen as the triumph of the braying ass. In a particular affinity, Bataille notes that "the existence of a sect of *licentious Gnostics* and of certain sexual rites fulfills this obscure demand for a baseness that would not be reducible, which would be owed the most indecent respect"—a rich, Bataillean paradox. Black magic, Bataille adds, has continued this tradition to the present day. He tells us that "Egypt in particular seems to have been an important center of production" of Gnostic stories during the third and fourth centuries. "Egyptian divinities or figures in an Egyptian style" were a frequent phenomenon, the acephalic god as Anubis, for example (52). For Bataille, Christianity is not enough. He is allied with those who find true dignity in ancient Egypt, a group that includes D. H. Lawrence and Norman Mailer.

Lawrence and Mailer think of ancient Egypt in terms of phallic sovereignty or mastery, a concept to which Bataille gives a vivid twist. Fundamentally, Bataille's sovereignty is a concept of consciousness. Since consciousness is instantaneous and fleeting, to be sovereign is a high-flown variety of immediate gratification, most notably in erotic situations. Yet we must bear in mind that Bataille does not oppose eroticism to formal thought as such. Eroticism can instruct philosophy, so to speak, since "the supreme philosophical question coincides with the summits of eroticism" (*E* 273). The result is ecstasy, even if—especially if—it is an experience of pain. Bataille thought of war as well as sadomasochism as, ideally, ecstatic experiences. They have in common the destruction of limits, the traditional philosopher's noose. Limit, project, deferred gratification, the myth of the moral life, Hegelian mastery—these give the conventional lie to the inevitable agony of living. Nothing is useful, everything is waste. Only transgression is real. We are near the solipsistic world of Sade. Convulsive laughter, Bataille suggests, will save us from solipsism. But as Sartre has said, Bataille tells us that he laughs, but he does not make us laugh (quoted in Conner 36). Whatever happened to Molière?

Bataille is contemporary in that he presents his madness as exemplary. "The world was his sickness," said his friend Jules Monnerot.[12] And Bataille confirms that his writing is an attempt at the "representation of a disorder."[13] Surya points out that Bataille loved Van Gogh because he was the first to paint sunflowers "wilted, burned, disheartening."[14] Bataille sees ruin rather than transcendence. As the critics have noted, the "abyss of funereal stars" in the graveyard love scene from *Blue of Noon* inverts the "starry sky" of Kant's second *Critique*.[15]

Bataille laments that "loss is the winner in the long run. Reproduction only multiplies life in vain, multiplies it in order to offer it up to death" (*E* 232). What follows from such cosmic pessimism? One might well ask, "How much credence can we give to a creep who can't look at a mattress without seeing a coffin?" But Bataille's passion and depth deny indifference. He invokes what the Roman Catholic Church calls "morose delectation," which occurs when the beauty of the object and sexual attraction have vanished and only their memory exists, in the form of "the halo of death" (237). This idea may serve as a means "of reconciling desire for the soul's salvation with the desire to be lost in the mortal bliss of an embrace." At the same time, "the desire for a desirable object is this time desire for an object with no charm of its own; it is the unintelligible and unconscious desire for death or at least damnation." Nor does Bataille disassociate himself from this vision. On the contrary, eroticism, he says, "is only fulfilled, only exhausts all its potentialities if it brings some degradation in its train, the horror of which will suggest the simple death of the flesh" (235).

For Bataille, "the aura of death . . . denotes passion" (21). Love itself spells suffering insofar as it is "a quest for the impossible." The consummation of two lovers "involves the idea of death, murder or suicide." Bataille is not clear about this until he talks about sacrifice or what he calls "sacred eroticism." Death releases in him a fantasy of unconditionality, a "full and limitless being unconfined within the trammels of separate personalities, deliverance through the person of the beloved." It is a strange, archaic, not to say cruel mind that seeks the sacred at the expense of human life. But the devaluation of ordinary human life is a primary assumption of his extremity. "The victim dies," Bataille tells us, "and the spectators share in what his death reveals." This, Bataille concludes, is "sacredness . . . the revelation of continuity through the death of discontinuous being to those who watch it as a solemn rite. Only a spectacular killing, carried out as the solemn and collective nature of religion dictates, has the power to reveal what ordinarily escapes notices" (22). What religion? What century? What millennium? Maybe there is progress in civilization after all. Bataille's "continuous" and "discontinuous" are metaphors more than they are concepts, an immoralist poetry of dehumanization and release. The passage recalls Lawrence's "The Woman Who Rode Away," in which the sacredness of masculine mastery is revealed. But Lawrence has the delicacy to give us a sacrifice that is self-imposed by an already estranged heroine.

"Eroticism," says Bataille, "is assenting to life up to the point of death" (*E* 11). Eroticism opens the way to death in that "death opens the way to denial of our individual lives" (28)—but why should we deny them? Bataille's erotic doctrine assumes a contempt for the lives we live, not merely the bourgeois, capitalist lives—Bataille is at this point well beyond his Marxist revolutionary phase—but any lives. Eroticism is, then, a form of destructive creation, a violent redefinition of human possibility. Poetry, eternity, death, and continuity he lists in sequence, commenting on his esteemed Rimbaud, whom he considers, rightly, as "one of the most violent of poets" (25). For Bataille, experience directs one to the insight that "underlying eroticism is the feeling of something bursting, of the violence accompanying an explosion" (93).

There is no doubt that something is bursting, perhaps with a sense of psychic joyful release; "explosion" is somewhat hysterical and melodramatic, the product of an unremittingly ferocious imagination.

"No one doubts the ugliness of the sexual act," according to Bataille (145). Yet this unseemly quality has a function. Like death, ugliness makes for anguish. The greater the (contained) anguish, "the stronger the realization of exceeding the bounds and the greater the accompanying rush of joy." The beauty of woman—"her humanity that is," he notes parenthetically—cannot prevent "the animal nature of the sexual act" from being "obvious and shocking." Beauty has nonetheless "a cardinal importance," since "to despoil is the essence of eroticism" (146). Taboos are transgressed, humanity is transfigured by anguish. The pull of death, Bataille concedes, is contingent to some degree on the persistence of life. Still, his central thrust is destructive. Sex may be beneficent (or animal), but eroticism, genital only in its origin, "is a sterile principle representing Evil and the diabolic" (230). The maudit prevails in his fiction as well as in his cultural criticism. Bataille holds that "divine life may be sought through death" (231). Mysticism lurks.

"I die because I cannot die," says St. Theresa. For Bataille, the death of not dying, the anguish of living, "is the ultimate stage of life" (*E* 240). He draws the connection between sexuality and religion, noting that "the longed-for swoon is thus the salient feature not only of man's sensuality but also of the experience of the mystics." But he has reached an ambiguous threshold: "It is hard to say whether the object of desire is the incandescence of life or death. The incandescence of life is death; death means an incandescence of life." Surely this is one of the more opaque passages in the history of the symbolism of light. For most thinkers, such as Freud, life and death are generally opposed —as are subject and object. Not quite so for Bataille. For him, there is a paradox in speaking of the "erotic object," since such an "object" implies for him the abolition of the limits of all objects. In Bataille, eroticism "shifts interest away from and beyond the person" but is nevertheless expressed by an object (130). Though he would deny it, Bataille remains doggedly metaphysical in an age that thinks of object choice in psychological terms. For all his emphasis on eroticism, he denies the reality of libido theory, "believing the concept of sexual energy to be a groundless fiction," though maintaining that "a non-predetermined sum of physical energy, expendable in several directions, always enters into sexual activity" (239 note 1). Bataille is not anchored in individual psychology, which helps to explain why his fiction is either thesis-ridden or expressionistic.

Bataille does see that though the "little death" of orgasm may be a desire to die, "it is at the same time a desire to live to the limits of the possible," which, however, yields to "the impossible with ever-increasing intensity" (239). This intensity, in our damned lives, ever veers toward the destructive, which has a fatal attraction. Bataille assumes "the turbulence and disastrousness of sexuality" and takes these to be "the essence of temptation." From a Freudian point of view, his is an intransigent moral masochism, regressed from morality to the Oedipus complex, which manifests itself not as superego but a desire for self-annihilation. There is in Bataille a need to self-destruct. Like Dostoevsky's gambler in Freud's eyes, Bataille seems compelled to work through a profound Oedipal guilt ad infinitum. Surya informs us that Bataille was, in fact, a gambler, "often with money, and sometimes with his life at Russian roulette."[16] "Temptation," Bataille tells us, "is the desire to fall, to fail, to faint, and squander all one's reserves until there is no firm ground beneath one's feet" (*E* 240). This is certainly consonant with his view of eroticism. But plaisir—pleasure, in the current French use of the word—suggests that temptation can be a much simpler experience, rhapsodic rather than anguished. It may suggest that dying into life is less profound than just living it, that creative destruction is secondary to creation itself, and that pleasure, finally, is more desirable than pain. Pleasure is, after all, more than bourgeois compromise.

Bataille acknowledges that "love of the sexual partner (a variant of marriage . . . often coinciding with it) changes sexuality into tenderness," and that "tenderness attenuates the violence of nocturnal pleasures" (242). But he feels that "the fundamental violence that makes us lose control always tends to disturb a relationship . . . to make us find in that relationship that death is near, and death is the symbol of all sensuality, even that modified by tenderness." Bataille, in short, never gives life its due. He posits a human nature in constant loss of control, an ego incapable of modulating definitively, an ineffectual culture sucked up by a dynamic nature. This is why he is nearly blind to the element of civilization in eroticism, the element of play, the psychological pas de deux. Violence may be expressed and sublimated in this play of eroticism that, far more often than not, displaces real violence, aggression, and ferocity. Bataille minimizes the artifice of the everyday, the propinquity of solution, in favor of the monolith of disintegration. He is mesmerized by death. His replacing the genitalia with a skull in the figure of Acéphale is, if not merely pathetic, silly. The symbolism is undoubtedly a joke, but—as Sartre said—we do not laugh. Bataille is the master of the unfunny joke.

In his review of *The Kinsey Report*, Bataille ridicules the American sexologist for seeing "guilty sexuality . . . as innocently material" (*E* 155). What disturbs him about *The Kinsey Report* is its confusion of "thingishness" with the sacred; he knows that in ancient Rome, *homo sacer* meant both "sacred man" and "accursed man." *The Kinsey Report* confuses the "profane" with "the momentous quality we sense in the secret violence of man or child." It is Bataille's great point of honor not to shrink from that violence. He argues that for the pagan, sacred things could be unspeakably foul; that sin was originally a taboo; and that the religious taboo is, in fact, sacred. It is clear to him that "the innermost depths of our nature . . . [are] revealed in so far as its accursed aspect is felt," for "our deepest truths come up to consciousness as something accursed and condemned, as sins in fact" (162–63). There is a problem here. Sin implies religious belief. And one is tempted to agree with Julia O'Faolain that "for the sake of reaching erotic rapture, [Bataille] held on to a sense of sin, which his loss of faith should have rendered impossible."[17] Bataille remains, one may say, emotionally originally sinful. He believes in taboos and their transgression. In any case, he would not have been the first to devise a philosophy in line with his odd sexual compulsions. Sade can get away with this more easily because he is a poet, whereas Bataille's *Erotism* is grinding philosophical discourse.

For Bataille, as we see, religion and eroticism are similar kinds of knowledge in that each "demands an equal and contradictory personal experience of prohibitions and transgressions" (*E* 39). Transgression is not the same as a back-to-nature or sexual liberation movement, where the prohibition is seen as unnatural—where there is, as it were, a taboo against taboos. Transgression suspends the taboo without repressing it, parallel to the Hegelian *aufheben*, meaning transcendence without suppression. We feel an anguish—another anguish—in violating the taboo since prohibitions are imposed from within. This is the experience of sin. Erotic inner experience, Bataille says, "demands from the subject a sensitiveness to the anguish at the heart of taboo no less great than the desire which leads him to infringe it." Though not orthodox, Bataille insists that "this is religious sensibility, and it always links desire closely with terror, intense pleasure and anguish."

Bataille's is a religious sensibility but finally a pagan one. For the pagan, Bataille notes, "religion was based on transgression and the impure aspects were no less divine than the opposite ones" (*E* 119–20). Christianity made impure sacredness the business of the profane world. In what he calls the Judeo-Christian devil (wrongly, in this case—there is nothing Jewish about Bataille's devil), we see transgression not as the basis of Satan's divinity but of his fall. Ever the modern rebel, Bataille insists that "nothing could stop Satan from being divine" (121). True transgression would have made clear what Christianity concealed, "that the sacred and the forbidden are one, that the sacred can be reached through the violence of the broken taboo" (126). So does eroticism reach its deepest intensity, stepping back only to leap further forward.[18]

Bataille's anthropology has a distinctly Sadean cast. "Corruption, or Evil, or Satan," Bataille tells us, "were objects of adoration to the sinner. Pleasure was essentially transgression, transcending horror, and the greater the horror the deeper the joy" (127). Such are Bataille's strange primitives. But they are not so strange to the readers of Sade. "The books of Sade," says Bataille, "expand these tales; they go much further but still in the same direction. It is always a matter of defying the taboo." All of this was done in the primitives according to rules. Primitive transgression was "organized" but, unlike the Sadean, "limited."

Bataille conceives of man's fate as a Sadean predicament. Given the isolated creature doomed to die, "violence alone, blind violence, can burst the barriers of the rational world and lead us into continuity" (140). Bataille's rational, ordered, or normal world is generally a simplification, sometimes even a cartoonish one, making his violence seem misplaced. "Degradation," he holds, "which turns eroticism into something foul and horrible" is brought on when transgression is impossible. Grim though it may be, degradation is nonetheless "better than the neutrality of reasonable and non-destructive sexual behavior." Bataille rarely lets up on his assault on the middle. Eroticism is the realm of transgression. And since "sexual excitement and ecstasy are always connected with an active sense of transgression," fighting and crime may have a sexual effect. (One recalls an Art, Murder, Sex t-shirt seen recently in New York.) But the Apollonian cannot—neither philosophy nor mathematics, nor "even poetic creation" (248 note 1), presumably of the non-Orphic variety. Bataille usually thinks of art in the service of transgression, art worth its Dionysian weight in gold—a sort of poetic potlatch, transcending the world of work and decency through the sovereign imagination. Art must have "the desire for the prodigal" or settle for being merely restrained, harmonious, Apollonian, and mediocre. Bataille could not conceive of a prodigal realism. Charles Dickens's *The Pickwick Papers* and Saul Bellow's *The Adventures of Augie March* would confound his categories. Nor could he conceive of a rage of goodness, as Dostoevsky did in *The Idiot*. Bataille has no sense that in the struggle for fictional sovereignty, there may be something that transcends transgression. He has no sense of innocence.

In his seminal essay, "The Notion of Expenditure," Bataille notes, sympathetically, that in "the practice of life . . . humanity acts in a way that allows for the satisfaction of disarmingly savage needs, and it seems able to subsist only at the limits of horror" (*V* 117). He laments the fact that, in what he considers the culture of utility, "violent pleasure is seen as pathological" (116). The "so-called unproductive expenditures: luxury, mourning, war, cults, the construction of sumptuary monuments, games, spectacles, art, perverse sexual activity (i.e., deflected from genital finality)" (118) are to him the core of being, immersed as they are likely to be in the destructive element. The energy level, he notes, is "infinitely greater" in these unproductive enterprises than in productive ones. In the case of competitive games, there are crowds of people responding intensely to passions beyond restraint. He notes, too, that tragedy is a form of unconditional expenditure, creation by loss and, therefore, close to sacrifice, which "is nothing other than the production of *sacred* things" (119). He emphasizes the ambiguity of the root meaning of sacred.

In "The Notion of Expenditure," Bataille focuses on the potlatch, or ceremony of the gift "offered openly and with the goal of humiliating, defying, and obligating a rival" (*V* 121). The great thing about the potlatch, however, is the waste, the "spectacular destruction of wealth." Bataille gives an example: "Relatively recently a Tinglit chief appeared before his rival to slash the throats of some of his own slaves. This destruction was repaid at a given date by the slaughter of a greater number of slaves." What Bataille seems to have in mind, even more than his admiration for savagery, is his loathing for the bourgeoisie. "Everything that was generous, orgiastic, and excessive has disappeared," says Bataille, because the bourgeoisie "has consented only to *spend for itself*, and within itself" (124). Gone is the old, generous, notion of public expenditure. The destructive, orgiastic drive of the potlatch—which, as Alan Stoekel says, Bataille considers "man's most fundamental need"[19]—is no more.

Bataille cannot and will not disassociate himself from violence. Most importantly, he asserts that "the domain of eroticism is the domain of violence" (*E* 16). Physical eroticism signifies "a violation bordering on death, bordering on murder," the dissolution of normalcy, the nakedness that disintegrates self-possession. "Repugnance and horror are the mainsprings of my desire," he confesses, insisting that "at bottom we actually want . . . the isolation, the threat of pain, the horror of annihilation" (60). Sexuality and death, he informs us in Sadean accents, are simply "the culminating points of the holiday [that] nature celebrates." The great advantage of sexual violence is that "like death itself, it overturns the structure of life," irrevocably in Bataille's view. He assumes "the violence of death" (106) as if no one ever expired peacefully, in the fullness of time and surrounded by the gifts of a civilized life.

In a striking image from "The 'Old Mole' and the Prefix *Sur*," which reminds the reader of Lawrence's earlier use of a similar image in "The Crown," Bataille compares a plant that "thrusts its obscene-looking roots into the earth in order to assimilate the putrescence of organic matter" with a man who "experiences, in contradiction to strict morality, urges that draw him to what is low, placing him in an open antagonism to all forms of spiritual elevation" (*V* 36). Bataille is drawn to images of waste, to what he calls "excremental fantasy." He has met resistance. At the outset of his career, André Breton condemned him as an excremental philosopher, shrewdly seeing a contradiction between his championing of the excremental and his reasoning about it. Can one really expect to be persuasive about a god who defecates? From time to time, Bataille sounds like a lunatic pedant out of something by Swift, as when he says: "We imagine that it is the stink of excrement that makes us feel sick. But would it stink if we had not thought it disgusting in the first place?" (*E* 58). When it comes to the odor of excrement, Bataille sees another miscarriage of culture. The implication is clear: what human beings need is life on all fours. The philosopher of excrement would like to recapture the salubrious air of estrum or, better yet, the golden age of ass sniffing.

There is no reality that civilization cannot accommodate, and even the insalubrious has its conventions. Pornography and obscenity come as naturally to Bataille as breathing. He does not elaborate much on the word *pornography*, perhaps because it implies, as in Lawrence's famous essay, "Pornography and Obscenity," a dirty way of looking at sex—that is, a derogatory way. For Bataille, the dirty is honorable (Dirty is the nickname of a well-regarded character), aggression showing its life. Bataille more often uses the word *obscenity*, perhaps because of its root meaning, "offstage." The stage is social normalcy—that is, lunacy. Offstage is where the real action is. The stage is where people are dressed. Obscenity is the realm of the naked. In this state, Bataille explains, "bodies open out to a state of continuity through secret channels that give us a feeling of obscenity. Obscenity is our name for the uneasiness which upsets the physical state associated with self-possession, with the possession of a recognized and stable individuality" (*E* 17–18). Bataille is a high-minded defender of "dirty books," even when the sexual context of obscenity is made more explicit. Considering the "continuity" of mortality and the disintegration of "individuality," Bataille concedes that "the key images of sexual activity" in obscenity are "finally" what separates "religious mysticism and eroticism," recognizing with pleasure that "the comparison . . . between manifestations of uncontrolled obscenity and the holiest of ecstasies is thought scandalous" (245). But he insists that "this repugnant sexuality is really nothing but a paradoxical way of giving greater point to an activity which in essence must lead to loss of control" (246). So the anguish of the mystic parallels the anguish of obscenity in its yield of sovereign freedom and bliss.

The ordinary world dissolves much as philosophy (in the sense of reasoned discourse) dissolves, much as the superfluous first-person pronoun dissolves. When it was not reality itself, it was alcohol that precipitated this state of mind in Bataille. He found affinity in Rimbaud's *je suis un autre* and that poet's attraction to the impossible—particularly in the despairing Rimbaud who went beyond literature. Bataille also found affinity in the sensuous mystics of Christianity, St. John of the Cross and St. Theresa of Avila. It was easy for Bataille to sympathize with "those for whom," as Connor puts it, "union with Godhead is less an accomplishment of the keenest minds, but akin to a marriage, or a surrendering." Connor notes that Bataille thereby engages a mystical tradition "divided against itself."[20] Clearly, Bataille is not on the side of the Platonists. Connor rightly holds that Bataille was not a mystic in the sense of transcending space and time, or even in the sense of believing in the mystery of existence. Nothing was painfully clear to Bataille, but everything was clearly painful except for the ecstasy that transcended the pain. In this he resembles Bernini's statue of St. Theresa. Yet her spasms, like those of the young Emma Bovary in Flaubert's famous novel, involve a deep repression that Bataille oddly excludes in his discussions of mysticism. That would involve him in psychoanalysis—which (despite an early, brief psychoanalytic experience), with its emphasis on libido and the structured I, has little interest for him. That would be submitting to what he considers the myth of Freud. With all this, Bataille remains, as Connor holds, less interested in the mystical experience than in the mystic's experience. Above all, Bataille was not interested in mysticism as revelation, or unity with God. His theology is, as Connor puts it, a mysticism of nonbelievers, mysticism without religion, even mysticism without mysticism in the sense that his view yields what he calls "nonknowledge" rather than meaning.

Bataille's outlook is not coherent. He gives us a rationalized explanation of experience while insisting that such an explanation is impossible. His views are based on empirical evidence that implies the existence of the coherent self he denies. The knowledge that he seeks—nonknowledge–is scarcely a knowledge that can be expressed. And it is at the least an ideational contradiction to write volumes on the virtue of silence. Those who do so fall back on the word in the end. To say that Bataille's incoherence is justified because he describes the essential chaos of experience is to give us the philosophical equivalent of the affective fallacy. The description of chaos requires order, the description of formlessness form, the description of unreason reason. Ironically, from time to time, Bataille admits the necessity of reason, even method; recognizes the consciousness of others; even accepts the need for ordinary morality. In these moments, he draws back from the extreme only to recover it. And the extreme remains dominant.

Bataille's ethics is that of the modern rebel. Ethics generally implies the "other," whom Bataille scarcely recognizes. It is in its nature telic, utilitarian, and compromising. The ethical good is Bataille's evil. At the same time evil is, for Bataille, good; admirably, energetically, and compulsively subversive; part of the sovereign morality of the instant. His ethical is the valued impossible, the courage to vault the abyss. Bataille's is an ethics without responsibility, an immoralism. He misses the poetry of morality partly because he wants just that, and partly because he fails to see it.

"Eroticism is the anti-matter of realism," says Sollers in his essay on Bataille.[21] So who needs the everyday, that straitjacket; who needs the normal, that Bastille to impulse; who needs psychobabble, that bourgeois lingo; who needs the "moral," that Judeo-Christian fantasy, that philosophical relic? The only thing to be said about the real world is that it is patently unreal. The human nature it unfolds is a fragment of culture, a linguistic interlude, its common sense a capitulation to the status quo.

The Francophile Susan Sontag gives us a subtle defense of pornography in just these terms. She sees pornography "degraded" because of "realism's standard," the nineteenth-century novel. For Sontag, "it is facile, virtually meaningless, to demand that literature stick with the 'human,'" favoring as she does "extreme states of human feeling and consciousness, those so peremptory that they exclude the mundane flux of feelings and are only congenitally linked to concrete persons—which is the case with pornography."[22] She cites the *roman nouveau* and William Burroughs, among others, as exemplary of the literature of extremity. "Extreme forms of art," she holds, "transcend social personality or psychological individuality" (44). But Joyce and Faulkner manage both the extreme form and psychology. Nor is it clear how the novels of Sade, for example, transcend psychological individuality—they barely comprehend it. The novels of Saul Bellow and the many writers he has influenced show that the human has not been consigned to the dustbin of obsolescence. In praising serious pornography as art, Sontag associates "deranged consciousness" too quickly with "originality, thoroughness, authenticity, and power." What is truest for her in pornography is "the aggressiveness of the intention." It aims at "disorientation, at psychic dislocation" (47). So it does, in its more artistic forms, in very much the terms that Bataille propounds. But when Sontag says that "the emotional flatness of pornography is . . . neither a failure of artistry nor an index of principled inhumanity" because "the arousal of sexual response in the reader *requires* it" (55), she is speaking about the pornography *simpliciter* of Sade rather than the stylized ritualism of Bataille's works that she most admires (*Story of the Eye* and *Madame Edwarda*). Even at that, she misses the significance of apathy or indifference in both Bataille and Sade.

Sontag's defense of pornographic art is cosily *enragé*. She holds that the writer's "principal means of fascinating is to advance one step further in the dialectic of outrage" (45). When she says that "he seeks to make his work repulsive, obscure, inaccessible," she is referring to qualities at which Bataille excels. And when she says that "the exemplary modern artist is a broker in madness," she informs us of this with a deadpan, insistent advocacy that makes us realize that excitement can be tedious, originality boring, and martyrdom narcissistic.

When she moves from the programmatic to the definitional, Sontag is on more solid ground. She defines Bataille's *Story of the Eye* (1928) and *Madame Edwarda* (1941) as pornography "insofar as their theme is an *all-engrossing sexual quest* that annihilates every consideration of persons extraneous to their roles in the sexual dramaturgy, and the fulfillment of this quest is depicted graphically" (60). She notes that "sheer explicitness about sexual organs is not necessarily obscene, it is only so when delivered in a particular tone." The tone in these two works is quite different, but there is something of a hysterical sameness to them. The earlier work is an all-too-youthful—Bataille himself called it juvenile—and the later work an all-too-middle-aged illustration of ferocity. Sontag broadly concurs with Bataille in saying: "It's toward the gratifications of death, succeeding and surpassing those of Eros, that every truly obscene quest tends" (60). She regards *Story of the Eye* as "the most accomplished artistically of all the pornographic prose fictions" of Bataille, and *Madame Edwarda* as "the most original and powerful intellectually," a judgment few would argue with. Sontag helps to define pornography, but she says little about how the works are Batailléan and how they are representative of the genre, scarcely bothering about the author's uniquely dramatic and thematic qualities.

A similar neglect obtains among some of Bataille's best-known French critics, a situation that the author helped (indirectly) to bring about. As Susan Rubin Suleiman says, the "theorists of textuality" (Barthes and Sollers) extend Bataille's notion of transgression to modern writing. *Écriture* to them means the kind of discursive writing that "exceeds the traditional boundaries of meaning, of unity, of representation," while it remains conscious of the logical rules it subverts, thereby paralleling Bataille's transgression-taboo continuum.[23] Suleiman rightly says that Bataille's pornographic works are metaphorical equivalents of key concepts, the fragmentary and incomplete nature of which Derrida called écriture because it denigrates meaning and authorial mastery. To the extent that a text is about the agonized perception of the void, it comments on absence of meaning. But Suleiman points out that these critics say little or nothing about the representational content of Bataille's fiction. (She also argues that Andrea Dworkin, on the other hand, sees only its representational quality, and from a programmatic point of view that reduces *Story of the Eye* to pulp fiction. As Suleiman puts it, Dworkin does not see the fiction but only the ideology she imposes on it.) Suleiman justly concludes that the *TelQuel* critics thereby passed over the sexuality displayed by Bataille on almost every page. It may be, then, that these works are available to what may be called a general criticism, one that balances thematic, imagistic, and psychological qualities.

Not that this kind of criticism is always clear. In writing about *Story of the Eye*, Germaine Brée expresses a typical view: "The incongruous nature and inexplicable succession of strange episodes defy definition."[24] But the aura of mystery that often surrounds *Story of the Eye* may be dispelled by a close reading of its imagistic content in relation to its theme. This is no peripheral concern in a work unified by images. That certain image clusters are prominent in the novel is not news, but the degree of coherence they bring to it deserves another look.

The liquid images, for example, expectedly shocking if vaguely nauseating, focus more uniformly than might be readily perceived on the maudit or degrading quality of the experience conveyed—a world in which nothing is clean or solid, a world permeated by a dirty flux. The experience dramatized is youthful, modern rebellion against authority (parents, church, asylum, life) that takes the form of sexual aggression. Nightmare picaresque, the novel is a clear instance of the literature of ferocity. In its fragmentary nature, its reliance on devices usually considered poetic, and its carefully manicured outrageousness, *Story of the Eye* delineates the lyrical line of ferocity. The story is about the sorrows of a trio—troilism is one of the orders of the day—consisting of a sadomasochistically inclined adolescent boy and girl and their very masochistic female friend. The first-person narrator is the young man; Simone is his girlfriend and Marcelle the third person. The liquid imagery constantly illuminates their relations. It is always symbolic of degradation, abjection, or disintegration, of oneself or the other. The saliva and semen of the first act of troilism, imposed on Marcelle, are indicative of her degradation, as is the rain—which does not serve its usual fertility function. When Simone pisses on her mother from the rafters—this does happen—we see the degrading of a figure of bogus authority. In fact, all authority is bogus. For the narrator, debauchery "soils not only my body and my thoughts, but also anything I may conceive in its course, that is to say, the vast starry universe which merely serves as a backdrop."[25] Transgression debases conventional or Kantian cosmology. However, the usual sadomasochistic slide into dirt, mud, and excrement in the novel is less exalted.

The most conspicuous and dramatic images, as Barthes and others have seen, are those having to do with the eye and its related objects here, the egg and the testicle. The relatedness is not as forced as it may first appear. Beyond their shared elliptical shape, consider the eye as perception, the egg as potentiality, and the testicle as potency. Together, they give Bataille a gold mine of positivity to negate. This is why he can play the images against one another or merge them in a theme and variations on negative transcendence. For Bataille, obscenity is a form of jouissance, transcending the mere plaisir that satisfies most people. They have eyes but do not see. "To others," says the narrator, "the universe seems decent because decent people have gelded eyes. This is why they fear lewdness . . . In general, people savor 'the pleasure of the flesh' only on condition that they be insipid; I cared only for what is classified as 'dirty' " (*Eye* 48–49). So speaks the emphatically retrospective "I" about his sixteen-year-old sovereign proclivities, thereby justifying them. The mixed metaphor—gelded eyes—integrates eye and testicle motifs in an especially concentrated (and repulsive) instance of Bataille's ferocity. What the benighted perceive is not in the service of admired aggression.

Transgression as torment does not take full hold here, as it does in *Madame Edwarda*. Breaking the taboo in *Story of the Eye* is often just a blast, as the expression goes, even if a self-consciously scandalous one. Suleiman says that "the drama of transgression occurs within the subject. ([Bataille] did not have a Catholic childhood for nothing.)"[26] There are many times, though, when Catholicism does not weigh heavily, when it is just part of the joke. It is almost as if Bataille's later theory of transgression developed in reaction to this "juvenile" part of the book. Still, fifteen years after its first publication, Bataille said: "I am as happy as ever with the fulminating joy of *Eye*" (SE 97–98). It expresses the wild, spontaneous aspect of sovereignty without doing full justice to the anguish of transgression.

Story of the Eye is a tale of perception so anguished as to be in a constant state of violent disintegration. In the struggle between Eros and Thanatos, Thanatos prevails. The theme of love in death and death in love connects all the strands of the narrative. Early in the story, the trio's car crashes into a cyclist, killing her. The event is shocking but not unique. "The horror and despair at so much bloody flesh, nauseating in part, and in part very beautiful," the narrator admits, "was fairly equivalent to our usual impression on seeing one another" (5). My love is like a red, red mangled cyclist! He understands Simone's involvement in the destructive element because it is basically his own: "On a sensual level, she so bluntly craved any upheaval that the faintest call from the senses gave her a look directly suggestive of all things linked to deep sexuality, such as blood, suffocation, sudden terror, crime; things indefinitely destroying human bliss and honesty" (6). A fatal car crash gives rise to these remarkable reflections, but it is a bullfight that gives them its most dramatic expression.

As aficionados of the bullfight and readers of Hemingway know, it is a notably alive form of aesthetic primitivism that ideally enacts the triumph of man over nature, or civilization over death. Needless to say, this is not the case in Bataille, where there is no triumph over death. The style and grace of the matador, the triumph of artistic control—in Hemingway's words, grace under pressure—and the expression of an Apollonian mastery over the threat of Dionysian destruction are the opposite of the reality that Bataille wishes to convey. Unlike Hemingway, Bataille does not understand the bullfight in its own terms. He writes, for example, that the bullfighter Granero "just barely eluded a frightful impact" (54). For Bataille, it is all death versus fragile life. For him the bullfight is, finally, the triumph of the destructive element in nature, and, subsequently, in man, in whom a sympathetic ferocity is evoked. The bullfight gone haywire is a perfect venue in Bataille's world for sadomasochistic release. Simone is fascinated by the bull "hurtling out of the bullpen like a big rat." The derogatory simile lets the reader know that nihilism has arrived in the arena. The fighting bulls are symbolic of a natural sadism heightened by culture. They are trained to sharpen their killer instinct, bred to be faultless monuments to masculine aggression.

As Bataille presents the bullfight, the first notable event is a male's destruction of a female. The horns of the bull plunge into the flanks of a mare, a "ludicrous, raw-boned mare... [with] vile bundles of bowels" (56). Simone is excited by this sadistic display: "Simone's heart throbbed fastest when the exploding bladder dropped its mass of mare's urine on the sand in one quick plop." We have in addition, then, the familiar urinary symbolism of degradation and disintegration. The plot thickens, sickens. Simone is in terror, "(which, of course, mainly expressed a violent desire) at the thought of seeing the toreador hurled up by one of the monstrous lunges of the horns." Bataille presents the bullfight as a sexual game enacted on the unconscious. So the bull's thrusts give "any spectator... that feeling of total and repeated lunging typical of the game of coitus." Moreover, Bataille holds, "the utter nearness of death is felt in the same way." He too sees the bullfight primarily as a sexual event, evoking a universal female masochism at the moment of the "prodigious passes." The narrator claims that "it is well known that at such thrilling instants the women jerk off by merely rubbing their thighs together" (56–57). More than any other remark in the book, this one shows the mental distance between the sixteen-year-old observing the event and the retrospective "I" describing it. We see a development in perversity. Bataille's bullring is a sexual tinderbox. Compare the relatively chaste Hemingway,[27] absorbed almost totally in the event. In *The Sun Also Rises* Lady Brett does fall in love with the bullfighter Romero, that civilized product and master of death, but no woman in Hemingway falls for the bull.

Simone desires one particular part of the bull, that ellipsoid of possibility, in this case potency: the testicle. The bull's balls, Bataille reminds us, are "glands the size and shape of eggs.... faintly bloodshot, like the glove of an eye" (*Eye* 60–61). Simone wants them, raw, "before me on a plate" (57). Salome wanted John the Baptist's head served up in similar fashion. In this nutshell contrast resides the decline of decadence. Our contemporary Salome, psychotic and nymphomaniacal rather than just pagan and spoiled, wishes to incorporate the sadistic body (as the testicle, still intact for her even though the bull has been killed) instead of merely subverting the spirit. This is the nature of her necrophilic cannibalism. She bites one of the balls in oral surrender and puts the second in her vulva, a proxy fuck.

Granero's killing of the first bull succeeds in bringing her real intercourse as well. The bloodlust of the protagonist couple is up, and the theatrics of mortality that the bullfight provides cast them into the erotic mode. Simone, the narrator tells us, "witnessed the killing [of the bull] with an exhilaration at least equal to mine" (60). Enough said. They step from "the filthy arena" into an outer courtyard full of "the stench of equine and humane urine . . . We stepped into a stinking shithouse"—in other words, the bower of bliss. "Our mouths cleaved together in a storm of saliva," says the narrator, underscoring the metaphorical liquidity of the scene. They come powerfully. But this is not paradoxical orgasm at the bullfight. After Granero's eye is pierced by the horn of the second bull, a scene enacting the triumph of death over civilization, "a shriek of unmeasured horror coincided with a brief orgasm for Simone" (64). Death, in the form of the bull, has the last laugh on Granero and helps make a woman out of the hysterical, androgynous Simone.

If one may impose Freudian terminology on Bataille, his work is an anguished celebration of id. Underlying this is an aggressive assault on superego, a faculty that plays a negligible part in Bataille's lopsided sense of ego. *Story of the Eye* is a monolithic assault on superego—what could be more ridiculous than the voice of moral authority?[28] Superego takes the familiar forms of parent and church, and neither has authority. Simone's mother is hapless, the narrator's father monstrous. The narrator "judged it provident to decamp and elude the wrath of an awful father, the epitome of a senile Catholic general" (17), thereby killing two birds with one stone. The church has no authority but is authoritarian. The crazy Marcelle asks the narrator for protection when her fantasized cardinal returns, making no distinction between asylum and church. Superego is a threat to her, the authority figure "the priest of the guillotine" (46). She is an impossible combination of piety and blasphemy. The narrator and Simone know how to blaspheme.

The final sequence of the narrative is a violent assault on the Catholic church. It is prefigured ironically in the visit of the narrator and Simone to what is claimed to be Don Juan's tomb at a church in Seville. The tour guide tells them that Don Juan is the church's founder. "After repenting," he says, Don Juan "had himself buried under the doorstep so that the faithful would trudge over his corpse when entering or leaving their haunt" (68). So much for libertinage. And, of course, since this is Bataille, so much for the authority of the church. Don Juan's supposed expression of guilt elicits in the dual protagonists "the wildest laughter."

The cataclysmic final episode of the work sees the priesthood violently degraded and, in the end, destroyed. In this Seville church there is a "blond priest . . . very handsome . . . (with the) pale eyes of a saint" (70). His white purity cries out for defilement, and the cry will soon be heeded. The young priest, Don Ammando, confesses Simone. The narrator confides: "I assumed this sordid creature was going to burst from his booth, pounce upon the impious girl, and flagellate her" (72). He is getting ready to knock the priest down. (His view of experience is often someone beating someone else.) But this is a Batailean church, so no such action is needed. Within breathing distance of the angelic priest, Simone masturbates in the confessional and then confesses it. She grabs his member. He does not resist. She sucks him off, then she and the narrator yank him out of the confessional. Simone slaps him ("the sacerdotal pig"), which gives him an erection. Degradation prevails. Accordingly, Simone pisses on his clothes while the narrator urinates in his nostrils. Simone strikes the priest in the head with the chalice. She and the narrator then make Don Ammando piss in the chalice and drink it. He is sexually aroused and masturbates on the host in the ciborium—Bataille's version of a Black Mass, Sade style. The priest then feels "rage and shame" and threatens "Spanish police . . . prison . . . the garotte" for Simone and the narrator (79). But superego will not prevail here.

O'Faolain observes that Catholic countries produce a particularly blasphemous pornography and the cases of Bataille and Sade certainly support that view. O'Faolain notes that France, sometimes called the first daughter of the church, is "the homeland of erotic writing."[29] The tendency to repression, the hierarchy of authority, the all-inclusiveness combined with its theatrical setting make the church an attractive target for the pornographer. The narrator, then, observes that the altar of the Seville church is "just right for sex" (*Eye* 79). The entrance of the church has paintings of decomposing corpses by Juan de Valdès Leal. In one, an eye is being gnawed by a rat. Bataille's nihilism puts this rat to anti-Christian use. The culmination of this scene can only be death. Sir Edmund, in his factual "English manner," informs Don Ammando that "men who are hanged or garrotted have such stiff cocks the instant their respiration is cut off, that they ejaculate. You are going to have the pleasure of being martyred while fucking this girl." This is a peculiarly insidious accommodation, in that the priest has been longing for martyrdom—to Bataille, every believer is an obsessive masochist. Simone and the narrator strangle him, Simone delivering the coup de grâce—the high point of her sadistic career. In appreciation, the priest's cock stands straight up. Ever the friend, the narrator puts the cock into Simone's vulva. She squeezes until the dead cock spurts inside her. She has, at last, literally made love to death, a macabre *liebestodt*, another necrophilic fuck. She is joyful. The narrator is ecstatic and, after some hesitation, mounts her "hard." Sir Edmund, having extracted an eye from the priest, somewhat pointlessly attempts to put it in Simone's ass. More appropriately, Simone puts it in her vagina, the triumph of id over superego, aggression over perception, sex over vision. The narrative ends with a chorus of liquidity. Ogling Simone's vagina, the narrator envisions the departed Marcelle's eye "through tears of urine" (84): Simone is pissing. A bizarre sympathy with disintegrated humanity, with mortality, prevails. Dressed in clerical garb to outwit the police, the narrator and Simone become fugitives in a fugitive world. A sort of eternal recurrence calms the experiential waters: "Each day, as a new character, I raped a likewise transformed Simone" (85). In Bataille, sexual aggression is another name for a renewed stability.

We have Bataille's reflections on the composition and personal background to this short, showy, difficult, much-praised work of pornography.[30] Since he began the work chiefly to get away from "the things I can be or do personally," that is, through mere personality, he at first thought that "the character speaking in the first person had no relation to me" (*Eye* 89). He tells us that the fiction was woven "out of two ancient and closely associated obsessions, eggs and eyes," with "the balls of the bull as independent." When a friend points out to Bataille that all three are the same shape, it effects "a profound region of my mind, where certain images coincide [this first commentary on the novel is called "Coincidences"], the elementary ones, the completely obscene ones, i.e., the most scandalous, precisely those on which the conscious floats indefinitely, unable to endure them without an explosion or aberration" (92). It turns out, then, that the book is personal in a deep, unexpected way. These remarks are altogether characteristic: profundity is equated with obscenity; consciousness is essentially violent.

In the second part of "Coincidences," we get a harrowing account of Bataille's father and his impact on the book. Paralyzed, syphilitic, his father urinated in a small container, his pupils pointed up as he did. Here is the origin of the author's obsessions with the eye and piss. In this activity, his father had a "completely stupefying expression of abandon and aberration" (93). Bataille is his father's son. Apparently in love with his father at an early age, he begins to hate him—"that supremely nauseating creature" (94)—at fourteen. The syphilitic is now howling mad. When his wife receives medical treatment in another room, he says, "Doctor, let me know when you're done fucking my wife." Bataille writes: "That utterance . . . in a split second annihilated the demoralizing effects of a strict upbringing [and] left me with something like a steady obligation, unconscious and unwilled: the necessity of finding an equivalent to that sentence in any situation . . . this largely explains *Story of the Eye*."

Suleiman's reading here is much to the point: "What the father suddenly reveals (or recalls?) to the son is that the mother's body is sexual. The knowledge that a 'strict upbringing' has always tried to repress, in a male child, is that his mother's body is *also* that of a woman. The recognition of the mother's body as female, and desirable—a recognition forced on the son by his blind but still powerful father—is thus designated as the source of the narrator's pornographic imagination."[31] Suleiman speculates that this is why it is on the woman's body that "the drama of transgression is played out. For the female body, in its duplicity as a sexual maternal and sexual feminine, is the very emblem of the contradictory coexistence of transgression and prohibition, purity and defilement, that characterizes both the 'inner experience' of eroticism *and* the textual play of the pornographic narrative."

But Bataille's agony is even more particularized and intense in these notes. He speaks of his mother to show us that his upbringing was an ideal nightmare. His mother was like Marcelle in some respects. His father went mad. His mother followed suit, "*at the end of a vile scene to which her mother subjected her in front of me*" (*Eye* 95). She is manic-depressive, with "absurd ideas of damnation and catastrophe." Bataille is afraid at one point that she might kill him in his sleep. From time to time, he would strike her and twist her wrists. She disappears, hangs herself in the attic, is revived. Bataille's art has fed on awful memories, in the process "acquir[ing] the lewdest of meaning" (96). A question arises: Because of his disastrous childhood, do we all have to be maudit? And obscenely so?

Bataille's second commentary, (written in 1943, fifteen years after the book's first publication) was ominously called "w.c." He explains that the pseudonym in the first editions of the book, Lord Auch, derives from a friend who instead of saying *aux chiottes* (to the shithouse) would say *aux ch*. In this context, Lord is the term for God in English. "Lord Auch is God relieving himself," Bataille tells us (*Eye* 98). Maybe it is better that he had not. In any case, it is a capstone to his excremental vision. "God sinking into it rejuvenates the heavens," he continues. And more: God "menuring with the majesty of a tempest, the face-grimacing, torn apart being IMPOSSIBLE in tears: who knew, before me, what majesty is?" (98–99). The integration of excrement and liquid is the final word on the God of degraded being, a Gnostic fantasy.

There are other spectacular revelations, not necessarily sequential or even clearly related. He confides that "I jerked off naked, at night, by my mother's corpse" (99), a scene incorporated into *Blue of Noon*. Eros and Thanatos go together in Bataille. In this appendix, he confesses some other Oedipal disturbances. Early in the novel itself, the narrator, rebelling against a repressive father, takes a bath in the father's bedroom, not a bad place to return to the womb—and then pockets his father's revolver. *Ma Mère*, which deals with an all but literal incest, is Bataille's most Oedipal work. His psychotic mother and Laure, his equally psychotic wife, parallel the riven women in his fiction.

Perhaps the most poignant of his revelations in "w.c." has to do with the abandonment of his helpless father in Rheims during the 1914 German advance into France. When the Germans evacuate the city, fear of their return drives his mother mad. After she recovers, they go to see Bataille's dying father, but it is too late: he had gone mad before the war. "So much horror," Bataille says, "makes you predestined" (100). Odd that he uses a theological word when he seems to mean determined. Whatever the word, he admits to a terrible vulnerability. In Oedipal terms, Bataille sees his piety phase (1914–20) as another attempt to abandon his father, who died refusing to see a priest. Yet as the years pass, he comes to a reconciliation of sorts with the man he once accused of making pederastic advances toward him. His pornography is his resolution of the Oedipus complex. "Today," he concludes, "I know I am 'blind' . . . I am man 'abandoned' on the globe like my father" (101). In his father's weakness, he finds strength. And in his mother's relative moral strength, he finds weakness. Surya tells us that when Bataille's mother died in 1930, he wrote in his journal: "Thank God my mother is dead. I am freed from the lie, from the hand capable of helping. My mother is dead, she who stifled."[32]

In this interpretation of *Story of the Eye*, I have gone against the current of poststructuralism by showing that Bataille's feeling of predestination is much more a psychological than a cultural determinism; that the author is present in the work; that the work is unified in terms of personally significant imagery; that it is well suited to thematic analysis, which clearly points to further unity; that the metaphysical quality of this expressionistic narrative is integrated with its imagistic and what might be called its psychological qualities; that, contrary to Barthes, the narrative is not primarily a setting for its precious metaphorical substance; that the erotic component is not simply rhetorical, nor machination in the sense used by Deleuze and Guattari; and that Bataille's obsessional experience deserves its due as such, which also means that it can be evaluated as a representation of experience. These remarks, of course, hold equally true for *Madame Edwarda*.[33]

Madame Edwarda is Bataille's poem of ecstasy. Lyrical, maudit, and inclusive, it is a mature rhapsody on doom. Ecstasy in Bataille *is* agony, the painful pleasure of an erotic squandering that is inseparable from transgression. Eroticism is not liberationist but a sovereign affirmation of violent impulse, the truth of the extreme. "Joy," says Bataille, "is the same thing as suffering, the same thing as dying, as death" (*M* 139). Horror, therefore, is the limit of ecstasy. For Bataille, a love story is a horror story, involving "an *unbearable* surpassing of being," analogous in this last quality to St. Theresa's agonizing ecstasy. Eroticism and mysticism are in this sense similar. "In this *insensate*— this mad-book," Bataille can claim, "we rediscover God" (141). But what sort of God is it that we shall find?

Because of the concentrated lyrical form of *Madame Edwarda* and its perverse, obscure content, a literal plot summary serves as a preface to critical analysis. This is a story narrated by a man who frequents whorehouses and, meeting the prostitute Madame Edwarda in Paris, has intercourse with her twice. After this, she puts on a mask and cape and slips away into the night along Rue St. Denis. Later the narrator finds her again, having convulsions; she finally hits him. Having exhausted herself, she goes with the narrator to Les Halles, the Parisian meat market, by taxi. She straddles the taxi driver in the back seat. The narrator watches them having sex, "lifeless" (157). He offers his reflections on the event, himself drowsy from having fallen asleep in the taxi.

Extravagant as this plot may seem, it is in a sense a familiar one to the reader of modern literature. Edwarda is "bored to death" (149). And the narrator confides that "our two mouths met in a sickly kiss." If this may seem like an intensification of T. S. Eliot's "young man carbuncular" scene from the century's most famous poem, Bataille helps to give this impression: "The room was packed with men and women and that was the wasteland where the game was played." Shortly after, under the Porte Saint-Denis, now sober in the night air, the narrator says: "I felt that I was free of Her"—he has acknowledged that, in her emptiness and absence, "she was GOD." He adds: "I was alone, as if face to face with black rock. I trembled seeing before me what in all this world is most barren, most bleak." In leaving the whorehouse, he has taken the wasteland with him. He never escapes it; in fact, its presence intensifies. Edwarda's convulsions, he later explains, "snatched me away from my own self, they cast my life into a desert waste 'beyond' " (155). But where Eliot considered the wasteland a form of dehumanization, Bataille considers it the essence of the human.

There is no permanence in this universe, but there is an absolute. "Anguish," Bataille says in the epigraph, "is the only sovereign absolute. The sovereign is a king no more, it dwells low-hiding in big cities" (n.p.). The only absolute, then, is the drama of disintegration in the face of the abyss. *Madame Edwarda* is the enlargement of such a moment, taking place in the purlieus of Paris, which might just as well have been one of Eliot's "unreal" cities. The sovereign moment can be mystical in its intensity, and the narrator evokes St. John of the Cross after Edwarda's collapse: "I let myself be absorbed into this unutterable barrenness—into this black night hour of the being's core no less a desert no less hostile than the empty skies" (155). Bataille inverts the Kantian universe (again): the narrator sees "above our heads, a starry sky, mad and void" (152). He does not doubt that Edwarda's "secret," after which he "lusted," was "death's kingdom" (153). The narrator gives perhaps the most vivid expression in Bataille to what convention considers original sin. He warns the reader that "he will only grasp me right whose heart holds a wound that is an incurable wound, who never, for anything, in any way would be cured of it" (155). There is a peculiar insistence here that is attributable to Bataille's pride in being doomed. He holds onto his suffering like a miser holding onto his gold. There is something tedious about this insistence, as if anguish were money in the bank. And it removes him from some of the Catholic ways of dealing with original sin.

The narrator's anguish at Edwarda's seizure leads to a movement typical of Bataille's fragmented world that he calls "sliding," which might be considered neutrally as psychological instability. "The vertiginous sliding which was tipping me into ruin," says the narrator, "had opened up a prospect of indifference" (156). Emotionally anesthetized, he is on his way from erotic partner to voyeur. This is not the exalted apathy of Sade. The narrator plays the voyeur in the taxi scene, after which he carefully observes Edwarda "drifting home from the 'impossible' " (157). Orgasm has taken her beyond limits, but further into the realm of anguish. She lives the "impossible": "the jet spitting from the root, flooding her with joy, came spurting out again in her very tears: burning tears streamed from her wide-open eyes." Eroticism is, finally, a denial of love, as it is curiously impersonal. The taxi driver as person is significantly insignificant, an object to her eroticized subject. "Love was dead in those eyes," comments the narrator, "a transparence where I read death's letters" (158).

Eroticism is the most intense response to death, and thus he can observe "her face swept in ecstasy." Her transfiguration is mystical, and therefore, in witnessing her "pain-wrung pleasure," he has the "exhausting impression of being witness to a miracle." The final turn of the screw is that his own disintegration neutralizes "the rapture of her whom in the deeps of any icy silence I called 'my heart'" (158). The words are carefully chosen. Bataille, or the narrator in this case, does not admit to love but to a sympathetic identity with the riven woman. And he does so not out of fire but out of ice, a passionate but self-annihilating temperament.

Sexually, the relationship of the narrator to Edwarda manifests itself as sadomasochistic. First, there is the narrator's sadistic attraction to the vulnerable Edwarda. He says: "My hands were holding Madame Edwarda's buttocks and I felt her break in two at the same instant" (149). He is attracted to her "thin voice . . . her slender body," both of which he finds "obscene"—that is, seductively destructive of normal perception. Similarly, he notes "her long obscene body." She intuits his perception in her extraordinary description of her cunt: "I guess what you want is to see the old rag and ruin" (150–51). In her own eyes, the overuse of her body by men and her suffering define her. Her life has been a kind of crucifixion, and the willing acolyte bends to kiss the sacred vaginal wounds. That she has been much used heightens her masochistic vulnerability and is the ultimate turn-on for her complicit sadist. But she bears the weight of her vulnerability to the point of breaking—having a convulsive seizure, to be exact—and her aggression inward turns outward. Suffering, she "displayed her behind, snapped her rump up"—as if this were symbolic of female aggression—and attacks the narrator, turning the tables on him: "She tore and hammered at my face, hit with clenched fists, swept away by a demented impulse to violence. I tottered and fell. She fled." The effort is too much, and she collapses—but just before she does, she says: "I can't stand any more . . . but you, you fake priest. I shit on you" (154). Her attempt to unman the narrator is at least temporarily successful. This reversal is implicit at the outset, given Edwarda's masculine variant name and given that she has called the narrator "Fifi," a feminine name sometimes applied to pet dogs. His apparent passivity in the face of her proclaimed divinity is enough to qualify him for a form of priesthood, bastardized though it may be, and on top of which she waves the excremental banner.

An antiphilosopher, Bataille writes pornography as a critique of reason. He says in a note to the preface of *Madame Edwarda* that "this definition of being and excess cannot repose upon a philosophical basis, excess surpassing any foundational basis," excess being "beyond all circumscribing restriction" (145, note 1). An irrationalist and a mystic of sorts, Bataille finds a tenuous permanence in activity that eludes rational categories—indeed, that eludes meaning altogether in the sense of purposively interpretable experience. So after Edwarda's collapse, the narrator says: "This nakedness now had the absence of meaning and at the same time the overabundant meaning of death-shrouds" (154). Absence of meaning is clear enough in Bataille. Overabundant meaning suggests a meaning beyond reason's ability to set right. Belief, as Bataille defines it, is another such overabundance: "GOD figured as a public whore gone crazy—that, viewed through the optic of 'philosophy,' makes no sense at all" (155). Bataille finds insight in the absence of sense or knowledge (*non-savoir*). Yet his narrator finds himself caught in a conundrum: "If nothing has any meaning, there's no point in my doing anything . . . in the end I'll have to let go and sell myself to meaninglessness, nonsense." This would be the ultimate masochism, for *nonsense* in this meaning "is man's killer, the one who tortures and kills, not a glimmer of hope left." The narrator let this part of the conundrum go without resolving it. From inertia, it seems, he returns to his clear obscurity: "I can't conceive of any 'meaning' other than 'my' anguish, and as for that, I know all about it. And for the time being nonsense. Monsieur Nonsense is writing and understands that he is mad." Characteristically, Bataille finds balance in imbalance, order in chaos. The narrator reaches for a conclusion, paradoxical though it may be: "But this madness, the meaninglessness . . . might that indeed be 'meaningful'?" His answer reflects Bataille's lifetime involvement with Hegel and Alexandre Kojève: "No, Hegel has nothing to do with a maniac girl's 'apotheosis.'" In other words, there is no Hegelian reason. Indeed Hegel is sorely lacking in not understanding *la part maudite*, the dark underside that to Bataille is the very essence of life. So the narrator is left with the enervating consolation of nonknowledge. "My life only has a meaning," he says, "insofar as I lack one," and he concludes, lamely: "Oh, but let me not be mad!" King Lear utters the same words but under much more compelling circumstances. There is something self-willed about Bataille's misery. It is at the nadir of what can only be called despair that the narrator utters his well-known, "GOD, if He knew, would be a swine." That is, God does not know; there is no divine omniscience; and, if there were, God would personify the dirtiest of beasts and the excremental vision. The narrator concludes his searing self-analysis by quoting from the religious tradition he repudiates. "O Thou my Lord," he beseeches, "(in my distress I call out unto my heart) O deliver me." "Out of the depths I cry out," *De profundis clamavi*, which derives from the Psalms, is the desperate and incongruous conclusion, if it can be called that, to the narrator's agony. But not quite the conclusion, for it ends with a typically Batailléan fillip: "Make them blind!" (159), a fragment of Oedipal revenge.

The narrator's resistance to meaning is a resistance to words themselves. The four parenthetical comments by the narrator deal with the inefficacy of words, but once more in a paradoxical way. "If you have to lay yourself bare," he says, "then you cannot play with words, trifle with slow-marching sentences" (156). But what else can one do? "Now more words," he sheepishly concedes. Bataille hides uncomfortably behind the obscurantist metaphor of silence. What he gives us is not the clarity of his vision but the experience of its anguished inconclusiveness.

[INTERCHAPTER]

BATAILLE ON SADE

As a writer and a thinker, Bataille is Sade's progeny. Sade is a constant presence in Bataille's mind, though to a considerable extent an evolving one. His earliest references to Sade associate the marquis with the excremental vision. In an early piece, "The Language of Flowers," Bataille thinks of Sade as a prisoner "who had the most beautiful roses brought to him only to pluck off their petals and toss them into a ditch filled with liquid manure" (*V* 14). (This story about Sade is apocryphal.) And the first of Bataille's three essays on Sade, "The Use Value of D. A. F. Sade" (cs. 1930), elaborates on the excremental theme as aggressive de-idealization.[1] Bataille argues that without a "profound complicity" with "the terrifying ruptures of what had seemed to be immutable," without "the fall into stinking filth of what had been elevated," without "a sadistic understanding of an incontestably thundering and torrential nature" (101)—well, what? The logic of this early essay may surprise the reader: "There could be no revolutionaries, there could be only a revolting utopian sentimentality." Bataille's first essay on Sade is a piece of the 1930s, and it is odd to see him link his ferocious master even indirectly with "the world triumph of socialism." His later, far more subtle essays on Sade, in tune with the anthropology of religion, make the point that Sade's value consists precisely in the fact that he has no use, that the nobility of his work begins with its being anti-utilitarian. But even in the 1930s essay, Bataille posits the emergence of a postrevolutionary reality marked by "a division between the economic and political organization of society on the one hand, and on the other an antireligious and asocial organization having as its goal orgiastic participation in different forms of destruction." This latter "use" is the actual Sadean one; it has to do with rebellion and passion rather than revolution and reason. Bataille states explicitly that "such an organization can have no other conception of morality than the one scandalously affirmed for the first time by the Marquis de Sade." Bataille announces: "Since it is true that one of man's attributes is the derivation of pleasure from the suffering of others, and that erotic pleasure is not only the negation of an agony that takes place at the same instant, but also a lubricious participation in that agony, it is time to choose between the conduct of cowards afraid of their own joyful excesses and the conduct of those who judge that any given man need not cower like a hunted animal, but instead can see all the moralistic buffoons as so many dogs." Bataille's anti-bourgeois immoralist animus—which he associates here with the failure of white consciousness and the coming of black revolutionary socialist consciousness—becomes somewhat more subdued in his mature writings but remains fairly constant, unifying his early and late visions.

Even more of a unifying force is his constant consideration of Sade. There is, for example, in *Erotism* generally the expected litany: libertines know the erotic value of murder; death is heightened by the licentious; pleasure is more acute if it is criminal, and the more abhorrent the crime, the greater the pleasure; murder is a pinnacle of sexual excitement; eroticism is to normal conduct what spending is to getting; setting limits to desires is the best way of multiplying them; the urge toward love, pushed to its limit, is an urge toward death. Bataille essentially agrees with Sade in thinking that "eroticism always entails a breaking down of established patterns . . . of the regulated order to our discontinuous mode of existence as defined and separate individuals" (*E* 18) but does not go so far as Sade in abolishing the middle. "In eroticism," Bataille holds, "less even than in reproduction our discontinuous existence is not condemned, in spite of Sade; it is only jolted." And, in as clear and modulated a statement as Bataille can make, he says that "what we desire is to bring into a world founded on discontinuity all the continuity [that] such a world can sustain. De Sade's aberration exceeds the limit" (19). The middle, in the mature Bataille of *Erotism*, is not entirely missing. It is totally absent in Sade, in Bataille's view, because "death . . . stands there more real than life itself." Bataille adheres to the ideas that everyone who can lay claim to being alive must to some extent indulge in extreme practices, and that the ultimate truth resides in these practices.

The mature Bataille considers himself a disciple of Sade who every so often defines himself by disagreement with the master. For example, Bataille makes more complex use of Christianity than Sade does. Bataille argues that Christianity "deepened the degree of sensual disturbance by forbidding organized transgression," as opposed to the organized transgression of primitive cultures, in which transgression implies reverence for the taboo. So when Baudelaire says that the unique and supreme pleasure of life lies in the certainty of doing evil, he is setting transgression in a Christian context. For as Bataille points out: "Evil is not transgression but transgression condemned. Evil is sin. Sin is what Baudelaire means" (*E* 127). The witches' Sabbath, the Black Mass, on the other hand, illustrates the "desire to sin." Bataille notes that Sade "denied Evil and sin [and] so had to introduce the notion of irregularity to account for the bursting of the sensual climax." Bataille's analysis seems inadequate at this point: Sade had other reasons to climax as well. In any case, Bataille is somewhat perplexed at the marquis's blasphemy since Sade "sensed the silliness of profanation if the blasphemer denied the sacred nature of the God that Blasphemy was intended to despoil. Yet he went on blaspheming." Still, Bataille sees a significance to Sade's blasphemy in view of the church's denial of "the sacred nature of erotic activity as part of transgression." Freethinkers like Sade denied what the church held divine as they ceased to believe in evil. For Bataille, this left them in a grave predicament: "Since eroticism was no longer a sin and since they could no longer be certain of doing wrong, eroticism was fast disappearing." This situation arose because "in an entirely profane world nothing would be left but the animal mechanism" (128), even if sin persists as a memory. Sade's kind of eroticism returns as "emotional eroticism, the most ardent kind," so that it "might gain what physical eroticism has lost"—that is, "an ecstatic lucidity . . . bound up with the knowledge of the limits of being" (129).

Bataille's second essay to focus on Sade, "De Sade's Sovereign Man," helps to delineate the character of "emotional eroticism." To do so, Bataille elaborates on his own notion of sovereignty, a psychological equivalent to the potlatch. Bataille points out, though, that Sade's "sovereign individual is no longer a man encouraged to his extravagance by the crowd" (*E* 167). And why should he be, since his victories no longer represent a public good in any sense? Indeed, Sade is more likely to be lynched by at least some of the people in the crowd, a probability about which Bataille seems totally oblivious. He does note that "Sade tried to use the privileges conferred on him by a feudal regime to further his passions." But he wrongly sees Sade as a Jacobin. Bataille notes the contradiction that Sade "propounded . . . a sovereign type of humanity whose privileges would not have to be agreed upon by the masses." To say the least. Yet Bataille is not much interested in Sade's political contradictions but in his transgression of limits. Indeed, the *droit de seigneur* is mild compared to the privileges Sade envisioned for himself. Sade's sovereign man, says Bataille, is "the man subject to no restraints of any kind," who "falls on his victims with the devouring fury of a vicious hound." Clearly, Bataille is using *sovereign* in a narrower, rather different sense here than when he defines it as a quality of consciousness. Yet he expresses his admiration in all seriousness. He does the same for Sade's writing, which "pushed back the limits of what was possible beyond the craziest dreams ever framed by man." The despot as model lover? Complete madness as an ideal? What Bataille wants to convey is that eroticism is one of the few authentic experiences; that harmony between sexual partners invalidates eroticism's "essential principle of violence and death"; and that communion between the participants "must be ruptured before the true violent nature of eroticism can be seen." He does distance himself somewhat from Sade, as if reconsidering his praise, but remains the faithful follower. He avers that Sade's "doctrine is not so wide of the mark as all that. It may deny the reality on which life is based, yet we do experience moments of excess that stir us to the roots of our being and give us strength enough to allow free reign to our elemental nature. But if we were to deny those moments we should fail to understand our own nature" (168). We would deny the denial of reason within us.

Though the modulating Bataille speaks here, his ruminations in this essay are often Sadean in their extravagance. As an example, there is the way in which Bataille elaborates on his nature-civilization antinomy. He tells us that "nakedness wrecks the decency conferred by our clothes" (170), apparently unaware of his melodramatic literalness. And he is astonishingly unaware that there is a decency in nakedness, not to mention a purity. He says that garments—apparently in spite of themselves—show the body "all the more disordered," a strange assertion. He is not speaking about the sexual suggestiveness that many clothing designers strive for, but about the inevitable elevation of the animal within the clothes. In a wild leap, Bataille adds: "Brutality and murder are further steps in the same direction." It takes a logical lunatic to equate taking someone's clothes off with taking someone's head off. Decency is not that indecent.

Bataille's Sadean nature is most clearly exhibited when he goes off the deep end. "Prostitution," "coarse language," "brutality," and "murder" all get him there. These show how "eroticism and infamy play their part in turning the world of sensuous pleasure into one of ruin and degradation" (170), which is, of course, a good thing. Sexual climax is not called the little death for nothing. "Our only real pleasure," says Dr. Waste, "is to squander our resources to no purpose, just as if a wound were bleeding away in us"—a really sick image, and far from the spirit of potlatch in its aspect of conspicuous waste as power. Why is this self-destructive purposelessness the only real pleasure? Because, Bataille tells us, "we always want to be sure of the uselessness or the ruinousness of our extravagance." "We want," according to Bataille, "a world turned upside down and inside out. The truth of eroticism is treason." Sontag would approve. Such are the fruits of modern rebellion.

Sade is the exemplar of this "ruinous" form of eroticism, which, in Bataille's view, involves the essence of the sovereign. For Bataille, this "emotional eroticism" exists primarily in pornography since "actual sovereignty . . . even in its worst moments falls far below the unleashed frenzy that de Sade's novels portray" (171). Moreover it is clear to him that Sade "himself was doubtless neither strong enough nor bold enough to attain to the supreme moment he describes." But he came closer than Bataille's remark would indicate, as recent biographies have shown.

How then does literary sovereignty differ from actual sovereignty in Bataille's view? He notes a paradox in the former. "Theoretically," he says, "denial of others should be affirmation of oneself, but it is soon obvious that if it is unlimited and pushed as far as it can possibly go, beyond personal enjoyment, it becomes a quest for inflexible sovereignty" (174), an impersonal quest since in Sade there is no self to affirm. Agreed. Concern for power, though, "renders real, historical sovereignty flexible." This is because "real sovereignty is not what it claims to be; it is never more than an effort aimed at freeing human existence from the bonds of necessity." And necessity is one concept that Sade never acknowledges, outside of the necessity of enacting sovereign desire. Bataille holds that Sade's sovereign man "has no actual sovereignty; he is a fictional personage whose power is limited by no obligations." But, I believe, he would have no obligations even if he were not a fictional character—Sade felt that he himself had none. Bataille's point is that the fictionality of Sade's sovereign man precludes the recognition by the slave (in Hegel's sense) upon which political sovereignty is finally dependent. The paradox is that though "free in the eyes of other people he is no less the victim of his own sovereignty." He is not free to accept mere plaisir, which Bataille characterizes as "a servitude in the form of a quest for wretched pleasures." This is so, says Bataille, because "Sade starts from an attitude of utter irresponsibility and ends with one of stringent self-control. It is the highest satisfaction alone [that] he is after" (175). In other words, he is after anguished eroticism, emotional sovereignty. "Excess," Bataille explains, "leads to the moment when transcendent pleasure is no longer confined to the senses, when what is felt through the senses is negligible and thought, the mental mechanism that rules pleasure, takes over the whole being" (173). This is a point well made and a good description of what happens in *Madame Edwarda*, but one may balk at making a wild encounter sound like a Hegel seminar. The very abstractness of Bataille's presentation, the totally sublimated enlargement of his experience, calls into question the authenticity of his sensual ethic. Has anyone strained so hard over sex?

Despite all the cerebral pyrotechnics, Bataille's conclusion does not reach beyond the point of romantic cliché. Having described the paradoxical heights of Sade's strange sensual journey, Bataille (following Blanchot) derives a tepid moral. "In the violence of this progression," he says, "personal enjoyment ceases to count; the crime is the only thing that counts and whether one is the victim or not is no matter, all that matters is that crime should reach the pinnacle of crime" (*E* 175). So this is Bataille's higher morality, a sort of Nietzsche on acid. Even Bataille seems disappointed in it. After all, he sees that Sade's sovereign man "does not offer our wretchedness a transcendent reality," in the usual sense of transcendence. And it seems cold comfort to him that "at least his aberration points the way to the continuity of crime! This continuity transcends nothing." It is the monotony of ferocity that "links infinite continuity with infinite destruction." This final flourish scarcely leaves Bataille immune to his own criticism.

Bataille's last essay on Sade shows an exhausted sophistication that has become increasingly defensive. "De Sade and the Normal Man" defines an almost ambiguous relationship between the two authors. It may be a reflection of Bataille's last marriage or his being old and sick. No longer the radical flame-thrower of his 1930s essay, "The Use Value of D. A. F. Sade," nor the proponent of Nietzschean desire of "Sade's Sovereign Man," Bataille here treats the "normal man" with so much deference that one might think he has thrown in the towel. When he notes that Sade "was not against the fool and the hypocrite as much as against the decent man, the normal man in all of us" (*E* 180), he is making a point about himself as well. He is right in saying that an extremist like Sade would find nothing so intolerable as a viable middle, but he is, in that "us," conceding that "normal" in some way includes himself. He would not have made even such a tangential concession in the 1930s, and along with the remarks in the essay on the mitigating tenderness of marriage, it would seem to be a recognition of the limits of ferocity. He goes so far as to say of the Sadean outlook: "Obviously, if it were taken seriously, no society could accept if for a single instant." But he really means literally, not seriously. In other words, Sade, like the author of *Madame Edwarda*, is a visionary whom we should not take literally. The problem with the visionary defense—

especially in fiction, which includes so much particularity—is that it seems to forget that the writer is giving us a vision of something. But Bataille does not make his stand here; in fact, there are more concessions. He has "no quarrel" with classifying sadism as pathological, though he points out that there is sadism in religion as well (e.g., sacrifice). Moreover, he concedes that "short of a paradoxical capacity to defend the indefensible, no one would suggest that the cruelty of the heroes of *Justine* and *Juliette* should not be wholeheartedly abominated." Why? Because "it is a denial of the principles on which humanity is founded. We are bound to reject something that would end in the ruin of all our works" (183).

Yet Bataille remains a true believer—in Sade. He is, willy-nilly, giving the normal-man school enough rope to hang itself. For Bataille, there has always been something wrong with "the principles on which humanity is founded." He notes that Sade's sovereign man "never even disturbed the sleep of the just for more than one moment" (178). Normalcy taken by itself, in short, is an illusion. And "the sleep of the just" is an ironically ambiguous phrase implying more sleep than justice. Indeed, a section heading of the essay simply announces "Vice is the deep truth at the heart of man," which sounds as if it were stolen from the Puritan black mass of "Young Goodman Brown." The subsequent praise of man's "irresistible excess which drives him to destroy," and the "divine or, more accurately, sacred significance" of that excess shows Bataille back in his usual groove. We are back to square one, the destructive element: "Our desire to consume, to annihilate, to make a bonfire of our resources, and the joy we find in the burning, the fire and the ruin are what seem to us divine, sacred. They alone control sovereign attitudes . . . which are gratuitous and purposeless, only useful for being what they are and never subordinated to ulterior ends" (185). We have here the useless value of D. A. F. Sade, in other words. It is with some irony that Bataille concludes that normal men would simply become old men without some sovereign excess, and "the normal man [should] know clearly what his sovereign aspirations are in order to limit their possibly disastrous consequences." But he has not made clear how the normal man can have aspirations that are truly sovereign. These two categories negate each other in Bataille, and blending the two has not been his mission up to this point. Bataille wants the normal man to "accept these [aspirations] if its suits him but not to push them any farther than he needs, and resolutely oppose them if his self-awareness cannot tolerate them."

Can there be a utilitarian sovereignty or a profane sacred, to use his terms? Can Bataille, in his own terms, produce a dialectical middle? I think not. He does not possess the language to do so. Though he does show respect for the taboo being violated, he does not possess a sufficiently complex view of "normal man." In any case, his fiction, devoted almost exclusively to the dramatization of the extreme, shows in its later expression a desperate melancholy rather than reconciliation. There is only the anguished recognition of an emptiness. Yet Bataille says in this essay that he differs from Sade in suggesting that there is "nothing here that could not be made to fit in with" normal man's point of view (185). After reading such a statement, one might even appreciate the integrity of Sade's uncompromising nature. Bataille does not seem to realize that having once opted for the wild horse, there is no alternative to riding him.

As a critic, Bataille says little about literature as such. He is, nonetheless, often interesting—even absorbing—when there is an ideational coincidence between his typical themes and the writer he writes about, as is the case with Sade. But Bataille is so saturated in his own thought that even here he becomes a moral ideologue of the aesthetic. Much powerful criticism does engage the moral imagination to some degree—as it should—but in Bataille one sees literary criticism as essentially the work of a writer struggling to define himself. His deep connection to Sade makes the struggle worth noticing.

9

HENRY MILLER

Henry Miller has not been taken seriously as a thinker, but perhaps he should be. There is even more reflection than sex in Miller, and his ideas are of a kind that clearly place him in literary consciousness. His speculative self is bound to his literary self—he is a writer who claims, however problematically, that there is no difference between himself and his central character, that he is not presenting art but life—and to the topography of a fictional world that even in its startling originality of incident, voice, and tone is, finally, culturally familiar. Consciousness releases the floodgates of expression in Miller when it is the consciousness of ferocity. The result is a stressed expression that manifests itself best in parts rather than in wholes—in sentences, images, and fragmented sections rather than architecture—as if inspiration and understanding came mainly in immediate utterance.[1]

The particular bite of the *Tropics* derives from this consciousness, a world in which apocalyptic dirt is assumed. A familiar passage in *Tropic of Cancer* reads: "'I love everything that flows,' said the great blind Milton of our times . . . I too love everything that flows: rivers, sewers, lava, semen, blood, bile, words, sentences . . . I love the words of hysterics and the sentences that flow on like dysentery and mirror all the sick images of the soul . . . I love everything that flows, everything that has time in it and becoming that brings us back to the beginning where there is never end: the violence of the prophets, the obscenity that is ecstasy, the wisdom of the fanatic, the priest with his rubber litany, the foul words of the whore."[2] This is copiously illustrative of Miller's language of denigration and disease, where rivers and sewers, words and bile, sentences and dysentery—in short, "the obscenity that is ecstasy" is fused into a dominant oneness. The lyricism of the *Tropics* at its most characteristic is a lyricism of aggression. "The scar which I leave on the face of the world will have significance," says the artist as mugger in *Black Spring*, and it must be admitted he was right.[3] For the Miller surrogate, the King James Bible seems to have been a collaboration with the Marquis de Sade. It "was created by a race of bonecrushers. It revives the primitive mysteries, revives rape, murder, incest, revives epilepsy, sadism, megalomania, revives demons, angels, dragons, leviathans . . . revives fratricide, regicide, patricide, suicide . . . revives the power, the evil, and the glory that is God" (*BS* 44). Amen! The meaning here lies mostly in the rhetoric, and the rhetoric is in the attitude. We are clearly dealing with a Bad Boy. Miller's rhetoric, deriving from Romantic rebellion, is tough yet is sometimes misconceived as pretty. The familiar "Coney Island of the Mind," for example, is not the buoyant image of threadbare unreality that some have taken it to be: "Evening is sordid, shoddy, thin as pasteboard. A Coney Island of the mind." Rather than buoyancy, the resonance is far closer to his wisecrack that Lourdes reminded him of Coney Island. Back in Brooklyn, he looks at the ocean, hears its "long uninterrupted adenoidal wheeze that spreads a cleansing catarrh over the dirty shebang," concluding that "everything is a lie, a fake. Pasteboard" (139–40). "Into the Night Life," the title of the piece from which this comes, tells us something about Miller's preferential locales; subjective landscapes are far more real for him than the stupid objective world.

The Miller surrogate, larky though he may be, has an often volatile temperament, and his utterances reflect a certain explosiveness. "The whole continent is a huge volcano," Miller writes; "Everywhere the same fundamental urge to slay, to ravage, to plunder."[4] So much for Europe. America is "a slaughterhouse," he says. At least, it would be if he could do what he wanted to his old neighborhood: "I look at people murderously. If I could throw a bomb and blow the whole neighborhood to smithereens I would do it. I would be happy seeing them fly in the air, mangled, shrieking, torn apart annihilated. I want to annihilate the whole earth. I am not a part of it. It's mad from start to finish . . . kill, kill, kill: kill them all, Jews and Gentiles, young and old, good and bad" (226). Luckily, Miller is powerless to affect anything in the obvious sense. But he can write and does have the greater power to change consciousness. He embraced the Dada Manifesto of 1918, which proclaims in revolutionary style: "Each page must explode" (quoted at 292). So most conspicuously do the pages of *Tropic of Capricorn*, a book he later called "the volcano's eruption."[5] As Philip Rahv has said, Miller was "naive enough" to take the Dada and surrealist "system of verbal ferocity at its face value" in adopting "their self inflationary mannerisms and outcries."[6] Even in the somewhat softer, distanced, analytic voice of *The Rosy Crucifixion*, the message is the same. In *Nexus*, Henry tells Mona: "The only way I can be myself is to smash things . . . Every word I put down now must be an arrow that goes straight to the mark. A poisoned arrow. I want to kill off books, publishers, readers." Having annihilated the respectable world, Miller is left with a familiar alternative of Romantic extremity: "I'd like to write for madmen . . . or for the angels."[7]

"Everything we are taught is false," said Rimbaud, and Miller wanted this epigram engraved on his tombstone.[8] "[Rimbaud] did not 'belong'—not anywhere," says Miller in *The Time of the Assassins* (Miller gets the title from a Rimbaud phrase), his 1946 critical appreciation of Rimbaud, adding: "I have always had the same feeling about myself."[9] More importantly, Rimbaud serves as an avatar of intransigence. Miller explains the shock of recognition: "My language, which had been shocking even as a child—I remember being dragged off to the police station at the age of six for using foul language—my language, I say, became even more shocking and indecent. What a jolt I got when I read that Rimbaud, as a young man, used to sign his letters—'that heartless wretch, Rimbaud.' Heartless was an adjective I was fond of hearing applied to myself. I had no principles, no loyalty, no code whatsoever" (*TA* 15). An antihero as far back as he can remember, Miller knows that honesty—that is, transgression—is the one essential. " 'We must be absolutely modern' said Rimbaud, meaning that chimeras are out of date," Miller explains. Commenting on the results of the Second World War, Miller notes that "the rotten edifice has crumbled before our eyes," a remark that might much more appropriately be made of the effects of the First World War. The Second World War had its heroes and villains, but Miller says never mind to all that. There is no sense of moderating distinction: "Either, like [Rimbaud], we are going to renounce all that our civilization has stood for thus far, and attempt to build afresh, or we are going to destroy it with our own hands" (33). Miller recognizes this destruction of the middle in Rimbaud and deems it heroic: "There was no in-between realm—except the false maturity of the civilized man. The in-between was also the realm of limitations—cowardly limitations" (155). One may legitimately ask whether there are any limitations that Miller would not consider cowardly. Rimbaud serves Miller as an occasion to produce maudit fortune-cookie platitudes: "the place for the genius is in the gutter" (69), "it is only at the gates of hell that salvation looms" (93), and "to earn salvation one has to become inoculated with sin" (103). More engaging is Miller's considering Rimbaud as a bomb that never quite went off. "Rimbaud," says Miller, is "like a volcano which, having spent its fires, becomes extinct." To Miller, even Rimbaud's waywardness is heroic: "This refusal to mature, as we view it, has a quality of pathetic grandeur" (149).

Taking an expression from Rimbaud, Miller calls *Tropic of Cancer* "my nigger book," by which he means it will be "the last word in despair, revolt and malediction" (*TA* 47). We can now see more clearly part of what attracted Mailer to Miller: in effect, the two are the first American self-proclaimed white Negroes, whose message is drenched in apocalyptic rhetoric. Miller waxes positively biblical in *Plexus*: "There will come from all corners of the earth, like the gathering of a whirlwind, a cry of exaltation. 'White man, your day is over! Perish like the worm! And may the memory of your stay on earth be effaced.'"[10]

Though this is more theatrical than anything in the hip Mailer, the iconography is very similar. In the *Tropics*, Miller manages to touch on the subject of murder gingerly, an alternative "lifestyle" as it were. "Only the killers seem to be extracting from life some satisfactory measure of what they are putting into it," he says (*TC* 10). Building on a phrase from Ezra Pound, he adds that "the age demands violence, but we are getting only abortive explosions. Men fall back on ideas, *comme d'habitude*."[11] Murder is a form of creativity for Miller, and he thinks of it as complementary to his work as a writer: "It will be enormous the Book. There will be oceans of space, in which to move about, to perambulate, to sing, to dance, to climb, to bathe, to leap somersaults, to whine, to rape, to murder" (24). Rape and murder may not be everyone's idea of fun, but Miller can get away with it because the more he talks the more obvious it becomes that he cannot perform these acts. The tone works against taking what he is saying literally. Yet in *Black Spring*, too, he thinks of murder as an ideal tendency. In his paean to the freedom of the streets, he notes: "Once you were free, wild, murderous" (*BS* 53). Apparently some of this aggression refers to his account of his early adulthood, when, in his disappointment about not yet saying anything concerning his own life, he thinks: "Ought to go back to the subway, grab a Jane and rape her in the street. . . . Ought to grab a revolver and fire point-blank into the crowd" (110). Later in the book, in a surreal fantasy, we see him mowing down a crowd with a gun (164). Even if not literal, these images suggest a meaning that is troubling enough. Also, there is an assumed misogyny in many of Miller's aggressive fantasies. In *Tropic of Capricorn*, he says: "Don't be disturbed if you see your neighbor going after his wife with a knife: he probably has good reason to go after her, and if he kills her you may be sure he had the satisfaction of knowing *why* he did it" (295). But generally women are the lesser of two evils, society being the greater. And sometimes women represent the voice of sanity, to the extent that this role for women is possible in Miller.

Miller has said that "hatred and vengeance" were the mainspring of *Tropic of Cancer*.[12] "Rome has to burn in order for a guy like me to sing," he holds (109). This self-conscious Nero lives easily in the apocalypse. In *Tropic of Cancer*, Miller and Boris are working on an anthology called *The Last Book*. He thinks of the project as "a bomb which, when we throw it, will set off the world." For some reason no one has been "crazy enough" to yet "put a bomb up the asshole" of our dying world, though it clearly "needs to be blown to smithereens" (*TC* 224). Seated in Paris, Miller sees the world "for the mad slaughterhouse that it is . . . The air is chill and stagnant, the language apocalyptic" (164). Indeed it is. Looking into "this fucked out cunt" of a whore—the epithet is Joycean—Miller receives an epiphany on his home turf: "If any man ever dared to translate all that is in his heart, to put down what is really his experience, what is truly his truth, I think then the world would go to smash, that it would be blown to smithereens and no god, no accident, no will could ever again assemble the pieces" (224–25). In Miller, the apocalypse comes from within. And in *Tropic of Cancer*, Miller is the man who dares. Considering that he is writing at about the time of Hitler's rise to power, Miller's apocalyptic fervor may be suspect: "Let us have more oceans, more upheavals, more wars, more holocausts." We then remember that this energy comes from an unlikely source: "Let us have a world of men and women with dynamos between their legs, a world of natural fury, of passion, action, drama, dreams, madness" (231). Let us have holocausts for the hell of it? Is the American contribution to the idea of apocalypse that it's furious fun, it's a blast? "I am dazzled by the collapse of the world!" writes Miller (*BS* 21). Playing variations on a theme, in *Tropic of Capricorn*, he says: "I am dancing the soul dance of white desperation, the last white man pulling the last trigger on the last emotion . . . I am the germ of a new insanity, a freak dressed in intelligible language" (*TCap* 121). Here we see Miller's most enduring role, the granddaddy of all freaks. "I will be the last man on earth," says Miller, "I will emerge from the show window when it is all over and walk calmly amidst the ruins. I will have the whole earth to myself" (201). Here Miller sounds like a bravado American version of Lawrence's Birkin in his devastated moments. "There was only one headline which still had the power to excite me," Miller writes in the nearly exhausted accents of *Plexus*, "and that was—THE END OF THE WORLD IS IN SIGHT!" (*P* 633). He adds with the curiously solipsistic certitude of his: "In that imaginary phrase I never sensed a menace to my own world, only to 'the' world." Miller seems always protected by the cocoon of an invincible subjectivity, oblivious to the resistance of reality.

Miller's ferocity yields an imagistic harvest of atomization and fragmentation. Nothing is unitary, whole, complete. In Yeats's words, "things fall apart, the centre cannot hold," and Miller is "the rough beast slouching." The language of the *Tropics* particularly gains from this perspective. The narrator of *Tropic of Cancer* is already full of the idea that "nothing is proposed that can last more than twenty-four hours. We are living a million lives in the space of a generation . . . The telephone interrupts this thought which I should never have been able to complete" (*TC* 10). He seems caught in a Heraclitean revolving door, which creates a problem for someone trying to write: "So fast and furiously am I compelled to live now that there is scarcely time to record even these fragmentary notes" (11). More humorously: "How the hell can a man write when he doesn't know where he's going to sit the next half hour?" (29). The sense of things falling apart haunts his love life as well. He thinks, when he and Mona make love after a long separation: "How good to feel her body again! But for how long . . . Will it last this time? Already I have a presentiment that it won't" (17). No, it won't. It can almost be said that theirs was a marriage of atoms, one contingent on its eventual disintegration. The fragmentary added to the fragmentary yields more of the fragmentary, as we shall see in discussing the marriage of Henry and June.

To speak of a particular striking image, Miller serendipitously comes across a book in a window called *A Man Cut in Slices*, or, in one meaning, a man seen from various points of view. The book uses the revolving narrator technique so well suited to the fragmentation of relativity. More than that, the image suggests the disintegrated consciousness of Hegel, the alienated consciousness that tears everything apart in the presumed task of redefinition. "You can't imagine how furious I am not to have thought of a title like that," Miller confesses (*TC* 36). (Actually, he had thought of the image earlier, in *Crazy Cock*, where the Miller surrogate Tony Bring is "a living being cut into slices,"[13] a victim of sharp dislocations.) The image appears crazily in a schizoid projection of Miller's in which the writer is an immoralist: "I tell no one why, after I had put everything down, I suddenly went home and chopped the baby to pieces . . . *Un act gratuit pour vous, cher monsieur si bien coupé en tranches!*" (*TC* 36). Miller easily slides into the idea of the gratuitous as murderous. How is this reconciled with his putatively sunny disposition? Does the fragmentary nature of reality produce a moral vertigo? Is it a world of fragments, a Deleuze and Guattari world? That this seems to be true can even be consoling to Miller: "Today more than ever a book should be sought after even if it has only one great page in it: we must search for fragments, splinters, toenails, anything that has ore in it, anything that is capable of resuscitating the body and soul" (232). Oh, for a slice of life, one might say. And if Paris elicits these fragments, the "atomic frenzy" (61) of New York is even worse.

So much enervation is in *Tropic of Cancer*. *Black Spring* suggests a kind of alternative: memory. But things in that book are not much different. "We live in the mind, in fragments," says Miller; "We no longer drink in the wild outer music of the streets—we remember only" (*BS* 9). In this book the fragmentation is meliorated by the days of his youth, which seem whole, some harmonious "music." Fragmentation may even be seen as a virtue, the fugitive being the essence of art and the artwork itself a mere imitation. Jabberwhorl Cronstadt says in *Black Spring* that "the moment you write a thing the poem ceases. The poem is the present which you can't define. You live it. Anything is a poem if it has time in it" (127). Similarly positive, Miller brags about "all my separate and immortal egos" (162). Is he making a virtue of necessity? Rather it seems the newfound confidence of a writer gliding into a second book rather than the hysteria of a writer creating his first—a hysteria mounting to megalomania, as when Miller announces that *Tropic of Cancer* will last a thousand years. Maybe so. In the last analysis, fragmentation is absorbed by Miller into aesthetic and personal style. "I had a thousand faces, all of them genuine," he says, even though it can be argued that there is hardly any convincing change throughout his work.[14] If anything, there is a monotony. But Miller insists that "wherever I was, whatever I was engaged in I was leading multiple lives." Jay Martin has said of *Tropic of Cancer*, which might have been called *A Man Cut in Slices*, that it is a set of "transparent cubist pieces . . . a self seen now this way, now that, a self existing only in its multiplicity" (293). While this is a fine statement in support of Miller's ostensible views, it skirts the fact that somehow we always come back to the irreducible, unmistakable Henry. Indeed, it might be said that Miller's most signal achievement is not the founding of a technique but the creation of a character.

Mona is his most elusive character. Trying to recapture a sense of her fugitive being in *Tropic of Capricorn*, he muses: "I forget what she looked like, what she felt like, what she smelt like, what she fucked like" (*TCap* 231). He adds: "She changed like a chameleon. Nobody could say what she was really like because with each one she was an entirely different person" (237). Nobody could say but Miller, who presents her in pieces. And there are times when she seems to elude even his devoted eyes. After Mara is exposed by her brother, for example, Miller thinks of the fifteen-year-old tragedienne in the picture and the current Mara of the dance hall. "Neither of them existed any longer," he says; "Nor did I perhaps" (*N* 179). It is clear that one of Miller's main motives for writing is to prove the reality of his existence—and hers.

Perhaps the most notable, although common, image of ferocity in Miller is shit. *Merde! Merde!* All is *merde*, as Gauguin said. Miller is surely a leading exponent of the excremental vision, at least the equal of Alfred Jarry. The phrase recalls Norman O. Brown's chapter on Swift in *Life against Death*. And Miller's use of language recalls Brown's contention that "shame and anality did not exist in the age of innocence" (*LD* 201) as well as Swift's line about "the golden age/to Gold unknown" (quoted at 201). Miller, in the eyes of the Millerites, is the contorted innocent, every wallow an indication of his vibrant saintliness. And Miller is an example of Brown's contention that "the human physical senses must be emancipated from the sense of possession, and then the humanity of the senses and the human enjoyment of the senses will be achieved for the first time" (318). Of course that age of innocence has not yet returned, and Miller may be found flaunting shit like a banner of contorted aggression. Our visionary receives illumination in contemplating a misused bidet. "What a miracle it would be," he opines with religious quavers, "if this miracle which man attends eternally should turn out to be nothing more than these two enormous turds" (*TC* 89). This vision is nihilistic: "That nothing was to be hoped for had a salutary effect upon me—nothing had been destroyed except my illusions." The last statement seems disingenuous since it is not clear that he had any at the time of the manifestation, which seems confirmatory rather than revelatory. But it is a manifestation nonetheless: "I could be no more truly alone than at this very moment. I made up my mind that I would hold on to nothing, that I would expect nothing, that henceforth I would live as an animal, a beast of prey, a rover, a plunderer." His conclusion Brown would applaud: "By what he calls the better part of his nature, man has been betrayed, that is all" (*TC* 90). This being so, aggression equates with survival. "If to live is the paramount thing"—and it is in Miller's view, and that of almost everyone else—"then I will live, even if I must become a cannibal" (*TC* 89). Ahead of his time, he then gives us a high-flown description of the Maileresque term: "I am only spiritually dead. Physically I am alive. Morally I am free." Morality without the spiritual is the Romantic morality of energy. The passage rings with the sense of individual destiny that permeates *Tropic of Cancer*.

Excrement, however, is merely another name for rage in Miller. In *Sexus*, he gets a mystical vision in—of all places—Brooklyn's Gayety burlesque theater, but he panics at the impossibility of communicating it. Beginning to itch "like mad," he looks around at the "meaningless pall" of the crowd and the theater itself.[15] He wants to shock, to yell—"*Shit! Hot shit!*"—but the passivity of the crowd prevents this: "They were dead, stinking dead, that's what. They were sitting in their own stinking shit, steaming in it . . . I couldn't stand it another second. I bolted" (*S* 311–12). Under the pressure of cracking, Miller gives us the word's more or less denotative meaning. Later, Miller is clearer: "*Caca*! The philosopher's stone of the industrial age. Death and transfiguration—into shit! every thought, every deed is cash registered" (471). The idea is Brownian. Miller sees utilitarian, conceptual man "bragging about the miracles of science, yet looking upon the world about as so much shit" (*P* 635). Miller is something of a Luddite, seeing all human progress as a bourgeois hoax. He can stand only so much unreality, and he gets the petit bourgeois version of it from his parents. Minor examples of it that they are, they are inevitably major to him, and they elicit the expected rhetoric as he smolders internally in ancient Brooklyn: "You want to nail me to the chair, make me listen to the shit-mouthed radio. You want me to sit and listen to your inane gossip about neighbors and relatives. You would continue to do this to me even if I were rash enough, or bold enough, to inform you in most definite terms that everything you talk about is so much horse shit to me. Here I sit and already I'm in it up to my neck, this shit" (*N* 106).

Generally, New York itself elicits the true, deep nausea. "In this vomit I was born and in this vomit I shall die," Miller once thought (*N* 169). When he comes back in 1940 as he writes in *The Air-Conditioned Nightmare*, he feels the old "disgust and nausea" about New York, "the most horrible place on God's earth."[16] There seems to be no corruption like the home grown. Filthy lucre is another instance, for Miller a particularly American corruption. In Europe with June he thinks: "In a way we were invaders. With our dirty American dollars" (*AN* 68). Brown would approve of the equation of dirt and dollars. (The Europeans themselves, however, do not seem to mind them.) Even June's irrepressible opening—"and now for the dirt"—conforms to the excremental standard. And it is extraordinary but expected that Miller, recalling images from Blaise Cendrars, says that "the next five lines will ever remain in my memory—extraordinary because the lines are more notable for a certain kind of violence than for anything else. 'On May 10th,' writes Cendrars of World War II, 'humanity was far from adequate to the event. Lord! Above the sky was like a backside with gleaming buttocks and the sun an inflamed anus. What else but shit could have issued from it? And modern man screamed with fear.' "[17] As a writer, then, Miller had an imagination full of visions of excrement. As an individual, he hated filthy toilets and kept house like a regular *putzfrau*. June ridiculed Henry's neatness as she ridiculed his relatively straight views of sex, considering both to be bourgeois excrescences.

But by and large for Miller the writer, cleanliness is the opposite of godliness. Rather, it is an illustration of what he takes to be Protestant anality. "My people were entirely Nordic, which is to say *idiots*," he says in a well-known passage; "They were powerfully clean. But inwardly they stank" (*TCap* 11). That is a typical Miller reversal. He remembers the domestic routine perfectly: "After dinner the dishes were promptly washed and put in the closet; after the paper was read it was neatly folded and then tucked away in the drawers." His parents' was an ethic of delayed gratification: "Everything was for tomorrow, but tomorrow never came." One can see the wish for immediate gratification and Miller's élan festering in this mesmerizing recollection of home. It resounds implicitly in the clarion aggression that opens *Tropic of Cancer*, where the Villa Borghese ambience suggests to him a connection between cleanliness and death: "There is not a crumb of dirt anywhere, nor a chair misplaced. We are all alone here and we are dead" (*TC* 1). Death and cleanliness coalesce again in a chilling image, when Miller describes a central trauma in his life, moving to a better neighborhood from the fourteenth ward: "At ten years of age I was uprooted from my native soil and removed to a cemetery, a Lutheran cemetery, where the tombstones were always in order and the wreaths never faded" (*BS* 53). So much for the living death of the Miller family's newfound respectability. Miller often takes a stand, but his stands may be boring. Take the *Black Spring* incident in which Miller invites home the self-styled Baron von Eschenbach, a customer at his father's tailor shop and a syphilitic. His wife, "one of my first" wives, is outraged: "How could you ask a man like that to sit at the same table with us?" (*BS* 88). She is worried not only about themselves but especially about their baby. The question is legitimate, but Miller soon explodes with rage. The baron is embarrassed. Miller says: "It made me feel so god damned ashamed of my wife that I could have strangled her on the spot." The aggression is misplaced, but Miller will always side with the "dirties" against the "cleans." He loathes the middle-class sense of propriety and will create his own alternative. He insists: "I shall be law and order as it exists in nature, as it is projected in dream. I shall be the wild park in the midst of the nightmare of perfection" (*TCap* 123).

In all these ways, Miller's ferocity may be considered an assault on what passes for civilized order, with the more sedately cultured being the more worthy of attack. We have touched on the white Negro as an instance of apocalyptic reality. But, for Miller, any nonwhite is superior, more human, than the European and American white. How could this not be the case, considering the extent of white rot? "I spit on the white conquerors of the world, the degenerate British, the pigheaded Germans, the smug self-satisfied French," says Miller (*TCap* 33). The alternative to this living death is life: "The little brown brothers of the Philippines may bloom again one day and the murdered Indians of America North and South may come alive." The condescending appellation for Filipino suggests that Miller may be more part of white consciousness than he realizes. And Miller's hope for the Indians has more to do with white self-hatred than with deep commitment to these people. His feelings for non-whites has a utopian cast. "I used to wonder, and I wonder still," he says, "whether essentially the Indian and the Negro will not get together, drive the white man out and re-establish Paradise in this land of milk and honey" (*P* 544). Miller is quite capable of the most dismal bromides on the subject: "White people lack spontaneity. When they laugh it seldom comes from the guts. Usually it's a mocking sort of laughter. The black man's laugh comes to him as easily as breathing" (562).

When it comes to high culture, Miller's preferences are similar. In Paris, for example, he expresses his strong preference for the Oceanic and African Exposition rather than the intellectualism of cubism, without realizing that cubist artists were influenced by primitive art, or that his own fragmented art is analogous to cubism. He writes in a letter that the exposition was the real thing, "the expression of peoples in various strata of civilization who have not been touched yet by the white heart rot of bogus white culture."[18] Too often Miller appears to be a mindless contrarian. In *The Colossus of Maroussi*, he says of the Acropolis: "I like the base of the Acropolis better than the Acropolis itself. I like the tumble-down shacks, the confusion, the erosion, the anarchic character of the landscape."[19] So he tacitly consigns this monument to Western consciousness to the rigid spirit of geometry. It seems odd that in Greece, Miller comes to the following conclusion: "I am done with civilization and its spawn of cultured souls" (*CM* 93).

The boy is the saving white grace. Miller notes that Spengler, in *The Decline of the West*, says that he owes something to Nietzsche's questioning faculty. "Was it so strange," Miller asks, "that in reading Spengler I began to appreciate all over again what truly wonderful thinkers we were as boys?" (*P* 620). But, alas, and predictably, "years of schooling destroyed the art." While schoolboy dialogue in Miller may be vivid enough, neither side of this distinction is notably dramatized. Rather, the hallowed haze of the fourteenth ward gives us a nostalgia thick enough to feed Miller's sentimentality-cynicism machine at full speed. Yet he remains faithful to the Romantic iconography of youth even in his later years. "Every genuine boy is a rebel and an anarch," he writes in *The Books in My Life*; "If he were allowed to develop according to his own instincts, his own inclinations, society would undergo such a radical transformation as to make the adult revolutionary cower and cringe."[20] Here we have the Reichean crusade of unrepressed children, a figure for the age of Aquarius. Miller is the harbinger of that late 1960s and early 1970s moment. Martin tells of an indigent Miller in Hollywood on Christmas Day 1941 speaking euphorically to two store clerks, who had "staked him to a meal of the leftover Christmas special in return for his offer to help them clean up . . . He spoke about the new age, the age of Aquarius, that was ready to dawn, when all that they had known of civilization—war and famine and books—would be wiped out for good, and a new, more human, age would begin."[21] Well, Aquarius has come and gone; it wiped out neither war nor famine—even though it made some laudable attempts—and it added to the proliferation of books.

Miller's animadversions on literature constitute his most curious anticultural stance. He is, after all, a writer, one who wrote so copiously and so endlessly that he has been called "a *voyou* with logorrhea,"[22]—a wildman with word sickness. (Both *voyou* and *logorrhea* are words that Miller used, as Rimbaud used "voyou" before him.) The famous beginning of *Tropic of Cancer* presents us with the paradox that his liberation as a writer came when he cast literature aside. "Everything that was literature has fallen away from me," he says. "There are no more books to be written, thank god" (*TC* 10). The sentiment must be deeply felt—where else does Miller thank God? Of course, God is a figure of speech. "This is not a book," Miller continues. Rather, it is some new, ferocious construct: "This is libel, slander, defamation of character. This is not a book in the ordinary sense of the word. No, this is a prolonged insult, a gob of spit in the face of Art, a kick in the pants to God, Man, Destiny, Time, Love, Beauty." Dismissal of the traditional abstractions is the condition of his emergence. Miller is writing anti-literature, proclaiming that "there is only one thing which interests me vitally now, and that is the recording of all that which is omitted in books." Obscenity, then, may mean honest inclusiveness. Miller is not merely interested in outrage; he wants experience—raw, ungenteel, un-ideal experience. So he can say: "What is not in the open street is false, derived, that is to say, *literature*." Whitman's "barbaric yawp" is Miller's literary precedent, along with Whitman's all-inclusive subjectivity, even if the open road has become a dead-end street. "For me the book is the man and my book is the man I am," says Miller (*BS* 21). The recently published *Crazy Cock*, one of Miller's early novels, sheds some light on what he is saying. In its genteel prose, it is merely literary, but in its focus on Miller's obsessive triangle it is "the man I am." Miller moves from the revolving point of view in *Crazy Cock* to the total subjectivity of *Tropic of Cancer*, becoming, richly, a writer of voice, a producer of literature. Kingsley Widmer's contention that Miller talks about life over literature but actually exalts literature over life makes much sense in this context.[23]

Less ambiguous than Miller's anti-literature is his anti-Americanism. America is the utilitarian, capitalist, scientific place, and therefore: "At the bottom of my heart there was murder. I wanted to see America destroyed" (*TCap* 13). Even more than Mailer, Miller sees an architectural obscenity as he looks at the "hideous buildings of New York . . . No stone was laid upon another with love and reverence; no street was laid for dance and joy" (68). Of course, that is not really true, and who is Miller to speak of reverence? Thinking of America as a whole, Miller says: "What I craved was to worship and adore." So Miller is the courtly lover at heart—no wonder America is not for him. He sees only "a wilderness of steel and iron, of stocks and bonds, of crops and produce, of factories, mills and lumber yards, a wilderness of boredom, of useless utilities, of loveless life" (*N* 326). His anti-American hymn, *The Air Conditioned Nightmare*, was published in 1941, a good year also for assault on America. Rather too confident that "Hitler will pass away," Miller points out that "we have our own dictator, only he is hydra-headed" (*AN* 18), adding that "as Democrats, Republicans, Fascists, Communists, we are all on one level" (21). Even less forgivable is his 1944 statement to an audience at Dartmouth College: "The Nazis are no different than you are. They're fighting for the same things that you're fighting for."[24] Miller's emphasis is on the basic decency of every human being. Least forgivable of all is his continuing to subscribe to a doctrine of moral equivalence even after the war, when all the atrocities were known. "Hitler, for all that has been said against him," Miller writes, "is hardly the brilliant, imaginative demon we credit him with being. He merely served to unleash the dark forces which we tried to pretend did not exist . . . In England and America we have far more realistic, far more ruthless types."[25]

Still Miller points to one American culture with pride, "the only culture we have been able to produce—the rich slave culture of the South" (*AN* 131). That was a rich culture, in some sense, but Miller's view of it is about as accurate as his prediction that "when this [Second World War] is over there will be an exodus to Europe such as this country has never seen" (49). He did not mean a flood of inquisitive tourists. Miller totally failed to anticipate the ascendance of the American cultural style in Europe, not that he would have applauded it or even admitted its existence. And he was forever confronted with the irony that the French—at least some of them—liked naive, generous Americans and dreamed of visiting New York. Above all, he was not yet aware of the great shift in attitudes toward sexual pleasure which took place during his lifetime and for which he came to be partly responsible.[26] As late as 1952, Miller can say: "I believe most earnestly that what repels Americans more than immorality is the pleasure to be derived from the enjoyment of the five senses" (*BML* 112). Small wonder that he sometimes acknowledged that he was out of touch with his own country. Yet there were other times when Miller—a man who pulled himself up by his Emersonian bootstraps, who often exhibited a Thoreauvian intransigence, and who considered Whitman the world's greatest poet and the only great writer America ever had—thought of himself as very American.

Though Miller is in the tradition of American personalism, the individual exaltation that comes from not striving that affirms the character of the unique self, his immoralism shows us how attenuated the strain of American Romanticism has become. The rhapsody of selfhood has become mere relief at survival, the Romantic buoyancy has become "a ferocious gaiety" (*TCap* 64). At the beginning of his best book, Miller proclaims: "I have no money, no resources, no hopes. I am the happiest man alive" (*TC* 1). The inveterate American optimism is perversely preserved in Europe because "here every man is potentially a zero" and "just because there is so little hope—life is sweet over here" (135). So speaks Miller in Paris, circa 1934. The individual is let loose in a world without meaning and without value. The expansion of the American Romantics has become a contraction, their generosity a hardness.

Miller's ferocious gaiety consists in being "unnaturally healthy, unnaturally indifferent" (*TCap* 64). So, for example, "if your best friend dies you don't even bother to go to the funeral; if a man is run down by a streetcar right before your eyes you keep on walking just as though nothing had happened." You expunge compassion, you develop a Sadean apathy, because you see compassion as a lie. You break the thread of connection, yet you are intact. "Loveliness is abolished," Miller holds, "because all values, your own included, are destroyed." You are beyond—or is it beneath?—good and evil. "Today I am proud to say that I am *inhuman*, that I belong not to men and governments, that I have nothing to do with creeds and principles," Miller announces (*TC* 229). Down with all of that, up with apathy; down with convention, up with nature. "I have nothing to do with the creaking machinery of humanity," he says. "I belong to the earth!" Where Lawrence was drawn to the impersonal, Miller espouses the inhuman, as cosmic gives way to immediate gratification. "I could no more think of loving Germaine than I could think of loving a spider," Miller says of a prostitute, precisely the simile used by Dostoevsky's underground man as he contemplates his prostitute. And like the underground man, Miller mocks the sublime and beautiful, thereby releasing an enviable energy of consciousness that enables him to claim that he has more life than the reader. Yet the spider metaphor is chilling, and it refers to a prostitute he likes! He does come back to her but apologizes to the reader for that loyalty: "And if I *was* faithful, it was not to Germaine but to that bushy thing she carried between her legs. Whenever I looked at any woman I thought immediately of Germaine, of that flaming bush which she had left in my mind and which seemed imperishable" (42). This is Miller's burning bush, the symbol of perpetual renewal. He is faithful to a distinctly pagan icon and to a miracle of his own choosing.

Breaking the moral umbilical cord causes problems of its own—notably, the problem of judgment. Take Curley, the seventeen-year-old who "had absolutely no moral sense, no scruples, no shame" (*TCap* 111). This is what Miller likes about him. He had "absolutely no sense of honor ... He would do anything in the world for me and at the same time betray me. I couldn't reproach him for it" (112). Given Miller's proclivities, he cannot call anyone to task. Nor can he be called to task. His friend Alfred Perlès found that he could not reproach Miller for his betrayals, since he would have done the same. As for Curley, "he wouldn't mind sleeping with his mother." Miller envies Curley his total lack of inhibition. He too is anti-Oedipus.

Hardened though Curley is, Miller's behavior upsets him. In a scene from *Sexus* that covers a period some years later, Curley is upset by Mona's attempted suicide and her sense of betrayal (Miller had gone to see his wife). Curley dismisses Miller's feeble claims of loyalty and faithfulness: "You should have been there holding her hand yourself. You're never there when anyone wants you. You were holding Maude's hand—now that she doesn't want you anymore. I remember how you treated her. I thought it funny then—I was too young to know better" (320). So Curley has matured. Miller has only grown older. "You ruin them! You destroy something in them, that's all I can say," Curley concludes. He is thinking also of Dolores at this point, in whom he had an unfulfilled interest, and whom Henry had left stranded, but his anger seems pure. Miller also suspects that Curley is interested in Mona, an automatic and, it appears, low attribution of motive. Many of the "scenes" in *Sexus* are an attempt by Miller to come to terms with what must be called his own guilt—there are all these accusers. But Miller seems impervious—the happy rock! When he makes a move on Maude's cousin Julie, who "was married now, just long enough, I figured, to want a change of rhythm" (390), he admits that "this speech couldn't be laughed off," but lets it go at that. Serious moral revaluation would be unthinkable. A farcical toilet flood is the dramatic resolution, with Miller master of the shitty, ignominious retreat.

Of course Miller is at his best as the heartless bastard, the moral imbecile, but this leaves the question of moral judgment, one that remains more insistent than ever in the light of recent biographies of Miller. It appears that there is less difference than we might want to think between the fictional Miller and the living Henry. A hallmark of the fictional Miller is his flouting of approbation, his constantly selling his birthright for a mess of pottage. In the *Tropics*, his wife cables him money from America, so he goes whoring. He sells his wedding ring for a meal. He tries to bum a nickel from a taxi driver and, when he cannot, gives him his fur-lined overcoat for it. To get money to take the subway to work in the morning, he swindles the blind newspaperman at the station. Caught in flagrant delectation with Mara by Maude, he feels that "everything has worked out splendidly" (*S* 192–93). When Mara chides him for leaving his daughter so willingly, he replies: "I could forget everybody if that were necessary" (215). A dentist works on his teeth for about fifteen months: "When the bill came I vanished" (410). The biographies suggest that most of this is fact. He was never happier, it seems, than when breaking a trust or refusing an offering. He took tuition money for Cornell University from his parents but never went, hiding out at Pauline's house and frittering the money away.[27] His friend Osborn gave him money for food, but he spent it on *Gauloises Bleues*. He signed a contract to get an advance on a book and gave the money away. He collected money for Alfred Perlès to go to Ibiza and spent it on himself (he then confesses to Perlès, who says that he would have done the same thing).[28] He wrote begging letters when he was frequently getting money from abroad. Probably the key to all this is the story that Perlès recounts: as a child, Henry would give away his Christmas or birthday gift, "sometimes the very day he received it."[29] His mother thought him wicked for this, and she may have had something there. How early it was that Miller developed his icy recalcitrance, his familiar *Je m'en foutism!* He did not want to make peace; the more prominent the occasion, the more delicious the embarrassment he could provoke.

Miller's recalcitrance might be viewed as a form of heroic honesty. Why befoul yourself with hypocritical gifts? Why accept things from people you reject? And Anaïs Nin is surely right in noting that Miller's "willed poverty" was "calculated, intentional, out of disdain for the bourgeois who holds a purse carefully."[30] (But to have carried this psychic trope throughout his life is a form of pathology. Even the generosity of his flush years—at the expense of his wife and children—may be seen as the flip side of pathology. As some biographers have pointed out, losing the persona of the impoverished rebel writer deeply depressed him.) Miller would defend his actions as the heroism of immoralism, the élan of the anti-hero: "Even if everything I say is wrong, is prejudiced, spiteful malevolent, even if I am a liar and a prisoner, it is nevertheless the truth and it will have to be swallowed" (*TCap* 13). The appeal is to authenticity, a quality that is presumably foreign to the everyday world. The problematic dossier of Miller the man remains. He pimped for his wife; he posed for pornographic photos; he wrote pornography (as did Nin) for a dollar a page (for example, *Quiet Days in Clichy* and "Mara-Mariguan"); he wrote a promotional brochure for a brothel and got a small commission for every American he induced to visit the place. This is the cold Henry who would often compromise himself—figuratively eat shit—in order to eat a meal. Miller thought that he was like Raskolnikov in Dostoevski's *Crime and Punishment*, but he was much more like the protagonist of *Rameau's Nephew*, the brilliant cynic, ludicrous sponger, and sometime pimp who challenges and revives the ethical "moi" of Diderot.

....

What, then, does Miller value? Any sailor on leave knows the answer. Miller called his protagonist "cuntstruck,"[31] and there are times when one may legitimately complain, as Peter Prescott did in his review of *Genius and Lust*, that "those parts of a woman that lie north of the navel and south of the knees are never closely examined."[32] At these moments, frequent enough in Miller, one feels that when the biographers get the facts straight they will prove that Miller was a midget. There are advantages to this perspective—Miller's rhapsody on cunts, for example (*TCap* 184). He may speak mindlessly of reverence elsewhere, but he is nowhere more reverent than in this hymn to the cunt, irreverent though it is. There are two sides to every story, and in an image from "Into the Night Life," a section of *Black Spring*, Miller gives us the other. He dreams that he is "walking up a treadmill behind a woman" (*BS* 136). This is the story of his life with the good ship woman, fore and aft. In the dream, Miller is taken by the woman's sphinxlike reality: "Written into her fleshless brow was the word sex stony as a lizard." Sex is his mystery, his purgatory, his rhapsody, and his comedy.

Miller is the master of nihilistic sexual comedy. Here he is example and influence. Take the wild scene where he clouts his wife for questioning his lateness. She goes to bed, and Miller screws his neighbor who, coming down to check the ruckus and be helpful to the wife, was bending over the bed. Later his wife cuddles up to him as he plans to take a day off for whoring. He then has his friend's wife. He thinks of many women, falls asleep, and has a wet dream (*TCap* 74–75). Miller considers himself a fucking machine, appropriating the impersonal energy of the dynamo to himself. Bergson argues that the essence of comedy was man acting like a machine, so there it is.

The comedy is, to be sure, degrading to women, yet the fact remains that Miller's comic energies are especially in evidence at just such moments. Curley, for example, "took pleasure in degrading [Valeska's cousin]. I could scarcely blame him for it, she was such a prim, priggish bitch in her street clothes" (*TCap* 180). Far more than Lawrence, Miller has the take-the-starch-out-of-them mentality. The cynical Curley excels at this, titillating even Miller. "Sometimes," we are told, "he'd stand her on her hands and push her around the room that way, like wheelbarrow. Or else he'd do it dog fashion, and while she groaned and squirmed he'd nonchalantly light a cigarette and blow the smoke between her legs . . . then very slowly and gently he shoved a big long carrot up her twat." Serves her right, "Miss Abercrombie and her high-toned Narragansett ways." Miller's Anglophobia mandates a Miss Abercrombie just as, in a strictly pornographic context, it mandates a Miss Cavendish in *Opus Pistorum*.

Probably the most memorable scene of this kind is Miller's encounter with the girl upstairs, a deaf-mute. "She was so obviously a simpleton," he writes, "that I didn't give her any notice at first" (*TCap* 181). Then again, "like all the others she had a cunt too, a sort of impersonal cunt which she was unconsciously conscious of." For just this reason she had hidden springs of desire: "I don't think I ever put my hand into such a juicy crotch in all my life." What else is there to say? Apparently, nothing: "Not a word out of us, as I say. Just a couple of quiet maniacs working away in the dark like gravediggers." A hilarious description, deriving its tang from metaphors of self-incrimination and unlikely work. Miller says, using the adjective precisely, that "it was a fucking paradise" and, as usual preferring body to mind, "I was ready and willing to fuck my brains out if necessary." He concludes along similar lines: "She was probably the best fuck I ever had. She never once opened her trap" (182). He hereby establishes a causal connection between great orgasm and mindlessness—*trap*, of course, meaning mouth, not vagina.

These scenes are so degrading to women and, one might add, to men that they have a certain archaic quality in contemporary America. Does Miller have an unsavory attitude toward what should be considered a tender relation? Absolutely, and he insists on it. "What I particularly wanted was to meet some low-down filthy cunt who hadn't a spark of decency in her," he informs us in a typical moment (119). Such cynicism can be redeemed only by art, if art is redemption. Language, tone, humor—these must be the arguments in Miller's defense. The sense of simultaneous erotic and linguistic release of *Tropic of Capricorn* is continued in *Sexus*. Miller makes love to Mara "right on the sidewalk under a big tree" (*S* 74) like Diogenes, who, as an old philosophy professor once said, performed in public the rites of Venus and was known as the dog. "I began to work on her like a plunger," says Miller; "I went off like a whale" (75). Images from the world of manual labor—plumbing or, at another point, riveting—and from the animal world are Miller's trademark. He describes one arduous encounter with Mara as being "like pushing a piece of still suet down a drainpipe" (180). His friend Carl says of a girl, "she's got a cunt like a suction pump";[33] elsewhere, Miller envisions "the whale with his six-foot penis in repose" (*TC* 2). He brags to Tania: "After me you can take on stallions, bulls, rams, drakes, St. Bernards" (5). Perhaps the hilarious nadir in lack of sentiment and in animal imagery is Miller's thinking of Maude as she feigns sleep: "It's wonderful to fuck your own wife as if she were a dead horse" (*S* 105).

Don't beat a dead horse, as the saying has it, but for Miller marriage is a dead horse made for beating, his most reliable joke. Miller's is the opposite of classical comedy, which rested on the acceptance of the socially axiomatic—as in Molière's *The Misanthrope*, where the eccentric Alceste is finally incapable of dealing with social sanity and is, in effect, cast out. Miller flays the axioms, especially the idea that marriage is a pillar of happiness. Molière's misanthrope gave way to Rousseau, a self-described *homme dechiré*, the original man in slices. That is, the misanthrope has become the agonized Romantic rebel. Has Rousseau morphed culturally into Henry Miller? Only if the ego has become the id. Alceste was laughed at; Rousseau is us—sympathetic but, at times, ridiculous; Miller laughs at. The eccentric has become the norm. Comedy has come full circle. In responding to Miller, we sympathize with heartlessness. No one laughs harder at Miller than himself. The rest of the world tends to be utterly ridiculous or too remote to really matter. This is Romantic solipsism, but with an American, optimistic twist. Miller is a misanthrope who loves life—or, rather, a misogynist who loves life. He may hate the people, but he loves the process. He denigrates the woman but glorifies the cunt. He is a desiring machine, a perfect Deleuze and Guattari schizo. In *Sexus*, the wife of a friend tells him: "You have the instincts of an animal; you make everything subservient to the desire to live . . . A woman wants love and you're incapable of love. If you were a lower type of man you would be a monster; but you convert your frustration into something useful. Yes, by all means, go on writing. Art can transform the hideous into something beautiful" (*S* 53–54). Beauty may not be the word, but she is right. Literature is ostensibly meaningless to Miller, but it is really his raison d'être.

Miller's hard humor rings a bell particularly with those who think of marriage as a farce, a disaster, or some combination of the two, and their number is legion. The painful laughs he elicits assume the modern disintegration. Then there is the suggestion that three hundred years from now, people will read *Othello* and die laughing, married love and fidelity having become the subject of farce. In this context, Miller has an eminent status. It is for the hopeless, divorced, but once-again romanced wife Maude to state the traditional view: "You never love me," she says, "*never*. You've treated me like an animal. You take what you want and you go. You go from me to the next woman—just as long as she'll open her legs to you. You haven't an ounce of loyalty or tenderness or consideration in you" (*S* 467). Furious, she hands him his sandwich and says she hopes he chokes on it. Miller's response is so ridiculously low that one laughs out loud: "As I brought the sandwich to my mouth I smelled the odor of her cunt on my fingers. I sniffed my fingers while looking up at her with a grin." Understandably, Maude says: "You're disgusting." She wonders why he still makes love to her, why he won't leave her alone. "I'm not making love to you," Miller answers; "It's not love, it's passion." True, it is not love, but since passion implies suffering within love, what he really means is sex or, to use an old-fashioned word, lust. Maude complains, rightly, that "you don't show any respect for me—for my person" (469), and then, great masochist that she is, she is torrid with him, for him. The description of their intercourse is one of the best in Miller: "I kept it up like a juggernaut. Moloch fucking a piece of bombazine. Organza Frigenza. The bolero in straight jobs" (474). The suggestion of blind devotion and cruel sacrifice in "juggernaut" and, again, appalling sacrifice in "Moloch" contrasts with the hymenal fabric of "bombazine" and "organza." (Miller coins *friganza*, which suggests frigging and picks up the vowel and consonant euphony of bombazine and organza.) The dance reference of *bolero* adds to the kinesthesia and assonance of the whole. Miller "seeketh only self to please, bind another to his delight, joys in another's loss of ease, and builds a Hell in Heaven's despite." Yet the Blakean context is rather elevated for Miller.[34] The scene ends with the following tableau of transgression: "I walked around the kitchen with my prick hanging out and helped her fix a cold snack" (475).With or without mayo?

These encounters give us vintage Miller: raunchy, spirited, heartless, hilarious. His style speaks eloquently for itself, but the moral vacuum precludes assent. Perhaps the issue comes to a head in one of Miller's *Sexus* reflections. He follows a woman in the subway who has "lithe, vigorous loins. Reminds you of someone, someone just like that, only with a different face. (But the face was never important!)" (*S* 316). The memory "of the ripple and flash of loins" persists, as does the image from childhood of "the bull in the act of mounting the cow." Miller concludes from this that "images come and go, and always it is some particular part of the body which stands out; some identification mark. Names—names fade out. Even the voice . . . But the body lives on, and the eyes, and the fingers of the eyes, remember." While one may—ought to—bridle at Miller's saying that the face was never important, one must admire his courage at insisting on the ultimate sexual reality of experience. Like Lawrence (with his insistence on the magic of touch), Miller is trying to straighten out a culture that has elevated soul or mind or respectability to the virtual exclusion of body. But Miller does so here to the virtual exclusion of face, name, and voice, surely a wretched excess. The mad logic of body over soul—his compensatory logic—is seen clearly in this harsh passage. When he seems to contradict this harshness, he does so in terms that belie the contradiction. For instance in *The World of Sex*, he says: "No matter how attached I become to a 'cunt,' I was always more interested in the person who owned it" (*C* 114)—as if this were something any serious writer would have to make clear! He does not seem to realize that his choice synecdoche is depersonalizing in itself, even with the quotes. Also, the metaphor of ownership implies a degrading concept of property. The truth is, as Miller himself argues, that in most cases he has lost the sense of face, a dehumanizing admission. Perhaps he gives us too many parallels to the animal world.

Even his friends were taken aback by Miller's callousness. Wonderful though many passages from *Tropic of Capricorn* are, the novel elicited a troubled response even from the spectacularly liberated Nin. She complained that the book reduces woman "to an aperture, to a biological sameness—except for June."[35] June, however, did not need the sex scenes and the scene involving her suicide attempt in *Sexus* (which are chronologically prior to the action of *Tropic of Cancer*) to react negatively to Miller's depiction of her. She read *Tropic of Cancer* and threatened to kill him.[36] And she comes off relatively well. His male friends too were troubled by his attitude toward women. Walter Lowenfels exclaims: "As for the poor girls! I never smelt anything more like garbage... How he hated them all, the vinegar of human kindness."[37] Even the cynical Perlès admits that in the course of his first long talk with Miller he "was frequently startled and shocked by the utter candor with which [Miller] described some of the more flagrant acts of betrayal and desertion, especially where women were concerned."[38]

The case for Miller can be made in terms of immediate gratification, and Miller makes it himself. "I want to become more and more childish and to pass beyond childhood in the opposite direction," he says (*TCap* 145), seeking to enter the realm of sexual infancy that Freud called the polymorphous perverse. Freud held that one should grow out of this phase, but Miller's position is that of the Freudian Left. "I want to go exactly contrary to the normal line of development," he insists, and "pass into a superinfantile realm of being which will be absolutely crazy and chaotic but not crazy and chaotic as the world about me"—the eternal justification of both the sexual and the political radical. And Miller is nothing if not a radical of anarchic impulses. For him, there is no alternative: "I have been an adult and a father and a responsible member of society. I have earned my daily bread. I have adopted myself to a world which was never mine . . . I want to pass beyond the responsibility of fatherhood to the irresponsibility of the anarchic man." An assault on reason is involved: "I want to outstrip the inventive man who is a curse to the earth." Above all, he would abolish the superego: "Everything which the fathers and the mothers created I disown," including, at this point, his own daughter. In returning to childhood, he returns to the kinesthetic world and, indeed, to the world of immediate gratification, "a world which I can always touch with outstretched arms, the world of what I know and see and recognize from moment to moment" (146). To touch with outstretched arms—something he could apparently never do with his mother.

Sexual experimentation, the realization of fantasy, satisfies the criterion of touch, reviving the sources of power. The troilism that takes place between Henry, Maude, and Cousin Elsie (a sweaty exercise in pornography and an unbelievable scene, considering the character of Maude) satisfies him in just this way. "There was such a feeling of freedom and intimacy that any gesture, any act, became permissible," says our randy bedroom Raskolnikov (*S* 480). Raskolnikov tries to abolish God; Miller tries to abolish bourgeois monogamy. Miller's paradise is a paradise of the polymorphous perverse. In *The World of Sex*, Miller speaks of "our dream life which offers a key to the possibilities in store for us"—that is, "the Adamic man." What are the characteristics of this American Adam? "For him," we are told, "there are no taboos, no laws, no conventions. Pursuing his own way, he is unimpeded by time, space, physical obstacles or moral considerations. He sleeps with his mother as naturally as with another. If it be with an animal in the field he satisfies his desire, he feels no revolt. He can take his own daughter with equal enjoyment and satisfaction" (*C* 115). Total deinhibition is the salve for all our ills—any kind of incest, bestiality. The resurgence of the id at all costs is the desideratum for this sexual Utopia, a tyrannical agenda. As for the world of the balanced ego, the implied Freudian world, Miller blasts the "medicine men . . . juristic fanatics . . . hair-shirted pedagogues and mystifiers who dominate the scene" and "would have us believe that to partake of a societal life the savage, the primitive being, as they call the natural man, must be hobbled and fettered." He blasts the benign view of repression and discards the usual view of sublimation. "All that is affected, in the name of Society, is the perpetuation of a great lie," he concludes (116). Where W. H. Auden could speak elegiacally of "Eros, builder of cities," Miller, commenting on Spengler's "late-city man,"[39] reverses Auden's emphasis: "And from the dead cock of this sad specimen arose the giant skyscraper with its express elevators and observation towers" (*TCap* 195). So much for Oedipus.

On the theme of delayed gratification, Miller is best not in his high-toned declamations but in his farcical encounters. There is no funnier scene in Miller than the one in which an insurance agent tries to sell him a life insurance policy, while Miller wonders how long it would be before he could take out a loan on the policy. "Supposing you should drop dead one day—what then?" says this commercial quintessence of bourgeois delayed gratification (*TCap* 313). With tears of laughter rolling down his face, Miller says: "Take a good look at me. Now tell me, do you think I'm the sort of fellow who gives a fuck what happens once he's dead?" Little does the good, plodding salesman know about screwing on sight or fucking a dead horse. "I don't think that's a very ethical attitude, Mr. Miller," he says. Miller responds: "Supposing I told you I don't give a fuck what happens to my wife when I die?" Some of the most delicious moments in Miller occur when the world of square benevolence meets the world of hip self-regard. In his fictional world, ethics is a form of garbage, the language of mediocrities. This scene is even funnier than Miller knows.

⁂

Any critique of Miller's crass sexuality must come to terms with June. Theirs is the ultimate fragmented relationship, yet it clearly is different from Miller's usual gestalt. "Day and night I thought of her, even when I was deceiving her," he writes in *Tropic of Cancer* (*TCap* 160). In this disjunction between feeling and act, we see the antihero in love. And Mona (the June character in the book, on whom Mona/Mara is based, is engaged in, among others, a serious lesbian relationship) may be saying pretty much the same thing when she thinks of him. Miller is honest about his cubist passion. He lives in "a Paris that has never existed except by virtue of my loneliness, my hunger for [Mona]" (162). (It is worth noting that June divorced Miller by proxy in Mexico in 1934, the same year *Tropic of Cancer* was published.) Miller's love is again magnified by a condition of ideal absence, his hunger for affection going back, it seems, to his unloved childhood in Brooklyn with the impossible mother. He seems pathetic in his adult reliving of an apparently inescapable separation anxiety. "When I realize [Mona] is gone," he says, "perhaps gone forever, a great void opens up and I feel that I am falling, falling, falling into deep, black space. And this is worse than tears, deeper than regret or pain or sorrow, it is the abyss into which Satan was plunged" (161). A touch of guilt reduces the pomposity. He can neither live with or without Mona at this point. Even in the later *Sexus*, Miller is still haunted by separation anxiety in his relation to the woman now called Mara. "To make absolute, unconditional surrender to the woman one loves," he says, "is to break every bond save the desire not to lose her, which is the most terrible bond of all" (*S* 9). And the figure of a desired mother, with his dependency on her, haunts the imagery of his devotion: "There was nothing I wanted to do except to put myself completely in her hands" (10). (Freudians would point out that both Mona and Mara mimic the word Mama.) Mara is "the one woman in the world whom I can't live without . . . [but she] knew that I was meant to destroy, that I would destroy her too in the end" (200–201). His dependency is inevitably a history of calamities.

A central cause of their fragmentary connection is the character of June herself. Miller writes of Mona: "She had her own wave length: it was short, powerful, disruptive. It served to break down other transmissions, especially those threatened to effect real communication with her" (*S* 432). Is it merely a dramatic irony that Miller is in love with someone he cannot communicate with (Nin, of course, was something else, but their communication was not particularly long-lived), or is it unconscious necessity? Part of June's fragmentary quality is her pretending to be what she is not—a Wellesley graduate, for example. She even lies about her dreams. That her flagrant lies increase Miller's love for her is an indication of his masochistic streak. Her lesbianism is a central part of the fragmentary quality of their relationship. Though they "lay rooted in [their] own bed . . . and fertilized the egg of hermaphroditic love" (437) in a sea of calm, her relationship with Jean Kronski is often pure hell for Miller. Again, did Miller somehow choose someone it would be impossible for him to love permanently? Is there some destructive parallel to his relationship with his mother, or some reflection of his poorly worked through Oedipal reconciliation with his father, the weak alcoholic with whom he could never really identify?

Sometimes Miller just seems caught up in the shower of atoms. Miller notes that as a social actor, Mona "could change with devastating swiftness from role to role" (*S* 507). After Mona and Stasia split, Miller is left dizzy and numb. "I don't think I have any feelings left," he says; "Anyway, I don't want to hear any more about love, ever" (*N* 151). His feelings have been atomized. And well they might be by a love object and patroness who, the biographers agree (along, apparently, with Miller's friends), was a borderline psychotic given to drug and alcohol abuse, a pathological liar who did not know the difference between right and wrong. The beauteous June was an immoralist's dream—or is it nightmare? According to Otto Rank, June was a multiple personality. For Rank, as Jay Martin puts it, June's "rapid transformations, her roles, must be understood as the absolute fragmentation of self: what she did in one case bore no relation to any other. June would hold herself sacred and yet give herself to temptations of any sort of corruption without noticing the contradiction." Perhaps, Martin speculates, "her multiplicity was meant to satisfy Henry's multiple needs."[40] No, but it did do that. Miller, as we have seen, considered himself a fragmented man, and birds of a feather fuck together.

Miller's sadomasochism also makes June the woman for him, as if his sadistic relation to most women (including his wives) found the necessary psychic balance in the masochistic aspects of his relation with her—the twisted *femme fatale* to his scurvy Bluebeard—as if his aggressive reaction to his mother's dominance included a self-lacerating need to submit to her authority and reenact his father's passivity. There are times when Miller seems an unlikely Myshkin to June's Nastasya Filippovna. "Certainly, her tales of her lovers were an aphrodisiac for him, even her deceits increased his passion," Martin correctly observes. "The masochist had found or created his sadist. Henry's divided attitude toward women, whom he regarded as either sacred or sluttish, found its exact equivalent in the way June presented herself."[41] The chameleon June was both madonna and whore.

June is a figure of mythic proportions as early as *Crazy Cock*, Miller's first fictional rendering of the odd triangle. "She rose," says Tony Bring, the Miller surrogate in the book, "and like a queen advancing to her throne, she approached him. His limbs were quaking, he was engulfed by a wave of gratitude and abasement. He wanted to fling himself on his knees and thank her blabberingly for deigning to notice him" (*CC* 28). Bring admits that "he was a cipher which they erased or not, as they pleased" (79), though he does, in a gesture of isolated aggression, lash out at the lover like a sexual McCarthyite: "Are you or are you not a pervert?" (106). The same situation—though in a more vivid, less "literary," language, a language of voice and sharper image—is rendered at the memorable conclusion of *Sexus*. Demoted, Miller thinks of himself as a dog. The lesbians come home together and Miller "wanted to dash in wagging my little tail and throw myself at their feet" (*S* 623). But he manages not to. When he overhears Mona swear to "the big one" that she never loved Miller and hears them "trying to do the man and wife act," Miller has a Dostoevskian fantasy of self-abasement: if he had barked then, "they would have kicked me around like a dirty cur." The unmanned Miller "began to menstruate. I menstruated from every hole in my body, deriving some humor from this physiological comedy" (624). So Miller the masochist may wind up a woman. The dog dreams that he wins a prize for one of the lesbians as an entry in a dog show. She picks him up and is going to take him to bed. "Woof woof!" he cries, in this nightmare involving his female dependency and dehumanization. In *Nexus*, Miller sees his relationship to Mona and Stasia analytically: "The more unwanted I was, the closer I stuck. The more I was wounded and humiliated, the more I craved punishment" (*N* 43). He tries to kill himself, but this too is a fiasco since his doctor friend had given him placebos. (In *Crazy Cock* there is another fiasco: he leaves a suicide note, but the June character does not bother to read it.)

Before the full impact of their lesbian relationship is apparent to him, Miller asserts: "I was quite willing to be made jealous if only I could witness this power she had of making others love her. My ideal—it gave me quite a shock to formulate it!—was that of a woman who had the world at her feet. If I thought there were men impervious to her charms I would deliberately aid her to ensnare them. The more lovers she garnered the greater my own personal triumph. Because she did love me, that there was no doubt about" (*CC* 326). But when—in view of her lesbian relationship—there is not just doubt but certainty, Miller is reduced to howling like a dog, one animal comparison he did not anticipate. The image of a woman with the world at her feet, then, includes him rather too obviously. What would Lawrence think? The masochistic tendency of this passage becomes masochistic obsession, and the words with which Miller concludes are hollow: "I did love her exclusively, only her, and nothing on earth would make me swerve" (327). The masochism involved in his fidelity to her polyandry would be breathtaking if his fidelity rang true. But it does so only fleetingly. Earlier in *Sexus*, Miller puts things in a more characteristic perspective. "I didn't give a fuck how many men were in love with her as long as I was included in the circle," he says (*S* 66), and we are once more in his familiar sliced universe. "I have never been jealous in my life," he asserts, shrewdly adding: "Maybe I had never cared enough." His conclusion is a flat contradiction of fidelity: "The really criminal thing is to make a person believe that he or she is the only one you could ever love." And his experience with her begins to degenerate into a "Where were you?" scene (69).

It is a psychological as well as a logical contradiction in Miller that his relations with women illustrate the madonna-whore complex. Mona/Mara is his richest portrayal in this vein, given that she is, in her dealings with men, the madonna as whore. Her permanent appeal, to the extent that this adjective can be used to describe Miller's feelings, resides to some extent in the realization that the relationship could not last. She is the madonna of innumerable rocks, his desired *femme fatale*. The whore part, as we have seen, is simpler, involving doing dirt on woman (a process that can be occasionally mixed with some benign feeling). Robert Ferguson sees only this part of Miller, holding with Nin that he could not relate to a woman as an equal and a friend, that relating to a woman meant dominating her, and that the truth is greatly at variance with the literary portrait of himself as the adorer of women and prophet of submission.[42] There is much truth to this, but it does not take the fictional evidence regarding June sufficiently into account.

The unambiguous madonna figure in his fiction is Cora Seward, his childhood love. "Why I didn't even think she had a cunt," Miller reflects late in life (*R* 126). She is "the divine, the unattainable Una Gifford, a thousand times more beautiful than MacGregor's prima donna, a thousand times more mysterious, and a thousand times beyond any reach of mine" (*N* 363). Miller is in his late teens, and Cora sits in an appropriately far corner of the room. She is the perfect woman, related to the good mother he had always longed for and occasionally comes across in a friend or relative. Earlier, MacGregor shrewdly observes: "If you were to run into her tomorrow, in the street, you'd probably run away from her," suggesting that there was not much to his longing. Miller responds: "Maybe I would. But that has nothing to do with it." She is an unattainable ideal, the Beatrice to his improbable Dante. Returning abruptly to the present, MacGregor says: "I'll give you two more years with this . . . this what's her name . . . Yeah *Mona*, Mona, Una . . . sort of go together don't they?" (*P* 468, ellipses in the original). Yes, they do, suggesting the one true faith, a sexual monism, Spenserian idealism capitulated to the Bower of Bliss. Is Una dramatically believable in a writer supersaturated in sex? Only as a madonna to his many whores, an index of unresolved sexual tensions going back to childhood. In the irresolution of his Oedipal turmoil, she is the ideal woman his mother never became. This is why, when in what he calls the ghetto, "in search of Jewish cunt," he can think: "What's a fuck when what I want is love?" (*TCap* 224). This brings on a vision of "Una with big blue eyes and flaxen hair." He sobs, enduring the pain of a permanent separation anxiety, realizing that *"you are alone in this world!"* (224–25). In his masochistic mode, Miller fantasizes about Una, "not the Una I had known, but a Una whom years of pain and separation had magnified into a frightening loveliness" (*S* 370). In his fantasy, "our lips with endless searching finally met, closed and sealed the wound which until then had bled unceasingly. It was a kiss that drowned the memory of every pain; it staunched and healed the wound"—his longed-for mother. But Una is soon with another and then transformed, in Miller's fantasy, into the matron "who belonged to another man, the Una surrounded by the spawn of wedlock." Nonetheless, Miller remains her abject, vaguely Dostoevskian, devotee: "From bar to bar I would wander, always looked on askance, always insulted and humiliated, often pummeled and kicked about like a sack of oats. Time after time I would find myself flat on the pavement, the blood trickling from mouth and ears, my hands cut to ribbons, my body one great welter of bruises and contusions. It was a terrible price I always had to pay for privilege of watching her take a breath of air. But it was worth it" (375). Miller is faithful at all costs to the women he never got and typically faithless to the many who were his wives. Ferguson notes that he takes Caryl Hill, whom he thought he would marry, to meet his wife Eve, "subjecting Eve to the same humiliations as Pauline Chouteau, Beatrice Miller, and June Miller."[43] Ferguson believes that Miller was not promiscuous or a conqueror but addicted "to the excitements of 'falling in love'" (337). He was both promiscuous and addicted.

But Ferguson is right in identifying Miller as an erotic solipsist, whose feelings about love were more important than any actual relationship. In the scene dealing with Mona's suicide attempt, there is no actual face-to-face dramatization because Miller is more concerned with his own responses to the event than the event itself. "To be truthful," he admits, "I forgot about my supposed personal loss and became absorbed in a rather blissful contemplation of the desirability of death. I began to think about my own death, and how I would enjoy it" (*S* 324). This is solipsism to the nth degree, a fag end statement of the irrepressible American Romantic optimism. Miller is aware of the absurdly paradoxical nature of the solipsistic component: "Then it came to me: only if she were dead could I love her the way I imagined I loved her!" And Miller is positively clairvoyant about the psychological asymmetry, the narcissism involved: "You did love her once, but you were so pleased with yourself that you forgot about her almost immediately. You've been watching yourself make love." Miller catches himself in the mirror of subjectivity and sees himself in a new light. He thinks he understands his relation to her suicide attempt: "You drove her to this in order to feel again. To lose her would be to find her again." Trying now to win her back, he says of himself: "You're grateful to those who make your heart bleed; you don't suffer for them, you suffer in order to enjoy the luxury of suffering." So we return full circle to the imperious woman with the world, or Miller, at her feet. As for ex-wife Maude, she is a mere decoy. "I didn't give a fuck about Maude" (325), he says in what is not exactly the right metaphor, though it does speak volumes about Miller's—and our culture's—evaluation of lovemaking as insignificance.

Clearly, there are two Millers, the Miller of self-abasement and the Miller of self-inflation. "My whole aim in life is to get near to God, that is, to get nearer to myself," he says (*TCap* 305). Somebody ought to tell him there may be a difference. His friend Osborn did, pointing out that Miller found no one's life important but his own. Miller agreed. His egomania stems from his contempt for the superego. He recalls that at sixteen: "I worked out an ideal universe . . . no money, no property, no laws, no police, no government, no soldiers, no executioners, no prisons, no schools. I eliminated every disturbing and restraining element. Perfect freedom. It was a vacuum—and in it I exploded" (*S* 495). He acknowledges that "I wanted a world made in my own image. I made myself God" (496). He believed this at sixteen. At twenty, he felt doomed but later feels that he retained these beliefs even as an adult, which he surely did. Mary Dearborn says that he possesses "an egotism so massive that one can almost forgive him for it, as one does a child."[44] It certainly would make him a more dramatic writer if he had a better idea of where he ended and the world began. Lack of dramatic effect has always been a problem in American personalism, for the simple reason, as Lionel Trilling puts it in his review of *The Henry Miller Reader*, that "in intense existence as personalism conceives it, there are no other people."[45] Trilling holds that "Miller is full of the ideal of human community, of human connection, and he writes descriptively about particular persons," but Trilling also sees that "in all his writing there is no hint of drama, not even in his fiction, no more than there is in Emerson, Thoreau, Whitman, or Anderson." Trilling contrasts Miller with Lawrence, who "has his own measure of transcendental longing . . . [and] can never for long detach himself from other people: with Lawrence it is always someone else who is decisive in the fate of the person, even if that fate is ultimate withdrawal and isolation."

What is personalism to culture is narcissism to psychology. Regarding Miller, two narcissistic images come to mind. In one, the Romantic solipsist tells us: "I have moved the typewriter into the next room where I can see myself in the mirror as I write" (*TC* 4). This was an energizing move for the egomaniac narrator of *Tropic of Cancer*. It is a wise man who knows his own needs, and Miller cannot get enough of himself. The other image, a more important one, involves the hypertrophy of self, in Quentin Anderson's phrase, familiar in Miller: "I saw an image of myself in the slot machine where the chewing gum was wracked up," says the Brooklynite at the Lorimer Street subway station (*S* 311). He is on the way to the Gayety burlesque. In the unlikely station Miller has had a three- or four-minute "seizure" of inspiration during which his ostensible ego disintegrates into a moment of total power fantasy: "A moment ago I had forgotten absolutely who I was: I had spread myself over the whole earth." Miller recognizes the danger of such psychological solipsism: "Had it been more intense perhaps I would have passed over that thin line which separates the sane from the insane. I might have achieved depersonalization, drowned myself in the ocean of immensity." In contrast with such a heady experience, the actual theater brings on the metaphorical excrement. Looking around at the "common clay," Miller is appalled. He views with contempt the "stinking dead" audience "sitting on their own stinking shit" (312). He bolts. Such fantasies of imperiousness and loathing are only an extreme version of his sadistic quality.

There can be little doubt that the psychological roller coaster of the Miller surrogate stems from the violence of his parents' relationship. Miller becomes conscious of this in his psychological discussions with Nin: "I see that in the women I loved there was always a dual nature—I prostrated myself before them, worshipped them, trusted them blindly, and I regarded them as cruel."[46] Such wild oscillation has much to do with Miller's inability to sustain a marriage for more than seven years, though this particular statement of it is too neutral to explain the ultimate contempt he felt obliged to show even to his relatively long-term female intimates. His mother was far more threatening than the mother in Philip Roth's *Portnoy's Complaint*, with her knife held high. Miller's mother goes one step further. When he comes home to "ask permission" to marry a woman twice his age (obviously there is some Oedipal significance here), "the old lady picks up the bread knife and goes for me" (*BS* 106). And, in the lurid, painfully funny scene where Miller, Mona, and Stasia arrive for Christmas dinner at his parents' home, he associates his mother with the hammer and the carving knife (*N* 103). Martin relates an earlier incident that, given Miller's tender age, was still more threatening: "In October of 1902, at the age of ten, he was suspended from grammar school for being incorrigible, a loafer, and a wild Indian . . . The cold blooded thrashing his mother administered to him on this occasion was calculated to put him back on the right track and it seemed to work for the rest of the school year."[47] It "worked" in unforeseen ways throughout Miller's life. Of course Miller was already a rebel: his mother was actually a physical threat. The young man Miller escapes the domestic madhouse and is out getting a dose of the clap "not to be there for the shindig, with mother and father wrestling on the floor and the broomstick flying" (*BS* 106). Broomsticks, of course, are a tool of witches.

Miller traces his rebellious nature, as he traces Rimbaud's, to the parental matrix, the cold, northern mother who never kissed or hugged him and the soft, part southern, alcoholic father. "Like Rimbaud, I too began at an early age to cry: 'Death to God!'" (*TA* 12). It was death to everything that his parents endorsed and approved of, "the superego world." Miller narrows it down even more: "The demon of revolt had taken possession of me at a very early age. It was my mother who implanted it in me. It was against her, against all that she represented that I directed my uncontrollable energy" (16). He would fantasize a wished-for mother—Karen Lundgren's, for example, or Aunt Caroline. His mother is "peeved" at his feelings about Caroline and considers him "ungrateful, a remark I never forgot, because I realized for the first time that to be ungrateful was perhaps necessary and good for one." The knowledge of ingratitude is the beginning of wisdom in Miller, and this is his personal start. In considering a Catholic girlfriend's concern with his sins, Miller muses: "What sins? . . . I rarely lied, except to my mother. I never stole, except from my mother. What had I to confess?" (*P* 240). Exacerbating his contempt is his mother's refrain: "Don't you think you'd better give up that writing and find a job?" (180).

It comes as no surprise that he idealizes his friend Roy Hamilton for having no family ties (*TCap* 150). In the moving "Reunion in Brooklyn," a returning Miller breaks down, "wept as I had never wept before," at the sight of his parents and their spotless house.[48] "It was," he says, "like a polished mausoleum in which their misery and suffering had been kept brightly burning." After his mother's mortifying treatment of Miller's sick father, she says with all the care an anal compulsive can muster: "Oh Henry, there's a thread on your coat" (115). His father—weak, ridiculed, formerly alcoholic—was occasionally tender toward Miller but was a constant humiliation to him. All this is the genesis of Miller's underlying contempt for women, as opposed to cunts.

Mona, apparently in sympathy with Miller, tells him that her father "was always helpless. My mother sucked the blood out of him. She treated him the way she treats me. Anything to have her own way" (*S* 239). But she adds in a new twist, designed to relate directly to the budding writer Miller: "I think he would have been a writer . . . You always wanted to write—why don't you do it? You mustn't sacrifice yourself for me." "No, let me sacrifice you," says one part of Mona, while the other says, "I will be your patron." With her stunning looks and her maternal support, Mona—or June—seems to be the ideal woman whom Miller had never had in his life. He remembers his first night dancing with June in a metaphor of maternal longing and dependency: "And so, in a swoon, I had let her carry me around the floor" (328). Yet much of June's description of her family life seems to be a fabrication. Martin points out that in another version her father, whom she said she loved, beat her.[49] Henry the sliced loves June the fragmented. They were made for each other.

"Every author I fall in love with I want to imitate. If only I could imitate myself," laments Miller (*N* 230). In this he actually succeeded. Art may be an imitation of life, as Aristotle said, but Miller's art is mainly an imitation of Miller. Certain aesthetic consequences accrue. Since, as George Wickes has put it, "Miller's method is rather like psychoanalysis" in that "he seems to be putting down everything he can remember about the period in hopes that some meaning will ultimately emerge from the mess,"[50] formlessness and repetition are weaknesses inherent in the procedure. There may be something heroic in Miller's willingness to conduct his psychoanalysis in public before there was money in the job, but it does have aesthetic consequences. Miller's chief flaw, as Frederick Crews observes in his review of *Genius and Lust*, is garrulousness, "an attempt to make exhaustiveness stand in place of significance."[51] A novel by Miller is a book unified by whatever Miller happens to be thinking—or so it often seems. "I thought of Melanie," he says, "whom normally, were I planning a book of my life, I would never have bothered to include. How had she managed to inject herself when ordinarily I scarcely gave her a thought?" (*S* 313). Good question, because he includes everything, hence her "significance." He then begins to contemplate the connection between "beauty," "insanity," and "varieties of the flesh" and says that he would get to the bottom of it "even if it took ten years to do" (315). It did but he did not. Often enough in Miller there is a disproportion between an event and the significance he imputes to it, as there is a disconnection between realistic notation and surreal elaboration. Characters are too often mechanically introduced to supply a sense of critique that Miller typically trumps with a florid speech of self-justification, although on other occasions he leaves the challenge unanswered and just moves on to something else. These characters, functional as they are, are often indistinguishable, and the dramatic is easily lost in the all-embracing subjectivity of the whole.

Particularly in reading the inflated enlargement of the Miller saga, *The Rosy Crucifixion*, one agrees with Miller—in a way that he did not intend—that his theme has become more and more inexhaustible. When he and Mona are asleep on the hard floor at Fletcher's place, one is overcome by the desire to let them lie there. When Miller tries to force "significance" the result may be tedious, as in his discourse on seeing and the artist (*S*270–73). At its worst, Miller's writing breaks down into the turgid ramblings of an autodidact (426–431). At these moments, he has an attack of the "positive": "*Everything lies ahead. The way is endless, and the farther one reaches the more the road opens up*" (430). This seems to be an indirect description and unwitting criticism of his method in *The Rosy Crucifixion*. The positive outbursts, which first surface in a major way in *Sexus*, are that much more incongruous in a book in which the sexual theme turns pornographic. Miller's claims for religious sanctity in the trilogy give one pause, as when he approvingly quotes the Russian mystic Fedorov as saying: "Each person is answerable for the whole world of fallen man" (*P* 637). Does he seem himself as answerable? He sees no irony in commenting: "My misfortune, metaphysically speaking, is that I was born neither in the time of Jesus nor in the Holy Russia of the nineteenth century." He does not seem to consider the implications of a reincarnation as Rasputin.

The problem of sentimentality becomes a major one in Miller's work beginning with *The World of Sex*. "A whore," we are told, "if treated right, can be the most generous of souls. Her one desire is to be able to give herself, not just her body."[52] While there is evidence in Miller to support this claim (for example, Mlle. Claude and Gervaise), there is more to refute it. And it is a little late in the day for the reader to take such a claim seriously. The whores of Paris were not deceived by Miller. When he was awarded the Légion d'Honneur in 1976, they staged a protest at the Elysée Palace. Like other Miller "marriages," this one was fragmentary.

We are told in *The World of Sex* that "love is the drama of completion and unification. Personal and boundless, it leads to deliverance from the tyranny of the ego" (*WS* 79–80). Miller may not be an authority on completion and unification in love. Yet he speaks of "a world transformed each day through the magic of love, a world free of death" (119). What occurs in later Miller is that a nice guy progressively replaces the ferocious, atomized, apocalyptic buffoon-savage, the persona that made him an important writer. In his later works, the hands are the hands of Miller, but the voice is that of Norman Vincent Peale. The Greeks spoke of *virtu* as the capacity that is most characteristically energizing. For Miller this capacity is the character of the literary outlaw.

The Colossus of Maroussi, impressive though it is in part, is also infected with sentimentality. "The joy of life comes through peace, which is not static but dynamic," says Miller, as if he were speaking from a pulpit (*CM* 205–6). But if this were possible, Miller as reverend would make his admirers grieve for the rebel they had lost. The impact that the Greeks have had on Miller's psyche, like his overall description of them, is in these ways unconvincing, another example of his tendency to split into extremes of negativity or positivity, cynicism or sentimentality. "For the first time in my life," he says, "I had met men who were like men ought to be—that is to say, open, frank, natural, spontaneous, warm-hearted." The result, claims Miller, is that "Greece had made me free and whole" (210). But Miller is much better in slices; a whole Miller is like having a whole salami. Despite the book's admirable evocations of ancient life in places like Mycenae and Epidaurus, Miller does not go far beyond the impressionistic transcendence of the sensitive tourist. And, as has been pointed out, one would not know from this book that many Greeks of the time were the impoverished victims of a dictatorial regime that they were unwilling to overthrow. Moreover, Miller chooses an odd time to romanticize Greece. Europe is falling apart; the Second World War is about to break out. So even in this distinguished travelogue, he exhibits in his choice of material the peculiar solipsistic vacuum that is his hallmark. Those who hold that *The Colossus of Maroussi* is Miller's best book—including some distinguished critics and, at times, Miller himself—must make this judgment in good measure on the basis of rescuing Miller for the cause of humanism, a sort of cultural death-bed conversion. But it is inconceivable to traduce the major energy of a career—his hilarious, nasty, phantasmagoric, uncompromising comedy, usually sexual—by claiming that its supreme achievement lies in the realm of humanistic expression. It might be nice if it did, but Miller is Miller. Even in his book on classical and contemporary Greece, the dominating Romantic presence of the *Colossus of Maroussi* is dwarfed by him.

If sentimentality is a problem even in the often engaging *The Colossus of Maroussi*, it becomes more of a problem in the prolix, often undistinguished books of his California years. Where *The Colossus of Maroussi* was anchored in a sense of place, classical Greece, *Big Sur* is anchored in what is, for Miller, less engaging turf: family and postwar friends. (Not a nature writer, Miller does not tell us much about the spectacular ambience of Big Sur itself.) Rather than classical Greece, what may come to mind is one of the sentimental interpolated tales from Fielding's *Joseph Andrews* that exalt benevolence. Miller is, finally, "good," and there may be something niggardly in taking him to task for displaying moral qualities found wanting in his ferocious works. But never was there clearer proof that literary judgment rests primarily on aesthetic function, and that morality counts insofar as it is absorbed in an aesthetic context, until that moment when all aesthetic assessments have been made in the mind of the critic. Then moral considerations remain essential to criticism—indispensable to evaluation and at the heart of the critical enterprise. These considerations are particularly relevant to Miller in that he undergoes a conversion to benevolence; the outlaw writer becomes in his later years the family-man writer and a repudiator of his own best work. Miller becomes an American! Old stinkfinger becomes the doting dad.

Toujours l'inconnu arrive as the French say—the unexpected always happens—but who would have expected the *larmoyant*!? As Miller notices the tops, marbles, spoons, and dishes of his kids (who have departed in a custody dispute), he admits that "each little object brought tears to my eye."[53] And when his son Tony says "shit," the impeccable dad says, "You mean caca, don't you son? Or *manure*?" (*Big S* 188). The once and future exponent of the excremental vision weeps with cleansing tears. He says of his little California children: "My eyes are moist with tears as I watch them move tenderly and reverently amid a swarm of golden memories" (21). In a sense, this is an extension of Miller's longtime sentimentality about youth, but the vague, metaphorical quality of the experience suggests a dangerously cloying quality. Miller can actually write: "Will they stand in reverie at the forest glade, where the little stream prattles on?" (22). Miller loves everything that flows, but his prose isn't flowing now. When the language is not trite, it is often just stale, as in the description of Butch riding Tony's bicycle: "Now and then he toppled off, but was up again in a jiffy" (105). The expression *in a jiffy* links Miller inexorably to the species Domestica Americanus, circa 1950.

At this time, Miller is living off the fat of the land, supplied with living quarters and more by materially well-off American friends. He is far from being the total obscurity he was in his early Paris days. Miller has said that being cut off with nothing was the most important thing that ever happened to him. His best writing has an edge of desperation. In 1950s California Miller is already something of a celebrity and somewhat pampered accordingly. "For the first time in my life I found myself surrounded by kind souls who were not thinking exclusively of their own welfare," Miller says (*Big S* 20). They were thinking exclusively of him. While friends demonstrated genuine generosity, Miller found himself in a vulnerable position for a narcissist, the celebrity center of attention gradually transforming himself into the indispensable guru. This process encouraged the sentimentalist in Miller.

Just as children will always be more elevating than adults to him, the poor will always be more noble than the affluent. So Miller says of his new environment: "Just as in Spain one finds the happiest children in all Europe, ragged, barefoot, naked though they often are, and generally filthy and starved—often beggars at three or four—so in Big Sur one has to go to the homes of the poorest family to find that joy and contentment, that spontaneity, that love of life, which the Lopez children ever exhibit" (*Big S* 112). Another sentence is even more cloyingly sentimental: "If I had to choose just one man with whom I would share the rest of my life in the midst of chaos and destruction, I would pick the unknown Mexican peon whom my friend Donner brought one day to clear the weeds in our garden" (118). He strikes Miller as being Christ-like, but Christ was among other things a demanding individual. Nowhere in Miller's writing is there the dramatization of a saintly peon. Nor could there be, given what makes him an engaging writer.

Rambling has always been a problem in Miller's fiction, but in the later, softer Miller, it becomes epidemic. More than ever, he makes exhaustiveness do the work of significance, which results in a new awkwardness, notably manifested in transitions. It often seems that Miller simply wants to write everything down. So he may say: "Here I must interrupt to relate what happened a few minutes ago when I was taking a nap" (126). It is not continuity that motivates Miller, but inclusion. Such transitions as "And now let us pass on to" (217) or "And now for the Essence" (223) are indications of a prolixity that has lost its bearings. These problems are apparent in *The Rosy Crucifixion* and become more pronounced in the California work, where the one-time literary rebel is reduced to quiet days in cliché.

In the moral reversal of his later years, the California octogenarian took a dim view of the voluptuary life. "Sexual revolution? Linda Lovelace?" he says to a 1976 interviewer, as if these two entities represented the identical reality. "Oh, I consider it a misfortune for us that we have created these things . . . Really I am amazed and disgusted . . . More and more I don't think the way I did when I wrote these books [the *Tropics*]. I don't give much of a damn for sex and all that business."[54] He laments the lack of "reverence" in the young. It is almost amusing to see Miller repudiate his metier and come out for positive thinking. The fullest defense of his reversal of values comes in the late *Reflections*: "When I reread passages from those books I'm most noted for even I am shocked by my use of language. Especially in regards to women and sex. I can well understand the rage women must feel having themselves talked about in such a crude manner. One would think that I despise women which couldn't be further from the truth. You see I created a monstrous character in my books and I gave him my name, Henry Miller. He's a demon, a rogue, a scoundrel . . . he thinks he's a great lover, when, in reality, he's a shitty lover! He's always too preoccupied with his own needs and desires to open himself up to the woman's needs. It was mostly exaggeration and bravado, you see? That character was me and *wasn't* me. It's as if there are two Henry Millers" (*R* 91). He concludes: "I was a much angrier man when I wrote those first books than I am today" (92). And, one might add, he was a far better writer. The major problem with this remarkably concessive statement is that there is no body of work that it infuses with anywhere near the same vividness as the work he repudiates. Miller is hardly the master of a moralistic perspective. How authentic is his newfound perspective, when it is not the driving energy in his fiction? It is fascinating to see Miller, in effect, come to the defense of Edmund Wilson, who, in an early review, detected some ironic distance between Miller and the hero of *Tropic of Cancer*. Miller violently repudiated Wilson's view at the time, insisting that there was no distance at all, that he was the character. Wilson, it seems, has had the last word. (But Wilson, taken aback at the immoralism of *Tropic of Cancer*, did not realize that Miller meant the reader to be sympathetic to it.) And Miller goes beyond even this admission of distance. He repudiates the rogue voluptuary whom most readers consider the heart of his achievement, particularly on—of all charges—the charge of insufferable narcissism.

Many critics hold the view that Miller is really a one-book man, and that book is *Tropic of Cancer*. Crews, for example, says that, as with most revolutionaries, Miller's reputation rests on one book; that after this major work, he went on to sure-fire stunts like sexual gymnastics, bombast against authority, and surrealistic fantasy; and that his opinion of himself and others undergoes a fatal softening.[55] Mailer too regards *Tropic of Cancer* as Miller's one major work and accepts the conventional wisdom that *The Rosy Crucifixion* in relation to the *Tropics* is twice as long and half as good. My own view is that *Tropic of Capricorn* is not too far behind *Tropic of Cancer*: though it does not sustain the manic, concentrated prose of *Tropic of Cancer*, it has at least as much of the diabolical hilarity and, in spots, a Rabelaisian lyricism that rivals the fierce tone of the earlier novel. *Black Spring* is too fragmented to be called a novel and, in any case, it is marred by a literary pretentiousness despite fine set pieces like "The Tailor Shop." And *The Rosy Crucifixion* has powerful moments, particularly the harrowing scenes of *Sexus*, but Miller is writing more and more about less and less. *The Rosy Crucifixion* becomes boring—even the author could not finish it.

Miller is a writer of the immediate sensual impression, and he uniformly produces the prose adequate to such a task only once, in *Tropic of Cancer*. *Black Spring*, *Tropic of Capricorn*, and *The Rosy Crucifixion* are more about his past. It appears that Miller is best at the present, not as good as a writer of the distantly retrospective. His consciousness does not soar in memory; his memory is not so richly transforming because his consciousness is not sufficiently complex. Moreover, as Kingsley Widmer says, the two decades devoted to *The Rosy Crucifixion* (actually, Miller was thinking about it as early as 1927 and "completed" it in 1959) were a "violation of Miller's own aesthetic," so that his "style of colloquial immediacy becomes dominated by triteness."[56] The major Miller is the literary outlaw, and Miller writing well was his own best revenge.

In 1965 *Publisher's Weekly* reported that of the five best-selling books in America, Miller had written three. The big sale years of *Tropic of Cancer* and

Tropic of Capricorn were already over, and the titles were the unlikely *The World of Sex*, a tepid defense popular, perhaps, because of its title; *Quiet Days in Clichy*, an admitted work of pornography; and *The Rosy Crucifixion*, which some considered Miller's masterpiece, his big book. The message is clear enough: America was starved for the literature of sexual liberation. And the winds of rebellion were beginning to stir. Only in a Puritan country could his writing have had such a liberating force, and only in a post-Marxist America could he stand as an avatar of revolution. Only after ideology had given way to antinomian gesture could his anarchic, salvationary subjectivity make him the ur-rebel without a cause. His sexual radicalism, laughable to Communist politicians in the East, found an audience in his once-despised America among the young who, following the Beats, were soon to be making revolution for the hell of it. They thereby cast Miller in a political context he never could have recognized. Raunchy, sneering, foulmouthed, laughing on the dung heap, Miller became an icon for the dirties. What were the *Weltschmerz* delicacies of Fitzgerald and Hemingway to the immoralist buoyancy of Miller for a generation hellbent on fun, the beginning of which was the destruction of straight authority. There was even the link of a dubious Eastern mysticism, a best-of-both-worlds religiosity that does not recognize that such mysticism is partly contingent on an overcoming of the erotic. Yes, Miller has had his day, his crazy decade or so. But the triumph of permissiveness has made his radicalism less urgent, and the rise of serious feminism makes his portrayal of women less acceptable.

In talking to colleagues about Miller as a writer of ferocity, I was struck by the questioning look I received from an occasional male colleague, as if Miller had no animosity toward women. Nothing speaks more clearly to the still fairly prevalent chauvinism assumed by our culture than the failure to see the misogynistic strain in Miller. It speaks to a feeling so general that some cannot perceive it. Those searching for an elevating meaning to sex in Miller's fiction will have a hard time finding it. In contrast to Lawrence, with whom he is sometimes compared, there is in Miller, as Kermode puts it, "no rebirth or escape from debased sexuality."[57] This is why, even in *Tropic of Cancer*, Kermode rightly sees a disparity between Miller's sense of mission and the antic bedroom disposition of the key episodes. Lawrence is talking about salvation. With the notable failed exception of Mona, Miller is talking about fornication, not salvation, and there is no such thing as a born-again fornicator. Miller remains, as Widmer puts it, a minor writer who has had a major influence.[58] His reputation has fallen (partly, it is true, through assimilation) because he hung too much on a small peg.

[INTERCHAPTER]

MILLER ON LAWRENCE

Even if it were not the underrated work of criticism that it is, Miller's study of Lawrence should be considered necessary reading merely because of its author and subject. Certainly in retrospect, the writing of *The World of Lawrence* was a literary occasion. A modern American novelist of sex writes a book about his English contemporary. Miller wrote and abandoned his study of Lawrence in the 1930s. (It was published for the first time in 1980, collected from essays, notes, and charts.) The then-unknown, unpublished, penniless, expatriated, middle-aged American pays homage to the well-known, prolific English writer who had recently died at the age of forty-four. Lawrence is a major modern writer whose most important work spans the period of high modernism, 1913–31. Miller, at that time an unknown, is a literary epigone, waiting—with a host of others in the dreary Paris well described by George Orwell in "Inside the Whale," his essay on Miller—for his career to be launched.

The idea for a book on Lawrence or Joyce first came from Miller's publisher, Jack Kahane, an enterprising man with a genuine admiration for Lawrence and for the soon-to-be-published *Tropic of Cancer*, who somewhat obviously linked Lawrence to Miller's novel in his own mind, not without the hope of turning a profit. Through association with the author of *Lady Chatterley's Lover* or *Ulysses*—neither work as good as *Tropic of Cancer* in Kahane's eyes—Miller would appear respectable, virtually immune to prosecution for obscenity.

Resenting the calculating aspect of the suggestion, Miller was nonetheless quick to take it up on its literary merit. What started out in his publisher's mind as a promotional pamphlet developed into a book that engaged all Miller's energies. "Henry has buried himself in his work," reports Anaïs Nin in her *Diary* for November 1932, and "has not time for June." She assesses the situation correctly: "He is asserting himself as a thinker, he is asserting his seriousness. He is tired of being considered a mere 'cunt painter,' and experimentalist, a revolutionary."[1]

The genesis of the work has been documented in outline by Evelyn Hinz and John Teunissen in the introduction to their edition of Miller's study. As they note, this study, which was to have been Miller's first book, turned out to be his last. Though the book is in places contradictory, incoherent, and repetitive, Miller's writing on Lawrence is considerably more valuable than Miller criticism would have led us believe.

Miller's original impulse was to consider both Lawrence and Joyce in a work of cultural criticism. However, the study outgrew Miller's control. As he wrote, he soon realized that though he really did not like Joyce (or Proust), he did—despite reservations about the Lawrence persona—like Lawrence. The shift to a focus on Lawrence alone came in May 1933; Miller had been working on the project since early 1932. Lawrence's essay "The Crown" was the turning point. Hinz and Teunissen give an odd rationale for this: "We must bear in mind that up until this time [Miller's] knowledge of Lawrence had been largely confined to his major novels and to secondary sources" (*TWL* 15). The word *confined* suggests that the essay is more important than the novels—including *Sons and Lovers* and, more particularly, considering the content of "The Crown," *The Rainbow* and *Women in Love*. In short, two of Lawrence's best novels! In what Miller called his "Passionate Appreciation" of Lawrence there is more passionate appreciation of "The Crown" (and the almost equally highly regarded expository work, *Fantasia of the Unconscious*) than for the novels that the study was written to illuminate. Surely there is a disproportion here. Indeed, Miller's lack of critical clarity on Lawrence's major novels is a disappointing one. "The Crown" is a great essay, and even late in life Lawrence claimed a central place for it in his work, but it is major because it explains the spirit of his fiction so well. Yet Hinz and Teunissen seem to endorse Miller's eccentric judgment when they mention the novels. In "The Crown, by contrast, he found a man, a profound thinker, and a visionary" (15).

The editors point out that the essay "was the kind of manifesto and testament that Miller had for the past eight years been struggling to formulate" (15). Miller needed explicit direction at this juncture in his career. But whether, as the editors claim, "Lawrence was the embodiment of many of the ideas which he had been developing on his own" (15) is a trickier proposition. Miller's appropriation of Lawrence is the subject of this essay.

Miller's advocacy of "The Crown" exhibits more enthusiasm than subtlety. Though, as far as Miller knows, nobody has heard of "The Crown," it is in his opinion "the most important thing that came out of the war . . . [Lawrence] never surpassed this utterance, nor equaled it indeed" (*TWL* 212). In a letter to Nin, Miller claims that the essay "is far and away the best thing Lawrence ever wrote," that "the language is matchless—reminiscent of the best in the Bible. The thought is superior to any of Jesus' sayings." A man with a mission, Miller feels that "it might have saved me a lot of work."[2] One part insight, one part euphoria, one part megalomania, Miller's utterance expresses a personal release, the shock of recognition. But how much of a recognition was it? The subject of "The Crown" is the meaning of dissolution, a theme central to the novels Lawrence is writing at that time, *The Rainbow* and *Women in Love*. Miller is roughly right in saying of these novels that "the former [shows] the disintegrative powers of corruption and the latter the creative powers" (*TWL* 120). But unlike Lawrence's best critics on the subject—Frank Kermode, Colin Clark, and George Ford—Miller has little to say about how the first half of this equation functions in these major works, and nothing to say about the more difficult second half. Like Murry, whose work on Lawrence is an obvious influence, Miller does not see how the sexual theme works here, how it is essential to the theme of resurrection. Like Murry, he rightly notes the importance of reduction but does not come to grips with it.

Part of Miller's difficulty in his book on Lawrence was his confusing Lawrence with himself: "I saw in his struggling my own struggle with the world. When he denounces the world I feel that I am denouncing the world too—in the very same words!" Miller almost felt that Lawrence was "dictating" the book to him.[3] It is remarkable that Miller, with his sense of vocation as sexual rebel in literature, took himself as solemnly as Lawrence did and thought of Lawrence as a surrogate, with the book on Lawrence an advertisement for himself. He exclaims: "It's not Lawrence—it's myself I'm making a place for!" (quoted in *TWL* 20). This very closeness made him more interested in Lawrence as an example, a representative man, than as a writer. His "passionate appreciation" suffers from a consequent asymmetry. Though Miller may have been too close to his subject to see it the way he should have, the real experience of reading Miller's study now is to realize how much he did see.

Though Lawrence and Miller differ in crucial ways, in others they were culturally aligned. The central point of connection is the attitude of ferocity that both assume toward the dominant bourgeois culture. Certainly at the phase of Miller's greatest creativity—the *Tropics*, especially *Tropic of Cancer*—he is even more the late Romantic rebel than Lawrence. "The world is always wrong," he writes a friend; "And I who says this, savagely, fanatically, blindly, obstinately, I know full well what hell there is in store for me with such an attitude . . . Never was there an age which a man could be less proud of than this" (quoted in *TWL* 17–18). In the living death of the 1930s, the negative is positive. Like Lawrence, Miller revels in the luxury of destruction, the violent apocalypse. Lawrence's symbol is the phoenix, which rises out of the ashes. Where do these ashes come from? Miller speaks of the "need" for "a holocaust of individual deaths" in order for "nascent forms" to "gain strength" (150). He sees no problem in the modernist sentimentalism that deaths will be "the loam, the top-soil, for the ideological flowering of the future" (150–51). For both authors at this point, history is apocalyptic, not cyclical. How rousing Miller must have found Lawrence's 1930 note to the second edition of "The Crown": "It is no use trying merely to modify present forms. The whole great form of our era will have to go" (*PII* 364). Given this mentality, Lawrence, on his part, would have understood Miller when he wrote: "Violence is its own justification, a pure thing, one of the purest things in life" (*TWL* 177).

Miller presents the personal genesis of his ferocity in *The Time of the Assassins*, where, as we have seen, he compares himself in an extended way to Rimbaud. The assassins are the beastly bourgeois who are mowing down the poets. Since ferocity holds uncompromisingly that "everything we are taught is false," (*TA* x) it may come as no surprise that Miller, rarely given to utterance about public events, says exaggeratedly in 1946: "Everyone is waiting for the great event, the only event which preoccupies us night and day: *the next war*" (35). Aware of his antecedents, Miller knows that the language of apocalypse is spoken not only by Rimbaud but "by Lawrence" and "by Céline, by Malaquais" (Mailer's one-time mentor). Almost traditionally, Miller feels that "we are coming to the end, and it is a catastrophic end which we face" (129).

In his monochromatic outrage, in his unlimited embrace of romantic cliché, Miller lends his rebel prestige to a new line of writers (William S. Burroughs and the Beats) and even academic critics (Leslie Fiedler and Ihab Hassan), whose radical innocence decries the conspiracy as they wait for the end. "We are talking a dead language . . . Communication is finished" (*TA* 67), says Miller in Rimbaudian accents, giving voice to the so-called literature of silence. Even when he celebrates language—Lawrence at his ferocious best, for example—Miller speaks of it as if it were basically an Apollonian restraint: "At its best, when he is swept along by his paroxysm of hate, there is in Lawrence's language so rich, so dark, at once so lucid and enigmatic, a direct and overwhelming appeal to the blood and soul of many as if he had surmounted all the barriers which language imposes, a direct appeal to the blood" (*TWL* 248).

Miller concludes with the ultimate compliment, admiration for the destructive element: "There are poison and fire in his words and a terrible naked beauty." Though this focuses on one central aspect of Lawrence to the exclusion of the tender, life-binding one, this earlier description from *The World of Lawrence* is more authentic and deeply felt than the somewhat formulaic negations of *The Time of the Assassins*. In Miller's 1946 study of Rimbaud, he can assert—somewhat anachronistically, and with a cloying self-pity—that "the place for the genius is in the gutter" (*TA* 69). Miller's delayed royalties are soon to make him an affluent rebel who takes up residence in one of the most enchanting—and bourgeois—areas of America, there to be lionized as one of the gurus of the California spirit.

In his later American years, Miller ignores a central aspect of postwar literary and intellectual culture: the viable revisionist liberalism that asserted itself. He says nothing about the strengths of a society that successfully opposed and defeated fascism and totalitarianism, even though many formerly radical writers had some good things to say about America and its culture. Miller lapsed into a long verbal silence.

Though it has its distinct limitations, his hardness and extremity is what is most valuable in Miller as novelist and critic. His very insistence on the iconoclastic, the antinomian, and the intransigent enables him to place Lawrence in a proper cultural perspective decades before the mid- to late 1950s, when a number of Morningside Heights critics rescued him from what F. W. Dupee has called the "Little England" moralism of F. R. Leavis.[4] In her admirable introduction to a collection of Lawrence's letters, Diana Trilling emphasized his visionary aspect and its limitations, asserting that he was not only interested in "a new way of acting but a new way of being," and, further, that he was a Utopian, that his sexual message could not be taken literally, that "there is no world for Lawrence's people, that they are isolated in their intensity, and that he doesn't permit *us* to live in the actual world . . . that he licenses sex only as a sacrament."[5]

In *The World of Lawrence*, well before the idea became something of a critical cause, Miller rightly links Lawrence with Nietzsche, who "seizes the hammer and ruthlessly smashes the old symbols, the icons, the dead letter of the law" (*TWL* 156). He rightly characterizes them as "the prophetic type. Men who prepare the ground for a new religious feeling" through their ideational work, which Miller identifies in Nietzschean terms as "the transvaluation of all values." He sees a coincidence of style in "Nietzsche the artist-philosopher, [and] Lawrence the philosopher-artist." (217).

If Lawrence is, in Miller's eyes, the prophet and seer, can the savior be far behind? The Lawrence-Christ parallel is one of the commonplaces of Lawrence criticism, one often enough encouraged and made explicit by Lawrence himself. Miller, like a number of the critics, is skeptical about Lawrence's assumption of this role: "In his moments of frenzied exaltation he is indeed a savior. But he cannot sustain the role . . . His voice grows hysterical . . . the voice of anguish, of a man crucified" (117). Miller sees himself in these roles, with the exception of that of savior. Though Miller tried to comprehend the universe, he does not, as he thinks Lawrence does, identify with it. He parts with Lawrence "in the effort to posit himself as universe, as God" (126). However, Miller, unlike Murry, does not take Lawrence literally: "Just as the ignorant disciples of Christ literally and vulgarly believed him when he promised a heaven and a resurrection, so Murry seems to have believed that Lawrence's promises would be literally fulfilled. He completely loses sight of the fact that it is only a great artist who can make these insane prophecies seem realizable" (226). The word *insane* does not carry its usual connotation in this context but implies a divine madness. Miller understands the Utopian element in Lawrence. Like Nietzsche, Miller says, Lawrence placed salvation on "the creation of a higher, fanatical, utopist idea . . . the only, even if utopian remedy" (191). Like Christ, Lawrence ultimately represented a sacramental ideal. This is why Miller calls "The Crown," *Fantasia of the Unconscious*, and *Apocalypse* Lawrence's "gospel," upon which "the works of future commentators will center" (233). The religious metaphor shows how much Lawrence was a matter of belief for Miller, how much he needed a didactic anchor. Yet Miller's quest for ideological direction was not quite a quest for religious salvation.

Miller thinks of Jesus and Nietzsche as "homologous types, precursors of the last Dionysian figure, Lawrence" (241), similar in their style of prophecy—which, for Miller, includes bitterness, wrath, and isolation. He thinks of the artist's immersion in the destructive element as the old drama of "Dionysus and the mysteries" on "a different level" (150–151). Though it was right for Christ to stress the spiritual, Lawrence, the modern Christ, sees that we have lived through "the life of mind and spirit" and that "there are left only the dark animal forces of life" (151). Though Lawrence is like Christ, Miller distinguishes him from "the neurotic-savior type who returns from the desert with a message of salvation, prepared to save man and to be offered up as a sacrifice" (159). But Lawrence did, in some sense do these things in his writing, typically in female personae: Lou Witt does go to something like the desert, and the woman who rode away does sacrifice herself.

Miller's sense of the artistic vocation parallels his sense of the visionary. He speaks axiomatically of the artist's "sworn and eternal opposition to mores and ideology"—and, without irony, of "his stubborn opposition to everything that exists" (148). It is obvious to him that the artist's "complete divorce from the common, outer, everyday profane, vulgar reality of the mass is his salvation and the salvation of art" (150). The artist is a sort of protestant who "can tolerate nothing but the dictates of his own conscience . . . He is obliged, therefore, to rule with tyrannical force. There is no ultimate distinction here between king, hero, saint, artist. At bottom he is the most tyrannical of all the creative types" (152). By this reading, there is a close link between art and sadism.

When Miller moves from Utopian iconoclasm to the actualities of art, he is on shakier ground. His notion of self-authorization is more Miller than Lawrence, as a reader of the *Tropics* can see. Miller himself points out that *Tropic of Cancer* is a triumph of the self over art, which explains the inchoate, rambling quality of his work. Lawrence's fiction, by contrast, is often structured to a point of moral intensity, which is the typically explosive climax. For all his egotistic self-dramatization, Lawrence was able to subordinate himself to literature—except in diffuse, self-focused failures like *Aaron's Rod* and *Kangaroo*. It is significant that Miller considers *Aaron's Rod* to be Lawrence's most important novel. It appears that Miller's alienation at this point in his life engenders a narcissism so deep as to make conformity to artistic necessity impossible. (Miller never fully emerged from this depth of narcissism as a writer.) This is why Miller really means it when he denies that *Tropic of Cancer* is a novel. He is close only to his own impulses. What Miller often gives us in form as well as content is literature as immediate gratification. Paradoxically, this is what made him an authentic influence. Miller's herky-jerk confusion of genres was later to be considered a hallmark of the experimental. Lawrence's intensely structured work, on the other hand, implies a strong superego, even if a reconstituted one. Dramatic necessity is an outcome of a writer's moral necessity. Miller's lack of superego is reflected in the endless amorphousness of a writer whose brilliance asserts itself in episodic fragments and lyrical bursts.

And when Miller attributes the artist-as-criminal persona to Lawrence, he is on even shakier ground. Lawrence himself never did that, despite near projections like Count Dionys. When he says that "in crime [Lawrence] experienced salvation" (247), Miller is indulging in fantasy. Miller simply equates artistic rebelliousness with crime, something a priest like Lawrence could never do. "The great crimes are committed in the heart by the pure at heart," Miller insists; "Compared with Tamerlane or Capone, Christ was a criminal of the first water" (115). Lawrence never makes so crude a distinction. It depends upon Miller's law: "The more abnormal he is—the more monstrous the more criminal—the more fecundating is his spirit." Miller does not distinguish between the necessity for artistic and moral change, or a justified iconoclasm, and the automatic assumption of a criminal posture. He often comments on the guilt his choice of profession entailed in a rigidly middle-class, German-American Protestant family, particularly with a mother like his. Hence, for him, artistic freedom is crime. But the world is not as stupid as his mother was. Though his ferocity enables him to see the essential subversiveness of Lawrence, Miller can become a victim of his own point of view.

Lawrence and Miller are writers best known for the erotic element in their work. What role does Miller assign to the Lawrencean woman? What is the essence of the other in the program of formidable isolation that Miller defines? Sex, after all, generally requires another person. Miller has next to nothing to say about tenderness in Lawrence. Yet he rightly sees woman as a threat to the Lawrencean hero's lordly independence. "It is because his creative instinct is so strong," Miller maintains, "that [Lawrence] is obliged to deny, at least in his art, the tyranny of her power" (*TWL* 54). Seeing that sex is the penultimate rather than the ultimate act in Lawrence, Miller says: "He looks to [woman] for his experience only in order to achieve his final isolation. The sex act is not the consummation or fulfillment—it is the point of departure." This is why love, marriage, and friendship all prove "insufficient," even "tortures." This last word he derives from Murry; other ideas about women, as we shall see, are also derived from Murry. Though Miller is right in saying that it is in *The Rainbow* rather than *Lady Chatterley's Lover* that "we witness this devastating, harrowing soul struggle" (54), he would have been even more right had he said *Women in Love*, with the marriage of Birkin and Ursula the clearest example of the struggle resolved in all of Lawrence. Miller's comments on Lawrence's most important novel are consistently wide of the mark, emphasizing the incongruous balance between ideational subtlety and critical inadequacy in his Lawrence study.

Yet Miller is clear in outline. He sees that Lawrence has none of the troubadour idealization of woman, none of the sense of surrender to a sublimated divinity manifest in the female. There may not be the conventional poetry of love, but there is the woman who is part of you. Miller does say that Frieda "is the woman who appears throughout (practically) all his books—the mysterious, unknowable, foreign woman whom Lawrence loved, if ever a man loved a woman" (33)—rather the way June Smith appears in his own work, the fated woman. Miller illustrates the tension between Lawrence and Frieda in the following example. Equating Frieda with Tanny of *Aaron's Rod*, he holds that Frieda was too much the modern woman. His reason for saying so is distinctly Lawrencean: she had "what every modern woman has—to her ruination—a stubborn will, a desire to play the man's role" (68). Miller says that this condition is made worse by Lawrence's dependence as an artist on woman, oversensitive to his own maladjustment in contemporary life. Miller is presumably speaking about himself as well, if one considers *The Rosy Crucifixion*. In the *Tropics* there are few signs of such a dependence.

Accordingly, Miller relishes Lawrence's advice to a young man about to be married; he finds it "astonishingly good—almost magnificent." Miller quotes from Mabel Dodge Luhan's *Lorenzo in Taos*: "Be alone always. Be gentle with her when she is gentle, but if she tries to impose her will on you, beat her!" (quoted in *TWL* 44). To Miller this seems "swell," the banal adjective linking him to common American male chauvinism in this respect. Further, Miller considers it the "essence of wisdom in man-to-woman matters." Moreover, this bromide seems to have come as a personal revelation: "I feel that if I had known that before," says Miller, "I might have averted so much trouble." He derives a particular satisfaction in knowing that "according to accounts he did beat the fat German woman up."

Miller overstates the case for Lawrence's difficulty with women. Birkin and Ursula, for example, are one of the convincing loving couples in modern literature. Following Murry, Miller treats Lawrence too much as a case. "His love of his wife," Miller says, "a love which is a continual torture to him, is nothing more than a love of self. Woman as a person, as the object of love, since he is powerless to give himself, to attach himself to her, he makes a force for evil, the devil which combats his spiritual masculine nature" (122). This is much too diagrammatic a view of Lawrence; it does not take into account, for example, his idea of constellated stars. And where Murry might oppose the spiritual to the physical, how can Miller? At least, how can the author of *The Rosy Crucifixion*? Part of the confusion in Miller's study is that he uses critical material he does not always assimilate. In Lawrence, the sexual is part of the spiritual. The spirituality of sexual love arises because woman is released as woman, just as man is released as man. This is dramatized in *Women in Love*, "The Fox," and *Lady Chatterley's Lover*—to name a few works from different periods of Lawrence's creative life. It is simplistic to say with Miller, and Murry before him, that Lawrence "can only grant the carnal, sensual love, passion based on fundamental antagonism—not spiritual love" (72). Moreover, this is a contradiction of what Miller says elsewhere in the study. Both are indispensable in much of Lawrence's work. Salvation may be individual, as Miller maintains, but it is not separate, and it cannot be arrived at alone. This is one of the mysteries of what Lawrence calls the greater life of the body.

Miller, following Murry, does not see clearly or consistently that physical love as an end in itself was death for Lawrence. He did see sometimes that, for Lawrence, physical love as a means to the end of cosmic self-definition, a Dionysian transfiguration, was the most elevated spiritual experience in life. Whether Frieda made this distinction is another question. There are many heroines in Lawrence, variations on Frieda, who are amenable to the hero's venture in spiritual definition. It is too easy to say, as Miller does, that Frieda resented "this superiority and death" stuff, as if Frieda was "the bitter stone of reality" (132). Miller adds: "This is why these Saviors never have wives! (Murry is quite right here. To play the Savior one must be a eunuch! One must marry God, the Spirit, etc. . . . because the wives give the Saviors away, expose their vital inner weakness, their divided self, their bisexual nature.) Frieda really broke [Lawrence's] back." Again, Miller follows Murry in treating Lawrence as a case study. Like Murry, Miller does not convincingly make the connection between the expository works that they both think are the great Lawrence— "The Crown" and *Fantasia of the Unconscious*—and the fiction that is the artistic embodiment of those works. In Murry's words, "the quick of Lawrence is in dissolution,"[6] but neither he nor Miller see the artistic power that Lawrence derives from that. This is why they regard the excessively didactic, artistically muddled *Aaron's Rod* and *The Plumed Serpent* rather than *Women in Love* or *St. Mawr* as Lawrence's "greatest" fiction. It is easy to understand why Miller was drawn to Murry's theme of mother fixation. With whatever Oedipal complications, Miller cut his mother off early in life. Consistent in his rebellion against the hard, loveless, castrating woman who was mom, Miller illustrates, as does Lawrence, what Freud called the universal tendency to debasement in the sphere of love. Dragging unconscious Oedipal tensions with him, where Miller loves he cannot desire, and where he desires he cannot love. Miller's first angelic love is an idealized pole that is more than balanced by the opposite pole of failed marriage and serial fornication. Much of Miller's love life, if that is the right word for it, can be seen in terms of the madonna-whore complex, the idealization of and revenge on the mean mother. Miller sees one aspect of the Oedipal malady, the inability to throw off the mother, as the psychological problem in Proust and Joyce as well as in Lawrence. Proust becomes a homosexual, Joyce sees the whore in woman, and Lawrence searches for a mythical man who is not a pervert, as Miller quaintly puts it. In *The Time of the Assassins*, he adds Rimbaud to his list of mother-troubled writers.

Miller's contempt for his mother is the obvious source of his misogyny. Considering the putative Anglo-Saxon propensity to consider woman man's equal partner and helpmate, Miller exclaims: "How ridiculous this business of listening to a woman!" (*TWL* 187). In *Fantasia of the Unconscious*, Lawrence states this idea a bit more subtly: "The woman who thinks and talks as we do is almost sure to have no dynamic blood-polarity with us" (*FU* 203). Is this male chauvinism or a case of *vive la différence*? For Miller, the reality has become so dehumanizing that insect imagery describes it most vividly: Woman "is crying for attention socially, politically . . . because she is actually eating up our world, appropriating it like the black widow spider, who after paralyzing its victim commences to suck its juices, raw and alive, or who in the midst of intercourse commences to eat. And that devout air of woman's today, her earnestness in pleading her cause, how like the praying mantis's hypocritical and deadly posture it is." Miller gets both famous bugs in, with a truly woman-hating hysteria. Not unexpectedly, he attributes this disaster to the "perversion of the maternal instinct in women," a phrase that strikes a personal chord. When this instinct is perverted, Miller holds, we see the "inimical, all-sufficient role of women . . . usurpation of man's role in life, when man does not throw off the yoke of swaddling clothes and the apron-strings, the root-malady in the case of Joyce, Proust and Lawrence," not to mention Caesar, the Czars, Pharaohs and Emperors. Down "mother domination"!

If Miller is more strident than Lawrence in his analysis of what the latter called cocksure women and hensure men, it is because he never had the passionate attachment to his mother that Lawrence once had and because he spent much of his life in uniform repudiation of the maternal. Strindberg was a favorite of both Henry and June. Miller does not consider Lawrence a misogynist in the sense that Strindberg was, commenting that Lawrence's "abuse goes out equally to man and woman" (*TWL* 188). Lawrence is, rather, an equal opportunity misanthrope. In Lawrence's life, however, Miller feels that the repudiation of woman was not successful, that "his wife leads him around by the apron-strings, as his mother did before her" (40). Miller finds in Frieda "the corruptive disintegrating aspect of the ideal-love mode . . . the tyrannical power of woman coupled with the comforting annihilation of her big womb and her draughts of death and forgetfulness" (122). Miller reduces Lawrence's relationship to Frieda to the death of physical extinction, escape, rather than to the creative death of artist-phoenix. But since Lawrence's life is intimately connected with his work, what then is he a prophet of?

Miller translates Lawrence's emotions into a theory of culture sexually considered. Man represents the civilizing process, woman nature. Yet it is woman's "deepest desire . . . to have the man make her aware of his superiority of vision and purpose," biologically bound as she is. "She herself is incapable of assuming this cultural role," Miller says; "She can only nourish it" (134). Woman "is amoral and uncivilizing, lethargy and night." Man's great fear, in Miller's view of Lawrence, is "the primal fear of his defeat at woman's hands . . . He triumphs cruelly when he enters her and makes her obey, but it is the short triumph of a moment or two" (185). Despite certain works of Lawrence's power phase—"The Woman Who Rode Away," for example—this last bit of psychomachia is more Miller than Lawrence, and more Mailer than either.

But is it only a middleweight like Miller speaking? Lawrence can be quoted to much the same effect. Ideally, Lawrence holds: "It is man's own religious soul that drives him on beyond woman to his supreme activity. For his highest, man is responsible to God alone . . . Hence Jesus, 'Woman what have I to do with thee?' " (*FU* 135). To Lawrence's chagrin, the modern world denies this ideal. "Now," Lawrence laments, "his consummation is in feeling, not action. Now, his activity is all of the domestic order . . . Instead of being assertive and rather insentient, he becomes wavering and sensitive," worshipping "pity and tenderness and weakness . . . [woman] grips the responsibility. The hand that rocks the cradle rules the world" (134). Woman "is now queen of the earth, and inwardly a fearsome tyrant . . . God help the man whom she pities. Ultimately she tears him to bits" (134). The violence of the image complements Miller's black widow spider. Lawrence's solution to the problem might have come from a Midlands pub—as, psychoanalytically speaking, it did, so much of his literary work after *Sons and Lovers* being an attempt at reclamation of his father's denied status as a man and at denial of his mother's role as an arbiter of civilized value. That smashed marriage bred a revolutionary, or, rather, a reactionary. "Take it all out of her," he urges. "Make her yield once more to the male leadership: If you've got anywhere to lead" (218). Take the starch out of her! Lawrence is united with his father at last, but then the father had nowhere to lead. Like Desdemona in *Othello*, the woman listens to the man's exploits, "all that she has missed" (220). The man must be more than the lover, he must be the "culture-bearer" (172).

If Lawrence's views on women coincide in certain key ways with those of a pub Englishman, like the proverbial Englishman, he only loves once. Despite his lashing out, he does, finally—in logic and in his own life—believe in marriage. This is a point never grasped by Miller because he could not find marriage a plausible solution to anything, although he tried many times. Constancy is an indication in Lawrence that sex is inseparable from a complicated, long-term, psychospiritual relationship. To the serial lover Miller, monogamy is inevitably thralldom, which is consistent with how he interprets Lawrence's relation to Frieda. Lawrence would have found appalling Miller's promiscuity and whoring, not to mention his many marriages. Miller does not quote Lawrence's saying: "After a false coition, like prostitution, there is not newness but a certain disintegration" (*FU* 141). For Lawrence, but not for Miller, this is the disintegration of death. The fundamental distinction between Lawrence and Miller is that Lawrence is a writer of sexuality or man-womanness even more than he is a writer of sex—the physical act is subsumed under the definition of man-and-woman; whereas Miller is a writer whose fantasy realism evolves far more from the sex act itself. Given this difference, it follows that Lawrence can easily sustain an elevated tone on the subject of intimacy. Indeed, he errs on the side of solemnity. Miller is generally not interested in the elevated tone, but on the rare occasions when he is, he can barely establish it. .

Lawrence amusingly contrasts his own intensity on the subject with that of "the French," and he might almost as well have been contrasting it with Miller's. Lawrence says that the Frenchman's "conception of sex is basically hygienic. A certain amount of copulation is good for you. *Ça fait du bien au corps*! . . . Well, it's more sane anyhow, than the Anglo-Saxon terrors."[7] According to Lawrence, the French rationalize sex and marriage. Miller makes note of Lawrence's view. He then observes that the French scorn Lawrence, who "strikes preeminently at the French stronghold, where the fight has been given up, where there is a grand indifference concerning women, where woman becomes the toy, the amusement, the wife who joins in and titivates [sic] the husband listening respectfully, but not seriously, playing a hypocritical role of 'friend' " (*TWL* 186). Miller believes that these are usually "marriages of convenience," with "patient mistresses" waiting to "provide the sexual orgies," and considers the whole arrangement "a happy compromise." Miller approves; Lawrence, of course, does not. Miller says that "at her best, the French woman resembles the Greek courtesan . . . she plays the trivial, insignificant role . . . She is not even regarded respectfully as a mother . . . she has been conquered by that masculine world the ancients represented" (189). This, in Miller's view, is all to the good, the wisdom of the ancients. Miller concludes with an almost verbatim Lawrencean twist: "The Frenchman knows that the woman who thinks as we do has no blood relationship with us." This is why sex in America and Russia is so dismal.

There is a curious doubleness in Miller's use of Lawrence, and it points to a central confusion in *The World of Lawrence*. On the one hand, Miller thinks of himself as an exponent of Lawrence's ideas on physical love; on the other hand, Miller's views actually correspond more closely to what they both identify as French. One can readily see why Miller felt so at home in Paris. Lawrence, of course, is basically mocking the "French" way. Yet both Miller and Lawrence express a certain contempt for the expectations of modern women, and both—as we have seen—accept to some degree a remarkably stereotyped chauvinistic, even misogynistic, relegation of woman to a form of inferiority. What Miller sees with special clarity in Lawrence is his sexual aggression and disgust, the angry husband-priest. In Lawrence this fierceness manifested itself as an arduous spiritual attempt to imagine figures of masculine power that are sometimes hard to distinguish from figures of impotence. In Miller there was failed love, serial infatuation, and endless compensatory amusement.

....

Alienation in marriage is the common thread between Miller and *Aaron's Rod*, which explains why Miller takes the novel to be Lawrence's central fiction. It is the work's theme and tone, surely, rather than its literary quality that accounts for Miller's deep involvement with and overvaluation of it. Most important is Miller's near identification with the situation of the central character. Miller describes *Aaron's Rod* as "the story of an artist who is strangled by domesticity, by the devouring female, and who is trying to liberate himself" (*TWL* 61). Though Lawrence would find this description sympathetic, there is a problem right at the beginning. For the "devouring" quality of Aaron's wife, Lottie, is not dramatized unless we assume that any economically disadvantaged wife and mother of two daughters making her ordinary demands is devouring merely by being what she is. On another level, and more convincingly, the novel assumes the failure of marriage, the impossibility of the spirit to define itself in the face of marital routine. If Miller understood anything, he understood this. It is his given as a writer. In *Aaron's Rod*, Miller finds Lawrence in a Millerian mode. Neither Lawrence nor Miller question why Aaron walks out on Lottie, nor do they ever seriously consider that there might be a moral issue. Man's freedom to split is axiomatic. Neither writer will become the victim their fathers were. Miller interprets Aaron in psychoanalytic terms: "One feels that Aaron's wife might be the unconscious portrait of Lawrence's mother, the woman whom he recognized as the lover and wife, the woman who had crippled him as a man, and whom again he takes revenge on unconsciously. It is not the portrait of his earlier loves, nor of Frieda. But it is the fundamental portrait, for Lawrence, of all women—in their role of mother, wife, destroyer etc." (62). Miller tells us that Aaron is "young Lawrence . . . [the] nascent artist, man of humble origins, sensitive, artistic, not yet aware of his destiny."[8] Miller loves Aaron's uncompromising isolation and finds his honesty heroic and lyrical, particularly when Aaron says: "I don't want to *care*, when care isn't me." Miller calls this "superb," the cry of the artist "who can not give himself completely, who withholds his love for creative purposes" (*TWL* 62). This eloquent cry might well be the motto of Miller's life. From one point of view, it suggests a heroic honesty that transcends what most people call feeling.

Yet Miller does not seem to be aware that his overvaluation of the novel is partly due to its misogyny. The hatefulness of Aaron's wife is assumed rather than dramatized. Moreover, hatred of women is in the air that Aaron breathes. Take his view of the flirtatious Jewish landlady. Although most of what she has displayed is social conscience—a sort of liberal, she speaks of the common good and funds for the education of children—Aaron perceives her to be "so loudly self-righteous, and so dangerous, so destructive, so lustful . . . Her and all women. Bah, the love game!" (*AR* 29). Or his reaction to being seduced by Josephine: "I did myself in . . . as if the bile broke inside me, and I was sick" (114). Rather than guilt, the strain of female physical proximity—a threat to his independence—is what disturbs Aaron. Or the narrator's parallel view of the Marchesa: "She would drink one drop of his innermost heart's blood, and he would be carrion. As Cleopatra killed her lovers" (345)—this of a woman whose occasionally clingy style might give a different message. When strident assertion takes the place of dramatization, Lawrence is in trouble, as he is in this book where he is too easily contemptuous.

Lottie, the name of Aaron's wife, seems to be an allusion to Lotte in

Goethe's *The Sorrows of Young Werther*, and the end of innocence. Home is where the hell is; children are a form of imprisonment. The themes are legitimate, as future divorce statistics confirm. And there is an occasional subtlety to Aaron's contempt, as when he contemplates "the infernal love and good will of his wife," and her "self-righteous bullying, like poison gas" (*AR* 32). It is clear from the simile that the Great War extended into the hearth. The writing has from time to time the sharp, satiric edge that the mature Lawrence found easy to command. But the disjunction between what is there in the book and what is assumed remains a problem. So does the consequent stridency. Aaron laments Lottie's "will, her will, her terrible, implacable cunning will!" But only an ordinary quality has been manifested. After he has left her, Aaron admits that in "a deadlock . . . both must be at fault" (200). He later admits to Lilly that the wife-beating he had engaged in is no solution.

Sounding rather like Lawrence in some of the darker moments of *Fantasia of the Unconscious*, the narrator of *Aaron's Rod* explains Lottie's mentality: "She, as woman, was the centre of creation, the man was but an adjunct. She, as woman, and particularly as mother, was the first great source of life and being, and also of culture. The man was but an instrument . . . It is the substantial and professed belief of the whole white world. Tacitly, they yield the worship to that which is female" (*AR* 201). It doesn't help the drama much that Lotte "never formulated this belief inside herself" (202). This is the heart of Lawrence's misogyny: not a hatred of woman as such, but a hatred of her nature distorted by civilization's collapse, so that woman has become the culture bearer. Lawrence's tendency to slip into religious metaphor underlines the spiritual nature of his thought. Aaron's resistance, like the narrator's, is a spiritual one, essential to his heartfelt definition of mankind: "Born in him was a spirit which could not worship woman: no, and would not." Aaron has the essential Lawrencean quality, "the arrogance of self-unyielding male," the lack of the definite article indicating a category rather than a case. Aaron will gratify Lottie sexually, but not in the sense that "she could envelop him, yield in her all-beneficent love." Hence her "outrage" from the beginning. He denies her queenly divinity, her "divine will and divine right" (205). Submission to love is, for Aaron, a form of suicide, "like jumping off a church-tower or a mountain peak" (209) or "degeneration into a sort of slime and merge" (211). No, instead the two individual constellated stars or, as Lawrence now puts it, Whitman's dalliance of eagles, "each bearing itself upon its own wings" (212).

The musical Aaron, not the most verbally articulate of men, does not express all this. In one of the most awkward passages in Lawrence, the narrator informs us that this is what Aaron would have said if he could. This is another example of assertion doing the work of dramatization. The narrator agrees with a hypothetical reader's objection to putting these thoughts in the mouth of a man not clever enough to think them, but maintains that they nonetheless take the form of self-conscious realization. What is clear is Aaron's sullen resentment, but resentment without dramatized clarity makes for a listless hero. Miller's need for moral support makes him overvalue a work expressing an attitude that asks for but does not earn our empathy.

Miller's high regard for this problematic novel stems in good part from his sympathy with Lawrence's sensibility, with the overall ferocity exhibited. He is right, I believe, in assuming that Lawrence is not critical of Aaron's negativism.[9] In addition to muffling the novel's sense of outrage, such a view implies that the author is in greater control of the loose, shrill narrative than he actually is. Aaron's harsh credo, expressed after his break with the Marchesa, is something with which the alienated, angry Lawrence and Miller would concur. Rejecting kindness, Providence, love, and harmony, Aaron says: "I believe in the fight and in nothing else," whether with woman or the world. "I want the world to hate me, because I can't bear the thought that it might love me" (*AR* 333). He feels a certain sympathy with Lilly, who "*knew* . . . and his soul was against the whole world" (365), especially when he says: "The anarchist, the criminal, the murderer, he is only the extreme lover acting in recoil" (372). Maybe so in some cases, but there must be a less destructive way of expressing love. And there must be a world not definable in terms of hate. Although Aaron has doubts about Lilly's tyrannical disposition—he suspects that Lilly won't allow a man to possess his own soul—he does not question this extreme view of love.

Despite Miller's affinity for independence to the death, he does express some doubt about the extremism of some of Lawrence's views, as he does about a simplification of them. "Murry's attitude and Lawrence's are wrong, absurd, impossible," he says; "The one makes life wholly dependent on a woman's love, the other tries to make life independent of her love" (*TWL* 64). But *Aaron's Rod* is not Lawrence's major work, and Miller remains an unlikely champion of togetherness.

There are, to be sure, a number of ways in which Miller sees himself reflected in the novel. Refuting Murry, he claims that "the theme of the book is not love or friendship between man and man. It is written to explain to himself [Lawrence] the necessity for obeying his own creative impulse, the Holy Ghost within himself . . . he is just recently married and already senses that his allegiance is not to the woman" (*TWL* 62). (See Kate Chopin's fiction for a similar sentiment from the woman's point of view.) Miller switches interchangeably between Aaron and Lawrence. Neither Aaron, the father of two, nor Lawrence is "just recently married," but Miller's comment could well describe his first marriage, an indication of the extent to which Miller is thinking about himself in dealing with this book. Aaron, like Miller, is a bohemian who won't accept ties to other people. Aaron uses words that Miller (or Lawrence) might have spoken: "I believe, if I go my own way, without tying my nose to a job, chance will always throw something my way: enough to get along with" (*AR* 226). Both writers share, then, a bravado nihilism and a profound indifference to convention.

Though Lawrence resisted "the modern" in the sense of intimate psychological description of petty lives, nothing could be more modern—or more appealing to the author of *Tropics*—than Lawrence's nihilism. *Aaron's Rod* contains an expression of disillusionment quite the equal in scope of more famous examples in *Lady Chatterley's Lover* or Hemingway's *A Farewell to Arms*. All three works express directly or indirectly the shock to Western consciousness caused by the First World War. Possessing the eloquence that Aaron lacks, Lilly speaks to the experience of loss of value: "The idea and the ideal has for me gone dead . . . The ideal of love, the ideal that it is better to give than to receive, the ideal of liberty, the ideal of the brotherhood of man, the ideal of the sanctity of human life, the ideal of what we call goodness, charity, benevolence, public spiritedness, the ideal of sacrifice for a cause, the ideal of unity and unanimity . . . the ideal of good, peaceful, loving humanity and its logical sequence in socialism and equality, equal opportunity or whatever you like" (*AR* 354). The sweeping quality of the negation is underscored by the political reference. We are often told that Lawrence was too interested in the personal and the religious to be political. But when he insists on translating his interests into political terms, one must be cognizant of the political uses to which he can be put.

The flagrant fascism of Lilly's ideas—something which escapes Miller—is a logical extension of Lawrence's modernist reductiveness. Lilly, whom Miller thinks of as the mature Lawrence's mouthpiece in this novel, agrees with Argyle's condemnation of "this democratic washerwoman business" (*AR* 352). Lilly agrees that "people are not *men*" (355). Lawrence describes them in the ominous imagery of dehumanization: "They are insects and instruments, and their destiny is slavery." Furthermore, they "will be brought to agree—after extermination." We see Lawrence's version of Dostoevsky's Grand Inquisitor when he writes of "inferior beings" committed to "superior beings." Levison, the Jewish liberal, sensibly objects, noting: "It'll take a bit of knowing, who are the inferior and which is the superior." Lilly replies: "Not a bit," assured of a voluntary acceptance that will be followed by "military power." All of this is chillingly prescient. Levison rightly surmises that it is all "the preposterous pretentiousness of a megalomaniac," at which point Lilly says, unconvincingly, that he would say the opposite with just as much fervor. An explosion bails Lilly—and Lawrence—out. To the very end, though, Lilly asserts Lawrence's doctrine of leadership and submission—this in Mussolini's Italy—leaving the detached Aaron to wonder: "And whom shall I submit to?" (377). The novel ends without an answer to this question.

Lawrence does not clarify Aaron's ambivalent relationship to Lilly. Indeed, Aaron's ambivalences are no more engaging than Lilly's. Rather than a dramatized ambivalence, there is largely a Lawrencean confusion. For example, Aaron breaks away from home life, yet "he hated the hard, inviolable heart that stuck unchanging in his own breath" (*AR* 57). But this does not amount to more than lip service to ordinary feeling. When Aaron vacillates about his affair with the Marchesa on the grounds of "some sort of connection" with Lottie "which it isn't natural, quite, to break" (*AR* 338), we see a feeble equivocation, since the connection has already been broken. The vague, hedging language here is telling. And when Aaron is tempted to follow Lilly, he thinks that he will yield on the bizarre ground that "yield he must in some direction or other" (366). He does not, finally, yield. Lawrence has written a novel in which undigested thematic material overwhelms an intriguing sense of character.

I cite these instances to underscore Miller's inability to see the inadequacy of Aaron as a character. Though the novel contains a fine rush of minor characters—brilliant in the case of Argyle—usually brought quickly in and out, the deeper Lawrence becomes, the less good he is. Miller sees no problem. For him, Aaron is Lawrence's most convincing hero. He views the book as giving deep insight into its author: "How well Lawrence understood the complete and fulfilled man, the mortally human man, we can see from the portraits of his heroes, and in particular that of Aaron Sisson" (*TWL* 61). Completeness and fulfillment are hardly qualities most readers would associate with Aaron, unless ditching one's family for individual freedom is considered the essence of these qualities in and of itself. Miller is too close to Aaron to see what Julian Moynihan has called his ethical inauthenticity (a quality he attributed to Lilly as well).[10]

In *Notes on Aaron's Rod*, Miller's brief, fragmentary study of the novel, he says that the story of Aaron and his wife is "exactly that of B—and myself. Lawrence is writing my story here" (*NAR* 17). He says this in reference to Aaron's recognizing that "he'd kill anything . . . [he] couldn't give himself," a description of the megalomaniac infantile. Miller notes that Aaron "so thoroughly detested his wife—and *Lottie* is a despicable creature, deserving of being ditched—that man has no business succumbing to pangs of conscience" (24). But is she so clearly despicable? Evidently, to the author of *Tropic of Cancer*. Aaron recognizes that in their deadlock, both he and Lottie were at fault. But, for Miller, Aaron cannot be at fault. He sees Aaron as "the man who achieves freedom of movement by renouncing his petty, imperious ego. Aaron Sisson, unlike Lawrence, does not hold himself up as an ideal, does not try to alter people or the world. But he will not allow others to alter him. Aaron Sisson proclaims in his own personality the majesty of his unique being" (*TWL* 129). Does Aaron have an imperious ego to renounce? It is his superego he tries to renounce. This is a significant confusion because for Miller the superego is seamlessly absorbed in the other faculties. Herein lies Miller's special, adverse charm. But Aaron has little charm and less majesty. *Majesty* is not the word even for the megalomaniac "I" of *Tropic of Cancer*. Miller's Aaron suffers from inflation by association.

Like Lawrence, Miller writes "art for my sake," so that he views his fiction as art for life's sake.[11] What is life, one may well ask. Yet, considering Miller as a critic, we see that this stance does give him access to what is problematic in high modernism. His advocacy of Lawrence lends support to his rejection of writers whom he considers modernists in the camp of life for art's sake, notably Joyce and Proust. Originally planned as a coda to *The World of Lawrence*, "The Universe of Death" stands as one of the best chapters in the book. Miller tells us that he took the title of this essay from Lawrence's *Fantasia of the Unconscious*.

In Joyce and Proust, Miller sees no spiritual reawakening—the most notable thing he does see in Lawrence. He sees in their art only the universe of death. "The revolution of the Word which [Joyce's] work seems to have inspired in his disciples," says Miller, "is the logical outcome of this sterile dance of death" (*TWL* 104). (Miller also attributes "the loss of sexual polarity" in Proust to "the soul's death" [99].) Here again Miller anticipates recent antimodernist criticism.[12] His attack on the aesthetic ideology of modernism rings true when he says: "With our latter-day exponents of head culture the great monuments are lying on their sides, they stretch away like huge petrified forests, and the landscape itself becomes *nature-morte*" (94). For their rarefied emotional quality, he calls the masterpieces of Joyce and Proust "these dead moons." It is oddly refreshing to see Miller faulting *Ulysses* and *Remembrance of Things Past* on axiological grounds. "In these epics," he argues, "everything is of equal prominence, equal value whether spiritual or material, organic or inorganic, live or abstract. The array and content of these works suggests to the mind the interior of a junkshop" (93). Joyce and Proust are "defeated men who escape from a cruel, hideous, loathsome reality into ART" (98). Miller's critical vulnerability manifests itself here, for if this is really what life is like—and he often enough agrees that it is—why not escape into art, especially the masterpieces of Joyce and Proust? One can make a more convincing case for the limitations of modernist aesthetic ideology, in criticism or in art itself, by denying rather than affirming its assumptions about the nature of reality.

In contrast to Joyce and Proust, Miller points to an affinity Lawrence has with Dostoevsky, a comparison that seems unlikely, on the face of it. Referring to Lawrence's essay "Aristocracy," Miller claims that Lawrence was "tremendously influenced" by Dostoevsky. The sun is to Lawrence what the moon is to Dostoevsky; the first is "the source of life," the second "the symbol of our non-being" (137). Whoever gets near to either is an aristocrat. The extreme of energy, the extreme of nihilism—both are poles of power in Lawrence, both vantage points of ferocity. As Miller says, "with the in-betweens [Lawrence] had no concern." Dostoyevsky's nihilistic characters are vividly alive to Lawrence, but he draws the line at the evil resonance of Stavrogin. Miller explains that as "a sun worshipper," as one with "the non-human, cosmic view of life," Lawrence saw Dostoevsky's negations as "death-loving." (138). Lawrence and Miller see the nihilist in Dostoevsky, but they do not see the moralist. They simplify him into another instance of ferocity.

Despite the rambling quality of Miller's study of Lawrence, several things clearly emerge from it. Miller reverses the usual procedure in being more concerned with Lawrence's doctrine than with his art. Like Lawrence, he writes criticism as an adjunct to his intellectual autobiography. But Miller does not succeed nearly as well as Lawrence in translating personal obsessions into cultural revelations. His study does have flashes of brilliant illumination, but there is often a gap between his cultural perceptions and the works of literature that Lawrence wrote. For Miller, as for Murry, the man was more important than the works. But we are interested in Lawrence's life because he wrote major works. It seems that Murry was settling the score of a fractious friendship. Miller is constructing a cultural icon, which often appears to be cast in his own image. But Lawrence is too big for the mold.

10

NORMAN MAILER

In Mailer, we can see how sexual radicalism evolves from a dissolving political radicalism. Mailer has spent a good part of his career making violence respectable. His justification for this, a familiar one, is that "individual acts of violence are always to be preferred to the collective violence of the state."[1] As if this were the only quality of the state, as if there were no personal responsibility for such acts. "The route to control could best masquerade under a conservative liberalism," says Mailer's proto-fascist General Cummings.[2] For a long time, Mailer thought that anyone who had anything good to say about America was an unwitting tool of fascism.

Beginning with *The Naked and the Dead*, Mailer denies the politics of civility, the reality of a liberal center. Some of Mailer's most interesting portraits have been liberals, and they all fit the same ideological mold. For this novelist, the function of the liberal is to vacillate. Spinelessness is the primary liberal characteristic in Mailer as early as *The Naked and the Dead*. Lieutenant Hearn is a character incapable of overcoming his advantages—wealth, class, a Harvard education. Though he is properly offended at the class inequities of army life and shows some spunk in asking to be transferred out of the division of the sadistic General Cummings, he is, Mailer tells us, Cummings's true soul mate: "There had been a time, many times when it would have appealed to whatever impulse there had been in him to . . . to do what Cummings was capable of doing. That was it. Divorced of all the environmental trappings, all the confusing and misleading attitudes he had absorbed, he was basically like Cummings" (*ND* 392). There is little in the narrative to support this assertion, but Hearn is a liberal and, *ipso facto*, irresolute. True, Hearn does want Cummings to approve of him again in his new active role, but there is a distinction between leadership and fascism. Hearn is equally critical of Marxism and fascism. He expresses the middle view and is therefore treated as something of a straw man by Mailer. No liberal would accept Cummings's formulation of liberal motives, yet Hearn agrees with them. For Cummings, there are two kinds of liberal, "the ones who are afraid of the world and want it changed to benefit themselves, the Jew liberalism sort of thing. And then there are the young people who don't understand their own desires. They want to remake the world but they never admit they want to remake it in their own image" (580). Suspicious of his own Faustian motives—"when he searched himself, he was just another Croft," (580) an improbable discovery as Croft is the proto-fascist sergeant—Hearn will give up his commission when he gets back to the United States. But we never get the chance to witness this gesture of decency because he is effectively murdered by Croft, who allows him to go unknowingly into a zone held by the Japanese.

Mailer's political point is clouded by Hearn's witlessness. Mailer's sexual view, however, is clear and consistent, if limited compared to its later thematic development. In *The Naked and the Dead*, Mailer is writing what is basically a naturalistic novel, so the sexual aggression is not yet self-conscious. As one would expect from a work in which, generally, social and natural forces dwarf the individual, or in which the individual is presented as a function of his biology, sexuality is usually seen as victimization or appetite. In the mean conditions of a company town, for example, Red Valsen is confined to Two-bit Annie. Wilson is the clearest example of the naturalistic self as mindless biological urge. There is more style, but not very different substance, in the wife-swapping of the officers and an added element of social contempt in the parties with lower-class women. Sex is seen here as social slumming, the obverse of the world of Martinez, for whom sex is social climbing. Class outrage, class embarrassment—these are the qualities of naturalistic fiction.

Though Mailer's sexual views are not yet developed in this work, one of his key oppositions is present in simple form: that of the stud and the Jew. As a counter to the rampant randiness of the gentile GIs, Roth and Goldstein are cartoons of prudery. "Women just aren't interested in it [sex]," they concur (56). Adjusted to his wife's frigidity, Goldstein believes that "children are what makes life worthwhile" (452). It is not without some justice that Gallagher—thinking of the million-dollar wound, the one that would send you home from war—says of his Jewish comrades in arms: "You could shoot 'em in the nuts and they wouldn't even know the difference" (429). Mailer spends a good part of his literary life making sure that he can never be taken for a nice Jewish boy from Brooklyn.[3]

Aspects of sexual violence become explicit in the portrayals of two characters in the novel. General Cummings's veneer dissipates in the bedroom as he mutters to his genteel wife: "I'll take you apart, I'll eat you, oh, I'll make you mine, I'll make you mine, you bitch" (416). At first she is "kindled" by this, but when she realizes that his aggression is a form of aloneness, something withers inside her. We know from Cummings's furtive encounter with Hearn, and his even more furtive encounter in a dark alley in Rome, that he is a homosexual, no casual matter in Mailer. "As a civilization dies," he tells us in his essay on Jean Genet, "it loses its biology. The homosexual, alienated from the biological chain, becomes its center."[4] His "only road back to biology," Mailer holds, "is to destroy Being in others." Mailer is speaking of the sexual act, which—as he sees it—turns a homosexual man into a woman. While Cummings never gets to impose his physical will on Hearn, he does impose his political will, destroying Hearn's "Being" in a sense more literal than the one Mailer alludes to, along with that of the platoon as a whole. The character of Cummings derives from Mailer's feeling that people in power were leading Americans into another war.

Sexual violence is most explicit in Croft, whose experience with women reinforces a social and perhaps innate meanness. Victim and victimizer, Croft is the first of Mailer's sadistic lovers, accompanying his orgasmic body rhythm with the phrase, "Crack . . . that . . . WHIP!" It is a given of *The Naked and the Dead* that marriages disintegrate. It could not be otherwise in a society so loveless, so ridden with inequalities of wealth and power. Croft's recourse is taking an occasional whore, whom he feels free to beat. When his wife, Janey, has an affair, he beats her, which elicits from her the unutterable: "That's one thing you ain't best in" (*ND* 163). A similar comment in *An American Dream* leads to murder. In the more passive idiom of *The Naked and the Dead*, Janey's remark drives Croft to enlist in the army. He can now crack his psychic whip over other men's wives, secure in the belief that women are whores, "deer to track" (64)—the metaphor suggesting a parallel between sex and killing. In *The Naked and the Dead*, the parallel remains only a suggestion.

The Naked and the Dead is as much a political novel as a war novel. The tawdry sex lives of the characters are symptoms of a diseased body politic, so much so that despite the near universality of sexual reference, the theme remains subdued, an index of a deeper aggression.

In this connection, the originality of *Barbary Shore*, Mailer's next novel, may be seen. Here Mailer handles the theme of sexual hostility more dramatically, putting it at the center rather than at an elaborately embroidered periphery. Political hysteria is the order of the McCarthyite day, with its attendant sexual dislocation. Mailer's discontent needs something subjectively deeper than naturalism, so he switches aesthetic gears to the Kafkaesque mode in a novel that blends nightmare with political allegory. "I wish," Mailer tells us with some bombast, "to attempt an entrance into the mysteries of murder, suicide, incest, orgy, orgasm, and Time" (*AdM* 99).

Barbary Shore is an instance of Mailer's political radicalism in its Trotskyite phase in that it presents Stalinism and capitalism as politically and morally equivalent at a time when revisionist liberals, quite rightly, were making a sharp distinction between them. Mailer sees a political chaos that is reflected in the sexual lives of his characters. His tendency to read political significance into sexual motives has become more pronounced. Once again, power in America is in the hands of the Right, and the women in this novel are in the hands of Hollingsworth, a sadistic FBI agent. Mailer may soon come to regard Hollingsworth's physical and verbal aggression as exemplary, but in this early novel the most obvious resonance is negative.

Politically, Hollingsworth triumphs over the fallen Stalinist McLeod, who is trying to redeem his sordid, murderous political past through Trotskyite theory, the first of Mailer's murderers to attain a certain grace. Hollingsworth's push for totalitarian conformity derives from a surprising source. "I'm not a political fellow," he says, "although I've always considered myself a sort of liberal,"[5] the route to control masking itself in a conservative liberalism. But the mask in Hollingsworth is far more apparent than the liberalism. His relationship to Guinevere, a series of one-night stands, culminates in an unlikely plan to get away together.

In what comes to be a Mailer mannerism, Guinevere has had some kind of sexual encounter with every major character in the book: Hollingsworth, who makes a woman out of her; Lovett, who is teased by her; Lannie, her lesbian friend; and McLeod, improbable husband and the father of her libidinous child.

The ideologically ravaged McLeod marries her to thaw himself out but "doesn't know that she's frozen too" (*Barb* 85). He wants to live with her like a family, despite the specter of baby carriages that haunts the land. Guinevere yawns, thinking of how little money he has.

Most ill of Mailer's sexually sick is Lannie, another disillusioned victim of the Stalinist collapse. For her, the FBI is indistinguishable from the Nazis, as are the Stalinists. Her beatings from Hollingsworth are proof that she is right. Later, in making unwilling love to Lovett, she cries: "Save me" (186) but then turns on him as a representative rapist, the narcissistic, sadistic male. "Does a boot know the ground it soils?" she asks. This image is used by Guinevere as well, but she still takes up with Hollingsworth after dissolving her meaningless relationship with Lannie.

The witness to and occasional participant in this sexual dislocation is Lovett. War casualty and psychic orphan, he is specially qualified by amnesia to observe and validate the grotesqueries of an almost unbelievable world. Although he describes himself as "without memory and henceforth privileged not to reason" (155), he is an avid reader of Marx and remembers that Marx was his Bible. Like Mailer, he links industrialism to sterility, musing: "The factories grew, the railroads were laid, the cities expanded, even into the twilight and the falling rate of love." Lovett never does find sexual love, only a dim memory of it with a woman at the seashore before the Korean War. He lives in a vaguely Kafkaesque world of victimization and will somehow bear the murdered McLeod's sacred object, the symbol of Trotskyite faith.

The political apocalypse that McLeod prophesied never came. The political content of the novel, weighing down its second half in abstraction, seems a form of scholasticism. The characters are figments of a melodramatic imagination, the prose undistinguished. The novel's value in Mailer's development is chiefly in its making sexual violence historically explicable and dramatically central.

One could almost have predicted Mailer's next novel, for *The Deer Park* fuses the political tensions of *The Naked and the Dead* with the spectacular negative sexuality of *Barbary Shore*. Mailer goes back to liberal-bashing, but in a more convincing way than in his first novel. He does this in the character of Eitel. Knuckling under to the House UnAmerican Activities Committee, Eitel ("I tell") at least grovels the way that some liberals really did. But even here Mailer tars with a thick brush. "In the end," says the one-time leftist screenwriter turned Establishment flunky, "that's the only kind of self-respect you have. To be able to say to yourself that you're disgusting."[6] So much for liberalism. The nonradical conscience has no chance against the Establishment; a revolutionary alternative is implied.

Mailer's strategy in *The Naked and the Dead* and *The Deer Park* is to draw up an indictment of all American society as totalitarian through an exposé of one of its parts. It is a dubious strategy in the war novel because there Mailer is delineating an institution that is in its nature authoritarian. Mailer's desire to join the Army to write the great novel of the Second World War is well-known. Luckily for him, he was sent to the Pacific theater (which disappointed him at the time); he later said that the density of European culture made it a relatively difficult novelistic subject for an American. There was another reason why he was fortunate not to have been sent to Europe: there the fascism was monolithic, and America was, strangely enough, fighting against it. What chance would Mailer's fascist general have had against Adolf Hitler? But Mailer did not misfire by much. The Army in the 1940s was a central American institution, and it may well have had its share of fascists. And the destruction of Hearn remains good narrative, if unconvincing politics.

In seizing on Hollywood as sink of iniquity, purveyor of tinsel, destroyer of minds and hearts, Mailer follows the then radical (and, one could argue, liberal) line. For him there is one overriding truth about Desert D'Or—it is totalitarian. Teppis is the Cummings of the movie world, the Big Brother who directs film companies and private lives with an equally heavy hand. Eitel is its Hearn, and Marion Faye—as we shall see—is its Croft. Sergius O'Shaughnessy, Mailer's bland surrogate, inhabits two separate worlds, the world of Palm Springs sex—heady but, finally, unreal—and the real world "where orphans burned orphans" (*DP* 45). The Hollywood novel has what the Army novel does not have, an originality of social perception; Mailer's eye catches much of the unreality of film colony life. The well-observed architecture and bar life of that midday midnight signals an inversion of the natural world, where appearance gives the lie to reality. Sergius can distinguish between the two but in a way that, in typical Mailer fashion, excludes the middle. We get one extreme or the other: the lush, enticing high of supersex ("I had pity for the hordes who could know none of this ... We were beyond all" [*DP* 120], says Sergius of his affair with Lulu) or the world of the brutally cast out; the world of possession or the world of dispossession.

A contempt for liberalism is more or less constant in Mailer's fiction for some time, for liberalism depends on the myth of an available middle, a way in American politics, whose nonexistence Mailer insists on to justify his radicalism. Only the radical and reactionary are real. Sameness, conformity, failure of individuality, the strange fruit of utilitarian rationalism—this is what Mailer sees in the middle, and what he rather loosely calls totalitarian. This is why he usually considers liberalism to be a form of totalitarianism. Like Marion Faye, when asked what is in the middle, Mailer might answer: "Slobs ... They always think what they have to think" (127–28). It is ironic that just as liberalism is making a critique of the liberal from within in the criticism of Trilling, the sociology of Shils, and the fiction of Bellow—making an assault on deterministic Utopias and simplistic progressivism—Mailer, either oblivious or in disagreement, attacks liberalism on the ground that it is deterministic.

In *The Deer Park*, Mailer remains the intransigent radical, but his radicalism takes a sharply different form in the character of Marion Faye. He is Mailer's first "white Negro," the hipster. Rebel and psychopath, Marion derives from the tradition of Romantic Satanism.[7] "Nobility and vice—they're the same thing," says Marion (128). "It just depends on the direction you're going . . . just so you carry it to the end." Here we have a virtual definition of negative transcendence. With his alcohol, drugs, and fast cars, a gun in his glove compartment, and a driver's license suspended long ago, Marion is beyond the law, beyond good and evil as they are customarily defined. In the context of the cynical, meretricious quality of Desert D'Or life, Marion's romantic criminality is seen sympathetically. The apocalyptic tendencies of Mailer's first two novels become explicit in Marion. Speeding through the atom-bomb desert to Mecca (Las Vegas), Marion yearns for the luxury of destruction: "So let it come, Faye thought, let this explosion come, and then another, and all the others, until the Sun God burned the earth. Let it come, Faye begged, like a man praying for rain, let it come and clear the rot and the stench and the stink, let it come for all of everywhere, just so it comes and the world stands clear in the white dead dawn" (139). That is a high price to pay for clarity, but a familiar one in the literature of ferocity. Small wonder this formidable character admires Sergius, who has killed people and has almost been killed himself. For Marion, and for Mailer at this point, death seems a more vivid energy than life, and Satan a more potent being than God.

After Eitel's vacillating delivers Elena into the hands of the bisexual Marion, the pimp performs a Black Mass on her body and the Satanist routs God. "To be pure," says Marion, "one must seek out sin itself, mire the body in offal so the soul may be elevated" (281). This Sadean hipster will run the world in the devil's name. God is not God, and love is "bullshit mountain," (286) a conclusion reached earlier by the disillusioned Sergius about marriage and everything else. In Mailer's world, apocalyptic sex has infected even the liberals, for when Elena discusses Marion's "weird" sexual habits in a letter to Eitel, she says: "There's one way he's like you, he thinks if he's doing something dirty, that's going to change the world or blow up the world or something of the sort" (264). In *The Deer Park*, Mailer replaces political radicalism with sexual radicalism, a notable shift.

Marion is an anarchist. However, his expression of anarchism does not take the political form of overthrowing established forms of government but the personal form of capsizing moral and social convention. The state, Mailer has come to think, will not wither away, Marxism has gone out with the refrigerator, and he turns his focus to the style of revolution rather than revolution itself. The major originality of *The Deer Park* is the incorporation of the hipster into a narrative that otherwise bogs down in the dizzying boredom of musical beds. Mailer is trying to make fictional capital out of the ore of libidinous impulse, the vein of orgy and orgasm that he first tapped in *Barbary Shore*.[8] His novels have moved from the constant awareness of sexual aggression in *The Naked and the Dead* to the central dramatization of some of its more spectacular manifestations in *Barbary Shore* and then to the creation of a character who is self-conscious about its role. Sex for Marion is not merely a symptom of social conditions but a reaction against them. He is the first of Mailer's sexologues. Marion's deification of sexual aggression implies a metaphysical truth, a negative transcendence of a politically enslaved golden ghetto, in which what should be a meaningful sexuality typically breaks down into random screwing.

In "The White Negro," his most important essay and part of *Advertisements for Myself*, Mailer enlarges his role as sexologue. He now sees sexual aggression as inevitably part of political and sociological activity and the hipster—the white man who imitates the desperate marginality of the presumed black style—as the new social type to put sexual aggression into effect. The hipster is Mailer's alternative to the middle. In one sense, the hipster is a resolution of the problem of Marion Faye, the failed Satanist. Regretting that he has been only a pimp, Marion will not force Elena to kill herself, as he had intended. He is, as it were, compromised by conventional views, pulled by the force of the middle. In "The White Negro," there is no such moral shilly-shallying.

Mailer's hipster knows that we all live under a triple tension: the concentration camps, the atomic bomb, and "slow death by conformity" (*AdM* 312). Totalitarian America and totalitarian Nazi Germany are quickly equated. Was the Holocaust, for example, a result of what Mailer calls "the insoluble contradictions of injustice?" And was it not, then, he wonders, an example of evil? But can it be equated to the U.S. bombing of Hiroshima and Nagasaki which, in its saving of a million American lives, was such a contradiction? And how close are we all to that "relatively quick death by the state as *l'univers concentrationaire*?" Would such considerations be uppermost in the mind of the hipster? Death by conformity was the more real issue, a legitimate concern for anyone—except, perhaps, the hipster. What Mailer is doing once more is legitimizing violence by assuming as axiomatic the essential violence of the state, keeping alive the idea of revolution in the form of gesture. In his critique of "The White Negro,"[9] Jean Malaquais rightly sees Mailer's hipster as an attempt to resurrect the myth of the proletariat.[10]

The decision of the hipster to encourage the psychopath in himself, "whether the life is criminal or not" (*AdM* 313), is Romanticism *in extremis*, a strident assertion of impulse at the expense of a society considered to be totally repressive. Mailer justifies the murder of a storekeeper by teenage hoodlums on the ground that it is the murder not only of a man but of an institution, private property; moreover, in bringing on the police, one is "daring the unknown." What price mystery? The phrase brings to mind his description of a killer grinding his heels into the face of a dying man: "Two people are engaging in a dialogue with eternity."[11] When he is justifying violence, Mailer sounds like a depraved Sunday school teacher. It becomes clear why he speaks of the hipster's search for love as the search for "the apocalyptic orgasm" (321), recalling Marion Faye's fantasy of blowing up the world. The hipster "drains his hatred" (321) in sex to mollify an assumed sadism so that he can "love" (320).

Mailer has Sade explicitly in mind when he says of his past-destroying, present-adoring Hip that "its ultimate logic surpasses even the unforgettable solution of the Marquis de Sade to sex, private property, and the family, that all men and women have absolute but temporary rights over the bodies of all other men and women—the nihilism of Hip proposes as its final tendency that every social restraint and category be removed, and the affirmation implicit in the proposal is that man would then prove more creative than murderous and so would not destroy himself" (328). Mailer does not see what a male chauvinist Sade is—in Sade, men have more rights than women—but he does see who his allies are. Sade is the patron saint of negative transcendence, a Utopianism that sees crime as sex, and he would have understood Mailer's rhapsodizing about "the paradise of limitless energy and perception just beyond the next wave of the next orgasm" (325).

If Mailer's version of Hip seems tendentious and militant compared to the benign, stoned privacy more accurately associated with it—which often works against sexual fulfillment—it is because of his inevitable political edge, his indictment of what he later comes to call liberal totalitarianism. "The liberal tenets of the Center are central," he laments; "All people are alike if we suppress the ugliness in each of us, all sadism is evil, all masochism is sick, all spontaneity is suspect, all individuality is infantile, and the salvation of the world must come from social manipulation of human material. That's why all people must tend to become the same."¹² It is as if the underground man had read Sade rather than Rousseau. Yet the middle found it relatively easy to absorb what used to be called perversity. And the next major wave of conformity was the wave of the infantile. In later years, Mailer laments that the hero of his vision has been reduced to the cocaine dealer. And, even in "The White Negro," Mailer is too complex not to see some possibility of a totalitarian underside to his heroic fantasy. But the main thrust of the essay is empathetic.

In writing *Advertisements for Myself*, Mailer is still in the 1950s and sees nothing in the middle other than the dead center of dullness. Typically, the middling life becomes a nostalgia for radicalism, psychoanalysis, a four-room flat in Queens, a career as a hack writer hiding a dim wish to be a novelist, a ten-year marriage, children, a titillation of pornography. Such is the scenario of Mailer's "The Man Who Studied Yoga," his story about the muddle in the middle. Sam Slovoda "is neither ordinary nor extraordinary . . . not young nor yet old, not tall or short . . . He is a mild pleasant-looking man who has just turned forty" (*AdM* 145). Mailer himself is more literally in Dante's middle of the journey, though as the first words of *Advertisements for Myself* state, he feels anything but: "I contain within myself the bitter exhaustions of an old man, and the cocky arguments of a bright boy. So I am anything but my proper age of thirty-six" (15). Slovoda, by contrast, does not have the tension of the extreme. He is not an exemplar of ordinary possibility but a satiric version of it.

Like the opening description of Sam, which focuses on the nondescript middle, the story is driven by a neutering rhetoric, with sentences that collapse into compromise. Sam is described as "straddled between the loss of a country he has never seen, and his repudiation of the country in which he lives" (161). He often tells himself "with contempt that he has the cruelty of a kind weak man" (146). He is not sure of the boundary between compromise and schizophrenia.

The crisis in the apparent calm occurs when a group of friends watch a pornographic movie called *The Evil Act*. In this movie, a sort of Sadean virgin initiate comes around to the point of view of her victimizers. "Let's do it again," she says (*AdM* 164). The question now is will these six respectable, professional, middle-class, largely Jewish people "perform the orgy which tickles at the heart of their desire"? The answer, of course, is no. After their friends leave, Sam and Eleanor do make love in front of the movie, and "one cannot say that it is unsatisfactory any more than one can say it is pleasant" (170). Sam is, in fact, aroused to performance, partly by the exemplary utterance of Frankie in the movie—"take that you whore." But he shrivels back into psychoanalytic worries and the pleasurable pain that years ago, before they met, Eleanor had partaken in such an orgy. Political passivity, sexual deflation—these are the wages of the middle class. Any sexual heroics will have to appear in the comic-strip prose that Sam turns out about "Bramba the Venusian and Lee-Lee Deeds, Hollywood Star" (171). The worst that can be said about Sam is that, neither sexual nor non-sexual, he masturbates for a living.

The other extraordinary story in *Advertisements for Myself*, and one of Mailer's best works, is "The Time of Her Time." Here for the first time in fiction Mailer finds a prose style adequate to his sexual aggression. "The Man Who Studied Yoga" made literary capital of the lack of just this quality in its admirable satiric thrust. "The White Negro" in its complex cadences, daring parallels and contrasts, and radical energy encased in a voice of historical doom is Mailer displaying apocalyptic aggression successfully for the first time in expository prose. (The Sorrows-of-Mailer "I" that cobbles *Advertisements for Myself* together is a lesser illustration of this originality.) These three short works make the book a watershed in Mailer's development. Ferocity is no longer just a theme but a point of view, and this will be reflected in his overcoming an admitted weakness in fiction, a sluggish narrative voice. In Marion Faye, Mailer was moving toward a new level of self-conscious dramatization, but he had not yet incorporated it into narrative voice. In Sergius of "The Time of Her Time," ferocity in Mailer finds its first poet.

"The Time of Her Time" is about the sexual initiation of Denise Gondelman—a nineteen-year-old, middle-class New York University student—into vaginal orgasm or sexually conscious time (the second *time* in the title). Before she meets Sergius O'Shaughnessy, the character from *The Deer Park* in a more psychologically secure incarnation as Greenwich Village stud and bullfight instructor, Denise is in her own psychoanalytic phrase "vaginally anaesthetized" (455). But not after, for Sergius is by his own description "the messiah of the one-night stand" (447), and Denise is the recipient of a wry salvation. Denise's Jewishness is no accident, for being Jewish means to Mailer a middle-class respectability that masks sexual inadequacy. Sergius has found in many Jewish women "a sort of 'Ech' of disgust at the romantic and mysterious All" (499), a quality that wars in Denise with putatively lesbian hysterics. That Denise has social pretensions, "a snotty elegance of superiority" (449), and a college-girl snobbery, and that this Jewess was "proud, aggressive, vulgar, tense, stiff and arrogant" (456), is every possible encouragement for Sergius to rise to the occasion. Class and sexual warfare merge as Mailer now sees everything in terms of the ass struggle. In Sergius, Mailer's prose takes on a new vividness. Denise's ways "inflamed the avenger of my crotch . . . I was a primitive for a prime minute, a gorged gouge of a working class phallus . . . I was one of the millions on the bottom, who had the muscles to move the sex which kept the world alive, and I would grind it into her, the healthy hearty inches and the sweat of the cost of acquired culture when you started low and you wanted to go high" (450). The prose is marked by a tone of hard worldliness, of sexual mastery manifested as an elegant Hip obscenity, a raunchy outlook elevated by a leaning toward the metaphysical, even the Utopian, as when Sergius speaks of "hefting those young kneadables of future power" (447). All is heavily underlined by a uniform sexual aggression. Sergius will "lay waste to her little independence" (451).

At first they make love merely "like two club fighters in an open exchange," knowing "neither the pain of punishment nor the pride of pleasure" (451–52). Making some impression on Denise, Sergius feels "the wanton whip-thrash of a wounded snake, she was on fire and frozen at the same time" (452). The prose in these examples tends to a euphuism so pronounced that, as in John Lyly, it amounts to the ornate celebration of a newly discovered language—which is precisely what it is. In Mailer's narrative, the inevitable ghost of Frankie appears. She kisses him so avidly that, Sergius confesses, "to my distant surprise . . . my hand came up and clipped her mean and open-handed across the face." She responds warmly to this but does not find the rhythm, and he is gone and, consequently, dangerous, with part of him "remaining cold and murderous because she had deprived me, she had fled domination which was liberty for her" (452). This last turn on the master-slave relationship was a war cry for feminists, though some of them have since come to have a certain affection for Mailer, for his supplying in his most characteristic moments so unyielding and transparent a definition of the enemy.

Denise is not without aggressive resources of her own. Repenting of having given the smug, irresistible Sergius her address and phone number, she socks him in the jaw. Nothing has come to conclusion that first memorable night, despite two heroic assaults on Sergius's part, and the second night is even more uneventful, leaving the metaphysical lover to feel like the central character of Kafka's *The Castle*—that tale, as he curiously puts it, "of the search of a man for his apocalyptic orgasm" (456). On the basis of this description alone, we can see the narrow lens Mailer uses to view the world of spiritual quest.

The third night is decisive. In that attempt at coupling, Sergius says: "I worked on her like a riveter, knowing her resistances were made of steel, I threw her a fuck the equivalent of a fifteen-round fight" (463). The first figure is out of Henry Miller; the second is pure Mailer. For all the pyrotechnics, however, Denise does not quite get there. He then holds her prone. As "she thrashed beneath me like a trapped animal," he enters "her symbolic and therefore real vagina." She achieves a kind of orgasm. But this isn't good enough, and Sergius turns her over and moves to—a wonderful combination of propriety and ruefulness—"love's first hole." Although she is teetering on the brink, she stops again until he says in her ear: "You dirty little Jew" (464). This ultimate assault on her solid middle-class identity does the job, but, ironically, Sergius at this point is too numb to reap the harvest. "Oh, Jesus, I made it, oh Jesus, I did," cries Denise, in a sobbing ecstasy. So we witness her conversion to Christianity as an orgasmic shiksa. But not quite: the morning after, she reverts to her Jewish middle-class roots in the form of what Sergius calls totalitarian psychoanalytic jargon, reducing the apparent Don Juan to the real homosexual. Yet Sergius cannot help admiring the killer in her.

Despite the brilliance of the three small jewels of *Advertisements for Myself*, which came out in 1959, Mailer had trouble creating a new novel. Between *The Deer Park* in 1955 and *An American Dream* in 1964 is a long and difficult period for Mailer as a novelist. It has often been suggested that the serial publication of *An American Dream* was how Mailer forced himself back into novel writing. Paying the bills also had much to do with it. What is more interesting is that when Mailer gets launched again, he returns to a version of the hipster. The more things change the more they are the same. Certainly not lumpen, Stephen Rojack is nonetheless the qualified psychopath, a man who finally follows his impulses no matter how destructive they may be. The victim of his rebellion against private property, tradition, and law, is not an anonymous storekeeper but his wife. Mailer's drift away from Marxism is indicated by the fact that in no way can Rojack be considered an updated version of the proletariat. Mailer now follows anarchic impulse wherever it may lead. There has also been an even greater change: as a reflection of the severity of conventional social restraints like marriage, now the apocalypse comes before the orgasm, and it comes in the form of murder.

Unlike the earlier hipster, Rojack has tried to work within the system, even the political system. A government major at Harvard, he has served in Congress with another war hero, John F. Kennedy. Rojack has, however, moved further to the left by bolting the Democratic Party and running for office in 1948 on the Progressive ticket led by Henry Wallace and Glen Taylor. After that defeat, he remains political in the broader sense, finding a niche on television as a professor of existential psychology. But in the struggle in Rojack's psyche between society and the moon, the moon wins. Rojack becomes totally immersed in his strange, extreme subjectivity.

Unlike the earlier hipster, Rojack has sought love in a mate, even various mates. He is no stranger to marriage, but he is a stranger to his current wife. Where Mailer's earlier psychopath may have found an outlet for his Romantic criminality in any representative of the Establishment, Rojack finds it in the elite essence of the power structure itself. This is what his wife represents. Her fancy moniker becomes a symbol of a general civilized depravity. Herself a victim of her super-rich father's incestuous desire, she in turn visits a brutishness on her spouse, the beleaguered Rojack. With her, he feels murderous—without her, suicidal. Considering his living death, his nausea in the face of experience, suicide becomes a heroic temptation to him. "Like a lion I would join the legions of the past and share their power," he thinks in the rather euphuisitic idiom of the novel's beginning. But the moment passes, and "nothing noble" remains[13]—nothing, that is, but murder.

There has been no woman in Mailer quite like Deborah, nor has there been another who is so clearly upper class. Mailer's macho types are so vulnerable in their erectitude that they are easy game for the promiscuous wife. Beginning with Croft, Mailer presents an anxiety of sexual performance so deep that it easily explodes into violence. Deborah, however, is Mailer's first total castrator. If there is one thing that elicits instability in Mailer, it is the powerful woman and the inconsequential man.

In his suicidal depression, Rojack is particularly vulnerable. His wealthy wife is the only achievement to which he can point. Furthermore, he needs her money for a possible run for the Senate in the distant future. The money is all the more troublesome in that she is more married to it than to him. These indirect instigations to assault are compounded by direct ones. Deborah knows how to hurt him. She belittles his status as a war hero and ridicules his new mistress: "What a big boy you must be to take up with a sparrow" (*AD* 25). In fear, Rojack kneels to kiss her hand, murmuring "I love you," but to no effect. She tells him of her bullfighter lover, asks for a divorce, and expresses distaste for his outré sexual proclivities, in which she has nonetheless engaged with other men. He slaps her face harder than he intended. She charges "like a bull," swinging her knee into his groin. Missing, "she reached with both hands, tried to find my root and mangle me" (30). He strangles her. Afterward, as if to affirm the justice of the murder, Rojack recalls the "pinch of pain" he had felt in navigating her Vagina Dentata. Even worse, he remembers what a superb, ballsy hunter of lion and bear she had been, and how she had degradingly taken him to hunt for moles and woodchucks, which he did not do very well. For Rojack, it seems, the reversal of male and female stereotypes justifies homicide.

Now a murderer, Rojack feels he is in a state of grace. He looks at himself in a mirror and thinks: "I had never seen a face so handsome" (38). This sick, sentimental glorification of murder is later endorsed by Cherry, who remembers that she "saw a man once after he had come back from a killing [who looked] like he'd been painted with a touch of magic" (175). Additionally, murder has its own rewards. Rojack informs us that murder is always sexual (although suicide never is), and as if to prove a point goes across the hall from his dead wife's room and takes the German maid, Ruta, in every possible way, exciting her by saying: "You're a Nazi" (44). Some sense of the immediate collapse of the novel may be seen in Rojack's musing that "she was becoming mine as no woman ever had, she wanted no more than to be part of my will" (45). The first perception is cliché, the second a ludicrously stereotypical grasping at masculine authority, the love object as maid.

His masculinity restored, Rojack is possessed by the superfluous desire to "kill her again." Now totally potent and dangerous, by way of departure Rojack "fired one hot streak of fierce bright murder" (56) into the ever-pliant Ruta as an exclamation point.

The novel breaks down in a plot involving detectives, the Mafia, the CIA, interrogation, staredown, and conspiracy. Rojack hears again the call of the middle, elicited by the image of Cherry, a Mafia mistress with a heart of gold, a spiritual virgin as her name indicates, a Sonia to his Raskolnikov. Even Mailer came to consider her a sentimental portrait. Trying to overcome his usual nausea, Rojack prays: "Let me love that girl, and become a father, and try to be a good man, and do some decent work. Yes God . . . do not make me go back again to the charnel house of the moon" (162). Richard Poirier finds this "incredibly moving,"[14] neglecting to point out that the very next sentence reads: "But like a soldier on six-hour leave to a canteen, I knew I would have to return" (*AD* 162). No more convincing is Rojack's almost conventionally religious assertion that love "was not a gift but a vow" (165). He had had hints of this before, even with Deborah, even with "girls I had known for a night and never knew again," which leaves one with the vision of nightly vows. With Cherry it is different. She confesses to him that she has had the time of her time with him, as he has already informed the reader that "for the first time in my life without passing through fire or straining the stones of my will, I came up from my body rather than down from my mind" (128). Cherry may be the answer to his inner divisions, the gulf between his hipster and middle-class selves. So she must be killed off somehow. Rojack lives in a world governed by extremity, as the two final confrontations prove. Shago Martin, a black jazz musician and former lover of Cherry, is a stud who has an aura of being in "a sexual round robin where the big people played. All the big Negroes and all the big Whites" (125). The banality of Rojack's power fantasy indicates a sharp reduction of the power scene. Even in his paranoia, General Cummings thought more seriously of the League of Omnipotent Men, a power elite. Sex as the power scene smacks of Hollywood vulgarity, to which Mailer has often been peculiarly subject. When Shago is replaced by Rojack in Cherry's affections, the black cocksman comes down hard on him: "She picks you, Professor, looking to square out, she's looking for something luke and tepid to keep her toes warm. You kissing them yet?" (192). Rojack stomps him.

In a rather mechanically contrived novel where a new character is introduced in each chapter to sing his aria, it is left to the climactic chapter for Rojack to meet Kelly, the fountainhead of corruption. In a way, Kelly seems a soul mate to Rojack. "There's nothing but magic at the top," Kelly says. For Kelly, too, the average man avoids God or the devil, "decides to be mediocre, and put up with the middle" (246). And Rojack is drawn by sexual emanations of troilism and bisexuality coming from Kelly. In the absurd bit of dramatic business with which the novel winds down, Kelly shows his true colors by nearly pushing Rojack to his death and is properly assaulted by Rojack in turn.

An American Dream is Mailer's most controversial work up to this point, having been extravagantly praised (by Richard Poirier and Leo Bersani) and roundly damned (by Philip Rahv and Elizabeth Hardwick). Yet even those who praise it usually do so with the understanding that it is something of a sport, a variation on Pop. If so, Mailer appropriates Pop effortlessly, having always had a special feeling for melodrama, Manichean struggles, erotic fantasies, and lurid cliché. Moreover, the excesses of the book are often illustrative of a certain kind of Pop, one involving a sympathetic portrayal of sexual violence and not another kind. Mailer's apologists ignore the question of why he found this kind so congenial, making him out to be a Flaubert of the crime-story set. "Nothing in the book . . . except the virtuosity of the writing itself indicates a way out of the nightmare Rojack seems to be telling," writes Bersani; "The *playfulness* of the novel is . . . the natural tone of a man for whom events have become strictly literary-novelistic situations to be freely exploited for the sake of a certain style and the self-enjoyment it perhaps unexpectedly provides."[15] All this makes the moral and psychological nexus of the novel far less important than it really is. Variation on Pop though it is, the book is obsessive Mailer and, by his own account, "realistic."[16] Why do apocalypse and orgasm open the floodgates of Mailer's style? Why not, say, family happiness?

While it is not true to say, as Rahv does, that all we learn from Mailer on the subject of murder is that it can be an exquisite sexual stimulant, it is true that we have murder without consequences, crime without punishment. As Rahv puts it: "Only in a hipster's fantasy is society so easily cheated of its prey and only in fantasy can the self became so absolutized, so unchecked by reality, as to convert itself with impunity into the sole arbiter of good and evil."[17] Whether the novel be realistic or fantasy realism, no amount of verbal pyrotechnics and Pop conventions obviates this criticism. The novel's violence is so typical of Mailer's concerns that despite the work's souped-up quality, its thematic tendency cannot be attributed to a flip absorption of Pop. Indeed, Mailer's penchant for guiltless violence and immoralism appears again and again in his work, in the name of some return of the instinctual or natural—as if rape and murder were primitive. Psychology and anthropology have taught us that this is not the case; that instincts are conservative; and that the id can be as tyrannical as any superego, the superego as repressed as any id. The white Negro is as much conditioned by pathology as he is liberated by spontaneity. Yet Rojack is beyond guilt. "The root of neurosis," thinks his surprisingly sympathetic father-in-law, the incestuous, murderous Kelly, "is cowardice rather than brave old Oedipus" (*AD* 235). After all, what could be wrong with Oedipus? Didn't he murder his father and fuck his mother?

The hero of Mailer's next fictional work—*Why Are We in Vietnam?*—fantasizes about doing both. He is described in rather dire terms by the family shrink as being "morally anaesthetized and smoldering with presumptive violence," as harboring "incest fixes, murder configurations, suicide sets, disembowelment diagrams and diabolism designs."[18] He is, in short, a typical Mailer hero. Anyway, the shrink is just "a nice Jewish fellow type" (*WV* 9) or "a fuckless wonder" (17). D. J., our disc jockey hero, bristles with libido. In this book, the super-American Texas psyche is anatomized by one of its own, who is also a white Negro. A reader of the Marquis de Sade by the age of fifteen and a follower of Burroughs, D. J. illustrates Mailer's view that through his obscenity, a man can discriminate between himself and repressive society. For Mailer, obscenity is sanity, the nobility, the humor of the common man under adverse conditions. In *Why Are We in Vietnam?*, such adversity is the air we breathe. The scabrous lyricism of the work allows Mailer to think that this "was the first time his style seemed at once very American to him and very literary in the best way."[19] To be sure, D. J. is not your common vilifier. He is a virtuoso, and this is Mailer's most *written* book, the one most dependent on sheer verbal performance, far more so even than *An American Dream*. The novella was written in one intense burst, where humor met with moral outrage. Obscenity, for Mailer, implies the socially meliorative. But how constructive can verbal sexual aggression be?

Like *An American Dream*, *Why Are We in Vietnam?* uses familiar plots as a peg for Mailer to hang his talent on. Faulkner's *The Bear*, with its rape of nature by predatory civilization, is the central romance that Mailer builds on here, even to the point of a final abandonment of civilized appurtenances. But the disproportion between nature and technology has become gross, and the motive for the hunt often grotesque. And there is no question of the initiation of an innocent—the book doesn't contain one. Added onto this romance are a few echoes of Hemingway's "The Short Happy Life of Francis Macomber"— the failure to shoot straight and to deal cleanly with a wounded animal, disgrace under pressure. Though, again, in Mailer there is a turn for the worse. Where Macomber comes of age, as D. J. does, Rusty only lies about it. How could it be otherwise, since he—a parody of Faulkner's Sam Fathers— represents the reality of plastic? D. J. feels murderous toward his father. Oedipally enough, he wants to kill him before (as well as after) Rusty's display of hypocrisy—out of pure high spirits, as it were. Mailer's metaphor is telling: "D. J. for the first time in his life is hip to the hole in his center which is slippery desire to turn his gun and blast a shot into Rusty's fat fuck face, thump in his skull, whawng! and whoong! with dead-ass butt of his Remington 721" (*WV* 144). Here the murderous impulse and lack of a center merge clearly into a nihilistic oneness. The mood is elevated, and why not? "Brilliance is next to murder, man" (219), quips D. J., illustrating Mailer's appalling sentimentality about the subject. When Rusty (he's rusting) falsely claims to have killed the bear, D. J. "couldn't sleep for fear he'd somnambulate long enough to beat in Rusty's head, so he got up" (167). It is not only the admirable D. J. who feels like a killer: God himself sends a message to the pristine wilds of Alaska. D. J. divines that "God was a beast, not a man, and God said, 'Go out and kill—fulfill my will, go and kill'" (219). The prophet hears strange voices. God is made to be an aspect of the fashionable negative transcendence.

But one ought not to assume that Mailer is D. J. at this point. Obviously, there is plenty of D. J. in Mailer. They speak the same language. Yet Mailer means to indict the whole super-Aamerican milieu, including to some extent even its white Negro aberration. Why are we in Vietnam? Because "Amurica" at its most "Amurican" produces sadists out to go beyond the limit—even Mailer's *machismo* is qualified here—witness the ethic of pro football and animal slaughter. It is a land so rife with technocratic totalitarianism that its prime characteristic is an aggression that feeds upon itself. In the novel, Vietnam is an afterthought and a logical extreme, the murderous conclusion to a murderous argument.

Both *An American Dream* and *Why Are We in Vietnam?* have climactic bisexual scenes that are anticlimactic concerning bisexuality. We have seen Mailer's negative view of homosexuality in his remarks on Genet. The white Negro then, who is bisexual, as is D. J. in tendency and Tex in fact, is—for all of Mailer's empathy—symptomatic of a dying civilization. The verbal obscenity remains justified, the necessary response to a larger obscenity, even though this response is itself indicative of sadistic excess. Which brings us to the final turn of the screw. Mailer's deepest sympathy is for precisely those characters who are doomed to aggression. His creative characters are violent and must be so; indeed, for Mailer creativity is a form of violence. His successful lovers are sadistic, even murderous. It is not for nothing that Sergius, in the masterly "The Time of Her Time," calls his penis "the avenger." It could not be otherwise in a society he judges to be monolithically repressive. In *Why Are We in Vietnam?* the rational, liberal part of Mailer cannot help condemning the killing in Vietnam, but the dark, subconscious Mailer, willy-nilly, goes along with its psychological necessity. D. J. is both creative and murderous, Croft imperious and violent, and Marion Faye romantic and sadistic. Killing Deborah gives Rojack "a view of . . . heaven;" it is like coming "in a woman against her cry" (*AD* 31). Here we have negative transcendence in all its black purity. Orgasm has often been associated with death, as a transcendence of time, but rarely with murder, as a destruction of the other. This is the wisdom of our Sade.[20]

In the nineteen years between 1964 and 1983, Mailer published no novel, though for ten of those years he worked on *Ancient Evenings* off and on. Ferocity diminished in him, and with it his ability, for a time, to explore what Gide called the wild darkness.[21] This loss is compensated for by the daylight reality of Mailer the journalist, but in that work the sense of apocalypse is not as intense. In *Armies of the Night*, Mailer realizes with regret that in any "final cataclysm" (*Armies* 94), he would be a victim not a leader, which does not prevent him from wishing for an American invasion of China. He has become a self-styled Left Conservative, critical of extremists on the Left (whose authoritarianism he underestimates) and Right (no underestimation here), yet insistent on the totalitarian quality of liberalism. Paradoxically, Mailer's incarnation as a public writer enables him to come back to character, in the person of himself, the worried, ambivalent, humorous, vaguely Whitmanesque citizen whose emergence accounts for much of the distinction and popularity of *Armies of the Night*. In achieving this persona, Mailer—with the help of a third-person substitute "I," half-hero, half-clown—unwittingly asserts the real value of liberalism.

Mailer's next nonfiction blockbuster, *Of a Fire on the Moon*, records with a peculiar mixture of excitement and melancholy that technocratic America has routed the antiplastic radicals. Those "princelings . . . of hip," with their "bellowings of obscenity like the turmoil of cattle," have fragmented into "informers, police agents, militants, angel hippies, New Left totalists . . . an unholy stew of fanatics, far-outs, and fucked-outs."[22] Sexual aggression seems to have become nightmare. If the hipster fantasists have lost their dream, the squares have produced fantasy. Technology, which tells us that black magic does not exist, has produced white magic in the form of the moon rocket. And how can literary machismo knock the biggest prick in the world? Mailer is confused. He cannot determine whether Neil Armstrong is devil or saint, or perhaps "twinsouled" (*FM* 398), or whether WASPs were savages or saviors. Nor can he now discern whether the devil represents science and plastic or marijuana—or both. Mailer sometimes considers his dualities as part of a Manichean struggle. But a Manichean who cannot make up his mind? Is Mailer offering dialectical depth or popular theology? Is he, in his own description, "the Nijinsky of ambivalence" (414), or just the Fred Astaire?

In *The Prisoner of Sex*, though, an exhausted Mailer is now willing "to cease thinking of himself as revolutionary."[23] The sexual theme reinvigorates him. What he considers the liberal totalitarianism of androgynous feminism arouses him to what is now a rather civilized aggression. Using a new version of an old argument—woman as the carrier of children is closer to nature than man is—Mailer justifies masculine dominance as a psychologically necessary counterforce to that closeness. Unisex behavior he sees as a form of sexual Stalinism in league with liberal utilitarianism and its rational quantification, its contraception, and its destruction of mystery and awe. He is now shocked by the polymorphous perverse. Much of the successful humor of the book derives from Mailer's realization that he is no longer a sexual Marxist but a sexual Tory. "Like all revolutions," he says of the sexual revolution in a 1986 interview, "it went off the rails."[24]

In psychological disarray, Mailer finds stability in an updated version of his "*l'univers concentrationaire*." To do this he goes to a literal, not merely a metaphorical, prison, in *The Executioner's Song*. He takes another try at the criminal, this time depending largely on fact to do the work of imagination. Keeping himself out of the book, he writes in a flat style, thereby deflecting the anticipated criticism that he was inflating murder again. The pathos of the criminal in Mailer's view is that psychopathology is a form of Romantic rebellion. But when Gary Gilmore murdered a gas-station attendant, are we supposed to believe he was entering into a new relationship with society? And Gilmore kills again, coming off clearly as a cold-blooded murderer. His love relationship, with its one-way suicide pact, remains dubious, one that was revived only when, imprisoned, Gilmore was basically inaccessible. And as Diane Johnson says, "to suggest disappointed love as an explanation for a Gary Gilmore is a somewhat irresponsible oversimplification."[25] In any case, Mailer's salvationary interest has shifted. The orgasm theme is muted.

Instead Mailer drifts toward the theological. Gilmore believed that he died to save his soul. Believing in karma and reincarnation, Gilmore thought that if he were executed, there would be no chance for his soul to expire before his body. Although Mailer grants that "it's possible he was a very evil man,"[26] he is taken by this "heroic element." In a telling metaphor, Mailer considers Gilmore "a failed movie star."[27] Could Mailer's attraction to Gilmore be based on the latter's celebrity? Possibly, since Mailer is quite capable of confusing celebrity with notoriety and tends to be struck by both. Mailer has said that by the end of the 1960s and into the 1970s "I felt more and more that I was no longer interesting as a subject to myself."[28] So he turned to other lives, even biography. But what was still interesting to him was his obsessions, as we see in this empathic portrait of a killer. It is interesting to see Mailer waffle on the Bernhard Goetz case. There is no room in Mailer's Romantic iconography for a middle-class killer.

Mailer's ambivalence about Gilmore makes for an engaging complexity. And his portrait of ordinary America reflects a love for that which Gilmore both embodies and destroys. Mailer confects a subtle blend of nihilism and decency. He says, surprisingly: "At one point I almost called this book 'American Virtue,' believe it or not. I was terribly tempted to, because I thought it was the true title."[29] But this became "impossible, because everyone would see it as a sardonic title." Mailer has an epiphany in supersquare Utah: "I learned something I never quite put into words before. I think in America we are all enormously concerned with being virtuous." Gilmore's execution highlighted this for Mailer: "You find people who may play a very small part in the execution of Gary Gilmore—yet they thought about it a great deal and they worried about it . . . Everybody wanted to do the right thing, and I thought that it might be that rather than that society is evil, maybe what it is is a sad comedy."

The distinction of Mailer's journalistic work derives from a complexity of vision that transcends ferocity. His daylight perceptions appear to be deeper than his nocturnal ones. And where *Armies of the Night* succeeds because he is so fully in it, *The Executioner's Song* succeeds because he is not. For Mailer in the past, there was no Left too *gauche*. He has now graduated from radicalism to liberalism, and, for many, this is his best work. But Mailer knows that his reputation as a writer in the long run will depend on the evaluation of his fiction. Will he be seen to have achieved such distinction in a work of art?

When, after a twenty-year hiatus, Mailer comes out with a full-length novel, *Ancient Evenings*, we see that fiction once again serves him as an occasion to release the sexual demons. At a fictional impasse in his contemporary America, Mailer finds an equal sexual darkness in ancient Egypt. Its erotic cosmos, Mailer stressed—not quite accurately—in interviews, antedates the Judeo-Christian tradition. And though he has said that he did not have contemporary America in mind, that he was striving for a total disorientation and a new psychology, many critics feel the novel has affinities to sexually liberated America and Mailer's obsessive sexual concerns. (And his reincarnation concerns as well, since he considers the Egyptian hereafter "close to my own.")[30] Mailer himself has said that it is a work that goes back to *Advertisements for Myself*, which canonized the importance of orgasm and titillatingly suggested the importance of orgy. Mailer's Egypt is beyond renunciation, even beyond death. Laws of nature and society are abrogated in favor of a narcissistic, infantile majesty. Though Mailer has been influenced by *The Book of the Dead*, he says nothing of the frequent appearance in that work of the word meaning "abomination" or "sin," which includes some of the more unusual sexual practices in his novel. True, Mailer can dodge this criticism by claiming that he is writing about the Egyptian feast of the pig. Menenhetet II tells us "on this night not only could we speak of matters considered improper on all other nights, but indeed, [we] were supposed to."[31] He thus creates a context of normal propriety. But, of course, Mailer chose this night as the subject of most of his novel, and propriety is scarcely the word for any part of it. The phrasing of Menenhetet's explanation—how "this night" is different from "all other nights"—is an (unintentional?) parody of a famous part of the Passover service (which, of course, celebrates the Jews' liberation from Egypt). If it reaches no other heights, this novel is certainly the apogee of Jewish de-identification.

In *Ancient Evenings*, Mailer presents a world without superego as he leaves no phallus unadored, no incest inhibited, no hole unentered. Ramses II, the major phallic presence and the pharaoh of the Exodus, has thousands of descendants, and the lower classes as well typically spend the night grunting and roaring with pleasure, "thereby encouraging the animals to join with their barks and screams and loving sounds" (*AE* 123), in remarkable animal unison. The precocious six-year-old narrator masturbates to the overwhelming scent of flowers, musing rather autistically: "I . . . did not know where the blooms of these flowers ended, and I began" (121), a crucial distinction that should be made much earlier in life. He recalls burying his nose into his mother, "higher and higher above her knees as I grew older" and admits: "I never knew such happiness as then" (227–28). Toward the end of the novel, in another incarnation, his incestuous wish is realized, no surprise in Mailer's ultimate game of musical beds. In the major public ceremony of the novel, Ramses II shows his immense erection to the populace, to tumultuous cheers. In a rapture of physical omnipotence, he says: "I am, I am all that will be" (503).

Mailer has always been drawn to figures who expressed masculine potency to the point of solipsism. "I hate everything which is not in myself," says not Ramses II but Croft (*ND* 164). Mailer's early admission of secret admiration for a violent character like Croft, startling then, makes clear sense in an overall view of his career.

Mailer has said of his ancient Egypt that "it's a world of dominance, where you find your place literally by whom you're doing it to,"[32] which puts an impossibly inflated importance on the sexual act and may explain why his paradise of the polymorphous perverse is a disintegrating one. Buggery once connoted rebellion for Mailer, who now presents it in a somber, elegiac tone. Mailer's Egypt is a place sated and diminished by its own fulfillments. Ferocity, contingent to some degree on social outrage, has lost its place. Mailer's career as an apocalyptic orgiast has come to a grinding halt.

Ideally a complement to love, orgasm in Mailer is often an alternative to it. There is usually the sense in Mailer that something is done to, rather than with, another. As a form, the novel demands more than fireworks and surfaces, which is why Mailer's best erotic work is in the short story and novella.

Sex is usually sexual aggression in Mailer, and sexual aggression a narcissistic rhapsody. In a great novelist of ferocity, such as D. H. Lawrence, sexual aggression is part of a sustained effort to realize one's own character through coupling—as in *Women in Love*, "The Fox," and *Lady Chatterley's Lover* (the latter a novel that Mailer said changed his life)—which is why aggression and tenderness are inextricably bound. Not so in Mailer. Great erotic fiction demands a pas de deux of development. Too often in Mailer, the couple is a man and his mannequin.

Moreover, viewing sex as the single index of one's spiritual condition implies an ideological simplification, a saved-damned, orgiastic-impotent dichotomy that assumes a rebellious elect, a salvationary scourge whose ferocity will lead to a cosmic kindling of the otherwise icy present. Though the case for an erotic cosmos carried a great, strained urgency in some of the moderns as a visionary antidote to sexual inhibition, the triumph of deinhibition has made the salvationary quality of orgasm appear less urgent. At the advent of the modern period, people were presumably deprived and hysterical; now they are sated and depressed. Promiscuity, unlike frigidity, seems to have no cure in libido theory. Easy access to sexual fulfillment may have less and less to do with love.

We need to assert that there are aspects of the spirit that have nothing to do with sex, and that there are aspects of sex that have nothing to do with anything but sex. It is not clear that public and private power often coalesce, nor is it clear that the apocalyptic is more necessary than civility to the salvation of our lives, assuming that they need saving. In witnessing the glare of sexual aggression in Mailer, his grasping for the Utopian primitive element, we view another light that failed.

Mailer has often said—to the consternation of many—that *Ancient Evenings* was his best work. It is, at least in quantity, the peak of his sexology phase, which in the last twenty years he has no longer pursued. Though now and again it has pursued him. *Ancient Evenings* is, whatever else, an original work. But, usually, when there is so great a disparity between a writer's expectation for a work and its actual public and critical reception, the air has escaped the balloon. With the notable exception of long stretches of *Harlot's Ghost*, Mailer's career as a major writer is over. The rest is cruising, the celebrity author writing merely interesting books to fulfill contractual obligations. After having gone all out, Mailer opts in his next work, *Tough Guys Don't Dance*, for the relative security of a literary convention: the mystery story. True, as one of the blurbs puts it, Mailer doing a mystery is like Julia

Child doing a hamburger. There is so much chopped meat in this book that hamburger may be an even more appropriate figure of speech than the reviewer intended. Mailer has not rid himself of ruddy gore. Yet the suspense, the revelation, and the story itself make the work seem almost conventional.

In *Tough Guys Don't Dance*, Mailer goes "Irish" again. Tim Madden is a tough guy, and it is easy for Mailer to create a tough-guy hero. In a novel whose very air is sadistic, our hero breathes well. He muses on sadism: "I was thinking that surgeons had to be the happiest people in the world. To cut people up and get paid for it—that's happiness."[33] He writes a note to himself that says: "the perception of the possibility of greatness in myself has always been followed by desire to murder the nearest unworthy" (*TG* 32), a Sadean perception that Madden tries in this instance to neutralize.

Along with this, we get Mailer's familiar macho paraphernalia of towers and parapets, though this time his hero, an amalgam of tough guy and would-be writer, thinks of Jones's biography of Freud and considers these structures as "doubtless an unruly attack of latent homosexual panic in myself" (100). He recalls the obelisk in Central Park, the graffiti in public toilets at the foot of the Washington Monument and, later, the Provincetown Monument. The homosexual theme is vivid in an encounter with the hulking, corrupt town police chief: "Homosexuality was sitting between Regency and me as palpably as the sweat you breathe when violence is next to two people" (147). In Mailer's world, it is often hard to imagine sex without violence. It does not make anything better that Madden's wife Madeleine, flays him by saying that Regency is a "stud . . . You never come near him" (181). Tears come to the eyes of our tough guy. Yet she has good reason to attack him. Had he not written about her, with Milleresque abandon: "Her cunt was more real to me than her face" (155)? This brought tears to her eyes. There is a suggestion of homosexuality in the fact that Madden leaves her for Patty Lareine because Patty is better at fellatio. Strong homosexual vibrations exist in scenes in *The Naked and the Dead, An American Dream, Why Are We in Vietnam?, Ancient Evenings, Tough Guys Don't Dance*, and, later, *Harlot's Ghost* and even *Oswald*. Mailer used to consider homosexuality an indication of a civilization losing its biology, but, beyond the first two works on this list, he treats it more empathetically. The frequency and heatedness of its appearance make one wonder where machismo ends and perversity begins for Mailer.[34]

Though in the murder mystery mode here, Mailer creates a character whose sleuthing is only distantly related to the ratiocination of a Sherlock Holmes. Tim Madden is a hard-drinking near-psychotic. Then there is the guilt. One of

Mailer's clever turns is having Madden, through a conspicuous amnesia, possibly be the perpetrator he is seeking. Madden has the Irish eloquence, usually the harsh kind. It is too bad, though, that the superb, somber descriptions of off-season Provincetown are largely wasted in a novel that sees Mailer at his usual game of musical beds, not to mention musical heads. There is quite a bit of decapitation. Almost everyone in the novel is capable of murder; even two of the ladies are killers.[35] But Mailer is still wallowing in sex. What the hell—it's only a mystery written for money, and for a deadline. It may be that Mailer needed a two-dimensional retreat from the "depth" of *Ancient Evenings*. It may be that after the symbolic lyricism, he wanted primitive suspense. But mystery-story titillation is not the answer.

In his next attempt at major fiction after *Ancient Evenings*, Mailer turns to history. It seems that, for Mailer, history is recent history. While his work has always been close to history, while his fiction has always had a political edge, it was history writ small. *The Naked and the Dead*, *Barbary Shore*, and *The Deer Park* are relatively private enactments of public realities. In *Harlot's Ghost*, we get history writ large: private life is subsumed by public event. History takes center stage. Furthermore, Mailer's characters are, in many cases, identified by actual name, in the style of E. L. Doctorow's *Ragtime*, thereby heightening the fictive quality of fact. Finally, Mailer does not now condemn or caricature complexity or ambivalence as liberal pusillanimity as he did in his earlier fiction. This sense of complexity, which for some time has distinguished his journalism, now distinguishes his fiction. The prose in *Harlot's Ghost* is sharper than that of, say, *The Naked and the Dead* in that the first-person narrator gives us a consciousness that can express this complexity and ambivalence through his own development. First person is Mailer's preferred narrative voice.

Harry Hubbard, the central character of this bildungsroman-cum-epistolary novel, is the protagonist as un-Mailer. WASP, genteel, for a long time virginal, polite, deferential, he illustrates, in the retrospective narrative, the ethnic joke: "What does the WASP say to his bride on their honeymoon night? 'I'm sorry, it won't happen again.'" Living in the shadow of powerful fathers—his biological father, Cal, and his surrogate father, Harlot (Hugh Montague)—Harry never harbors a radical thought. Although in the 1950s Mailer had a radical's view of the CIA—he was even part of an organization to expose it[36]—that was partly because he saw the Cuban missile crisis as an immediate danger to the United States; here he can treat the CIA with a fascinated, if ambiguous, empathy. His novel about the CIA is positive in the intensity of his absorption in its milieu seen from the inside. Research, typically a hindrance to imagination, serves here as a stimulus, as it did in *Ancient Evenings*. If Mailer takes some of his most vivid tableaux from books about the CIA, he nonetheless makes them his own. He is displaying a literary love. The novel is a tribute to a privileged segment of WASP America, with its freedom, power, intelligence, wealth, Ivy League education, genteel swear words, proud way of using last names as first names, ideal of service, dedication to protecting and defending the United States, and even its controlling paranoid element couched though it may be in facade and seclusion. Mailer hardly gives an idealized portrait of this class. But the novel, one may say, is a tribute even to its blunders, the excesses of a notable—hence, for Mailer, fascinating—aggression.

Writing about WASPs is nothing new for Mailer, but here it is full-blown. He is, perhaps, the only American Jewish novelist to have no Jewish central characters (except Jesus). Jewish de-identification has always had a strong pull for Mailer, as it has for some of his amorous fellow American Jewish novelists. Mailer seems to have one-upped them in real life by marrying a Church.[37] In *Harlot's Ghost*, he married the church called the CIA. And he has to live with it. Not quite surprisingly, though, Mailer's WASP protagonist is actually one-eighth Jewish (this seems to be a favorite fraction of his), as were Rojack and Tim Madden, and that Jewishness is an emblem of their moral courage and of Mailer's own fractional Jewish identity. Harry's residual Jewishness lies in not liking anti-Semitic jokes and in making an occasional Jewish one. He may be part Jewish, but he is all WASP.

As un-Mailer, Harry is a sophisticated version of the Establishment cop. The once typically Dionysian Mailer gives us a restrained narrative consciousness. Not wishing to speak about Harlot's death, which remains a mystery— Did he really die, or did he defect? And if he died, who killed him and why?— Harry finds himself in an atypical place for a Mailer protagonist: "I felt I had finally retreated to the middle of myself, to the clear logical middle of myself, and if my emotional ends had been consumed, so was the middle stronger ... drunkenness is the abdication of the ego and mine had just surfaced like a whale. I felt considerable need to recognize all over again just how sane I could be, which is to say, how lucid, how logical, how sardonic, how superior to everyone's weaknesses, including my own."[38] The one-time apostle of id feels the attraction of ego, which, of course, implies a superego that it reconciles to id. Indeed, the WASP milieu that Mailer depicts is known for, among other things, the seriousness with which it takes superego, sometimes to excess. The one-time apostle of extremity is drawn to the middle. Of course, Mailer is not Harry—or any of his other narrators—but he is accepting of him as a sympathetic narrative intelligence. Mailer is drawn to the virtues of a new type, the citizen hero. This is a reversal. Is it an example of maturity (in his seventies), or of decline?

"I adored America. America was a goddess," says Harry (*HG* 184). His enthusiasms tend to be civic, even patriotic. "Although I am a moral person," he says in his nice, old-fashioned way, he is willing to die for "ultimate purposes"—that is, for his country (164). This positive feeling is not an aberration. When he considers the ex-marine Gus Sonderstrom, whose "underlying passion is to be virtuous," he thinks, a bit defensively this time: "Maybe it's late and I'm sipping too much *fundador* but suddenly I love America" (444). The defensiveness makes one wonder whether the invention of Harry is Mailer's way of expressing an America-loving alter ego, the most appropriate tribute to WASP America. At the same time, Mailer's narrator goes from innocence to experience—as Harry's qualified affirmation indicates—when he undergoes various CIA manipulations and adventures. What is noteworthy is that his experiences do not corrupt him. That is, his narrative function is to develop a sufficiently elastic consciousness. He is involved, believing, tainted, and redeemed. His is, after all, a public life, secretive though it may be, and his morality is a matter of public trust more than private knowledge. Mailer is sufficiently empathetic.

As a novelist, Mailer is also interested in how public life merges with private life. Private life in Mailer often means sexual life. Here too Harry may sound like the un-Mailer. "Libido may be an inner conviction," thinks Harry in the midst of a sexual fantasy, "but libido rampant is megalomania" (757). The author of *Ancient Evenings* may have learned something. To be sure, innocent Harry does not remain a virgin for long. Yet his torrid tumbles with Mrs. Sally Porringer come with the guilt of having not thought of Kittredge, "for whom I had saved myself . . . forever removed from my first taste of all-out frenzy and lust" (449). Lust—who would have thought that this compromising word would appear in a Mailer novel? Harry wonders, Mailer-style, whether lust is not "the release of mediocrity in oneself," but subsequently the un-Mailer thinks that "a new mediocrity had been ingested just as much as the old had been purged" (467). Fans of Mailer the sexologue need not lose heart, since Harry the virgin is soon enough transformed into Harry the cocksman. In a Mailer bildungsroman, bildung begins in the bedroom. In saying that "randy mustang" Sally "would be honored best for introducing me to my true and natural estate, which was to love women at large" (574), as a sort of ambassador for fornication as it were, Harry displays the Maileresque overweenied pride. His affair with Sally, though, is generally smartly done because it does not risk too much, even when he thinks he is being raped. His subsequent affair with Modene Murphy (aka Judith Exner), whatever its intention, functions best as a plot device to get Harry closer to John F. Kennedy, then running for president (and to Sam Giancana and Frank Sinatra), so close that the sexually adept Harry can say: "I could have welcomed Jack Kennedy into bed with us at the moment" (804). That Mailer must indulge his predilection for orgiastic fantasy even in a political novel is perhaps to be expected. But he quickly, if slavishly, returns to the power context and a possible presidential victory. Harry continues: "If Jack won, then I, by the intermediary of her body, would still have touched immortality" (812). Mailer considers this reflection to be a sign of latent homosexuality. The Modene sequence is unconvincing. Can anybody care that Harry is mourning her loss, when he hears about her having sex with JFK and Sam? Mailer's typical narrative strategy—when in doubt, fuck 'em out—is especially insipid in the Modene affair. Still, as a narrative device the sequence has much value. Her taped phone conversations bring public notables down to the level of believable gossip, not to say vulgarity. Mailer can thereby deflect his own tendency toward celebrity worship. When it comes to stars, Mailer can be light-headed.

In *Harlot's Ghost*, sexual aggression reflects political aggression but is subordinate to it. Harlot is Harry's "surrogate father" (13), and he comes wrapped in an enigma: is he an authority or an authoritarian? "Our real duty is to become the mind of America," he tells Harry. This position is even more problematic because of Mailer's belief that the true espionage artist draws on his paranoia. In a preliminary to the novel—an essay written many years before its publication, when Mailer was at an early stage of his CIA research—he is still explicitly fearful of "the overall domination of an invisible second government."[39] The 1976 essay is called "A Harlot High and Low" (referring to a translation of Balzac's *Splendors and Miseries of Courtesans*). The word *harlot* is also considered more explicitly: "What a country we inhabit. What a harlot. What a brute."[40] This is a whole truth in the essay (Mailer is writing about the CIA and Watergate) and a half-truth by the time he writes the novel. Apparently living with the CIA made judgment more complex. Moreover, the Cuban missile crisis involved more difficult choices.

The protagonist of *Harlot's Ghost* has his own difficulties. Neither of Harry's two fathers—Cal and Harlot, real and surrogate—gives him much comfort. Their years in the CIA have made them all the more intractable. Harlot holds that the putative Soviet move toward peaceful coexistence and consequent split with hard-line Communist China is mere disinformation. Castro will make overtures. Communism will appear human. Hence Castro must go. Cuba, which used to be minor, can now become major. Mailer, soft on Castro to the end in any case,[41] takes a dim view of this. Yet Harlot's gesture of confirmation is Maileresque: he goes rock climbing. Harlot has taught Harry something about becoming a man. He has also taught him much about integrity in presumed opposition to CIA profiteering from privileged information. Harry's real father, Cal (a name that brings Calvinism to mind) Hubbard, along with Helms and Harlot, torpedoes Castro's possible overtures to the United States in order to sabotage rapprochement (which Mailer seems to want desperately). Cal, less subtle than Harlot, even thinks that JFK and Castro are in cahoots in some Catholic plot. Cal is a hard-nosed, hard-muscled, hard Right, hard-on. At fifty-three, he is enough of a sexual threat to take Modene from Harry. Harry himself takes away the wife of his surrogate father, whose marriage to Kittredge is CIA family. Harry feels ambivalence but finally rejects both fathers. For a writer who rejects Freud, as Mailer does (and as Kittredge does, even though she quotes him sympathetically in the formulation of her own tedious views), Mailer has here an unusual amount of Oedipal underplay. If wishes could kill, this would have been a bloodier book.

Kittredge Gardner, Harlot's longtime wife, becomes Harry's wife and apparent true love. But she functions more as a narrative presence than as a lover. The novel is sometimes unwieldy in its attempted integration of public and private themes. In the loose, baggy Operation Mongoose section (about the plot to assassinate Castro), Kittredge functions as a political analyst rather than an intimate of Harry's. Their relationship is less believable because they hardly see each other. And the beginning chronological postscript seems virtually disconnected from the rest of the novel, even though Mailer is impressive in his description of portentous place for the third consecutive novel. (Sometimes it is a bit much, as when Harry is half-certain that he will be in a wreck.) Maybe it has become a necessary starting-up ritual for Mailer.

For all the politics in the novel, Mailer is no longer turning the world upside down; he is now sympathetic to a vaguely Protestant religious dualism: "Heaven and Hell, God and the Devil" (*HG* 155) are what Kittredge believes in. Her sexual relations are an illustration of this dualism—"devil's heaven" (14), as she earlier puts it to Harry. There is nothing apocalyptic here, just spicy domesticity. Her dumping Harry for Dix Butler is dramatically undeveloped, though the latter, a sadistic bisexual, will bring her back to the anal thrills she ostensibly resists. In a reverse turn on ferocity, Dix (as if he has more than one penis) gets "shit-face" with the double agent Chevi Fuertes in the shower, reaming him, sticking his face in a shitty toilet. Aggression here is an expression *of*, not *against*, the Establishment. That Harry feels a repressed bisexual attraction toward Dix is meant to indicate WASP decadence. Dix is present in one of Harry's sexual fantasies as part of a threesome. The sexual has its political dimension. "One difference between you and me," Dix says to Harry, "is that I understand our profession. You have to be able to turn yourself inside out" (290). So the CIA is a political version of the polymorphous perverse. This seems to be a major part of Mailer's fascination with it. As for polymorphous perversity in sex itself, Dix is an able representative, as are Kittredge and Harlot and, Mailer tells us, the many homosexuals in the intelligence services of the United States, Great Britain, and other countries.

Harlot recommends having a heterosexual relationship to the homosexual Rosen, an exceptionally bright CIA operative. He recommends it as a way of rising in the CIA. Rosen says that "decent women inspire nothing in me" (1093). Harlot thinks this nonsense, pointing out that "there is no greater pleasure than that obtained from a conquered repugnance." Rosen says: "You are quoting the Marquis de Sade," as had Marion Faye on this point in *The Deer Park*, in a less genteel manner. The tone is very different, lighter in *Harlot's Ghost*. Harlot, of course, is aware that he is reversing Sade's argument when he suggests the virgin solution to Rosen, and he does so in a tone that reverses Marion's solemnity—despite his own Sadean proclivities. So Sade has become for Mailer a symbol not of rebellion but of conformity.

The sadomasochism in this book is not the sole prerogative of the WASP Establishment. Some of the best parts of the CIA narrative involve the Montevideo sexual comedy of Boris and Zenia Masarov and, subsequently, Zenia and Georg Varkov, as well as the Pedro Peones sequence (about the police chief who likes being spanked). These are on a par with the Hintertur (the German word means "back door") chapter depicting a sleazy gay sex club in Berlin. Sexual aggression in this book is not apocalyptic but emblematic. It is typical of what Mailer presents—sympathetically—in this book as WASP decadence, though is far from being exclusively WASP.

There are other vivid touches and sequences in the novel: the fascinating story of Yakovlev and Dzerzhinsky, who do not know whether they are dealing with the truth or a lie; the character of Billy Harvey; the hacienda in Uruguay that sits ten miles from its front gate; Mailer's ear for genteel WASP expletives like "Hell and soda water," "my suffering little toe," and "my Aunt Mary"; his greater narrative voice sophistication, as when the Silverfield men marry golden gentile women; the fine use of the historical present in the journal of the Bay of Pigs; Modene and her friend Willi's unintended humor in their dialogue on the tapes; and the use of epistolary form to modify the bildungsroman so that it can include as a perception by Harry or Kittredge much that would not otherwise fit in this loose, baggy monster of a novel. Mailer is, to say the least, a mature craftsman here, as demonstrated by his organization of a monumental amount of narrative possibility—although the organization works best from Berlin to the Bay of Pigs sequences. Linking all this is an intelligence that sees things with a more level-headed gaze, penetrating deeper into the meaning of his material than Mailer has typically shown. Despite its flaws, *Harlot's Ghost* may be judged the most absorbing of his three very long novels. Its underlying force comes from the fact that it presents us with an institution—the CIA—that justifies Mailer's paranoia yet enables him to transcend it. He chooses a slice of history that was made for leftist assault—the memory of CIA illegalities, the Bay of Pigs fiasco, the assassination plots against Castro—but renders the experience with a depth that does not permit him to give in to such assaults.

Mailer's involvement with JFK and the Cuban missile crisis resulted next in *Oswald's Tale*. He is once again the journalist-researcher, this time writing a book about what everyone knows. So Mailer complicates the obvious by writing a fascinating preliminary section on what few know, the life of Oswald and Marina in Minsk. This section manages to defamiliarize front-page newspaper material, and at the same time it is a mesmerizing portrait of dismal if respectable Soviet life. We see the extent to which the secret police infiltrate everyday life—a touchingly perceived everyday life—the extent to which they are assumed as an everyday presence. The simple, Russified English of this half of the book makes the strange somewhat familiar.

We see Oswald's two loves—the Soviet Union and Marina—the first short-lived, the second stillborn. Mailer gives us a portrait of the sadist as a young dog. Oswald was a wife beater. This behavior is subdued until his reincarnation in Texas, where his Communist past is particularly suspect. There he starts beating the diminutive Marina regularly, with increasing violence: not just slapping her, but using his fists. He even beats her when she is pregnant. To complicate things, he thinks, wrongly, that an old beau of hers is waiting in the wings. It is one of those horrific cases. A neighbor says: "I think that man over there is going to kill that girl."[42]

Marina says: "Your beating shows me your upbringing" (*OT* 365). Oswald replies: "Leave my mother out of this," and strikes Marina harder. But we cannot leave his mother out of this. Oswald was born posthumously: Robert E. Lee Oswald died while Marguerite was pregnant with their son. Oswald slept in the same bed with his mother until he was ten or eleven. With a mother like Marguerite, it was not hard to overcome incestuous attachment. He had no respect for her; she had no authority over him. Oswald was a truant, and he struck his mother. A perceptive psychiatric social worker says of this "emotionally starved, affectionless youngster" that "he acknowledged fantasies about being all-powerful and being able to do anything he wanted," including "hurting or killing people." Another Oswald observer comments: "He and he alone was entitled to that which was forbidden to everybody else" (517). The seeds of Sade sprout in unexpected places, unless one sees *force majeur* as impotence pretending to be omnipotence. (Mailer imagines Oswald sporting a Hitler mustache.) This latter is surely the case with Oswald, a cipher of a man, a Raskolnikov without a university. Oswald is American, however, so he has the moxie to shoot for the stars, as it were, not just a little old lady. And Raskolnikov's ax seems primitive in our technological culture. Above all, Oswald the American is a practical killer, not merely a theoretical one. He is an assassin, not just a murderer. It is chilling when a representative of the "Fair Play for Cuba Committee," which exists to "foster Communist ideals" (594), informs us that Oswald said: "President Kennedy should have been assassinated after the Bay of Pigs" (625). The head of the Moscow Passport and Visa Office had said of foreigners who applied to live in the Soviet Union: "Ninety-nine percent of them were disturbed" (46), an apparently accurate assessment. Nor is Oswald "proficient in Marxist-Leninist theory" (79).

His mother, of course, thinks her son is just wonderful. "I happen to know, and know some facts, that maybe this is the unsung hero of this episode," she says of the assassination (711). She thinks her son worthy of burial in Arlington Cemetery. She thinks that the Secret Service and Marina were in a plot to kill Kennedy. Marina, meanwhile, thinks "part of the guilt is" Marguerite's. Mailer agrees, considering that "every malformation, or just about" of Oswald's character "had its root in her" (789). In *The Naked and the Dead*, Mailer gives much weight to environmental determinism. The older he gets, the more psychological he becomes. His categories are, on occasion, Freudian, but there is no fear of his crossing the line into Freudianism.

Despite its psychological subtlety, in the end *Oswald's Tale* shows us Mailer's expected preference for political categories over psychological ones. After all, how can Oswald be totally wrong, since Mailer has a soft spot in his heart for Castro and Cuba and thinks that American policy toward Cuba is basically stupid? "Whether [Oswald] was an assassin with a vision or a killer without one... whether an act of vision is mindless or is a cry of wrath that rises from a skewed heart maddened by his own vision of injustice" makes "some difference to our commonweal," says Mailer (198). Yes, but what difference? *Vision* is not the word that describes Oswald's mentality. It implies ennoblement, something akin to art, a justified ferocity. Mailer's killers are likely to be artists of some kind, autodidacts or intellectuals—Jack Abbot, Gary Gilmore, and Rojack. Sadism too easily implies ennoblement for him. (Oswald has the added advantage of having a powerful mother, albeit a cartoon of one, and an absent father.) Mailer wishes to perceive this "killer as tragic rather than absurd" (198). Raskolnikov knew that he was no hero but a "louse." Mailer cannot help thinking of his louse as something of a hero, the writer's last link to the sentiments of the revolutionary Left. So he tries to elevate Oswald. "What is never taken seriously enough in Oswald," he says, "is the force of his confidence that he has the makings of a great leader" (555). Apparently we do not take seriously enough the force of his delusions. Oswald elicits a residual sympathy in Mailer. "Who among us," he asks, with misplaced dramatic effect, "can say that he is in no way related to our own dreams?" Mailer concludes the thought and the book by saying: "If it had not been for Theodore Dreiser and his last great work, one would like to have used 'An American Tragedy' as the title for this journey through Oswald's beleaguered life" (791). But Dreiser the naturalist thinks of Clyde Griffiths as a victim of environmental circumstance. So, though Dreiser did not see it this way, *American tragedy* is an oxymoron. Mailer, however, sees Oswald nostalgically as the last flicker of a noble politics, in its ideal rather than actual bureaucratic sense. Fortunately, his book—a fairly derivative portrait of Oswald—is far better than its concluding wisdom.

Oswald's Tale is Mailer's last American book. With the Kennedy-CIA-Oswald events, he has exhausted the American theme. In fiction, he moves to archetypal if historical figures, Jesus and Hitler. Mailer takes pride in writing about figures of a certain dimension—JFK, Marilyn, Picasso, Jesus, and Hitler—but with the exception of *Marilyn*, potboiler though it is, the literary results are small. The Hitler book, *The Castle in the Forest*, is notable in being an oblique extension of the Maileresque ferocious. It is also of considerable formal interest in that Mailer writes in a genre he has never before used, the family chronicle. Mailer's most vivid fiction—"The Time of Her Time," *An American Dream*, and *Why Are We in Vietnam?*—has been dramatic. Even in the sprawling, naturalistic *The Naked and the Dead*, he shows a gift for the intensification of scene, for a crescendo of action. Character is defined by action, action by character. Mailer typically excels as a fiction writer when the context is secluded, the plot is lurid, and his hero is up against the clock. Mailer narrative typically exists in dramatic time. But the family chronicle is a narrative that gives an illusion of timelessness and space, as in George Eliot and Tolstoy. Time is chronological rather than dramatic, attuned to a generational rhythm and a seasonal progression.

It thus seems strange to see Mailer functioning in a narrative world defined by its counter-dramatic rhythms. Equally strange is his choice of subject: the creation of Hitler. Mailer exhibits narrative daring in managing the incipiently demonic in a pastoral setting, describing the childhood milieu of the world's greatest mass murderer. Mailer gives us Hitler's family in slow time. Given the author's denial of things Freudian, it is doubly odd, even contradictory, that he proceeds in a Freudian pattern: from Mom and Pop Hitler to toilet training, the primal scene, and sibling rivalry. Indeed, the Mom and Pop show is the main part of the story, as it tends to be in Freudian psychoanalysis. As in Freud, Mailer's primary focus is on Pop.

The most vivid character in the novel is Alois Heidler (later Hitler), Adolf's father. As noted in chapter 6, the historian Robert Waite depicts Alois as an intimidating brute who beat his wife and his children—and even his dog, until it wet the floor.[43] At one time young Adolf took 230 cracks of the cane. Of such scenes are murderers made, Waite quotes a psychoanalyst as saying. Alois had a picture of himself placed so as to dominate the house. His children could not address him in the familiar *du* but had to call him *Herr Vater* (Mr. Father).

His sadism was matched by his randiness. His female relatives were among his amatory conquests. Hitler's mother Klara was Alois's niece and his blood-daughter. Mailer's *Waldviertal* backwater is quite the bangeroo equal of *Peyton Place* or, for that matter, *Ancient Evenings*. In short, from historian to novelist an extraordinary transformation has taken place. Waite's Sadean slob becomes Mailer's Sadean cavalier. "The husband has been called a brute, but he's just macho," says Mailer, a strange judgment given what appears to be the historical evidence. For much of his career, Mailer could not have conceived of the libertine square, but in his eighties he presents one admiringly.[44] His contemporaries were less generous, however. Coming from a part of Europe where, according to Waite, inbreeding and incest was not uncommon, Alois's sexual exploits were such that "they drew mixed reviews. Some villagers were shocked by his infidelities, others indifferent, others a bit envious."[45] Mailer spares no detail in delineating these exploits. Even at the beginning of his book, Joanna, Klara's mother, speaks the familiar Maileresque words to husband Alois: "You have made me feel as I have not felt before."[46] She is now orgasmic. Mailer's two-year old Adi witnesses "the bull roar" of his father's voice and the "soft" cries of his mother, "full of the oddest torture, cries that spoke of joy soon to come," following which he witnesses his father "sitting on her face!" Even the missionary position seems sadistic, with "his big belly slapping on her belly." It is also dehumanizing: "She was grunting like a dog. So full of contentment: 'You beast, you are an ugly man, you are an animal you!' and then again, 'You, yes, you, *ja, ja, ja.*' There was no question. She was happy. *Ja!*" (*CF* 96). Even before Rojack and Ruta, Mailer has been an exponent of the "Ja-Ja" school of orgasm: the sadistic stud takes all.

Finding elegant women too difficult, the extracurricular Alois contents himself with maids and cooks. There were days "when he made love to each of the three women he could look upon as regulars" (38). He has fancy sex with many. Mailer loves him. So does the narrator, one of the devil's minions. "We may remember," the narrator says, "that the last time we saw Alois, he was burying his nose and lips in Klara's vulva, his tongue as long and demonic as a devil's phallus. (Be it said: we are not without our contributions to these arts.)" (98). Decades ago, Mailer may have announced his graduation from sexologue to a role in the larger world, but he can never really give up that role. Here it appears with the heavy levity characteristic of the narrative voice.

With all this, Alois is not sufficient to Mailer's sexual imaginings. Therefore he introduces Der Alte. Alois is based on biography, while Der Alte is entirely fictional. An expert beekeeper and teacher about bees to Alois, Der Alte responds to the destruction of his beehive not with the expected weeping but with "a rare sweetness [that] returned to his loins. This was the first such sugaring of his body he had felt in years" (262). Murder is always sexual, Rojack opined; apparently, so is violent extinction of any kind. But this is just a harbinger of things to come. Der Alte serves Mailer's apparent need for what might be considered ritual homosexuality. He fellates the very young Alois Jr. Even the devil-narrator is "repelled" (282). Alois Jr. is himself full of "disgust" with his partner. Mailer goes into lurid detail: cunnilingus excites Alois Sr., analingus Der Alte. For a moment we seem to be in Mailer's Egypt. The buttocks of the young boy "began to feel like the portals of a beauteously endowed temple. He would wait until his pleasure rose high enough to be ready to explode, and then would turn to give it all to the old boy's gullet" (285). Knowing such things, Alois Jr. feels disgust for his father's awe of Der Alte. In *Ancient Evenings*, even in *Harlot's Ghost*, such homosexual pyrotechnics have a thematic relevance far more clear than in this novel, where they seem something of a formality—Mailer clearing his throat, as it were.

There is one new dimension in this display of sex. For the first time, Mailer gives us the perspective of an old man and even of an aged man on these matters. The old Alois Sr. muses that he had "no interest in the cooks and maids at the Gasthof. Worse, they seemed to have no interest in him. Nor did he mind it" (387). When he thinks of the possibility of reincarnation as a reward for having been "one hell of a licentious knight," he realizes, as must Mailer, that this idea "kept you out of the quicksand of growing old" (338). Sex has become something of a fading meteorite, which does not prevent Mailer from continuing to describe it when it is in full trajectory.

Mailer's usual music seems muted. Though the excremental vision is still operative, it is blurred. We see it through the labored insight of the narrator. "As a devil," he says, "I am obliged to live intimately with excrement in all its forms, physical and mental" (98). He speaks of "emotional waste" but also "caca itself." He notes that as devils, "we live in shit and work with it. So, we often look to comprehend a marriage through the eye of the cloaca—and I will add, that is not the worst way, since parenthood is not only the crown but the outhouse of marriage" (98–99). This last is a lugubrious metaphor, but considering that the novel leads to the first sadistic flowerings of a very young Hitler, not without its point.

"All that spiritual excrement!" the narrator exclaims and sighs, admitting that "strange shifts into love occur . . . aeration is offered to what has been an airless union" (303). Can there be a more jaded endorsement of marriage?—marriage as a therapeutic punching bag or the ultimate in mud therapy? It may be that his six marriages and eight children fathered by him have worn Mailer down. His writing was once going to change the world. This psychic exhaustion is reflected in his prose. Confronted with the difficulty and expense of beekeeping, Alois Sr. takes psychic stock: "All the same, he did feel a cautious optimism. April had come. Flowers were sprouting, the walnut trees, the oaks, the plum trees, the beeches and cherry trees, the maples and apple trees were in bloom. There would be a host of flowers in the meadow" (202). "Cautious optimism" is taken from American political talk. But can it be Mailer writing about "a host of flowers in the meadow"? It makes one nostalgic for the high-wire tension of some of his earlier prose.

Nor does the leaden opening of the novel help, with its arcane speculation about the virtues of incest. And where is all Mailer's honey gathering going? It is a way of solving the problem of multiple points of view, but at considerable cost. When Philip Roth, in *American Pastoral*, gives us the process of glove manufacturing as a symbol of civilized effort, it is moving. But Mailer's beekeeping goes on and on, to no particular effect other than the foreshadowing of disaster. Even Alois Sr. seems bored by the subject when Der Alte talks about how "timing" is so important in the beekeeping process. "You told us already," Alois says (274). So he has.

Mailer's is the first attempt to write a fictional account of Hitler's childhood. "I knew from the beginning I wanted to do just the childhood," he says; "In fact, originally I was going to end the book when he was three years old. It was going to be more about his family than about him, mainly because of my age."[47] It was probably much more than his age. Waite points out that little is known of the Hitler of four or five years of age, let alone two or three.[48] Mailer's novel is another example of his adherence to what is basically a Freudian paradigm, despite his often expressed antagonism to Freud. Take the Ja-Ja primal scene. Mailer writes that Adi has no doubt "that his mother is betraying him" (*CF* 97). But Mailer gives us a crude version of the Freudian. Freud is not so much interested in the mother's enjoyment, but in her having sex at all. In Mailer, two-year old Adi is furious because his father is, as it were, a better stud. "He would never forgive her," says the narrator. Adi nips at his mother's breast in anger during feeding time, the beginning of his oral sadism. In a more ominous Freudian turn, the favored younger brother, Edmund, is fatally injected with measles by the young, sick Adi, who turns out to administer a kiss of death. This sibling rivalry development is fictional.

"There's no rational explanation of Hitler," says Mailer.[49] There is, for him, only a supernatural one. Mailer did not devise his celestial war for this novel: he has been thinking in these terms virtually all his career. His concepts are scarcely original. His denial of an omniscient, omnipotent God and, accordingly, an ex nihilo creation, goes back to ancient Gnosticism. His account of God as vulnerable, even weak, does so as well. In Mailer, God and the devil are locked in an equal struggle for the soul of man. This comes to be called Manichean, although he calls it, in his loose way, existential—that is, you do not know the outcome. But Hitler presents Gnostic Mailer with a problem. Mailer does not want his characters to say "the devil made me do it," but he nonetheless defuses questions of individual moral responsibility by seeing causality in terms of Manichean struggle. His projected three-volume work would have moved toward but would not have reached the Holocaust, which is not comprehensible in terms of the small theological drama that Mailer presents. The devil says as much.

Mailer's war between the gods does not convince. His God is fatally compromised. The narrator says the "presence of a colleague (probably unwanted in the first place) had to reduce His sense of His own stature" (*CF* 153). One might ask then why capitalize *His* (twice in one sentence) in the first place? Why assume a transcendence when none exists? In his characterization of God, the devil unwittingly contributes to this lack of stature: "I may make my mistakes," God says, "but I do pay attention to who wins. That is the best way to discover what works" (215). Mailer's God is an empiricist. The emphatic levity of the narrative voice is reinforced by that of the devil himself.

Mailer's narrator is present at the creation of little Adolf Hitler, stationed in a bedroom, "an officer of rank in the finest Intelligence service that has ever existed" (68). Mailer has had good luck with intelligence in *Harlot's Ghost*, where it serves a political function. But making theology a form of conspiracy is a symptom of paranoia. Moreover, Mailer's theological strategy just does not work. J. M. Coetzee has remarked that Mailer's Adolf is "not satanic, not even demonic, simply a nasty piece of work."[50] That is, Mailer to the contrary notwithstanding, the book works better as psychology than as theology. Mailer's next novel in the projected trilogy was to have featured Hitler's relationship to Geli Raubal. We will now never know exactly what Mailer would have made of this relationship, but that it speaks clearly to a spectacular sadomasochism is pertinent to the argument presented here. In his sexologue phase, Mailer thought this nexus was heroic; he now sees it largely as pathology. This is part of a sadness he felt in the last decades of his life.

[INTERCHAPTER]

MAILER ON MILLER

The first thing to be said about *Genius and Lust*, Mailer's anthology of Miller, is the most obvious: it is virtually a symmetrical counterpart to the earlier Lawrence Durrell anthology, *The Henry Miller Reader*.[1] Published in 1959—not long before the court decisions on *Lady Chatterley's Lover* and *Tropic of Cancer*, which greatly liberalized the obscenity laws in Great Britain and the United States—the Durrell anthology reflects its era. You would never know from Durrell's collection that explicitly rendered sexual experience was central to Miller's fiction, or even a part of it. Judicious, decorous, even representative in its way, the collection shows us how fine and various a writer Miller can be without his main subject. The mere pagination tells most of the story. In a lengthy anthology, Durrell devotes just twenty-four pages to *Tropic of Cancer*, twenty-five to *Black Spring*, none to *Tropic of Capricorn*, and only four to the mammoth *Sexus*—the volumes that most critics consider the heart of Miller's fiction. There are twenty pages (a character sketch) from *Plexus* and none from *Nexus*. In other words, the Miller of renown, of the *Tropics* and *The Rosy Crucifixion*, is represented by a total of seventy-three pages, or about 23 percent of the text. There are 247 pages from Miller's other works, largely nonfiction. Not having a free hand, Durrell focuses on local color, which includes an excerpt of the ghetto description from *Sexus* and two lyrical evocations of Paris from *Tropic of Cancer*; on self-contained pieces that are more autobiographical than fictional; on literary essays; and on portraits of fellow writers or artists.

Having the advantage of free reign, Mailer essentially reverses Durrell's ratios. Seventy-six percent of his anthology is from the *Tropics* and *The Rosy Crucifixion*, with sixty-three pages from *Tropic of Cancer* (just ten pages less than Durrell's entire selection from the six main books), twenty-nine from *Black Spring*, and seventy from *Tropic of Capricorn*. By far his largest single-volume selection is from the notorious *Sexus*, which gets 174 pages in Mailer's most remarkable redesign. If in his aggression and randiness, Miller is some sort of clownish bull, Mailer is going to present him in all his horniness.

To see precisely what Mailer is doing, we must take a look at his actual selections. The opening section, "Genius," consists entirely of selections from *Tropic of Cancer*. Mailer begins with the "I will dance over your dirty corpse" opening lyricism of the first seven pages[2]—in other words, with Miller's phallic megalomania and hyperbolic cunt painting. *Tropic of Cancer* begins with a bang—several, in fact—and the colloquial quality of this familiar metaphor suggests the common equivalence of sex and aggression that Miller assumes. The second early selection (*TC* 11–19) gives us the splendor of Parisian misery, the ambiguity reinforced by the "wild consumptive notes of hysteria, perversion, leprosy" (17) of Mona, the *femme fatale* Miller loves. This selection gives us Paris as problem rather than elegy and supports the novel's opening note of Romantic reversal. The next selection (36–43), again in contrast to Durrell, gives us seedy Paris, "the full squalor of the scene" (37), concluding with a hymn to the cunt inspired by an unsentimental prostitute whom, like the underground man, Miller writes "I could no more think of loving . . . than I could think of loving a spider" (42). Durrell's prostitute selection, "Berthe," from *Quiet Days in Clichy* (later redone by Miller in *The Rosy Crucifixion*), is almost sentimental by comparison; in it, Miller drops his stony persona. Next, Mailer again focuses on Parisian squalor, hunger, dirt, cockroaches, and lice (*TC* 65–68), concluding with what might have been a great scene in a better novelist: Miller finds a concert ticket in a bathroom but—famished, "panic-stricken," an outsider among the respectables—he lets the dramatic opportunity slide into some ready-made surrealism.

Where Mailer's selections have so far emphasized Miller's negative lyricism, his final two examples from *Tropic of Cancer* give us narrative in the more conventional sense. First, there is the adventure of Kepi in the bordello. A follower of Gandhi and a married father of eight, Kepi is a freeloader who "has absolutely no ambition except to get a fuck every night"—a man after Miller's own heart. Kepi mistakes a bidet for a toilet. Oddly, Mailer presents the vaguely nauseating narrative for its own sake, leaving out the crucial manifestation that Miller receives from it. Mailer excludes the explicit nihilism of the excremental vision, one of the most important passages in Miller. Is it that the residual moralist in Mailer could not face up to such stark disillusionment?

He is more judicious in his final editorial choice, the raunchy Miller–Van Norden–Carl sequence. This is by far Mailer's longest selection from *Tropic of*

Cancer and the best narrative sequence in the novel. In contrast, Durrell's main narrative selection is the Dijon episode, which—except for Miller's well-received disquisition on the love life of the elephant—is free from sexual reference. Mailer's selections clearly delineate the randy and raucous, the solipsistic and anti-literary, the filthy and ferocious. He does not select the more enigmatic reflections on Mona; the elevated, picture-book Paris of Durrell; or the concluding, positive lyricism.

Mailer's *Black Spring* choices are less coherent, as they would have to be, considering the fragmentary nature of the book, which is much more of an anthology of essays and autobiographical fragments than a work of fiction. The book is made for Durrell's anthology because it is so much a collection of fragments. Any anthology is such a collection to some degree, but Mailer is trying for more coherent effects, bound together, of course, by his critical commentary. Durrell has virtually no such commentary; it is Miller who makes the comments in his anthology. In *Black Spring*, Miller is, despite his denigration of literature, more self-consciously literary in a conventional sense than in *Tropic of Cancer*. So Durrell's selection of "The Fourteenth Ward" and "A Saturday Afternoon" fits perfectly with his taste for the literary and for local color. The first passage gives us an artsy, vaguely Proustian evocation, with purple prose ascending to surrealism; the second is a ramble rather than an essay on the history of literature as the history of subjectivity. Mailer makes a relatively long selection from the fine autobiographical set piece called "The Tailor Shop." One may wonder what this mellow piece is doing in Mailer's chapter dubbed, after Miller, "Crazy Cock." In fact, the selections and interchapter material in *Genius and Lust* are not always well integrated. Mailer's essay is a paean to sexuality, but the selection deals only tangentially with that subject. After a fine, lengthy evocation of his first scene of employment and its attendant parental sorrows, Miller "crazy cocks" a deceased customer's mourning wife and, later, his own angry, pregnant spouse.

The "Crazy Cock" selections from *Tropic of Capricorn* are abundantly illustrative of Mailer's descriptive rubric. Reversing his usual sequential pagination, Mailer begins with a spectacular eight-page sequence from the latter part of the novel (*TCap* 176–84). Here is Miller's lyricism of the cunt in full flower, beginning with Hymie's curious, elongating lovemaking procedures; continuing with Curley's string of half a dozen women, including a virtuosic, endlessly pliable cousin; and culminating with Miller and "the girl upstairs," a deaf-mute whom Miller considers "probably" the best lay he has ever had. Considering

Mailer's interests, it is surprising that he did not include Miller's subsequent catalog of cunts (194–96). Yet we are clear on the subject of crazy cock.

The remaining "Crazy Cock" selections appear according to their place in the narrative. First is a long selection focusing primarily on the memorable Cosmodemonic Telegraph Company, which deals only tangentially with sexual pyrotechnics (Miller offers jobs to women for sexual favors) (*TCap* 16–40). This is another of a number of selections in the anthology that do not relate very directly to the interchapter material. But the next two selections support the section's title. In the first, Miller has intercourse with Valeska while his wife is having an abortion (57–60); in the second, a tour de force of madcap speed and steaminess, Miller is the epitome of crazy cockery. He clouts his wife, screws a neighbor and then his wife, plans on going whoring, thinks longingly of another woman, and winds up the day with a wet dream. Miller derives metaphysical wisdom from this, considering it as being one with impersonal nature. He speaks of nature's womb rather than that of any particular female, which does not prevent his resumption of activities on the usual female material (a young girl, then a sleeping Egyptian Jewess) (70–86).

The "Narcissism" section signals a shift in pace and tone, as Mailer selects now from *Tropic of Capricorn* with something else in mind. Rather than ribald picaresque, we get something more ambitious—an attempt at psychological seriousness, the character of Mona. The *Capricorn* examples of Mona are brief: Mona as elusive other (*TCap* 237–39) and as dream girl *femme fatale* (339–45). By far the largest part of "Narcissism" comes from *Sexus*. Mailer is right to focus on the watershed quality of this book. First, it is in keeping with his aim of diving into the dirt, for *Sexus* goes beyond the obscene into the pornographic. Second, and more important, *Sexus* enables him to deal centrally with Mona/Mara, the love of Miller's life and the bane of his existence. Mailer thereby makes some of his acutest critical comments on the nature of narcissism. In focusing on the erotic element in Miller in this way, Mailer is able to confront head-on the most important female other of his emotional and literary life. Yet Mona is not even mentioned in the Durrell anthology. As Mailer engagingly puts it: "What Miller has bogged into . . . is the uncharted negotiations of the psyche when two narcissists fall in love" (*GL* 186). His selections inevitably point out the especially "electric" and "empty" quality of such a relationship (189).

The first excerpt (*S* 9–13) shows a Miller plagued with separation anxiety when he thinks of Mona/Mara and with hostility when he thinks of his wife, two unconscious parallels to Miller's relationship to his mother. In the second selection (16–21), Miller and Mona/Mara make wild love in a taxi, yet there is mutual fear and a sense of fatalism. The third selection (69–79) is full of torrid lovemaking as well, this time in the open air, and made more spicy by a "where were you" scene at the dance hall. Tenderness is not the characteristic note. "I worked on her like a plunger," Miller says, in an image that will not be lost on Mailer the riveter (via the stud in "The Time of Her Time"). As if it were taken from "Crazy Cock" rather than "Narcissism"—though either will do—Mailer's next selection (*S* 113–27) presents the foursome of Miller, Mara, Ulric, and Lola. Miller then performs "last rites" on the rejected wife, Maude. The fifth section (131–50) switches gears to the revenge fantasy of old man Carruthers. Miller's manhood seems secure but is somewhat undercut by Mara's trip to the country with two girlfriends (the lesbian theme is introduced). Selection six (178–84) mingles description of exhausted sex and hideous landscape, a combination Mailer finds especially appealing. The next selection (190–98) is the *in flagrante delicto* scene, Stanley's setup of his friend Henry, which ironically does work out well—Miller is freed from a life of marital servitude. Yet the next excerpt (208) reveals Miller's confusion. He loves Mona but laments: "I do not possess her." And he never will.

The next two selections in "Narcissism" present Miller with moral ambiguities he cannot handle as a novelist. Remarkably, they go uncommented on by Mailer. In the ninth selection (211–16), Miller tells Mona that he is willing to stop visiting his daughter if it bothers her. Mona, partly reacting to her own isolation as a child, blurts out that she would never leave a child. Miller's world-well-lost sentiment then rings hollow. Unable to dramatize complicated emotion that isn't comic, Miller lets this scene go. If Miller is seen here as a moral neuter, he unwittingly presents himself in the next selection (273–88) as a moral idiot. After meeting Maude's Victorian challenge, Miller hears that Mona has tried to kill herself. Not particularly impressed by this news, Miller has sex again with Maude. The next selection (300–307) presents the paradox that Maude now has sexual possession of Miller because he is not hers—which appeals to the author of *The Deer Park*. The twelfth selection (318–20) drifts back to the moral crux: Mona tried to poison herself because Miller cannot control himself. It is not at all clear that Miller learns anything from this experience. In the equally crucial thirteenth selection (323–33), Miller analyzes his own narcissism, imposing a pattern of permanence on their love that, in fact, is not there.

The fourteenth selection (438–448) skips to a later part of the novel, the almost self-contained story of Mona's rape, a harrowing tale about which the ever-loving Miller is skeptical—it might be a cover for the cause of possible venereal disease. That such disease may have lesbian origins is the wry suggestion of the following selection (455–59). The sixteenth selection (465–488) is one of the wildest in Miller. Our hero is at it again with his ex-wife, in a hilarious scene in which hate and physical attraction go hand in hand. No wonder the scene also evokes the shit standard. After a torrid troilism episode, Maude says: "I love you." In the seventeenth selection (503–13), Mona gets a job as an actress and wants to marry Henry, a curious marriage of solipsists. An impossible marriage, it would appear, since, as Mailer tells us in his commentary for the solipsist: "What is in his mind is more real to him than himself, and vastly more real than any of the people who come and go in his life" (*GL* 410). The eighteenth and final selection (*S* 524–43) moves to the elegiac description of the ghetto, the one selection from *Sexus* where Miller and Durrell overlap somewhat. Where Durrell gives nothing more than a brief lyrical description, Mailer's selection goes on to describe Mona as a Jew and lover, making the case for the centrality of body and soul in this relationship, as far as this is possible for a solipsist. Surely Durrell's anthology is impoverished by her total exclusion.

While one may quarrel with some exclusions in Mailer's generous selection from *Sexus*, its inclusiveness makes such objections beside the point—with one conspicuous exception. Mailer's exclusion of the lesbian climax that culminates in Miller's masochistic fantasy of degenerating into a dog leaves out the most dramatic part of the novel, and a crucial psychological part as well. Of course there are space limitations in any anthology, and hard choices to be made, but nothing could justify this total exclusion in a selection so large—nothing, that is, but the special view of an anthologist with an eye for the final integrity of crazy cock macho. This distorts Miller as well, not allowing him to resolve his own crises.

The *Sexus* selection is so large that it may give the impression that Miller's earlier work leads up to this one, and his later work is what comes after it. But Mailer does not believe this, valuing *Tropic of Cancer* as Miller's best work. Nor is *Sexus* his most representative work. It is his most pornographic work of serious fiction and at the same time, as part of *The Rosy Crucifixion* trilogy, one of his most psychologically ambitious (and one of his longest); these factors in themselves, as well as the corrective factor it supplies in the Miller world to Durrell's anthology, are why Mailer chose so extensively from it. His emphasis is appropriate as *Sexus* really is a central Miller work, and perhaps

Mailer felt he had to insist on this to make it clear. *Tropic of Cancer*, the distantly second largest selection, is a much shorter work and, more importantly, familiar turf. But if one were reading Miller for the first time in this anthology, the emphasis on *Sexus* is overdone. It is possible, though, that most people who read the anthology did so to see how Mailer would do it. Rather well, I think.

Given the brief, fragmentary quality of virtually all the remaining selections and the fact that most of what comes after *Sexus* in the anthology was written after the *Tropics* and *Sexus*, the rest is something of an anticlimax. This conclusion is reinforced by the quality of Mailer's commentary, which leads up to the brilliance of "Crazy Cock" and "Narcissism" and then tails off into the final five relatively modest critical performances. Even the gross measurement of page numbers tells us something about where Mailer's major effort lay. The first five commentaries (all excellent criticism but "Status") take up fifty-five pages, the last five just thirty-three.

The "Surrealism" section is taken mostly from *Tropic of Capricorn*. The first selection (*TCap* 295–96) gives us what was once considered outrageous verbal play. Let's do something live, even if destructive, Miller concludes. It is a bit difficult to understand how the next selection (333–39) is illustrative of surrealism. A rather listless account of Miller's early love live—pure idealism or pure lust—does not seem to belong here. But when one considers Mailer's comment that being in lustful congress with a woman you hate is the origin of surrealism, the selection seems plausible. The next surrealist selection (346–48) presents Venus as Lilith, whose lies Miller believes in. The final two selections come from *Black Spring*. First there is the dazzling Cronstadt wordplay inspired by Joyce (*BS* 115–29), then a sadistic doctor fantasy that seems to have influenced Burroughs (143–46).

There is not much to be said about the section called, in a forced joke, "Grease." The selections from *The Colossus of Maroussi* focus on the character of Katsimbalis. The relation between commentary and text seems marginal. Mailer does make the intriguing—and more or less true—point that the book is not top-drawer Miller because it is not obscene. The next section, called "Henry the First," is culled from *The Air Conditioned Nightmare*. It consists of most of a hilarious set piece (*AN* 97–108), which Durrell also includes, involving Miller's tribulations with an old car, plus an extraordinarily sympathetic account of southern aristocratic life and architecture (205–17). Miller thinks it far more human than the money culture. The next section, "Domestic Misery," contains what is perhaps Miller's most powerful explicitly autobiographical writing, "Reunion in Brooklyn," from the collection *Sunday after the War*. This is one place where Durrell's anthology is superior, for the simple reason that he includes the whole heart-rending account of Miller's visit to his parents. Should one wish to make the case that Miller is a domestic realist, one would begin here—and perhaps end here. In this piece, Miller's sense of rage and disintegration remains in the confines of the ordinary. The second "Domestic Misery" selection, from *Big Sur* (177–91), is a tonal counterpart. We are given a light sketch of Miller as paterfamilias, a sort of fantasy Victorian to the point of tears. Of course, the wife gets possession of the children after Miller throws in the sponge. The final section, "Portraits," begins with the memorable portrait of Conrad Moricand from *Big Sur* (275–87), followed by a very funny account of the klutzy Miller as roofer from *Plexus* (322–44). Mailer seems to derive an unusual pleasure in seeing cocksure Henry at the mercy of the mechanical. The next selection is Elfenbein's monologue from *Nexus* (276–86). A lyrical Jew and raconteur, Elfenbein is one of a number of philo-Semitic portraits in Miller. Mailer then goes back to *Sexus* (385–91) for an incident that could almost have fit in the "Crazy Cock" section: but friend Julie puts him off. This sequence includes more of Miller's comic klutziness—and an overflowing toilet, a scene that J. P. Donleavy seems to have remembered in *The Ginger Man*. Mailer's second *Sexus* selection (150–57), which is very funny, concerns MacGregor's indifferent wife, the embattled Tess Malloy. "Portraits" concludes incongruously with a general description, a "portrait" of a diseased capitalist America. That also concludes the book. Mailer wouldn't have it any other way.

It is clear that once the reader gets through Mailer's "Narcissism" section, the rest of his anthology, for all the good things in it, might just as well have appeared in Durrell. In other words, Mailer's book falls into two separate parts: Miller as the ferocious fornicator, and the amiable Henry. While both strains are present in Miller, this hedging of bets may be considered a weakness in the anthology because the major aim of Mailer's criticism of Miller is an illumination of his ferocity. We now turn to a consideration of this criticism, the most important critical writing Mailer has done.

Mailer has been taken down for using Miller as a form of self-aggrandizement, for indirectly flattering the macho, so important in his own literary profile. And there are times when the commentary is too idiosyncratically Mailerian to be a description of Miller. For Mailer, it is axiomatic that man's alienation from nature and his consequent dread of woman (who, because of mysterious child-bearing powers, is not alienated) "made men detest women, revile them, humiliate them, defecate symbolically upon them, do everything to reduce them so that one might enter them and take pleasure of them" (*GL* 93). But Miller's misogyny is a psychological, not a metaphysical, compulsion, stemming from the "dominant mother, ineffectual father" syndrome (which Mailer feels to a lesser degree) rather than a never-to-be-assuaged sense of romantic grievance. When Mailer compares "the power relation of sex" to a street fight in which one man beats another's head against the ground, he is striking a note alien to Miller. And Mailer gives a grimly sadistic twist to this relation in his power description of fellatio: "The tastes are ground into the other's mouth and cowardice is expiated by going down" (176). This mentality has more to do with Mailer's Rojack or Ramses II than with any Miller persona. Even the Miller of *Sexus*, socking it to Victorian Maude, which is as close as Miller comes, is getting even in a bedroom sort of way, sadistic in tone but without Mailer's brutality. Mailer rightly observes: "He detests his wife but loves to fuck her." If Mailer were sticking to his metaphysical guns, he would have to say that Miller screws her so well because he detests her. Mailer's "but" suggests a meliorating reality that runs counter to violent custom. Mona is only the most obvious refutation of the simply sadistic pattern; various whores and an occasional girlfriend also refute it.

Mailer's emphasis is rather too combative in other judgments as well. He says: "There is nothing in literature to compare to the accounts [Miller] gives in *Tropic of Cancer* and *Sexus* of making love to other women—they read like round by round AP wire stories" (*GL* 179). This is close in some cases; Miller does compare one coupling to wrestling, though not with Mailer's bellicose tone. In Miller it is another variation on a theme, an incarnation of phallic celebration. He does not, for example, feel hostile to Tania (only to her not belonging to him) but to her listless cocksman of a husband. Fight metaphors apply perfectly well to, say, "The Time of Her Time" ("I threw her a fuck the equivalent of a fifteen-round fight" [*AdM* 463]). Combat does not really apply to Miller for the additional fact that his women do not fight back. A more relevant metaphor is circus—*maximus*, of course.

While some Mailer protagonists actually murder women, no Miller characters do. Though Miller has his share of romantic clichés, the sexy murderer, a Mailer favorite, is not one of them. The killer is Mailer's ultimate image of male potency, sexier than the athlete, whose potency is merely physical. This is because Mailer's view of sex is essentially sadistic. "Something in a woman wishes to be killed went the old wisdom," says Mailer, a new exponent of the old and the wise; "She would like to lose the weakest part of herself, have it ploughed under, ground under, kneaded, tortured, squashed, sliced, banished, and finally immolated. Burn out my dross is the unspoken cry of his girls" (*GL* 180). Once again Mailer is grimly theoretical in describing a man who is as often as not just fucking around. Moreover, in saying that to be a woman is to be a masochist, Mailer is overlooking a strong masochistic streak in Miller himself, without which he could not have been impaled on Mona for so long. Miller, one recalls, loves the book title, *A Man in Slices*. And, Mailer's commentary to the contrary notwithstanding, in Miller it is not always the male who impales. Far more than Miller, Mailer "is in sex for the kill" (180). Mailer's theoretical misogyny is that of an ex-Marxist still settling the social power score. Miller's is that of the common man, as much true-blue American flouting of respectability as it is neurotic protest against the mother.

Though Mailer's depiction of Miller is self-serving in these ways, the main value of his criticism is that it does demonstrate Miller's underlying ferocity. If Mailer seems to be gilding the lily in the extremity of his literal claims, his metaphors often ring true: Miller "makes love to his ex-wife like a pirate opening a chest or a terrorist blowing up factory, a sex murderer whose weapon is his phallus" (*GL* 180). However dangerous Miller's penis may be, though, it is never lethal. Certainly in his relation with Maude, "it is social artifice he would slay first, and hypocrisy, and all the cancers of bourgeois suffocation. 'Take that, you cunt,' is his war cry." Well, it is, but unlike Mailer, Miller is not typically on the warpath. Not having Mailer's tendency to slip into the luridly melodramatic, Miller is not reducible to comic-book rhetoric. Miller's sexual aggression is social as well as psychological, but it does not have Mailer's violent edge. Miller does not have the heroic imagination: he survives in the cracks.

Mailer writes: "It is as if Henry Miller contains the unadvertised mystery of how much of a monster a great writer must be" (*GL* 10). For Mailer, the mystery is necessarily monstrous or bestial. Miller writes about his own ferocity in more measured terms. "One reason why I have stressed so much the immoral, the wicked, the ugly, the cruel in my work," Mailer quotes him as saying, "is because I wanted others to know how valuable these are, how equally if not more important than the good things" (quoted at 17). The statements of Mailer and Miller do not quite jibe. Miller's is humanistic by comparison.

Mailer's criticism is at its most convincing in describing Miller's negative epiphanies. He rightly says that Miller "is a demon at writing about bad fucks . . . So he dived into the sordid, and portrayed men and women as they had hardly been painted before . . . he can even write about the whipped-out flayed heel-ground butt of his own desire for a whore, about fucking when too exhausted to fuck and come up with a major metaphor" (85). The epiphany comes through the activity in a transcendental relation: "One crazy fuck begets another—this is the message, over and over. One is connecting into the electrical system of the world" (91). Here we have an instance of negative transcendence, the inversion of value traditionally conceived to achieve countervalue, which is a hallmark of ferocity. Mailer quotes Miller on this point: "Perhaps a cunt, smelly though it may be, is one of the prime symbols for the connection between all things" (quoted at 93), a sentiment echoed less graphically by Mailer at the end of *The Deer Park*. If one lacks the sense of personal presence in Miller, the sense of a face, Mailer finds this a virtue. Indeed, he comments eloquently on the absence: "In all his faceless, characterless, pullulating broads . . . their cunts are always closer to us than their faces" (*GL* 94). Just so. Yes, it is a peculiar adoration that Miller feels at this nether shrine. Without Mailer's womb envy, without deviously ascribing to woman "the power and the glory," as Mailer does, Miller arrives in more homespun fashion at the higher impersonality. Faces do not seem to matter much to these lower theologians. Mailer is describing himself more than Miller but is not far from the mark in saying: "It is the mirror of how we approach God through our imperfections, *Hot*, full of the shittiest lust." The final adjective is the last refinement of negative transcendence.

For Mailer, it is precisely Miller's eccentric angle of vision that makes him an influential figure. We have become accustomed to the negative honorific. We value Miller because, in Mailer's words, "there is honor in the horror, and metaphor in the hideous" (16). Forget harmony, proportion, restraint, the properties of an Apollonian sense of beauty. Miller's prose is the product of outrage, full of explosive Sadean élan. Mailer waxes Elizabethan in describing Miller's writing as "a wildwater of prose, a cataract, a volcano, a torrent, an earthquake" (9).

In this overstatement, Mailer expresses his weakness for the volcanic: literature must explode. Never mind that Miller is equally at home in the routine movement of a quiet river, metaphor of the neutral life force, the flux that negates the titanic ego. Yet Mailer is basically right about the *Tropics* and *Sexus*. Miller did anticipate, indeed influence, the landscape of a good deal of contemporary American writing, "the big-city garbage can of bruises, migraines, static, mood chemicals, amnesia, absurd relations and cancer," as

Mailer puts it (*GL* 9); "Turn on, tune in and drop out was old hat to Henry—he had been doing it all his life." Miller never took drugs and thought those who did were pathetic, but he is the vague granddaddy for American dropouts. Mailer praises Miller for elevating the shit standard, exulting in what Miller could do with it compared to a shitless wonder like Henry James. It took immigrant stock and Brooklyn to bring the language back to its basal force as a mirror of the apocalypse. "With the exception of Hemingway," Mailer maintains, Miller "has had perhaps the largest stylistic influence of any twentieth-century American author," citing *Naked Lunch*, *Portnoy's Complaint*, *Fear of Flying*, and his own *Why Are We in Vietnam?* as apt illustrations. Mailer is right here, but perhaps too right, given that what he says reminds us of Frederick Crews's remark that Mailer will never produce a book like *Tropic of Cancer*, "which mark[s] out fundamentally new possibilities for fiction."[3]

Mailer does have reservations about Miller, and, considering Miller's subject matter, they are serious. "He could be poetic about anything and everything except fucking with love," Mailer says, adding parenthetically and half-ironically: "(of course it is fair to ask: who can?)" (*GL* xiii). Considering the centrality of June Smith to his fiction and his life, Mailer must lament Miller's "failure to create her" (xii). For all his enthusiasm, Mailer sees that Miller's inability to focus on "the one subject which cried out to him . . . what is to be said of love between a man and a woman?" makes him a less important writer than D. H. Lawrence. While this statement is generally just, it is not quite fair. For while Mailer sees a certain weakness in Miller's writing as "invariably an evocation of some disembodied and divine cunt," he might just as well point to the works in Lawrence that are an evocation of some disembodied phallus, like *Aaron's Rod*, "The Lady Bird," and "The Woman Who Rode Away." Both writers are to some degree in thrall to the higher impersonality. Because of this lack in Miller, Mailer holds that "one cannot grasp the core of Henry Miller" himself (183). He believes that Anaïs Nin's description of June Smith refers to Miller as well. Nin sees June's self as "brilliance and strangeness . . . enormous ego, false, weak, posturing, [that] lacks the courage of its personality" (quoted at 183). But we do know Miller, all too well—we know him ad nauseam—and what Mailer prefers to characterize as an enigma is Miller's failure to attain the heroic stature that the sexual adventurer must, according to Mailer's logic. Fucking as the answer is, after all, a dead end.

Mailer also has clear reservations about Miller's prose. Like everyone else, he shakes his head over Miller's garrulousness. Miller may yet go down in history as the Polonius of the sexual revolution. Commenting on Miller's intended masterwork, *The Rosy Crucifixion*, Mailer regrets that "'I-got-laid-and-it-was-wondrous' is the opening theme and by the end not one new philosophical connection has been laid onto the first lay" (*GL* 186). Mailer is a *Tropic of Cancer* loyalist, an ardent admirer of its explosive prose. Yet for him even the relatively straightforward *Tropic of Capricorn* is artsy, overwritten, and an example of "all forms, all manners, even all vices of avant-garde writing" (369). Even Mailer rejects the facile verbal apocalypse of *Black Spring* —"the great sun of syphilis is setting" (quoted at 368) etc. Again like everyone else, Mailer sees a further stylistic deterioration in Miller's later work, making special note of the qualified success of *The Colossus of Maroussi*, though he judges it—rightly, I believe—not to be one of Miller's best works because it is not obscene. It is nice to have Miller in the humanist camp, but that is not his real home.

Mailer comments often and well on Miller's style but says little about structure, maybe because there is so little to talk about. Indeed, Miller's amorphousness as a storyteller is one quality that Mailer does comment on: "We can suspect that Miller hated to obey the narrative line of the novel. It is as if he would be conforming then to all the demands of the machine, of the American machine" (502). This equation cannot be justified. Even before Kant, we have known that the realm of literature is not that of the machine. It is more appropriate to say that Miller's plots are inept because his work contains no morally structured sense of action, because his own moral bearings—where they exist at all—are so unstable. Since Mailer agrees with Nin's tough judgment that Miller had no philosophy, only sentiments, he might have made this connection for himself.

Given Mailer's reservations, it is not surprising that his more extravagant endorsements of Miller's stature are unconvincing. Invoking Melville and Faulkner for stylistic comparison and Marlowe and Shakespeare for imagistic comparison does not do Miller much good. But Mailer is right in emphasizing style and image as special strengths of this fundamentally lyrical writer. Nor is it clear that Miller is a writer of incomparably larger dimension than Robert Frost. When Mailer maintains in 1976 that, despite this, Miller would never be invited to read from his work on Inauguration Day (not, one may assume, unless Gary Hart were elected president), we perceive that Mailer is again thinking at least as much about his own situation as he is about Miller's. And while *Tropic of Cancer* is a work of note and has been an influence, it is not, as Mailer contends, one of the ten or twenty great novels of the twentieth century. Nor is it better than anything by Fitzgerald. Mailer's preference of *Tropic of Cancer* to *The Great Gatsby* tells us as much about the sexual corner into which he has backed himself.

All things considered, Mailer's lengthy commentary remains the best piece of criticism he has written. It is wrong to regard it as primarily a piece of literary politics, a prolonged exercise in self-inflation disguised as adulation. Why is it not a perfectly legitimate and sometimes brilliant redefinition of tradition by a particular individual talent? Mailer underestimates Miller's value as a literary critic (some of the Lawrence criticism, for example, should be far more interesting to him than it is precisely because of its insight into Lawrence's ferocity), as an autodidactic thinker of fragmentary illuminations (Durrell's anthology is more representative on both counts), and as a wry connection to classic American Romanticism. But his arguments are always engaging. Mailer's Miller is a legitimate recognition, a concord of the discordant.[4]

CONCLUSION

THE NAKED AND THE CLOTHED

We have elaborated on the theme of ferocity in individual writers and intellectuals who have had an influence on the American literary climate in the middle of the twentieth century. The Beat movement had a similar impact, and its best novel is William Burroughs's *Naked Lunch*. Published in Paris in 1959 and in the United States in 1962, the Supreme Court of Massachusetts declared it not obscene in 1966. Many critics regard it highly. One of its defenders in the Massachusetts trial was Norman Mailer. Mailer said that it had "enormous importance to me as a writer" and that Burroughs "might have been one of the greatest geniuses of the English language if he had never been an addict."[1] When it comes to writers of ferocity, Mailer is given to hyperbole. There is no question that *Naked Lunch* was important to him as a writer, especially as he wrote *Why Are We in Vietnam?* However, that Mailer work is more conventional than *Naked Lunch* in having a beginning, a middle, and an end. It is a narrative in time, partly because of its other influence, Faulkner's *The Bear*, and even more because Mailer feels an instinctive obligation to storytelling as a novelist. Burroughs has no such feeling in *Naked Lunch*; it is a narrative in space, fragmentary and formless. It is a theme and variations rather than a linear narrative. Its cut-up technique was, for this mother, the invention of necessity. He did not have to worry about structure. Further, Allen Ginsberg played Pound to his Eliot, even participating in *Naked Lunch* far more actively than Pound did in *The Waste Land*, putting the mass of manuscript material together by collating and integrating letters, autobiographical fragments, narrative sketches, and comedy routines. This from a mass of manuscript material stained by God knows what. So while Mailer is enamored of Burroughs's talent, he admits that he cannot call *Naked Lunch* "a great book like *Remembrance of Things Past* or *Ulysses* because of the imperfection of its structure" (*NL* xiv). There are several other reasons, but Mailer then gives a good description of Burroughs's power. "There is a sense in *Naked Lunch* of the destruction of the soul," he says, "which is more intense than any I have encountered in any other modern novel. It is a vision of how mankind would act if it was totally divorced from eternity" (xvii). Burroughs, it seems, brings out the latent theologian in Mailer, as well as the aesthetically attuned psychologist. Burroughs avoids sentimentality "by attaching a stringent, mordant vocabulary to a series of precise and horrific events, a species of gallows humor which is a defeated man's last pride, the pride that he has, at least, not lost his bitterness." Fair enough. Mailer gleans a moral in Burroughs: "At the end of medicine is dope; at the end of life is death; at the end of man may be the Hell which arrives from the vanities of the mind." More than any other work, *Naked Lunch* gives us "the vanities of the human will ... the excesses of evil which occur when the idea of personal or intellectual power reigns superior to the compassions of the flesh," according to Mailer (xviii). There are innumerable works that give us more about the vanities of the will than *Naked Lunch* does. And when Mailer is talking about compassions of the flesh, he is talking more about himself than about Burroughs, for whom compassion is not the word. Mailer is more on target when he speaks about death, the equation of civilization and destruction, the subversion of the ego by the id, and the ferocity of an imagination that takes no prisoners because there is no one who is not imprisoned.

Naked Lunch met a certain antinomian literary expectation, which Burroughs has described as the literature of delirium. "I apparently took detailed notes on sickness and delirium," he says. "I have no precise memory of writing the notes which have now been published under the title *Naked Lunch*" (xxxvii). (The title was suggested by Jack Kerouac.) Burroughs defines *naked* as a "frozen moment when everyone sees what is on the end of every fork." This is another instance of the stripping away of civilized forms, forms that he judges to be sadistic. He attacks capital punishment, for example, an ultimate form of control: "If civilized countries want to return to Druid Hanging Rites in the Sacred Grove or to drink blood with the Aztecs, let them see what they actually eat and drink. Let them see what is on the end of that long newspaper spoon" (xliv–xlv). Here is the lunch again, and the fork or spoon is the news from civilization. But Burroughs himself is obsessed (in *Naked Lunch* and elsewhere) with hanging rites and their subsequent ejaculations, the life-in-death psychodrama of sadomasochistic desperation. Nor is he averse to drinking blood, metaphorically speaking. Violence is the glue that keeps his fragments together; there is no balm like ferocity. Burroughs has said: "If I really knew how to write, I could write something that someone would read and it would kill them."[2] He may have succeeded.

It can safely be said that Burroughs does not sentimentalize. No angel-headed hipsters appear in *Naked Lunch*. There is nothing transcendent about "junk" because "a rabid dog cannot choose but bite," as Burroughs says in a typical downward comparison (*NL* xxxix). He suggests legalized, supervised use of morphine as a solution to drug addiction.

But the novel contains no such hope. Its familiar opening words—"I can feel the heat [the police] closing in"—strike the note of paranoia with which this novel resonates. If the narrator (Burroughs's surrogate) escapes from the "narcotics dicks" at the opening, he murders two in the last fragments. Law and order is most eloquently expressed in the words of a sadistic, redneck sheriff. After all, hipsterism is the stoned version of the unconditioned self. Burroughs's obsession with the depredations of control has filtered down into the expression "control freak." Control is the origin of his most vivid comic daymares. His sadistic merry-go-round typically involves surgeons, policemen, and addicts. Sometimes the gallows humor is gallows humorless (e.g., when the Mugwump strangles the boy with a noose, observing his ejaculations and humping the dead body). Jack the Ripper and the Boston Strangler fit in as casual references. The juiced prose, particularly eloquent in its description of American drag, can be downright awful, even when it resembles a haiku (for example, "pieces of murder fall slow as opal chips through glycerine"[3]). Burroughs kicked his drug habit but kept on writing. Literature was his homeopathic cure. Literature and one other thing: he commented in a film interview that he owed his subsequent good health to the orgone box.

Mailer is not quite right about death being the end of life for Burroughs. Death is present virtually at the beginning. Burroughs saw heroin addiction as a death wish and saw the whole world addicted to death, most notably the bourgeois world, the Midwestern, middle-class, middle-age world of his early traumas. He does not believe that this world can be transformed by words. In the *Semiotext(e)* issue on schizo culture, he says: "Words are still the principal instrument of control."[4] So we see Burroughs as one of Frank Kermode's neo-modernists, a mutant who is against language, art, ethics, and form.[5] Burroughs thinks declarative sentences are a mistake because he has nothing to declare. He is a model of Deleuze and Guattari's schizo, even to the point of phylogenetic regression. In one funny passage in *Naked Lunch*, Burroughs introduces the talking asshole. Diderot had a talking vagina in *The Indiscreet Jewels*, a more intriguing and civilized form of comic possibility. But it isn't quite right for Burroughs if it isn't shitty. At the core of his aesthetic excrementalism (comparisons with Swift are apt) is a moral nihilism. Just as *Naked Lunch* is a conglomeration of words without meaning in the old sense, it is a tale of crime without punishment. The murder of the police officers (of course, in the context of the novel they "deserve" it) Hauser and O'Brien by the Burroughs surrogate goes unpunished. "Nothing is true, everything is permitted," says a sympathetic character in Burroughs's *The Wild Boys*, a violent, fiercely misogynistic work. What is denied by Dostoevsky is affirmed by Burroughs. Burroughs anticipates Foucault in subjecting everything, including language, to power games. So even though Burroughs achieves an imaginative release in literature, it is a compromised grace in which "ultimate freedom means a society constructed of sadistic and masochistic relationships, fantasy living through pleasure-pain situations of inflicting and receiving."[6] And though Burroughs gives us a cry from a tortured heart, his lack of personal affect gives us what Jennie Skerl calls a literature that is autobiographical but not subjective.

To the extent that Burroughs is Dr. Benway, a professional sadist, the cure may be worse than the disease. How much har-har horror can the reader take before the verbal pyrotechnics fizzle into a limb fallen asleep? Just when we think we have seen everything, something really new appears that out burrows Burroughs, that goes so deeply into horrific violence that we really do not want to get the joke. It must be a joke. *Naked Lunch* and Bret Easton Ellis's *American Psycho*[7] give us characters devoid of inner life. In Burroughs evil is external; in Ellis it is a habit attached to a social sleepwalker. The self has disintegrated into nightmare fragments. Ellis's masterstroke is to present radical sexual aggression not as rebellion but as the logical consequence of conformity, a conformity so deep that people are often taken for someone else. Ellis draws no Marxist moral from this. His hero, often referred to as "the boy next door," far from looking like a junkie walks out of the pages of *GQ* (he takes fashionable cocaine). Where Burroughs's point was to be naked, Ellis's is to be clothed. No other novel spends so much of its time on the splendor of clothing—designer clothing, at that. It is one of the generosities of bourgeois culture to attribute artistic profundity to the soul of a haberdasher. That or one of the glaring weaknesses of bourgeois materialism. In Ellis, charisma has been transferred to the material world, since it has nowhere else to go. When there is no inner world, the outer world takes over. Because of this disproportion, realism becomes a form of surrealism. Which is more fantastic, *Naked Lunch* or *American Psycho*?

The pleasures of *American Psycho* are decadent ones and are given satirically by Ellis. He embodies that much of the reality principle. A lady friend spells Patrick Bateman's initials out in a birthday sushi arrangement, disturbed that "the tuna looked too pale" (*AP* 9). His two main girlfriends go to business school in Geneva and Lausanne. He buys magazines that have already been delivered to him through his subscription. He has three phone lines. He films part of his murder of a woman on his "Sony palm-sized Handy cam" (246). He and a lady friend drink "an expensive California Cabernet Sauvignon" with mahi-mahi and pilot fish (the only chink in Ellis's formidable yuppie armor that I can discern—a white wine is called for). One of his two girlfriends uses Evian to make ice cubes. The other complains "about weight she hadn't gained" (281). Summering in the Hamptons, she "went back to the city three times that last week . . . once for a manicure and pedicure and facial, the second time for a one-on-one training session at Stephanie Herman, and finally to meet with her astrologer." She is questioned by Bateman about why she helicopters into the city. This is the one point in the novel where even he is bothered by so much excess. " 'What do you want me to do' she shrieked, popping another dietetic truffle in her mouth, 'Rent a *Volvo*?' " Like the Marxist, the society snob has a rich contempt for the middle class.

The pleasures of *American Psycho* derive from the slyly observed detail, defining the distance, however slight, between the author and his maniacal central character. These details illuminate the point where money meets a numbered anality, where conspicuous consumption meets the superclean, the superordered. There are Bateman's Interplak toothbrush, with its speed of 4,200 rpm, that "reverses direction forty-six times per second" (26); his creams, moisturizers, mousses, and brush; and his envy of Owen's "perfect, even part" and "tan scalp" (148). Bateman is upset when drizzle ruins his hair. When he takes money out of a particularly simpatico ATM, the bills are "crisp, freshly printed twenties, and I delicately place them in my gazelleskin wallet so as not to wrinkle them" (163).

Bateman is not without a culture hero: Donald Trump, the presiding spirit of 1980s luxe. If Trump likes the pizza at Pastels, so will Bateman—though as it turns out, he does not. His one priority is to get invited to the Trumps' Christmas party aboard their yacht. The Young Republicans have a bash at

Trump Plaza. They read *The Art of the Deal*. In an echo of the national anthem, Bateman looks "admiringly" at "Trump Tower, tall, proudly gleaming in the late afternoon sunlight" (385). There it is, in all its phallic significance, the symbol of yuppie heaven. (The question of Trump's real standing with the top-level business community and with serious economists never comes up; nor does his publicity-hound reputation for meretricious behavior.) Trump's standing as a moneymaker, at least in the popular yuppie mind, and his mastery of cold cash (made in real estate but later lost, in part, in the gambling industry) imply a capable sadism, though it is not until his later incarnation as an American pop mogul—a commodity in a world of commodification—that Trump becomes a television icon whose emblematic utterance is "You're fired!"

Like Freud, Ellis blends money, anality, and sadism. His friend Price works at Pierce and Pierce. The crocodile loafers that Bateman sports not only make the man, they make him in a predatory idleness. Bateman gives himself a pedicure—obsessive cleanliness again—and tortures his small dog almost in the same breath. Not given to charity, he gouges out the eye of a homeless black man who upsets his delicate emotional equilibrium. Although he does not find the American Nazis on a television show charming, he does not find them "unsympathetic" either (156). A sociable sadist, at a party he serves his friends a urinal cake disguised in cheap chocolate syrup (the only cheap thing he buys). Homosexuals bring out his sadistic edge; for Bateman every homosexual is a "faggot." He despises the gay pride parade—an image of self contempt? He fucks the bleeding mouth of one of his recent female victims. There are, I think, seventeen of them in the narrative time of the book, and others offstage. This, of course, is the most horrific sadism in the book. His Uzi is a "symbol of order" (346).

Bateman's anality elicits the usual excremental reference. "I feel like shit but look great," he says (343), showing that everything but his emotional life, if you can call it that, is under control. His designer wardrobe produces an apparently immaculate effect. If clothing, which covers nakedness, is a symbol of civilization, we can see what civilization has come to: an elegant decadence in a moral vacuum. Bateman always feels his clothes are a straitjacket. The world is not right, and he feels dehumanized. In his relationship with Evelyn, he fantasizes "women giving birth through assholes," a reduction of procreation to something close to shit. If shit is here, can the apocalypse be far behind? He fantasizes "the total destruction of the world" because "it's an isolation ward that serves only to expose my own severely impaired capacity to feel." This leaves him with the usual sadistic impulse: "I suddenly imagine Evelyn's skeleton, twisted and crumbling, and this fills me with glee."

Bateman is Narcissus as Bluebeard. He kills women because they don't matter. In all of fiction, he is the male character who looks at himself in the mirror most. He cannot get enough of "how good I look" (11), even if it means staring at his reflection in a glass table. He admires his abs more than he admires any woman. He comes from California. He is often said by critics to be characterless, yet who else would say: "I wish I *had* switched mousses because since I last saw my hair, seconds ago, it feels different, as if its shape was somehow altered on the walk from bar to table" (231). Bateman's narcissism may be lost in trivialities, but it has a power base. He wants Evelyn to call him "King," though he never tells her so. For him, narcissism is the norm. He likes Whitney Houston's "The Greatest Love of All" because, he says, "since it's impossible in the world we live in to empathize with others, we can always empathize with ourselves" (254). Can one empathize with oneself? The narcissistic Bateman can.

His narcissism recalls Freud's tyrannical primary narcissism, that of the infant who sees the world as indistinguishable from his needs. But it also recalls the more conventional meaning, an egotist so bound up in his impulses as to make the rest of the world serve them. Bateman has the requisite dysfunctional family—a father who is a son of a bitch, to whom Bateman cannot talk; an institutionalized mother; and a brother he wants to avoid. "I'm a child of divorce," says Bateman; "Give me a break" (215). His favorite television program, "The Patty Winters Show," broadcasts an interview with "a man who set his daughter on fire while she was giving birth" (347). It is no fun being a kid in Bateman's world, or even an embryo. The child's world is subsumed by violence or sex. Tuning into another Winters program, Bateman listens to the hostess ask a child of eight or nine, "But isn't that just another name for orgy?" (382). This is not the book to read for Oedipal resolution, with one possible exception. Bateman makes obscene phone calls to female students at the Dalton School, whispering lasciviously: "I'm a corporate raider . . . I orchestrate hostile takeovers." Then, sucking air like a rhinoceros in heat, he mutters "bitch." The fear he elicits turns him on, maintaining his erection, "until one of the girls . . . asked, unfazed, 'Dad, is that you?'" (162).

American Psycho is another twentieth-century novel with a negative credo. For Bateman, the wasteland is an interminable state of mind. He notes that "where there was nature and earth, life and water, I saw a desert landscape that was unending" (374). He notes that "it did not occur to me, *ever*, that people were good or that a man was capable of change or that the world could be a better place through one's taking pleasure in a feeling or a look or a gesture, of receiving another person's love or kindness. Nothing was affirmative." Since he considers desire "meaningless," like a true disciple of Sade, he lives the idea that "sex is mathematics." Bateman affirms nothing but a nihilistic vacuum: "Fear, recrimination, innocence, sympathy, guilt, waste, failure, grief, were things, emotions that no one really felt anymore. Reflection is useless, the world is senseless. Evil is the only permanence. God is not alive. Surface, surface, surface was all that anyone found meaning in" (375). For him, profundity is another name for superficiality. A negative narcissist, Bateman says, "*I am simply not there.*" But he is there enough to know that "I want my pain to be inflicted on others" (377). Like Hemingway and Lawrence, Bateman makes disillusion with civilization his credo and rationale. But where the negative credo of a Frederick Henry and a Connie Chatterley reflected a complex irony deeply felt, Bateman's is the monochrome monologue of a slob.

In the epigraph to the novel, Ellis quotes from Dostoevesky's introduction to *Notes from the Underground* to the effect that such persons as the underground man "not only exist in our society, but indeed must exist, considering the circumstances under which our society has been generally formed."[8] The underground man would dissent from this bit of determinism. He is, after all, heroic in the sense that Hegel uses to describe the base heroism of the disintegrated consciousness. As we have seen, the essence of the underground man's attraction is encapsulated in his saying: "I have more life in me than you."[9] Bateman could truly say: "I have more death in me than you." The difference is between self-lacerating rebellion and self-lacerating conformity. Like the underground man, Bateman breaks down once and admits to the attraction of the good: "I just want to be loved," he cries out in what may be the funniest line in the book. He has just killed an anonymous girl—"this girl, this meat is nothing, is shit" (*AP* 345). Yet the theme of love and goodness has been running through the novel as a slight ironic thread in the form of the *Les Miz* ads he sees from time to time. And it functions as a partial explanation of his emotionally splitting in two again toward the end of the narrative, when— after violently repudiating these qualities—he now dotes on Huey Lewis and the News and tunes like "Walking the Kid," "Doing It All for My Baby," and "Hip to be Square" (359). He feels this moral euphoria right after committing a series of murders. Splitting is apparent in the second epigraph to the novel as well, which quotes Miss Manners: "That's what civilization is all about—doing it in a mannerly and not antagonistic way." Deleuze and Guattari were wrong. "In civilization there have to be some restraints. If we followed every impulse, we'd be killing one another."[10] Miss Manners or Pop goes the humanist. It may be a sign of Bateman's wish for the civilized life that he has been seeing a psychiatrist for two months.

In a review of *American Psycho*, Norman Mailer states that "the book is disturbing in a way to remind us that attempts to create art can be as intolerable as foul manners."[11] It seems odd to have Mailer, the writer of often lurid fiction, on the side of Miss Manners. (However, Mailer displayed surprisingly gracious manners, even at a first meeting.) Mailer's real disappointment in Ellis's work is that "the first novel to come along in years that takes on deep and Dostoyevskean themes is written by only a half-competent, narcissistic young man" (221)—as opposed to, say, the fully competent, narcissistic middle-aged author of *An American Dream*. I am not sure that either *An American Dream* or *American Psycho*—both books purporting to be about our nation and both giving us crime without punishment—has all that much to do with Dostoyevsky, in whose *Crime and Punishment* crime is punished, and guilt and the superego have great force. For Mailer, it appears, mad violence is intrinsically profound. Mailer is not so much upset by Bateman's predilection for killing women as he is by Bateman's being such a stick, so unbelievable a character, which makes his mayhem simply a form of butchery. "We cannot go out on such a trip," he argues engagingly, "unless we believe we will end up knowing more about extreme acts of violence, knowing a little more, that is, of the real inner life of the murderer" (221). To say, however, that Mailer's Rojack gives us that may not be saying much. Then, too, Ellis can argue that the point is that Bateman does not have an inner life to relate. He is representative of the new so-called blank fiction. All exterior, he is not committed to anything other than self-gratification. He is, as Mailer argues, a monster. Perhaps Mailer's real objection is that Bateman may be Sadean, but he is not a rebel, not transgressive. He is not Maileresque. If one wants to shake American society to its core, Mailer argues axiomatically, "one has to have something new to say about the outer limits of the deranged" (221). Redemption through violent madness is typical of ferocity. It may make for grim, episodic pornography, but Ellis does not think in terms of even an attempt at redemption.

Mailer can only assume that Ellis disapproves of Bateman, raising the interesting question of Ellis's connection to his subject matter. In interviews, Ellis comes across like Bateman's alter ego, the nice boy next door. He has said that the novel is a critique of the male mentality, that he loves women, that it is not really a book about violence, and that he is not interested in murder but in the corruption of the rich.[12] The good, daytime Ellis denies any essential connection with his nocturnal obsessions. He writes satire, Ellis says, which is true—but what form does the satire take? Certainly not the kind deriving from embattled moral certitude. If Ellis is almost accidentally involved with fantasies of lurid sadism, why do they pursue him not only in this book but in others that he has written? I recall a typical session with Ellis at the New School, in which he gave the eerie impression of being the only one in the large hall who did not understand his own work. Or perhaps he was not willing to understand it. With all the misogynistic destruction of women in Ellis, his mask as women's best friend is particularly artificial. Women come off even worse in Ellis than they do in Burroughs. Some critics think that Burroughs literally got away with murder. Ellis is apparently attempting a version of that feat in disguise.

Is Ellis interested in the corruption of the rich? He is—this is a source of his self-incriminating satire—but not in the quasi-Marxist way that Mailer suggests. "When an entire new class thrives on the ability to make money out of the manipulation of money, and becomes obsessed with the surface of things," says Mailer, "that is with luxury, commodities, food, and appearance—then, in effect, says Ellis, we have entered a period of the absolute manipulation of humans by humans: the object correlative of total manipulation is coldcock murder" (159). Reducing the world of finance to "the manipulation of money," then the grim "absolute manipulation" and, finally, the sinister "total manipulation" is a ghost from Mailer's Marxist past. Ellis is not so much interested in capitalism as he is in its cultural consequences, in which he is complicit. His novel gives us satire as self-laceration. *American Psycho* is not about class warfare. The proletariat, in the form of taxi drivers or maids, elicits Bateman's uniform contempt. Indeed, his contempt for the poor, as Mailer notices, is exceeded only by his contempt for the homeless, who bring out his extreme sadism as easily as a woman or a "faggot," and for the same reason: vulnerability elicits the most violent cruelty in Bateman. He is, as the title indicates, a psychopath. Ellis's Bateman is about hot-cock murder.

The literature of ferocity justifies itself by evoking a moral vacuum to which it must desperately respond. In doing so, it typically creates a moral vacuum larger than the one that brought it into being. Given the extremity of this vision (or these visions), the necessary cultural counterweight is a wild man in the wilderness, a moralist infused with a sense of prophecy. If one considers the intellectual landscape, Philip Rieff, whom we know from his earlier incarnation as a distinguished interpreter of psychoanalysis, fits the description. Rieff has been described by one of his followers as a neglected sociologist, and in a profession increasingly dominated by data, maybe he is—at least, as neglected as a Benjamin Franklin professor of sociology at the University of Pennsylvania can be. If Rieff has been neglected, it is also because he is a moralist, even something of a traditionalist. He courageously runs against the currents of deconstruction and postmodernism that have until recently dominated the literary and intellectual discourse of the last few decades. At the end of the 1960s and beginning of the 1970s, he writes *Fellow Teachers*,[13] a powerful work of social criticism, which more explicitly than any other serious work of discourse addresses the problem of moral exhaustion or, perhaps, of vacuity produced by the tradition of ferocity and modernism in general. As a self-styled "Jew of culture," Rieff addresses himself to his fellow secular rabbis (*FT* 198). In *The Triumph of the Therapeutic* (1966), Rieff had noted that "elites before our own were predominantly supportive rather than critical of culture as a moral demand system (*TT* 33). Admonitions were the expectable predicates of consolations, he says; that is what is meant, nowadays, by "guilt culture." Gone are those days, at least for high culture, but Rieff wishes to have them back in some new form. He misses what he calls "the civilization of authority." In the culture of modernism, all "positive" communities appear "either fraudulent or stupid." The negative community holds sway.

Freud is partly responsible for this. His psychoanalysis is the origin of the therapeutic mode. In a letter to Marie Bonaparte, he writes: "The moment a man questions the meaning and value of life he is sick, since objectively neither has an existence" (quoted in *TT* 34). Rieff himself ridicules "value" as a relative construct but endorses it emphatically as an actual synthesis, as the indispensable element in culture. In his landmark 1959 study *Freud: The Mind of the Moralist*, which did so much to establish Freud as a central figure in modernism, Rieff nonetheless draws back from the moral neutrality of psychological man. "Psychological man may be going nowhere, but he aims to achieve a certain speed and certainty in going," Rieff says; "The important thing is to keep going" (*TT* 41). In this way, psychoanalysis supported the rise of the James Dean, rebel without a cause, syndrome: "You don't go anywhere, you just go." Of course, ever since Romanticism the journey has been more important than the goal. In the United States during the nineteenth century and the early part of the twentieth, *experience* meant seeing the world. By the middle of the twentieth century, it had come to mean getting a kick. So has Lambert Strether's exigent injunction to little Bilham in Henry James's *The Ambassadors* to "live . . . live all you can" been reduced to a trip on a motorcycle.[14] Rieff is no fan of experience in either of these meanings. For him, *experience* is just another name for indirection. Freud has made this longtime American situation worse. "There is no doctrine of maturity like that of Freud," Rieff says, "with its acceptance of meaninglessness as the end product of analytic wisdom" (*TT* 43). This is a harsh judgment, even to some extent in Rieff's own terms. Freud wants some kind of inner balance, and the ego is not as weak in Freud as Rieff makes it out to be. Moreover, though Freud did not advocate morality, he often assumed it. The problem in society today, as Rieff now sees it, is one of moral failure. "By mid-century," he says, "the old established controls are enunciated so vacuously, and in such hollow voices, that they sound like remissions" (238).

This statement from *The Triumph of the Therapeutic* is fully illuminated in *Fellow Teachers*. As a Jew of culture, Rieff may not believe in God, but he does believe in "god-terms" (*FT* 48)—moral truths that define a culture, that make it a well of authority in a desert of meaninglessness. (He cites John Barth's *The End of the Road* and Pirandello's *The Rules of the Game* as illustrations of the afflicted weightlessness of that desert.) The biblical landscape has a haunting propriety in this sense. Because it had such moral authority, "ancient Israel constituted a high culture, although its arts, science and technologies were not remarkable" (*FT* 68). Ancient Israel had the Moses that we miss. The Israelites' "God-terms" were neither "functional" nor "mythic," they were just true. Rieff holds that "in the absence of a supreme interdictory Figure, another Moses, with his disciples, a defense by Jews of culture against our democratic orgiasts may be reordered . . . by a revival of severe codes of law" (162). At least this much would be established: "There is no crime without punishment" (167). For the ancient Israelites, belief in God manifested itself as poetic justice. Rieff looks around him and is depressed. He sees the "revolutionary acts" of Don Juans in their "erotic arenas" as examples of the new "freedom," that which "has come to mean a break through inhibiting civilities characteristic of high culture" (168). The Nietzschean "transvaluation of values" has had "its American climax" as a "valuation of all sexuality." Rieff notes with irritation that "nothing is [considered] perverse" (184).

Rieff may seem like a contemporary version of a prophet from the Hebrew Bible, and he quotes it approvingly. He says of his late memorable essay, "By What Authority?": "This essay is a wordy version of proverbial wisdom, said better in Proverbs 27:20: 'The nether world and Destruction are never satisfied; so the eyes of men are never satisfied.' "[15] Further, his idea of authority is exemplified by God's saying: "I am that I am." There is no cultural relativism here. Yet in Rieff, Jerusalem (including not only Jewish but also some Christian texts) is often tempered by Athens.

Rieff's view of authority is based on a tripartite distinction that first appears in *Fellow Teachers*. The first and central term is interdiction. These are moral limits, which he holds to be "the primary forms of high culture, not the arts and sciences" (*FT* 69).[16] Since the social and the psychological differ, interdicts are not to be confused with repressions. An interdict is based on a creed; a repression is never a precept. "Meaningful interdicts must be taught; we humans are not born with them," Rieff holds. "On the contrary, the human is born criminal," he says, in a bold proposition that is not so far from the primary narcissism of Freud's tyrannical infant, and darker than the Hebraic view Rieff professes to support. Rieff holds that "to praise the infantile is to praise criminality," doubtless thinking of our eroticized culture's glorification of immediate gratification. Who, then, will be ready for the showdown at high noon? "You and I, fellow teachers, are the real police, whether we like it or not," he writes (93–94). He is thinking, of course, of professors of philosophy, broadly speaking, not professors of orgy or criminality. Like the professor of philosophy whom Raskolnikov should have had, Rieff says: "We know it is to our humanity that everything is not permitted." Anyone who has "come to terms with God" understands this negation. The existence of the necessary intellectual elite is contingent on a sense of limits. "High culture, for which we teachers must stand if we are to stand for anything," he says, "is an establishment of bounds, a fixing of doors and bars in place—and yet, no imprisonment" (109). Contrary to popular opinion, Jesus was "a tremendous recognizer of the interdicts. He tells us that he came explicitly to deepen law, which he thought had grown too external, not to abolish it" (121). If this were not enough authoritative testimony, Rieff quotes his greatly admired Plato, who speaks of "the goddess of limit." It seems to be the fate of this goddess to be perpetually besieged. In any case, Plato describes in *Philebus* a situation familiar to anyone in Rieff's cultural situation. "Seeing in insolence and all manner of wickedness [a] breaking loose from all limit, in point of pleasure and self-indulgence," the goddess "established the limit of law and order, of limited being; and you say this restraint was the death of pleasure: I say it was the saving of it" (quoted in *BWA* 248). In denying the rule of pleasure, Rieff's idea of authority rescues pleasure from itself.

The second of Rieff's moral triad is remission. Remissions are "positive acceptances: what is not done—yet within the culture and in particular circumstances, done" (*FT* 73). He concedes that the way of the world requires this plasticity. All men benefit. Remission can be as harmless as dreaming. But as authority, which it commonly is in contemporary life, remission lacks force and vitality. As we have seen, this is particularly a problem in post-Freudian therapy and theory, where interdiction is actively undercut and where, consequently, the superego realities that Freud advocated are greatly diminished. In his presumptive moral neutrality, then, Freud is hoist on his own petard. Value-free scientists are even more remissive. "Equally remissive," Rieff observes, "our *artists/apostles* are equally helpless; they can only mount more and cheaper assaults on experience."

They can only encourage the transgressive, the third term of Rieff's triad. Transgressions are the direct subverters of interdicts, as anyone who has read this book knows. "No is the forbidden word in the enlightened parental vocabulary," says Rieff (122). This is the beginning of "anything goes," which commands authority for want of any other. Norman Brown is an illustration. Rieff rejects the idea that Brown can be considered holy because "a holy man cannot be a rhapsode of transgression, except as he leads us on to deep down interdicts, repressions freshly achieved" (197). But the aim of Brown is "to break us of the transgressive sense," so that his "exercises of erotic health must end in violence." Mailer is another illustration. Rieff considers "The White Negro" to be "the ur-text of our cultural revolution." In that essay, Mailer advises us "to escape the restraints of our inherited culture" by imitating blacks. Rieff considers Mailer "the finest blackface comedian of our time . . . who insults real blacks by his imitations," reducing them to "the most slavish intellectualized fantasies of the primitive" (103, note 65).

For Rieff, modernism advocates a "kind of naked life in which everything is exposed and nothing is revealed. How we moderns love to undress" (55). Indeed *modernism* has been defined as the labor of denudation. Even lunch must be naked. Rieff holds that "like everything else, flesh must be taught," seeing that "nowadays as Revolution . . . it is taught as if beyond criticism." Spirit, on the other hand, is "untaught." Teaching flesh "in all its expressible varieties . . . amounts to sado/masochistic activism." It certainly does in the literature of ferocity. Rieff sees a world in which people of the sexual ethic "cry that they have been banished out of the garden and try to strip down to what they consider flesh, as if in protest against their banishment." Of course, the significance of the banishment from prelapsarian bliss escapes them. The naked do not understand the clothed. They do not understand that "to remain alive, as humans, we are required to dress and there is no dress without memory of how our ancestors dressed. Adornment, the dressing up of existence, is inseparable from historical memory" (183–84). Civilization, in other words, transcends nature, gives it meaning, endows it with social value. In Yeats's adjectives, what matters is accustomed, ceremonious.[17] In his interpretation of the Fall, Rieff steers a middle course between the Scylla of Brownian utopianism and the Charybdis of Augustinian original sin.

What Rieff pines for—from what some consider his position on the Freudian Right—is a new incarnation of a sacred order, the revivification of the cultural superego. (Rieff himself is reluctant to be described as a Freudian.) He wants to put Humpty Dumpty together again. "In superego," he says, "we see the ghost of the sacred order," in aggression, the ghost of transgression. Authority has been reduced to therapy in the modern displacement of the interdictory, permissive, and transgressive "entirely from the sacred to the psychological" (*BWA* 239). We have lost Freud's "piety of mind," which—in *The Ego and the Id*, for example—"marches out to the progressive conquest of the id" (243). The superego is the necessary hinge, but it is now the wobbling pivot. "To make any new beginning at the necessary old science, of limits," says Rieff, "we can begin only by recognizing that our barbaric enlightenments have deinhibited the agency of inhibition: superego." Rieff rises to a literary eloquence. "The superego has not declined," he maintains, "it has undergone a metamorphosis. That agency made too active in any cause, rather than constraining, incites; modern criminals and would-be revolutionaries are not creatures of 'impulse,' as in the nineteenth-century imagination but . . . driven creatures of high principle, militants of this immediacy and that. Rapists grow didactic. Apostles of the body flaunt their principles . . . It is a resolutive contradiction in terms for the superego to express itself chiefly in transgressive activity. Such activists of easy principle are one price we are paying for packaging authority entirely inside quotation marks" (*FT* 43). Even before the nineteenth century, Sade exemplified these truths. Rieff here indicts the literature of ferocity. This outlook has attempted to bury Freud, who remains by comparison a noble figure for Rieff, a defender of high culture, a skeptic of "infinite openings of possibility" (216). For Rieff, "Freud maintained a sober vision of man in the middle, a go-between, aware of the fact that he had little strength of his own, forever mediating between culture and instinct . . . Maturity, according to Freud, lay in the trained capacity to keep the negotiations from breaking down." And even if Freud has fought a losing fight, "the exemplary cast of Freud's mind and character is more enduring than the particulars of his doctrine. In culture it is always the example that survives, the person is the immortal idea" (31). These are generous words, but they are somewhat vague and certainly not adequate to a Freudian. Heinz Kohut, to some degree, supplies a therapeutic rationale that supports Rieff's assessment: parents who were once too close are now distant. The consequent lack of an ego ideal or ideal object makes for a weak superego.

The problem of authority is the problem of faithlessness. And for Rieff, "art is our repository of faithlessness" (*BWA* 231). But for him, "a work of art is a moralizing form; moved as we are by it, no work of art can be neutral in the eternal war of culture. Art is the most subtle form of social direction." We are confronted with a momentous either-or: "Art deepens the thrust of culture into character, creating ever greater loyalties to the godheads most fully alive in (and only in) their deepest order, or, as in its present extremity, art subverts that order, goes down to murder its own godheads, and often, to mock its own use of god-terms." The literature of ferocity offers illustrations in abundance. Visionary though he is, Rieff sees the utility of art, for "it is interior space that is first reshaped, preliminary to the reshaping of social order" (*FT* 20). Rieff argues that "in a true culture, a genius is not considered a criminal, nor is criminality honored as genius" (46). He goes so far as to say that art not only should not, but cannot, subvert authority. "Imagination is creative," he argues moralistically and heretically, "only when in its true guilt, it subserves the interdicts. This is the imagination of priestly theorists—of Dostoevsky in *The Devils*, for example." The alternative is clear: "When the imagination grows transgressive, then it expresses itself in brutalities, however technically refined." In contemporary literature and film, "transgressiveness, the form of revolution, has taken the content of sexual display. The director of an art work becomes an honorary phallic swordsman and rhapsode of violence." Obviously, Rieff has not given up, but he needs help. "It is conceivable," he writes, "that, with enough scientific research and literary freedom of inquiry, the old interdicts (against economic exploitation, or incest, or murder, or unchastity, for random examples) can be revived."[18] He adds with somewhat uncharacteristic modesty, "but I doubt revival by force of intellect" (*FT* 100–101). To this last caveat, one should add that the passionate quality of Rieff's intellect makes his work an illustration of the literary freedom he longs for.

His insistence on authority has been interpreted as his awaiting the Second Coming of Himself. His apocalyptic negation of transgression glosses over differences between, say, Sade and the later Bataille, or Miller and Lawrence (though in the second pair he obviously does make a distinction). Sex may be spiritualized, even if not from above. The lower, to use Rieff's terminology, may have its own higher. Is what he gives us a plainly needed heterodox cultural conservatism, or the hysteria of a closet fascist? The former, I believe. He remains somewhat vague about how his vision would be enacted in the dull everyday world, and he is self-admittedly better at diagnosis rather than cure. But as an elegist of the Freudian moment, a prophet of cultural disintegration, and a thinker who is critical of the idea that everything is a construct, Rieff strikes a profound chord. No one can accuse him of being mindless, even less of being soulless. He raises a crucial question: Why are momentous—indeed, in his sense, sacred—concepts like law and order considered to be, in a cartoon reduction, the unique province of a redneck sheriff? Rieff describes a topsy-turvy world that too often sees out as in, and in as out; down as up, and up as down; black as white and white as black; bad as good, and good as bad. He presents a forceful critique of the assumed reversalism of the literature of ferocity and helps to dispel the miasma generated by deconstruction.

Rieff's stance, in its own extremity, succeeds better as prophecy than possibility. His contention that moral limits—rather than the arts and sciences—are the primary forms of high culture reverses the flow of culture in the modern era. Yet he concedes that the "old interdicts" can be revived by "enough scientific research and literary freedom of inquiry" (*FT* 101). Rieff's predicament is moving. My still closer sympathies are with writers whose humanistic oeuvre[19] mediates between sexual pleasure and morality, between the inner voice and the object, and between extremity and its opposites—most notably Bellow, Updike, and Roth.[20] So late in the dispensation of romanticism, this literature of self-regard often takes a comic turn. In their individuated ways, the careers of these novelists, among others, enliven and elevate the middle even when going beyond it, to give us versions of reality that more truly represent the complexities, responsibilities, and vulnerabilities of post-Puritan America.

NOTES

INTRODUCTION

1 Saul Bellow, *Herzog* (New York: Viking Press, 1964), 164.
2 Quoted in Lionel Trilling, "The Fate of Pleasure," *Beyond Culture* (New York: Viking, 1965), 76–77. Trilling refers to Wallace Fowlie's *Rimbaud* (New York: New Directions, 1946).
3 Lionel Trilling, *Sincerity and Authenticity* (Cambridge: Harvard University Press, 1972), 56.
4 Barbara Ann Schapiro's study of intersubjectivity in Lawrence notes the shift in feminist criticism of Lawrence from censorious to dialogic. Millett and her followers, in Schapiro's view, cast Lawrence as "a sadistic pornographer" (*D.H. Lawrence and the Paradoxes of Psychic Life* [Albany: State University of New York Press, 1999], 2). As she argues, the case is far more complicated.
5 Michel Foucault, *Madness and Civilization: A History of Insanity in the Age of Reason*. Trans. Richard Howard (New York: Vintage, 1965), 52–53, 56.
6 Norman O. Brown, *Life Against Death* (Middletown: Wesleyan University Press, 1959), 78.
7 Henry Miller, *Tropic of Cancer* (New York: Grove, 1961), 339.
8 Henry Miller, *Tropic of Capricorn* (New York: Grove, 1961), 145.
9 Philip Rieff, "By What Authority?" in *The Problem of Authority in America*, ed. John P. Diggins and Mark E. Kann (Philadelphia: Temple University Press, 1981), 239.
10 Daniel Fuchs, *Saul Bellow: Vision and Revision* (Durham: Duke University Press, 1984).

CHAPTER 1. FREUD AND THE POSTWAR TEMPER

1 Peter Gay, *Freud: A Life for Our Time* (New York: Norton Anchor Books, 1989), 568.
2 Eli Zaretsky, *Secrets of the Soul* (New York: Knopf, 2004), 83. Freud's sense of America was somewhat more complicated than Gay describes it. Zaretsky points out that Freud said professional failure in Vienna would have meant going to America, and that he thought his invitation to lecture at Clark University in

America was "an honorable call." Freud also thought, however, that once the Americans realized the sexual basis of his ideas he would be "up shit creek" (quoted 81). Yet he described his American reception as "the realization of an incredible daydream" (82). It was his first public appearance as a psychoanalyst. In Europe, he "felt like someone excommunicated, here I saw myself received by the best as an equal" (quoted 82). In 1939, Zaretsky tells us, Freud advised Arnold Zweig to emigrate to the United States rather than to England. America, said Freud, "seems to me an anti-Paradise, but it has so much room and so many possibilities, and in the end one does come to belong to it. Einstein told a friend recently that at first America looked like a caricature of a country, but now he feels himself quite at home there" (quoted 235).

3 Quoted in Ernest Jones, *The Life and Works of Sigmund Freud* (New York: Basic Books, 1953), 3:280.
4 Sigmund Freud, *Studies on Hysteria*, Standard Edition, 2:305. All quotations from Freud, unless otherwise noted, are from *The Standard Edition of the Complete Psychological Works of Sigmund Freud*, translated from the German and under the general editorship of James Strachey, in collaboration with Anna Freud, and assisted by Alix Strachey and Alan Tyson (London: Hogarth, 1953–74), 24 vols. Rpt. 1991.The work is designated as *SE* in the text.
5 Quentin Anderson, *The Imperial Self* (New York: Knopf), 1971.
6 Reinhold Niebuhr, "Human Creativity and Self-Concern in Freud's Thought," in *Freud and the Twentieth Century*, ed. Benjamin Nelson (New York: Meridian, 1957), 259–60.
7 Ibid., 261.
8 Ibid., 270.
9 Philip Rieff, *Freud: The Mind of the Moralist* (New York: Viking, 1959), 272.
10 Ibid., 314.
11 Ibid., 323.
12 Zaretsky, *Secrets of the Soul*, 305.
13 Rieff, *Freud*, 328.
14 Lionel Trilling, *Freud and the Crisis of Our Culture* (Boston: Beacon, 1955), 39.
15 Ernest Jones, *The Life and Works of Sigmund Freud* (New York: Basic Books, 1953), 1:27.
16 Gay, *Freud*, 491.
17 Jones, *The Life and Works of Sigmund Freud*, 1:27.
18 Almost. A recent *New York Times* article—Ralph Blumenthal, "Hotel Log Hints at Elicit Desire that Dr. Freud Didn't Repress," December 24, 2006, points to evidence of an assignation with his wife's sister, thereby confirming the long-lived rumor about that extramarital relationship.
19 Susan Sontag, *Against Interpretation and Other Essays* (New York: Delta Dell, 1966).
20 Jack Spector, *The Aesthetics of Freud: A Study in Psychoanalysis and Art* (New York: McGraw Hill, 1977), 141–42.

21 T. S. Eliot, "'Ulysses', Order, and Myth," in *Selected Prose of T. S. Eliot* (London: Faber and Faber, 1975), 175–78.
22 Rieff, *Freud*, 214.
23 Jeffrey Abramson, *Liberation and Its Limits: The Moral and Political Thought of Freud* (New York: Free Press, 1984), 1.
24 Ibid., 2.
25 Rieff, *Freud*, 247.

CHAPTER 2. FREUD AND OTHERS ON AGGRESSION

1 Edward Bibring, "The Development and Problems of the Theory of the Instincts," *International Journal of Psycho-Analysis*, 22 (1941): 104.
2 Although Freud used the word *Thanatos* in conversation, he never did in his writings.
3 Many scholars have distinguished between instincts and drives. Ernest Jones, for example, points out that the German word *Trieb* is "less committal than the English 'Instinct,' which definitely implies an inborn and inherited character" (*The Life and Works of Sigmund Freud* [New York: Basic, 1953], 2:317). Rather than instinct, one may consider "urge," "impulsion," "or the more colloquial and expressive American 'drive.'" While Freud considers neither instinct nor drive entirely satisfactory, he prefers the former because it emanates from the interior of the body. In "Instincts and Their Vicissitudes," Freud had defined instinct as "the demand made upon the mind for work in consequence of its connection with the body" (*SE* 14:127). Heinz Hartmann, Ernst Kris, and Rudolph M. Loewenstein (*The Psychoanalytic Study of the Child*. International Universities Press [New York: International Universities Press, 1949], 4:9–36) prefer the term *instinctual drive*, which is to a human what instinct is to an animal. They hold that there are no relevant id and ego functions in animals, while these are all-important in humans. Psychoanalysts generally think that instinctual drives are modified by culture. Biologists consider instincts to be specific to particular patterns of behavior, whereas drives may not be so limited. Therefore, *drive* is the more appropriate term to apply to Freud's work. In recent decades, there has been a shift from instinct and drive theory to object relations theory, another category developed by Freud.
4 Albert J. Solnit, "Aggression: A View of Theory Building in Psychoanalysis," *Journal of the American Psychoanalytic Association* 20, no. 3 (1972): 436–37.
5 Leo Bersani, *The Freudian Body: Psychoanalysis and Art* (Berkeley: University of California Press, 1986), 20.
6 Philip Rieff, *Freud: The Mind of the Moralist* (New York: Viking, 1959), 222.
7 Bersani, *The Freudian Body*, 40.
8 Ibid., 23.
9 Rieff, *Freud*, 326.

10 Ibid., 326.
11 Ernest Jones, *The Life and Works of Sigmund Freud*, 42.
12 Max Schur, *Freud: Living and Dying* (Madison, Conn.: International Universities Press, 1972).
13 Otto Fenichel, "A Critique of the Death Instinct," in *The Collected Papers of Otto Fenichel, First Series*, ed. Hanna Fenichel and David Rapaport (New York: Norton, 1953), 366.
14 Robert J. Stoller, *Perversion: The Erotic Form of Hatred* (London: Maresfield Library, 1986), 13.
15 Stoller elaborates on this idea in *Perversion*. He likes to distance himself from Freudian abstraction (for example, the Oedipus complex and the superego) but is nonetheless heavily dependent on it. He thinks that Freud's emphasis on the parent-child relationship is "the most powerful and explanatory social learning theory of human development ever proposed" (19). Arising from hatred of a dominant or tyrannical mother, perversion arises as a way of coping with one's gender identity. Perversion, a fantasy put into action, preserves erotic pleasure. Its origin is blighted heterosexuality. At its core is a desire to harm others. (It differs from aberration in which erotic techniques are used as a complete sexual act that differs from the culture's view of normalcy. Aberration is not the product of conflict.) In perversity, Oedipal threats are decisive. In this form of hatred, one wishes to harm the object. In an act of revenge, childhood trauma is turned into adult triumph. The need to repeat unendingly "comes from one's inability to get completely rid of the danger, the trauma" (7). The psychodynamic view that perversion is motivated is resisted by those whose primary field is the genes, the brain, hormones, conditioning, and bell curves.

    Stoller raises an interesting question. Given Freud's description of Oedipal conflict and the pitfalls of libidinal development, can powerful sexual excitement exist without brutality? He makes a parallel, as Freud did, to jokes. Normal development demands infantile frustration "in order to permit the separation that will result in the ego functions and identity necessary for coping with the external world." Frustration, then, is an essential tool that "creates a reservoir of unconscious hatred, coping with which helps determine successful or maladaptive personality development." Thus even much of heterosexual behavior might have a touch of the perverse. Yet, as Freud basically said and Stoller confirms, "mastery, that most gratifying experience often comes about through restitution for passively suffered frustration by creating fantasies, character structures, or modes of activity that in their most primitive form are brutal, but that, filtered through a process of sublimation, may end up far removed from the original hatred" (89). Stoller goes so far as to ask, "If hostility could be totally lifted out of sexual excitement there would be no perversions, but how much living sexuality would be possible?" (89). His view of perversion turns almost euphoric when he says that "perversion is one more masterpiece of the human intellect" (106), serving as it does the evolutionary purpose of human survival. The child continues his development; life goes on. There is triumph out of disaster. "Orgasm," he says, "is not merely discharge or even ejaculation but a joyous, megalomanic burst of freedom from anxiety (analogous to the release of great laughter following a beautifully executed joke, where the build-up of hostile intent is suddenly fractured, with laughter the outcome)" (107). Another analogy: art—like sexual excitement—is "the search for {controlled, managed} ambiguity" (117). In short, given the Oedipal situation, perversion is necessary. It "allows cruelty and hatred in the family to be contained before they become too destructive" (216), channeling it, Stoller says archly, into "calmer currents of the imagination, such as religion, art, pornography, and daydreams" (218).

A later study by Stoller, *Pain and Passion: A Psychoanalyst Explores the World of S & M* (New York: Plenum, 1991), is tonally different, darker in coloration. Stoller has lost his way, at least in his conclusion. In *Pain and Passion*, Stoller, who writes well and has a sense of humor, can still sound like the buoyant writer of the earlier book. For example, he can give us an image as striking (if not quite as original) as it is relevant to his argument: "At the center of erotic excitement is buried, like the irritant to be surrounded by the pearl, a memory of original, undefended trauma, and . . . the pearl (excitement) is the successful encapsulation and transformation of the original trauma" (247). But, after giving us a gallery of vivid but sick patients, he seems depressed himself. After all his effort, he concludes with a view of destructiveness as evil. Rough eroticism does not help that much. "Most of us," he says, "sado-masochistically, try at times to live morally, that is, to play our games consensually, a condition we call *love*" (294). But he argues that we don't usually succeed. The psychological faith he once had seems to have fled: "psychic defenses—signs and symptoms we willfully construct—contain the triumph of evil: self-deception and deceiving others, trust undone" (294).

16 Stuart Asch, "The Analytic Concepts of Masochism: A Reevalution," in *Masochism: Current Psychoanalytic Perspectives*, ed. Robert A. Glick and Donald I. Meyers (Hillsdale, N.J.: Analytic Press, 1988), 95.

17 Arnold Cooper, "The Narcissistic Masochistic Character," in *Masochism: Current Perspectives*, ed. Robert A Glick and Donald I. Meyers (Hillsdale, N.J.: Analytic Press, 1988), 117–38.

18 Anita Phillips, *A Defense of Masochism* (London: Faber and Faber, 1988), 3.

19 Leo Bersani, "Foucault, Freud, Fantasy, and Power," *GLQ: A Journal of Lesbian and Gay Studies* 2, 1–2 (1995): 25.

20 Otto Kernberg, "Clinical Dimensions of Masochism," in *Masochism: Current Perspectives*, ed. Robert A Glick and Donald I. Meyers (Hillsdale, N.J.: Analytic Press, 1988).

21 John K. Noyes, *The Mastery of Submission* (Ithaca: Cornell Univeristy Press, 1997), 32.

22 Bersani, "Foucault, Freud, Fantasy and Power," 15.

23 Ibid., 25.
24 David Couzens Hoy, ed. *Foucault: A Critical Reader* (New York: Oxford University Press, 1986), 16.
25 Lawrence Stone, "An Exchange with Michel Foucault," *New York Review of Books* 31 March 1983:43.
26 Michel Foucault, *Madness and Civilization*, trans. Richard Howard (New York: Random House, 1988), 198.
27 Michel Foucault, *Madness and Civilization: A History of Insanity in the Age of Reason*, trans. Richard Howard (New York: Vintage, 1965), 52–53, 56.
28 Michel Foucault, *The History of Sexuality*, trans. Robert Hurley (New York: Random House, 1990), 1:5.
29 James Miller's excellent biography, *The Passion of Michel Foucault* (New York: Simon and Schuster, 1993), presents Foucault as a dramatic instance of the death instinct, a man who considers that dying from the experience of love is to experience the ultimate passion. Was his dying of AIDS suicidal? Potentially, Miller thinks. Overall, he holds that Foucault's project is to make of human life an experience of hatred and aggression. Though Foucault rejects the Freudian death instinct as biology, he accepts it as history. Like Bataille, he is a philosopher maudit. Miller's book documents the extent to which sadomasochism coalesced with Foucault's intellectual life. Like his master Nietzsche—or Socrates, for that matter—Foucault lived his thought. David M. Halperin objects that "by so thoroughly personalizing Foucault's thought, Miller in effect depoliticizes it" (*Saint Foucault* [New York: Oxford University Press, 1995], 174). Inevitably, perhaps, to some degree. By and large, however, Halperin does not object so much to Miller's modus operandi—which is not so far from his own—but to the fact that Miller does not regard Foucault's life and politics as exemplary. Halperin, of course, does.
30 Halperin, *Saint Foucault*, 94.

CHAPTER 3. WILHELM REICH

1 Philip Rieff, *The Triumph of the Therapeutic* (New York: Harper Torchbook Edition, 1968), 149. This book is designated as *TT* in the text.
2 Wilhelm Reich, *The Function of the Orgasm*, trans. Theodore P. Wolfe (New York: Noonday Press, 1942), 168. This book is designated as *FO* in the text. Except where otherwise noted, references to other Reich works will be from the Noonday Press editions, which will have the following designations in the text: *CA* for *Character Analysis*, trans. Theodore P. Wolfe (1949); *SR* for *The Sexual Revolution*, trans. Theodore P. Wolfe (1962); *MC* for *The Murder of Christ*, written in English (1966); and *LLM* for *Listen, Little Man!* trans. Ralph Mannheim (1974; repr. New York: Orgone Institute Press, 1948).
3 Frederick Crews, *Out of My System* (New York: Oxford University Press, 1975), 160.
4 Charles Rycroft, *Wilhelm Reich* (New York: Viking, 1972).

5 Susan Sontag, *Against Interpretation* (New York: Delta Dell, 1966).
6 Charles Rycroft, *Wilhelm Reich* (New York: Viking, 1972), 60.
7 As a sexual visionary, Reich was sure to have a literary following. Saul Bellow is the most prominent, though hardly the most devoted, of these. In *Henderson the Rain King*, Bellow gives us a central character who is looking to be provoked into salvationary explosions. But Bellow was already post-Reichian, and Henderson's therapy in the hands of the Reichian Dahfu is rendered in terms of experience that goes well beyond orgasm. Henderson's numerous ticks, his longing for a figure of authority (but it is moral authority), and most spectacularly, the farcical expression of body as animal formula are Reichian in origin, as when Reich says, "peculiarly enough, such a formula usually derives from the animal kingdom, like 'fox,' 'pig,' 'snake,' 'worm' " (*FO* 269). Bellow chooses a lion. The Reichian chest pressure deriving from the feeling of worthlessness, of being submerged, is even more reminiscent of Tommy Wilhelm of *Seize the Day*. Bummidge's "humanitis" in *The Last Analysis* derives from Reich's "familitis." Bellow was under Reich's spell for a while—and still retains an occasional Reichian phrase in his essays, like "the great noise"—but soon enough came to consider him paranoid. His friend Isaac Rosenfeld remained mired in his orgone box for too long. Neither, of course, were writers of "ferocity."

It was Norman Mailer who remained for a long time Reich's true and triumphant disciple. Mailer's cult of orgasm, genital salvation, and belief in the emotional plague as the true source of cancer all show Reich's influence, most explicitly acknowledged in *Advertisements for Myself*. Given what Reich would have called Mailer's phallic narcissism—shown in the compulsion of a number of his male characters to master women aggressively and to rack up the scores—there is some question as to whether Mailer is a Reichian disciple or a Reichian case. He certainly thought of himself as the former and was, in any case, deeply involved with Reichian therapy.

Not so William Burroughs, although another writer of ferocity. In *Nova Express*, he makes glib reference to orgone energy and the orgone box. The philosopher of the genital is seen, improbably, in the service of homosexuality and drug addiction. But Reich condemned drug addiction and refused to treat homosexuals. *Yage Letters* makes equally incongruous use of Reich. Burroughs says that the child prostitute boys of Peru "are the least character armored people I have ever seen. They shit or piss anywhere they feel like it. They have no inhibitions in expressing affection." Even the "average *non queer*" boys seem to enjoy homosexuality (William Burroughs and Allen Ginsberg, *Yage Letters* [San Francisco: City Lights, 1963], 40). This Reichian scenario has enormous comic possibilities, but the often funny Burroughs is here too close to the facts to give his fantasy free reign. There is a certain amount of character armor of which Reich would approve, even endorse. Reich, with his emphasis on the genital, is remarkably free of images of defecation and urination. A rare exception occurs in his assault on the average man: "It is the fate of great achievements, born from a way of life that sets truth before security, to be gobbled up by you and excreted in the form of shit" (*LLM* 64).

8 Renan is a nineteenth-century French historian of religion who saw religion from a relativistic perspective. *Life of Jesus* is his best known book.

CHAPTER 4. NORMAN O. BROWN

1 Norman O. Brown, *Life against Death* (Middletown, Conn.: Wesleyan University Press, 1959), 175. This work is designated as *LD* in the text.
2 Norman O. Brown, *Apocalypse and/or Metamorphosis* (Berkeley: University of California Press, 1991), 2. The work is designated as *AM* in the text.
3 Norman O. Brown, *Love's Body* (Berkeley: University of California Press, 1966), 187. The work is designated as *LB* in the text.
4 Frederick Crews, *Out of My System: Psychoanalysis, Ideology, and Critical Method* (New York: Oxford University Press, 1975), 229.
5 Ibid., 29.
6 This memorable formulation is taken from John Middleton Murry's *Jonathan Swift: A Critical Biography* (London: Cape, 1954).
7 Quoted from Jonathan Swift's "The Lady's Dressing Room," in Norman O. Brown, *Life against Death*, 188.
8 Quoted from Swift's *Gulliver's Travels*, in Brown, *Life against Death*, 189.
9 *LD* 92, quoting William Empson's essay on Swift in *Some Versions of Pastoral*.
10 Quoted from Swift's *A Tale of a Tub* and its appendix "The Mechanical Operation of the Spirit," in Brown, *Life against Death*, 193.
11 Crews, *Out of My System*, 36.
12 Susan Sontag, "Psychoanalysis and Norman O. Brown's *Life against Death*," *Against Interpretation and Other Essays* (New York: Delta Dell, 1966), 257.
13 Georges Bataille, *Visions of Excess*, ed. Allan Stoekl, trans. Allan Stoekl with Carl Lovitt and Donald M. Leslie Jr. (Minneapolis: University of Minnesota Press, 1985), 8.
14 Crews, *Out of My System*, 37.
15 *LB* 91: "Tarry awhile, you are so beautiful," from Goethe's *Faust*.
16 Lionel Trilling, "The Fate of Pleasure," in *Beyond Culture* (New York: Viking, 1965), 72.
17 Ibid., 81.
18 Ibid., 84.
19 Bataille, *Visions of Excess*, 144.
20 Quoted in Philippe Sollers, "The Roof," *Writing and the Experience of Limits*, ed. David Hayman, trans. Philip Barnard with David Hayman (New York: Columbia University Press, 1983), 117.
21 Paul Zweig, *The Heresy of Self-Love* (New York: Basic Books, 1968).

22 Eugene Goodheart, *Desire and Its Discontents* (New York: Columbia University Press, 1991), 140.
23 Ibid.
24 Ibid., 19.
25 Bataille, *Visions of Excess*, 142.

CHAPTER 5. DELEUZE AND GUATTARI

1 Gilles Deleuze and Félix Guattari, *Anti-Oedipus: Capitalism and Schizophrenia*, trans. Robert Hurley, Mark Seem, and Helen R. Lane, with a preface by Michel Foucault (Minneapolis: University of Minnesota Press, 1983), 118. The work is designated as *AO* in the text.
2 Félix Guattari, "Everybody Wants to be a Fascist," *Semiotext(e)* 2, no. 3 (1977): 87. The work is designated as "Everybody" in the text.
3 René Girard, "Delirium as System," in *"To Double Business Bound": Essays on Literature, Mimesis, and Anthropology* (Baltimore: John Hopkins University Press, 1978), 113.
4 Peter Rudnytsky, *Freud and Oedipus* (New York: Columbia University Press, 1987), 338. Sophocles is mentioned once in the text itself (*AO* 267), but not in any way that subverts Rudnytsky's observation.
5 Freud refers to the miraculating rays but not to the miraculated anus. His point is not to elevate homosexuality but to show its connection to paranoia in a patient with a strong feminine identification who is struggling with dementia. What with Artaud and Schreber to help get their argument off the ground at the beginning of their book, Deleuze and Guattari have a special interest in the exemplary homosexual.
6 The work is Paul A. Baran and Paul M. Sweezy's *Monopoly Capital: An Essay on the American Economic and Social Order* (New York: Monthly Review Press, 1966).
7 The authors' brackets.
8 Rudnytsky, *Freud and Oedipus*, 340.
9 Sylvère Lotringer and Bill Hellerman, "Philip Glass Interview," *Semiotext(e)* 3, no. 2 (1978): 183.
10 Norman O. Brown, *Life against Death* (Middletown, Conn.: Wesleyan University Press, 1959), 18.
11 Félix Guattari, "Psycho-Analysis and Schizo-Analysis," *Semiotext(e)* 2, no. 3 (1977): 78.
12 Ibid., 85.
13 Abbie Hoffman, *Revolution for the Hell of It* (New York: Dial, 1968).
14 Sherry Turkle, *Psychoanalytic Politics* (New York: Basic Books, 1978).
15 Alice Jardine, "Women in Limbo: Deleuze and His Br(others)," *Sub-Stance* 44–45 (1984): 47.
16 T. J. Adamowski, "Kingdom of Desire," *Canadian Forum* 58, no. 33 (1978): 34.

17 Jay Cantor, "Review of *Anti-Oedipus Capitalism and Schizophrenia*, by Gilles Deleuze and Felix Guattari," *New Republic*, December 24, 1977: 37.
18 Girard, "Delirium as System," 102.
19 Lionel Trilling, *Sincerity and Authenticity* (Cambridge: Harvard University Press, 1974), 160.
20 Sylvère Lotringer, "Libido Unbound: The Politics of 'Schizophrenia,'" *Semiotext(e)* 2, no. 3 (1977): 7. Lotringer also holds that "the events in France have proven that revolution is possible even in a highly industrialized capitalist society," not aware, apparently, of the difference between an uprising and a revolution, and that, by 1973, the "revolution" had failed.

INTERCHAPTER 1. DELEUZE AND GUATTARI ON LAWRENCE AND MILLER

1 D. H. Lawrence, *Aaron's Rod* (New York: Avon, 1960), 209. The work is designated as *AR* in the text.
2 D. H. Lawrence, *Psychoanalysis and the Unconscious* (New York: Viking, 1960), 15. The work is designated as *PU* in the text.
3 D. H. Lawrence, "We Need One Another," in *Phoenix: The Posthumous Papers of D. H. Lawrence*, ed. Edward D. McDonald (London: Heinemann, 1961), 192. The work is designated as *Ph* in the text.
4 D. H. Lawrence, *Fantasia of the Unconscious* (New York: Viking, 1960), 161. The work is designated as *FU* in the text.
5 Lawrence's allusions to madness are conventional. He does not elevate it to an honorable status. He asks his "dear reader" rhetorically: "Do you think you're as obvious as a poached egg on a piece of toast, like the poor lunatic" (*FU* 67)? And Deleuze and Guattari's submerged metaphor of the unconscious as a repressed proletariat ready for the revenge of the "machine" in a material world is not in the same universe as Lawrence's pedestrian working man who should know his master. "I would like him," says Lawrence, sounding much like Lilly, "to give me back the responsibility for general affairs, a responsibility he can't acquit" (149).
6 Henry Miller, *Tropic of Cancer* (New York: Grove, 1961), 257.
7 Henry Miller, *Sexus* (New York: Grove, 1965), 425–31. A number of their quotations from Miller are repeated, particularly a quote from Miller's satiric treatment of psychoanalysis in *Sexus*, which appears three times—as well as three more times in Seem's brief introduction.
8 *AO* 298, quoting Miller's May 7, 1936, letter to Michael Frankel in *Hamlet*, 2 vols., ed. Henry Miller and Michael Fraenkel (Santurce, Puerto Rico: Carrefour, 1939), 1:124–26.

CHAPTER 6. THE MARQUIS DE SADE

1 See Hans Jonas, *The Gnostic Religion*, 2nd ed. (Boston: Beacon, 1963).
2 Simone de Beauvoir, "Must We Burn Sade? introduction to the Marquis de Sade," *The 120 Days of Sodom and Other Writings*, comp. and trans. Austryn Wainhouse and Richard Seaver (New York: Grove, 1966), 61.
3 Maurice Blanchot, "Sade," introduction to the Marquis de Sade, *Justine, Philosophy in the Bedroom, and Other Writings*, comp. and trans. Richard Seaver and Austryn Wainhouse (New York: Grove, 1965), 42.
4 Marquis de Sade, *Juliette*, trans. Austryn Wainhouse (New York: Grove, First Evergreen Edition, 1976), 256. The work is designated as *Jul* in the text.
5 Maurice Lever, *Sade: A Biography*, trans. Arthur Goldhammer (New York: Farrar, Straus and Giroux, 1993), 355.
6 Ibid., 321.
7 Beauvoir, "Must We Burn Sade," 56.
8 Ibid., 52.
9 Ronald Hayman, *De Sade* (London: Constable, 1978), 89.
10 Alphonso Lingis, "Translator's Introduction," in Pierre Klossowski, *Sade My Neighbor* (Evanston, Ill.: Northwestern University Press, 1991), ix.
11 Marquis de Sade, *Justine, Philosophy in the Bedroom, and Other Writings*, comp. and trans. Richard Seaver and Austryn Wainhouse (New York: Grove 1965), 341. *Philosophy in the Bedroom* is designated as *PB* in the text.
12 Beauvoir, "Must We Burn Sade," 62.
13 Ibid., 7.
14 Sean Manchester, *Mad, Bad, and Dangerous to Know: The Life of Lady Caroline Lamb* (London: Gothic Press, 1992), 49.
15 Quoted in Ronald Hayman, *Marquis de Sade: The Genius of Passion* (London: Constable), 123.
16 Lever, *Sade*, 204.
17 Blanchot, "Sade," 54.
18 Beauvoir, "Must We Burn Sade," 29.
19 Roland Barthes, *Sade, Fourier, Loyola*, trans. Richard Miller (New York: Hill and Wang, 1976), 33.
20 Eugene Goodheart, *The Skeptic Disposition in Contemporary Criticism* (Princeton: Princeton University Press, 1984), 75 note 31.
21 Barthes, *Sade, Fourier, Loyola*, 8.
22 Philippe Sollers, *Writing and the Experience of Limits*, ed. David Hayman, trans. Philip Barnard with David Hayman (New York: Columbia University Press, 1983), xxiv.
23 Andrea Dworkin, *Pornography: Men Possessing Women* (New York: Perigee, 1981).
24 Steven Marcus, *The Other Victorians* (New York: Bantam, 1967).
25 Richard von Krafft-Ebing, *Psychopathia Sexualis: With Special Reference to the Antipathic Sexual Instinct; A Medico-Forensic Study* (New York: Paperback Library, 1965).
26 Gray, I gather, has interviewed Bach. For a more detailed description of some of

the material given here, see Sheldon Bach and Lester Schwartz, "A Dream of the Marquis de Sade: Psychoanalytic Reflections on Narcissistic Trauma, Decomposition, and the Reconstitution of a Delusional Self," *Journal of the American Psychoanalytic Association*, (1972): 451–75.

27 Francine du Plessix Gray, *At Home with the Marquis de Sade: A Life* (New York: Simon and Schuster, 1992), 157.
28 Quoted in Laurence L. Bongie, *Sade: A Biographical Essay* (Chicago: University of Chicago Press, 1998), 93.
29 Gray, *At Home with the Marquis de Sade*, 25.
30 Bongie, *Sade*, 73.
31 Lever, *Sade*, 13.
32 Klossowski, *Sade My Neighbor*, 158.
33 Lever, *Sade*, 14.
34 Ibid., 51.
35 Marcus, *The Other Victorians*, 254.
36 Lever, *Sade*, 116.
37 Beauvoir, "Must We Burn Sade," 25.
38 Barthes, *Sade, Fourier, Loyola*, 124.
39 Marquis de Sade, *The 120 Days of Sodom and Other Writings*, comp. and trans. Austryn Wainhouse and Richard Seaver (New York: Grove, 1966), 497. The work is designated as *D* in the text.
40 Beauvoir, "Must We Burn Sade," 60.
41 Barthes, *Sade, Fourier, Loyola*, 25.
42 Jane Gallop, *Interactions: A Reading of Sade with Bataille, Blanchot and Klossowski* (Lincoln: University of Nebraska Press, 1981), 15.
43 Ibid., 17.
44 Annie Le Brun, *Sade: A Sudden Abyss*, trans. Camille Naish (San Francisco: City Lights Books, 1990), 46.
45 Marcus, *The Other Victorians*, 273.
46 Robert G. L. Waite, *The Psychopathic God: Adolf Hitler* (New York: Basic Books, 1977), 155. Of course, the rise of the Third Reich had much to do with politics and ideology. Hitler's pathology was nonetheless part of the puzzle.
47 Ibid., 70.
48 William Blake, "The Marriage of Heaven and Hell," *Selected Poetry and Prose of William Blake*, Northrop Frye ed. (New York: The Modern Library, 1953), 134.
49 Quoted in Waite, *The Psychopathic God*, 81.
50 Ibid., 267.
51 Ibid., 51.
52 Melanie Klein, *Contributions to Psychoanalysis: 1921–1945*. International Psychoanalytical Library. No. 34 (London: Hogarth Press, 1948).
53 Marquis de Sade, *Justine, Philosophy in the Bedroom, and Other Writings*, comp. and trans. Richard Seaver and Austryn Wainhouse (New York: Grove,1965), 457. *Justine* is designated as *J* in the text.

54 *Juliette* ends on a similar, even more brutal, mockery of poetic justice. After being dragged off for an orgy, Justine is sent out into a storm by her tormentors, friends of Juliette, to show "how the powers above reward piety and goodness." A thunderbolt "entering by way of her mouth, had burst out through her vagina" (*Jul* 1190), in a more sexually demonic display of godhead. She is dead. The powers that be have "left [her] ass untouched," only to have it defiled in a sodomistic display by her tormentors. Juliette feels justified in her pursuit of vice.

55 Beauvoir, "Must We Burn Sade," 38.
56 Edmund Wilson, "The Documents on the Marquis de Sade," *New Yorker*, September 18, 1965, 210.
57 Angela Carter, *The Sadean Woman* (New York: Pantheon, 1988), 49.
58 Leon Charney, *Sexual Fiction* (London: Methuen, 1981), 48.
59 Ibid., 46.
60 Gray, *At Home with the Marquis de Sade*, 357.
61 Hayman, *De Sade*, 129.
62 Blanchot, "Sade," 67.
63 Ibid., 66.
64 Le Brun, *Sade*, 191.
65 Ibid., 89.
66 Barthes, *Sade, Fourier, Loyola*, 137.
67 Beauvoir, "Must We Burn Sade," 26.
68 Astryn Wainhouse, foreword, Marquis de Sade, *Juliette*, trans. Austryn Wainhouse (New York: Grove, 1976), x.

CHAPTER 7. D. H. LAWRENCE

1 Paul Delany, *D. H. Lawrence's Nightmare* (New York: Basic Books, 1978), 177. The work is designated as *LN* in the text.
2 Saul Bellow, "Where Do We Go from Here: The Future of Fiction," *Michigan Quarterly Review* 1, no. 1 (Winter 1962): 27.
3 Quoted in D. H. Lawrence, "A Propos of *Lady Chatterley's Lover*," in Lawrence, *Phoenix II: Uncollected, Unpublished and Other Prose Works*, coll. and ed. with an introduction and notes by Warren Roberts and Harry T. Moore (London: Heinemann, 1968), 515. *Phoenix II* is designated as *PII* in the text.
4 D. H. Lawrence, *The Complete Short Stories* Vol. 1 (New York: Penguin, 1976), 111. *The Complete Short Stories* is designated as *SS* in the text.
5 D. H. Lawrence, *Four Short Novels* (New York: Penguin, 1976), 59. *Four Short Novels* is designated as *FSN* in the text.
6 D. H. Lawrence, *St. Mawr and the Man Who Died* (New York: Vintage, 1925, 1928), 20. The work will be designated as *St.M* or *MD*, as warranted.
7 D. H. Lawrence, *The Plumed Serpent*, introduction by William York Tindall (New York: Vintage, 1951), 431. The work is designated in the text as *PS*.

8   D. H. Lawrence, *Lady Chatterley's Lover*, introduction by Mark Schorer (New York: Grove, 1957), 338. The work is designated in the text as *LCL*.
9   Philip Rieff, "Two Honest Men," in *D. H. Lawrence Sons and Lovers: Text, Background, and Criticism*, edited by Julian Moynahan. (New York: Viking Critical Library, 1968), 524. The work it refers to, D. H. Lawrence, *Sons and Lovers* (New York: Viking Critical Library, 1968), is designated as *SL* in the text.
10 D. H. Lawrence, *The Rainbow*, introduction by Richard Aldington (New York: Viking Compass, 1961), 190. The work is designated in the text as *R*.
11 D. H. Lawrence, *Collected Letters of D. H. Lawrence*, ed. Harry T. Moore (London: Heinemann, 1962), 1:579. The work is designated as *CL* in the text.
12 D. H. Lawrence, *The Letters of D. H. Lawrence*, ed. with an introduction by Aldous Huxley (New York: Viking, 1932), 200.
13 George Ford, *Double Measure* (New York: Norton, 1965), 168–69.
14 D. H. Lawrence, *Women in Love* (New York: Viking Compass, 1960), 5. The work is designated as *WL* in the text.
15 D. H. Lawrence, *Kangaroo* (New York: Compass, 1960), 75. The work is designated as *K* in the text.
16 D. H. Lawrence, *Apocalypse*, introduction by Richard Aldington (New York: Penguin, 1976), 61. The work is designated as *A* in the text.
17 Frank Kermode, "D. H. Lawrence and the Apocalyptic Types," in *Continuities* (New York: Random House, 1968), 134.
18 Mabel Dodge Luhan, *Lorenzo in Taos* (New York: Knopf, 1935), 61.
19 Aldous Huxley, introduction to D. H. Lawrence, *The Letters of D. H. Lawrence*, xii.
20 Cornelia Nixon, *Lawrence's Leadership Politics and the Turn against Women* (Berkeley: University of California Press, 1986), 85.
21 See Mario Praz, *The Romantic Agony*, trans. Angus Davidson, Second Edition. Forward by Frank Kermode (Oxford: Oxford University Press, 1970).
22 Aldous Huxley, ed., *The Letters of D. H. Lawrence* (New York: Viking, 1932), 199–201.
23 In his introduction to *The Book of the Dead: The Hieroglyphic Transcript of the Papyrus of Ani* (New Hyde Park, N.Y.: University Books, 1960), translator E. A. Wallis Budge tells us that the ball the scarab rolls "contains not its eggs but dung that is to serve as food for its egg, which it lays in a carefully prepared place" (133). The early Egyptians thought that the sun was the scarab's offspring because they thought the dung contained the egg. The cult of the beetle was far older than that of Ra, the sun god of Heliopolis. Budge notes that scarabs "fly during the hottest part of the day, and it was this peculiarity which probably caused the primitive Egyptians to associate them with the sun" (168). He says: "The Egyptians believed that the beetle was an incarnation of Khepera, and imagined some resemblance between the ball of food for the larva which it rolled over the ground and the ball of the sky, which . . . was rolled across the sky by him" (169).
24 There are numerous examples of the unresolved Oedipus complex in Lawrence's early work. Alfred Durant is so much the mama's boy that "a strong sensitiveness

had kept him from women ... that she was a palpable woman made it impossible for him to touch her" (*SSI* 164). Freud speaks of psychic impotence. Alfred "felt as if he were not physically but intrinsically" impotent. Bertie Reid of "The Blind Man" is quite capable of adoring women so long as he does not have to approach them physically. Paul Morel of *Sons and Lovers* must avow to his mother that he does not love Miriam; son and mother then kiss fervently. Brother William abuses his betrothed in front of his mother and can feel passion only for a woman he holds in contempt. Tom Brangwen in *The Rainbow* has some compromised sex with loose women but is physically incapable with nice ones.

25 David Ellis, introduction to *The Complete Poems of D. H. Lawrence* (Hertfordshire: Wordsworth Editions, 2002), 4.
26 Mark Gertler, on whom Loerke is very loosely modeled, has a similar but more explicitly sexual work. Lawrence characterized the sexuality in it as "utterly impersonal and sterile ... an endless round of mechanical futility" (quoted in *LN* 259).
27 Some of what Lawrence might have thought about Loerke may be gleaned from the manuscript of an epilogue fragment in which Loerke and Gudrun have broken up and she is living in Frankfurt with her infant son by Gerald.
28 Colin Clarke, *River of Dissolution: D. H. Lawrence and English Romanticism* (New York: Barnes and Noble, 1969), xi. The work is designated as *RD* in the text.
29 Colin Clarke, "Critical Exchange on 'Lawrence Up-tight' Four Tail-pieces," *Novel* 5, no. 1 (1971): 60.
30 Harry T. Moore, *The Intelligent Heart* (New York: Black Cat Grove, 1962), 103.
31 Frieda Lawrence, *Not I but the Wind* (New York: Viking, 1934), 4–5.
32 Luhan, *Lorenzo in Taos*, 69.
33 Quoted in Nixon, *Lawrence's Leadership Politics and the Turn against Women*, 165.
34 Ibid., 47.
35 Ibid., 118.
36 David Cavitch, *D. H. Lawrence and the New World* (New York: Oxford University Press, 1969), 67. Cavitch attributes the crystallizing of this strong tendency in Lawrence to an event in 1923: "When Frieda visited her family in Germany, Murry accompanied her to the continent, and there she proposed that they have an affair. He wrestled with his conscience and refused her, only because, he believed, it would have been disloyal to Lawrence ... just when he felt most isolated, his wife left him and offered herself to the one man to whom Lawrence looked for the manly love that would, in his eyes, confirm his masculinity. Murry's transformation from symbolic brother-lover to father-aggressor dangerously externalized Lawrence's fear of men which underlay his homoerotic desires. Perilously at the edge of a breakdown, Lawrence was pushed further towards effeminacy as the only way to win manly love—and deeper into defensive hatred of the male power that attracted him" (147–48).
37 Jeffrey Myers, "D. H. Lawrence and Homosexuality," in *D. H. Lawrence: Novelist, Poet, Prophet*, ed. Stephen Spender (New York: Harper and Row, 1973), 139.

38 Quoted in Edward Nehls, ed., *D. H. Lawrence: A Composite Biography* (Madison: University of Wisconsin Press, 1955–57), 1:162.
39 Eugene Goodheart, *The Utopian Vision of D. H. Lawrence* (Chicago: University of Chicago Press, 1963), 169.
40 Eliseo Vivas, *D. H. Lawrence, The Failure and Triumph of Art* (Evanston, Ill.: Northwestern University Press, 1960), 112.
41 Kermode, "D. H. Lawrence and the Apocalyptic Types," 135.
42 Huxley, introduction, xxvii.

CHAPTER 8. GEORGES BATAILLE

1 In Brown and Bataille we are dealing with a modernist appropriation of Heraclitus. Despite his occasionally prophetic tone, Heraclitus did not embrace the apocalyptic mysteries. Although he did speak of war and strife, he did not wish for destruction. He believed in what Brown and Bataille deny, a god of reason, the reign of law, and a music of the spheres, even though these may contradict the spirit of a cosmic unity deriving from strife.
2 Georges Bataille, "The Practice of Joy before Death," in *Georges Bataille: Visions of Excess Selected Writings 1927–1939*, ed. Allan Stoekl, trans. Allan Stoekl, with Carl R. Lovitt and Donald M. Leslie Jr. (Minneapolis: University of Minnesota Press, 1985), 236. *Georges Bataille* is designated as *V* in the text.
3 Brown is referring here to his chapter called "Fire," written during the week of the 1963 Cuban missile crisis.
4 Norman O. Brown, "Love Hath Reason, Reason None," manuscript based on a lecture given at Boston University, December 15, 1993.
5 Georges Bataille, *Erotism: Death and Sensuality*, trans. Mary Dalwood (San Francisco: City Lights Books, 1986), 90–91. The work is designated as *E* in the text.
6 Jane Gallop, *Thinking through the Body* (New York: Columbia University Press, 1988), 102.
7 Philippe Sollers, "The Roof: Essay in Systematic Reading," in *Writing and the Experience of Limits*, ed. David Hayman, trans. Philip Barnard with David Hayman (New York: Columbia University Press, 1983), 118.
8 Peter Tracey Connor, *Georges Bataille and the Mysticism of Sin* (Baltimore: Johns Hopkins University Press, 2000), 111.
9 Georges Bataille, *The Trial of Gilles de Rais*, trans. Richard Robinson (Los Angeles: Amok, 1991), 12. The work is designated as *GR* in the text.
10 Michel Surya, *Georges Bataille*, trans. Krzysztof Fijalkowski and Michael Richardson (London: Verso, 2002), 29.
11 Connor, *Georges Bataille and the Mysticism of Sin*, 110.
12 Quoted in Surya, *Georges Bataille*, 288.
13 Quoted in Connor, *Georges Bataille and the Mysticism of Sin*, 71.
14 Surya, *Georges Bataille*, 125.

15 Connor, *Georges Bataille and the Mysticism of Sin*, 97. See Georges Bataille, *Blue of Noon*. Trans. Harry Mathews (New York: Urizen, 1978).
16 Surya, *Georges Bataille*, 58.
17 Julia O'Faolain, "Erotic Fantasy," *London Magazine*, June–July 1977, 26.
18 For confusions in Bataille's use of *sacred* and *profane*, see Suzanne Guerlac, " 'Recognition' by a Woman!: A Reading of Bataille's *L'Erotisme*," *Yale French Studies* 78 (1990): 95.
19 Stoeckel, xvi.
20 Connor, *Georges Bataille and the Mysticism of Sin*, 30.
21 Sollers, "The Roof," 119.
22 Susan Sontag, "The Pornographic Imagination," in *Styles of Radical Will* (New York: Dell, 1969), 42. Sontag has since reversed her *enragé* sympathies with cultural nihilism. She became disillusioned with the avant-garde and transgressiveness of the late 1960s and early 1970s, and its assault on high culture. She came to write fiction that deals with the social personality and psychological individuality that earlier she wished to transcend. What happened to Solidarity in Poland and her own encounter with contingency in the form of illness has helped to dispel her radical Utopianism. She is, however, best known for her earlier radical stance.
23 Susan Rubin Suleiman, "Transgression and the Avant-Garde: Bataille's *Histoire d'Oeil*," in *Subversive Intent: Gender, Politics, and the Avant-Garde* (Cambridge: Harvard University Press, 1990), 76.
24 Germaine Brée, "The Break-up of Traditional Genres: Bataille, Leiris, Michaux," *Bucknell Review* 21, nos. 2–3 (1973): 8.
25 Georges Bataille, *Story of the Eye*, trans. Joachim Neugroschel (San Francisco: City Lights Books, 1987), 49. The American translation is based on the 1928 edition. The work is designated as *Eye* in the text.
26 Suleiman, "Transgression and the Avant-Garde," 82.
27 For a very different view of bullfighting in Bataille, see his essay review, "Hemingway in the Light of Hegel." Translated by Ralph Vitello. *Semiotext(e)* Vol. 2, no. 2, 1976:5–16. The original essay review appeared in *Critique* No. 70, March 1953. Here, Bataille sees bullfighting as as a reflection of the world of masters, "the old flash of sovereignty." Hemingway's sovereignty is aesthetic; Hegel's is historical. Bataille respects both.
28 There is one point in the novel where the narrator acts, incongruously, as superego. Simone wants to sit on a dish containing the bull's balls. Her exhibitionism is further piqued by "all these people watching" (*Eye* 63). (The event recalls an earlier incident in which she sits on a plate of milk.) The narrator insists that "it really was totally out of the question." Why he does so is not quite clear. Still, Simone makes an authority figure out of him, if only for a moment.
29 O'Faolain, "Erotic Fantasy," 23.
30 I am not persuaded by the recent supersubtle suggestion that the sections called part 2 are a literary ploy. The final sections strike me as too agonizing—and

consistent with Surya's biographical account (although he draws on them)—not to be as true as memory will allow.
31 Suleiman, "Transgression and the Avant-Garde," 85.
32 Quoted in Surya, *Georges Bataille*, 11.
33 Georges Bataille, *My Mother, Madame Edwarda, The Dead Man*, trans. Austryn Wainhouse (London: Marion Boyers, 1995). The work is designated as *M* in the text.

INTERCHAPTER 2. BATAILLE ON SADE

1 George Bataille, "The Use Value of D.A.F. de Sade," in *Visions of Excess: Selected Writing, 1927–1939*, ed. and trans. by Allan Stoekl (Minneapolis: University of Minnesota Press, 1985), 91–102.

CHAPTER 9. HENRY MILLER

1 For example, there were four drafts of *Tropic of Cancer*, the first twice as long as the final version.
2 Henry Miller, *Tropic of Cancer* (New York: Grove, 1961), 232. The work is designated as *TC* in the text.
3 Henry Miller, *Black Spring* (New York: Grove Press, 1963), 21. The work is designated as *BS* in the text.
4 Henry Miller, *Tropic of Capricorn* (New York: Grove, 1963), 42.The work is designated as *TCap* in the text.
5 Henry Miller, undated letter to Lawrence Durrell, in *Art and Outrage: A Correspondence about Henry Miller between Lawrence Durrell and Alfred Perlès, with an Intermission by Henry Miller* (New York: Dutton, 1961), 31.
6 Philip Rahv, "Sketches in Criticism: Henry Miller," in *Henry Miller and the Critics*, ed. George Wickes (Carbondale: Southern Illinois University Press, 1963), 83.
7 Henry Miller, *Nexus* (Paris: Obelisk, 1960), 231. The work is designated as *N* in the text.
8 Quoted in Henry Miller, "Preface," *Time of the Assassins: A Study of Rimbaud* (New York: New Directions, 1962), x.
9 Henry Miller, *The Time of the Assassins* (New York: New Directions, 1946), 6. The work is designated as *TA* in the text.
10 Henry Miller, *Plexus* (New York: Grove, 1965), 565. The work is designated as *P* in the text.
11 Ezra Pound, "Hugh Selwyn Mauberley," in *Personae* (New York: New Directions, 1926), 188.
12 Henry Miller with Michael Frankel, *Hamlet* (Paris: Carrefour, 1939–43), 1:354.
13 Henry Miller, *Crazy Cock* (New York: Grove Weidenfeld, 1991), 114. The work is designated as *CC* in the text.

14 Jay Martin, *Always Merry and Bright: The Life of Henry Miller; An Unauthorized Biography* (Santa Barbara, Calif.: Capra, 1978), 293.
15 Henry Miller, *Sexus* (New York: Grove, 1965), 311. The work is designated as *S* in the text.
16 Henry Miller, *The Air Conditioned Nightmare* (New York: New Directions, 1945), 12. The work is designated as *AN* in the text.
17 Henry Miller, "Blaise Cendrars," in *The Henry Miller Reader*, ed. Lawrence Durrell (New York: New Directions, 1959), 346.
18 Henry Miller, letter to Emile Schnellock, quoted in Martin, *Always Merry and Bright*, 184.
19 Henry Miller, *The Colossus of Maroussi* (New York: New Directions, 1941), 43. The work is designated as *CM* in the text.
20 Henry Miller, *The Books in My Life* (New York: New Directions, 1952), 82. The work is designated as *BML* in the text.
21 Martin, *Always Merry and Bright*, 382.
22 Frank Kermode, "Henry Miller and John Betjman," in *Henry Miller: Three Decades of Criticism*, ed. with an introduction by Edward Mitchell (New York: New York University Press, 1971), 89.
23 Kingsley Widmer, *Henry Miller* (New York: Twayne, 1963), 142.
24 Quoted in Robert Ferguson, *Henry Miller: A Life* (New York: Norton, 1991), 291.
25 Miller, "Blaise Cendrars," 234.
26 In this sense, Miller's influence was long-term. The sociologist Lillian Rubin writes about daughters "engaging with ease and aplomb in sexual behaviors their mothers didn't dare dream of." One of these daughters told her the following "without a trace of embarrassment or self-consciousness": "I was about 16 and I had this friend—not a boyfriend, a boy *friend*—and I didn't know what to give him for his birthday, so I gave him a blow job" (Lillian B. Rubin, *Erotic Wars* [New York: Harper Perennial, 1990], 14). Miller's prose is quite compatible with working-class metaphor which here invigorates the language of a student at the University of Michigan.
27 Ferguson, *Henry Miller*, 21.
28 Henry Miller, *Reflections*, ed. Twinka Thiebaud (Santa Barbara, Calif.: Capra, 1981), 34. The work is designated as *R* in the text.
29 Alfred Perlès, "My Friend Henry Miller—Paris, 1930," in *Henry Miller and the Critics*, ed. George Wickes (Carbondale: Southern Illinois University Press, 1963), 6.
30 Quoted in Ferguson, *Henry Miller*, 210.
31 Martin, *Always Merry and Bright*.
32 Peter Prescott, "In the Torrid Zone," LXXIV (November 15, 1976), 109. *Newsweek*.
33 Henry Miller, *"Quiet Days in Clichy" and "The World of Sex": Two Books* (New York: Grove, 1978), 83. The work is designated as *C* in the text.

34 William Blake, "The Clod and the Pebble," in *Selected Poetry and Prose of William Blake*, ed. Northrop Frye (New York: Modern Library, 1953), 37.
35 Quoted in Ferguson, *Henry Miller*, 258.
36 Martin, *Always Merry and Bright*, 273.
37 Walter Lowenfels, "A Note on *Tropic of Cancer*—Paris 1931," in *Henry Miller and the Critics*, ed. George Wickes (Carbondale: Southern Illinois University Press, 1963), 17.
38 Perlès, "My Friend Henry Miller—Paris, 1930," 9. Miller seemed to relish the role of complete bastard. A favorite movie of his was *Five Easy Pieces*, in which Jack Nicholson plays a Miller type who is cynically focused on a dumb woman whom he can abuse as she grovels. He also engages in meaningless sex with others. Coming from a "good family," he has had a falling out with his father, with whom he cannot communicate because the old man has become a mute. We are never told what made the central character convert to immoralism (in the process of which he gave up on his musical talent) or why he is so full of hate. A key missing part, if my memory of the movie serves, is that the mother gets no significant mention. The movie ends with a memorably cold scene in which Nicholson's character leaves his car at a gasoline station when his foolish lady friend goes to the ladies' room. He hitches a ride out of her life. Walking out on the woman is a paradigmatic Miller act and accounts for much of his attraction to *Aaron's Rod*.
39 From Oswald Spengler's *Decline of the West*. For a fuller explanation in Miller see *Plexus* (New York: Grove, 1965), 526, 633–39.
40 Martin, *Always Merry and Bright*, 272.
41 Ibid., 84.
42 Ferguson, *Henry Miller*, chap. 15.
43 Ibid., 332.
44 Mary Dearborn, *The Happiest Man Alive: A Biography of Henry Miller* (New York: Simon and Schuster, 1991), 310.
45 Lionel Trilling, "Angels and Ministers of Grace," *Mid-Century* no. 7 (December 1959): 8.
46 Quoted in Martin, *Always Merry and Bright*, 284.
47 Ibid., 14.
48 Henry Miller, "Reunion in Brooklyn," in *The Henry Miller Reader*, ed. Lawrence Durrell (New York: New Directions, 1959), 99.
49 Martin, *Always Merry and Bright*, 82.
50 George Wickes, *Henry Miller*, Pamphlets on American Writers (Minneapolis: University of Minnesota Press, 1966), 39.
51 Frederick Crews, "Stuttering Giant," *New York Review of Books*, March 3, 1977, 9.
52 Henry Miller, *The World of Sex* (Paris: Olympia Press, 1959), 44–45. The work is designated as *WS* in the text.
53 Henry Miller, *Big Sur and the Oranges of Hieronymous Bosch* (New York: New Directions, 1957), 191. The work is designated as *Big S* in the text.

54 Quoted in Martin, *Always Merry and Bright*, 482.
55 Crews, "Stuttering Giant," 9.
56 Widmer, *Henry Miller*, 85.
57 Kermode, "Henry Miller and John Betjman," 89.
58 Widmer, *Henry Miller*, 158.

INTERCHAPTER 3. MILLER ON LAWRENCE

1 Quoted in Henry Miller, *The World of Lawrence*, ed. Evelyn J. Hinz and John J. Teunissen (Santa Barbara, Calif.: Capra, 1980), 13. The work is designated as *TWL* in the text.
2 Henry Miller, *Letters to Anaïs Nin*, ed. and with an introduction by Gunther Stuhlmann (New York: Putnam, 1965). The work is designated as *LAN* in the text.
3 Quoted in Jay Martin, *Always Merry and Bright: The Life of Henry Miller; An Unauthorized Biography* (Santa Barbara, Calif.: Capra, 1978), 288–89.
4 F. W. Dupee, "Leavis and Lawrence," in *The King of the Cats*, 2nd ed. (Chicago: University of Chicago Press, 1984), 202. Dupee's review was originally published in 1956.
5 Diana Trilling, introduction to *The Selected Letters of D. H. Lawrence*, ed. Diana Trilling (New York: Farrar, Straus and Cudahy, 1958), xxvii–xviii. See also Eugene Goodheart, *The Utopian Vision*, based on a Ph.D. dissertation directed by Lionel Trilling.
6 John Middleton Murry, *Son of Woman: The Story of D. H. Lawrence* (London: Cape, 1931), 123.
7 D. H. Lawrence, "Introduction to These Paintings," *Phoenix* (London: Heinemann, 1961), 562.
8 Henry Miller, *Notes on Aaron's Rod* (Santa Barbara, Calif.: Capra, 1980), 120. The work is designated as *NAR* in the text.
9 Lawrence's review of Hemingway's *In Our Time*—published in 1927, three years after *Aaron's Rod*—singles out "Soldier's Home" for special praise. The story parallels the nihilism of *Aaron's Rod* in a more innocent milieu. It too addresses the question of alienation experienced by ordinary man. On being asked, the disillusioned Krebs tells his mother he does not love her. Like Aaron, "he doesn't love anybody and it nauseates him to have to pretend that he does." Lawrence asks, in words that echo *Aaron's Rod*, "If he really *doesn't* care, then why should he care?" (D. H. Lawrence, "Review of *In Our Time*," in *Phoenix*, 361).
  In *Notes on Aaron's Rod*, Miller observes that Murry (who had written a book on Dostoevsky) and Lawrence discussed Dostoevsky a great deal, and that Stavrogin is the one character Lawrence mentions again and again. Lawrence can't bear Stavrogin's power of evil, "and so he tries to make a petty, malevolent little devil of Stavrogin—*biting people's ears*" (*NAR* 27). Miller is disappointed in Lawrence's perception of Stavrogin's act "because Stavrogin does it so un-deliberately as in a

trance. Such a great Slav Hamlet, Stavrogin is!" In contrast, Miller notes, "here, in *Aaron's Rod*, Lawrence is playing the Hamlet himself and he is so feeble, so petulant." Comparison with Stavrogin reduces Miller's opinion of *Aaron's Rod*.

10 Julian Moynahan, *The Deed of Life* (Princeton: Princeton University Press, 1963), 97.

11 D. H. Lawrence, *The Letters of D. H. Lawrence*, ed. James T. Boulton (Cambridge: Cambridge University Press, 2000), *I 491*.

12 To take one example I am especially familiar with, I was struck by Miller's description of the negative outcome of the religion of art in the same terms and metaphors that I used (several years before I came across *The World of Lawrence*) to describe it from a point of view sympathetic to the fictional enterprise of Saul Bellow, in my critical study, *Saul Bellow: vision and revision*. For example, Miller also spoke of the cold monumentality and moonlike emotion. Miller also contrasted the aesthetic ideology of modernism to Dostoevsky, although in a way very different from my own.

CHAPTER 10. NORMAN MAILER

1 Norman Mailer, *Advertisements for Myself* (New York: Berkley Medallion, 1966), 328. The work is designated as *AdM* in the text.

2 Norman Mailer, *The Naked and the Dead* (New York: Rinehart, 1948), 556. The work is designated as *ND* in the text.

3 There is no fear of that. Mailer's readings at the YMHA, for example, reflect his Sadean proclivity for making doodoo on the altar. There, in the ambience of Isaiah and Jeremiah (and culture, generally speaking), Mailer made a scene at each of his few appearances over the years: by reading the lines, "So long / as / you / use / a knife / there's / some / love left," from his poem about wife stabbing; by reading from the Ruta scene in *An American Dream*, followed by a strong sample of obscenity from *Why Are We in Vietnam?*; and by wallowing in the gore of the Battle of Kadesh from *Ancient Evenings*. It should be said that the reading from his novel about Jesus was, in this sense, uneventful.

4 Norman Mailer, *Cannibals and Christians* (New York: Delta, Dell, 1966), 210.

5 Norman Mailer, *Barbary Shore* (New York: Signet, 1951), 196. The work is designated as *Barb* in the text.

6 Norman Mailer, *The Deer Park* (New York: Berkley Medallion, 1955), 260. The work is designated as *DP* in the text.

7 He is "apparently based on Mickey Jelke, a rich, overweight oleomargarine heir indicted for running a Manhattan call-girl operation" (Mary V. Dearborn, *Mailer: A Biography* (New York: Houghton Mifflin, 1999), 101.

8 The play version of *The Deer Park* is even more Sadean than the novel. In the play, a more jaded Sergius recalls the action of Desert D'Or as a scene from hell that "reveals that love may be murder, and murder an act of love" (*The Deer Park: A*

Play [New York: Dial, 1967], 58), a line that does not appear in the novel. Since no one in the play is murdered, Sergius's message remains cryptic. Marion does try to get Elena to overdose, but this is not an act of love—nor is his initial reluctance to do so. In the play, Marion makes an explicit sexual proposition to Eitel, who turns it down in a gesture of indirect defiance: "It's what all the people who run the machine want us to be. Queer" (101). Marion responds, somewhat incoherently since he is Elena's occasional lover: "We have to take it from each other in order to defy the fury of the murderous cunt" (102). In one recollection of his Korean War exploits, a relaxed Sergius tells the geishas: "I got the cruelty to make you happy" (161), a Sadean intensification of the original line in the book: "I have the cruelty to be a man" (*DP* 198), referring to his bombing prowess and his consequent abstention from geishas. In *Deer Park: The Play*, Sergius can be brutal and misogynistic; he can talk about "sawing away on some slut" (161). In the expansion of Sadean motifs, Zenlia, Don Beda's partner in orgy, is a more developed character, reflecting a coprophilic wisdom. She speaks of two kinds of monarchs: "Those who eat their mistresses' dire flop and those who don't. The second variety is not easy to live with. They know nothing of perfume" (160). Marion still wants love mired in offal, but the apocalypse at the end of the play is not sexual—it is the explosion of the atom bomb.

Another major shift is Eitel's rejection of Elena in terms similar to those expressed by Munshin in the novel. In *Deer Park: The Play*, Eitel finds Elena "socially ... hopeless ... [a] social cripple!" (121). He sees himself as "a rebel who loathes himself because he has done so little to change the monstrous world." Although he marries Elena after her failed suicide attempt and they succeed in having a child, Eitel dies of ennui.

Mailer struggled with versions of *The Deer Park* off and on for eighteen years, as if he thought his life as a major writer depended on it. Perhaps it did. As late as a 1987 interview, Mailer says that *The Deer Park* was his best novel, a title he usually reserves for *Ancient Evenings* (and, on at least one occasion, *An American Dream*). See Michael Ventura, "Dance of a Tough Guy," reprinted in *Conversations*, 390.

9 Jean Malaquais, "Reflections on Hip," in Mailer, *Advertisements for Myself*, 332–35.
10 Ibid.
11 Eve Auchincloss and Nancy Lynch, "An Interview with Norman Mailer," *Mademoiselle*, February 1961, 162.
12 Norman Mailer, *The Presidential Papers* (New York: Putnam, 1963), 202.
13 Norman Mailer, *An American Dream* (New York: Dial, 1965), 12–13. The work is designated as *AD* in the text.
14 Richard Poirier, *Norman Mailer* (New York: Viking, 1972), 154.
15 Leo Bersani, "The Interpretation of Dreams," in *Norman Mailer: The Man and His Work*, comp. Robert F. Lucid (New York: World, 1971), 176.
16 Quoted by Robert Solotaroff, *Down Mailer's Way* (Urbana: University of Illinois Press, 1975), 112.

17 Philip Rahv, "Crime without Punishment," *New York Review of Books*, March 25, 1965, 3.
18 Norman Mailer, *Why Are We in Vietnam?* (New York: Berkley Medallion, 1967), 9. The work is designated as *WV* in the text.
19 Norman Mailer, *Armies of the Night* (New York: Signet, 1968), 61–62. The work is designated as *Armies* in the text.
20 In conversation with me at a PEN meeting in New York, on June 19, 1983, Mailer confirmed that he once thought of doing a book on Sade and that he had told Jacqueline Kennedy, then, I gather, his editor, of his intention to do so. "It's impossible," Mailer told me. "That was from a period when I said anything that came into my head. I was thinking of it. But then it would have meant getting involved with reading a lot of books in hard French." Mailer expounded on the subject in an astonishing way: "Sade is interesting. He says, if you want to kill a man, why not kill him?" We were having a casual, serious, cordial conversation. This is too good to be true, I thought. Should I argue with him or let him go on? Why not just kill a man! (I tried to remember where, exactly, Sade said this.) Because it's wrong. Responding perhaps to my wide-eyed silence, Mailer went on: "Of course, that's tyranny." I agreed and asked him if he took Sade's political ideas seriously. Was Sade really interested in revolution? Or did he use his politics as a smokescreen to legitimize his sexual fantasies, his real subject? Mailer answered: "He was interested in sex. The revolutionary ideas were probably a reaction to the aristocrats who did him in. He was in the Bastille. His mother-in-law was after him. He had some mother-in-law! But his political ideas were important." I said, referring to the Bastille, "He was one of nine prisoners. Spent years incarcerated. He wrote *120 Days of Sodom* secretly in the Bastille. His political ideas break down. He was a tyrant, a total narcissist." Mailer seemed to agree, but on curious grounds. "He was a buggeree—that's important," Mailer said. "There's a big difference between being a bugger and a buggeree." I was willing to take his word for it—it seemed obvious enough—though I wondered how Mailer could be so sure of this distinction as it applied to Sade. There was evidence of both in the works and the biographies, Mailer said. "Yes," I said, "but he was everything." Mailer said: "What I like about him is that he carried the logic of his experience to its extreme conclusions." Just so. The gentlemanly Mailer bought me a drink. Apparently, Mailer's conversation with Kennedy did not go well. When Norman Podhoretz proposed a 1969 dinner party for her, "she accepted on the condition that Mailer not be invited" (Dearborn, *Mailer*, 250).
21 Gide, Andre. "Henry James," in *The Question of Henry James*, ed. F. W. Dupee (New York, Holt and Co., 1945), 251–52.
22 Norman Mailer, *Of a Fire on the Moon* (New York: Signet, 1971), 385. The work is designated as *FM* in the text.
23 Norman Mailer, *The Prisoner of Sex* (New York: Signet, 1971), 35.
24 Quoted in Jennifer L. Farbar, "Mailer on Mailer," in *Conversations with Norman Mailer*, ed. Michael Lennon (Jackson: University Press of Mississippi, 1988), 348.

25 Diane Johnson, "Murder and Mailer," *New York Review of Books*, December, 6, 1979, 4.
26 Quoted in John W. Aldridge, "An Interview with Norman Mailer," in *Conversations*, ed. Lennon, 294.
27 Quoted in Farbar, "Mailer on Mailer," 348.
28 Quoted in Michiko Kakutani, "Mailer Talking," in *Conversations*, ed. Lennon, 264.
29 Quoted in William F. Buckley Jr. and Jeff Greenfield, "Crime and Punishment: Gary Gilmore," in *Conversations*, ed. Lennon, 239–40.
30 Quoted in Michael Ventura, "Dance of a Tough Guy," in *Conversations*, ed. Lennon, 387.
31 Norman Mailer, *Ancient Evenings* (New York: Warner, 1983), 214. The work is designated as *AE* in the text.
32 Quoted in Bruce Weber, "Mailer's Flight to Ancient Egypt," *Harper's Bazaar*, May 1983, 104.
33 Norman Mailer, *Tough Guys Don't Dance* (New York: Ballantine, 1984), 32. The work is designated as *TG* in the text.
34 Mailer told Selden Roman: "My answer to my Women's Lib critics is: of course I'm a latent homosexual. But I choose, as Sarte puts it, to be heterosexual" (quoted in Dearborn, *Mailer*, 120). Tone counts for much in a statement like this, and Mailer may not mean what he appears to be saying. However, as Dearborn points out, one may ponder the significance of the following: Mailer stabs Adele in the back and belly, "narrowly missing her heart," penetrating her cardiac sac, when she calls him "you little faggot" (quoted in ibid., 163).
35 This gives the author much satisfaction. Mailer says: "When one person is more murderous than the other in the act of love, they are left, male or female, with an intolerable tension that keeps one from real satisfaction" (quoted in Ventura in *Conversations*, ed. Lennon, 389). This means that Mailer is not much of a follower of Sade after all. In any case, he believes this only half the time.
36 The organization was called the Fifth Estate and had as part of its mission the outing of CIA operatives. "I cringe when I think of the name now," says Mailer (quoted in Dearborn, *Mailer*, 410). Dearborn writes of the standing ovation that Mailer received from a CIA audience for a speech on nuclear proliferation and terrorism. Some agents, however, were shocked by his reference to "wet jobs" (assassinations), considering them wrong or illegal. Others said that "the agency was never involved in the kind of riotous excess and sex" that Mailer describes in the novel. In the face of continued illegalities, some former agents were disturbed at Mailer's friendly meetings with CIA leaders (see ibid., 415).
37 Barbara Norris, Mailer's sixth wife, "after consulting with Mailer would choose a new last name, Church. Norman likes few things as much as the prerogative of renaming a woman himself" (Dearborn, 337).
38 Norman Mailer, *Harlot's Ghost* (New York: Ballantine, 1991), 60. The work is designated as *HG* in the text.

39 Norman Mailer, *Pieces and Pontifications* (Boston: Little, Brown, 1982), 203.
40 Ibid., 203.
41 This is more personal than political, as Mailer's soft spot for what he likes to call "larger than life" figures goes beyond ideology. Hence he can say in an interview: "Charles de Gaulle and Castro were the only two heroes of the modern world" (quoted in Dearborn, *Mailer*, 304).
42 Norman Mailer, *Oswald's Tale: An American Mystery* (New York: Ballantine, 1995), 496. The work is designated as *OT* in the text.
43 Robert G. L. Waite, *The Psychopathic God: Adolf Hitler* (New York: Basic Books, 1977).
44 In her recent memoir, *A Ticket to the Circus* (New York: Random House, 2010), his wife, Norris Church Mailer, reports that Mailer did not remain faithful to her but resumed his libertine ways for eight years of his old age. She thought of leaving him but preferred, in the end, to have a ticket to the circus.
45 Ibid., 132.
46 Norman Mailer, *The Castle in the Forest* (New York: Random House, 2007), 31. The work is designated as *CF* in the text.
47 Quoted in Ron Rosenbaum, interview with Norman Mailer, "Oh, the Devils He Knows," *Moment*, June 6, 2007: 34.
48 Waite, *The Psychopathic God*, 145.
49 Quoted in Ron Rosenbaum, interview with Norman Mailer, "Oh, the Devils He Knows," *Moment*, June 6, 2007.
50 J. M. Coetzee, "A Portrait of the Monster as a Young Artist," *New York Review of Books*, February 15, 2007, 11.

INTERCHAPTER 4. MAILER ON MILLER

1 Henry Miller, *The Henry Miller Reader*, ed. Lawrence Durrell (New York: New Directions, 1959).
2 Henry Miller, *Genius and Lust: A Journey through the Major Writings of Henry Miller*, comp. Norman Mailer (New York: Grove Press, 1976). All quotes from Miller are from the editions cited in previous chapters. Only quotes from Mailer's introduction to *Genius and Lust* use page numbers from that volume, which is designated as *GL* in the text.
3 Frederick Crews, "Stuttering Giant," *New York Review of Books*, March 3, 1997, 9.
4 For what it is worth, here is Miller's view of Mailer's criticism, first as it appeared in fragmentary form in *The Prisoner of Sex* and then in *New American Review*: "I started to read it but I couldn't stand it . . . you see, I hate the New York type—the ultra-sophisticated, analytical, critical of everything . . . I've started to read his stuff, but it's too much, I can't stand it, I don't like that kind of writing" (quoted in Jay Martin, *Always Merry and Bright: The Life of Henry Miller; An Unauthorized Biography* [Santa Barbara, Calif.: Capra, 1978], 488). Two points should be made. Miller could rarely stand any criticism but his own. And though he regarded his

own criticism as appreciation, it was sometimes quite complex—one might say, in the New York manner.

CONCLUSION

1 Norman Mailer, excerpts from "*Naked Lunch* on Trial," William Burroughs, *Naked Lunch* (New York: Grove, 1966). William Burroughs, *Naked Lunch* (New York: Grove, 1966), xiv. The work is designated as *NL* in the text.
2 Quoted in Jennie Skerl, *William S. Burroughs* (Boston: Twayne, 1985), 79.
3 William Burroughs, *Naked Lunch* (New York: Black Cat Grove, 1966), 232.
4 William Burroughs, "The Limits of Control," *Semiotext(e)* 3, no. 2 (1978): 38.
5 Frank Kermode, "The Modern," in *Continuities* (New York: Random House, 1968), 11.
6 Quoted in Tony Tanner, "Rub Out the Word," in *City of Words* (New York: Harper and Row, 1971), 133.
7 Bret Easton Ellis, *American Psycho* (New York: Vintage, 1991). The work is designated as *AP* in the text.
8 Quoted in ibid., epigraph.
9 Fyodor Dostoevsky, *Notes from Underground and The Grand Inquisitor*, trans. by Ralph Matlaw (New York: Dutton, 1960), 115. Quoted in Lionel Trilling, "The Fate of Pleasure," *Beyond Culture* (New York: Viking, 1965), 81.
10 Ellis, *American Psycho*, epigraph.
11 Norman Mailer, "Children of the Pied Piper," *Vanity Fair* 54, no. 3 (March 1991): 159.
12 Bret Easton Ellis, interview, The New School, ca.2003.
13 Philip Rieff, *Fellow Teachers* (New York: Harper and Row, 1973). The work is designated as *FT* in the text.
14 Henry James, *The Ambassadors* (New York: Harper's Modern Classics, 1948), 149.
15 Philip Rieff, "By What Authority?" in *The Problem of Authority in America*, ed. John P. Diggens and Mark E. Kann (Philadelphia: Temple University Press, 1981), 229. The work is designated as *BWA* in the text.
16 Peremptory though it may sometimes be, Rieff's secular traditionalism can be flexible. He cites Lionel Trilling as the primary object of the assault on authority, though, as he must know, Trilling would not agree with his preferred placement of interdictions vis-à-vis the arts and sciences. As Norman Brown says, Trilling is "the Jew of culture whose Moses is Matthew Arnold"—if it isn't Sigmund Freud (Norman O. Brown, "Rieff's *Fellow Teachers*," *Salmagundi* 24 [fall 1973]:41). Rieff values a certain hardness in Trilling, and a certain sense of distinction. He quotes with firm approval from "Mind in the Modern World," Trilling's Jefferson Lecture: "Implicit in the concept of mind is the idea of order, even of hierarchy, the subordination of some elements of thought to others. And in the carrying out of the enterprises of mind a hierarchy of persons prevails—those who are recruited to

such undertakings must rise from the ranks . . . Such personal gratification as mind affords is likely to be of the postponed kind" (quoted in *Fellow Teachers* 199, note).

Brown expresses an even greater flexibility toward Rieff in his lecture. Though Rieff sees Brown as part of the problem, Brown's reaction to *Fellow Teachers* is as follows: He is "greatly impressed and deeply stirred" (34) at what he considers Rieff's anticipating "the return of the gods" (36) and rediscovering the necessity for the category of the sacred. He notes that "although Rieff explicitly adjures prophecy, he's a great apocalyptic prophet in this piece" (37). The generous Brown, sympathetic to apocalypse, holds that "this piece of writing feels as if it were the explosive birth of a nova, a new star which sheds light all over the place."

17 William Butler Yeats, "A Prayer for My Daughter," *Collected Poems of W. B. Yeats* (New York: Macmillan, 1952), 187.

18 Who said chastity is dead? Not in the technological culture of contemporary civilization, as Reay Tannahill reports: "Virginity restoration is known nowadays (in Tokyo, at least) as 'hymen rebirth.' Between thirty and forty thousand such operations are estimated to be carried out in Japan every year, mostly on girls about to be married; more than 80% of Japanese men still demand a virgin bride. Plastic surgeons use sheep gut to construct an artificial hymen, and the date of the operation has to be carefully calculated as the sheep gut dissolves within a month. A delayed wedding means the operation has to be done again" (*Sex in History*, rev. and updated ed. [Chelsea, Mich.: Scarborough House, 1992], 374, note).

19 My essay "Bellow and Freud" distinguishes between quite distinct liberal humanisms, the Freudian and the Bellovian. *Studies in the Literary Imagination* 17 (Fall) 84:59–80.

20 For a study of the relationship between pleasure and morality in American Jewish writers, see my essay "Identity and the Postwar Temper in American Jewish Writing," in *A Concise Companion to Postwar American Literature and Culture*, ed. Josephine Hendin (Oxford: Blackwell, 2004), 238–62.

INDEX

Aaron's Rod (Lawrence), 88–94, 277, 279–80, 284–90, 343
Abramson, Jeffrey, 22–23
Advertisements for Myself (Mailer), 300–305, 314
Aggression, 1, 5, 7, 11, 20, 24, 28, 45–49, 55–56, 62–63, 103, 110, 114, 116, 147, 149, 151–52, 170, 187, 206, 209, 213, 221, 232, 235, 239, 295, 311–12, 318, 322, 360; distinguished from mastery, 25; creative, 165; transcendent, 194
Air-Conditioned Nightmare, The (Miller), 240, 244
Ambivalence, 24–25
America, 11, 245, 284, 311, 314, 320, 362
American Dream, An (Mailer), 8, 305–10, 317, 326, 354
American Psycho (Ellis), 5, 349–55
Anal organization, 30, 55–59, 104, 111, 127, 196, 241, 351
Ancien régime, 3, 103, 112, 114, 143
Ancient Evenings (Mailer), 9, 311, 314–18, 320, 327–28
Anderson, Quentin, 13, 261
Antinomian, 7, 9, 16, 21, 40, 103, 108, 132, 138, 145–46, 187, 270, 347
Anti-Oedipus (Deleuze and Guattari), 65, 67–87
Apathy, 137, 209, 220, 245–46
Apocalypse, 6, 41, 62, 148, 151, 156, 177, 187, 195, 235–36, 265, 274, 301, 311, 315–16, 343, 351, 395
"Apocalypse" (Brown), 53
Apocalypse (Lawrence), 156, 276
Apocalypse and/or Metamorphosis (Brown), 194
Apollonian, 4, 27, 53–54, 59, 107, 195, 204, 212, 342
"A Propos of *Lady Chatterley's Lover*" (Lawrence), 162
Aristotle, 14, 108
Armies of the Night (Mailer), 311–12, 314
Art, 2–3, 19–20, 29, 59, 74, 97, 176–77, 204, 243, 250, 263, 277, 361–62
Artaud, Antonin, 37, 70, 72–73, 77–79, 97, 101
Asch, Stuart, 31
Auden, W. H., 10, 254
Authoritarian, 6, 36, 41, 43, 214, 298, 312, 321
Authority, 9, 19, 22, 36, 38, 40–41, 47, 173, 183, 185, 187, 211, 215, 321, 356–59, 361
Autobiographical Study, An (Freud), 18
Avante-garde, 2, 3, 108, 140

Balzac, Honoré de, 83–84, 321
Barbary Shore (Mailer), 4, 295–97, 300, 318
Barthes, Roland, 107–8, 116–17, 210–11, 218

"Base Materialism and Gnosticism" (Bataille), 198
Bataille, Georges, 1–7, 40, 45, 57, 60, 63–66, 194–231, 361
Baudelaire, Charles, 225
Bear, The (Faulkner), 310, 346
Beats, the, 13, 16, 99, 120, 147, 270, 274
Beauvoir, Simone de, 103–6, 116–17, 130, 144
"Belle Dame Sans Merci, La" (Keats), 64
Bellow, Saul, 2, 10, 51, 145, 204, 209, 298, 322
Bersani, Leo, 5, 25, 27–28, 32, 35, 72, 308–9
Beyond Culture (Trilling), 3
Beyond the Pleasure Principle (Freud), 25, 28
Bibring, Edward, 24
Big Sur (Miller), 266
Black Spring (Miller) 232, 235, 238, 241, 248, 269, 332
Blake, William, 6, 53, 72, 74, 122, 141, 179
Blanchot, Maurice, 103, 137–38
Blank Fiction, 9, 354
"Blind Man, The" (Lawrence), 172
Blue of Noon (Bataille), 218
Bongie, Laurence L, 111–13
Books in My Life, The (Miller), 243
Bourgeois, 1, 71, 108–9, 144, 154, 176, 195, 202, 225, 240, 248, 254, 348–49
Brée, Germaine, 210
Brown, Norman O., 5, 16, 27–28, 47, 53–66, 80, 194–96, 239–40, 359–60, 389 n. 16
Burroughs, William, 5–9, 120, 208, 274, 309, 338, 355
"By What Authority" (Rieff), 357–61
Byron, George Gordon, 106

Camus, Albert, 77, 121
Cantor, Jay, 86
Capitalism, 6, 9, 40, 55, 57, 68, 74–77, 99–100, 145

Carlyle, Thomas, 179, 181
Carter, Angela, 131
Castle in the Forest, The (Mailer), 326–31
Cavitch, David, 163, 192
Character Analysis (Reich), 43, 45–46
Character armor, 43
Charney, Leon, 131–32
"Child is Being Beaten, A" (Freud), 30–32, 126
Christ, 48–49, 55, 93–94, 167, 185, 192, 197, 276, 278
Christianity, 13–14, 31, 54–55, 60, 69, 77, 96–97, 102, 138, 156, 194–98, 204, 207, 225, 358
Civility, 2, 4, 8, 21, 103, 316, 357
Civilization, 2, 6–10, 21, 44, 55, 58, 61, 92, 136, 147, 152–53, 155, 179, 189, 202, 206, 212–14, 227, 234, 242–43, 282, 286, 295, 310, 347, 353–56, 360
Civilization and Its Discontents (Freud), 24–25, 33, 41–42
Clarissa (Richardson), 129, 133, 141
Clarke, Colin, 163, 178–81, 183, 185, 273
Colossus of Maroussi, The (Miller), 242, 265
Comedy, 8, 249–51, 257, 266, 314, 348, 359
Common sense, 1, 53
Confessions, The (Rousseau), 64
Conformity, 4, 6, 9, 12, 298, 300, 302, 323, 349, 353
Connor, Peter Tracey, 197–99, 207
Cooper, Arnold, 31
Crazy Cock (Miller), 244, 257
Creative destruction, 4, 10, 145, 169, 195, 202
Crews, Frederick, 43, 53–54, 264, 269, 343
Crime, 3, 7, 46, 102, 105–9, 112, 116, 135, 197–98, 204, 225, 229, 278, 301, 358, 361
Crime and Punishment (Dostoevsky), 354, 358
"Crown, The" (Lawrence), 146, 156, 164, 182, 206, 272, 276, 280

Cruelty, 7, 40, 76–78, 136–37, 141, 181, 194, 196, 355
Culture, 1, 3, 5–6, 15–19, 47–48, 51, 56, 58, 63, 102, 202, 206, 213, 241, 243, 275, 356–61

Dean, James, 149, 356
Dearborn, Mary, 261
Death instinct, 24–28, 33–34, 41, 49, 61–63, 72, 76, 110
Deconstruction, 5–6, 25–26, 72, 77, 356, 362
Deer Park, The (Mailer), 8, 297–300, 305, 318, 323, 336
Defense, 30–31, 43–44, 111
Delany, Paul, 145, 162, 192
Deleuze and Guattari, 5–6, 9, 65, 67–101, 219, 251, 348
Derrida, Jacques, 210
"De Sade and the Normal Man" (Bataille), 229–31
"De Sade's Sovereign Man" (Bataille), 226–29
Descartes, René, 14, 26, 31, 65, 80
Desire, 65–72, 76–84, 94, 101, 107, 199–201, 225, 226, 228, 353
Determinism, 13–14, 18, 27, 52, 218, 298, 325
Diderot, Denis, 248, 349
Dionysian, 4, 6, 32, 41, 53, 57–60, 107, 147–48, 166, 194–95, 212, 276, 280
Don Giovanni (Mozart), 106
Dostoevsky, Fyodor, 62–63, 136, 178, 204, 246, 248, 257, 259, 289, 291, 319, 353–54, 361
Drives, 24–25, 29
Dreiser, Theodore, 326
Dupee, F. W., 275
Durrell, Lawrence, 332–35, 337–39, 345
Dworkin, Andrea, 109, 210

"Economic Problem of Masochism, The" (Freud), 33

Ego, 5–9, 13–25, 31, 42–43, 52, 56, 60, 64, 67, 69, 72, 77, 79, 90, 94–96, 164, 171, 195, 202, 214, 250, 254, 265, 290, 319, 347
Ego and the Id, The (Freud), 5, 24, 26, 31, 42, 360
Ego psychology, 5, 24–26, 43
Egypt, 9, 91–92, 96, 136, 166–67, 177, 190, 198–99, 314–16, 328
Eighteenth Brumaire of Louis Bonaparte, The (Marx), 85
Eighties, 350
Eliot, T. S., 1, 13, 20, 154, 219–20
Ellis, Bret Easton, 5, 9, 349–55
Emerson, Ralph Waldo, 13, 64, 245, 261
Engels, Friedrich, 83–84
Eros, 10, 24, 28, 42, 54, 59, 62, 165, 174
Eroticism, 6–7, 32, 34, 39, 66, 92, 117, 119, 136, 144–45, 152, 160, 165, 175, 187, 192, 196–208, 219–21, 225–28
Erotic transcendence, 4, 60, 166, 197
Erotism (Bataille), 196–208
Essentialist, 17, 21, 40
Eve of St. Agnes, The (Keats), 63
Excremental vision, the, 3, 26, 55–56, 78, 118, 178, 198, 206, 211, 214, 217–18, 221–22, 224, 239–41, 261, 267, 299, 329, 333, 343, 349, 351
Executioner's Song, The (Mailer), 313–14

Fantasia of the Unconscious (Lawrence), 41, 94–95, 182, 272, 276, 280–81, 286, 290
Farewell to Arms, A (Hemingway), 288
Fascism, 67, 70–71, 77, 99, 288, 293, 298
Faulkner, William, 13, 151, 209, 310, 346
Fellow Teachers (Rieff), 59, 358–62
Fenichel, Otto, 28
Ferguson, Robert, 258–60
Ferocity, 1, 4, 6–10, 20, 27, 29, 37, 40–41, 51, 58, 66, 70, 100, 145, 151, 153–56, 164, 178, 187, 201–2, 209, 211, 213, 237, 241, 265, 273, 278, 287, 291, 311, 314–16, 326,

Ferocity (*cont.*)
329, 334, 341–42, 345–48, 354–56, 359–62; as institution, 43; *jouissance* and, 196; as narrative point of view, 303
Fifties, 12–13, 15–16, 18, 267, 302, 318
Flaubert, Gustave, 2, 207
Ford, George, 151, 163, 178, 273
Forties, 11–12, 18, 298
Foucault, Michel, 5–6, 35–39, 70, 135, 349
Fowlie, Wallace, 3
Fox, The (Lawrence), 146, 158, 280, 316
Frank, Waldo, 147, 156
Freud, Sigmund, 3–6, 10–22, 24–44, 47, 52–58, 61–65, 68, 71–76, 80–81, 86, 92–96, 109, 112, 121, 124–27, 194–95, 201–2, 207, 214, 253–54, 280, 317, 322, 325, 327, 330, 351, 356–62
Freud and the Crisis of Our Culture (Trilling), 16
Freudian Body, The (Bersani), 25
Freud: The Mind of the Moralist (Rieff), 15–16, 21, 25–28, 356
Fromm, Erich, 13, 127
Function of the Orgasm, The (Reich), 41–51
Future of an Illusion, The (Freud), 19

Gallop, Jane, 117–18, 196
Gay, Peter, 11, 17
Genital organization, 5, 30, 35, 37, 46–47, 53, 58–59, 72, 109, 205
Genius and Lust (Mailer) 248, 264, 332–45
Girard, René, 69, 87
Gnosticism, 64, 102–3, 198, 218, 330
Goodheart, Eugene, 65, 108
Gray, Francine Du Plessix, 111–13, 134

Hamlet and Oedipus (Jones), 100
Harlot's Ghost (Mailer), 317–24, 328, 331
Hartmann, Heinz, 24–25, 43
Hayman, Ronald, 105, 137

Hegel, G. W. F., 3, 199, 203, 222, 228–29, 237, 353
Héliogabale (Artaud), 78
Heliogabolus, 96, 135
Hemingway, 9, 155, 212–13, 310, 343, 352
Henry Miller Reader, The (Durrell), 332–34, 337–39, 345
Heresy of Self-Love, The (Zweig), 64
Hinz, Evelyn, and John Teunissen, 272
Hipster, 8, 299–301
History of Sexuality, Vol. I (Foucault), 37–38
Hitler, Adolf, 6, 53, 70–71, 121–28, 236, 244, 327, 329–31
Hobbes, Thomas, 137, 196
Holbach, Baron von, 104–5
Honest consciousness, 3–4
Hoy, David Couzens, 36
Humanism, 2, 5, 10, 17–20, 34–35, 39, 45, 64, 68, 73, 86, 100, 193, 266, 344, 354, 362
Huxley, Aldous, 163, 193

Id, 5–6, 8–9, 13–16, 25, 42, 64, 67, 72, 76, 106, 171, 195, 214, 216, 250, 254, 309, 319, 347, 360
Imagination, 7–8, 65, 82, 105, 107, 135, 204, 313, 318, 361
Impersonality, 161, 167, 189–91, 227, 343
Individual (Individuality), 16, 22, 83, 90–91, 94, 98, 170, 225, 301
Inhibitions, Symptoms, and Anxiety (Freud), 112
Interpretation of Dreams, The (Freud), 100
Instincts, 24–25, 28–29, 33, 34, 40–44, 48–52, 55, 136, 360
"Instincts and Their Vicissitudes" (Freud), 24
Irony, 60, 150

Jardine, Alice, 85
Jews (Jewish), 20, 91, 203, 294, 303, 305, 309, 314, 319, 337, 356–58

Job, 128–29
Johnson, Diane, 313
Jones, Ernest, 17–18, 28, 317
jouissance, 7, 32, 196, 211
Joyce, James, 2, 20, 209, 272, 281, 290–91
Juliette (Sade), 114, 118, 141–44, 229
Justine (Sade), 128–34, 229

Kafka, Franz, 82, 296–97, 304
Kangaroo (Lawrence), 153–54, 162, 277
Kant, Immanuel, 14, 199, 211, 220
Keats, John, 63–64, 141, 178
Kermode, Frank, 9, 156, 163, 193, 270, 273, 348
Kernberg, Otto, 33
Kinsey Report, The, 202–3
Klossowski, Pierre, 14
Kohut, Heinz, 64, 361
Krafft-Ebing, Richard von, 4, 120

Lacan, Jacques, 67–68
Lady Chatterley's Lover (Lawrence), 2, 59, 146–47, 155–56, 161–63, 173, 178, 182–83, 187, 193, 271, 278, 280, 288, 316, 332
Ladybird, The (Lawrence), 146, 166, 172, 178–79, 190, 343
Laing, R. D., 77, 87
Lamb, Caroline, 106
La Rouchefoucauld, 53, 116
Law, 103–4, 108, 118–19, 132, 136, 138–39, 241, 299, 305, 348, 357–58
Lawrence, D. H., 1–9, 32–33, 41, 45–47, 54, 59–60, 63, 87–99, 145–93, 199, 206, 236, 246, 252, 258, 261, 270–92, 316, 345, 353, 361
Lawrence, Frieda, 184, 279–80, 282
Leavis, F. R., 163, 275
LeBrun, Annie, 120, 144
Lever, Maurice, 103–4, 106, 113–15, 138
Liaisons Dangereuses, Les (Laclos), 131
Liberal (Liberalism), 8, 23, 42, 44, 131, 294, 296–98, 301, 311–12, 318; denial of, 293; Foucault and, 25; moderation, 1; repression, 108; revisionist, 12, 21
Liberation (sexual), 5–6, 22, 26, 51, 135, 138, 144, 197, 219, 270, 314
Libido, 28, 33, 42, 56, 65, 67, 75, 77, 83–84, 100, 201, 207, 300, 309, 316, 320
Life against Death (Brown), 56–61, 65
Libertine, 3, 7, 63, 102, 105–6, 111, 113, 115, 129–30, 132, 135, 138, 142, 163, 214, 225, 327
Limitless, 4–7, 25, 27, 57, 65–66, 70, 74, 82, 106, 113, 134–35, 194, 200–201, 228, 301
Limits, 1, 8, 10, 13, 15–16, 20–22, 40, 58, 61, 65, 70, 74, 82, 99, 198, 225, 358, 360, 362; Freud and, 4
Lingis, Alphonso, 105
Listen, Little Man (Reich), 41, 51
Louis XV, 105, 113, 115
Love, 25–26, 30, 32, 47–48, 50, 52, 55, 64, 69, 89, 93–94, 114, 116, 123, 148, 152, 158, 161–93, 200, 202, 212, 216, 219–20, 225, 243, 280, 284, 286–87, 301, 306, 315–16, 322, 337, 343, 353
Love's Body (Brown), 53, 58–59, 65, 69, 194–95
Luther, Martin, 55, 62

Madame Edwarda (Bataille), 8, 65, 209, 212, 219–23, 229
Madness and Civilization (Foucault), 36–37
Mailer, Norman, 1–5, 8, 16, 45–46, 63–64, 105, 107, 199, 235, 239, 269, 282, 293–348, 354, 359
Malinowski, Bronislaw, 50
Ma Mère, (Bataille), 218
"Man Who Studied Yoga, The" (Mailer), 302–3
Manichean, 50, 85, 308, 312, 330
Man Who Died, The (Lawrence), 49, 150, 159, 161, 185, 189–91

Marcus, Steven, 109–11, 120–21
Marcuse, Herbert, 16, 57
Martin, Jay, 243, 256, 263
Marx (Marxism), 1, 7, 13, 21, 39–40, 50, 56, 71, 74, 76–77, 86, 99, 194, 196, 200, 270, 294, 297, 299, 305, 312, 341, 349–50, 355
Masochism, 26, 29–35, 47, 66, 111, 115, 126–27, 132, 170–71, 174–76, 202, 211, 213, 215, 221–22, 251, 256–58, 301, 341
Maturity, 4, 8, 12, 26, 59, 234, 320, 357, 360
Mechanism, 51, 67–69, 82, 90, 95, 98, 101
Mein Kampf (Hitler), 121, 124–25
Michelangelo, 20, 90
Middle, 1, 84, 145, 204, 225, 229–30, 234, 293, 298, 300, 302, 307–8, 319, 360, 362
Middle class, 1, 3–4, 15, 131, 134, 303, 305, 313, 348, 350
Millenarianism, 12, 51, 179
Miller, Henry, 2–3, 5, 8–9, 45–46, 63, 86, 88, 99–101, 232–92, 361
Millet, Kate, 5, 363 n. 4
Mind, 2, 30, 40, 389–90 n. 16
Misanthrope, The (Molière), 250
Modernism, 2, 4, 7–9, 19, 21, 32, 40, 63–64, 69, 79, 97, 102, 130, 135–36, 145, 151, 155, 165, 183, 187, 219, 234, 251, 274, 288, 290, 347, 356, 359
Money, 11, 56–57, 103, 155, 247, 350–51, 355
Monnerot, Jules, 199
Moore, Harry T., 184
Moral life, 8, 20, 23, 40, 199, 208, 355–58, 362
Moral realism, 14–15
Moses, 20, 141, 153, 357
Moses and Monotheism (Freud), 20
Murder of Christ, The (Reich), 48, 50–51
Murry, John Middleton, 191, 273, 276, 278–80, 287, 292, 370 n. 6

Narcissism, 5, 6, 33, 44, 49, 56, 58–59, 64, 68, 73, 111, 159, 168, 190, 209, 260, 267, 269, 277, 296, 315–16, 335–36, 352–54, 358
Nature, 6–7, 13, 15, 21, 37, 40, 48, 50, 58, 63, 72, 80, 83, 102, 104, 118, 130, 134–39, 147, 188, 202, 206, 212–13, 227, 241, 282, 310, 312, 352, 360
Naturalism, 2, 8, 294–96, 326
Negative transcendence, 3, 8, 33, 62–63, 106–7, 198, 211, 299–301, 310–11, 342
New Introductory Lectures (Freud), 43
Nexus (Miller), 233, 257
Niebuhr, Reinhold, 13–15
Nietzsche, Friedrich, 6–7, 9, 22, 53–54, 64, 69, 73, 88, 92, 93, 101, 103, 114, 121, 136, 145, 149, 156, 193, 195, 275–76, 357
Nihilism, 8–9, 194, 249, 288, 291, 301, 310, 313, 333, 349, 353
Nin, Anaïs, 248, 258, 262, 271, 273, 343–44
Nirvana, 27–28, 61–62, 66, 195
Nixon, Cornelia, 163, 185–86
Normalcy, 5, 21, 29–30, 35, 39, 58, 196, 204, 229–30
Notes from the Underground (Dostoevsky), 353
Notes on Aaron's Rod (Miller), 289–90
"Notion of Expenditure, The" (Bataille), 205
Noyes, John, 35

"Odor of Chrysanthemums, The" (Lawrence), 162
Obscenity, 8–9, 55, 206, 211, 216, 221, 232, 243, 304, 309–12, 338
Oedipus Complex, 6, 15, 18, 20, 27, 30–31, 34–35, 38, 41, 47, 64, 68–78, 81, 89–99, 123, 125, 127, 202, 218, 259, 280–81, 309–10, 322, 352
O'Faolain, Julia, 203, 215
Of a Fire on the Moon (Mailer), 312
"Old Mole and the Prefix *Sur*, The" (Bataille), 206
120 Days of Sodom (Sade), 117–20, 134

"On Narcissism" (Freud), 24
"On the Universal Tendency to Debasement in the Sphere of Love" (Freud), 168
Orphic, 6, 194
Original Sin, 13–15, 197, 203, 220, 360
Oswald's Tale (Mailer), 317, 324–26
Other Victorians, The (Marcus), 109–110

Pamela (Richardson), 132–33
Paranoia, 36, 39, 70–71, 76, 80, 82, 85, 104, 125, 308, 319, 321, 331, 348
Perlès, Alfred, 246–47, 253
Perversion (Perversity), 29–30, 63, 70, 106, 108, 127, 140, 163, 165, 167–68, 175, 205, 213, 257, 302, 317, 357
Phenomenology of Mind (Hegel), 3
Philebus (Plato), 358
Phillips, Anita, 31–32
Philosophes, 3, 104, 117, 128–29, 134, 136
Philosophy in the Bedroom (Sade), 105, 122, 134–40
Plaisir, 7, 196, 202, 211, 228
Plato, 14, 134, 207, 358
Pleasure, 10–11, 35, 38–39, 49–50, 62–63, 80, 103–4, 108–9, 132, 137, 195, 202, 211, 221, 225, 227, 358
Pleasure Principle, 34, 41, 61, 63, 110, 195
Plexus (Miller), 235
Plumed Serpent, The (Lawrence), 146, 154–56, 159, 161–62, 172, 186, 280
Poetics (Aristotle), 108
Poirier, Richard, 307–08
Politics of Experience, The (Laing), 77
Polymorphous perverse, 6, 10, 30, 58, 60–61, 64–66, 109, 134, 142, 144, 253–54, 312, 315, 323
Pornography, 2, 5, 47–48, 102–3, 106, 109, 115, 121, 125, 132, 134, 206, 208–10, 215, 217–18, 221, 227, 302, 335
"Pornography and Obscenity" (Lawrence), 206

Postmodernism, 7, 9, 74, 356
Potlatch, 7, 196, 204–5, 226–27
"Practice of Joy Before Death, The" (Bataille), 194
Pre-Romantic, 3, 134
Prescott, Peter, 248
Primitive (Primitivism), 4, 7, 33, 44–45, 51, 54, 145, 204, 212, 225, 233, 242, 304, 309, 316, 359
Prisoner of Sex, The (Mailer), 312–13
Proust, Marcel, 272, 281, 290–91
"Prussian Officer, The" (Lawrence), 33, 45, 146
Psychoanalysis, 4, 6, 10–21, 26, 35–40, 43–44, 50, 53–55, 58, 62, 67–71, 83, 85, 94–95, 138, 207, 263–64, 285, 302–5, 356
Psychoanalysis and the Unconscious (Lawrence), 41, 92, 94, 166–67
Psychopathic God: Adolf Hitler, The (Waite), 121–28
Puritan, 13, 59, 133–34, 145, 270

Queneau, Raymond, 21

Rahv, Philip, 308–9
Rainbow, The (Lawrence), 147–51, 156–57, 164, 172, 182, 272–73, 278
Rank, Otto, 256
Realism, 29, 208, 283, 309
Reality Principle, 79, 103, 111, 350
Reason, 4, 14, 54, 60, 86, 92, 105, 195, 206–7, 221–22, 224, 227
Rebellion, 1, 3–4, 9, 16, 43, 47, 120, 149, 152, 196, 211, 233, 305, 353
Reflections (Miller), 268
Reich, Wilhelm, 5–6, 37, 40–52, 58, 67, 69, 81, 85, 100, 243
Religion, 15, 18–19, 33, 90–91, 96–97, 102, 128–29, 150, 187, 193, 197, 203, 207, 230
Remembrance of Things Past (Proust), 291, 346

Repression, 6–7, 9, 15, 20, 21, 30–31, 34, 37, 40–43, 47, 50, 52, 54–62, 65–69, 74, 76, 81, 94, 106, 108, 194, 197, 207, 215, 254, 301, 309, 358

Revolution (Revolutionary), 1, 21, 37, 40–41, 43, 65, 69, 76–86, 108, 144, 194, 224, 233, 269–72, 299–300, 312, 326, 357, 359, 361

Richardson, Samuel, 129, 133–34

Rieff, Philip, 5, 9, 15–16, 21, 23, 25–28, 40, 43, 47, 147, 169, 356–62, 389 n. 16

Rimbaud, Arthur, 3, 8, 78, 135, 200, 207, 234, 274–75, 281

Robbe-Grillet, Alain, 144

Romantic (Romanticism), 7–8, 16, 40, 44, 63–65, 70–75, 91, 96, 99, 105–6, 121–22, 135–38, 141, 146, 150, 163, 178, 239, 243, 245, 260, 299, 301, 345, 356

Rosy Crucifixion, The (Miller), 233, 264, 268–70, 279

Roth, Philip, 262, 330

Rousseau, Jean-Jacques, 64, 118, 250, 301

Rudnytsky, Peter, 71, 79, 102, 105

Rycroft, Charles, 44–45, 49, 50

Sade, Marquis de, 1, 3, 6–9, 37, 45–46, 53, 55, 63, 102–44, 198, 203–6, 209, 215, 220, 224–32, 245, 301–2, 309, 311, 317, 323, 325, 342, 353–54, 360–61

Sade, Fourier, Loyola (Barthes), 108

Sadism, 9, 29–35, 40–50, 55, 63, 66, 78–79, 104, 106, 109–10, 113, 115, 126, 136, 141, 170, 174–76, 197, 213, 221, 229, 233, 256–57, 261, 274, 295, 301, 311, 317, 324–25, 327–28, 340, 347–49, 351, 355

Sadomasochism, 5–9, 30–39, 121, 124, 126, 163, 168, 170, 199, 211, 213, 221, 256, 323, 331, 347, 359

St. Mawr (Lawrence), 146, 157, 159, 162, 186–90, 280

Sartre, Jean-Paul, 199, 202

Schizoanalysis, 68–71, 79–80, 92, 101

Schizophrenia (Schizo), 6, 47, 61, 68, 70–86, 302

Schnitzler, Arthur, 17

Self, 1, 6, 17–18, 22, 34, 39, 61, 66–67, 81, 85, 91, 98; illimitable, 4; romantic, 135; structured, 5

Seventies, 1–2, 12, 22, 144, 243, 313, 356, 379 n. 22

Sex, 2, 3, 7, 35, 37–38, 44, 47, 50, 68, 95, 97, 102, 149, 152, 155, 161–63, 167–68, 186, 196, 201, 204, 206, 229, 241, 259, 268, 271, 278, 283, 294, 301, 316, 329, 352–53, 362

Sexual aggression, 2, 8, 9, 34, 37, 46, 66, 164, 171, 182, 184–211, 216, 284, 294–97, 300, 303–4, 310, 312, 316, 321, 323, 333, 341, 349

Sexuality, 5, 16, 21, 23, 26, 29, 37–38, 42, 56, 139, 145, 159, 163, 170, 174, 181, 186, 188, 201–2, 283, 294, 303, 357

Sexual Politics (Millet), 5, 365 n. 4

Sexual Revolution, 6, 41, 313, 344

Sexus (Miller), 32, 247, 251–58, 264, 269

Shakespeare, William, 17, 283

Sixties, 1, 16, 18, 59, 73, 77–78, 84–85, 108, 144, 194, 243, 313, 356, 379 n. 22

Skerl, Jennie, 349, 389 n. 2

Solipsism, 7, 8, 51, 60, 69, 105–6, 114, 117, 122, 128, 137, 149, 151, 173, 190, 199, 236, 251, 260, 266, 315, 334, 337

Sollers, Philippe, 108, 196, 208, 210

Solnit, Albert, 25

Sons and Lovers (Lawrence), 32, 52, 89, 94, 156, 183–84, 186, 272

Sontag, Susan, 59, 208–10

Sorrows of Werther, The (Goethe), 4, 286

Sound and the Fury, The (Faulkner), 151

Spector, Jack, 19

Spengler, Oswald, 242, 254

Stalinism, 71, 295–96, 312

Stoekel, Alan, 205

Stoller, Robert, 28–34, 266–67 n. 15

Stone, Lawrence, 36
Story of the Eye (Bataille), 8, 209–19
Stuck, Franz von, 125
Sublimation, 6, 7, 14, 54–56, 61, 66, 118, 147, 174, 194, 254, 279
Suleiman, Susan, 210, 212, 217
Sun Also Rises, The (Hemingway), 213
Superego, 5–10, 13–14, 18, 27, 31–34, 40–42, 65, 69, 71–72, 76, 107, 135, 214–18, 253, 277, 290, 309, 315, 319, 354, 359–60, 361
Surrealism, 9, 20, 119, 338
Surya, Michel, 198–99, 202, 218
Swift, Jonathan, 55–56, 58, 206
Symbolism, 60, 150, 159, 165–66, 201, 211, 213, 246, 351

Tears of Eros, The (Bataille), 197, 207
Theresa, Saint, 31, 201, 219
Thirties, 11, 16, 194, 224, 229, 274
Three Essays on the Theory of Sexuality (Freud), 26, 30
"Time of Her Time, The" (Mailer), 46, 303–5
Time of the Assassins, The (Miller), 234, 274–75, 281
Tocqueville, Alexis de, 13
Totalitarianism, 71, 76, 275, 296–98, 300, 302, 305, 312
Totem and Taboo (Freud), 20
Tough Guys Don't Dance (Mailer), 316–18
Tradition (Traditionalist), 9–10, 97, 243, 305, 356
Tragedy, 13, 16, 27, 71, 101, 205, 326
Transgression, 8–9, 109, 190, 201, 203–5, 210, 212, 225–26, 234, 354, 359–60, 361
Trilling, Diana, 275
Trilling, Lionel, 3–4, 13, 16–17, 62, 63, 261, 298, 389 n. 16
Triumph of the Therapeutic, The (Rieff) 40, 42, 44, 356–57
Tropic of Cancer (Miller), 2, 8, 232, 236–39, 241–44, 253, 255, 261, 269–73, 276, 290
Tropic of Capricorn (Miller), 233, 236, 238, 250, 252
Turkle, Sherry, 85
Twenties, 11–13, 59, 86

Ulysses (Joyce), 20, 271, 291, 346
Unconscious, 6, 14, 16–20, 23, 26, 30, 32, 36, 41–44, 49, 56, 58, 68–70, 77, 80, 83, 92, 94–98, 101, 110, 149, 175, 200, 213, 256
"Use Value of D.A.F. Sade, The" (Bataille), 224–25
Utopianism, 1, 5–6, 12–13, 21, 40–41, 49–51, 58, 61, 65, 69, 72, 86, 97, 108, 110, 136, 224, 242, 254, 275–76, 298, 301, 304, 316, 360

Violence, 1, 3–6, 27, 40, 43, 57, 63, 66, 102–3, 108, 113, 123, 127, 129, 135, 145, 148, 151, 174, 181, 187, 194–95, 198–206, 214, 216, 274, 293, 300, 306, 309, 311, 317, 341, 347, 349, 352, 354–55, 361
Visions of Excess, 198, 205–6, 224–25
Vitalism, 49, 67, 82–83, 97–98, 101, 149–50, 156, 193
Vivas, Eliseo, 193

Wagner, Richard, 122–23, 127
Wainhouse, Austryn, 144
Waite, Robert G. L., 121–28
"We Need One Another" (Lawrence), 92
"White Negro, The" (Mailer), 8, 107, 235, 300–303, 359
Whitman, Walt, 243, 245, 261, 286, 312
Why Are We in Vietnam? (Mailer), 8, 309–11, 326, 343
Wickes, George, 263
Widmer, Kingsley, 269–70
Wild Boys, The (Burroughs), 349
Wilson, Edmund, 131, 268–69

"Woman Who Rode Away, The" (Lawrence), 33, 88, 158–59, 160, 186, 200, 282, 343

Women in Love (Lawrence), 7, 33, 147, 149, 151–52, 157–58, 161–62, 164–78, 181–86, 191–93, 272–73, 278, 280, 316

Wordsworth, William, 141, 178

World of Lawrence, The (Miller), 271–84

World of Sex, The (Miller), 252, 254, 265, 270

Yeats, W. B., 237

Zaretsky, Eli, 11

Zweig, Paul, 64

DANIEL FUCHS IS A PROFESSOR EMERITUS OF ENGLISH AT
THE CITY UNIVERSITY OF NEW YORK'S COLLEGE OF STATEN ISLAND.
HE IS THE AUTHOR OF *SAUL BELLOW: VISION AND REVISION* AND
THE COMIC SPIRIT OF WALLACE STEVENS.

....

LIBRARY OF CONGRESS CATALOGING-IN-PUBLICATION DATA
FUCHS, DANIEL
THE LIMITS OF FEROCITY : SEXUAL AGGRESSION
AND MODERN LITERARY REBELLION / DANIEL FUCHS.
P. CM.
INCLUDES BIBLIOGRAPHICAL REFERENCES AND INDEX.
ISBN 978-0-8223-4992-1 (CLOTH : ALK. PAPER)
ISBN 978-0-8223-5005-7 (PBK. : ALK. PAPER)
1. LITERATURE, MODERN—20TH CENTURY—HISTORY
AND CRITICISM. 2. AGGRESSIVENESS IN LITERATURE. I. TITLE.
PN771.F79L56 2011
809'.933538—DC22
2010039879

www.ingramcontent.com/pod-product-compliance
Lightning Source LLC
Chambersburg PA
CBHW061341300426
44116CB00011B/1947